SUB-PATENT INNOVATION RIGHTS

This ground-breaking work delves into the world of sub-patent intellectual property rights, exploring utility model and similar protection offered by over 100 countries worldwide. Drawing on the expertise of leading scholars from around the globe, this volume provides a comprehensive analysis of sub-patent protection systems, comparing and contrasting statutory frameworks, registration requirements, corporate strategies, and litigation tactics. The book also highlights current policy debates surrounding these systems, including their potential to promote local innovation and economic development, proposals for cross-border harmonization, and their interaction with increasingly integrated litigation systems. This book is an invaluable resource for scholars, attorneys, historians, economists, and anyone dealing with complex international intellectual property matters. This title is also available as Open Access on Cambridge Core.

Jorge L. Contreras, the James T. Jensen Endowed Professor for Transactional Law at the University of Utah S.J. Quinney College of Law, is an internationally recognized expert on intellectual property law and practice. He is the author or editor of twelve prior books and more than 150 scholarly book chapters and articles. Before entering academia, he was a partner at a major international law firm where he practiced transactional intellectual property law in Boston, Washington, DC, and London.

Sub-patent Innovation Rights

UTILITY MODELS, PETTY PATENTS AND INNOVATION PATENTS AROUND THE WORLD

Edited by

JORGE L. CONTRERAS

University of Utah

CAMBRIDGE
UNIVERSITY PRESS

CAMBRIDGE
UNIVERSITY PRESS

Shaftesbury Road, Cambridge CB2 8EA, United Kingdom

One Liberty Plaza, 20th Floor, New York, NY 10006, USA

477 Williamstown Road, Port Melbourne, VIC 3207, Australia

314–321, 3rd Floor, Plot 3, Splendor Forum, Jasola District Centre, New Delhi – 110025, India

103 Penang Road, #05-06/07, Visioncrest Commercial, Singapore 238467

Cambridge University Press is part of Cambridge University Press & Assessment, a department of the University of Cambridge.

We share the University's mission to contribute to society through the pursuit of education, learning and research at the highest international levels of excellence.

www.cambridge.org
Information on this title: www.cambridge.org/9781009478120

DOI: 10.1017/9781009478113

When citing this work, please include a reference to the DOI 10.1017/9781009478113

First published 2025

A catalogue record for this publication is available from the British Library.

Library of Congress Cataloging-in-Publication Data
NAMES: Contreras, Jorge L., editor
TITLE: Sub-patent innovation rights : utility models, petty patents, and innovation patents around the world / edited by Jorge L. Contreras, University of Utah.
DESCRIPTION: Cambridge, United Kingdom ; New York, NY : Cambridge University Press, 2024. | Includes bibliographical references and index.
IDENTIFIERS: LCCN 2024023516 (print) | LCCN 2024023517 (ebook) | ISBN 9781009478120 (hardback) | ISBN 9781009478090 (paperback) | ISBN 9781009478113 (epub)
SUBJECTS: LCSH: Patent laws and legislation. | Patent licenses. | Technological innovations–Law and legislation | Inventions.
CLASSIFICATION: LCC K1505 .S83 2024 (print) | LCC K1505 (ebook) | DDC 346.04/86–dc23/eng/20240527
LC record available at https://lccn.loc.gov/2024023516
LC ebook record available at https://lccn.loc.gov/2024023517

ISBN 978-1-009-47812-0 Hardback
ISBN 978-1-009-47809-0 Paperback

Contents

PART III THE FUTURE OF SUB-PATENT INNOVATION RIGHTS

Contributors

Lionel Bently (BA Law, University of Cambridge). KC (hon). Professor of Intellectual Property Law (Herchel Smith), University of Cambridge and professorial fellow of Emmanuel College, Cambridge.

Magnus Buggenhagen (MSc, PhD candidate, Technische Universität Berlin). Principal Consultant, LexisNexis Intellectual Property Solutions/LexisNexis IPlytics GmbH.

Daniel R. Cahoy (JD, University of New Hampshire; BA, University of Iowa) Robert G. and Caroline Schwartz Professor and Professor of Business Law, Pennsylvania State University Smeal College of Business.

Alessandro Cogo (PhD, Università di Pavia; PhD, Ludwig-Maximilians-Universität München; JD, Università degli Studi di Torino). Associate Professor, IP & Business Law, University of Turin.

Jorge L. Contreras (JD, Harvard Law School; BSEE and BA, Rice University). James T. Jensen Endowed Professor for Transactional Law and Director of the Program on Intellectual Property and Technology Law, University of Utah S.J. Quinney College of Law. Visiting Professor, University of Minnesota Law School.

Lisa van Dongen (LLM, Tilburg University) Postdoctoral Researcher at the Institute for Information Law (IViR), University of Amsterdam.

Thibault Gisclard (PhD, Sorbonne & Max Planck Institute; MS, University of Nancy). Associate Professor of Intellectual Property Law and Comparative Law, University of Lille.

Jussi T. S. Heikkilä (DSc, University of Jyväskylä). Adjunct Professor, LUT University.

Martin Husovec (PhD, Ludwig Maximilian University & Max Planck Institute; Masters and Bachelor, Pavol Jozef Safarik University). Associate Professor, London School of Economics and Political Science.

Mark D. Janis (JD, Indiana University; BS, Purdue University). Robert A. Lucas Chair and Professor of Law, Director, Center for Intellectual Property Research, Indiana University Maurer School of Law, Bloomington.

Sang Jo Jong (Law degree, Seoul National University; PhD, London School of Economics). Professor of Law, Seoul National University School of Law.

Timo Minssen (Jur. Dr., LLLic., LLM, MICL, Dipl. Jur.). Professor of Law and Managing Director and Founder of the Center for Advanced Studies and the Collaborative Research Programme in Biomedical Innovation Law (CeBIL), University of Copenhagen (UCPH). LML Research Affiliate, University of Cambridge.

Maikon Oliveira (BA, MA, Universidade Federal do Paraná; MBA, Pontifícia Universidade Católica do Rio Grande do Sul). Partner and Head of the Area of Patents and Innovation Management, Baril Advogados Associados.

Lynda J. Oswald (PhD, University of London; JD, MBA, AB, University of Michigan). Louis & Myrtle Moskowitz Research Professor of Business and Law and Professor of Business Law, University of Michigan Stephen M. Ross School of Business.

Peter Georg Picht (PhD, LLM, Yale). Professor for Business, Competition and Intellectual Property Law, University of Zurich; head of the Center for Intellectual Property and Competition Law (CIPCO), University of Zurich. Research Fellow Max Planck Institute.

Dan Prud'homme (PhD, Macquarie University; LLM and PgC, University of Edinburgh Law School; MPP and BA, University of Maryland College Park). Assistant Professor, Florida International University (FIU) College of Business.

Marco Ricolfi (LLM, Yale Law School; JD, Turin University). Professor of Business Law and Intellectual Property, Turin Law School.

Matthew Rimmer (PhD, University of New South Wales). Professor of Intellectual Property and Innovation Law, Faculty of Business and Law, Queensland University of Technology.

Isaac Rutenberg (PhD, California Institute of Technology; JD, Santa Clara University; BS, Colorado School of Mines). Associate Professor of Information, Communication, and Technology Policy and Innovation, Strathmore University; IP Advisor, CIFOR-ICRAF.

Luca Schirru (LLM, American University Washington College of Law; MSc, DSc, PPED/UFRJ). Executive director and researcher at Brazilian Copyright Institute (IBDAutoral). Professor, specialization program on Intellectual Property Law at the Pontifical Catholic University of Rio de Janeiro.

Jens Schovsbo (LLD, PhD, University of Copenhagen). Professor in Intellectual Property Law, Center for Information and Innovation Law (CIIR), University of Copenhagen.

Brad Sherman (BEco, LLB, LLM, PhD). ARC Laureate Fellow and Professor of Law, University of Queensland.

Rafał Sikorski (Law degree, Adam Mickiewicz University; LLM, Central European University, PhD, Adam Mickiewicz University). Professor of Law, Adam Mickiewicz University.

Tine Sommer (LLD, PhD, LLM). Professor of Intellectual Property Law, Department of Law, Aarhus BSS, Aarhus University.

Martin Stierle (Dipl.-Jur., University of Bayreuth; LLM, University of California Berkeley; PhD, LMU Munich). Associate Professor, Faculty of Law, Economics and Finance (FDEF), University of Luxembourg.

Uma Suthersanen (LLB, University of Singapore; LLM, PhD, Queen Mary University of London). Director, Queen Mary Intellectual Property Research Institute and Chair in Global Intellectual Property Law, Queen Mary University of London.

Masabumi Suzuki (LLB, University of Tokyo; LLM, Harvard Law School). Professor of Intellectual Property, Faculty of Law, Waseda University.

Marian Weber (BLaw, MArts, University of Zurich). Research assistant, University of Zurich.

Yu Yang (PhD, Fudan University; European Master in Law and Economics, Erasmus Mundus Scholarship). Associate Professor, School of Global Governance, Shanghai University of International Business and Economics.

Foreword

Utility models, also known as petty patents, innovation patents and by various other names, are a long-established form of intellectual property right. Thus some national regimes date from as long ago as the late nineteenth or early twentieth century. They are also an increasingly widespread form of protection, now to be found in over a hundred countries. They are also an internationally recognized form of protection, notably by the Paris Convention for the Protection of Industrial Property since the Washington Act of 1911. As was first recognized in Uma Suthersanen's pioneering study for UNCTAD in 2006, utility models are a form of protection which may be particularly suitable for developing economies. In developed economies, it is common for there to be cyclical debates as to the advantages and disadvantages of such rights, and in particular whether, as some supporters claim, they foster innovation by small and medium-sized enterprises. For example, Australia introduced petty patents in 1979, reformed and re-named them innovation patents in 2001, but abandoned the system in 2021. Finally, utility models can interact with other rights, as was recently highlighted by the decision of the Grand Chamber of the Court of Justice of the European Union in Case C–382/21 P *European Union Intellectual Property Office* v. *KaiKai Company Jaeger Wichmann GbR* [EU:C:2024:172] (holding that an application for a Community-registered design could claim priority from a design right or utility model filed in another Contracting State of the Paris Convention in the preceding six months, but not from a patent).

Despite the ubiquity and significance of utility models, they have until now attracted very little attention from scholars. Jorge Contreras is therefore to be congratulated in taking the initiative of editing this volume. He has assembled an international team of distinguished scholars who, between them, have gone a long way to remedy the previous neglect of this important topic. There are chapters by national experts which explore the present or past laws of fifteen countries. In addition, there are cross-jurisdictional contributions which provide an overview of such systems, prospects for harmonisation at least within the European Union, interaction with other aspects of the intellectual property system and their economic impact. As such, the book can be whole-heartedly recommended to anyone with an interest in this corner of intellectual property law.

Richard Arnold
Royal Courts of Justice, Strand, London.

Preface

Patents are important tools for innovation policy. They incentivize creation and dissemination of new technical solutions and help to disclose their working to the public in exchange for limited exclusivity. But in addition to patents, more than one hundred countries around the world offer a "lesser" form of protection for innovations known variously as utility models, technical designs, petty patents, innovation patents, short-term patents, which this volume refers to collectively as "utility models."

Utility models have been contemplated alongside patents by the Paris Convention for the Protection of Industrial Property since 1911. Yet neither the Paris Convention nor any other major international agreement explicitly delineates the scope of utility model protection, which is left largely to the discretion of national and regional jurisdictions. The result of this lack of formal treaty guidance is a diverse set of utility model rules that lack significant harmonization across countries and regions and which have ebbed and flowed over time.

Despite their long history and widespread adoption, utility models remain, as Professor Mark Janis observed more than two decades ago, "a backwater of intellectual property." Compared to the large body of scholarly literature in other areas of intellectual property law, there is scant literature concerning utility models, and only a handful of empirical studies that focus on them.

This volume represents the first book-length study of utility models and other forms of sub-patent innovation protection around the world. It compares, contrasts, and critically analyzes these forms of protection in a range of jurisdictions while shedding light on the manner in which utility models are utilized by innovators and industry.

The international collaboration of scholars and legal practitioners that resulted in this volume began in February 2022. It involved several online workshops during the summer and fall of 2022, as well as a workshop hosted by the London School of Economics and Political Science in February 2023. Preliminary results of this collaboration were presented at the European Policy for Intellectual Property (EPIP) conference held Krakow, Poland, in October 2023, as well as other conferences and symposia around the world.

Several chapters of this volume include empirical analyses of filing, assignment, and litigation data available from national patent offices, the World Intellectual Property Organization (WIPO), and IPLytics, a private patent analytics firm with which we have collaborated. Other chapters present statutory and regulatory analysis of local filing rules, case histories, and the experience of practitioners in this area. On the basis of these comparisons, we present conclusions, or at least offer hypotheses, regarding the relative effectiveness of utility model systems in achieving their purported goals, and the degree to which such systems can or should be harmonized to a greater degree.

We hope that this volume will become a definitive resource for intellectual property attorneys, patent offices, regulators, policymakers, academics, and judges who are confronted with these enigmatic and ever-changing forms of legal protection.

We are grateful to Matt Galway, Jadyn Fauconier-Herry, Balamuthukumaran Pasupathy, and the rest of the production and editorial staff at Cambridge University Press for helping bring this volume to fruition.

1

Utility Models and Other Forms of Sub-patent Protection*

Jorge L. Contreras, Martin Husovec, and Matthew Rimmer

More than 100 countries around the world offer a form of innovation protection "below" that of patents.[1] These forms of protection are known variously as utility models, technical designs, petty patents, innovation patents, short-term patents, registration patents, and the like.[2] For the sake of convenience, in this book we refer to all such forms of sub-patent innovation protection as "utility models."

While national rules regarding the scope, availability, and issuance of utility models vary from country to country, most utility model regimes offer protection for tangible products, with many, but not all, jurisdictions excluding processes, biological materials, and computer software from the scope of protection. The duration of utility model protection ranges from five to fifteen years, with most countries offering ten years of protection.[3] In most countries, utility model applications are not formally examined and must simply disclose the product in question.

Given the lack of examination, obtaining utility models is generally viewed as faster and cheaper than obtaining patents.[4] This combination of speed and cost, in theory, makes utility models potentially attractive to small and medium enterprises (SMEs) that cannot afford to obtain full patent protection.[5] Similar considerations have also been raised as advantageous to innovators in low-income countries.[6] As one commentator observed of Germany's utility model system, which dates to

* Portions of this chapter are adapted from Jorge L. Contreras and Magnus Buggenhagen, Standards Essential Utility Models, 64 *Jurimetrics Journal* 1 (2024).

1 As of February 2024, WIPO lists 83 different governmental offices that issue utility model registrations including several regional offices. WIPO 2023b.

2 *See* Suthersanen 2019, 4 (discussing nomenclature).

3 *See* Richards 2010, table 1.

4 Prud'homme 2014, 17 Chart 2 (comparing official costs of utility models versus patents in China and various European countries) and 48–49.

5 *See* Prud'homme 2014, 10–11; Suthersanen 2006, 7–8.

6 *See* Prud'homme 2014, 10–11; Suthersanen 2006, 7–8.

1891, utility models were from the beginning intended to benefit small businesses and innovators who lacked the resources to seek full patent protection:

> A utility model patent is a "little patent," or the "patent of the small business man." Its value lies in the rapid protection of short-lived innovations. It is intended to promote the development or further development of articles of use, articles of mass consumption, for which it has always had special significance . . .[7]

Despite their long history and widespread adoption, utility models remain, as Professor Mark Janis observed more than two decades ago, "a backwater of intellectual property."[8] Compared to the large body of scholarly literature on patents, copyrights and other areas of intellectual property law, there is scant literature concerning utility models, and only a handful of empirical studies that focus on them.[9]

This book seeks to fill that gap with a series of chapters focusing on some of the key jurisdictions in the development of utility model law and regulation, followed by chapters that consider the efficacy and impact of utility models more broadly for innovation, litigation, and economic development.

1.1 ADOPTION OF UTILITY MODEL PROTECTION AROUND THE WORLD

The concept of the utility model was first introduced in Great Britain via an 1843 Act that allowed applicants to register the shape and configuration of useful articles of manufacture – a complement to an 1842 act protecting ornamental product designs.[10] Given a range of perceived conflicts with the patent system and little use by practitioners, the UK statute was formally revoked in 1919.

Germany, in contrast, embraced the concept of utility models during the late nineteenth century as a necessary form of legal protection for "small inventions" – useful improvements of products such as clothing, hand tools, and housewares.[11] Utility models, in the German framework, fit somewhere between existing protections for fashion designs, which were purely aesthetic, and patents, which required a higher showing of novelty. In 1891, the German legislature enacted its first statute protecting the utility model, or *Gebrauchsmuster*.[12]

Japan and Poland followed shortly after Germany in enacting utility model protections on the German model during the early twentieth century,[13] with other

[7] Naumann 1958, 802–803.

[8] Janis 1999, 152.

[9] *See* Chapter 2 (empirical literature).

[10] For a detailed account of this historical development, see Chapter 3 (UK).

[11] For a detailed account of the history of utility model protection in Germany, see Chapter 6 (Germany and Switzerland).

[12] Ibid.

[13] *See* Chapters 8 (Poland) and 12 (Japan).

jurisdictions across Europe, Asia, and Latin America implementing utility model systems throughout the century. Some utility model systems, such as Finland's, were introduced as recently as 1992, and Australia's petty patent system, the first of the twenty-first century, was enacted in 2001 (and has since been dismantled, as discussed below).

Jurisdictions around the world continue to experiment with utility model protection, and proposals for utility model systems have been periodically made in the United States,[14] the European Union,[15] Pakistan,[16] India,[17] and other countries.

At the same time, some countries that once had utility model systems have discontinued them due to perceived conflicts with the general patent system or their failure to achieve desired goals. Thus, the Netherlands, which adopted a "short term patent" system in 1995, eliminated that system in 2008.[18] Belgium abolished its "small patent" system in 2009.[19] Australia established a system of "petty patents" – but then replaced that system with a new model of "innovation patents" in 2001. It formally discontinued that system in 2021 after significant policy debate.[20]

And though major industrial jurisdictions including Germany, France, Italy, Japan, and Korea still offer utility model protection, utility models are utilized most heavily in China, where more than 98 percent of the approximately three million worldwide utility model applications were filed in 2022.[21]

From a comparative perspective, there is a great profusion and diversity of utility models of patent protection. There is ongoing debate as to whether there should be international harmonization in respect of utility models of patent protection.

1.2 UTILITY MODELS UNDER INTERNATIONAL AGREEMENTS

1.2.1 *Paris Convention*

Utility models are expressly contemplated alongside patents by the Paris Convention for the Protection of Industrial Property, which added language concerning utility models in 1911.[22] Yet the Paris Convention does not require that signatory states

[14] *See* Chapter 16 (United States).
[15] *See* Chapter 20 (EU harmonization proposals).
[16] *See* Grosse Ruse-Khan 2012.
[17] *See* Swamy 2022, Sheikh 2022, Sharma and Kumar 2018.
[18] *See* Prud'homme 2014, 11.
[19] *See* Prud'homme 2014, 11–12.
[20] Chapter 10 (Australia).
[21] WIPO 2023a, 62 table A61 (2,950,653 Chinese utility model applications versus worldwide total of 3,010,510 utility model applications).
[22] Paris Convention for the Protection of Industrial Property, Art 1, ¶ 2, July 14, 1967, 21 U.S.T. 1583, 828 U.N.T.S. 305 ("The protection of industrial property has as its object patents, utility models, industrial designs, trademarks, service marks, trade names, indications of source or appellations of origin, and the repression of unfair competition.")

adopt utility model protection or explicitly delineate the scope of that protection, which is left largely to the discretion of signatory states.

The principal effect of the Paris Convention on utility models is to require that signatories grant national treatment to applicants for these rights, meaning that they may not discriminate between domestic and foreign applicants or among applicants from different countries.[23] This requirement tends to prevent states from making utility model protection available only to national applicants or to small entities – both of which could be argued to foster the policy goals of utility model protection, but which may not be implemented in the face of national treatment obligations.[24]

The Paris Convention also requires that if a party files a utility model application in a signatory state, then other signatory states must give that party the benefit of that original priority date if they file locally within 12 months of their initial filing.[25]

1.2.2 *TRIPS Agreement*

Unlike the Paris Convention, the 1994 World Trade Organization (WTO) Agreement on Trade-Related Aspects of Intellectual Property Rights (TRIPS Agreement) does not cover utility models.[26] According to one leading commentator, this omission was intentional.[27] But while utility models are not expressly authorized under the TRIPS Agreement, they are not prohibited by it either. Accordingly, as observed by Uma Suthersanen, WTO members "are free to formulate or reject utility model protection as they see fit," provided, of course, that they comply with national treatment obligations under the Paris Convention, which are incorporated into TRIPS.[28]

1.2.3 *European Union*

In the 1990s, observers in the European Union[29] began to note that the different sets of utility model laws in EU member states could have a negative impact on the integration of the European single market, the free flow of goods within Europe,

[23] Paris Convention, Art 2:1.

[24] *See, e.g.*, Chapter 8 (Poland), Section 8.3 (noting possibility of foreign applicants to "hijack" this IP right intended to benefit local filers).

[25] Paris Convention, Art 4.

[26] Agreement on Trade-Related Aspects of Intellectual Property Rights, April 15, 1994, Marrakesh Agreement Establishing the World Trade Organization, Annex 1C, 1869 U.N.T.S. 299 [TRIPS Agreement].

[27] Gervais 2008, 337–338 (TRIPS Agreement was intended to cover only standard patents and not utility models).

[28] Suthersanen 2019, 6. Utility models have also been recognized in certain bilateral and multilateral trade and investment agreements. *See* Grosse Ruse-Khan 2013, 5–6; Suthersanen 2019, 6–7.

[29] A detailed account of EU efforts to harmonize the law of utility models can be found, with citations, in Chapter 20.

and a reduction of competition among European companies. In 1995, the European Commission published a Green Paper on the possibility of harmonizing European utility model law, and in 1997 issued a proposed Directive on the protection of utility model. The proposal was updated in 1999, but work on the proposal was suspended in 2000 due to disagreements among member states, notably the United Kingdom. The proposed directive was formally withdrawn in 2006 as the Commission focused its attention on the development of a unitary patent system. Yet in 2013, one year after the European Parliament's enactment of regulations on the unitary patent, the Commission again turned its attention to utility models, commissioning a study of the economic impact of utility models on European markets, which was published in 2015.

Utility models are not included in the recent European legislation concerning the Unified Patent and Unified Patent Court (UPC),[30] and several countries that participate in the UPC system also maintain national utility model systems.

1.2.4 *Patent Cooperation Treaty*

Despite the absence of utility models from these substantive international agreements, utility models are covered by the World Intellectual Property Organization (WIPO) procedural Patent Cooperation Treaty, which enables the coordination of filings in various countries offering utility model protection.[31] WIPO also provides guidance to member states in respect of the advantages and disadvantages of utility models.[32] Despite the availability of PCT applications for utility models, filings in many countries remain predominantly local and are made directly through a national filing office.[33] This suggests that many utility models are filed in only the country of origin, and are not the subject of international filing campaigns, as are many patents.

1.2.5 *Bilateral and Regional Trade Agreements*

In addition to the international agreements noted above, several bilateral and regional trade agreements contemplate utility model protection.[34]

1.2.6 *Regional Filings*

Members of three multinational regional alliances may obtain regional utility model protection with a single filing. These alliances include the Andean Community,

30 *See* Chapter 17 (UPC).
31 Patent Cooperation Treaty.
32 *See* WIPO 2024a.
33 *See* Chapter 8 (Poland), Section 8.2.
34 *See* Grosse Ruse-Khan 2012, 11–15.

ARIPO (the African Regional Intellectual Property Organization), and OAPI (the African Intellectual Property Assn).[35] Such regional protection may, in some cases, be obtained in lieu of, or in addition to, protection at the national level.

1.2.7 *Utility Models and Sustainable Development*

The United Nations 2030 Agenda also provides an important context in which to consider utility models of patent protection. SDG 9 of the UN Sustainable Development Goals seeks to "build resilient infrastructure, promote inclusive and sustainable industrialization and foster innovation." Target 9.b calls for parties to "support domestic technology development, research and innovation in developing countries, including by ensuring a conducive policy environment for, inter alia, industrial diversification and value addition to commodities."

In this context, there has been consideration of whether utility models may provide better adapted systems of intellectual property for developing countries, least developed countries, small island states, and landlocked countries. There has also been discussion of alternative models of promoting research and development in developing countries. These considerations are discussed in greater detail in Section 1.4.2.

The United Nations Development Programme (UNDP) has been interested in the promotion of grassroots innovation as an inclusive path to development.[36] To this end, the UNDP has set up a network of Accelerator Labs to help crowd-source and distribute sustainable innovation – a project that has led to discussion about what model of intellectual property would be best suited to deal with grass-roots innovation.[37] Numerous commentators have suggested that utility models may offer certain advantages in this regard, as discussed below.

1.3 CHARACTERISTICS OF UTILITY MODEL PROTECTION

While utility model protection varies from country to country, utility models share key characteristics. This section highlights some of the similarities and differences of utility model protection in various jurisdictions.

1.3.1 *Eligible Subject Matter*

It is a common perception that utility models are intended to cover relatively simple product design features or "minor improvements" that do not rise to the level of

[35] *See, e.g.*, Chapter 15 (Kenya).

[36] www.undp.org/acceleratorlabs/publications/grassroots-innovation-inclusive-path-development

[37] *See* Sander 2023 ("What surfaces over and over again is the question: how to handle intellectual property? It is a pain point for innovation in UNDP – with no clear solution.")

inventiveness of patents.[38] For example, the original German utility model system was originally directed toward physical products (i.e., those that possessed "spatial form," or *Raumform*).[39] Thus, as recently as 2021, utility models in Germany were registered for inventions such as neck pillows (DE202021001064U1), Christmas tree stands (DE202021000981U1), drinking straws (DE202021103855U1), and a novel "mobile dog waste collection aid" (DE202021003254U1). However, the German spatial form requirement was eliminated in 1990. Germany now permits utility model protection for chemical and electrical, in addition to mechanical, designs, resulting in what Mark Janis refers to as "a scope of eligible subject matter essentially congruent to that of the regular patent regime."[40] Thus, recent German utility models include a "communication control chip" (DE202021106098U1), a "circularly polarized cylindrical two-port MIMO dielectric resonator antenna device for 5G applications" (DE202021105303U1), and a "payment system with the option of transaction-specific rights control" (DE202021000532U1) – inventions that could easily be envisioned as the subjects of ordinary patent protection. This convergence of utility model and patent coverage has occurred in several jurisdictions. Thus, whereas the Danish law as originally enacted in 1992 was aimed at simple devices such as hand tools and kitchen utensils, in its current form the statute covers "any creations," including in "chemistry, pharmaceuticals, mechanical and electrical engineering."[41]

As a result, many utility models today are virtually indistinguishable from patents, at least at a textual level.[42] Yet other jurisdictions continue to limit the subject matter for which utility model may be obtained, often excluding methods and processes, chemical compositions, and software.[43]

1.3.2 *Examination*

One of the key differences between utility models and patents is in the process and substance of their examination. While patents are typically examined by a governmental office that has technical expertise and applies strict patentability criteria to claimed inventions, in many countries utility models are granted on a registration basis, in which no substantive examination is undertaken by the granting authority,

38 *See* Radauer et al. 2019, 771 ("one of the oldest, means to address the patent cost barrier for SMEs, is the creation of a second-tier patent system by means of introducing a utility model (utility model), i.e., a second layer of IP rights akin to patents, but with less stringent patentability criteria.")

39 *See* Chapter 6 (Germany and Switzerland).

40 Janis 1999, 164.

41 *See* Chapter 4 (Denmark).

42 *See* Heikkilä and Lorenz 2018, 697 ("there exists a subset of utility model filings linked to inventions that are important enough to pass the threshold for patent protection.")

43 *See* Productivity Commission (Australia) 2016, 243, table 8.2 (comparing scope of protection in various countries).

or in which an examination assesses only novelty but not nonobviousness.[44] These differences often result in the issuance of utility models in a manner that is more rapid and less expensive than that of patents.[45] Thus, while average prosecution times (the period from filing through issuance) for patents range from two to four years,[46] utility models are often issued in a matter of months.[47] However, the reduced examination given to most utility models could make their validity less certain than patents and might not confer on utility models the presumption of validity that is given to patents in many jurisdictions.[48]

Further complicating the picture, jurisdictions have periodically altered their examination standards for utility models. For example, as noted in Chapter 12, with the improvement of Japanese industry's technological capabilities and other factors, patent applications began to outnumber utility model applications around 1980, and the number of utility model applications declined sharply from 1985 onward. In response, the utility model system was extensively revised in 1993, including the abolition of substantive examinations, with the aim of making the system more attractive by ensuring that the system provides early protection for technologies with short life cycles. And as discussed in Chapter 11, China continues to consider adjustments to its utility model examination procedure and standards in order to reduce the number of "low quality" utility models that are issued.

1.3.3 *Validity Challenges*

Utility models can be subject to validity challenges either in administrative or judicial proceedings. Administrative cancellation proceedings are typically brought before the governmental office that issued the utility model.[49] In some countries, such challenges may not be brought until the utility model is issued (i.e., pre-grant challenges are not available).[50] In court, the validity of a utility model may be challenged as a defense when the utility model is enforced against an alleged infringer.[51]

1.3.4 *Conversion*

While utility model systems in most countries are distinct from the patent systems of those countries, several countries permit the conversion of patents and patent

[44] *See* Productivity Commission (Australia) 2016, 243 table 8.2 (comparing jurisdictions); (Radauer et al. 2019), 777–778.

[45] *See* Radauer et al. 2015, 3; 2019, 771–772 ("The highest benefit for users of the utility model system is, practically across all countries, speed").

[46] *See, e.g.*, Singer 2022 (average U.S. patent pendency in 2022 was 25.7 months); Productivity Commission (Australia) 2016, 242 (average one-month processing time for Australian innovation patent and 6 months to several years for standard patent); Mao and Thomas 2022 (providing estimates of timing for multiple jurisdictions).

[47] *See* Bianchin 2021; Kilpatrick Townsend 2022; Radauer et al. 2015, 148.

[48] Radauer et al. 2015, 148.

[49] *See* World Intellectual Property Organization 2023b.

[50] *See, e.g.*, Productivity Commission (Australia) 2016, 242, table 8.1.

[51] *See* WIPO 2023b.

applications into utility models and vice versa.[52] For example, if a patent application has been rejected on the basis of prior art over which the claimed invention is found to be obvious, the patent application may be converted into a utility model application to obtain the benefit of the lower examination standard.[53] In countries such as Italy, this conversion may be made both to national patents, European patents, and new unified patents.[54] In other countries, such as Germany and Denmark, UMs may be "branched off" from a pending patent application, with the benefit of the first filing's priority date.[55]

1.3.5 *Enforcement*

The ability of holders to enforce utility model varies around the world. In a few jurisdictions, utility models may not be enforced in litigation; rather, the holder must seek a substantive examination or convert them to patents before they are enforced.[56] But in most jurisdictions, utility model may be enforced directly once they are issued.[57]

Some jurisdictions that permit the direct enforcement of utility model impose precursor requirements to enforcement. Japan, for example, requires that the holder of a utility model obtain a technical opinion from the Japanese Patent Office regarding the compliance of the enforced utility model with the requisite statutory requirements,[58] and France requires that the holder of a utility model obtain and provide a search report to the accused infringer.[59]

Even with such requirements, utility models are frequently litigated in some jurisdictions. One Dutch researcher found in 2003 that Dutch "registration patents" – largely equivalent to utility models – were litigated 2.7 times more than ordinary patents.[60]

As with patents, remedies for infringement of utility model may include monetary damages as well as injunctive relief to prevent an infringer from continuing its infringement. The enforcement of utility model has led to significant awards in some cases. For example, in one 2016 case, the owner of a Japanese utility model claiming a "toe support pad" was awarded monetary damages of approximately US$1.2 million.[61] And in a Chinese case that was heard by the Supreme People's Court, the successful enforcer of a utility model claiming the design of a selfie stick obtained a damages award of RMB 1 million, followed by the filing of a "massive number of lawsuits" against other manufacturers of this popular consumer product.[62]

[52] *See, e.g.*, Chapter 5 (France).
[53] *See* Chapters 7 (Italy), and 17 (Unified Patent Court).
[54] *See* Chapter 7 (Italy).
[55] *See* Chapters 4 (Denmark), 6 (Germany and Switzerland), and 17 (Unified Patent Court).
[56] *See, e.g.*, Advisory Council on Intellectual Property (Australia) 2015, 8 (owner of Australian innovation patent can enforce rights only after substantive examination and certification)
[57] See Radauer et al. 2015, 32.
[58] Chapter 11 (Japan); Kilpatrick Townsend 2022.
[59] Chapter 5 (France); Kilpatrick Townsend 2022.
[60] van Engelen 2004, 26–30.
[61] Chapter 12 (Japan).
[62] Chapter 11 (China).

In some jurisdictions, utility models have been used to tactical advantage in litigation.[63] As discussed above, in Germany, a utility model may be branched off from a pending patent application. As a result, applicants may file utility models strategically in order to obtain quick protection for inventions that are making their way through the slower patent issuance system. Utility models can then be enforced against alleged infringers before the issuance of the corresponding patents, often resulting in the entry of an injunction barring the infringer from continuing to make or sell infringing products.[64] Protection can then be extended for an additional ten years once the corresponding patent issues. Moreover, as explained by one commentator, the scope of utility model claims in Germany may be "tailored" to an infringer's products even after an infringement lawsuit has been filed.[65] That is,

> the owner has the opportunity to file new claims during the infringement proceedings and to adapt or even shift the scope of protection in view of the infringer's defence. The owner of the German utility model can thereby make very specific limitations, which are generally considered to be too restrictive in the framework of patent examination proceedings without the knowledge that the product may be at risk of later attack.
>
> Moreover, these tailored claims are only binding between the parties, as no limitation declaration is required vis-à-vis the public. In other words, the German utility model owner could assert other correspondingly tailored claims against another infringer using the entire disclosure of the utility model.[66]

Given the potential for tactical litigation uses of utility model such as these, some commentators have questioned the usefulness and advisability of utility model systems. The Australian government, for example, noted that Australia's version of utility model, "innovation patents," was frequently "used strategically, either to target alleged infringers of standard patents or to increase uncertainty over the scope of rights for competitors."[67] In fact, the "high level of uncertainty" associated with utility model protection has been cited as a tactical *advantage* for utility model holders seeking to enforce their rights in litigation.[68]

63 Bianchin 2021 ("One of the main advantages of a German utility model is the various tactical options in its enforcement in infringement proceedings, which make it a highly flexible tool in the IP portfolio.")

64 Radauer et al. 2015, 32–34.

65 Bianchin 2021.

66 Ibid.

67 Productivity Commission (Australia) 2016, 239, 255.

68 Bianchin 2021 ("As long as the protectability of the utility model has not been officially examined, it is often difficult for third parties to assess the extent to which the utility model is or could be legally valid without considerable analysis effort of their own. In practice, it has been shown that this hidden effect of a German utility model often leads to a significant competitive advantage for the owner.")

1.4 ASSESSING UTILITY MODEL SYSTEMS

Utility model systems have emerged in a range of countries – large and small, rich and poor – over the past century and more. As noted in Section 1.1, countries have had different experiences with their utility model systems, leading some to modify their systems significantly and some to abolish those systems entirely, all while other jurisdictions consider implementing utility model systems for the first time. As such, it seems important to assess the success of utility model systems in achieving the goals for which they were developed.

1.4.1 *Assessment Tools and Methodologies*

There are few existing empirical methodologies for assessing the performance of utility model systems. The first of these was developed by Dan Prud'homme (2017a), who designed a methodology for assessing both systemic strictness and appropriability for four Asian "latecomer" jurisdictions (China, Japan, South Korea and Taiwan). He found that the strictness of the systems in each of these jurisdictions increased over time, suggesting that these jurisdictions "have pursued a dynamic catch-up strategy of transitioning from imitative to more sophisticated technological development by increasing both strictness and appropriability-strength of utility model regimes in conjunction with increasing knowledge accumulation and, to some extent, technological capabilities."[69] Prud'homme extends this analytical methodology to twenty-five different jurisdictions in Chapter 21, finding evidence of an inverted U-curve between utility model accessibility and usage whereby a moderate amount of accessibility may lead to more filings than a low or high level of accessibility.

In 2023, Jussi Heikkilä introduced a novel key performance indicator (KPI) approach to assess national utility model systems on the basis of numbers of filings, filer characteristics, the interaction between utility model and patent systems, and issuance timelines.[70] He applies this methodology to the case of Finland in Chapter 9.

The remainder of this Section 1.4 briefly outlines some of the interrelated policy drivers that have been used to justify utility model systems: the incentivization of sub-patentable innovation, the support of SMEs, the promotion of local industry, and the bolstering of developing economies.[71] It then considers the implications of utility model protection for intellectual policy more generally.

[69] Prud'homme 2017a, 67.

[70] Heikkilä 2023a, 8–10.

[71] Further discussion of the motivations and rationales for utility model protection can be found throughout this volume. See, e.g., Chapter 9 (Poland), Chapter 20, Section 20.4 (European harmonization), Chapter 22 (low-income countries).

1.4.2 *Protection of Sub-patentable Innovation*

Utility model statutes were originally enacted to offer protection for technical designs and improvements that fall below the level of patentable invention, but which are functional and thereby do not qualify for more traditional design protection. For example, as discussed in Chapter 4, the Danish utility model law was originally enacted in 1992 to cover hand tools, kitchen utensils, and similarly simple products. Without utility model protection (i.e., in jurisdictions that only offer patent protection), these innovations would remain unprotectable. And given that, by some accounts, a large number of welfare-enhancing innovations are cumulative or incremental in nature, the lack of legal protection leaves these innovations vulnerable to appropriation without compensation.[72] This vulnerability, in turn, reduces incentives to produce such innovations, thereby reducing overall social welfare. This, at least, is the theory.

Yet, as noted in Section 1.3.1, the scope of many utility model statutes has expanded beyond the simple product design features that they were originally enacted to protect. Thus, some critics have charged that while utility models may offer firms additional means for protecting product features and litigating with competitors, these benefits are largely additive to existing patent or other forms of protection and may not actually serve to increase innovation at all. In fact, it could be argued that any socially valuable innovations worthy of protection can be protected by ever-expanding patent, copyright, trademark, design,[73] trade secret, plant breeder,[74] and other forms of intellectual property,[75] rendering utility model protection either superfluous (for valuable product features) or excessive (inasmuch as they protect trivial product features that fall below the novelty or inventiveness threshold required for patentability or other forms of protection).

And far from being harmless, the extension of exclusive rights to these minor features withdraws them from the public domain so that they may not be utilized as the basis for further improvements or innovations. Jerry Reichman observed a quarter century ago that, at least in the United States, "property-based rules do not and cannot work" for small-scale innovations because "[t]hey return to the first comer too little or too much, they impede follow-on developments, ignore the significant contributions of the public domain, balkanize the knowledge base, and increase transaction costs."[76] Thus, as Reichman suggests, the protection of these

[72] See Dutfield and Suthersanen, 2007, 35–36; Grosse Ruse-Khan, 2013; Suthersanen 2006, 6.

[73] See Church et al. 2021 (noting 11 EU design rights cases also raising utility model claims in four countries).

[74] The Australian innovation system had certain provisions dealing with potential conflicts with plant breeders' rights.

[75] See Wilkof et al. 2023 (discussing multiple areas of overlapping IP rights including utility models).

[76] Reichman 2000, 1797. See further discussion in Chapter 16 (United States).

product features through exclusionary utility model rights may decrease overall innovation and social welfare.[77] Reichman's solution is to allow the creators of minor innovations to receive compensation for their use, but to remove their ability to exclude others from that use (i.e., a liability rule, rather than a property rule system).[78] Others have similarly argued that utility models, if granted, should be subject to compulsory licensing regimes.[79] But it is not clear that even these limited protection regimes are necessary. As Suthersanen, Dutfield, and Chow have observed, "[n]ot everything created under the sun must be awarded intellectual property protection."[80] In many cases, the judicious refusal of intellectual property protection on minor innovations may ultimately inure to the public benefit. Such may be the case with utility models, at least in some contexts.

1.4.3 *Supporting SMEs*

As discussed in the introduction to this chapter, the German *Gebrauchsmuster* was introduced in the nineteenth century in order to help individuals and small businesses by offering them a quick and inexpensive route to the protection of minor product features and improvements. Many utility model systems since have likewise sought to foster innovation by SMEs that cannot afford the time or expense of seeking patent protection for each of their innovations.[81]

It is clear, as the chapters in Part I illustrate, that utility model protection can be obtained more quickly and cheaply than patent protection. Yet there is little actual evidence that SMEs in countries that offer utility model protection have benefited significantly from that protection, or that these SMEs have engaged in more, or more valuable, innovative activity than SMEs in countries such as the United States and the United Kingdom, which lack utility model protection.[82] As noted in Chapter 16, the United States offers a range of procedural benefits to SME patent filers including reduced fees, which could potentially offer SMEs cost savings comparable to those offered by utility models but with the benefit of stronger patent protection (for those inventions that qualify).

Moreover, as noted in Chapter 2 (Section 2.2.3), in several of the jurisdictions studied in this volume, the primary filers of utility model applications are large

77 See also Grosse Ruse-Khan 2012, 29 (eliminating utility model protection may "have positive welfare effects in terms of keeping such innovations free in the public domain for everyone to use").

78 Reichman 2000.

79 Boztosun 2010, 431.

80 Suthersanen et al. 2007, 18.

81 The difficult question of why governments should support patenting and innovation by SMEs is beyond the scope of this chapter.

82 See Grosse Ruse-Khan 2012, 27 (noting lack of empirical verification of assumptions regarding the usefulness of utility model protection to SMEs).

international firms such as Ford Motor Company and Siemens, rather than SMEs. One notable exception is China, in which the vast majority of utility model filings are made by local entities that do not appear to have significant international operations.

1.4.4 *Promoting Local Industry*

Related to the support of SMEs, utility models are often promoted by policy makers for their potential to foster local and domestic innovation.[83] Moreover, as observed by Grosse Ruse-Khan, "for countries which are net-importers of IP protected goods, encouragement of local industry to produce more IP-protected goods is important to reduce dependency on imports. This would equally reduce a trade deficit in IP-protected goods – and in turn reduce royalty outflows."[84]

As noted in Chapter 2 (Section 2.2.3), the vast majority of utility model filings in most countries are made by domestic entities. Yet, large international firms have also availed themselves of utility model protection in many countries, often emerging as the largest filers for utility model protection. This phenomenon is certainly evident with respect to utility models that are declared as essential to industry standards (see Chapter 18), which are dominated by multinational firms such as Interdigital and Samsung. But foreign utility model filings are not limited to large multinational firms. As noted in Chapter 9 (Section 9.2.1), Finnish firms trading with partners in Germany, Sweden, Russia, China, and other jurisdictions have also taken advantage of utility model filings in these countries.

In some jurisdictions foreign firms have been seen to make the greatest use of sub-patent protection. In Australia, for example, the system of petty patents, and its successor regime of innovation patents, were justified in terms of promoting local innovation by individual inventors and SMEs. However, Australia ultimately determined that the system had outlived its usefulness and was not providing significant benefits to the national economy. It elected in 2021 to discontinue its system entirely.[85]

1.4.5 *Utility Models and Economic Development*

As discussed in Chapter 22 and elsewhere in this volume, utility models, compared to patents, have been viewed as particularly attractive for innovators in low-income

83 See Grosse Ruse-Khan 2012, 29 (noting connection between goals of supporting SMEs and fostering local innovation), WIPO 2024. Given national treatment obligations under international treaties such as the Paris Convention and the TRIPS Agreement (see Section 2.1), local interests cannot be too explicitly favored by these protection regimes.

84 Grosse Ruse-Khan 2012, 30.

85 See Chapter 10 (Australia).

economies given their lower threshold of originality and modest cost. In 2023, twenty-three of forty-six UN-designated least-developed countries had utility model protection systems.[86]

In 2006, Suthersanen authored a landmark study for the United Nations Conference on Trade and Development (UNCTAD) on the potential benefits of utility model systems for innovators in low-income economies and for low-income countries themselves. Her work (upon which she expands in Chapter 22) has led many commentators to believe that utility model systems can both foster innovation in and attract foreign investment to these countries. As one recent UNCTAD report notes, "[w]ith generally less stringent compliance requirements compared with patents or industrial designs . . ., simpler application procedures and shorter terms of protection, [utility models] present a more accessible form of IP protection that can enhance technological learning in [least-developed countries (LDCs)] with less advanced technologies."[87] Indeed, the report goes on to equate the *absence* of utility model protection as a significant negative factor for least-developed economies:

> Without second-tier IP protection systems like utility models, there are fewer incentives for domestic firms and foreign investors to invest in the development of local product innovations. Since innovation is crucial for production and to develop a local knowledge base, the absence of protection for minor inventions could affect the ability of LDCs to convert knowledge and new ideas into wealth and social benefits.[88]

A 2015 report commissioned by the European Commission also acknowledged the potential benefits of sub-patent protection to developing economies, noting that "in catching up economies, particularly in Japan and also in Korea [i]t has been shown that utility models facilitated the development of local industry, by incentivising small improvements on existing state-of-the-art technologies from developed countries."[89] The report goes on to note, however, that "once the economies matured, the utility model lost much of its supportive function for this inward international technology transfer."[90] Thus, the benefits of utility model systems may be temporary – useful when an economy is at an early stage of development, but dropping off once it achieves a level of maturity.

86 UNCTAD 2023, 17.

87 UNCTAD 2024, 7.

88 UNCTAD 2024, 7

89 Radauer et al. 2015, 1–2. *See also* Suthersanen 2019, 24 ("when the national economy and its industries reach higher levels of technological capacity, as in Japan and certainly Australia, it does appear that the disadvantages outweigh the perceived advantages").

90 Radauer et al. 2015, 1–2. *See also* Suthersanen 2019, 24 ("when the national economy and its industries reach higher levels of technological capacity, as in Japan and certainly Australia, it does appear that the disadvantages outweigh the perceived advantages").

1.4.6 *Credibility of Utility Model Systems*

Whatever their intended benefits, utility model systems have been criticized in their implementation. Observers have noted that the lack of examination of utility model applications has led to the registration of spurious "innovations" such as the infamous wheel design in Australia.[91] The lack of examination and low cost of utility model applications has also prompted massive registrations in China, leading to the general view that utility models are "low quality" forms of protection.[92]

In addition, the strategic use of utility models in jurisdictions such as Germany and Denmark, where "branching off" can be used to obtain enforceable rights over inventions that are the subject of pending patent applications,[93] the convertibility of failed patent applications into utility models and vice versa in jurisdictions such as Italy,[94] and the declaration of unexamined utility models as "standards essential patents" as to which royalties may be collected from implementers of technical standards such as Wi-Fi and 5G,[95] lend further support to arguments that utility models are legal constructs that may be used to the tactical advantage of sophisticated firms, but do little to advance the policy goals for which they were created.

For all of these reasons, utility models may be suffering from a crisis of legitimacy – one that may lead additional jurisdictions to abandon this form of protection in favor of more stringent patent protection or domain-specific sub-patent protection.

1.4.7 *Broader Implications for Intellectual Property Policy*

By illuminating aspects of utility model protection across the globe, this volume offers a few lessons for wider intellectual property policy. Unlike nontraditional intellectual property rights in several countries that are directed to the protection of minor innovations in specific industries, such as semiconductor topographies, databases, or vessel hulls,[96] utility model rights have broader application. Paradoxically, this broader application makes the case for harmonization of utility model protection weaker because policymakers around the world struggle to agree upon their exact mission in the economy and society.[97]

From this perspective, the utility model is a curious example in the family of intellectual property rights. Untethered to one predominant justification or clear use case, utility models sometimes aimlessly flow in the river of intellectual property and

[91] See Chapter 10 (Australia).

[92] See Chapter 11 (China).

[93] See Chapter 6 (Germany and Switzerland).

[94] See Chapter 7 (Italy).

[95] See Chapter 18 (standards-essential utility models).

[96] See discussion in Chapter 16 (industry-specific protections in the United States). See also Bambauer 2024.

[97] See Chapters 19 (lack of harmonization and business models), 20 (harmonization efforts in the EU) and 21 (heterogeneity across borders).

yet survive for decades on the books. As such, they appear to lack a clear and motivated constituency of beneficiaries.

Uma Suthersanen sees this as a feature and not a bug. In Chapter 22, she encourages policymakers around the world "to choose existing rationales and/or expand the justifications for [utility model] laws which best suit the local conditions," such as different innovative practices. Yet unlike secondary forms of IP that are not expressly included under the TRIPS Agreement, such as databases, utility models may not be structured explicitly to preference local or national interests given the requirement for national treatment under the Paris Convention (see Section 1.2.1).

The analysis offered by the authors in this volume also invites reconsideration of how we speak about the bigger family of intellectual property policies in general. Behind this broad, unifying term hides a diverse range of sharp and blunt tools. In Europe, for instance, horizontal instruments, such as the IP Enforcement Directive, treat all IP rights equally. For the critical stage of granting remedies, the legislature pretends that all protected subject matter, including national utility models, have the same societal value. This approach, however, seems misguided. The unique raison d'etre and limitations of each IP right should be considered by the judiciary and authorities that extend the power of remedies to any instrument. This problem is not limited to the remedial stage of the design of IP policies.

A failure to appreciate the strength and seriousness of protected innovations can backfire in other tangible ways. For instance, when China adopted a top-down policy to spur innovative activity, it encouraged patents and utility models alike to be widely embedded into social policies, such as secondary education, career advancement, internal migration, and criminal incarceration.[98] Individuals immediately seized this opportunity by exploiting the weaknesses of the utility model system to obtain related rewards without actually innovating. Had the legislature appreciated that strong ex ante screening should be a key precondition for the linkage of social benefits with the award of IP rights, many gaming strategies could have been avoided.[99]

1.5 CONTENTS OF THIS VOLUME

Following the introductory material in this chapter, Chapter 2 offers empirical data regarding utility model filings around the world.

Next, Part I (Chapters 3–16) provides details regarding utility model regulations, filings, and litigation in a number of key jurisdictions around the world. In Europe the United Kingdom's 1843 utility design statute, the world's first utility model

[98] Heng et al. 2024.

[99] As noted in Chapter 11 (China), the Chinese utility model system has been made more stringent in response to critiques like these.

regime, is of significant historical interest and is addressed in Chapter 3. Chapters 4–9 then address existing utility model systems in a number of small and large European jurisdictions: Denmark, France, Germany (and Switzerland), Italy, Poland, and Finland. In addition, Chapter 9 applies a unique analytical "key performance indicator" framework to the Finnish utility model system. Chapter 10 offers a comprehensive political and legal history of the Australian invention patent system, which was abolished in 2021. Chapter 11 then turns to China, the largest issuer of utility models today, and Chapters 12 and 13 cover Japan and South Korea, two other significant Asian jurisdictions with a long history of utility model issuances. Chapters 14 and 15 then turn to two significant "developing" economies, Brazil and Kenya, and their unique utility model systems. Finally, Chapter 16 turns to the United States, which does not have, and has never had, a general utility model system, but which offers sub-patent protection in several specific vertical markets (semiconductor topographies, boat hull designs, etc.), and in which more general sub-patent protection systems have been debated for decades.

Part II addresses ways that utility models are currently being used in national and international systems. Chapter 17 covers utility models in the new Unified Patent Court in Europe. Chapter 18 explores the characterization of utility models as "standards essential patents" within international standards bodies. Chapter 19 then turns to corporate strategy in utility model filing and enforcement.

Part III takes a broader view and offers syntheses of utility model systems in different contexts. Chapter 20 recounts the long history of efforts to harmonize the law of utility models in the European Union and develops recommendations and predictions regarding the fate of harmonization efforts in the future. In Chapter 21, Dan Prud'homme empirically assesses the accessibility of utility models across twenty-five different jurisdictions. And Chapter 22 concludes with Uma Suthersanen's survey and assessment of the success of utility model systems in fostering innovation and economic development in low-income countries.

2

Overview of Worldwide Utility Model Filings, Litigation and Activity

Daniel R. Cahoy, Jorge L. Contreras and Lynda J. Oswald

The global landscape of existing utility model rights is a helpful starting point to the discussion on utility model innovation policy at the country level as well as company strategy. WIPO data indicates that approximately 3 million utility model applications were filed globally in 2022, a growth rate of 2.9 percent from the previous year and close to the global total of 3.5 million applications for standard patents.[1] Only about one-half of the world's countries provide for utility model systems, yet companies from around the world acquire these rights. Utility models are important players in the intellectual property (IP) environment, and the unique qualities of the system and differential representation require specific analysis.

In this chapter, we review existing empirical data and present additional data regarding utility model filings and litigation worldwide. Our purpose is to provide background and context for the more detailed discussion in the remaining chapters in this book.

2.1 REPRESENTATION OF UTILITY MODEL SYSTEMS ACROSS THE WORLD

As detailed in subsequent chapters, utility model systems are generally less harmonized than standard patent rights in terms of subject matter coverage, length of protection and the process for securing the rights. Such differences might lead one to suspect that utility models are marginalized as a global right. To be sure, the right is conspicuously absent in major IP markets such as the United States, Canada, the United Kingdom and India. On the other hand, utility models are protected in seventy-five countries and regional patent offices.[2] Although many of

[1] WIPO 2023a, 7.

[2] The World Intellectual Property Organization lists seventy-five issuing authorities, though Australia recently phased out its system. WIPO 2023b. Additionally, Taiwan has a utility model system, but it is not listed by WIPO because the country is not recognized by the United Nations.

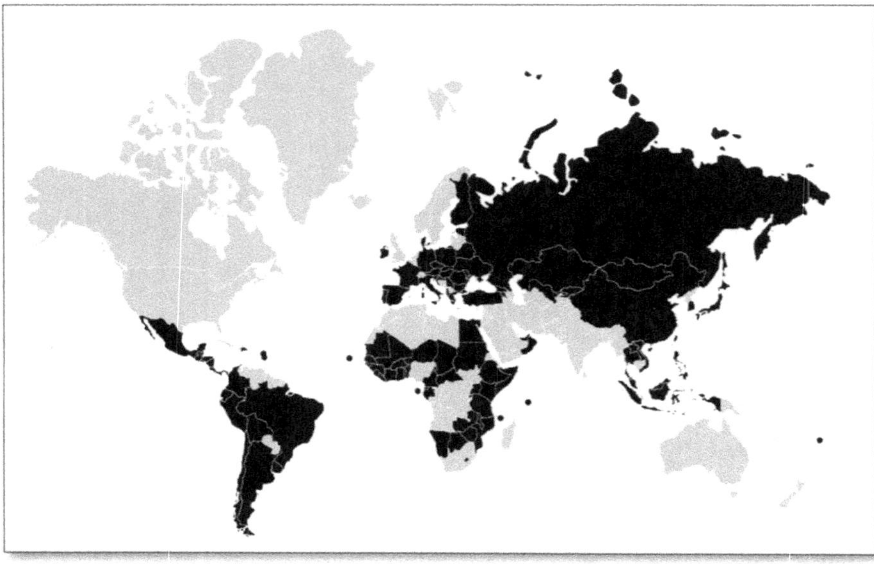

FIGURE 2.1 Countries with utility model protection in 2023 (WIPO 2023b)

these countries are small, together they represent a significant portion of the global economy. Specifically, utility models are in force in countries generating about one-half of the world's economic output by GDP.[3] Although not ubiquitous, utility model protection can hardly be described as rare (see Figure 2.1).

The creation of a utility model system is a matter of national choice. Utility models are not mentioned in the primary international IP treaty, the 1994 TRIPS Agreement.[4] The Paris Convention for the Protection of Industrial Property does recognize the existence of utility models but does not oblige members of that treaty to provide such protection.[5]

Even within major trading regions, there is disparity. For example, the United States, Canada and Mexico share sufficient trade synergies to have entered into the North American Free Trade Agreement (NAFTA)[6] and, more recently, the US-Mexico-Canada Agreement (USMCA),[7] but only Mexico has a utility model system.[8] Several members of the European Union (EU), such as Luxembourg and

3 World Bank 2023.
4 TRIPS 1994.
5 Paris Convention for the Protection of Industrial Property, art. 1, ¶ 2, July 14, 1967, 21 U.S.T. 1583, 828 U.N.T.S. 305.
6 NAFTA 1992.
7 USMCA 2019.
8 Pemberton and Soni 1992.

Sweden, do not have utility model systems, but others, such as Germany, France and Italy, do.[9] Although trading regions may share some goals for IP protection, they do not necessarily see eye-to-eye with respect to utility model protection.

2.2 DESCRIPTIVE STATISTICS ON UTILITY MODELS

2.2.1 *Existing Studies*

Over the years, a small amount of empirical literature concerning utility models has emerged.[10] Suthersanen (2006) offers empirical data on utility model filings in Germany, Japan, Korea, China, Malaysia and Taiwan. Suthersanen et al. (2007) collect contributions including empirical data on utility model filings in Singapore, Australia, Japan, Korea, China, various ASEAN nations and Mexico. Both of these foundational works seek to assess the effectiveness of utility model systems as promoters of local innovation, particularly in emerging economies. Relatedly, Heikkilä (2023) develops a set of key performance indicators (KPIs) for utility model systems based on a literature review and the public statements of governmental issuing offices.

Utility models have also been the subject of a handful of more recent studies focusing on business strategy and innovation theory. Kim et al. (2012) analyze Korean utility model filings to assess their contribution to firm performance. Cao et al. (2014) compare firms' filing behavior for inventions protected in both the United States and China. Heikkilä and Lorenz (2018) study the strategic utilization of utility models by German firms, while Heikkilä and Verba (2018) explore the structures and characteristics of European patent families that include utility models. Cahoy and Oswald (2021) use US patent priority data to assess the degree to which firms elect to pursue patent versus utility model protection for similar innovations. Finally, Zhang (2022) investigates the frequency with which utility models are litigated in China and the characteristics that make both patents and utility models more likely to be litigated.

2.2.2 *Utility Model Filings by Country*

To provide an updated picture of the global utility model landscape, we used data provided by the World Intellectual Property Organization (WIPO)[11] as well as the IPLytics platform (now a part of Lexis-Nexis).[12] As an official United Nations organization, WIPO makes available filing data from the patent offices of its 193 member states.[13] The IPLytics database includes patent and utility model filing

9 Prud'homme 2014.
10 For an excellent overview of the literature, see Heikkilä 2023a, § 2.
11 WIPO 2023d.
12 https://platform.iplytics.com
13 WIPO 2023e.

TABLE 2.1 *Top 20 utility model applicants, 2021 and cumulative 1990–2021*[a]

Country	2021 rank	2021 utility model	1990–2021 rank	1990–2021 utility models (n = 23,515,896)
China[b]	1	2,852,219	1	19,839,834
Taiwan	2	15,162	5	515,008
Germany	3	10,576	4	569,205
Russia	4	9,079	6	234,215
Australia	5	7,844	12	42,943
Japan	6	5,238	3	679,994
Ukraine	7	4,425	7	147,980
Turkey	8	4,490	11	53,555
Korea[c]	9	4,009	2	806,739
Thailand	10	3,762	13	42,039
Indonesia	11	3,249	18	15,844
Spain	12	3,091	8	96,124
Brazil	13	2,578	9	92,245
Italy	14	2,019	10	88,093
Philippines	15	1,799	17	22,316
Czech Republic	16	1,104	15	39,134
Poland	17	779	14	40,415
Mexico	18	706	19	15,556
France	19	673	24	8,910
Hong Kong	20	552	23	9,032

[a] All data sourced from WIPO, other than data for Taiwan, which is sourced from IPLytics.
[b] References to "China" refer to the Peoples Republic of China, excluding the special administrative areas Hong Kong and Macau and Taiwan (Republic of China).
[c] References to "Korea" refer to the Republic of Korea.

data from 98 national and regional patent offices.[14] These databases were queried between March and May 2023.

From 1990 to 2021, inclusive, approximately 23 million applications for utility models were filed, with approximately 17.7 million filed between 2012 and 2021, inclusive (Table 2.1).

As indicated in Table 2.1, China is by far the jurisdiction in which the most utility models are filed. In 2021 alone, there were 2.8 million Chinese utility model filings out of a global total of 2.9 million (97.6 percent), and from 1990 to 2021, collectively, there were 19.8 million Chinese utility model filings out of a global total of 23.5 million (84.4 percent). The growth of Chinese utility model filings is discussed in greater detail below.

Other than China, several jurisdictions, including Germany, Korea, Japan, Taiwan and Russia, have consistently had significant numbers of utility model

[14] IPLytics, IPlytics Platform Data Sources 5, https://platform.iplytics.com/pdf/IPlytics_DataSources_EN.pdf.

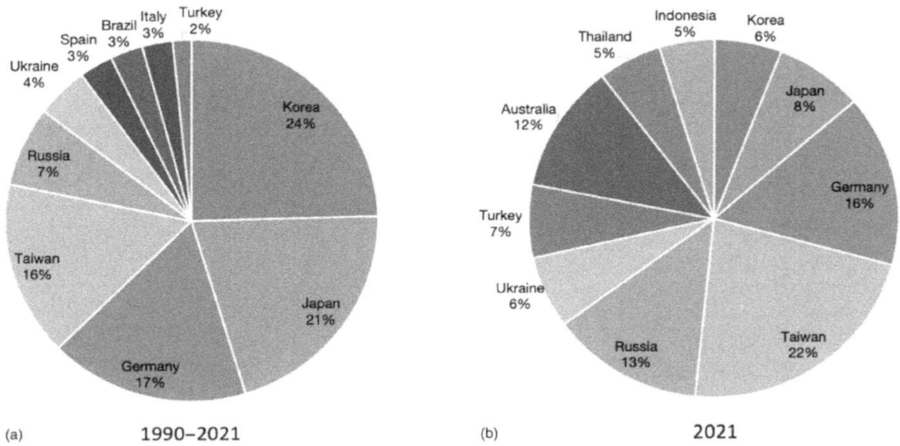

FIGURE 2.2 Top 10 utility model filing jurisdictions (excluding China), 1990–2021 and 2021

filings. Figure 2.2 shows the top 10 jurisdictions for utility model filings in 2021, as well as cumulative utility model filings for the period 1990–2021.

Figure 2.2 highlights a number of notable shifts in utility model filings over time. First, Korea and Japan, both early leaders in utility model filings, have dropped in ranking, leaving Germany and Taiwan as the highest filing jurisdictions after China. Countries in Central Europe and Asia Minor, including Russia, Ukraine and Turkey, as well as smaller Asian countries such as Thailand, Indonesia, Philippines and Hong Kong, have increased their rankings at the expense of European jurisdictions such as Spain, Italy and Poland. Some of these trends are examined in greater detail below.

Figure 2.3 illustrates filings for utility models during the 1990s, when four jurisdictions dominated the filing of utility model applications: China, Germany, Japan and Korea, representing 1.5 million of 1.7 million total filings worldwide (89.5 percent). This period marks the beginning of China's rise to become the dominant jurisdiction for utility model filings.

From 1990 to 1993, China, Germany and Korea had comparable levels of utility model filings, with Japan leading by a significant margin. A statutory change in Japan in 1993 led to a sharp decrease in Japanese filings.[15] From 1995 to 1997 Korea was the utility model filing leader but was overtaken by China in 1997 with approximately 50,000 filings to Korea's 46,000.

As shown in Figure 2.4, annual Chinese filings began to increase rapidly in the early 2000s, breaking the 100,000 mark in 2003 (representing 52 percent of all filings worldwide).

[15] See Chapter 11 (Japan).

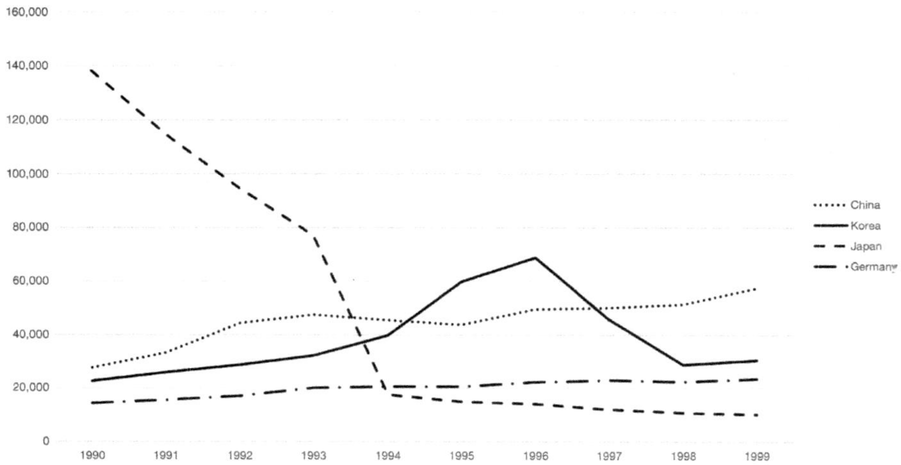

FIGURE 2.3 Utility model filings 1990–1999 in top 4 jurisdictions

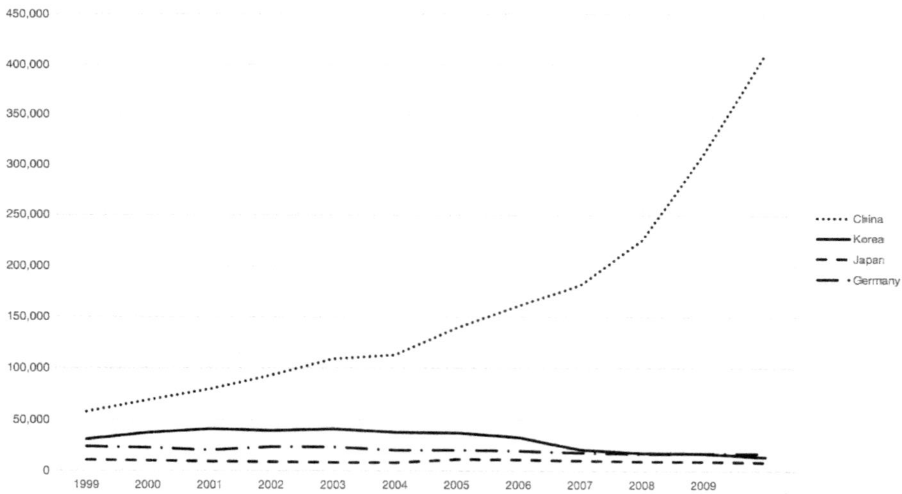

FIGURE 2.4 Utility model filings 1999–2009 in top 4 jurisdictions

In 2011, China's 585,000 utility model filings represented 87.2 percent of the 671,000 filings worldwide and in 2021, China's 2.8 million filings represented 97.6 percent of the global total. The reasons for China's rapid embrace of utility model filings has been discussed in the literature and is beyond the scope of this article.[16]

As a result of China's massive surge of utility model filings, analysis of activity in the rest of the world can only be understood if Chinese filings are omitted. Thus,

[16] *See, e.g.*, Prud'homme 2014.

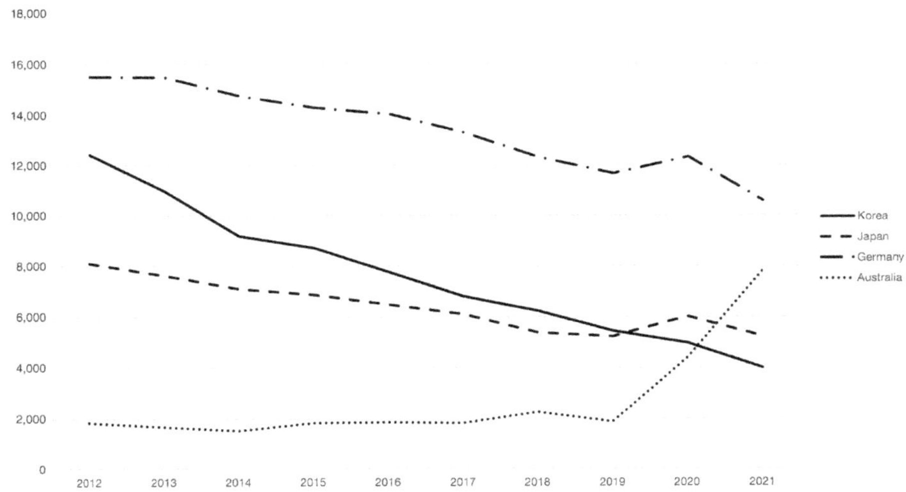

FIGURE 2.5 Utility model filings, 2012–2021, top 6 jurisdictions (excluding China)

from 2012 to 2021, approximately 424,000 filings in the top six jurisdictions other than China (Australia, Germany, Japan, Russia, Korea and Ukraine) accounted for 55 percent of non-China filings during that period. These filings reveal a few interesting trends shown in Figure 2.5.

As shown in Figure 2.5, with the exception of Australia, filings in each of these countries declined during the period; this decline ranged from a 32 percent (in Germany) to 68 percent (in Korea). Australia is the exception, possibly because, as noted above, Australia abolished its innovation patent system in 2021 and beginning in 2019 filers sought to obtain as much protection as possible while it was still available.

2.2.3 *Utility Model Filers*

The utility model systems of certain jurisdictions appear to be more attractive to foreign filers than others. For example, the vast majority of Japanese utility model filers are firms headquartered in Japan. From 2000 to 2022, of the top 30 applicants for Japanese utility models, only two were non-Japanese (Foxconn (Taiwan)[17] and Applied Materials (US)). Filings in Japan are also exceptionally distributed, with the top 1,000 filers representing only 8.4 percent of total applications during that period. A similar pattern appears to exist in China, where the vast majority of utility model

[17] Foxconn is a Taiwan-based conglomerate that, for purposes of this chapter, is used as an umbrella designation for Hon Hai Precision Industry Co., Fushikang (Kunshan) Computer Connectors Co. and Sharp.

applicants appear to be local Chinese firms, although the very large number of Chinese utility model filings make this observation difficult to verify empirically.

In Germany, on the other hand, 10 of the top 30 utility model applicants are foreign-based, including the top filer, Ford Motor Co., whose 1959 applications are nearly double the number of applications by the second highest filer, Siemens (1,028).[18] Other non-German applicants in the top 30 are based in the United States, Hong Kong, Taiwan, Korea, Japan and Italy.[19] German utility model applications are dispersed across a large number of applicants, with the top 1,000 applicants representing approximately 73,000 of 313,000 applications from 2000 to 2022 (23 percent), but far less so than Japan.

Because domestic applicants are traditionally the single largest group in any country, they can obscure global trends reflecting business strategy. Only 0.5 percent of the 3 million utility model applications filed globally in 2022 were made by non-residents.[20] Further, a simple count of top filers or most prominent originating countries will be dominated by the domestic filers in the top utility model country, China, which accounted for 98 percent of global filings in 2022.[21]

A potentially more interesting consideration is the strategy of global filers who look outside of their own countries. When one excerpts domestic filings from each country and considers the global trend, the surprising result is that even though the United States has no utility model system, US residents are among the top-three most represented non-domestic applicants across the world (see Figure 2.6). This suggests that utility model rights may have strategic value outside of a particular innovation system.[22]

2.2.4 *Litigated Utility Models*

The frequency with which utility models are enforced or challenged in administrative proceedings (which, for the sake of convenience, we refer to as "litigated") has not been studied. This section provides initial descriptive statistics concerning litigation and challenges of utility models.

From 2000 to 2022, we identified approximately 30,000 utility models that were the subject of judicial proceedings, including both administrative challenges and court litigation.[23] These figures do not include utility models that were subject to

[18] Ford may have a particular business strategy favoring utility models. See Chapter 19.

[19] Cahoy and Oswald have found that, as of 2017, firms based in the United States, Japan, China, Germany, Korea and Switzerland filed the greatest number of utility model applications outside of their home jurisdictions. (Cahoy and Oswald 2021).

[20] WIPO 2023a, 8.

[21] Ibid. at 21.

[22] Japan, China and Germany do have utility model systems; hence, some of their firms' foreign filing activity may stem from the efficiency of extending domestic filings rather than a global strategy.

[23] The IPLytics database, which we utilized in this study, does not distinguish between litigation in judicial proceedings and validity challenges at patent offices and other administrative

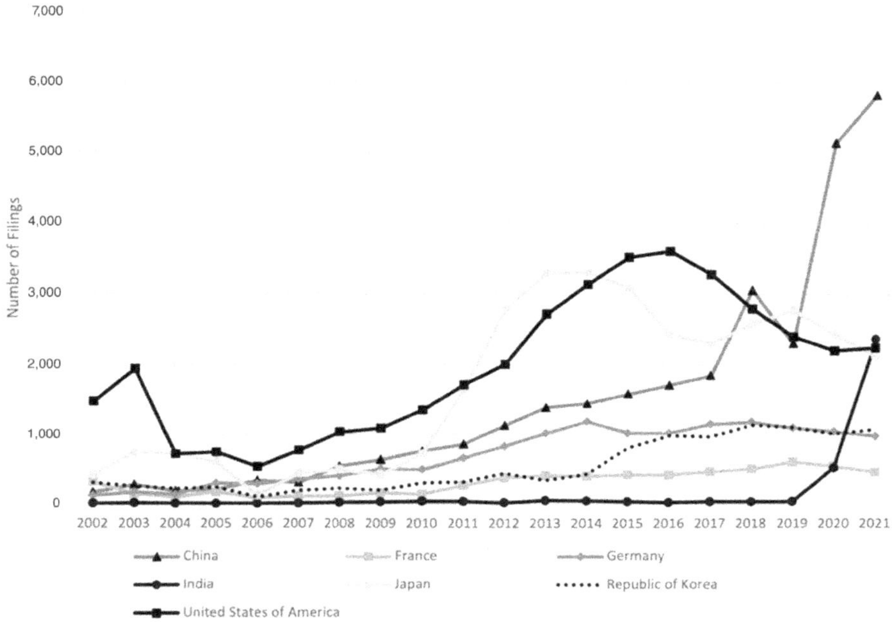

FIGURE 2.6 Non-domestic filings by residents of top-filing countries (WIPO 2023d)

arbitration proceedings. As shown in Table 2.2, litigated utility models can be found across a wide range of jurisdictions, from large, developed economies to small and developing ones.

Consistent with its position as the leading jurisdiction in terms of overall utility model filings, China is also the site of the greatest number of utility models subject to litigation (69.5 percent). This being said, this share is significantly lower than China's share of overall utility model filings during this period (95.6 percent). As such, China appears to have a somewhat lower rate of litigation than other jurisdictions.

Other jurisdictions in which large numbers of utility models are filed (i.e., Germany, Japan, Russia, Korea) also lead the rankings for litigated utility models. Nevertheless, there is a "long tail" of jurisdictions in which utility models are litigated but relatively few utility models have been issued. For example, Finland, with 79 litigated utility models, ranks 13th in terms of litigated utility models, but only 23rd in terms of overall utility model filing during the period. Moreover, some

tribunals. Moreover, some jurisdictions whose sub-patent systems are referred to by names other than "utility models," such as the now-discontinued "registration patents" in the Netherlands, are not identified by IPLytics as utility models, even though such rights may have been subject to significant litigation activity.

TABLE 2.2 *Jurisdictions where utility models were litigated, 2000–2022*

Jurisdiction	Litigated utility models	Jurisdiction	Litigated utility models
China	21,018	Peru	22
Germany	2,589	Chile	21
Japan	1,377	Austria	14
Russia	1,292	Bulgaria	14
Taiwan	1,213	Colombia	13
Korea	911	Hungary	11
Brazil	512	Australia	6
Turkey	341	France	6
Czech Rep.	257	Philippines	4
Spain	249	Costa Rica	4
Italy	101	Estonia	4
Poland	97	Argentina	3
Finland	79	Romania	2
Denmark	36	Greece	1
Slovakia	36	Moldova	1
Ukraine	25	Portugal	1

jurisdictions that rank fairly high in terms of utility model issuance (e.g., Australia, France, Philippines) have very little utility model litigation, and Thailand, Mexico and Hong Kong, which ranked 11th, 17th, 19th, respectively, in terms of utility model issuances during the period, had no reported utility model litigation during the period.

A wide range of parties have been involved in utility model litigation, with no individual party holding more than 0.2 percent of total utility models subject to litigation (either as the plaintiff or defendant). Of the twenty firms holding the largest number of utility models subject to litigation from 2000 to 2022 (ranging from 22 to 63 utility models), three were Taiwanese and seventeen were Chinese. Even among the top 50 holders of litigated utility models, the large majority were Chinese (including Segway, the former US manufacturer of personal mobility devices, now a Chinese-held firm), along with a handful of Taiwanese and Japanese firms.

PART I

Utility Model Laws and Practices around the World

3

The Rise and Fall of the United Kingdom's Forgotten Utility Model

The Utility Designs Act 1843

Lionel Bently and Brad Sherman

As discussed throughout this volume, utility models are a form of intellectual property law that offer protection for 'minor inventions' through a regime similar to the patent system.[1] The German *gebrauchsmuster*, introduced in the 1891 Utility Models Act, is widely regarded as the prototype for such second-tier protection.[2] Indeed, Hausser (1987) said that 'the utility model, as an industrial property right, was "invented" in Germany'.[3] Utility models have also been seen as foreign to the United Kingdom. The Department of Trade and Industry's Green Paper on *Reform of the Law relating to Copyright, Designs and Performers' Protection* (1981), a follow up to the Whitford review of the British law of copyright and designs, declared that the United Kingdom has 'set its face' against such a scheme.[4] In this chapter, we argue that while it has often been suggested that utility models are a product of late nineteenth-century German thinking and that they are foreign to the United Kingdom, utility model protection was first introduced to the United Kingdom in the Utility Designs Act 1843.[5] As such, it is clear that utility model protection has a long-established (albeit somewhat tarnished) pedigree in British law and that utility model protection came into force in the United Kingdom some fifty years before its German counterpart. In this chapter we highlight the key features of the Utility Designs Act 1843, the way the Act was received, and speculate on the reasons why the Act was forgotten.

1 Turner 2019.
2 On the German *gebrauchsmuster*, see Chapter 6. See also Isay 1932; Stringham 1935; Mott 1963; Vossius and Hallman 1985, 129–168; Hausser 1987, 314; Kretschmer 1987, 780; Liesegang 1992; Grosse Ruse-Khan 2012, 38–46; Königer 2017.
3 Mott 1963 233; Hausser 1987; Segade 2008, 135; Grosse Ruse-Khan 2012, 38.
4 Segade 2008, 135.
5 6 & 7 Vict., c. 65. This has occasionally been recognised. *See e.g.*, Ladas 1975, 949 (Great Britain may have been the first); Chen 1983; Weston 1983, 372, [15]; Llewellyn 1996, 3, n. 14.

3.1 THE BACKGROUND TO THE UTILITY DESIGNS ACT

In the early part of the nineteenth century, patent law in the United Kingdom, which was a blend of custom, prerogative, statute law and judicial intervention, was a mess. As the 1829 Select Committee investigation revealed, there was uncertainty over what was protectable, over the nature and function of specifications, and of the role of claims and drawings.[6] Moreover, the system for the administration of patents that existed at the time was complex: in order to obtain a patent for the whole of the United Kingdom, patent applications had to be lodged in offices in London, Edinburgh and Dublin. In order to obtain an English patent,[7] applicants needed approval from at least eight offices.[8] The upshot of this was that the procedure for the grant of patents was both time-consuming and costly. As the *Report on the Signet* concluded in 1849, 'the number of successive stages through which a patent for a new invention must pass before its final completion is productive of great trouble, delay and expense to the party seeking the grant, without any corresponding benefit to the public'.[9] Furthermore, it was very difficult to ascertain the nature of pre-existing patents because existing patent specifications were (until January 1, 1849) deposited in any of three offices (Rolls, Petty Bag and Enrolment) so all three had to be searched in order to ascertain whether an applicant's invention was new and therefore whether any resulting patent would be valid.[10] The complex nature of patent administration not only meant that it was very difficult to ascertain the nature of pre-existing patents,[11] it also had knock-on effects for the cost of a patent, which in the 1830s might be as much as £250 or £300.[12] One commentator, using the soubriquet 'Vindicator', bemoaned in 1835 the 'exorbitant fees demanded, paid to and received by certain automatons who represent certain antiquated bags and things, whose vested interests are deemed sacred'.[13]

If obtaining patents was problematic, so too was their enforcement, which could be very expensive and time consuming.[14] Although interim injunctions were readily granted in relation to patents that had subsisted for some time,[15] infringement was

6 Report from the Select Committee on the Law Relative to Patents for Inventions (1829) 3 PP.

7 Bottomley 2014b.

8 SCLPI 1829, 48–49 (Francis Abbott); Report on Signet 1849, ix; MacLeod 1988, 76; Bottomley 2014a, esp. 36–39 (detailing the 10 stages), 40–41 (describing stages for Scotland and Ireland). A popular account was provided by Dickens (1850, 73–75).

9 Report on Signet 1849, ix.

10 Following the Act to regulate certain Offices in the Petty Bag (1848) specifications were enrolled at the Enrolment Office of the Court of Chancery. Prior to that, most specifications were entered at the Rolls Chapel.

11 But cf. Bottomley 2019 (highlighting the wide dissemination of patents through journals).

12 Bottomley 2014b, 61; 2014a, 61–62 (putting cost at £145 for England, £90 for Scotland and £145 for Ireland).

13 Vindicator 1835.

14 Hindmarch 1851, 1–2 (summarising three problems of procedure, cost and enforcement).

15 Bottomley 2014a, 127–130.

determined through proceedings at law, which required a trial (at so-called 'nisi prius') and was then usually subject to legal review by the relevant court (Common Pleas, Exchequer or Queen's Bench) sitting in full (with the possibility of further trials and further reviews). However, to obtain relevant evidence, proceedings first had to be commenced in Chancery seeking 'discovery'. Writing to the *Morning Chronicle*, Cornelius Ward (a woodwind instrument maker who had patented a drum and a flute) cited a situation where a patentee decided against litigating 'for fear of the direful expense and hopeless chicanery of law'.[16] And at a meeting of the Inventors Patent Law Reform League early in 1851, the chairman reported an instance of litigation over a patent for military drums that had lasted for five and a half years at an expense of £7,000.[17]

A second significant aspect of the intellectual property landscape was the early system of protection for designs.[18] In the late 1780s, protection was provided by Parliament to the designers of patterns for printed calicos, linens, cottons and muslins.[19] While this protection was initially limited to two months, in 1794 it was extended to three months.[20] By the 1820s and 1830s, calls were made for extension of these laws to cover a wider array of designs and for the lengthening of the term of protection. In the 1830s this movement for reform was linked to arguments for reform of the law and administration of letters patent, through proposals for the introduction of laws of 'art and manufacture'.[21] While it ultimately proved impossible to obtain any real reform of patents, the push for the protection of designs bore fruit in the form of the Design Registration Act 1839,[22] which provided up to three years protection, on registration, to designers of the shape and configuration of any article of manufacture.

While the 1839 Design Registration Act brought about a number of significant changes, it was soon replaced by two new Acts. The first was the Ornamental Designs Act 1842, which gave protection to designs for purpose of ornamenting any article of manufacture.[23] The other Act, which was passed the following year, was referred to variously as the Utility Designs Act, the Non-Ornamental Designs Act, the Utility Registration Act, the Configuration Act, the Registration Act, and (perhaps facetiously) 'the Useful Act'.

16 Ward 1850; Anon 1850e, 5 (editorial) (costs of litigation). Ward had obtained an injunction from the Vice-Chancellor in 1843 to restrain Thomas Key from infringing the drum patent, but at the trial in 1847, Cresswell J. instructed the jury to find there had been no infringement. On the cost of litigation in courts of law in this period, see Polden 1999, 8.

17 Anon 1851b.

18 Bently 2018, 177–183.

19 27 Geo. 3, c.23 (1787).

20 34 Geo. 3, c.24 (1794).

21 Sherman and Bently 1999, 104–105.

22 2 Vict., c.17 (1839).

23 5 & 6 Vict., c.100 (1842).

The main impetus for reform was that the designers of patterns for cloth printing, previously protected automatically under the Calico Printers Acts, decided that they were prepared to accept registration as the quid pro quo for extension of the term of protection from 3 months to 9 months.[24] At the same time, the Registrar of Designs, F. B. Long, took the opportunity to rectify problems in the operation of the 1839 Registration Act.[25] The vague language of that Act, which *The London Journal of Arts and Sciences* described as 'an undigested chaos of confusion, inutility and obscurity'[26] had led to the registration of many designs for objects of utility (some of which were enforced successfully, as in *Grassby v Westerdale* (Patrington petty sessions 1842),[27] while others were treated as invalidly registered: *Evans v Harlow* (Stockport Borough Court 1843)). In response, the Registrar recommended that the Board of Trade remove the incentives to register such shapes as ornamental designs by establishing a separate regime. The Board of Trade did this through the Utility Designs Act.[28]

The Utility Designs Act 1843 (UDA) protected 'any new or original Design for any Article of Manufacture having reference to some purpose of Utility, so far as such design shall be for the Shape or Configuration of such Article'. Protection under the Utility Designs Act 1843 (as under the 1839 and 1842 Acts) required application to the Design Registry and, once granted, lasted for three years. The application was required to include a title, two drawings of the design, and such description in writing as was thought necessary to render the same intelligible.[29] According to the rules, the description was required (i) to indicate the useful purpose; (ii) distinguish the several parts of the design by reference to letters, figures or colours; and (iii) indicate which parts were not new and original.[30] The drawings were to be no more than 24 inches by 15 inches and 'on a proper geometric scale' (UDA 1843, s. 8). The price of registration was £10.[31] Importantly, and in contrast to the Ornamental Design Act 1842, registrations were – like patent specifications – open

[24] Sherman and Bently 1999, 63–73, 77–79.

[25] On this, see Report of Registrar of Designs to the Board of Trade (November 3, 1841); First Report 1853.

[26] Anon 1840.

[27] The only report, in the *Mechanics Magazine*, incorrectly identifies the defendant as 'John Westerdale Owthorne' but it was John Westerdale, a wheelwright, of Owthorne.

[28] Anon 1850h, 144; Sherman and Bently 1999, 79–85.

[29] UDA, s. 8. Even greater flexibility was added by the 1850 Act, s. 11 (according to which the registrar could dispense with drawings and accept a written specification) and Copyright of Designs Act 1858, s.5 (allowing submission of portion of an article of manufacture). *The Practical Mechanic's Journal* called the former 'an utter absurdity': Anon 1850c, 159.

[30] First Report 1853, 485; UDA, s. 8.

[31] Johnston Committee 1962, 127. For criticism of this as too high, see Grafton 1846. From 1851, provisional registration for 1 year was permissible at a cost of a mere 10 shillings. See First Report 1853, 487–488.

to the public,[32] and the titles of all the registered useful designs were widely circulated.[33] However, copying of the designs was not permitted until the rights had expired.[34]

The scope of the new right was defined and its enforcement regulated by reference to the Ornamental Designs Act.[35] This meant that the right was infringed by applying 'any such design, or any fraudulent imitation thereof for the purpose of sale, to ... any article of manufacture, or any substance' or publishing, selling or exposing for sale any such article or substance to which the design had been applied, knowing that consent had not been given to such application. In addition to proceedings for damages, and in Chancery for an injunction, remedies included the recovery of penalties of £5–£30 per offence (though not to exceed £100 per person per design), as well as costs, by way of an action for debt, an action on the case, or by way of summary proceedings before two magistrates.[36] Fifteen years later, the county court was also explicitly given jurisdiction to hear cases and award damages.[37]

3.2 RECEPTION OF THE UTILITY DESIGNS ACT

The Utility Designs Act 1843 received a mixed reception. While some commentators welcomed the new regime, others, who complained that the Act was anything but transparent,[38] likened it to an attempt to present a picture to one ignorant of anatomy by using 'dry bones'.[39] Beyond these criticisms of the nature and form of the Act, a more serious dispute arose as to the relationship of the utility design system to the patent system: a matter over which the 1843 statute said nothing. The question of the relationship between the two legal regimes, which became more heated as the Utility Designs Act increased in popularity,[40] was played out in tracts, textbooks and in such specialist periodicals as the *London Journal of Arts and Sciences*, the *Repertory of Patent Inventions*, and the *Mechanics' Magazine*. While views on this matter varied somewhat, they fell into two general approaches.

On one hand, commentators such as Alexander Prince, Joseph C. Robertson (Editor of the *Mechanics' Magazine*) and Thomas Turner (barrister and legal

32 UDA, s. 10.

33 First Report, 509 ff (list to December 31, 1853).

34 That said, some of the registrations, with images, were published in journals such as the *Patent Journal and Inventors' Magazine* under the title 'specifications of articles registered': (1846) 1, 438–439; (1846–1847) 2, 910–911.

35 UDA 1843, s. 6.

36 ODA 1842, s. 8 (penalties), ss. 12–13 (costs).

37 Copyright of Designs Act 1858, s. 8.

38 Anon 1843a, 143–147; S.Y. 1844a, b; Webster 1851, 82; First Report 1853 in (1854) 28 PP 269, 463, App. N.

39 Anon 1847c; Anon 1847e, 368.

40 By 1850 the number of registrations had risen to 476 per annum, which was much the same as the annual number of patent grants.

commentator) took the view that the Utility Designs Act and the patent system were alternative ways of protecting mechanical devices. Under this view, applicants could elect between the protection offered by the Utility Designs Act, which cost £10 for three years of protection throughout the whole nation and the patent system, which cost £300 but lasted for the longer term of 14 years. As the *Mechanics' Magazine* explained:

> We look upon it as a real boon conferred on the Genius and Industry of the people – as their Act of Emancipation from much, if not the whole, of that enormous load of oppression, which our wretched and monstrously expensive system of patent law has for ages imposed on them it is, in truth, an Act for the Protection of New Inventions of all classes and degrees (with a very few exceptions), those of the higher as well as those of least value; an Act, the benefit of which will be felt, and we doubt not, gratefully recognised in every workshop and every working nook of the United Kingdom. It is, in a word, AN ACT FOR MAKING PATENTS CHEAP.[41]

Other commentators such as William Carpmael (patent agent), William Spence (patent agent) William Hindmarch (barrister) and Thomas Webster (1811–1875, barrister and from 1865 QC) took a different view, arguing that the subject matter of each system was essentially distinct. In particular, they suggested that the Utility Designs Act merely protected the form of an article, whereas patent law protected the 'principle' by which an invention worked, that is, its 'function'.[42]

The divergence of opinion played an important role in the way the Utility Designs Act was perceived, utilised and evaluated. For example, the way the Act was interpreted influenced the way its success was measured. For those who took the view that the Act was 'an act to make patents cheap', its success was judged in terms of whether it offered a speedy, simple and cheap system of registration: irrespective of what was actually registered. As such they welcomed the registration of table lamps, ball cocks, heel tips, screw wrenches, sash fastenings, weft distenders, light reflectors and pneumatic life preservers which occurred in the first month of the Act's operation.[43] For those who took the view that the Utility Designs Act merely protected the form of objects, most of these registrations were thought to be mistaken and worthless.[44] Carpmael called the Act 'a perfect curse' that had

[41] Anon 1843b, 164; Billing and Prince 1845.

[42] Spence 1847b, 11; Hindmarch 1851, 25. Yet others took a middling position, arguing that 'some inventions' could be protected under either regime, but quite how many was less clear. Anon 1847e, 367 (William Newton); Report on the Signet 1849, 63, Q. 1118 (evidence of William Newton); SCPB 1851, Q. 1103 (Alfred Newton) (suggesting that a great many inventions fell into the overlap); Anon 1848b, 276–277 (critiquing Spence's narrow view); Anon 1851d (William Johnson, a Glasgow patent agent, critiquing Carpmael's narrow view).

[43] Anon 1843c. The representations can be found at TNA: BT 45/1.

[44] Hindmarch 1846, 25; Spence 1847a, 16.

produced 'most pernicious results.'[45] According to Webster, registration was tantamount to robbery.[46]

3.2.1 *The Nature of the Conflict*

At one level, the conflict over the appropriate scope of what ought to be registered under the 1843 Act was expressed in two different though related ways. The first turned on the notions of 'form' and 'principle'. For the proponents of the narrow view, the scope of the Utility Designs Act was confined to the outward or visible form of the object registered. It was said that form only extended to encompass principle – which was taken as the primary concern of patents – in the very limited circumstance where the form of the article happened to be the only shape that could be used to perform the function in question. This meant, for example, that while the Utility Design Act could protect the form of the stem or oil vessel of a table lamp, it could not protect any new way of raising the wick in the lamp or supplying the lamp with air.[47] Given the belief that utility model protection was limited to the visible exterior form of objects while patent protection extended to principles, and that form and principle were readily separable, those who favoured the narrow view were able to deny that there was any real overlap between the two systems of protection.[48] In contrast, the proponents of the broad view of the Utility Designs Act took a different view of the 'form/function' dichotomy. For these commentators, the divergence between form and principle was much less clear. As Robertson, writing in the *Mechanics' Magazine*, explained:

> We really see it as a matter of some difficulty to imagine any cases of mechanical improvement which will not come within the exceedingly comprehensive terms of this Act. Such an invention as Watt's great discovery of condensing in a separate cylinder might possibly fall without the line; but the direct-setting engine, the oscillating engine, and a score of others of the like character, would as undoubtedly fall within it. All paddle-wheels, and all stern-propellors would be most clearly included. So would all agricultural machines; all railway bars, chairs, sleepers etc; all wood pavements. In short, mere processes only, and such chiefly as are of chemical description, will be excluded.

Arguing that every principle presumed some understanding of form, it was said that the two concepts were inseparable. Or, as Turner said, 'you cannot have principle without special form, more than you can have respiration without lungs'.[49]

[45] SCPI 1851, Q. 191, p. 30 (evidence of Carpmael).

[46] SCPB 1851, Q.105, p. 26 (evidence of T. Webster); Webster 1851, iii–v.

[47] Carpmael 1846, 4–5.

[48] Spence 1851, iv–vi.

[49] Turner 1849, 63. See also Civis 1845 ('every variation of shape resolves itself into some sort of mechanical action or effect'); Liverpool Financial Reform Association 1851, 8 ('form, in many cases, embraces a principle of action.')

The second issue that distinguished the conflicting views of the Utility Design Act related to the way the design was represented. More specifically, it turned on a difference of opinion over how the visual and textual elements of the design registration were construed and the relative weight that each played in determining the scope of the property protected. It is important to recall that when registering a design, applicants were required to include three things: a title, two drawings of the design which were to be no more than 24 inches by 15 inches and on a 'proper geometric scale', and such description in writing as was thought necessary to render the same intelligible. In practice, the representations varied, with many (especially those prepared by registration agents) including lengthy written explanations of the drawings. For example, Registration Number 9, for an improved ball cock (Figure 3.1) (which had been drafted by Joseph Robertson) included two figures and the following description:

> Fig. 1 is an external view of the ball cock. Fig. 2 is a sectional view. A is the water supply pipe. B is the ball cock which is connected to the supply pipe by means of a spur C and hinge D . . .
>
> CLAIM
>
> The parts of the said design which are not new or original are the branch A of the supply pipe and the ballcock B. The parts claimed as new are FIRST the spur C and hinge D by which the ballcock B is attached to the branch A of the supply pipe and SECOND the branch A2 of the supply pipe with the valve box F and Valve G attached thereto.[50]

When proponents of the narrow construction of the 1843 Act spoke of the outward form of objects, they meant the visible form which was represented in the drawings of the design. In this situation visual representation was assumed to have two characteristics: first, it was believed that drawings were capable of being appreciated and understood by any viewer; there was no specific knowledge or skill required to interpret the visual element of the design application. Secondly, the drawing or visual representation operated to confine protection to the detailed specific embodiment that was found in the registration. In this context, the textual features of a utility design application, which the Act required applicants to submit in order to render the drawing intelligible, were seen to perform the limited role of enabling the new and old elements of the shape to be differentiated: the text played no role whatsoever in understanding the drawing and thus determining the property protected. In contrast, these commentators believed that patents captured the essence of the invention – the principle – through the medium of text, that is, the patent specification: a document which was interpreted from the standpoint of the

[50] TNA: BT 45/1/9.

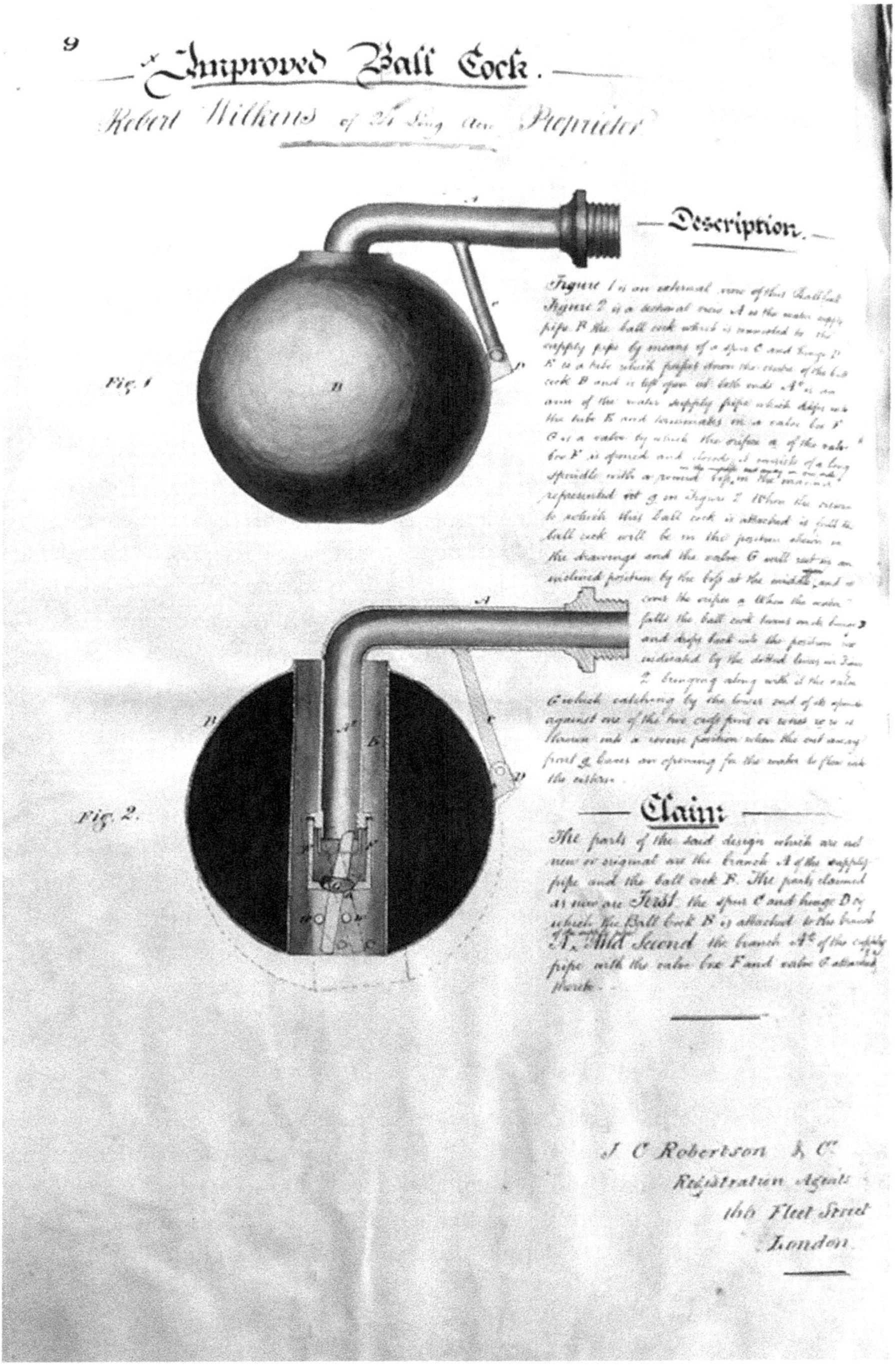

FIGURE 3.1 Improved ball cock, registered on September 9, 1843, by Robert Wilkins (with J. C. Robertson and Co as registration agent): BT 45/1/9

community skilled in the art and in such a way that the protection encompassed multiple embodiments.

While those who favoured a narrow reading of the 1843 Act prioritised the visual representation of the design over its textual supplements, opponents of this approach took a more open view of the relationship between the visual and the textual. Moreover, for this group the roles of the divergent techniques of representation – visual and textual – were by no means as fixed as the proponents of the narrow view made out. That is, they did not think that there was a single, universal relationship between text and image. Instead, they were able to imagine diverse ways in which text and image might interact in identifying an intangible object or subject matter of rights.

Proponents of the more expansive view of the 1843 Act differed from those who construed it more narrowly in two more specific ways. First, some of those who favoured a more open interpretation of the 1843 Act argued that visual representation was not as confined, specific and limiting as had been suggested. Importantly, this meant that the protection offered to registered designs extended to include geometrically different shapes which were functionally equivalent. This more expansive understanding of visual interpretation was based on the idea that visual representations did not require universal understanding. Rather, the visual representations were to be interpreted by a skilled community, a community which would understand the essential rather than the accidental shape of the article.[51] As one commentator observed,

> [T]he essential and important shape and configuration of an article of utility is not by any means necessarily outward and manifest, but may be such as can only be carefully appreciated by persons conversant with articles of its class . . .

In addition, based on the idea that 'a word gives the essential principle of a shape',[52] it was also suggested that while visual images were capable of being interpreted in different ways, the text which was attached to the drawings informed the way the image could be construed. Specifically, it was argued that the text tied down the meaning of the visual image, allowing the image to constitute the basic representation of even functional attributes of the protected design.[53]

3.2.2 *How Are We to Understand This Conflict of Views?*

In part, the conflict that took place over how the Utility Designs Act was to be construed can be traced to the fact that different groups had different understandings of how the image–text relationship was understood. In this sense, the experiences of the Utility Design Act are consistent with the view that the relationship between the visual and the textual is not determined by some universal truth: either system of

[51] S.Y. 1844a, b.
[52] Turner 1849, 63.
[53] Cf. Barthes 1977a, 25; 1977b, 39.

representation is interchangeable, though equally in a specific context each could be mutually exclusive.[54]

While it is clear that the social environment of the mid-nineteenth century was capable of sustaining different understandings of how the image–text relationship was to be understood, this leaves open the more difficult question: how are we to make sense of the differences which took place at the time? Although at a general level the specificity of the image–text inter-relationship can be explained as a site where political, institutional, economic and social antagonisms played themselves out,[55] there are a number of more specific explanations for the differences.

3.2.2.1 Interests

One way to see the differences over techniques of representation and their interpretation is as a battle for money and power between two distinct groups: established patent agents who promoted a narrow interpretation of the 1843 Act, and a new class of 'registration agents' and aspiring patent agents who advocated for a broad construction of the Act.

ESTABLISHED PATENT AGENTS The parties who developed and peddled a narrow interpretation of the 1843 Act were for the most part established patent agents.[56] Although persons designating themselves as patent agents can be traced to the late eighteenth century,[57] in the 1840s there were only between seven and ten patent agents in London: William Carpmael and Moses Poole (from 1821, operating from 'The Patent Office', 4 Old Square Lincoln's Inn); William Newton (from around 1818, operating from the 'Office for Patents' at 66 Chancery Lane); Joseph Clinton Robertson (from around 1828); Paul Rapsay Hodge (from around 1831); Frederick W. Campin (from 1838, at 156 Strand); William Spence (from 1839); Charles Barlow and Philip Le Capelain; and a few others.[58] While there were no legal barriers preventing a person from calling themself a patent agent, it was difficult at this time to establish a profitable foothold. As a result a number of those who described themselves as patent agents were subject to bankruptcy proceedings.[59] In response to the difficulties, many 'patent agents' combined their patent work with other

54 Mitchell 1984, 5; Crary 1990, 6.

55 Mitchell 1986.

56 See generally Dutton 1984, ch. 5; Van Zyl Smit 1985.

57 For example, James Poole (father of Moses): Dutton 1984, 86; Bottomley 2014a, 67–68; Murfitt 2017, 85.

58 Report on Signet 1849, 15, Q. 368 (Campin) (suggesting 10 patent agents in 1848); Robertson in Report on Signet 1849, 70, Q. 1242 (Robertson); SCPB 1851, 83, Q. 475 (Hodge); Anon 1846a (indicating 14 patent agents in London); Anon 1850d; Turner 1851, 98; Newton 1879, ch. 10; Edmunds 1890, v.

59 For example, in 1842, Edwin Twizell Gough of the Strand and George Dellanson Clark; in 1847 George Drysdale Dempsey; and, in both the 1840s and 1850s, Masta Joscelin Cooke. The latter, at least, seems to have been a consequence of failed business ventures.

occupations such as editing journals: Joseph Clinton Robertson was editor of the *Mechanics' Magazine*; Luke Hebert was editor of *Register of Arts and Journal of Patent Inventions*; William Newton was the proprietor and editor of the *London Journal of the Arts and Sciences*; George Dellanson Clark was proprietor of *The Inventors' Advocate*; Charles Barlow and, successively Philip Le Capelain and Edward Haynes, operated the *Patent Journal and Inventors' Magazine*; while William Johnson, a Scottish patent agent, ran the *Practical Mechanics' Journal*. (In fact, in the case of Robertson and Johnson, they were involved in editing their journals before practising as agents).[60] Many of those offering their services as patent agents were solicitors, chemists or civil engineers with other sources of income;[61] others combined acting as agents with the patenting and exploitation of their own inventions.[62]

Amongst the established patent agents, the most vociferous advocate of the narrow interpretation of the 1843 Act was William Carpmael, who was recognised as 'the most eminent and successful agent of the day'[63] and who claimed he had 'half the business'.[64] Carpmael was widely respected: the professor of machinery at University College, Bennet Woodcroft called Carpmael 'a patent agent of great experience and talent'[65] – indeed both had frequently given expert evidence in patent cases. More sceptically, according to the barrister Thomas Turner, Carpmael and Poole looked on themselves as 'licensed gamekeepers of the manor of useful art and the registerers as so many poachers'.[66]

One of the consequences of a utility model regime that was permitted to operate as an alternative to the patent regime would have been to undermine the practices of patent agents. The reason for this was that the esoteric knowledge that was required to navigate a patent through the complex patent system – one of the unique commodities that patent agents purveyed – would have been rendered valueless. As a result, Turner observed, '[p]robably, if it were left to them, they would contract the limits of utility in form till nothing visible were left'.[67]

The suggestion that it was the self-interest of the established patent agents which led them to argue for a narrow reading of the Utility Designs regime is consistent

60 Anon 1866.

61 For example, George Shaw, who would become Birmingham's leading agent, was a chemistry professor at Queen's College medical school: Anon 1904; Benjamin Pickever Wilme, whose career as an agent never took off, was a civil engineer and wrote a handbook on mapmaking; John Yonge was an attorney.

62 For example William Baddeley (d. 1867): Timbs 1868, 281–282.

63 Report on Signet 1849, 51, Q. 901 (barrister Thomas Webster).

64 Report on Signet 1849, 28, Q. 627. This claim is borne out by Bottomley (2014a), 65–66 (calculating relative shares of the business from the Privy Seal account books as Poole & Carpmael (43 per cent), Newton & Co (24 per cent) and Robertson & Co (13 per cent).

65 SCPB 1851, 237, Q. 1687.

66 Turner 1849, 49.

67 Turner 1849, 49.

with their opposition to the reform of the patent system.[68] For example, Carpmael's partner, Moses Poole, told the 1829 Select Committee on Patents that he could not 'see any defect in the present law' of patents – a view which corresponded closely with his interest in maintaining the advantage he had gained from his lengthy experience navigating the system. In the middle of the century, when patent law was variously described as a 'heap of injustice and extravagant persecution',[69] 'a stain upon the character of the nation',[70] and a 'disgrace to the intelligence of the country',[71] Carpmael obdurately maintained the stance that the patent system 'works very well' and that 'the law could not be better than it is'.[72] Although Carpmael repeatedly denied that his views on law were informed by his business interests,[73] when considering the related issue of patent law reform, contemporaries were sceptical that patent agents would be able to offer disinterested advice. Giving evidence to the 1851 Select Committee on bills to amend patent law and practice, Henry Cole explained that the Society of Arts had excluded patent agents from being involved in its reform proposals: 'they were not the parties who had to pay or to suffer; but the parties who gained by the patent system, and lost nothing'.[74]

REGISTRATION AGENTS In contrast, one factor which may have influenced the likes of Alexander Prince and Joseph Robertson, who favoured the broader view, was that they had developed substantial practices acting as agents for registrants (in Robertson's case, in addition to a substantial practice as a patent agent). In fact, Prince played an important role in advocating for what became the 1843 Act itself: he was so aggrieved by the temporary removal of protection at the Design Registry by the 1842 Act that he sent a petition to Board of Trade.[75] This pleaded that the memorialists were aggrieved that applications that would have been registered under the 1839 Act had been rejected by the Designs Office on the ground the applications were not 'strictly and sufficiently ornamental'; despite the fact that there had been no suggestion that the 1842 Act was intended to restrict the scope of registrable designs. Once the Utility Designs Act was up and running, Prince was quick to get involved: as agent, he filed the first two applications, and five out of the first ten. Of the first 100 registrations under the Utility Designs Act, Prince acted as agent for

68 SCLPI 1829, 82 (Moses Poole); see also Carpmael 1832, ch. 8; SCPB 1851, 10, Q.72; Webster 1852, 5 n.(a).

69 Anon 1850b.

70 Brewster 1850.

71 Robertson 1846, 175n. Anon 1850i ('disgraceful to the statute book of a wise and enlightened nation'); Webster 1853, 16 ('vicious' system had 'received the unqualified condemnation of every disinterested person').

72 SCPB 1851, 29 Q 128; 80 Q. 471.

73 SCPI 1851, 10–11, QQ. 72–75.

74 SCPB 1851, 260, Q. 1845.

75 BT/1/413, June 29, 1843 ('The Prince Memorial').

21 of the applicants while Robertson acted for 24.[76] Although we do not know what they charged, these agents obviously had a pecuniary interest in the success of the regime. Other, more traditional patent agents were less involved in registering designs: William Newton had a smaller but steady practice doing so; and William Spence drafted a few applications each year. As far as we have been able to ascertain, the names of the leading patent agents, Carpmael and Poole, do not appear anywhere in the register.[77]

BARRISTERS What about the barristers? Following a rapid expansion in the size of the bar, competition for work was so great that the decade of the Utility Designs Act was widely dubbed 'the hungry forties'.[78] Out of fear that there would be a simultaneous reduction in court business, many barristers opposed procedural reform, such as the establishment of the County Court as a cheap forum for civil litigation (Polden 1999, ch 1). Did the prospect of a cheap tribunal, namely proceedings before magistrates, when compared to lucrative patent proceedings (with long trials, frequently the subject of multiple sets of further proceedings at law and in Chancery, and typically involving larger teams of counsel), affect barristers' attitudes to the Utility Designs Act?

In general, barristers favoured a narrow construction of the scope of the Act. For example, figures such as Thomas Webster and William Hindmarch, who were to become the pre-eminent patent barristers of the middle decades of the century, interpreted the 1843 Act in the same way as Carpmael and Spence.[79] That said, the view of the bar were not unanimous: the Chancery barrister, Thomas Turner,[80] was much more open-minded about the Utility Design Act, offering views that at least took account of those of Robertson and Prince.

Was Webster's stance one of self-interest? By the time of the 1843 Act, Thomas Webster (who had done a degree in mathematics at Cambridge) was a member of

[76] BT 45/1. For Prince, see BT 45/1/1, 2, 4, 5, 8, 14, 15, 20, 25, 33, 41, 46, 47, 55, 62, 65, 71, 76, 79, 92. For Robertson, BT 45/1/9, 10, 16, 17, 19, 26, 29, 31, 32, 37, 38, 42, 44, 45, 48, 52, 54, 63, 64, 84, 86, 95, 99, 100.

[77] Based on browsing BT 45/1–7, 9, 12 and 14. Prince's name disappears by the fifth volume, and the work at 14 Lincoln's Inn Fields was taken over by J. C. Haddan. Prince reappears as an agent in BT 45/12 as Green and Prince 4 Trafalgar Square (e.g. BT 45/12/2317) and very strongly in BT 45/14, though that partnership with Thomas Green was dissolved in September 1852. By contrast, Robertson sustained his position over the first decade as the leading 'agent for registration.'

[78] Anon 1851c; Cocks 1983, 57, 88 (in the decade between 1835 and 1845, the bar expanded from 1,300 to 2,317); Hay and Snyder 1989, 46; Polden 1999, 44; 2010, 1017 ff.

[79] See also Whitworth 1848, 287. Whitworth had no personal interest: he was an equity draftsman and conveyancer.

[80] He appeared in *Sealy v Browne* (Rolls Court 1843) and *Burnett v Smith* (VC 1844).

the common law bar[81] and practiced on the Northern Circuit. Given the industrial centres of the North, Webster was able to specialise in patent cases. In 1844, for example, he was involved in at least three patent trials in Liverpool,[82] five in London,[83] and two 'en banc' hearings consequent upon trials conducted in 1843.[84] Thus, although it is clear that in 1844 Webster had a thriving patent practice, it is doubtful that he would have lost much if any of this business as a result of the Utility Designs Act. In section III we discuss the case law under the Act, including 24 sets of proceedings before magistrates for infringement (see Appendix 1). In most of the cases, both complainant and defendant were legally represented,[85] usually by a barrister, sometimes by two: William Clarkson, a highly regarded criminal barrister,[86] appeared in eight of the eighteen cases where the reports mention counsel; while patent barristers Thomas Webster, Benjamin Rotch and William Hindmarch were counsel in ten of the cases. Webster appeared (usually alone) in seven trials in Utility Design Act design cases between 1843 and 1852,[87] and in one case that was heard in Queen's Bench, *Margetson v Wright*. It is true that the trials were shorter (patent trials were commonly 3–5 days) and the consequential hearings proportionately fewer, but it is probably the case that the low value of the innovations in issue meant that few if any of these disputes would have made it to Chancery for discovery or preliminary relief, let alone to nisi prius for trial.

The magistrate's cases do, however, suggest an explanation for Webster's trenchant critique of the 1843 Act. While, as in patent cases, Webster tended to represent the complainant, in this environment he was generally unsuccessful. Although formally victorious in *Margetson*, the defendant paid the fine and continued to manufacture the products (leading to further unsuccessful proceedings before the Vice-Chancellor and in Queen's Bench). The one Utility Design Act case in which Webster succeeded – *Kennedy v Coombs* – was the only one in which he

81 Despite being a member of the common law bar, Webster appeared in Chancery cases: e.g. before the Lord Chancellor and Master of the Rolls, sitting together in *R v Newton*, May 28, 1845, and the following year in *Rubery v Barr* (VC 1845).

82 *Pow v Taunton and Holt* (nisi prius, Liverpool Assizes 1844); *Bentley v Fleming* (nisi prius, Liverpool Assizes 1844); *Crosskill v Grounsell* (nisi prius, Liverpool Assizes 1844).

83 *Bentley v Carver* (nisi prius, Westminster 1844); *Mangnall v M'Alpine* (nisi prius, Guildhall 1844); *Muntz v Foster* (nisi prius, Westminster 1844); *Woodcroft v Reyner* (nisi prius, Guildhall 1844); *Russell v Ledsam* (nisi prius, Westminster 1844).

84 *Nickels v Haslam* (Common Pleas 1843); *Stead v Williams* (Common Pleas 1844).

85 In *Motte v Lancaster* (Guildhall Police Court 1850), Alderman Challis advised the complainant to seek professional advice in drawing up an information to avoid technical defects that had marred the complaint). Cf. Bentley 1998, 22 (rare for lawyers to be involved in summary cases in general).

86 Anon 1856.

87 *Vine v Johnson* (Worship Street Police Court 1843); *Welch and Margetson v May* (Guildhall Police Court 1844); *Wolferstan v Warner* (Guildhall Police Court 1844); *Kennedy and Asprey v Coombs and Finlay* (Marlborough Street Police Court, London 1845); *Besley and Thorowgood v Gallie* (Guildhall Police Court 1848); *Margetson v Wright* (Guildhall Police Court 1848); *Gregory v Armstrong* (Thames Police Court 1851).

represented the defendant. In Webster's experience, owners of designs rarely won through, whereas, at least in patent trials before juries, patentees nearly always succeeded.[88] No wonder, then, that Webster thought registration worthless.

Giving evidence to the Select Committee on the Protection of Inventors Bill in March 1851, Webster expressed his dissatisfaction with proceedings before magistrates under both the Ornamental Design Act and Utility Design Act (SCPI 1851: 31–32, Q. 201):

> Nothing can be worse than the tribunal; the justices are the great difficulty . . . it is so difficult, that I have in many cases advised parties not to attempt it; and where it has been attempted, there has been a failure, in the majority of cases, from technical objections . . . nothing can be worse than going before the justices.

If Webster's views on the Utility Design Act aligned with his professional interests, they also reflected his experiences as an advocate.

3.2.2.2 Professional Territory

Another way of reading the dispute over the interpretation of the 1843 Act is as a battle over professional territory and reputation. In this context, it is important to remember that patent agents, who were regarded as a 'comparatively recent self-instituted amphibious body (half lawyer half man of science),'[89] occupied an ambiguous and uncertain position (especially as regards the legal profession).[90] Indeed, until July 1, 1889 (when a requirement of registration was introduced by section 1 of the Patent, Designs and Trade Marks Act 1888) anyone could – and many did – set themselves up as 'patent agents'. This was particularly problematic at a time when reform of the system was being considered and reputation was the key to influence.[91] Given their unprotected status, it is unsurprising that established patent agents would turn upon newcomers presenting themselves as 'registration agents' calling them an obscure and motley crowd of incompetent, unprincipled persons – a 'mushroom class'[92] – who hang and prowl round the outskirts of the patent profession.[93] Amongst those charlatans, one who was directly referred to was Alexander Prince – one of the two key registration agents in the early years of the 1843 Act's operation, memorialist to the Board of Trade and co-author of a text

88 In contrast, as another barrister, Matthew Davenport Hill, explained to the Select Committee on the Patent Bills, in patent cases 'verdicts are almost uniformly for the patentee'. SCPB 1851 279, Q. 2001.

89 Anon 1850d, 321.

90 Turner 1850, 98; Anon 1851a, 'Invasion' (patent agency 'an anomalous offshoot' of the legal profession). The Post Office Directory for London for 1847 listed 26 'Patent and Design Registration Agents' including 7 solicitors.

91 Van Zyl Smit 1985, 99.

92 Anon 1850d, 323; 1858b, 486.

93 Anon 1850d. This was to continue as a theme: Cunninghame 1894, Preface.

advocating a broad interpretation of the 1843 Act.[94] Like many, Prince's business was precarious and he faced bankruptcy in 1849, 1858 and again in 1868.[95] In an attempt at self-aggrandisement, the established patent agents suggested that the upstarts who promoted the utility designs system lacked the education, skill and experience necessary to obtain efficiently and securely a patent grant. In the absence of some bar to a man 'taking the cloth',[96] the effect of the introduction of the simple registration machinery would have been to create an opening for these new entrants. Whether or not they really lacked the esoteric knowledge of established patent agents, they would have been able to make a living from representing inventors.[97]

3.2.2.3 Political Motivations

While concerns with finance and reputation go some way towards explaining the differing views over the 1843 Act, they only provide a partial picture. For example, while Robertson's promotion of the utility model system as an alternative to the patent system was motivated in part, by self-interest, he was also fired by a political fervour to support the working class and saw the new system as a way to open up the possibility for all inventors to acquire technological properties. Robertson had established the *Mechanics' Magazine* with Thomas Hodgskin,[98] who has frequently been seen as a 'Ricardian socialist'.[99] In the 1820s, Robertson had been a driving force behind the establishment of the London Mechanics' Institute (Hodgskin 1859; Anon 1859b), an initiative that sought to give mechanical operatives a chance for self-education (Flexnor 2014, 41). Robertson's political drive to remove obstacles facing the working classes to self-betterment, and thus to ensure their due reward for their ingenuity, may have constituted his primary motive for promoting the Utility Design Act as 'an Act for making patents cheap' (or what we would now think of as a utility model regime).

Views about the Utility Designs Act were intertwined with debates about the desirability of reducing the costs of patenting. As already noted, much of the criticism of the existing patent system focussed on the price of patents, with one particular focus being the accessibility of the system for the poor and working classes. For many commentators, it was this group of 'operatives' that were the 'real innovators',[100] and the price of protection needed to be reduced to reward those who really

[94] Billing and Prince 1845.

[95] Anon 1868. In the 1850s Prince went bankrupt with debts of £50,000, having attempted to exploit certain patents including one for imitation leather. See Anon 1858a.

[96] Anon 1850d, 323.

[97] It was objected that they had advertised that patent rights could be obtained for a smaller sum. Carpmael 1846, 14.

[98] Flexnor 2014, 72 ff.

[99] Claeys 2000, but cf. Mingardi 2021, who sees Hodgskin as a working class libertarian.

[100] SCPB 1851, 248, Q. 1782 (Isambard Kingdom Brunel stating that most inventions came from 'practical operatives.')

warranted it. For example, patent agent Paul Hodge favoured cheap patents precisely because 'many inventions among the operatives of this country, who very often are the real inventors, would be encouraged to take out patents'.[101] An Editorial in the *Morning Chronicle* in 1850 bemoaned the fact that the exorbitant price of patents prevented the real inventors from obtaining their due reward.[102]

For others – typically those who opposed the registration of utility designs – protection through exclusive rights was seen as something that ought only to be granted to really meritorious inventions, and price was a way of ensuring that minor inventions were not protected. For example, Carpmael denied that allowing operatives to gain patents or other rights would in practice benefit them: he told one Select Committee that 'a patent to a poor man is generally a curse'.[103] In addition, Carpmael adhered to the view that 'cheap patents would be highly pernicious to the country'.[104] Carpmael worried that reducing the cost of registration would lead to a proliferation of patents, which would in turn increase the difficulties of clearing rights and getting business done. In many respects, his concerns parallel those of recent times in relation to patent thickets, non-practising entities and the so-called 'anti-commons'.[105]

The debate over 'poor inventors' was in turn linked to concerns over the desirability of servants gaining exclusive rights that could affect the master's investments. For Carpmael, opening protection up to 'operatives' was fraught with danger. This was because it was the masters who were the inventors and the Utility Design Act presented an unfortunate mechanism that allowed servants to interfere with their master's 'property'. Most of those debating the Utility Design Act and patent reform would have been aware of cases such as *Haynes v Brown* and *Brown v Wigram*, which concerned a windlass or capstan for use with a ship's anchor, that illustrated the confusion that could arise. Haynes, White and Bevis had been in the service of Thomas Brown when, as Charles White claimed, he was asked to make a windlass for different sizes of chain, and in response he made a model of a capstan which he gave to Brown. Subsequently, White, Haynes and Bevis registered the design under the Utility Design Act (on March 29, 1847), licensed the use of the design to a shipbuilder called Wigram at Blackwall, and brought proceedings in the Guildhall Police Court against their former employer, Brown, for infringement. Brown, who in the meantime (on April 20, 1847) had acquired a patent (it seems after effectively opposing White's own patent application before the Attorney General on around

[101] SCPB 1851, 83, Q. 477. Also 88, Q. 518 (Hodge). See also SCPB 1851, 212, Q. 1493 (Fothergill).

[102] Anon 1850e, 5.

[103] Report on Signet 1849, 31, Q. 693 (Carpmael). For details as to how Carpmael dealt with 'poor inventors', by appraising their contribution and, if meritorious, linking them with capitalists, see SCPI 1851, 26, Q. 185.

[104] SCPB 1851, 30, Q. 137 (Carpmael).

[105] Heller and Eisenberg 1998.

April 8–10),[106] successfully resisted the proceedings for infringement (arguing that the design was not new and unpublished at the date of registration).[107] Brown, in turn, brought an action against Wigram, for infringement of the patent in December 1850, which Wigram defended by relying on the earlier registration by White et al.[108] The two cases were largely determined according to (what some contemporaries regarded as a dubious interpretation of) the substantive questions of publication and novelty, but both courts were made conscious of the master–servant dynamic, in particular the opportunity the Utility Design Act presented for opportunistic registration by aggrieved, disloyal or departing servants.[109]

That said, a number of commentators who took a similar analytical line to Carpmael on the protection afforded by the Utility Design Act diverged from him on the matter of the desirability of cheap patents or something like a utility model regime. Chief amongst these was William Spence, who in publications in 1847 and 1851 argued in parallel with Carpmael that the registration of designs under the Utility Design Act could not afford the protection that registrants hoped for. However, Spence was sympathetic to the idea of what he called 'little patents' (1847b: 11, 1851: iv). As he explained in his evidence to the Select Committee on the Patent Bills in 1851:

> My notion is this, that we require two sorts of patent, a short patent and a long patent. I have all along thought that the Legislature had a good object in view, as I stated in my former evidence, in the Utility Designs Act, but I can only recognise in that an intention in the right direction, and not a purpose carried into effect.[110]

Spence elaborated his ideas further in a letter to Aris's *Birmingham Gazette*.[111] In a similar vein, Webster, though critical of the Utility Design Act, favoured reduction in the cost of patenting. Indeed, giving evidence to the Select Committee on the Protection of Inventors (1851), Webster asserted that the popularity of the Utility Design Act was itself a reason why the price of patents should be reduced.[112]

3.2.2.4 Patent Culture

A final explanation relates to what one might call 'patent culture', that is the assumptions and ways of thinking of the established patent professionals.[113] More

[106] GB 11666 (April 20, 1847) ('Machinery for raising and lowering weights (capstans)'). The specification, enrolled on October 20, 1847 was published in *The Patent Journal and Inventor's Magazine* (October 30, 1847) 524.

[107] *Haynes v Brown* (Guildhall Police Court 1848).

[108] *Brown v Wigram* (Exchequer 1850).

[109] Charles Barlow and Payne, patent agents and the editors of the *Patent Journal and Inventors' Magazine*, were especially critical: Anon 1848a, 335.

[110] SCPB 1851, 139, Q. 867 (Spence).

[111] Anon 1847b, 4.

[112] SCPI 1851, 32, Q. 201.

[113] Cf. Gooday and Wilf 2020.

specifically, the culture with respect to drafting and interpretation of letters patents – the representation of the intangible – made it difficult for patent agents to feel comfortable with the machinery of the Utility Designs Act. While drawings were not required as part of the patent specification, by the 1830s they were commonly used.[114] However, patent practice treated drawings in the specification as playing a secondary role as *illustrations* rather than aids to understanding 'the principle' of the patent.[115] The job of identifying the invention in its full breadth was one for the written description, including claims (which, while not yet required, were increasingly common). In contrast, the drawing was an example, a representation of 'an embodiment', a particular instantiation, or, as one commentor put it, a kind of 'test of the truthfulness' of the description.[116] Such views, when transported unmodified into the Utility Designs system, led to a view that design representation only supported a very limited property (whereas, as we have seen, proponents of broad interpretation of the Utility Design Act treated the textual description as pinning down the open meaning of the representations).[117]

3.3 JUDICIAL AND ADMINISTRATIVE RESPONSES

Although the 1843 Act allowed the Registrar to reject non-ornamental shapes from the register of ornamental designs under the 1842 Act, the Registrar was unable to reject an application from the utility designs register on the ground that the application was properly the subject of a patent.[118] Nevertheless, shortly after the 1843 Act came into force on September 9, 1843, the Registrar issued a noticed stating that no design

> will be registered, the description or statement respecting which shall be suggestive of a claim for any such mechanical action, principle, contrivance or application.[119]

Quite what was the legal basis for this notice (and the practise it purported to foreshadow) is unclear,[120] but the notice was influential. *The London Journal of the Arts and Sciences*, edited by the patent agent William Newton, which had regarded the scope of the Act as ambiguous,[121] narrowed its position in response saying that

[114] Spence 1847a, 72.
[115] Godson 1823, 119; Spence 1847a, 72–73.
[116] Spence 1847a, 72–73.
[117] Turner 1851, 100 ('The description [in a utility design] explains the drawing and defines the points claimed.')
[118] First Report 1853, 481.
[119] Bowen 1843. In other respects, the Registrar left the decision as to what to register entirely to the applicant: Sherman and Bently 1999, 93.
[120] Cf. First Report 1853, 481 (registrar has no power to refuse application as long as rules are complied with). That said, see Anon 1846b, 297–299 (reporting that Registrar had refused to register application as lacking novelty).
[121] Anon 1843a.

interpretation of the Utility Design Act as protecting inventions involved a 'misconception',[122] and after listing the titles of designs registered under the 1843 Act, repeatedly warned readers of the dangers that these registrations were invalid.[123] The Registrar's notice had also emphasised that decision to register was a matter of personal risk for applicants.

As the patent agent William Spence pointed out, the subject matter and scope of protection under the Utility Design Act was not a matter that could be resolved administratively: it turned on the judicial interpretation of the Act. Unfortunately, a clear resolution of the different interpretations was unlikely. This was because proceedings to enforce the rights of registrants could be brought before magistrates and most complainants chose that course. If the Utility Design Act was an act to make patents cheap, and in the absence (until 1846) of a cheap county court,[124] there was a certain logic to their being enforced in the police courts which were thought of by some as a 'poor man's court'.[125]

It was the view of contemporaries that the 1843 Act had not generated a great deal of litigation.[126] In the period between 1843 and October 1852 (when the Patent Law (Amendment) Act 1852 came into operation), there were at least twenty-four sets of proceedings before magistrates for infringement under the Utility Design After Act (see Appendix 1). All but one (*Twigg v Kemp* (Public Office, Birmingham 1848)) were brought in London, including sixteen at the police court in the Guildhall. Just under half of the cases resulted in the defendant being fined – though the convictions in *Motte v Welch* and *Dixon v Bessell* (1850 Guildhall Police Court) were overturned. The fines were mostly £5, often referred to as the 'mitigated penalty' applicable where the accused undertook not to repeat the offence, but in at least one case, *Margetson v Wright*, the defendant made no such undertaking and the penalty (a mere 20 shillings) was insufficient to deter further infringements. Complainants do not seem to have sought to exploit the potential for very significant penalties through cumulation of the fine on a per article basis (up to a maximum of £100).[127]

The issue of the relationship between design and patents was raised in many of the design cases by defendant's counsel. The argument was usually made that the subject-matter for which protection was being sought was properly a matter for the patent regime and thus the registration was invalid. In *Wolferstan v Warner* (Guildhall Police Court 1845), concerning an improved boiler tap (Figure 3.2), William Clarkson argued that

[122] Anon 1843d.
[123] Anon 1843e.
[124] Polden 1999, ch. 1.
[125] Davis 1984, 315. For proposals in the 1830s to use the justices for civil claims, see Hanly 2006, 260.
[126] SCPB, 407.
[127] Anon 1843c.

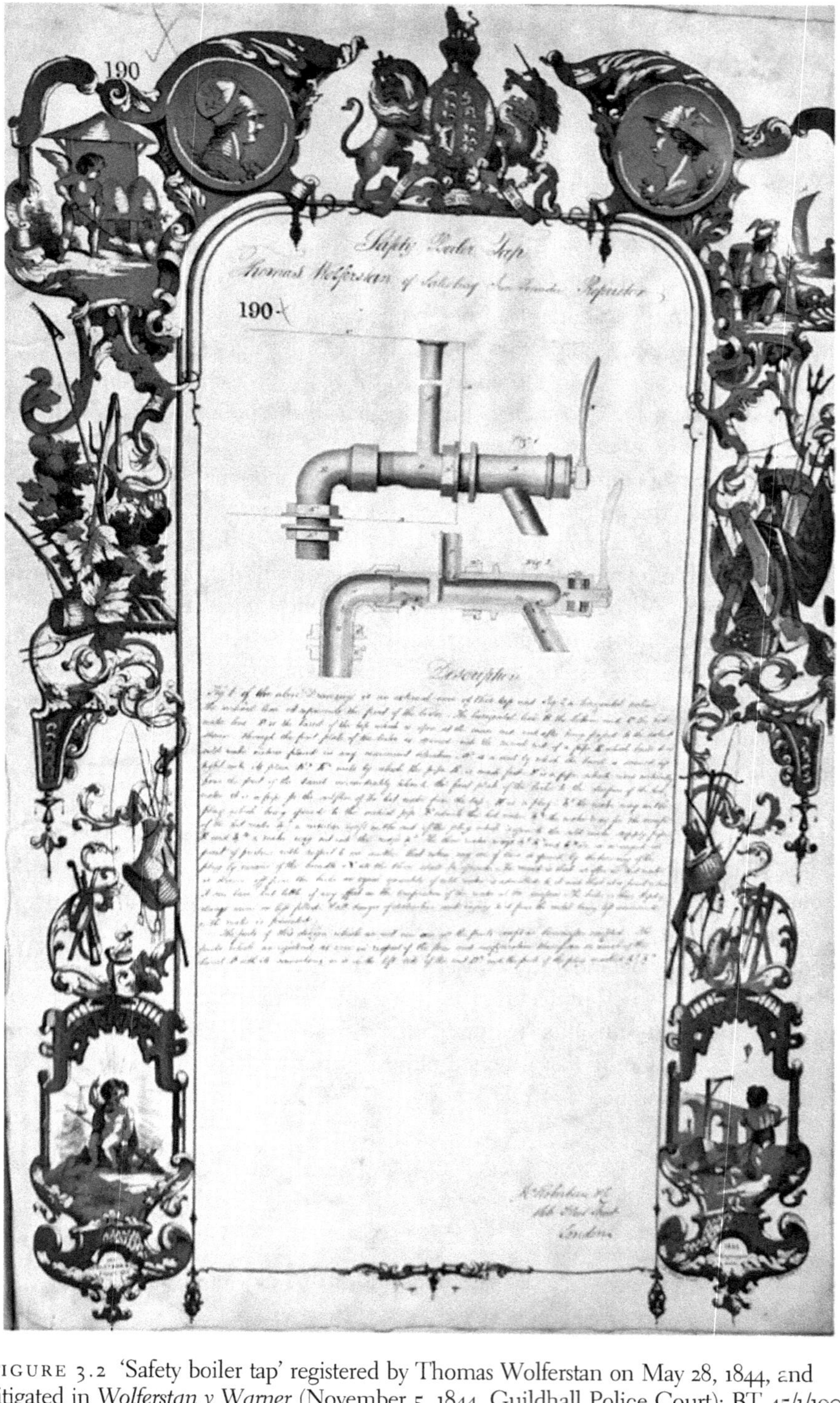

FIGURE 3.2 'Safety boiler tap' registered by Thomas Wolferstan on May 28, 1844, and litigated in *Wolferstan v Warner* (November 5, 1844, Guildhall Police Court): BT 45/1/190

> by endeavouring to evade the expense of taking out a patent at an expense of as many pounds as he had paid shillings for the registration, had overreached himself. The part for which registration had been obtained was a mechanical contrivance, and not a mere change of form or configuration, to which alone that act applied.[128]

The defendant raised other objections (including that the designs were different in important ways, and that the complainant had not marked all the taps sold with the word 'registered' as required by the 1843 Act). Although the magistrate dismissed the summons, the aldermen refused to explain their decision, so it was not clear whether doubts about whether the tap was eligible for protection influenced the decision (and the arguments of counsel were a subject of trenchant criticism in the *Mechanics' Magazine* (1844) 41: 331).

In *Webb v Hughes* (Guildhall Police Court 1847), the claimant's registration (Figure 3.3) related to a tray for storing lace ribbon; the defendant registered (Figure 3.4) and sold an improved version adapted to store more lace.[129] Clarkson, again appearing for the defendant, argued that the 'Act had reference only to matters of form. It was nothing that the same principle or idea was taken, if the form and means were different. Principles were protected by patent law, and mere shape by the registration law'.[130] The argument did not seem to land: the magistrates declined to decide the case, one thinking there was infringement, the other finding that the defendant's design was sufficiently different from Webb's and as such that there was no infringement.[131] In *Haynes v Brown* (Guildhall Police Court 1848), concerning the design of a windlass controller, Benjamin Rotch and William Clarkson argued that as the complainant had themselves applied for a patent, the registration under the Utility Design Act was evidently invalid:

> the whole thing being the proper subject of a patent as a new mechanical action, the registration under an Act which respected only new forms of known articles of utility was a nullity ... the Registration Act did not, and was not intended to supersede the patent law.

The magistrate dismissed the complaint, but on the basis of the absence of novelty of the design (given prior disclosure).

In three cases, the magistrates seem to have taken the broad view of the Act. In *Fox v Evans*, (Guildhall Police Court 1848) the magistrates found infringement of the complainant's 'Alarum for time pieces' (Figure 3.5) because the defendant reproduced the dial, even though the defendant's version had no alarm. The magistrates, Aldermen Finnis and Lawrence, were unmoved by the fact that the clocks involved different mechanical mechanisms. In *Dixon v Bessell* (Guildhall

[128] Anon 1844.
[129] BT 45/5/977, registered on February 25, 1847.
[130] Anon 847a, 383.
[131] Anon 1847d.

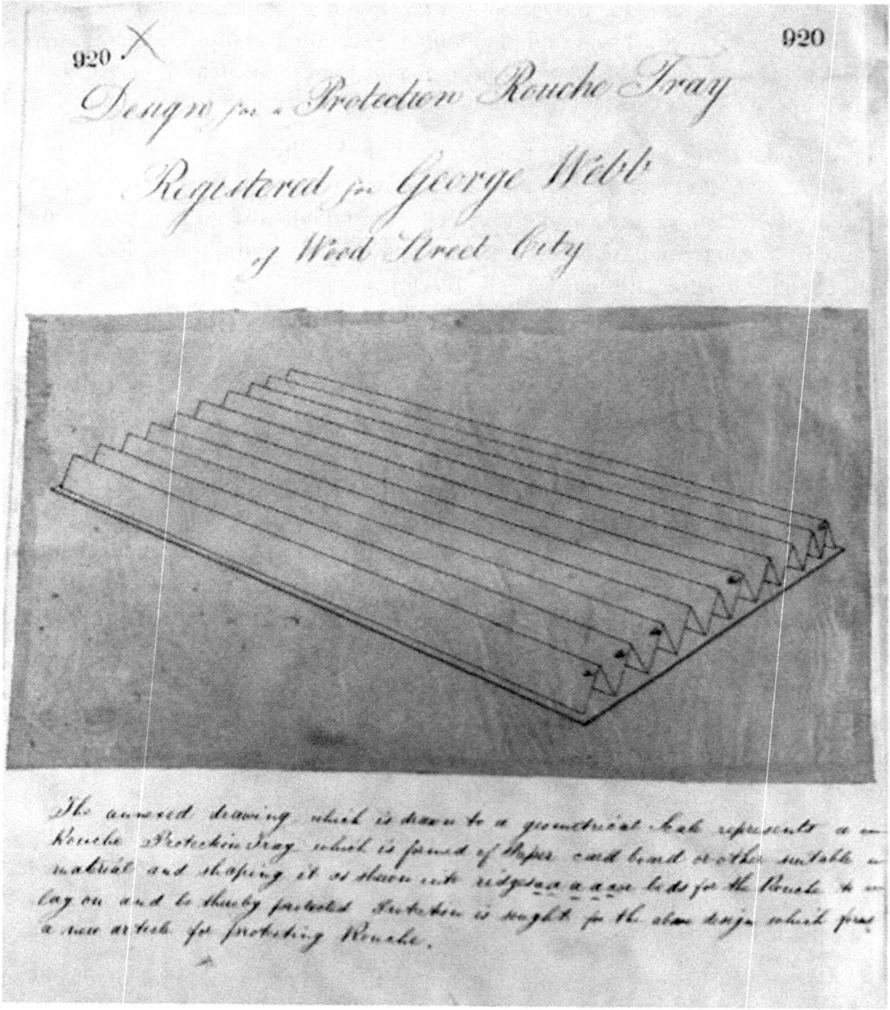

FIGURE 3.3 'Protection rouche tray' registered by George Webb on January 13, 1847, and litigated in *Webb v Hughes* (April 12, 1847, Guildhall Police Court): BT 45/5/920

Police Court 1850), in relation to a ventilator in a window (Figure 3.10), Alderman Wilson expressed the view that Dixon's design was so ingenious that he deserved at least seven years protection and the defendant had engaged in 'bare-faced piracy'. In neither *Fox* nor *Dixon* was the defendant represented by counsel, and likely the tribunal was not exposed to the narrow reading of the Utility Design Act. In contrast, in *Motte v Welch* (Guildhall Police Court 1850), concerning a registered design for an improved portmanteau (Figure 3.6), the defendant's counsel explicitly argued that as the improvements involved the use of rivets rather than sewing and the use of

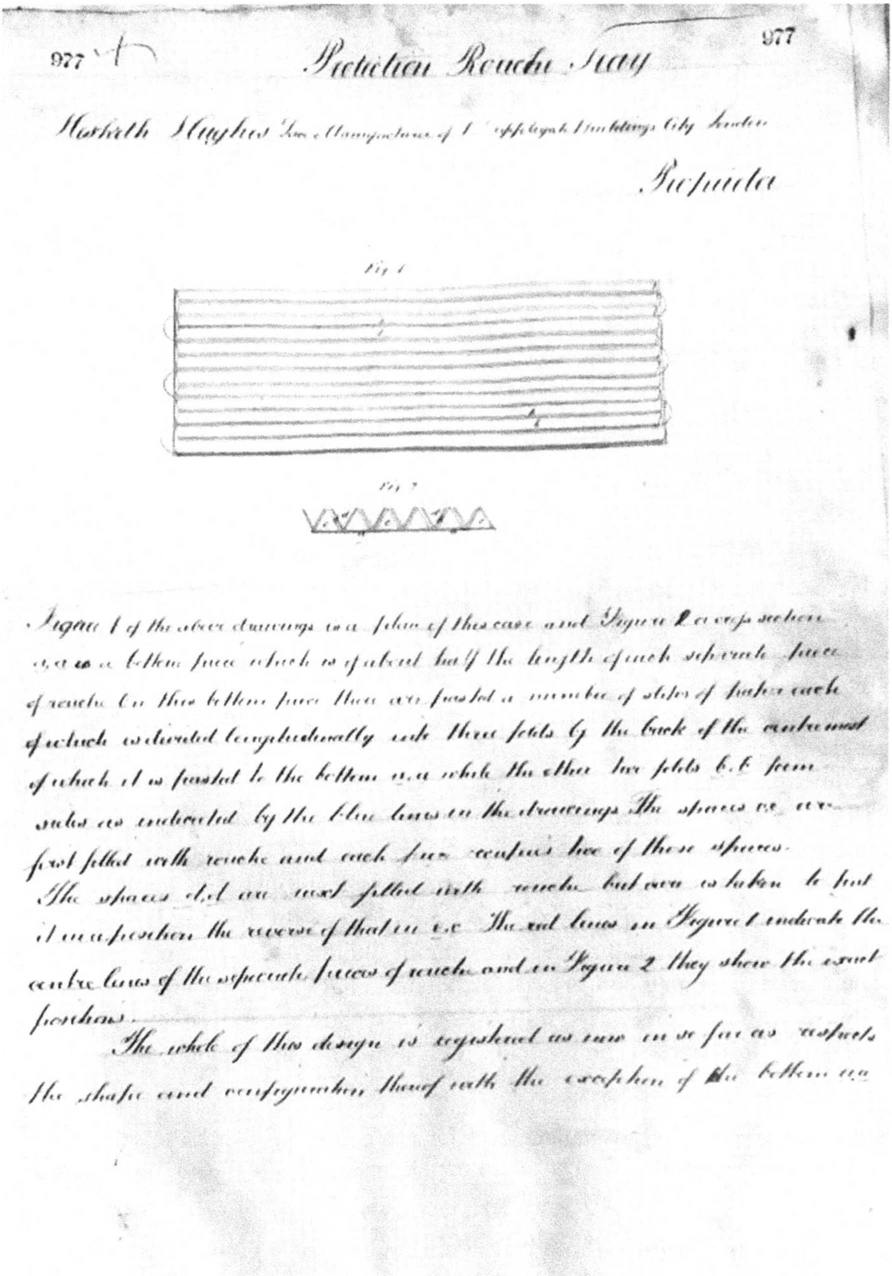

977 977

Protection Rouche Tray

Hosketh Hughes [illegible] Manufacturer of [illegible] City London

Proprietor

Fig 1

Fig 2

Figure 1 of the above drawings is a plan of this case and Figure 2 a cross section a,a,a is a bottom piece which is of about half the length of each separate piece of rouche. On this bottom piece there are fastened a number of slips of paper each of which is divided longitudinally into three folds b the back of the centremost of which it is fastened to the bottom a,a while the other two folds b.b form sides as indicated by the blue lines in the drawings. The spaces c,c are first filled with rouche and each piece confines two of these spaces. The spaces d,d are next filled with rouche but care is taken to put it in a position the reverse of that in c,c. The red lines in Figure 1 indicate the centre lines of the separate pieces of rouche and in Figure 2 they show the exact positions.

The whole of this design is registered as new in so far as respects the shape and configuration thereof with the exception of the bottom a,a

FIGURE 3.4 'Protection rouche tray' registered by Hosketh Hughes on February 25, 1847, and litigated in *Webb v Hughes*: BT 45/5/977

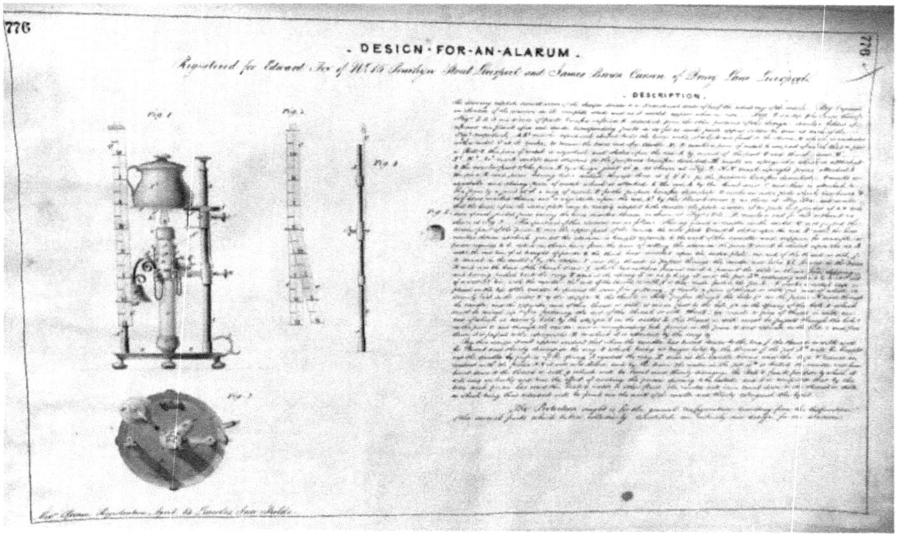

FIGURE 3.5 'Alarum for time pieces' registered by Edward Fox and James Brown on July 25, 1846, and litigated in *Fox v Evans* (May 6, 1848 Guildhall Police Court): BT 45/4/776

one piece of leather, rather than several, there was no new shape and thus no new design. Nevertheless, having heard copious evidence, Alderman Challis found for the registrant.

Sometimes a narrow view of the Utility Design Act clearly motivated the decision of the tribunal. In *Kennedy and Asprey v Coombs and Finlay* (Marlborough Street Police Court 1845), the registration, which was drafted for the complainants by J. C. Robertson & Co, was for 'an improved portable ink and light box for writing desks and travelling cases' (Figure 3.7). The novelty lay in the hinging which enabled the lid of the box to be thrown back without pulling its base from the case. The experienced magistrate, John Hardwick, seems to have accepted Thomas Webster's submission that the novelty was a matter of mechanical contrivance rather than a new design in shape or configuration. Dismissing the information, the magistrate explained:

> The articles are nearly the same, except, for a particular use, there is a slight change of mechanical contrivance. I entertain very strong doubt as to the novelty of design, for the purposes of these proceedings.

In *Woolley v Warner* (Guildhall Police Court 1845), the dismissal of the action also seems to have turned on the view that the registered design was really an invention outside the Utility Design Act. The registration was entitled 'Improvements in the shape and configuration of lamps and apparatus connected therewith for the burning of oil of turpentine, camphine, naptha etc.' (Figure 3.8).

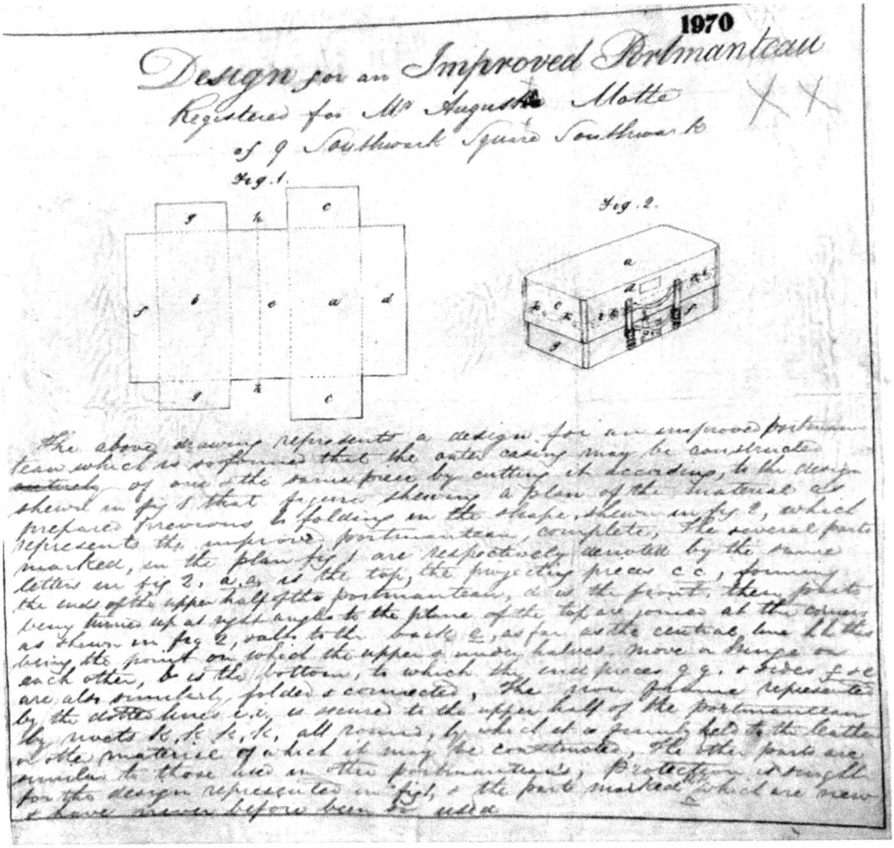

FIGURE 3.6 'Design for an improved portmanteau' registered for Auguste Motte on July 23, 1849, and litigated in *Motte v Welch* (March 30, 1850 Guildhall Police Court) and *Motte v Lancaster* (June 19, 1850 Guildhall Police Court) : BT 45/10/1970

The description identified which of the different components were new and old. In defence, Clarkson argued that 'any new mechanical action must, it is clear, be the subject of a patent'. Benjamin Rotch, counsel for the complainant, responded that he did not admit that. Nevertheless, the information was dismissed. Alderman Hughes Hughes – who, unusually for an alderman, had something of a legal background[132] – said he was satisfied that 'it was a new application of a mechanical action and not a mere alteration of form or configuration', a conclusion with which Alderman Charles Farebrother agreed.[133] The decision received some criticism in

[132] He had been an attorney in the Court of Common Pleas and later a barrister, though it is unclear whether he practiced in the latter capacity: www.historyofparliamentonline.org/volume/1820-1832/member/hughes-hughes-william-1792-1874

[133] Anon 1845.

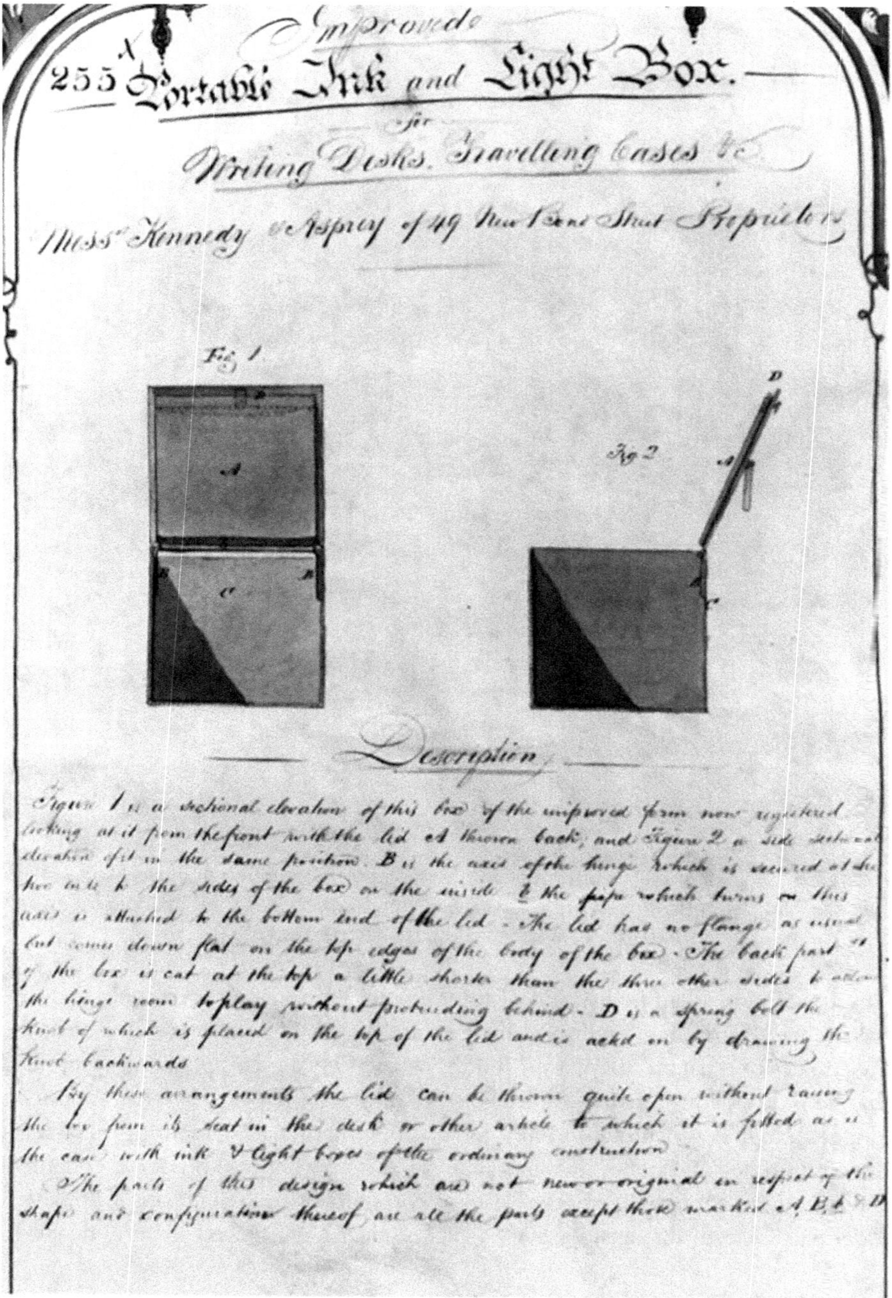

FIGURE 3.7 'Improved portable ink and light box' registered for Francis Kennedy and Charles Asprey on August 27, 1844, and litigated in *Kennedy and Asprey v Coombs and Finlay* (February 15, 1845 Marlborough St Police Court): BT 45/2/255

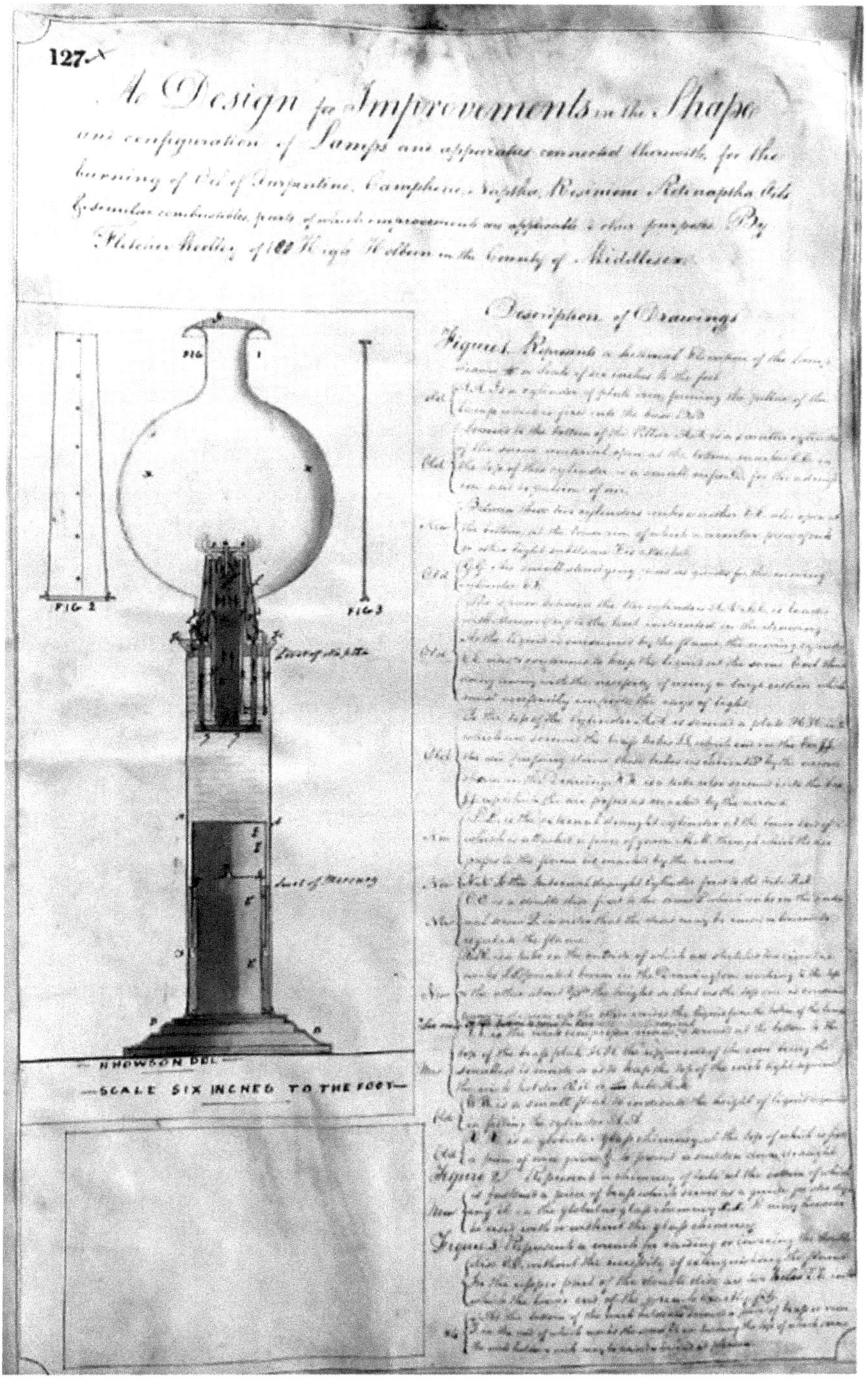

FIGURE 3.8 'Improvement in the shape and configuration of lamps' registered for Fletcher Woolley on February 21, 1844 (and litigated in *Woolley v Warner* (March 22, 1845 Guildhall Police Court): BT 45/1/127

Robertson's *Mechanics' Magazine*, albeit attributed to 'Civis of Gray's Inn Square'.[134] When reflecting on the fact that many of the prosecutions in the police courts had been unsuccessful, the barrister Thomas Turner explained that this was attributable to 'fastidiousness about mechanical action, etc.'

A writer in the legal journal *The Jurist*, using the initials 'G.S.', referred to the 'known incompetency' of the justices,[135] adding that 'such functionaries are naturally averse to be troubled with discussions for which they are so little qualified by education or habit'. The aldermen who sat in the police courts at the Guildhall were often businessmen rather than lawyers[136] and, despite having a legal clerk,[137] frequently seemed uncomfortable with their responsibilities. Writing to the *Mechanics' Magazine* after the first two decisions of the aldermen, S.Y. observed that 'the persons appointed by the Act to settle disputed points, are those most likely to prove unable to comprehend the merits of the question on which they have to decide, and [...] are in every way irresponsible for their decision'.[138] Reflecting this, the Guildhall judges seemed to have looked for ways to avoid dealing with the complaints. As Turner put it, the aldermen took 'prejudices and crotchets on the points of interpretation that arise'.[139] Thomas Webster gave a similar assessment to the Select Committee on the Protection of Inventors Bill (in March 1851) that[140]

> there has been a failure, in the majority of cases, from technical objections ... I have been before almost every magistrate in London, and, with one or two exceptions, I have always had the matter shirked, either upon some technical objection, or, if that has been got over, it has been said, 'there is an alternative

[134] Civis 1845.

[135] G.S. 1850. See also Anon 1847d (critiquing the tribunal and proposing a separate and competent tribunal for adjudication on scientific matters); Anon 1850g ('a very unfit arena' and favouring use of the county court); Liverpool Financial Reform Association 1851, 9 ('incompetency of the tribunal for the duties imposed upon it').

[136] Select Committee on Metropolis Police Offices 1837, 129, Q. 1223 (evidence of E. G. Wakefield); Select Committee on Metropolis Police Offices, 1838, p. 117, Q. 1212, p. 119, Q. 119 (Sir Peter Laurie). For example, Charles Farebrother, involved in three of the cases, was from a firm of auctioneers. In contrast, the stipendiary magistrates at the London police courts (such as Bow St, Worship St, Marlborough St and Hammersmith) were required to be barristers of seven years standing and given a salary of up to £1,200 per annum: Metropolitan Police Court Act 1839, 2 & 3 Vict., c.71, s. 3, s. 9. Of the four stipendiary magistrates who decided cases on the UDA, the most notable as a legal expert was Peregrine Bingham, who had operated as a law reporter of cases in the Court of Common Pleas between 1819 and 1840, before taking up a post at Worship Street (1840–1846) and later Marlborough Street police courts (1846–1860): Anon 1864. Outside London, a stipendiary magistrate was required to be a barrister of at least five years' standing. See Polden 2010, 1004–1012.

[137] Select Committee on Metropolis Police Offices, 1838, p. 117, Q. 1210, 119, QQ. 1219–1220 (Sir Peter Laurie) (on abilities of two clerks, Hobler and Paine); 144, QQ. 1594, 1598 (J. H. Eliot).

[138] S.Y. 1844a, 330. Also S.Y. 1844b.

[139] Turner 1851, 105.

[140] SCPI 1851, 31–32, Q. 201. See also First Report 1853, 493.

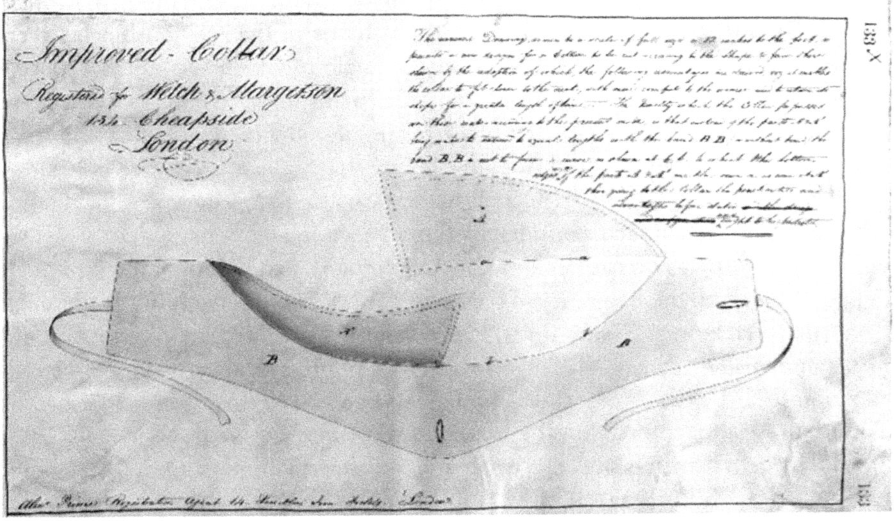

FIGURE 3.9 'Improved collar' registered for Welch, Margetson & Co on February 29, 1844, and litigated in *Margetson v May* (October 1844 Guildhall Police Court): BT 45/1/133

remedy; you can bring an action at law'; so that, practically, the rights are constantly being defeated.

There was certainly evidence to support such a conclusion. In an early case, *Margetson v May* (Guildhall Police Court 1844), concerning the design of a shirt collar (Figure 3.9), one of the magistrates, Alderman Charles Farebrother, an auctioneer, had been inclined to dismiss the proceedings because the matter was too trivial (though he was persuaded by his colleague not to do so).[141] In *Wolferstan v Warner* (Guildhall Police Court 1845), the aldermen concluded that the complainant had not established its case, but when counsel asked in what respect, the alderman, Sir George Carroll, a stockbroker, refused to explain. In contrast, other magistrates thought that the issues were so serious that they were better dealt with elsewhere. In *Besley v Gallie* (Bow Street Police Court 1848), dismissing the summons on a technical point (that it was not sent to the defendant's residence as opposed to its business premises), the Bow Street Magistrate, barrister David Jardine (d. September 1860), said he thought the matter 'far too important to be disposed of by a magistrate in a summary way. It was quite foreign to the general business of the police courts'.[142]

[141] But cf. *Boswell v Denton* (Guildhall Police Court 1845) (ODA case, Alderman Moon suggesting it was a matter for the court of Chancery).

[142] Turner 1851, 105.

One can easily imagine that the magistrates were ill at ease, as the cases often involved difficult points of law (particularly in terms of the relationship between patents and the Utility Design Act), whereas their usual diet would have been making findings of fact.[143] Moreover, the magistrates may have also resented the amount of time the cases were taking: the magistrates had plenty of work and were used to resolving matters speedily – 'the justice that was meted out at the police courts could be very abrupt'.[144] Certainly those that reported the cases on designs noted that they consumed a considerable time.[145] On the other hand, it may be that some of the tribunals overcame their initial discomfort, particularly at the Guildhall Police Court given the frequency of hearings.[146] In *Motte v Welch* (Guildhall Police Court 1850), Alderman Challis initially asked counsel to present more evidence and in his conclusions explained that he had given 'a great deal of time and careful attention to this case, in order that it might not be said he had decided hastily'.[147] The result was overturned, but the tribunal had certainly done its best.

While patent barristers such as Turner and Webster might have been able to point to instances such as these to justify their criticisms of the magistrates, their views might also have been informed by the fact that the day-to-day operation of magistrates was unfamiliar to them. Magistrates were used to exercising a wide degree of freedom which they often used to ensure that the outcome was consistent with their vision of their role.[148] One wonders whether the criminal barrister William Clarkson would have shared Webster's view: the reports identify him as counsel in nine such prosecutions, four times for the complainant and five for the defendant, with a 75 per cent success rate (six wins, two losses, the ninth case being undecided). He probably had a better idea as to how to present cases to magistrates. Moreover, one might wonder what a criminal law barrister might have made of the practice of trying patent cases before juries (the value of which were increasingly questioned during the 1840s).[149] Even with the widespread use of special juries,[150] the outcomes were hardly always satisfactory. In *Ward v Key* (nisi prius, 1847), for example, the jury initially ignored Cresswell J.'s instruction to find that the defendant had not infringed, finding (as it seems all juries did at that time) for the plaintiff patentee.

143 On the regular diet of assault, petty theft, drunkenness, vagrancy, etc., see Davis 1984, 316–321 Auerbach 2021, ch. 1.

144 Davis 1984, 313. With respect to the Guildhall Police Court, it was suggested that the aldermen didn't always give enough time to their duties: Select Committee on the Metropolis Police Offices 1838, 143–144, QQ. 1592–1593 (evidence of J. H. Eliot).

145 *Haynes v Brown* (Guildhall Police Court 1848) (3 hours); *Webb v Hughes* (Guildhall Police Court 1847) (3 hours); *Motte v Welch et al* (Guildhall Police Court 1850) (evidence of fourteen witnesses heard over two days).

146 But, outside this specific field, the aldermen had been criticised for their inconsistency: Select Committee on the Metropolis Police Offices 1838, 145, Q. 1607 (evidence of J. H. Eliot).

147 *Motte v Welch et al* (Guildhall Police Court 1850).

148 King 2006, 22–39.

149 Hanly 2006, 261–262.

150 Oldham 1987.

However, the jury revisited the matter when the judge explained to it that if it did not so find, the members would face the prospect of being compelled to hear the defendant's witnesses. Evidently, the lengthy and hugely costly processes of patent litigation were not guaranteed to produce just results.

Perhaps most significantly, the magistrates were not a suitable vehicle for establishing precedent. Not only were the cases reported inconsistently and sparingly in the newspapers,[151] the magistrates rarely reserved judgment and never offered more than the briefest of reasoning. While many of the outcomes were noted in periodicals of interest to inventors (such as Robertson's *Mechanics' Magazine* or Newton's *London Journal*) and made their way into commentaries, these were not as precedents so much as indications of the inclinations or instincts of these tribunals. It is fair to say that the magistrates mostly preferred the narrow interpretation of the Utility Designs Act of the likes of Carpmael to the broader reading of Robertson and Prince – but whether this was because they wanted to minimise this part of their workload, avoid the consequences of wrongfully convicting a defendant,[152] or because they thought this was the best interpretation of the statute, is difficult to say.

There was no appeal from the magistrates,[153] but proceedings could be taken to have their decisions quashed by way of the writ of certiorari,[154] and an authoritative view of the Utility Design Act was most likely to come from such decisions. This was the course of action taken by the defendants in *Motte v Welch* (Guildhall Police Court 1850) and *Dixon v Bessell* (Guildhall Police Court 1850). In *R v Welch* (Queen's Bench 1851), Lord Campbell overruled the magistrates' decision because of a technical defect, but in *R v Bessell* (Queen's Bench 1851) the Court ruled on the scope of the Utility Design Act. The design in issue was for a 'ventilator', that is a mechanism for opening the pane of a window (Figure 3.10). As can be seen, the drawings indicate the overall operation of the system for opening the window and focus in detail on the form of the screw. Apart from describing how the various components (pane, frame, screw and pulley) interacted, the textual component specified that '[t]he part or parts of this Design which are not new or original are all the parts and apart from the purposes thereof **What is Claimed** as new is the general configuration and combination of parts marked A, B, b, D, c, e, a, c exclusively of Figs 5.6. and which are subsidiary or illustrative'...). Quashing the conviction, the court held that Dixon's design was not within the statute because in

[151] Davis 1984, 317 (citing Sir Thomas Henry, the Chief Magistrate of the Metropolitan Police Courts who explained that cases on pawnbroking went unreported: 'In every police court there are fifty to sixty cases in a day, and the reporters, perhaps, select the one case which would most likely interest the public.' Select Committee on Pawnbrokers, 1870, 170, Q. 3600).

[152] As was found to have occurred in *Dixon v Bessell* (1850 Guildhall Police Court) leading to a successful damage claim for £100 for false imprisonment against Alderman Samuel Wilson – 'a highly respectable magistrate' – in *Bessell v Wilson* (nisi prius 1852, aff'd Queen's Bench 1853).

[153] Bentley 1998, 24 (noting that a general right of appeal from magistrates was first introduced in 1857).

[154] King 2006, 31–33.

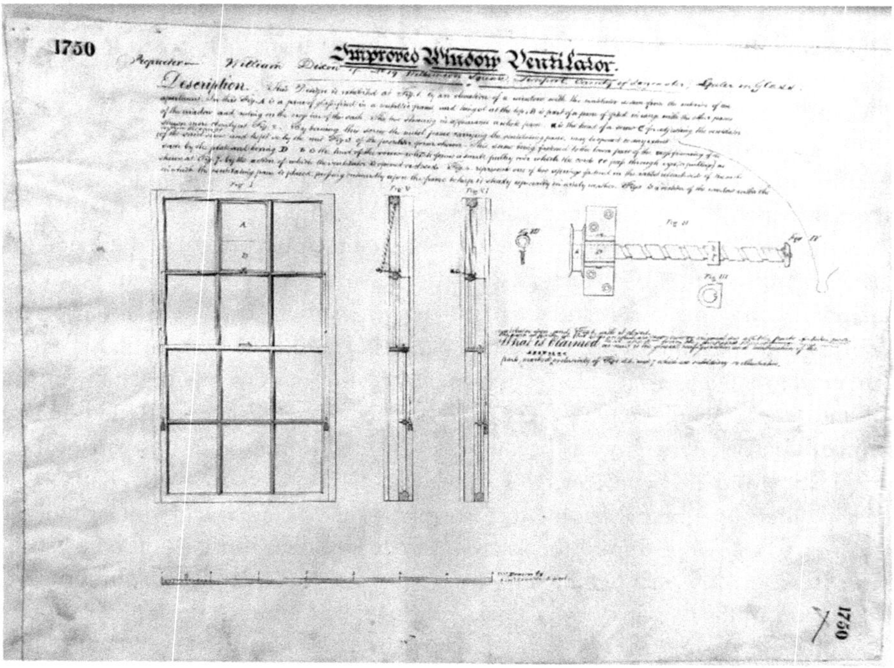

FIGURE 3.10 'Improved window ventilator' registered by William Dixon on January 26, 1849, and litigated in *Dixon v Bessell* (October 1, 1850, Guildhall Police Court): BT 45/9/1750

the description it specified the design as being a combination of features to produce a result and thus was not dependent on the specific shape or configuration of those features. Indeed, the Court observed that the same effect could be produced using different shapes and that had Dixon's protection been limited to the shape then Bessell, who used a different shape of screw, would not have infringed. The potential importance of the holding was apparent to patent agent Frederick Campin who suggested that it placed 'some hundreds' of registrations 'at the mercy of the pirate'.[155]

The only case in which the alternative route to the magistrates,[156] that of using the superior courts, was taken was *Margetson v Wright*, which concerned the design for a 'Protector label' with a metal eyelet that prevented the label being ripped off (Figure 3.11). The defendant had registered its own version, the 'Direction label' (Figure 3.12). The complainant succeeded in summary proceedings and was

[155] Campin 1851.

[156] After 1847, there was a further possibility – proceedings in the County Courts – and this avenue was used in at least one ODA case in the period: *Coalbrookdale Co v Page* (Warwickshire County Court 1851). For detail on such proceedings, see Polden 1999, ch. 1. The court was mostly perceived as a venue for reclaiming debt, though gradually, as damages limits were increased, became a more attractive venue for torts. See Smith 1969.

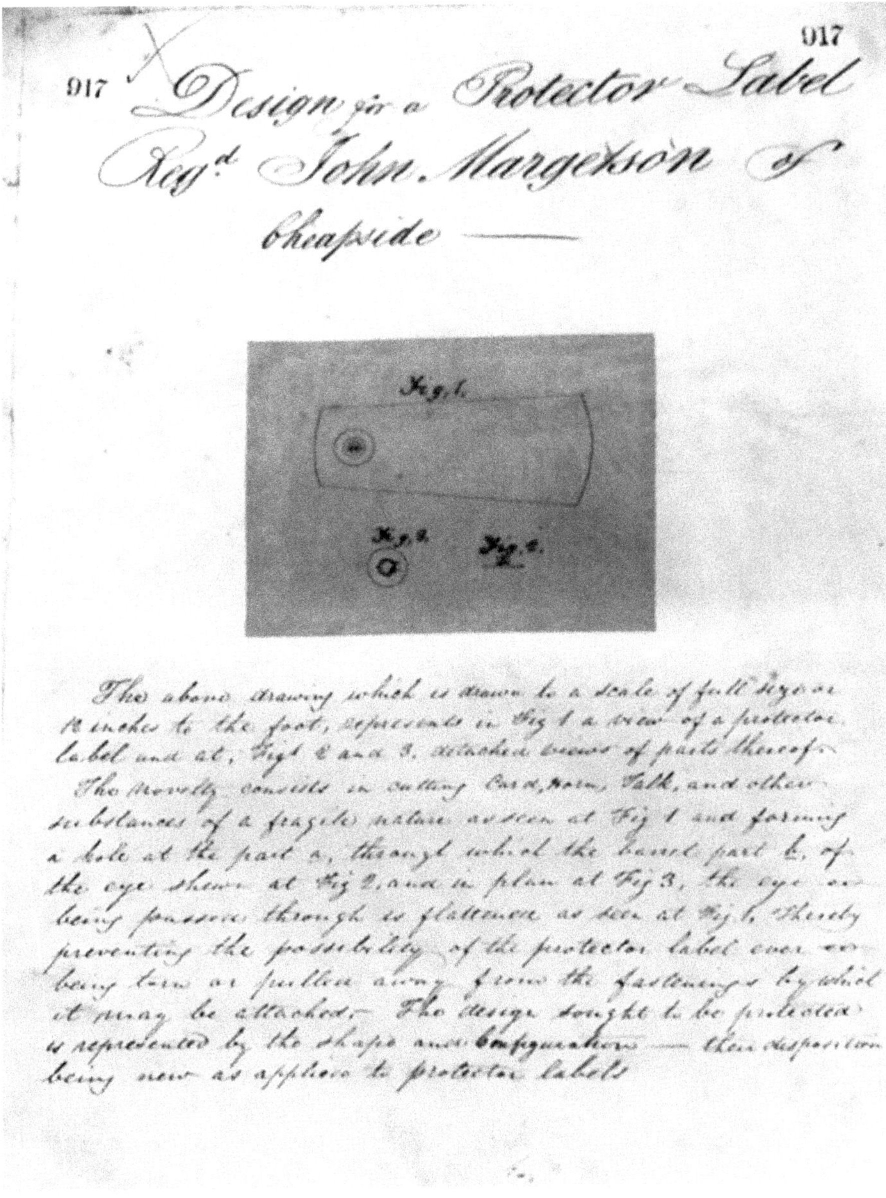

FIGURE 3.11 'Protector label' registered by Margetson on January 9, 1847, and litigated against Wright in the Guildhall Police Court on June 3, 1848: BT 45/5/917

awarded 20 shillings.[157] Nonetheless this did not prevent the defendant from continuing to make and sell its label. Margetson therefore issued a bill for an injunction.

[157] *Margetson v Wright* (Guildhall Police Court 1848).

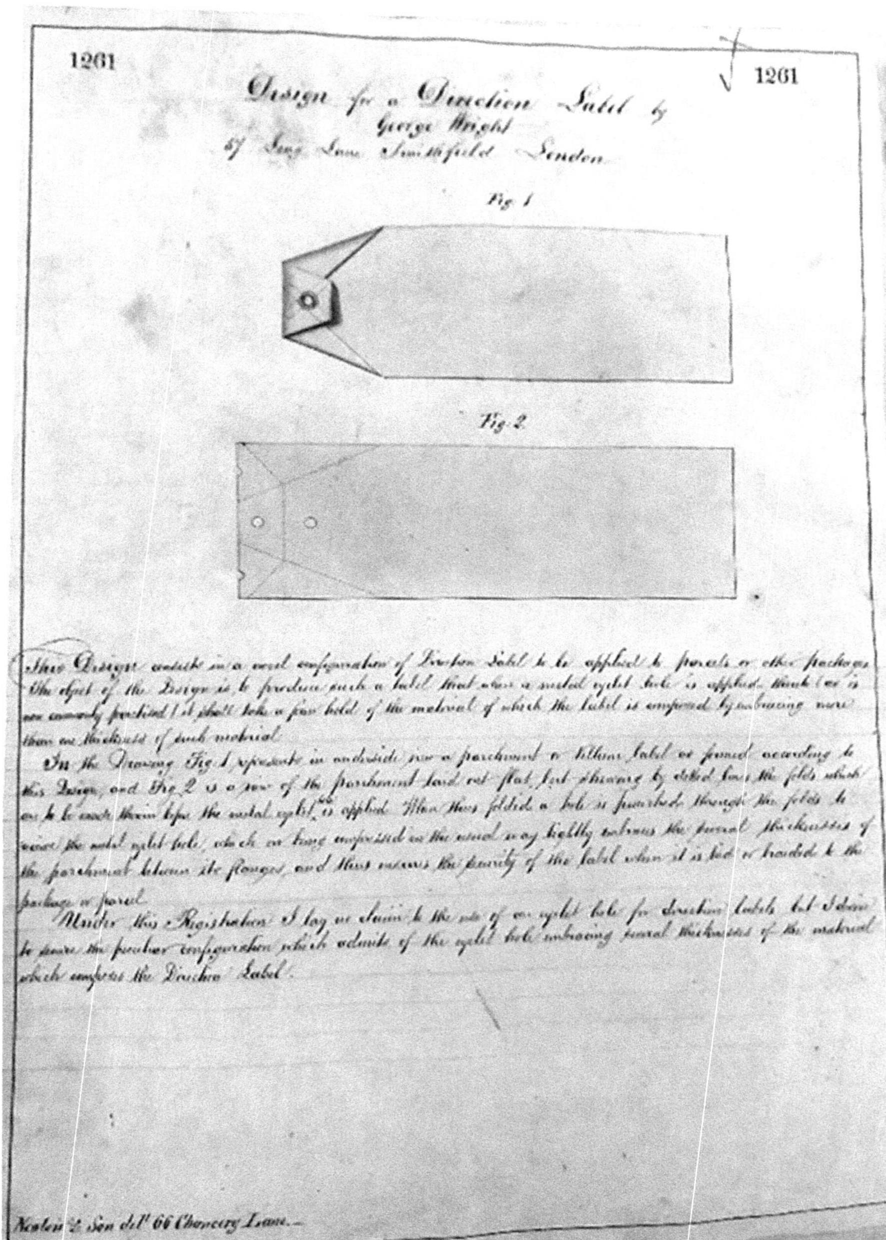

FIGURE 3.12 'Direction Label' registered by George Wright on November 17, 1847, and said by Margetson to infringe his registration in the Guildhall Police Court on June 3, 1848, as well as subsequent proceedings in Chancery and common law: BT 45/7/1261

When the Vice-Chancellor (Knight-Bruce) refused to grant injunctive relief,[158] Margetson sought to establish his rights at law. Unfortunately, in proceedings before Denman LCJ, sitting with a common jury out of term, the defendant was able to prove the availability of the design before the date of registration.[159] The authority thus gave no guidance on the interpretation of the Utility Design Act.

Two other cases concerning Utility Design Act registrations were brought in the common law courts for money owing under licensing arrangements and tried at nisi prius: *Millingen v Picken* and *Rogers and Beedle v Driver*. In both cases, the defendant sought to justify non-payment of licensing money ostensibly owed under the contracts by asserting that the registration was invalid. The more complicated of the two cases, *Millingen*, related to a parasol which could be opened using a single hand. The defendant had entered an agreement to make and sell the parasol. However, the defendant considered the design to fall within scope of an earlier patent for 'Constructing umbrellas and parasols' owned by Joseph Barker and wrote to parasol manufacturers, under Barker's name, asserting this.[160] The agreement between Millingen and Picken contained a penalty clause, for £100, should Picken do anything to prejudice Millingen's right and title. The plaintiff brought proceedings claiming that it was entitled to the sum. Millingen won at trial, but before the Court of Common Pleas en banc, Serjeant Byles argued that:

> the invention ... was a mechanical contrivance, and, therefore not within the meaning of [the Utility Design Act], which pointed only to pattern, shape, or configuration of the article manufactured, or for the ornamenting, thereof. He argued that the invention was the subject of a patent, and not of copyright.

Tindal LCJ initially awarded the rule *nisi*, but on June 3, 1845, the Court en banc affirmed the verdict stating that the defendant was not free to defend the action by claiming the plaintiff was not entitled to the registration. The case, therefore, ultimately provided no clarification as to the scope of the Utility Design Act.

In *Rogers and Beedle v Driver*, Beedle had invented a shape of brick, twice the size of a normal brick but with a cylinder cut out so that when laid against a corresponding brick the combination created a channel that would allow the passage of air (Figure 3.13).[161] Calling the design the 'universal ventilating brick', Beedle had entered into a partnership with Rogers to exploit it. They licensed Driver to make the bricks for the Southampton area, Driver in return promising a fee of £100 plus a

[158] *Margetson v Wright* (Vice-Chancellor 1848).

[159] *Margetson v Wright* (Queen's Bench 1849).

[160] Patent Specification 7357 (April 29, 1837). Barker would later seek injunctive relief against Millingen: *Barker v Millingen* (Vice-Chancellor 1845) (Shadwell V-C, dissolving injunction initially granted on June 6, 1845).

[161] Anon 1849a (describing registration); Anon 1849b (with illustration).

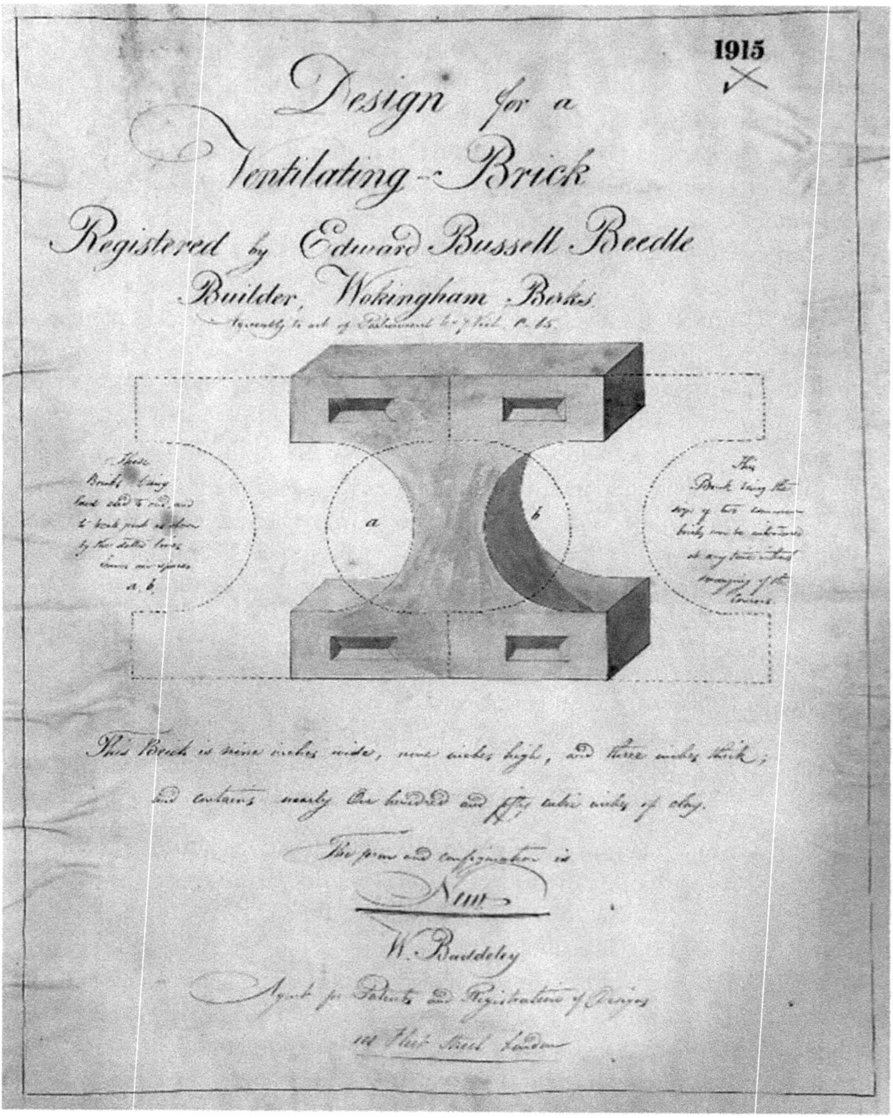

FIGURE 3.13 'Ventilating brick' registered by Edward Beedle on and litigated in the Berkshire Lent Assizes, 1850, in *Rogers and Beedle v Driver*: BT 45/10/1915

7 per cent royalty on sales. When Driver failed to pay the full fee, Rogers and Beedle brought an action at Berkshire Assizes for the remainder. Driver sought to argue that the registration was invalid on various bases including that the subject matter was properly that of a patent, and thus not registered design. Patteson J said he could see no reason why the statutory right should not be available for matters that were also

patentable,[162] and the full court of Queen's Bench agreed. Without offering a conclusive view as to whether the brick was patentable, the judges were unanimous that there was no reason to think that the patentability of an article precluded its registration under the Utility Design Act.

It is hard to assess the impact of the 1843 Act. Writing in 1851, Thomas Turner noted that 'we have very little of an authoritative nature to guide us in deciding what proportion of the registered designs might have been or may be maintained'.[163] One 'eminent member of the bar' had, by 1850, apparently expressed the opinion that 'it is impossible to protect any machine, or portion of a machine, under [the Act]' leading one commentator to suggest that only one in ten had been validly registered.[164] Some thought the uncertainty merely an opportunity for 'puffing and pretence'.[165] Others offered more positive appraisals. Charles Barlow and Philip Le Capelain, patent agents, agents for registration and editors of the *Patent Journal and Inventors Magazine* argued that while the 1843 Act was 'singularly obscure and indefinite' nevertheless it 'has worked well, and conferred incalculable advantages on inventors'.[166] As we have seen, registrants succeeded in a reasonable proportion of cases and, magistrates frequently adhered to their own sense of justice. *The Builder* anticipated that in future reform proposals 'Justice will be done to the Registration Act as an irregular improvement in, or rather substitute for, the law as it stands – as a "small patent law" in short, as the public have not been slow in making it.'[167]

According to the Society of Arts, the Act had a very positive effect on the morality of 'inventors'. Although offering no empirical evidence, the Society of Arts was convinced that manufacturers respected the registrations, irrespective of their validity.[168] Clement Johnson, the successor to F. B. Long as the Registrar of Designs, claimed that 'on the whole the Act has worked to the satisfaction of inventors and the public in general.'[169] In particular,

> however theoretically imperfect the system of registration may have been, that practically a degree of protection was afforded at a cheap rate to . . . minor inventors, and secured to many a property in their own invention, which, without the existence of the system, must have been totally lost.[170]

[162] *Rogers and Beedle v Driver* (nisi prius, Berkshire Lent Assizes 1850).
[163] Turner 1849, 24 'the Act has, on the whole, worked well.' Liverpool Financial Reform Association 1851, 8 (estimating that only 1 in 3 registrations was valid).
[164] Anon 1850c, 560.
[165] Anon 1850a.
[166] Anon 1847c.
[167] Anon 1850f.
[168] SCPB, 407.
[169] First Report, 482.
[170] First Report, 482.

3.4 THE DEMISE OF THE UTILITY DESIGN ACT

While the parameters of the subject matter of the Utility Design Act and its relationship to patentable subject matter remained undefined, after 1852 the level of concern with the overlap between the two regimes waned rapidly. This was because of the reform of patent administration which simplified the patent system, united the three patents of England and Wales, Scotland and Ireland into one, and established a central patent office. Most importantly, reductions in the cost of a patent to £25 for three years enabled the patent system to compete with a £10 Utility Design Act registration.[171] Although some had suggested that if the patent system was reformed that the Utility Design Act should be abolished,[172] others suggested that it should be left to die a natural death,[173] which was what happened. Following the patent reforms, utility design registrations fell to about 100 per year after 1860 (a number maintained until 1883), while patent registrations increased exponentially after 1852 (prompting further reflection on the desirability of making patents even cheaper).

With fewer registrations, fewer cases were reported.[174] With no significant developments in the jurisprudence on the Utility Design Act in the next three decades, the precise boundary and the degree of overlap remained uncertain. In 1872, giving evidence to a further Select Committee on Letters Patent, Bennett Woodcroft, the clerk to the Commissioners of Patents (established under the 1852 Act), observed that there were many patents that had been taken out that were 'properly the subjects for the registration of designs' and that 'many inventions go to the Design Office, which belong to the Patent Office'.[175] In line with this, treatises continued to warn of the dangers of assuming that protection under the Utility Design Act was in some way equivalent to that of a patent;[176] nonetheless, the practice continued.

In 1883, it was decided to merge the Ornamental and Utility Designs Acts into a single regime.[177] The Memorandum which accompanied the Patents, Designs and Trade Marks Act 1883 acknowledged that prior to 1883 many matters that were

[171] An Act for amending the Law for granting Patents of Inventions, 15 & 16 Vict., c. 83. See Norman 1851, v (predicting reform of patent law would reduce interest in the 1843 Act); Webster 1852, 11. Reform of the patent system was heavily influenced by the design registration experience. See, SCPB 1851, App. E, 410; The Society of Arts 'Inventions Registration and Protection Bill 1851: '[it] is expedient to extend to inventors the protection afforded to Designs.'

[172] SCPB 1851, 166, Q. 1099 (Alfred Newton).

[173] SCPB 1851, 167, Q. 1101 (Thomas Webster).

[174] *Loveridge v Gray, Bailey and Bartlett* (Birmingham Public Office 1861), *Holder v Osborn* (Birmingham Public Office 1862), *Taylor v Cowley* (Birmingham Public Office 1868), *Wright v Wells* (Balsall Heath Police Court 1875); *Wolverson v Law* (Birmingham Public Office 1877).

[175] SCLP 1872, 70, Q. 1325.

[176] Murdoch 1867, 13; Copinger 1870, 219; Craig 1879, 46, 52.

[177] Patents Designs and Trade Marks Act 1883 (46 & 47 Vict. c.57) ('PDTMA'). The jurisdiction of the magistrates was also abolished.

patentable had been protected under the Utility Design Act.[178] As Joseph Chamberlain, the President of the Board of Trade, told the House of Commons, the Utility Design Act

> had been largely used in order to obtain what we might call a cheap patent, because under [the Act] a mechanical invention could be registered for a period of one year's provisional and three years complete registration, for a sum of £10. Practically, registration under these provisions constituted a patent for four years for the sum of £10.[179]

However, because the 1883 Act reduced the costs of patents to £4, the attraction of design registration (at £10) disappeared: 'such useful designs as embrace a mechanical action would be treated as subject matter for a patent'.[180]

The implication from this was that the 1883 reform was not intended to change things substantively; the Registry would be simplified by removing the formal classification that relied on the distinction between shape, etc., which served the purpose ornament versus utility. As the barrister Edward Daniels observed, the distinction between the two forms of design 'was abolished'.[181] Nothing in the move implied that if an applicant were to choose the now more expensive design protection over patenting, that utility of form would not remain a consideration in the assessment of the novelty of a design or its infringement.

Whatever the intention, the effect of the merger of the Ornamental and Utility Designs Acts did have important consequences. This is because, in practice, administrative changes and judicial interpretation ended the feasibility of using the design regime as a utility model scheme: it was not so much the 'distinction' between ornamental and utility designs that was abolished so much as the category of utility designs itself.

On the administrative side, presumably anticipating that such applications would no longer occur because of the cheapening of patents, the implementing apparatus for the registration of designs was altered so that it no longer provided for the application to include a title, let alone 'such description in writing as was thought necessary to render the same intelligible'.[182] As Edmunds explained, 'no elaborate explanation by the author of the design is required or allowed'.[183] Moreover, while under the Utility Design Act, the drawings were to be 'on a proper geometric scale',[184] the drawings required under the 1883 Act only needed to enable the registry

178 Quoted in Daniels 1884, 69.
179 Hansard (HS), Vol 278, col 349–350 (April 16, 1883) (Second reading of Patents, Designs and Trade Marks Bill).
180 Quoted in Daniels 1884, 69.
181 Daniels 1884, 69. See also Fulton 1894, 141.
182 UDA, s. 8.
183 Edmunds 1895, 56.
184 UDA, s. 8.

to 'identify the design'.[185] While the 1883 Act still required a statement as to the 'nature of the design',[186] rule 9 of the Design Rules 1883 interpreted this as merely an indication of whether the design related to 'pattern', 'shape', or 'configuration' and an indication as to the method by which the design was to be applied to the article. Importantly, too, the 1883 Act conferred on the comptroller the power 'if he thinks fit, to refuse to register any design presented to him for registration'.[187] Thereafter, the Office could reject applications that it thought inappropriate, for example because the application appeared to relate to mechanical actions or principles. Finally, under the 1883 Act, all designs were secret – so that if useful designs had remained protected a person could incur penalties even though they could not have known of the registered design.[188]

In effect, the post-1883 design regime was no longer structured to function as a utility model. This is vividly illustrated by comparing the registrations under the 1843 Act with a registration under the 1883 regime.

On November 10, 1884, Walker, Hunter & Co registered a design for a fire door (Figure 3.14).[189] As is evident, the representation used under the 1883 Act had no text (whereas those used under the 1843 Act had plenty of text). Elsewhere in the register book, under 'Statement of Design' Walker, Hunter & Co wrote 'range fire door with moulding on to fit. Moulding forming front of range. Shape to be registered'.[190] There was nothing to indicate the function of the moulding beyond the words 'to fit'. (The entry in the newly published *Official Journal of the Patent Office* was even less informative, referring just to the registration number, proprietor, date of registration and class).[191] As we will see, this change in form had implications for the judicial interpretation of the scope of protection afforded by a representation.

The administrative changes fed into judicial interpretation of the scope of eligible subject matter under the Patents, Designs and Trade Marks Act 1883. With the exception of one or two first-instance decisions,[192] the courts began to develop case law that limited the potential to protect the function or functional components of an article through design registration. The first judicial move in this direction was to declare that the purpose of any particular shape was irrelevant and that novelty and infringement were to be assessed simply by 'the eye'. The second was to re-evaluate the relationship between design and patents and bit by bit to embrace the principle that anything that could be patented was ipso facto not protectable as a design.

[185] PDTMA, s. 48.
[186] PDTMA, s 47(3).
[187] PDTMA, s 47(6).
[188] PDTMA, ss. 22, 52 and 88; Edmunds 1895, 69–70.
[189] BT 50/21.
[190] BT 51/9.
[191] Anon 1884, 1087.
[192] *Tyler v Sharpe* (1894), 36.

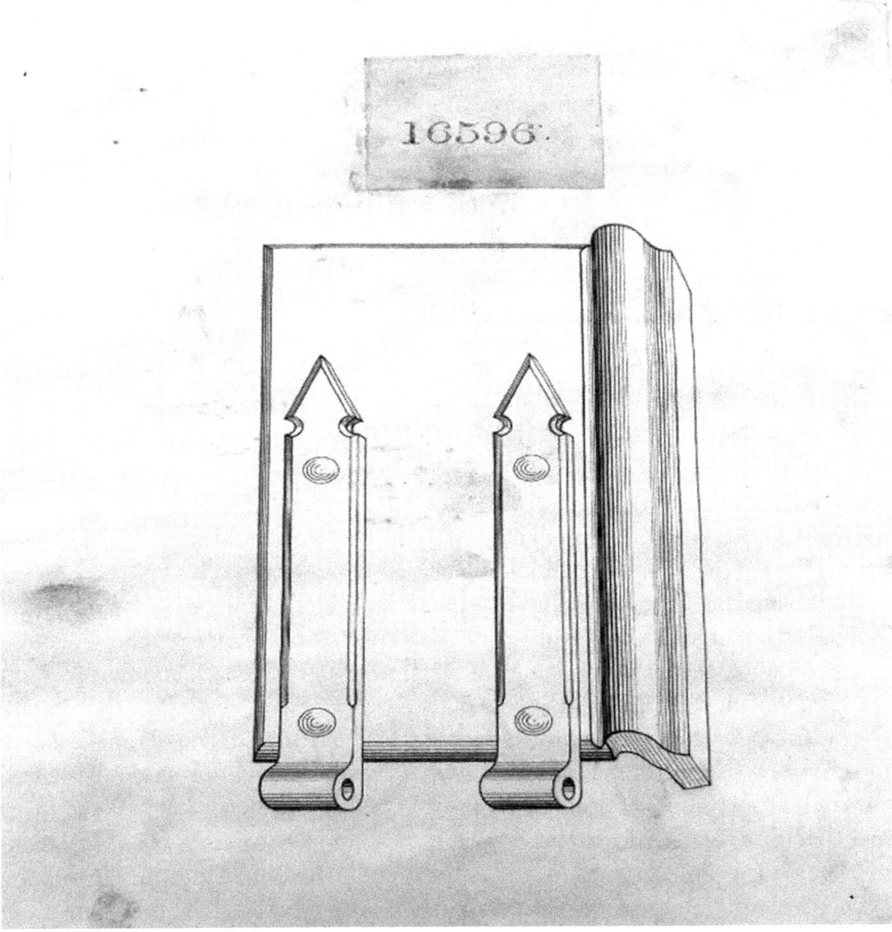

FIGURE 3.14 Walker, Hunter, & Co's registration under the Patents, Designs and Trade Marks Act 1883, dated November 10, 1884, litigated in *Walker, Hunter, & Co v Hecla Foundry* (1889 House of Lords): BT 50/21/16596

The first move was taken by the House of Lords in its 1889 decision in *Walker, Hunter, & Co v Hecla Foundry* (1889 House of Lords). In this case the claimants registered a design for a fire door for a kitchen range, with the representation as set out at Figure 3.14. The key characteristic of the door was the moulding on the door, which the registrant claimed operated to exclude cold air from the range (a function that would not have been obvious to a non-expert from looking at the representation). As already noted, the text accompanying the registration indicated that protection was for 'the shape' of the door but said nothing about function. While the court below had treated the purpose of the moulding as being relevant to determine whether the defendant's fire door infringed (so that any suitable moulding would infringe), the House of Lords indicated that this was not the correct approach. Instead, they said that the purpose of the shape was an irrelevant consideration: all that mattered was the similarity of shape viewed by the eye. As Lord Herschell stated, 'I do not think the object which the designer has in view in adapting the particular shape, or the useful purpose which the shape is intended to serve, or does serve, ought to be regarded in considering what is the design protected'.[193]

In many ways, this reasoning was the inevitable consequence of the changes in the administrative rules which precluded the possibility of claim-like descriptions that had been commonly used under the Utility Design Act. In the absence of such statements, courts would either have had to identify the purpose of a design from circumstantial matters, or treated the purpose of the shape as being irrelevant to its legal evaluation. The House of Lords chose the latter approach. The ruling meant that the 1883 Act had been more than a mere formal merger of two classes of ornamental and utility designs into one (as Chamberlain had put it). The removal of the textual aspect of the representation had deprived the courts of a key feature that had facilitated the identification/interpretation of designs.

By leaving the appraisal of any registration or alleged infringement to the 'eye' alone,[194] the merger effected in 1883 assimilated the scopic regime of representation/interpretation to that of the Ornamental Design Act. In *Hecla Foundry*, Lord Watson declared that the decision of the House of Lords in *Holdwsorth v McRea* (1867 House of Lords), a case decided under the Ornamental Design Act, was equally applicable to the 1883 Act. In this case, the issue was whether depositing a specimen of a fabric pattern had been satisfactory for the purposes of section 5 of the 1858 Act. All members of the House of Lords held that the registrant had complied with the Act and as a result that the design protected was for the entire combination of features in the sample. Lord Westbury elaborated further: 'the appeal is to the eye, and the eye alone is the judge of the identity of the two things. Whether, therefore, there be piracy or not is referred at once to an unerring judge, namely, the eye, which takes the one figure and the other figure, and ascertains whether they are or are not the same'.

As there was nothing 'below the surface', it was assumed that no explanation was required as to the meaning and purpose of ornament. Lord Westbury's test was premised on the belief that vision was universal and self-explanatory, requiring neither education nor expertise.[195] In this context, it was the judge who determined similarity by comparing features side by side. As David Fulton explained, 'the Court will not look beneath the surface, but must find the reasons for registration apparent

[193] *Walker, Hunter v Hecla* (1889), 558.

[194] See also *In re Clarke* [1896] 2, ch 38.

[195] Cf. *Cooper v Symington* (High Court, Ch. D. 1893), 264, 265, 267 ('expert eyesight' which 'receives evidence'). In practice the parties were permitted to lead whatever evidence they chose: Edmunds 1895.

to the eye'.[196] The indirect effect was to exclude many functional features from consideration at all because they would go unnoticed to the 'universal' as opposed to the trained or informed 'eye'. As Baron Pollock indicated in *Moody v Tree* (High Court 1892), small changes to shape or configuration which achieved functional effects could be disregarded if they were not 'pleasing to the eye'.

The second move was to frame the concept of design within the broader context of other industrial property rights (a concept recognised internationally in the Paris Convention of 1883 and implicitly in domestic legislation enacted that same year). More specifically, judges started to define design protection by reference to patent protection, giving the latter some sort of historical precedential and normatively superior status. In this characterisation, patent protection was recognised as historically and normatively prior while design law was seen as a legislative supplement. As a result, whatever the purpose of design law may have been, it could not have been intended to overlap with the subject matter of patents. If subject matter were patentable, it ipso facto should not be regarded as falling within the field of design protection. This mode of thinking tallies with what we have referred to elsewhere as the 'denigration of design'.[197]

This form of reasoning can be seen most clearly in *Moody v Tree*. The case, which concerned a registered design for a basket (Figure 3.15), had initially been heard at Kent County Court, where a jury ruled the claimant's design to be novel. The Court allowed the defendant to apply to the Divisional Court for a ruling on whether, even though new, the registration related to a design, and the superior court concluded it did not. Below the representation of the basket the applicant had indicated that the pattern involved the osiers being worked in singly and all the butt ends being outside.[198] The Divisional Court concluded that this described a mode of construction, not a design. Baron Pollock (a survivor from the pre-Judicature Court of Exchequer, though now in the High Court) initially expressed some discomfort in dealing with design protection 'in consequence of the novelty of this Act of Parliament, which in one sense is founded on patent law, but in another sense is entirely distinguishable from patent law'.[199] However, having satisfied himself that 'the Act with which we are dealing now is founded upon a different basis to the Patent Act', Baron Pollock reasoned that 'the Designs Act was intended *to add to* the Patent Act by making that which was not patentable – the subject of a design'. In contrast to previous authorities that had foreseen the possibility of overlap, Pollock utilised the historical priority of patent law to interpret the concept of design as necessarily excluding material that was patentable. Concurring, Vaughan

[196] Fulton 1902, 294.

[197] Sherman and Bently 1999, 163.

[198] Although this is stated in the report, the surviving register contains no such text. And the entry in the *Illustrate Official Journal* refers only to the number, class (III), proprietor's name and address and the date of registration: Anon 1891, 568.

[199] *Moody v Tree* (1892), 336.

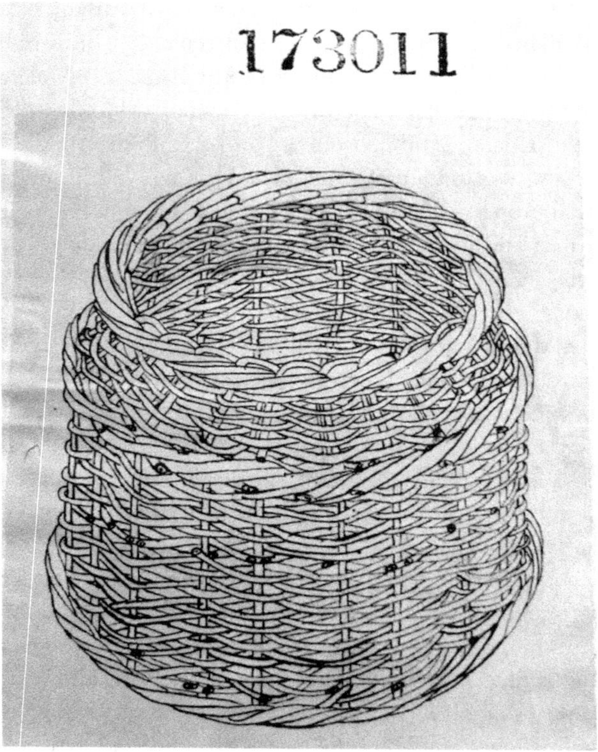

FIGURE 3.15 Thomas Isaac Moody's registration of a design for a basket, dated June 17, 1891, and litigated in *Moody v Tree* (High Court 1892): BT 51/64

Williams J. argued that 'it was not the intention of the Act of Parliament that processes which could not, either for want of novelty, or want of utility, or some other reason, be protected as patent rights should be protected by reason of ... the provisions contained in this Statute with reference to designs'.[200]

These judicial manoeuvrings reinforced the perception that the protection of 'useful designs' had been abolished in 1883. In 1930, looking back, the Chair of the Sargant Committee observed that 'in 1883 registration of such [utility] designs was abolished, and that since that date registration had been possible only in respect of ornamentation'.[201] In turn, these judicial manoeuvrings also prepared the ground for statutory amendment of the definition of 'design'. Following a report of the Board of Trade in 1916,[202] judicial limitations were statutorily confirmed by the introduction of an exclusion from the registered design system of 'any mode or principle of

[200] *Moody v Tree* (1892), 336.

[201] Minutes of 29th Meeting, June 25, 1930.

[202] The Board of Trade's Committee, chaired by Lord Parker, was never published officially, though some of it has recently been transcribed: Johnson 2017.

construction or anything which is in substance a mere mechanical device'.[203] With these exclusions, the utility design regime was finally brought to an end.

3.5 FORGETTING THE UTILITY DESIGNS ACT 1843

Almost immediately after the final vestige of the 1843 Act was removed from British law in 1919, there were calls for the introduction of some kind of short-term, cheap and speedy protection for minor innovations in the United Kingdom. The first came in 1928 in the form of a report by the British Science Guild,[204] a pressure group made up of scientists keen to have scientific insight incorporated into public policy.[205] Entitled, *Reform of British Patent System*, the committee led by the electrical engineer, William Eccles, proposed the introduction of a 'short term patent' for new and useful variations of known constructional forms and arrangements and compositions characterised by new ingredients, but not for processes.[206] The proposal was rejected by a governmental committee established by the Board of Trade,[207] though it regarded the question as 'one of the most important and most controversial subjects' that it had to consider.[208] The question was raised again in the early 1960s in another departmental inquiry on industrial design (the Johnston Committee), which indicated that though the question was a 'live one' it was outside the Committee's terms of reference. The idea was rejected again in the Banks report in 1971. Despite what might have been regarded as a conclusive rejection, just over a decade later a Green Paper issued by a committee headed by the then Chief Scientific Officer to the Cabinet Office recommended adoption of a regime of 'registered inventions'.[209] The recommendation did not, however, make it onto the statute book.[210]

Despite the persistent interest in some sort of utility model through the twentieth century, none of the various proposals or reports built upon the Utility Designs Act

[203] Patents and Designs Act 1907–1919, s. 93, as amended by Patents and Designs (Amendment) Act, 1919, s. 19. In *Tecalemit Ltd v Ewarts Lts (No. 2)* (High Court, Ch.D. 1927), 506, Moritz KC submitted that this changed the words of the statute 'but the law remained the same'.

[204] For internal consideration even earlier by the Board of Trade see Temple Franks (1912) and Hatfield (1912).

[205] MacLeod 1994.

[206] British Science Guild 1928, 22–24.

[207] Sargant Committee 1931, 81–86. In fact, in its submissions to the Committee, the representatives put the case much less forcefully, stating 'While there is in some quarters a strong demand for the introduction of what we have called "short-term patents" – i.e. monopolies intermediate in character between patents and registered designs – account must be taken of certain difficulties': BT 209/282.

[208] Sargant Committee 1931, 81, [371].

[209] Nicholson Committee 1983.

[210] Department of Trade and Industry, *Intellectual Property and Innovation* 1986, 15–18, [3.4]–[3.16].

1843.[211] Instead, the German *gebrauchsmuster* was consistently used as the legal model for the proposed new rights.[212] The *gebrauchsmuster*, introduced in 1891 to fill the 'gap' perceived to exist between registered designs (which were limited to aesthetic appearance) and the high level of inventiveness necessary to merit patents,[213] protected 'working appliances or articles of utility, or parts of the same in so far as they serve the object of the work or use through a new shape or arrangement'. Even though the *gebrauchsmuster* was itself very likely inspired by the British precursor,[214] it was the German version that had become the key reference point in the United Kingdom.

Why was the Utility Designs Act so quickly forgotten? One potential reason for this is strategic: whether one supported or opposed proposals for a second tier of protection, the 1843 Act probably offered little to buttress one's case. For supporters, the experience of the 1843 Act could hardly have been presented as a huge success. While the German *gebrauchsmuster* proved to be as popular as patents in terms of registrations,[215] after 1852 there were rarely more than 100 utility designs registered each year in the United Kingdom. Moreover, the fact that the *gebrauchsmuster* was a feature of the law of an important foreign trade rival had rhetorical force: the fact that the *gebrauchsmuster* benefited and supported German innovators was a strong argument for its adoption in the United Kingdom.[216] For opponents of the adoption of a utility model in UK law, the experience of the 1843 Act might have enabled them to argue 'we tried it, and it was a failure'. However, as we have seen, it would have been difficult to assert that it had clearly been a resounding failure.[217] For those aware of the history, it might have been better to ignore the British experience and instead emphasise that the German *gebrauchsmuster* was linked to distinct features

[211] The records of the Parker Committee of 1916 do include a Memorandum by W. J. Tennant of patent agents Boult, Wade & Tennant in which he observes 'The reinstatement of the old design patent is very often spoken of as desirable': BT 209/485.

[212] British Electrical Allied Manufacturers Association 1916; British Science Guild 1928, 22, [25]; Sargant Committee 1931, 82, [374]; Johnston Committee 1962, 104–105, [164]; Banks Committee 1972, 145, [491] (also referring to Japan); Nicholson Committee 1983, 20, [4.7] (as well as those of Japan, France, Italy and Australia).

[213] Isay 1932, 268ff.

[214] The language and concept are close, and we are told the German government carefully reviewed the laws of the United States, France and Great Britain: Osterrieth 1912, 196. Weston 1983, 372, [15] who called the Utility Designs Act 'the forerunner of German Gebrauchsmuster'.

[215] Hatfield 1912 (reporting that in 1909 there were 44,411 patent applications in Germany and 52,933 applications for *gebrauchsmuster*); British Science Guild 1928, 24, [30].

[216] Recommendations of the British Electrical Allied Manufacturers Association 1916 in BT 209/486. However, the Comptroller had considered and rejected the idea four years previously (Temple Franks 1912) and was not open to reconsidering it.

[217] Charles Sargant, who had declared himself opposed to adopting a British *gebrauchsmuster*, said he found a paper produced by the committee secretary, R. W. Luce, on 'previous British legislation re utility designs' to be 'not very conclusive': Minutes of 28th Meeting, June 4, 1930, 3, [5].

of German law and procedure – for example the high standard of patent examination – which made its adoption in the United Kingdom unnecessary or problematic. (Interestingly, perhaps, nothing was said at this point about divergent approaches to the drafting of claims and their interpretation.) This would also have allowed more xenophobic opponents to characterise the utility model not only as unnecessary or undesirable, but also as intrinsically foreign.

While strategic decisions to remember history selectively and to ignore inconvenient aspects from the past help to explain the absence of references to the 1843 Act, the collective amnesia is more likely as much a consequence of prevalent ways of thinking about intellectual property law. As we described in *The Making of Modern Intellectual Property Law*, by the end of the nineteenth century a particular way of thinking about 'intellectual property law' had fallen into place, according to which the field was divided into particular branches – patents, copyright, designs and trademarks – each with its own self-image and logic.[218] By the last decades of the nineteenth century each branch had its own treatises, many of which remain today – volumes by Copinger and Scrutton on copyright; Terrell, Edmunds, and Frost on Patents; Edmunds on designs. The distinctness of these categories was further cemented through the twentieth century, for example by way of international and regional arrangements for registration. In this categorisation, the history of the Utility Designs Act was included in the category of history of design law (even if only as a historical aberration),[219] whereas proposals for utility models and short-term patents were conceptualised within the field of patent law. As a result, the 1843 Act was simply not part of the 'memory' of British patent law.[220]

The dominance of such a way of thinking about the shape and nature of the law is evident in many of the twentieth century documents that considered introducing a utility model law into the United Kingdom. For example, in arguing for the adoption of a British *gebrauchsmuster* the British Science Guild said that 'the new body of law that must be created should preferably conform to *the model of patent law* rather than of design law'.[221] The Sargant Committee's response, rejecting the proposal, argued that the entire idea of a 'useful design' was confusing, if not self-contradictory, because the very word 'design' implied in law the protection of appearance rather than utility.[222] The Committee went on to suggest that the confusion arose because 'patents' and 'designs' were placed within the same legislation – a curious comment given that the Committee was itself charged with reviewing the law of patents and designs but one entirely consistent with the idea that the different branches of 'intellectual property' comprise distinct regimes with

218 Sherman and Bently 1999, chs. 5–8.

219 Edmunds 1895, 8–9, with Act at 211. Copinger 1893, 485.

220 It is not mentioned in Edmunds 1890 (even though he also authored a treatise on designs), Frost 1891, or Terrell 1884.

221 British Science Guild 1928, 22, [26] (emphasis added).

222 Sargant Committee 1931, 82–83, [378]; a better term was 'useful devices'.

their own ontologies, epistemologies, teleologies and histories.[223] When the Johnston Committee was asked by various parties in 1961 to consider recommending the introduction of a 'utility model',[224] it regarded the matter as falling beyond its terms of reference:[225] presumably conceiving the issue to be one for the 'more important' branch of patent law rather than design law.[226] The Committee's historical review of legislation had mentioned the protection of 'useful designs' under the 1843 Act,[227] but clearly did not think this sufficient to consider utility models as falling within 'law relating to protection of industrial designs'.[228] Perhaps least surprisingly, the Banks Committee, with its focus on patent law treated the proposal as a 'petty patent' entirely within the normative (and implicitly historical) framework of patent law.[229] Even though the Nicholson Committee came to a very different conclusion from Banks, the framing was the same, even if the language 'two-tier patents' and 'registered inventions' was slightly distinct.[230] It seems likely that the dominance of the modern framework for intellectual property thinking, coupled with the characterisation of *gebrauchsmuster*/utility models/petty patents as properly belonging within patents, goes a long way to explaining why most commentators and policy-makers have failed to draw a connection between these various proposals for reform and the forgotten Utility Designs Act of 1843.

[223] Sargant Committee 1931, 83, [378].
[224] Johnston Committee 1962, 104–105, [164].
[225] Johnston Committee 1962, 105, [164].
[226] Johnston Committee 1962, 6.
[227] Johnston Committee 1962, Appendix B, 127.
[228] Johnston Committee 1962, 2 (terms of reference).
[229] Banks Committee 1972, 145, [491].
[230] Nicholson Committee 1983, 20, [4.7].

APPENDIX 1 *Cases under the Utility Design Act 1843*

Hearing date	Complainant	Defendant	Subject	Tribunal	Counsel	Outcome
December 28, 1843	Vine	John Johnston, 30 London Wall, Regn No 34	'Churn'. Regd. September 28, 1843; BT 45/1/20 (registered to Attwood, Wimble and Warne)	Worship St. Peregrine Bingham.	Webster for C; Gurney for D[a]	Dismissed (absence of novelty).
October 1844	Joseph Welch and John Margetson, haberdashers, 134 Cheapside	Mr May, Moorgate St, hosier	'Improved collar.' Regd. February 29, 1844; BT 45/1/133	Guildhall. Aldermen Charles Farebrother and William Hughes Hughes	Webster for C. Lott (a solicitor) for D[b]	Fined £5.
November 5, 1844	Thomas Wolferstan, Salisbury	John Warner & Sons, Jewin Crescent, Cripplegate, brassfounder	'Safety boiler tap.' Regd. May 28, 1844; BT 45/1/190	Guildhall. Sir George Carroll and Alderman John Johnson	Webster for C; Clarkson for D	Dismissed. No reason provided.
February 15, 1845	Francis Kennedy and Charles Asprey, 49 New Bond Street	Coombs and Finlay	'Portable ink and light box.' Regd. August 27, 1844; BT 45/2/255	Police Court, Marlborough Street, London. Mr John Hardwick[c]	Simons for C; Webster for D	Dismissed (absence of new shape/ configuration; only novelty lay in mechanical contrivance).
March 22, 1845	Fletcher Woolley, 180 High Holborn	John Warner, Crescent, Jewin St	'Improvements in the shape of lamps and apparatus connected for the burning of oil of turpentine etc.' Regd. February 21, 1844; BT 45/1/127	Guildhall (Aldermen Charles Farebrother and William Hughes Hughes)	Rotch for C; Clarkson for D	Dismissed: claim related to mechanical action rather than shape.

(*continued*)

Hearing date	Complainant	Defendant	Subject	Tribunal	Counsel	Outcome
October 27, 1845	Luke Williams, Upper Marylebone St, ironmonger	William Rimell, King St, Hammersmith (quick boiling kettle, Regd. August 22, 1845); BT 45/3/524	Concave bottom tea-kettle. Regd. January 13, 1845: BT 45/2/347	Thomas Paynter, Magistrate. Hammersmith Police Court		Dismissed as D's design was substantially different.
March 12, 1846	Joseph Guise, Margaret St, Spa Fields, London	Thomas Walsh, Half Moon Passage, Aldersgate St	Regd. January 24, 1845; BT 45/2/358	Aldermen Challis and Hughes Hughes	Clarkson for C; Humphrey for D	£5 and 40 shillings cost.
April 12, 1847	George Webb, Wood St, City (lace manufacturer)	Hosketh Hughes, lace manufacturer (Regd. February 25 1847); BT 45/5/977	Protection Ruche Tray. Regd January 13, 1847; BT 45/5/920	Guildhall. Sir James Duke and Alderman Michael Gibbs.	Payne for C.[d] Clarkson and Wordsworth for D.	Dismissed without prejudice.Judges were divided on merits.
December 31, 1847	Vincent Price, 33 Wardour Street	George Chambers, Upper Thames St	'Improved Economical Ironing Stove'. Regd. February 8, 1847;BT 45/5/954.	Guildhall. Aldermen Samuel Wilson and Charles Farebrother	Clarkson for C; Ballantine for D	Dismissed.
February 19, 1848	George Lister Haynes, Charles White & Charles Bevis, of 61 Backchurch Lane, Whitechapel	Thomas Brown of Tower Hill	'Windlass'. Regd. March 29, 1847; BT 45/6/1020 [controller' for use in anchoring ships]	Guildhall. Aldermen Michael Gibbs and Francis Moon	Wolrych for C; Clarkson and Rotch for D	Dismissed as lacking novelty.
May 6, 1848	Fox, hairdresser/perfumer, St Georges Circus, Blackfriars Rd. The	Jeremiah Evans, furnishing ironmonger, King William St	'Alarum for time pieces'. Regd. July 25, 1846; BT 45/4/776	Guildhall. Aldermen Thomas Finnis and William Lawrence		D fined £5, 4 shilling costs. Infringement though no

	registration was effected by 'Edward Fox and James Carson, both of Liverpool'					evidence of copying.
June 3, 1848	John Margetson, Cheapside	George Wright, Long Lane, Smithfield (Regd November 17, 1847; BT 45/7/1261 for 'Direction Label')	'Protector label'. Regd. January 9, 1847; BT 45/5/917	Guildhall	Webster for C; Bodkin for D[e]	D fined £1.
November 20, 1848	George Twigg, Powell St, Spring Hill Terrace, Birmingham	Smith and Kemp, Brearley St, Birmingham	'Double rim button'. Regd. February 11, 1848; BT 45/7/1351	Public Office, Birmingham. S. Thornton, Mayor and James James	Slaney for C[f]; Harding for D	Dismissed.
December 29, 1848	Robert Besley and William Thorowgood, letter founders, Aldersgate, London	Gallie	'The Courthand Printing Type'. Regd. February 11, 1847; BT 45/5/957	David Jardine, Bow Street	Webster for C; Hindmarch for D	Dismissed (on basis defendant resided in Scotland).
March 30, 1850	Auguste Motte, 9 Southwark Square, London	Joseph James Welch et al. (of Welch & Margetson)	'Improved portmanteau'. Regd. July 23, 1849; BT 45/10/1970	Guildhall, Alderman Thomas Challis	Clarkson for C; Hawkins for D	£5 and costs.[g]
June 19, 1850	Auguste Motte, 9 Southwark Square, London	Robert Lancaster, Bread St	'Improved portmanteau'. Regd. July 23, 1849; BT 45/10/1970	Guildhall, Alderman Thomas Challis	–Hawkins for D[h]	Dismissed (information misdescribed the invention).

(*continued*)

Hearing date	Complainant	Defendant	Subject	Tribunal	Counsel	Outcome
October 1, 1850	William Dixon of Liverpool, dealer in glass	John Bessell of Farringdon St, London	'Improved window ventilator'. Regd. January 26, 1849; BT 45/9/1750	Guildhall, Alderman Samuel Wilson.	Hindmarsh for C; D not represented	Fined £30 for each offence plus £10 costs.[i]
October 9, 1850	Thomas Ryan Pinches27 Oxendon St, Haymarket. Die sinker and engraver	William Leschallas (also Le Challas),32 Budge Row, Wholesale stationer	Purse envelope. Regd. June 26, 1850; BT 45/12/2350	Guildhall. Alderman Thomas Sidney	Clarkson for C; Watts for D	£5 plus costs.
Same	Same	Joseph Addenbroke2 Bartletts Passage. Holborn (envelope maker)	Same	Same	Not stated	20 shillings and £5 costs.
Mar 8, 1851	Alfred Gregory	Herman Harbusch Armstrong, 184 St George St, Wellclose Sq	A safety plate for a ship's scuttle. Regd. April 20, 1850; BT 45/12/2274	Thames Police Court. Edward Yardley	Webster for C; Simpson (solicitor) for D	Dismissed: D's not an imitation of C's.
May 5, 1851	Samuel Levy Samuels and Jonas Engel,Wholesale parasol manufacturers, Mumford St, Milk St, Cheapside	Foster, Porter, & Co, Wholesale parasol manufacturers, 47 Wood St, Cheapside	'Fleur de lis Parasol'. Regd. by Alexander Grant, March 27, 1850; BT 45/12/2242	Guildhall. Alderman Francis Moon	Huddlestone for C; Clarkson for D	£5 with £7 costs.
May 24, 1851	Same	Thomas and James Venables, linendrapers, High St, Whitechapel	Same	Worship St Police Court	Huddlestone for C; Solicitor for D	£5 with £5 costs.

May 15, 1852	Samuel Scowen and Rowland M.H.S. White, 9 Noble St. Warehouseman/ cravat manufacturer	Weston	'The Aptandum Collar'. Regd. April 16, 1850; BT 45/12/ 2265	Clerkenwell Police Court. Mr Corrie	Thomas Jones for C; Streeten for D	Withdrawn.
October 1852	Adolphus Biddell, 11 St John Square Clerkenwell	Rogers and De Costa, Commission agents (or hawkers?) Hutchinson Avenue, Petticoat Lane, London	'Alarm door and window wedge'. Regd. February 19, 1851; BT 45/14/2697	Guildhall. Alderman Moon	Hawkins for C; Lewis for D	£10.

[a]Probably Russell Gurney (1804–1878), son of Baron John Gurney.
[b]Probably Thomas Lott (d. July 28, 1869) of Bow Lane.
[c]Although the Act referred to two justices, one of 'Jervis' Acts' of 1848 allowed for a single magistrate to hear a case: An Act to facilitate the Performance of the Duties of Justices of the Peace 1848, s. 30.
[d]Probably Joseph Payne, who would later serve with William Bodkin at the Middlesex Sessions.
[e]William Henry Bodkin MP, d. 1874.
[f]Probably Robert Agliouby Slaney, M. P. (1791–1862).
[g]Quashed in *R v Welch* (Queen's Bench 1851).
[h]Possibly Sir Henry Hawkins (1817–1907), later Lord Brampton, who was a junior barrister at this time.
[i]Quashed in *R v Bessell* (Queen's Bench 1851). For enforcement of the penalty, see *Morning Advertiser*, November 2, 1850, p. 4; *London Evening Standard*, November 2, 1850, p. 1.

4

Utility Models in Danish Law

Tine Sommer, Timo Minssen[*] *and Jens Schovsbo*

In Denmark, a specific Act for the protection of utility models was introduced by Act No. 130 of 26 February 1992. The regulation of utility models in Danish law has been elaborated in close connection with Danish patent law. Even though the rules are enacted separately, the wording of the Patent Act and the Utility Model Acts is very similar. The close interaction between the two systems is built into the design of the Acts. For example, branching-off from a patent application or patent under opposition to a utility model application is permitted. The core area for utility models is the protection via registration of "minor inventions", so-called *creations* (Danish: *frembringelser*). These differ from "real patents" (Danish: *opfindelser*) mainly by having a lower threshold for "inventive step". Whereas a patentable "invention" must differ "essentially" (Danish: *væsentligt*) – a "creation" should only differ "distinctly" (Danish: *tydeligt*) from the state of the art. Moreover, utility model protection can be obtained without substantive examination whereas patent protection always requires a full evaluation both of the formal and substantive requirements. The term of protection for utility models is less than that of a patent. Since 1998, there has been a decline in the demand for utility model protection in Denmark.

4.1 THE REGULATION OF UTILITY MODELS IN DENMARK: BACKGROUND

The first Danish act for the legal protection of utility models was adopted in 1992.[1] Prior to this, Danish law only provided protection for the technical features of

[*] Minssen's research for this chapter was supported by a Novo Nordisk Foundation Grant for a scientifically independent International Collaborative Bioscience Innovation & Law Programme (Inter-CeBIL programme – grant no. NNF23SA0087056).

[1] Act No. 130 of 26 February 1992 and Consolidated Act No. 367 of 9 June 1998. An English language version of the Act can be found at https://wipolex-res.wipo.int/edocs/lexdocs/laws/en/dk/dk174en.html

products or useful and technical methods, etc. via the Patent Act. Moreover, it was generally assumed almost as a *dogma* that utility could not be protected against imitation via any of the existing legal systems otherwise aimed at promoting innovation in product designs such as the Industrial Designs Act, the Copyright Act or the (liberal) protection afforded by the Marketing Practices Act. It was therefore quite a novelty when the Utility Model Act was introduced and an extra dish of exclusivity was added to the already quite impressive Danish smorgasbord (Danish: *smørrebrødsbord*) of exclusivity provisions.

The Utility Model Act basically aims at serving the needs of small and medium sized enterprises (SMEs) which were active in certain areas of innovation, for example hand tools and kitchen utensils.[2] Protection was lacking, in this area. For hand tools and other such types of invention made by SMEs, patent protection would often be overly burdensome in terms of costs and effort, and a shorter term of protection might well suffice. Moreover, the Act was intended to filling the gap between industrial designs law (focused at a the shape of products) and utility patent law (focused at a product's technical function (utility)). The perceived gap between a product's "form and function" was most likely exacerbated by the tradition in Denmark (indeed in the Nordic countries) for "functional design" where – as it is normally stated – "form follows function". The protection of minor technological advances and minor inventions featured highly on the statutory rationale for the utility model protection in Denmark as did the lack of substantive examination. In addition, utility models can be obtained more rapidly and at lower cost than patents. In short, utility models are a cost-efficient, faster and easier way to obtain sui generis protection aimed at the needs of SMEs.

The 1992 Act was amended in 2007.[3] At first blush, the changes appear to be substantial, but in fact they had more to do with form than content. Whereas the 1992 Act simply referred to the Danish Patent Law Act, the 2007 Act abandoned this approach. Since 2007 the Utility Models Act has been an independent Act in addition to the Patent Act. In terms of content, most of the provisions of the Consolidated Utility Models Act No. 91 of 29 January 2019 and the Danish Consolidated Patents Law Act No. 90 of 29 January 2019 have identical wording. The Utility Models Act is supplemented by a Ministerial Order on the examination and other processing of utility model applications and registered utility models.[4]

[2] Lovforslag nr. L 119 af 20. november 1991, L 49 Forslag til lov om brugsmodeller af 9. november 2005, Lise Østerborg, Indledende bemærkninger til indførelse af brugsmodelbeskyttelse i Danmark, NIR 1984, pp. 18–24, Roth and Niels Holm Svendsen, Lov om Brugsmodeller m. v. i U 1992B223, and Niels Holm Svendsen in NIR 1993/2, p. 237 ff., Jens Schovsbo, Ny dansk lov om brugsmodeller: En oversigt i NIR 5/2006, 489 ff., Jens Schovsbo, Morten Rosenmeier, Clement Salung Petersen, Immaterialret, 2024, p. 427 ff. DJØF, Palle Bo Madsen, Immaterialret, Jurist- og Økonomforbundets forlag, 2020, p. 183 ff.

[3] Act No. 1431 of 21 December 2005 and Act No. 538 of 8 June 2006.

[4] Danish Ministerial Order (2006).

4.2 PROTECTABLE SUBJECT MATTER AND SUBSTANTIVE CRITERIA

Today, the protection of a utility model is not only relevant to those areas of innovation that were anticipated when the first Act was adopted in 1992. The scope of the Act has expanded beyond its original focus on hand tools, etc. Today, the subject matter for which protection can be obtained is open ended, as in the Patent Act: "Any creations" can be protected (unless specifically exempted, see below). Thus, apart from physical products, protection is open within every field of technology including chemistry, pharmaceuticals and mechanical and electrical engineering.

The substantive criteria for obtaining protection for utility models are novelty, "inventiveness" ("distinctly" different), and industrial application. The Consolidated Danish Utility Models Act states:

> Any creation which is susceptible of industrial application and which provides a solution to a technical problem [. . .] can be registered as a utility model.[5]

As mentioned above, the word *creations* reflects the intent – from a linguistic viewpoint – to distinguish the subject matter from that of "inventions" in patent law. Importantly, the word "creation" should not be understood as suggesting an element of "creativity" (or "originality") in copyright's sense as a precondition for obtaining protection. "Creation" in the Utility Model Act is simply meant to differentiate between "real inventions" (which may be protected by patents) and "small inventions" which may be protected only as utility models.

"Novelty" should be understood in the same way in both the Patent and the Utility Model Acts. Thus, whether something is "novel" is assessed on the principles of universal (absolute) novelty. It is against this that the creation must "differ distinctly" to be protectable. Even if it differs "essentially" from the state of the art, the doors to the Patent Act open, too.

The inventive step criterion in the Patent Act implies that inventions differ *essentially* from the state of the art. Creations on the other hand need only differ *distinctly* therefrom to qualify for utility model protection.[6] It can be difficult to measure the exact content of this requirement but trivial, obvious or insignificant differences from the state of the art will not be sufficient.

Some doubt remains as to the exact profile of "the person skilled in the art", and whether one should apply the same standards as in patent law or different ones. Precedent is scarce. However, administrative practice and case law from the Danish Maritime and Commercial High Court seem to suggest that for the assessment in utility model law, the person skilled in the art should be expected to have a more narrow focus when compared to patent law and to include only the exact scope of

5 Section 1(1) of the Consolidated Utility Models Act No. 91 of 29 January 2019.

6 Paragraph 2, subsection 1 of the Consolidated Danish Patents Law Act No. 90 of 29 January 2019, and paragraph 5, subsection 1 of the Consolidated Utility Models Act No. 91 of 29 January 2019.

the claimed creation and (very) little beyond. The combination of a "narrow" scope of the person skilled in the art with a "low" threshold may lead to a very broad scope of protection and might be hard to align with the starting point that "trivial, obvious, or insignificant differences" from the state of the art do not suffice. Also, it would seem to depart from the starting point of parallelism with patent law to rely on a different type of skilled person in utility model law. So far, the Danish Supreme Court has not decided on the matter, so the nature of utility model law's "person skilled in the art" remains unclear at the moment.[7] The assessment of inventiveness regarding utility models is based on the problem-and-solution-approach (known from patent law).

According to Section 2(1) and subsection 2 (ii), creations cannot be registered as utility models if they relate to war material or to *methods*.[8] At this point, the scope of the Act differs from the Patent Act where methods can be (and to a large degree are) protectable. The modification on methods is further qualified in subsection 3, which states:

> Notwithstanding subsection 2 (ii) it shall be possible to register a utility model for products for use in any such methods, including substances and compositions for use in methods for the treatment of the human or animal body by surgery or therapy or diagnostic methods practiced on the human or animal body, or products obtained by microbiological process or other technical processes.

It is not quite clear why the Act does not follow the lead of the Patent Act on the issue of methods. For some technologies – chemical and computer programs – the effect of the limitation is to reduce the scope of protection offered significantly. Arguably, method claims might be much more complicated to draft when compared to product claims. Many of the SME creators envisaged by the Act would therefore find it hard to draft the claims themselves. Furthermore, even if they did succeed in drafting them, such claims might not provide a suitable basis for future infringement suits. It was probably to avoid such complications that the legislator simply decided to shut the door on method claims and to leave it only for patent law.

4.3 UTILITY MODEL STATISTICS

During the first 10 years after the act came into force (1992–2002), approximately 4,500 utility model applications were filed in total. In 1994, with a total of 471 applications, interest in the newly instituted legal protection peaked. Since then, interest in utility model applications has declined, and it reached a low ebb in 2022 with only 85 applications. More than 60 percent of applicants are Danish (Table 4.1 and Figure 4.1).[9] From 2013 to 2022 the average was 118 utility model grants per year (Table 4.2 and Figure 4.2).[10]

7 Schovsbo et al. 2024, 437 ff.
8 Schovsbo et al. 2024, 435 on the allowability of product-by-process claims.
9 DKPTO 2023.
10 164 in 2013 and 90 in 2022.

TABLE 4.1 *Utility model applications (DKPTO 2023)*[11]

Submission year	Utility model applications in total	Danish applications	Percentage Danish applications (%)
2013	197	157	80
2014	185	146	79
2015	158	120	76
2016	146	113	77
2017	132	100	76
2018	92	70	76
2019	110	78	71
2020	140	105	75
2021	118	76	64
2022	85	53	62

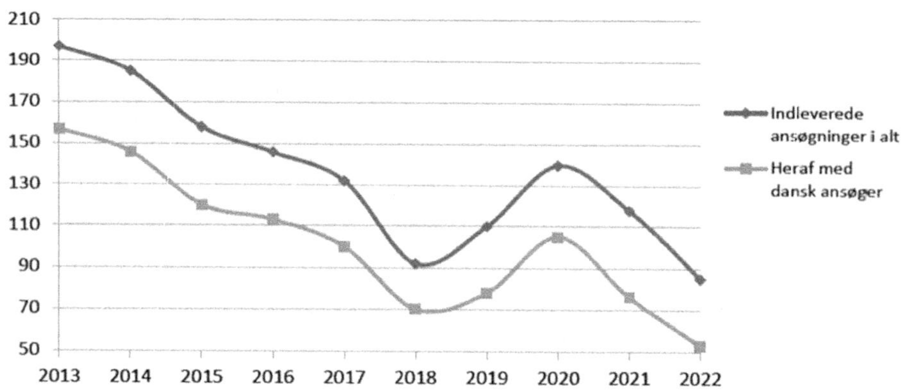

FIGURE 4.1 Number of utility model applications (total number of applications and applications with a Danish applicant)

The Danish empirical data from IPLytics on utility models from 1992 to 2009 and the empirical data from the DKPTO from 2010–2012 made up a total of 7,416 grants (Table 4.1 and Table 4.3). The data therefrom also clearly verifies a sheer decline in the demand of utility model protection.

Based on the IPLytics' data in Table 4.4, one may also notice that (major) users from 1992 to 2009 were to be found in industries limited to mechanical engineering, consumption and process engineering (civil engineering (consumption), machine tools, electrical machinery, process engineering (special equipment), medical technology (instruments), furniture games).

[11] Utility model applications for 2010 (198), 2011 (171) and 2012 (161) (DKPTO 2020).

TABLE 4.2 *Granted utility models (DKPTO 2024 b)*

Registration year	Registered utility models in total	Danish applicants	Percentage Danish applicants (%)
2013	164	127	77
2014	159	126	79
2015	147	110	75
2016	126	91	72
2017	120	92	77
2018	108	78	72
2019	80	59	74
2020	101	69	68
2021	85	52	61
2022	90	59	66

TABLE 4.3 *Danish utility model applications by year (IPLytics)*

Year	Number of applications: total 5868
1992	276
1993 (1994) 1995 (1996) 1997 (1998)	512 (418) 427 (418) 421 (404)
1999 (2000) 2001 (2002)	382 (326) 301 (328)
2003 (2004) 2005 (2006) 2007	299 (282) 246 (263) 236
2008 (2009)	

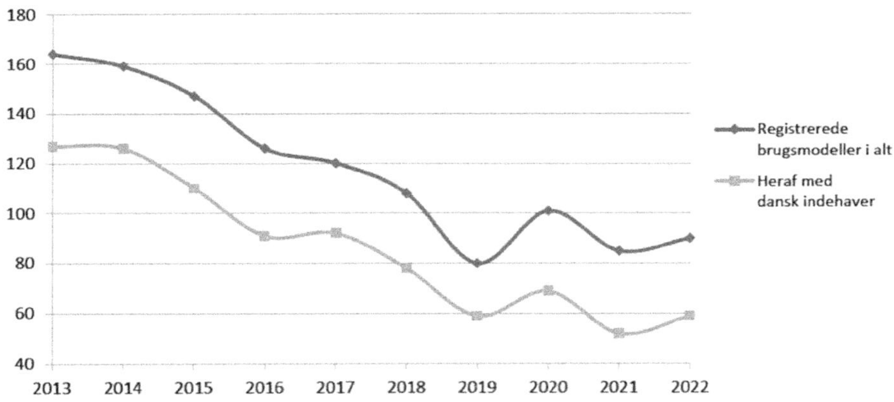

FIGURE 4.2 Total number of registrations with a Danish applicant

Utility models (issued and published applications) are searchable and accessible in a database administered by the Danish Patent and Trademark Office (DKPTO).[12]

[12] https://onlineweb.dkpto.dk/pvsonline/Patent.

TABLE 4.4 *Number of Danish utility model patents per application year, by industry (IPLytics 1992–2009)*[13]

Industry	Year/number of applications
Chemistry, pharmaceuticals	(1992: 13) 1993: 15 (1994: 16) 1995: 10 (1996: 8) 1997: 12 (1998: 3) 1999: 18 (2000: 21) 2001: 13 (2002: 16) 2003: 17 (2004: 10) 2005: 8 (2006: 21) 2007: 15 (2008: 6) 2009: 8 (2010: 21) 2011: 7 (2012: 8) 2013: 20 (2014: 7) 2015: 4 (2016: 5) 2017: 5 (2018: 6) 2019: 9 (2020: 9) 2021: 4 (2022: 2)
Consumption	(1992: 49) 1993: 93 (1994: 66) 1995: 75 (1996: 69) 1997: 74 (1998: 74) 1999: 60 (2000: 69) 2001: 71 (2002: 52) 2003: 65 (2004: 56) 2005: 59 (2006: 44) 2007: 47 (2008: 36) 2009: 23 (2010: 38) 2011: 27 (2012: 31) 2013: 23 (2014: 10) 2015: 15 (2016: 10) 2017: 11 (2018: 13) 2019: 10 (2020: 13) 2021: 12 (2022: 3)
Electrical engineering	(1992: 14) 1993: 30 (1994: 33) 1995: 37 (1996: 32) 1997: 30 (1998: 38) 1999: 30 (2000: 28) 2001: 27 (2002: 34) 2003: 17 (2004: 23) 2005: 15 (2006: 21) 2007: 19 (2008: 11) 2009: 19 (2010: 16) 2011: 14 (2012: 16) 2013: 8 (2014: 11) 2015: 10 (2016: 3) 2017: 10 (2018: 6) 2019: 13 (2020: 8) 2021: 8 (2022: 2)
Instruments	(1992: 26) 1993: 38 (1994: 40) 1995: 37 (1996: 42) 1997: 31 (1998: 26) 1999: 32 (2000: 22) 2001: 19 (2002: 28) 2003: 19 (2004: 23) 2005: 17 (2006: 26) 2007: 26 (2008: 9) 2009: 18 (2010: 14) 2011: 9 (2012: 12) 2013: 15 (2014: 7) 2015: 7 (2016: 6) 2017: 8 (2018: 3) 2019: 9 (2020: 11) 2021: 7 (2022: 4)
Mechanical engineering	(1992: 37) 1993: 59 (1994: 50) 1995: 42 (1996: 34) 1997: 45 (1998: 38) 1999: 45 (2000: 28) 2001: 32 (2002: 30) 2003: 35 (2004: 32) 2005: 23 (2006: 28) 2007: 29 (2008: 27) 2009: 14 (2010: 18) 2011: 15 (2012: 17) 2013: 14 (2014: 6) 2015: 2 (2016: 4) 2017: 12 (2018: 8) 2019: 9 (2020: 9) 2021: 3 (2022: 1)
Mechanical engineering, machinery	(1992: 54) 1993: 94 (1994: 71) 1995: 83 (1996: 87) 1997: 90 (1998: 82) 1999: 74 (2000: 53) 2001: 51 (2002: 55) 2003: 52 (2004: 52) 2005: 53 (2006: 48) 2007: 35 (2008: 39) 2009: 20 (2010: 28) 2011: 25 (2012: 30) 2013: 22 (2014: 15) 2015: 5 (2016: 11) 2017: 14 (2018: 18) 2019: 16 (2020: 16) 2021: 6 (2022: 3)
Other fields	(1992: 31) 1993: 83 (1994: 66) 1995: 77 (1996: 76) 1997: 77 (1998: 93) 1999: 71 (2000: 68) 2001: 47 (2002: 61) 2003: 60 (2004: 41) 2005: 44 (2006: 41) 2007: 44 (2008: 26) 2009: 25 (2010: 23) 2011: 19 (2012: 22) 2013: 18 (2014: 5) 2015: 2 (2016: 3) 2017: 7 (2018: 13) 2019: 10 (2020: 8) 2021: 1 (2022: 1)
Process engineering, special equipment	(1992: 52) 1993: 100 (1994: 76) 1995: 66 (1996: 70) 1997: 62 (1998: 50) 1999: 52 (2000: 37) 2001: 41 (2002: 52) 2003: 34 (2004: 45) 2005: 27 (2006: 34) 2007: 21 (2008: 22) 2009: 26 (2010: 21) 2011: 15 (2012: 19) 2013: 28 (2014: 12) 2015: 10 (2016: 13) 2017: 12 (2018: 8) 2019: 12 (2020: 15) 2021: 11 (2022: 3)

[13] As Table 4.4 illustrate trends in (major) users of the system, we have used the data from IPLytics 1992–2022. However, the data from IPLytics are inconsistent with those from the DKPTO (2010–2022).

Industry	Year/number of applications
Waste and wastewater	(1992: 0) 1993: 0 (1994: 0) 1995: 0 (1996: 0) 1997: 0 (1998: 0) 1999: 0 (2000: 0) 2001: 0 (2002: 0) 2003: 0 (2004: 0) 2005: 0 (2006: 0) 2007: 0 (2008: 0) 2009: 0 (2010: 0) 2011: 0 (2012: 0) 2013: 0 (2014: 1) 2015: 0 (2016: 0) 2017: 1 (2018: 0) 2019: 0 (2020: 0) 2021: 0 (2022: 0)

When registered, utility models are published on the digital platform https://tidender2.dkpto.dk/ (Dansk Brugsmodel Tidende), cf. Section 21(1) and below for international utility model applications under the Patent Cooperation Treaty (PCT) designating Denmark.[14]

4.4 GRANTING PROCEDURE

Utility models are granted by the Danish Patent and Trademark Office (DKPTO) by a simple registration procedure. The granting procedure requires the applicant to file an application for the registration of a utility model containing a statement of the subject matter for which protection is sought.[15] In addition, the creation must be described or shown in a manner sufficiently clear to enable a person skilled in the art to carry it out. As for creations involving the use of biological material, a sample can be deposited.[16] Additional details regarding the procedure are described in Part 3, Section 19 of the Order no. 1605 of 8 December 2006, requires that the claims contain a statement of novelty and the state of the art, which can be made in the form of a reference to the description, including drawings or photographs.[17]

The simple registration procedure entails only a cursory examination. Hence, novelty and inventiveness need not be assessed ex officio by the DKPTO.[18] In 2023, the Danish Maritime and Commercial High Court ruled that the DKPTO is not obligated to consider ex officio the risk of double

[14] Espacenet 2024.

[15] Part 2 and Section 14 of the Consolidated Danish Utility Models Act (2019). An international utility model application under the Patent Cooperation Treaty (PCT) can be filed, and in its capacity of receiving Office the DKPTO shall receive, check and transmit international applications accordingly, cf. Part 3 and Section 26(2) and Part 8, paragraph 41(1) of the Order on the Examination and Other processing of Utility Models Applications and Registered Utility Models.

[16] Sections 14(2) and 15(1) of the Consolidated Danish Utility Models Act (2019) and Part 4, Section 24 of the Order no. 1605 (2006).

[17] Sections 19(2) and 19(1)(ii)(iii) of the Consolidated Danish Utility Models Act (2019).

[18] Ibid. Section 19(1).

patenting for utility models, cf. U 2023.2178 SHR. To file an application, the applicant shall pay a fee, and he can request an optional examination if an additional fee is paid according to Section 19(2). In doing so, the requirement of novelty and inventiveness, cf. Section 5, must be examined before registration. For a detailed description of the examination procedure, see order No. 1605 of 8 December 2006.[19]

Except for the lack of substantive examination, the granting procedure for both patents and utility models are rather similar. The applicant may also claim priority of a previous patent or utility model application according to Article 4 of the Paris Convention ('convention priority'), provided that the subsequent application is filed within 12 months from the date of filing the previous application.[20]

If the application complies with the requirements, the creation will be registered and a notification published by DKPTO, Section 21(1). As a rule, the creation will not be registered earlier than 15 months from the date of filing the application.[21] Accordingly, by then the files shall be available to the public, even if the creation has not been registered, Section 24(1). Most utility models are registered prior to the statutory 15 months of publication, but the registration is not effected prior to the publication. Upon a request by the applicant, the publication or registration may be effected earlier.[22] In contrast, the files of a patent application will be available as of the date on which the patent is granted, cf. Section 22(1) of the Consolidated Danish Patent Law Act. However, according to subsection 2, the statutory requirement for publication is 18 months from the date of filing even if a patent has not been granted. By request, the publication of the grant can be postponed until the 18 months' limit has expired. Measuring pendency for utility models and patents will have to take the above differences into account. However, there is no publicly available empirical data on the differences in pendency for utility models and patents.

4.5 FEES, DKPTO

The basic fee per application is 2,000 DKK (approx. 250 EURO), and the basic fee for subsequent filing of a Danish translation of an international application is 1,100 DKK (approx. 147 EURO).[23] The basic fee for resumption is 400 DKK (approx. 53

[19] For international (PCT) utility models applications, see Part 3 of the Consolidated Danish Utility Models Act (2019).

[20] Section 11(1) of the Consolidated Danish Utility Models Act (2019).

[21] Section 24(1).

[22] Section 24(2).

[23] When proceeding with an international utility model application designating Denmark, the applicant shall pay the prescribed fee to the DKPTO and file a translation into Danish within 33 months from the international filing date or, if priority is claimed, from the priority date.

EURO) and for re-establishment 3,000 DKK (approx. 400 EURO). If the applicant requests substantive examination before or after a registration, the basic fee is 4,000 DKK (approx. 530 EURO).

Utility model protection lasts three years from the date of filing and may be renewed for further two periods of three or four years, respectively, against payment of the prescribed fees.[24] The maximum term of protection is ten years. The renewal fee for the first period is 2,000 DKK (approx. 267 EURO) and for the second period 3,000 DKK (approx. 400 EURO). Renewal fees paid after the expiry of the registration period concerned will be increased by 20 percent.[25] Finally, the basic fee for publication of notice of amended registration and publication of amended text amounts to 1,000 DKK (approx. 133 EURO). The basic fee for appeal is 5,000 DKK (approx. 667 EURO).

4.6 THE ADMINISTRATIVE APPEAL PROCEDURE AND REVOCATION BY A COURT DECISION

As a utility model can be registered without substantive examination, it is not possible to file an opposition with the DKPTO, as is the case for granted patents.

A utility model registration may be revoked by a court decision on the grounds listed in Section 47(1): *if* the registration has not been effected in accordance with the basic requirements in Sections 1 to 5, *if* the description of the creation is not sufficiently clear, or *if* the application has been amended after it has been filed or *if* the scope of protection has been extended after the registration. The division between DKPTO and the courts is clear as the courts cannot rephrase the claims.[26]

Revocation proceedings may be instituted by any person.[27]

After a utility model registration has been granted, any person may file a request with the DKPTO for examination of the registration, cf. Section 50(1). The request for examination may only be based on the grounds for revocation referred to above (Section 47(1)). If proceedings are instituted before the courts prior to a final decision from the DKPTO, the DKPTO will suspend the examination until the case has been finally decided unless the request has been filed by the proprietor of the utility model, Section 50(4).

Finally, the applicant may appeal the final decision of the DKPTO to the Board of Appeal for Patents and Trademarks. The same applies to the proprietor of the

If the application is written in Danish, the applicant shall file a copy of the application within 33 months.

24 Section 38(1) of the Consolidated Danish Utility Models Act (2019) and the renewal of registration shall be advertised.

25 Section 39 (1) payment of renewal fees.

26 U 2019.3126 Ø.

27 Section 47(4) of the Consolidated Danish Utility Models Act (2019).

utility model when a utility model registration is revoked entirely or partially after a request for examination of the registration under Section 50.[28] Appeals must be filed no later than two months after the DKPTO has notified the party which is affected by the decision, cf. Section 25(2). Other parties having an interest in the decision may file a similar appeal no later than two months after the publication of the decision. The decision of the Board is final and cannot be appealed to any other administrative authority.[29]

Once the decision has been brought before the Board of Appeal, it may not be brought before the courts until the decision from the Board has been given.[30]

4.7 UTILITY MODEL INFRINGEMENT, DAMAGES AND INJUNCTIONS

Utility models may be enforced against an infringer in court. However, only the injured party may institute proceedings, unless the institution of proceedings is required in the interest of the public, cf. Section 54(4). It follows from Section 54 (1) that any person who intentionally or with gross negligence infringes the exclusive right conferred by a utility model registration shall be punished with a fine. The penalty may increase to imprisonment of up to 18 months if the infringement has been committed intentionally and under aggravating circumstances unless heavier penalty is provided for by Section 299b of the Danish Penal Code (where the range of penalty is up to 6 years). Aggravating circumstances are considered to exist if a significant and obviously unlawful profit is intended by the infringement.

As for monetary damages, it is stated that any person who intentionally or negligently commits utility model infringement shall pay (i) a reasonable compensation, and (ii) damages for any further injury, which the infringement has caused, inter alia the loss of profit suffered by the injured party and the illicit profit obtained by the infringer, cf. Section 55(1) and (2). Additional compensation may also be fixed to the injured party for non-financial injury, cf. Section 55(3).

The infringed party may also claim that a product infringing a utility model shall be (i) withdrawn from the market, (ii) removed definitively from the market, (iii) destroyed, (iv) surrendered to the injured party or (v) altered in a specified manner, all at the expense of the infringer, cf. Section 56(1) and (3).

A prohibitory or mandatory injunction may be granted according to Section 413 of the Danish Administration of Justice Act, if the party applying for the injunction

[28] Section 25(1).

[29] Section 25(4).

[30] The case law from the Board of Appeal is available at https://apv.naevneneshus.dk (in Danish). The Maritime and Commercial High Court case law can be found at https://domstol.dk/om-os/english/.

proves on a balance of probabilities or by clear and convincing evidence: (i) that the party holds the right for which protection by way of a prohibitory or mandatory injunction is sought; (ii) that the conduct of the opposing party necessitates the granting of the injunction; and (iii) that the ability of the party to enforce its right will be lost if the party has to await a full trial.

The court may decide that the granting of a prohibitory or mandatory injunction is to be conditional on the party providing security for any detriment and disadvantage inflicted on the opposing party because of the injunction, cf. Section 415.

In connection with a temporary injunction, the party that believes it has been injured can request the bailiff's court to carry out preservation of evidence with the other party, just as the party can be required to provide information, cf. Part 29 a Responsibility for finding and presenting evidence in the case of infringement of intellectual property rights, etc. of the Danish Administration of Justice Act.

4.8 BRANCHING-OFF FROM A PATENT APPLICATION OR PATENT UNDER OPPOSITION

Utility models and patents are closely connected in Danish law. An applicant can file applications and combine protection in several ways. It is possible to file an application for the same creation/invention combining an application for a utility model with an application for a patent, which can be filed at the same time. Double protection is only possible if all requirements stated in the act are fulfilled. Hence, a registered utility model may pave the way for injunctions long before a corresponding patent is issued.

Furthermore, as a right of priority, for the purpose of Section 5(1) and (2) and Section 9, the applicant may also claim priority of previous patent or utility model applications filed in or for a state party to the Paris Convention, provided that the subsequent application is filed within 12 months from the date of filing the previous application.[31]

Finally, a patent application may be used as a basis for a utility model application. Thus, a patent application may be used in whole or in part as a basis for a utility model application in respect of the same creation. The priority date of the patent application may be relied upon for the application for the utility model, cf. Section 12(1). The branching-off is provided by Section 13 of the Ministerial Order no. 1605 of 8 December 2006 on the Examination and Other Processing of Utility Model Applications and Registered Utility Models, which states that a patent application

[31] Section 11(1) of the Consolidated Danish Utility Models Act (2019).

may be used as a basis for a utility model application for up to ten years from the date of filing the patent application or from the date which is deemed to be the date of filing. In this regard, a patent application for Denmark means (i) a Danish application; (ii) an international application proceeded with in Denmark; (iii) a European patent application designating Denmark and (iv) a European patent application converted into a Danish patent application.

5

Utility Models in French Law

Thibault Gisclard

In France, *certificats d'utilité* were introduced by the Law n°68-1 of January 2, 1968. According to article L. 611-2 of the French Intellectual Property Code, French *certificats d'utilité* are regulated by the same rules as French patents, with the main exceptions being a shorter duration, the absence of a requirement for a research report, and the lack of opposition proceedings.

5.1 HISTORICAL BACKGROUND

Certificats d'utilité (hereinafter utility certificates) were created in 1968 as a way for inventors to obtain protection for their invention, but with fewer requirements than full patents.[1] Notably, utility certificates can be granted by the French Intellectual Property Office, called INPI (*Institut National de la Propriété Industrielle*) without providing any research report on the elements of the state of the art that can be taken into consideration to assess the patentability of the invention. An influential author has suggested that utility certificates were introduced as "petit (small) patents" in order to increase the prestige of regular patents.[2]

However, it should be noted that in the past, regular patents, introduced just after the French Revolution by the law of 5 Vendémiaire An IX, did not require any examination of priority, merit or success of the inventions, and patents were therefore always designated as "SGDG" (*sans garantie du gouvernement – without guarantee of the government*). Their validity could only be assessed by the courts.

The French Patent Law of 1844 maintained the absence of prior examination, and it was only in 1968 that the examination of patents was introduced through a

[1] *Certificats d'utilité* should not be confused with provisory patent applications, which have been created by Law no. 2019-486 of 22 May 2019 and Decree no. 2020-15 of 8 January 2020, nowadays codified in Articles R. 612-3-1 and R. 612-3-2 of the French Intellectual Property Code.

[2] Mathely 1974, 196.

research report. However, even then, for more than fifty years, the effectiveness of that provision has been very limited: indeed, the INPI could only refuse to grant a patent if the research report showed that the invention was manifestly lacking in novelty.[3] In other words, there was still no substantial examination by the INPI of the novelty or nonobviousness of the invention.

It follows that, until very recently, these former French full patents were, in practice, as regards their examination, not very different from utility certificates of the time, even though a research report was formally required for patents as part of their application.

The examination of novelty and inventive step for French Patents only became greater with the enactment of the *loi n° 2019-486 du 22 mai 2019 relative à la croissance et la transformation des entreprises*, also known as the *loi PACTE*, which allows the INPI the right to refuse to grant a patent for an invention that does not comply with the requirements of novelty or inventive step.[4] Thus, the research report is now of practical use during application proceedings before the INPI, since its content can lead to the refusal of the patent, and it is not a mere formal requirement anymore. However, and rather strangely, that legislative reform also applies to utility certificates and therefore allows the INPI the right to refuse to grant a utility certificate for lack of novelty or inventive step, although a research report is not required, and will in practice not be provided to the office at that stage, which practically prevents an effective examination of these requirements.

Therefore, since 2020, utility certificates have become somewhat different from patents in practice, since the absence of a requirement of a research report as part of the application proceedings can be of practical use for inventions that are nonnovel or that lack an inventive step. Indeed, the research report that is requested for patent applications can now be used by the INPI to refuse to grant a patent, whereas a utility certificate might still be granted, although the INPI is also supposed to examine the requirements of novelty or of the inventive step for utility certificates, because of the references which are needed in order to examine these requirements are not required for a utility certificate.

5.2 APPLICATION PROCEDURE

The application procedure for a utility certificate follows the rules of a patent application, except for the requirement of research report, and that no opposition proceedings are possible. Indeed, article L. 611-2 of the French Intellectual Property Code states that "the provisions of this chapter relating to patents shall apply to utility certificates with the exception of those laid down in Article L. 612-14, the first paragraph of Articles L. 612-15 and L. 612-17 and Articles L. 613-23 to L. 613-23-6".

[3] French Intellectual Property Code, former Article L. 612-12, 7°.

[4] French Intellectual Property Code, Article L. 612-12, 7°, which points to Article L. 611-10, 1° referring to the novelty, inventive step, and industrial application requirements.

The application for a utility certificate is therefore regulated by Articles L. 612-1 et seq. of the French Intellectual Property Code. According to Article L. 612-2 of the French Intellectual Property Code, the filing date of the [utility certificate] application is the date on which the applicant has filed documents that contain: (a) an indication that a [utility certificate] is sought; (b) information identifying or communicating with the applicant; and (c) a description [...] or a reference to a previously filed application under conditions prescribed by regulation.

The invention must be set forth in the [utility certificate] application in a manner sufficiently clear and complete to enable a person skilled in the art to carry it out.[5] The claims define the subject matter of the protection sought. They must be clear and concise and based on the description.[6]

Additional details concerning the content of the application are provided by Article R. 612-3 of the French Intellectual Property Code, which states that the [utility certificate] application shall comprise a request for the grant of a [utility certificate], the model for which shall be laid down by decision of the Director General of the National Institute of Industrial Property, and to which shall be annexed: (1) a description of the invention, accompanied, where appropriate, by drawings; (2) one or more claims; (3) an abstract of the technical content of the invention; and (4) where appropriate, a copy of the earlier filings.

After filing, the conformity of the utility certificate application with the legislative and regulatory provisions referred to in Article L. 612-12 is formally examined by the Director of the Institut National de la Propriété Industrielle, according to Article L. 612-11 of the French Intellectual Property Code.

Notably, Article L. 612-12 of the French Intellectual Property Code states that any application for a [utility certificate] shall be rejected, in whole or in part: [...] (4) the subject matter of which is an invention that is not patentable under Articles L. 611-16 to L. 611-19; (5) whose subject matter cannot be considered as an invention within the meaning of Article L. 611-10, paragraph 2; (6) whose description or claims do not allow the application of the provisions of Article L. 612-14; (7) whose subject matter is not patentable within the meaning of Article L. 611-10, paragraph 1; (8) whose claims are not based on the description [...]. If the grounds for rejection affect the [utility certificate] application only in part, only the corresponding claims will be rejected. In the event of partial noncompliance of the application with the provisions of Articles L. 611-17, L. 611-18, L. 611-19 (4° of I) or L. 612-1, the corresponding parts of the description and drawings will be deleted ex officio. Therefore, although in theory, an application for a utility certificate where the invention is not novel or lacks an inventive step should be rejected, the INPI might, however, encounter serious difficulties for seriously examining these requirements without any research report, which the law does not require for utility certificates.

5 Ibid., Article L. 612-5.

6 Ibid., Article L. 612-6.

The next step is the examination of the invention by National Defense. The Minister in charge of Defense is authorized to take cognizance of patent [and utility certificate] applications at the National Institute of Industrial Property, on a confidential basis. Inventions that are the subject of patent [and utility certificate] applications may not be disclosed and freely worked until authorization has been granted to that effect.[7] During this period, patent [and utility certificate] applications may not be made public, no true copy of the patent [or utility certificate] application may be issued without authorization, and no transformation of a patent into a utility certificate or vice versa may be initiated, and no publication of the invention may be initiated. These authorizations, which shall be granted by the Director of the National Institute of Industrial Property on the advice of the Minister responsible for defense, may be granted at any time, and the first authorization shall be acquired as of right at the end of a period of five months from the date of filing of the patent [or utility certificate] application.[8]

Afterwards, the application for a utility certificate is published, according to Article L. 612-21 of the French Intellectual Property Code.

Only then can the utility certificate be granted. The title (certificate) shall include the description, if applicable, the drawings, and the claims.[9]

Utility certificates are now issued for a period of ten years from the date of filing of the application.[10] Before the law of May 22, 2019, and its implementation decree n°2020-15 of January 8, 2020, the duration of a utility certificate was only six years from the date of filing of the application. Utility certificates that have been issued for less than six years before January 10, 2020, the date of publication of the implementation decree, have their duration extended to ten years.[11]

As of 2024, the filing fee for a utility certificate are 26€ for an online application. The delivery fee is 90€, and the annual tax varies from 38€ for the second year to 220 € for the tenth year.[12] In case the utility certificate is used in court proceedings for infringement, and only in that case, a research report will be required, which will add 520€ to the cost.

5.3 PRACTICAL USE OF UTILITY CERTIFICATES

In 2022, there were 673 applications for utility certificates made to the *Institut National de la Propriété Industrielle*, which corresponds to only 4.5 percent of all French patent applications. In addition, on that year, only 5 of these utility

[7] Ibid., Article L. 612-9.
[8] Ibid., Article L. 612-8.
[9] Ibid., Article L. 612-17.
[10] Ibid., Article L. 611-2.
[11] According to the INPI, in 2020, 70 percent of eligible utility certificates have been extended.
[12] In case the tax has not paid by the owner, the utility certificate will lapse: see, e.g., French Cour de Cassation, Commercial Chamber, 23 February 1993, n°91-15.376.

certificates were transformed into regular patents, whereas there were 188 transformations of utility certificates into regular patents in 2021 and 137 in 2020, which were the first two years following the legislative reform allowing that possibility.

The number of applications seems to be slightly increasing, since, in 2005, only 390 applications for utility certificates were made, whereas in 2010 this number had increased to 484, and reached its peak to 1019 in 2020.

In practice, according to the INPI, in 2010, 44 percent of the applicants for utility certificates were French, whereas 30 percent of applicants were from China, Taiwan and Hong-Kong.

5.4 PUBLICATION OF UTILITY CERTIFICATES

Like patents, utility certificates are published in the *Bulletin officiel de la propriété industrielle* (BOPI).

Article L. 612-21 of the French Intellectual Property Code provides that the Institut National de la Propriété Industrielle shall ensure publication, under the conditions defined by decree in Council of State, by mention in the BOPI, by making the full text available to the public or by dissemination by means of a data bank or distribution via computer storage medium the file of any application for a patent or utility certificate at the end of a period of eighteen months from its filing date or from the priority date if priority has been claimed, or, at the request of the applicant, before the expiry of that period.

French utility certificates are also available in public databases, notably in the Espacenet database of the European Patent Office.

5.5 EFFECTIVENESS OF UTILITY CERTIFICATES

Although utility certificates are granted by the INPI without any research report, and therefore without any serious possibility for the office of examining of the requirements of novelty and inventive step, it should be noted that these "paper tigers" can only produce actual legal effects if they are valid, which notably means that they concern an invention which is new, which involves an inventive step and which is susceptible of industrial application.

For this reason, infringement proceedings before courts require the owner of the utility certificate to provide the research report that is mandatory for the granting of a Patent.

Article L. 615-6 of the French Intellectual Property Code provides that in infringement proceedings brought pursuant to an application for a utility certificate, the applicant shall file a research report drawn up under the same conditions as the report provided for in Article L. 612-14 (i.e., for a patent application).

That research report and the challenging of the validity of the utility certificate by the presumed infringer will allow the court to check whether that utility certificate is valid, and therefore whether or not to allow it to be asserted.

Although license agreements of utility certificates[13] technically do not require a research report, the validity of such license agreements can be challenged in court proceedings, on the basis of the nonvalidity of the utility certificate, for example, for lack of novelty or inventive step. Indeed, a judgment of the Paris Court of First Instance stated that a license agreement and an assignment of a utility certificate were void for lack of purpose (*"absence d'objet"*: former article 1126 of the French Civil Code) since the owners of this utility certificate had not proven the novelty and the inventive step of the invention protected by the licensed utility certificate.[14]

Unlike the French patents, opposition proceedings are expressly excluded for French utility certificates by Article L. 611-12 *in fine* of the French Intellectual Property Code.

Therefore, the validity of a utility certificate can only be challenged in court proceedings. According to Article L. 611-12 *in fine* of the French Intellectual Property Code, Article L. 613-25 relative to challenging the validity of a French patent in court is also applicable to French utility certificates. This means that the [utility certificate] shall be declared invalid by a court decision: (a) if its subject matter is not patentable under Articles L. 611-10,[15] L. 611-11[16] and L. 611-13 to L. 611-19;[17] or (b) if it does not set forth the invention in a manner sufficiently clear and complete for a person skilled in the art to carry it out; or (c) if its subject matter extends beyond the contents of the application as filed or, where the [utility certificate] has been granted on the basis of a divisional application, if its subject matter extends beyond the contents of the original application as filed; or (d) if, after limitation [...], the scope of protection conferred by the [utility certificate] has been increased.

5.6 ENFORCEMENT OF UTILITY CERTIFICATES AGAINST INFRINGERS

Utility certificates may be enforced against an infringer before the Paris Court of First Instance.[18] As already mentioned, this requires the owner to request a research report for that utility certificate. Indeed, Article L. 615-6 of the French Intellectual Property Code provides that in infringement proceedings brought pursuant to an application for a utility certificate,[19] the applicant shall file a search report drawn up under the same conditions as the report provided for patent applications.

[13] See, e.g., French Cour de Cassation, Commercial Chamber, 19 September 2006, n°04-17.932.

[14] Paris Court of First Instance of 13 June 2013, n°11/04424.

[15] Which deals with nonpatentable inventions.

[16] Novelty requirement.

[17] Mainly dealing with public policy.

[18] Article D. 631-2 of the French Intellectual Property Code, which refers to the Article D. 211-6 of the French Code of Judicial Organization.

[19] According to Article L. 613-1 of the French IP Code, exclusive rights [patents, utility certificates, SPCs] start from the application date. However, according to Article L. 615-4, infringements made prior the publication of the application or to the notification of the application to a third party cannot be actioned. Furthermore, the court cannot decide upon infringement until the patent [or utility certificate] has been granted (Paris Court of appeal, 25 April 2001).

As regards the proof of infringement, the very efficient French proceeding called *Saisie-contrefaçon* can be used for establishing infringement of a utility certificate.[20] This specific form of action can be ordered by the president of one of the specialized courts in whose jurisdiction the action is brought.[21] The order need only include a simple request and recitation of the utility certificate to be enforced.[22]

The *saisie-contrefaçon* proceedings are detailed by Article L. 615-5 of the French Intellectual Property Code, which first states that infringement may be proven by any means. It then adds that, to this end, any person having standing to sue for infringement shall be entitled to have an infringing product, or document describing it, seized for evidentiary purposes. This seizure may be conducted in any place and by any bailiffs, and if necessary assisted by experts appointed by the plaintiff. The court may order, for the same evidentiary purposes, a seizure of a detailed description or materials and instruments used to manufacture or distribute the allegedly infringing products or to carry out the allegedly infringing processes.

The remedies that are available against an infringer of a utility certificate are the same as for the infringement of a patent.[23]

Therefore, the rules concerning the determination of damages are provided by Article L. 615-7 of the French Intellectual Property Code, which provides, in accordance with the European Directive 2004/48 of April 29, 2004, on the enforcement of intellectual property rights, that in determining damages, the court shall take into account separately (1) the negative economic consequences of the infringement, including the loss of profit and loss suffered by the injured party; (2) the intangible harm caused to the injured party; and (3) the profits made by the infringer, including the savings in intellectual, material and promotional investments that the infringer has derived from the infringement. Finally, the court may, as an alternative and at the request of the injured party, award a lumpsum as damages, and that this sum, which is not exclusive of the compensation for the intangible harm caused to the injured party, shall be greater than the amount of the royalties or fees that would have been due if the infringer had requested authorization to use the right infringed.

In addition, products recognized as infringing and the materials and instruments that were used primarily for their creation or manufacture may be recalled from commercial channels, permanently removed from those channels, destroyed or

[20] For an example, see French Cour de Cassation, Commercial Chamber, March, 29, 2011, n° 09-16.330 and 09-68.144.

[21] These judicial courts referred to in Article D. 631-2 of the French Intellectual Property Code. In practice, these can only be on first instance, the Tribunal Judiciaire de Paris (Paris Court of First Instance), and, on appeal, Paris Court of Appeal.

[22] Article R. 615-2 of the French Intellectual Property Code.

[23] In addition, customs enforcement is also possible for French utility certificates: see Article 2, 1, k) of the EU Regulation n°608/2013 of the European Parliament and of the Council of June 12, 2013, concerning customs enforcement of intellectual property rights.

confiscated for the benefit of the injured party.[24] The court may also order any appropriate measure to publicize the judgment, in particular its posting or publication in full or in excerpts in the newspapers or on the online public communication services that it designates, in accordance with the terms that it specifies. Naturally, these measures are ordered at the expense of the infringer.

In addition, injunctions can be issued by the courts.[25]

However, it should be noted that utility certificate enforcement proceedings seem to be very rare in practice. In any case, since such proceedings would in practice imply discussion of the validity of the utility certificate, and hence raise the same issues of fact and law as a full patent litigation, the cost of litigating a utility certificate would probably be as high as the cost of a full patent litigation.

5.7 CONVERSION BETWEEN UTILITY CERTIFICATES AND FULL PATENTS

Under the recent *loi PACTE* and the decree n°2020-15 of January 8, 2020, effective as of January 11, 2020, it is possible to convert a utility certificate application into a French patent application. Before this, a patent application could be converted to a utility certificate but not the reverse.

Accordingly, Article L. 612-15 of the French Intellectual Property Code now provides that an applicant may convert its application for a patent into an application for a utility certificate under conditions laid down by regulation, but also that an applicant may convert its application for a utility certificate into an application for a patent, within a time limit and according to a procedure specified by regulation.

Additional details are provided in the regulatory part of the French Intellectual Property Code. According to Article R. 612-53, and subject to the provisions of Article R. 612-31, the request for conversion of the utility certificate application into a patent application must be made in writing at any time during the period eighteen months from the filing of the utility certificate application or from the priority date if priority has been claimed and, in any event, before the start of the technical preparations, provided for in Article R. 612-39, undertaken with a view to publication of the utility certificate application. Where the patent application is the result of the conversion of a utility certificate application in accordance with the provisions of the second paragraph of Article L. 612-15, the search report fee shall be paid within one month of the date of receipt of the request for conversion.[26] Likewise, a request for conversion of a patent application referred to in Article R. 612-3 into an application for a utility certificate maybe made in writing at any time during the period of eighteen months from the filing date or from the priority date if priority has been

[24] Article L. 615-7-1 of the French Intellectual Property Code.
[25] See Gisclard and Py 2022.
[26] Article R. 612-54 of the French Intellectual Property Code.

claimed and, in any event, before the start of the technical preparations provided for in Article R. 612-39, undertaken with a view to publication of the patent application.[27]

As a result, conversions between patents applications and utility certificates applications are now possible in both directions. This means that an invention which is novel and involves an inventive step can be protected at first with a utility certificate application, which can shortly after be converted to a full patent application, since it deserves it. Conversely, an invention which is either not very promising from an economical point of view, or which might not comply with the requirements of a patent (e.g., because it is obvious) can be "downgraded" and still be the subject of a utility certificate application, even though there is now a (rather theoretical, at least if the research report has not been made yet) risk of rejection of that utility certificate application because of the lack of novelty or inventive step, and, even if granted, that utility certificate will only be effective in a court proceeding if the invention is novel, nonobvious, and the research report has been made at that later stage.

Utility certificates are therefore not necessarily third-rate patents: indeed, they can also be a step towards a full patent.

5.8 PRACTICAL USE OF UTILITY CERTIFICATES

Utility certificates are designed and mostly used for inventions that have a shorter lifespan, in order to lower the costs and delays compared to regular patents.

However, the protection is shorter (ten years instead of twenty years), and the research report is still required a posteriori if the utility certificate is asserted in infringement proceedings, which means the cost of the research report is not avoided, but only delayed until the litigation stage (for those few utility certificates that are eventually litigated).

The new procedure to convert a utility certificate application into a patent application may allow utility certificates to constitute an intermediate step before an applicant incurs the expense of obtaining a regular patent.

A key use of utility certificates is to prevent, on the grounds of lack of novelty,[28] a third party from applying for a patent in France concerning the same invention. Utility certificates can also be used to obtain international priority for applications made by the owner of the utility certificate.[29]

[27] Article R. 612-55 of the French Intellectual Property Code.

[28] French Cour de Cassation, Commercial Chamber, 27 September 2017, n°15-23.246.

[29] For an example highlighted in a litigation, see Paris Court of First Instance May 7, 2015, n° 13/16172. Conversely, the owner of a foreign utility certificate can use it as a priority for the application of a French utility certificate: see, for a German utility model used as a priority, French Cour de Cassation, Commercial Chamber, March 29, 2011, n°09-16.330 and n°09-68144.

In a more questionable way,[30] utility certificates can be used to obtain protection for inventions that would not meet the requirements for a regular patent, taking profit from the lack of research report at the application stage, which does not allow for an effective control of novelty and inventive step, and of the lack of opposition proceedings. For this reason, in such cases, a utility certificate might still be granted by the INPI, although that invention doesn't comply with the legal requirements (novelty, inventive step, etc.) for a utility certificate. However, such a utility certificate will be held invalid in court because the defendant will, at that stage, be able to prove that it did not satisfy the legal requirements. This strategy might be used by the inventor either ab initio, or through a conversion from a patent application, but before the research report for a patent application has been issued, since an already issued unfavorable research report can now be used by the INPI to reject the application for a utility certificate if the invention lacks novelty or inventive step. In such cases, utility certificates may be used (abusively) as leverage in negotiation against small entities or weak competitors.

30 Compare with a decision which considered as an act of unfair competition the use of the words "patented" for an invention which was only protected by a utility certificate, French Cour de Cassation, Commercial Chamber, October 24, 2000, n°98-12.563, since it wrongly implied that the duration of the protection was longer.

6

Utility Models in Germany and Switzerland

Peter Georg Picht and Marian Weber

6.1 GENERAL OVERVIEW

In Germany, the utility model is a type of intellectual property right that provides protection for novel and useful inventions. It is governed by the German Utility Model Act (*Gebrauchsmustergesetz* – GebrMG) which was enacted in 1891, making it the oldest still-existing utility model system in the world.[1] Utility models grant the right holder exclusive control over the use and commercialization of an invention for a period of ten years from the date of filing, subject to the payment of annual renewal fees. In a way, the utility model is the "little sister" of a full-fledged patent (also called a "petty patent"), protecting the same type of subject matter (technical inventions) with a more limited scope (discussed in more detail below).

The origins of the German utility model date back to the late nineteenth century, a period of rapid industrialization in which industry endorsed strong legal protection for its innovations. After the introduction of the first German patent law in 1877, it was soon recognized that patent law might not be suitable for all types of inventions and that an additional protection regime for inventions with less stringent protection requirements was desirable.[2] Unsurprisingly, demand for utility models was high from the outset. Just about two weeks after the German Utility Model Act entered into force on 1 October 1891, sixty-eight utility models had already been applied for in different technical categories.[3] Today, approximately 10,000 utility models are issued in Germany each year,[4] predominantly in the construction sector (mechanical engineering and machinery), followed by transport, furniture, games, electric

[1] Heikkilä and Lorenz 2018, 8. The Act was amended by Decree of 28 August 1986; last amended on 10 August 2021. We recognize, of course, the older utility design system established in the UK in 1843, but which is no longer in existence (see Chapter 3).

[2] Suthersanen 2016, 15.

[3] DPMA 2024a.

[4] DPMA 2024b.

machines and devices, and medical technology.[5] All registered utility models are accessible in a searchable database administered by the German Patent and Trademark Office ("*Deutsches Patent- und Markenamt*"; DPMA).[6] After a peak of utility model grants in the late 1990s, a general downward trend in applications can be observed which seemingly corresponds to a downward trend in the filing of patent applications.[7] Some scholars propose far-reaching adjustments to the utility model protection system.[8] Others wonder whether the use of utility models will intensify, for example, for the protection of standard-essential technology that tries to escape patent and competition law's stricter FRAND licensing guardrails.[9] So far, however, German utility model law and use have proven rather stable.

6.2 PROTECTION AND GRANTING REQUIREMENTS

According to § 1 (1) Utility Model Act, utility model protection requires an invention that is new, industrially applicable, and embodying an inventive step.

6.2.1 *New Invention*

Just as patents, utility models protect only inventions of a technical nature and not, for instance, aesthetic creations of form, works of art, scientific theories, mathematical methods, or software (§ 1(2) GebrMG). In contrast to patent law, neither processes (§ 2(3) GebrMG) nor biotechnological inventions (§ 1(2) GebrMG) can be protected by utility models.

The invention is considered "new" if it does not belong to the state of the art at the priority date (§ 3(1) GebrMG). Prior art for a German utility model is only what has been made available, prior to the filing or priority date, to the public either by written description or by prior use in Germany (§ 3 (1) GebrMG). This is narrower than German patent law which considers prior art whatever is known to the public worldwide through written or oral description, use, or in any other manner (§ 3 PatG).

6.2.2 *Inventive Step and Industrial Applicability*

In particular because the historical legislature intended the utility model to protect smaller inventions and technical designs, the traditional interpretation, which still prevails in the legal literature, considered "inventive step" to require a lesser degree

5 DPMA 2024b.

6 The database can be accessed online: https://register.dpma.de/DPMAregister/pat/basis

7 Boschert 2014, 144; Heikkilä and Lorenz 2018, 10.

8 Takenaka 2021c (suggesting inter alia abolition of the written description requirement and removal of owner exclusivity in favor of statutory licensing rights).

9 See Chapter 16 (Standard-Essential Utility Models).

of inventive performance than the "inventive activity" stipulated in § 1(1) German Patent Act.[10] Generally speaking, this interpretation considers it sufficient if the person having ordinary skill in the art (PHOSITA) – this concept is largely the same as in German patent law[11] – makes the invention by reflecting on the prior art beyond a routine employment of his skills and prior art.[12]

Since 2006, however, the German Federal Court of Justice (*Bundesgerichtshof* – BGH), the highest first-instance court in utility model matters, has held that the inventiveness threshold is the same for patent and utility model law.[13] The BGH points out,[14] in particular, that a threshold even lower than the one currently applied in patent law would risk permitting an excessive monopolization of trivial achievements. The rather limited differences in the level of protection between patents and utility models would not justify such extensive utility model protection. The legislative intent of easier access to utility model protection is sufficiently observed by the narrower concept of prior art, which prevents the grant of a utility model for truly nonnovel inventions. As reflected by the BGH's decision, "inventive step" is a matter of law, albeit one that strongly depends on the factual circumstances of the case, and high instance courts can, thus, review it on appeal.[15]

Industrial applicability is assumed if the invention can be made or used in any area of commerce or agriculture (§ 3(2) GebrMG).

6.2.3 *Limited Pre-grant Examination*

In the application procedure for a utility model, the German Patent and Trademark Office (*Deutsches Patent- und Markenamt*; DPMA) does not assess novelty, inventive step, or industrial applicability of the invention (§ 8(1) GebrMG). If the application complies with the formal requirements of §§ 4, 4a, 4b GebrMG, the utility model is granted as an "unexamined IP right",[16] entered in the Utility Model Register, and published in the Patent Gazette (§ 8 Section 1 GebrMG). Because of this limited pre-grant examination, the registration procedure to obtain a utility model is (as of 2021) completed after 4.2 months on average.[17] This is much faster than the patent granting procedure which is usually completed after approx. 2.5–3 years.[18]

[10] Mes 2013, 140.
[11] BpatG GRUR 2008, 689 – *Scharnierkonstruktion*.
[12] BPatG GRUR 2006, 489 – *Schlagwerkzeug*; 2004, 852 – *Materialstreifenpackung*.
[13] BGH GRUR 2006, 843 – *Demonstrationsschrank*.
[14] See, from the lead decision, BGH GRUR 2006, 843 para. 18 seq. – *Demonstrationsschrank*.
[15] BGH GRUR 2012, 378 Rn. 16 – *Installiereinrichtung II*.
[16] DPMA 2017, 4.
[17] DPMA 2024c. See also Heikkilä and Lorenz 2018, 10.
[18] DPMA 2024d.

6.3 APPLICATION PROCESS AND ASSOCIATED COSTS

According to § 4, 4a GebrMG the application for a utility model is filed with the DPMA. The DPMA provides an application form for the registration of a utility model on its website.[19] The application must be accompanied by a description of the known prior art and the structure and advantages of the applicant's invention. The description may be supplemented by one or more technical drawings. The application must contain claims which delineate the essential features of the invention and determine the scope of protection (§ 4(3) GebrMG). There also is a novelty grace period pursuant to § 3(1)(3) GebrMG that caters to the need, for example, of individual inventors or R&D companies, to disclose inventions early on, prior to filing.[20] Due to the grace period, protection is still available if an inventor applies for a utility model registration within six months after the publication of the invention.[21]

In principle, anyone can file a utility model application without the need to involve an attorney. However, applicants not domiciled in Germany must be represented by a duly authorized attorney.

6.3.1 *Branching-Off*

A utility model cannot be turned into a patent, by application or otherwise, and vice versa. However, an important statutory mechanism for combining patent and utility model protection is known as "branching-off" (*Abzweigung*) applications under § 5 GebrMG. Such applications allow an applicant to claim the filing and, if applicable, priority date of a previously submitted patent application also for a subsequent utility model application provided the latter application concerns the same invention. Technically, the applicant provides a written declaration together with the utility model application referring to a previously submitted patent application with effect for the Federal Republic of Germany.[22]

However, there is controversy on the interpretation of what is considered the "same" invention. According to a narrower interpretation, the invention is considered the "same" if there is a literal correspondence and content identity between the submitted documents describing the invention for, respectively, the patent and the utility model application.[23] According to another opinion, the invention is the "same" if the subject matter of the branched-off utility model application is readily

[19] DPMA 2024e.

[20] German Bundestag, Drucksache 14/2879, 10 March 2000, 13.

[21] § 4a (1) GebrMG.

[22] The procedure in which the patent is sought is irrelevant for that matter. For example, the previous patent application could have been requested via a national application according to the German Patent Law, a European application according to the European Patent Convention [EPC], or an international application according to the Patent Cooperation Treaty [PCT].

[23] I.e. identity of documents (*Unterlagenidentität*); see also Schennen GRUR 1987, 22, 226.227; Mes 2020.

recognizable, to a person skilled in the art, in the related patent application.[24] The different views can have implications, for instance, regarding foreign language patent applications – literal conformity of the application documents cannot be achieved in such settings. This somewhat formalistic outcome suggests, in view also of the branching-off mechanism's rationale to facilitate parallel patent/utility model protection (cf. also below V.), the broader concept of the "same" invention as the more convincing one.[25]

The Federal Court of Justice has held[26] that even a utility model application the subject matter of which goes beyond that of the referenced patent application can claim the priority date of said patent application to the extent the two applications overlap. This, as it were, extensive reading of the branching-off concept does not consider the overlapping utility patent application to be invalid, as previous practice[27] would have.

6.3.2 *Costs*

For a utility model application, a filing fee of EUR 40 is due within three months from filing the application. In the case of an electronic application, the filing fee is EUR 30. Fees for maintenance[28] of the utility model are due after three, six, and eight years. If the respective maintenance fee is paid not at all, not in time, or not in full, the utility model lapses.[29]

6.4 CHALLENGING VALIDITY

According to § 15(1) GebrMG anyone can challenge a registered utility model and request its cancellation[30] either (a) if the subject matter of the utility model is not eligible for protection according §§ 1 to 3 GebrMG; (b) if the subject matter of the utility model has already been protected on the basis of an earlier patent or utility model application; or (c) if the subject-matter of the utility model goes beyond the content of the application in the version in which it was originally filed. If the grounds for cancellation concern only part of the utility model, the cancellation takes effect only to that extent. If the subject matter of the utility model is challenged for lack of eligibility, the court evaluates the substantive criteria of novelty, inventive

[24] BPatGE 35, 1 = GRUR 1995, 486; see also BPatGE 39, 10; BPatG Mitt. 1996, 211, 213; Mes 2020.

[25] See also Kraßer, GRUR 1993, 223, 226, 227; Goebel, GRUR 200, 477, 428 f.

[26] BGH GRUR 2003, 867.

[27] BPatGE 34, 14 = GRUR 1993, 963; Mes 2020.

[28] DPMA 2024f.

[29] DPMA 2024c.

[30] A request for cancellation of the utility model must be filed with the German Patent and Trademark Office, in writing, and contain a statement of the facts on which it is based (§16 GebrMG).

step and industrial applicability during the procedure. This ex post review thus steps in for a full-fledged ex ante examination of the utility model.

The utility model division of the German Patent and Trademark Office decides validity challenges by way of a formal decision (§17(3) GebrMG). This decision can be appealed to the Federal Patent Court and, ultimately, to the Federal Court of Justice (§ 18 GebrMG).

The relatively low threshold for a validity challenge, especially broad standing, renders utility models considerably less resilient than patents and has, for this reason, attracted some criticism.[31] On the other hand, the easier assailability of utility models may counterbalance the lower requirements for obtaining a utility model, especially the lack of a full-fledged ex ante examination.

6.5 ENFORCING UTILITY MODELS

A utility model can be enforced against an infringer in court according to §§ 24 seq. GebrMG. Any person who, without the consent of the proprietor of the utility model, manufactures, offers for sale, puts on the market, uses, imports, or possesses a product which is covered by the subject matter of the utility model may be sued by the proprietor for an injunction if there is a risk of repeated infringement (§ 24(1)(1) GebrMG). The right to injunctive relief already exists if there is a substantiated threat of a first offence (§ 24(1)(2) GebrMG). Neither the motives of the (possible future) infringer[32] nor fault on its part[33] matter. However, the right to injunctive relief is limited by the proportionality defense (§24(1)(3) GebrMG): Insofar as the claim would, due to the special circumstances of the individual case and the requirements of good faith (*Gebote von Treu und Glauben*), lead to a disproportionate hardship for the infringer or third parties that cannot be justified by the exclusive right of the rightsholder, the rightsholder is to receive only an appropriate financial compensation (*angemessener Ausgleich in Geld*). The claim for damages, however, remains unaffected (*unberührt*) by the proportionality defense (§24 (1)(5) GebrMG). This provision was introduced in utility model law together with an equivalent provision in German patent law in August 2021,[34] thereby transposing existing, but still developing, case law[35] regarding a proportionality defense into statutory law.[36]

In case of fault, the infringer of a utility model is also liable for damages (§ 24(2) GebrMG). When assessing damages, courts may also consider the infringer's infringement profit (§ 24(2)(2) GebrMG). According to § 24 (2)(3) GebrMG, the

[31] Boschert 2014, 144; Brack 2009, 11.

[32] Mes 2020, § 24 GebrMG, Rn. 41 et seq.

[33] Judgment of the German Federal Court of Justice (BGH) of 6 July 1954, I ZR 38/53, BGHZ 14, 163 (170).

[34] Entwurf eines Zweiten Gesetzes zur Vereinfachung und Modernisierung des Patentrechts.

[35] BGH, 10 May 2016, X ZR 114/13 – Wärmetauscher ("Air Scarf").

[36] On the discussions around this revision, see, e.g., Picht and Karczewski 2022, 159 et seq. with further references.

claim for damages may also be calculated based on the amount that the infringer would have had to pay as reasonable remuneration if it had obtained permission to use the invention ("license analogy").

Furthermore, the rightsholder may demand the destruction of infringing products (§ 24a(1) GebrMG), as well as their recall and definitive removal from the channels of distribution (§ 24a(2) GebrMG). These claims are equally subject to a proportionality requirement which takes the legitimate interests of third parties into consideration (§24a(3) GebrMG).

The holder of a utility model can also require the infringer to provide information on the origin and the distribution channels of the infringing products (§24b(1) GebrMG). Further claims go to the production of specific documents or to inspections (§24c(1)(1), (2) GebrMG). If there is a legitimate interest, the court may grant the winning party permission to publish the judgment at the expense of the losing party (§ 24e GebrMG).

Intentional infringement – including the exercise of rights conveyed by a granted patent which results in the infringement of a previously granted utility model – can, upon request by the rightsholder or in case of sufficient public interest, be punished under criminal law with up to three years of imprisonment or a fine (§25(1) GebrMG), for commercial activity up to five years imprisonment (§ 25(2) GebrMG). The attempt is punishable as well (§25(3) GebrMG).

6.6 COEXISTENCE OF UTILITY MODELS AND PATENTS

Both utility models and patents protect technical inventions, and they share protection requirements, such as novelty, inventive step/activity, and industrial applicability. The German legal framework allows for the usage of both patents and utility models in a combined or complementary fashion.[37] This "two-tiered patent system"[38] can be used better to coordinate the protection of inventions, for example, by using a joint priority date (c.f. § 5 GebrMG).

As outlined above, utility models, unlike patents, do not require a substantive ex ante examination of novelty, inventive step, or commercial applicability to be granted, making the application process much simpler, faster, and cheaper. On the other hand, they provide a much less reliable legal position as challenges have a higher likelihood of success.[39] Self-assessment costs regarding a utility model's validity (e.g., in preparation for a potential infringement litigation) may even reduce or remove the utility model's cost advantages over a full-fledged patent that issues only after full examination.[40] Against this background, utility models are in practice often used by rightsholders that eventually want to obtain a patent but

[37] Boschert 2014, 139.
[38] Heikkilä and Lorenz 2018; Liesegang 1992, 3.
[39] Heikkilä and Lorenz 2018; Radauer et al. 2015; Suthersanen 2006.
[40] Mes 2020, § 49 GebrMG, Rn. 3.

need to quickly secure rights during the period between the patent application and the grant of the patent.[41] Holding a utility model for the same invention can also prove advantageous in litigation if the patent applicant wishes to fight an infringement during the patent application procedure.[42]

6.7 UTILITY MODELS IN SWITZERLAND?

Under Swiss law there does not exist a utility model. Swiss patents are, essentially, subject to the same protection requirements as German patents.[43] However, the protection requirements of novelty, inventive step ("non-proximity"; *Nicht-Naheliegen*), and industrial application are not examined prior to the grant of a Swiss patent.[44] In this regard, the Swiss patent is similar to the German utility model. Hence, to obtain greater legal certainty, many Swiss inventors do not file for a Swiss (national) patent but instead seek a – fully examined – European patent, granted under the European Patent Convention and whose scope of protection they opt to extend to Switzerland.

To make the Swiss patent more attractive to users and to better comply with international standards, a revision of Swiss patent law is currently under way, with a view to introducing a patent (alternative) that will have a substantive examination system covering novelty and inventive step. Early in the legislative process, the introduction of an unexamined utility model complementing the patent was on the table as well. During the consultation process, however, the idea was dropped because stakeholders preferred the stronger protection offered by the current patent without full-fledged ex ante examination.[45] Instead of introducing two separate intellectual property rights, the draft now favors a flexible design[46] of the new patent right: Upon filing an application, the IPI will conduct obligatory research on the state of the art and publish its finding in a report.[47] During the application process the applicant will have the option to request a full-fledged examination of the patentability requirements, including novelty, inventive step, and commercial applicability.[48]

In January 2023 the Swiss Parliament began deliberations on the revision of the Patent Law. As of this writing, the outcome and timeline seem open.[49]

41 Boschert 2014, 143.
42 Brack 2009, 6.
43 Articles 1, 14 Swiss Patent Act.
44 Article 59(4) Swiss Patent Act.
45 Botschaft zur Änderung des Patentgesetzes vom 16. November 2022, BBl 2023 7, 10.
46 Recitals on the amendment of the Patent Act, 19.
47 nArticle 57a Swiss Patent Act.
48 nArticle 58b (4) revSwiss Patent Act.
49 www.parlament.ch/de/ratsbetrieb/suche-curia-vista/geschaeft?AffairId = 20220078.

7

Utility Models in Italy

Alessandro Cogo and Marco Ricolfi[*]

Utility models fall within the definition of "Industrial Property" provided for by Art. 2 of the Industrial Property Code (IPC) enacted by legislative decree 30/2005. Accordingly, their protection follows the general rules established by the Code for all industrial property rights (Art. 1–6; Art. 117 ff.), the provisions specifically dedicated to utility models (Art. 82–86), as well as the rules governing patents to the extent they are compatible with the specificities of utility models. Of limited relevance appear Articles 2592 and 2594 of the Civil Code, which offer a summary of the basic rules governing this intellectual property right.

7.1 SOURCES OF LAW AND HISTORICAL DEVELOPMENT

The first law protecting designs and models dates back to 1868.[1] It granted a two-year exclusive reproduction right to the "inventors" of "new industrial designs and models" upon deposit and subject to revocation in case of failure to work the design or model within the first year from grant. Absent a definition of "designs and models", it remains disputed whether the law referred to ornamental creations only, or to functional ones too.

Over the first three decades of the twentieth century, considerable efforts were made to reform the laws protecting intellectual property.[2] The outcome was Royal Decree 1602/1934, which separately addressed utility models, on one hand, and ornamental designs and models, on the other, in its Titles III and IV, respectively.

[*] Sections 7.1, 7.2, 7.3, 7.4.4, and 7.4.5 were written by Alessandro Cogo; Sections 7.4.2–7.4.3 by the authors together. This chapter is based on extensive bibliographical research (minimally reflected in the footnotes and references list) performed by Giorgio Ribero.

[1] Law 4578/1868.

[2] *See* Jannoni Sebastianini 1936, 1 ff. For information on the preparatory works specifically regarding utility models see Vanzetti 2008, 189 ff.

Although it never entered into force,[3] the Royal Decree of 1934 substantially influenced the next generation of laws aimed at establishing a comprehensive and coherent system of protection for industrial property. Industrial designs and models became the subject matter of a separate law, namely Royal Decree 1411/1940, which replicated with minor amendments the rules on utility models and ornamental designs and models of the law of 1934.

Royal Decree 1411/1940 remained in force until the enactment of the IPC, which regulates utility models today. During its life, the Royal Decree underwent three major reforms. First, the law 265/1977 extended the term of protection from four to ten years in the case of utility models, and fifteen years for ornamental designs and models. Second, the law 60/1987 reshaped the relationship between utility models and patents with the introduction of the possibility of transformation of applications for patents into applications for utility models, and vice versa, and conversion of invalid patents into utility models, and vice versa. Third, the Legislative Decree 95/2001, by implementing Directive 98/71/EC on the legal protection of designs, reformed entirely the rules applicable to ornamental designs and models. The nineteenth-century legislative scheme, in which new utilitarian and ornamental features of industrial products faded into a blurred and indistinct legal concept, got finally, and completely, overhauled.

7.2 SUBJECT MATTER

According to Article 82 IPC, utility model protection can be issued for new designs that confer particular efficacy or convenience of application or use to machines, or parts thereof, instruments, tools, or any other object, such as new designs which consist of particular shapes, arrangements, configurations, or combinations of parts. It follows from this definition that utility models cannot protect methods[4] and are of little to no relevance for products whose formal configuration does not impact functionality.[5] Indeed their relevance is fundamentally restricted to the field of mechanics and excludes chemical, biological, and similar innovations.

7.3 REQUIREMENTS FOR PROTECTION

Utility models must be "new", as required by Art. 82 IPC. Despite the silence of the law, it is generally accepted that novelty should be understood in absolute terms.[6]

[3] In fact, entry into force required the approval of a regulation which was never adopted.

[4] *See*, e.g., Franzosi 2008, 159; Di Cataldo 2012, 288. Product-by-process claims are nonetheless admitted: cf. *Bosch v Candy* (Cass. 8510/2008).

[5] Cf. Vanzetti 2008, 197, who considers not protectable by utility models chemical, biotechnological, electronic inventions, as well as second use inventions.

[6] See Fazzini 2019, 583 f.

This follows from the reference made by Art. 86 IPC[7] to provisions dealing with patents, which are also applicable to utility models, so long as the provisions are compatible. The compatibility of these provisions seems to be fulfilled in the case of novelty, considering that Art. 82 IPC mentions it without providing a definition.

According to a view adopted early on in the jurisprudence and never abandoned, utility models also need to show some sort of originality. Again, this follows from the reference made by Art. 86 IPC to provisions regarding patents, among which is the requirement of inventiveness regulated by Art. 48 IPC. However, this requirement must be adapted to the specific subject matter of utility models, which – following the definition provided by Art. 82 IPC – consists in a configuration of a known product conferring particular efficacy or convenience of application to it. In the courts' view, the matter here is not to evaluate the nonobviousness of an invention because, by definition, a utility model is not an invention, that is, the solution of a technical problem, which entails the creation of new scientific knowledge through discovery of a cause–effect relationship that translates into a new product. What utility models protect is an innovative concept which relates to the configuration of a known product and enhances its efficacy or convenience of application. Therefore, the question to be answered is whether such new configuration originates from the application of elementary technical rules or from a banal combination of preexisting inventions or models. Some degree of inventiveness and the overcoming of technical difficulties are required.[8]

7.4 RELATIONSHIP TO PATENTS

As already mentioned, utility models cannot protect methods. In this respect, any potential overlap between utility models and patents is avoided.[9] In the remaining cases, it has always proven difficult to master the relationship between these two kinds of intellectual property rights. Hurdles have emerged over the years, though.

7.4.1 *Patents and Utility Models under the Law of 1934*

In 1934, utility models were meant to provide cheap, easy-to-obtain, quickly granted, and short-lasting protection to "little inventions", within a context in which it was envisaged that patent applications were gradually to become subject to substantive examination and opposition procedures. The idea was to follow the example of Germany,[10] whose extraordinary industrial development had been helped, in the view of contemporary literature, by a well-functioning patent system, which offered

7 *See* above, Section 7.1.

8 *See Gipron v Masters* (Cass. 19688/2009).

9 Di Cataldo 2012, 288.

10 See Chapter 6 (Germany and Switzerland).

utility models as a convenient alternative to full patent protection. Utility models were seen as an innovation of the German Patent Office, which effectively limited its backlog in the examination of patent applications by channeling lesser innovations to the simpler registration system provided for utility models.

Following an approach that continues today, utility models were regulated by reference to the law on patents, absent specific rules and subject to a compatibility requirement.[11] However, the fact that patents and utility models shared the same rules did not mean that overlap was necessarily allowed. On the contrary, the introduction of utility models as a separate intellectual property right, distinct from both patents and ornamental designs and models, was seen as an improvement made possible by a greater understanding of the specific characteristics that make such innovations different in kind.[12]

Early on, the idea took ground that utility models and ornamental designs protected new formal configurations of existing goods impacting their functionality or aesthetics, while patents covered inventive ideas giving birth to new products[13] – an approach that forecloses overlap between utility models and patents.

This view seemed to be confirmed by a rule that allowed the simultaneous filing of a patent application and a utility model application, which would be considered only if the Patent Office refused to grant, entirely or partially, the patent.[14] Indeed, such a rule – allowing so-called "alternative applications" or *Hilfsanmeldungen* as labeled under the German system – seemed to imply that the same innovation could not be double patented, that is, protected by both a patent and a utility model. Such a rule would have made little sense if patents and utility models could have had the same subject matter: considering that utility models conferred shorter and narrower protection compared to patents, what difference would it make if someone decided to pay more fees to get this protection in addition to a patent? The only convincing reason that could justify the impossibility (at least in theory: see *infra*) of prosecuting two applications for the same innovation was therefore the existence of a "qualitative difference" regarding the subject-matter of patents and utility models, one that could justify the conclusion that a certain innovation can only fall in one category or the other.

Moreover, a transitional provision stated that patent applications filed (but not yet accepted) before the entering into force of the new law would yield the grant of a utility model, instead of a patent, if their "subject-matter had the characteristics of a utility model".[15] This appears to be another sign that there is a qualitative difference

[11] Cf. Art. 65 R.D.1602/1934.
[12] Cf. Jannoni Sebastianini 1936, 60.
[13] This approach is represented even in the literature preceding the 1934 reform: see, e.g., Ghiron 1929, 90 and 118–119.
[14] Cf. Art. 60 R.D. 1602/1934.
[15] Art. 138 R.D. 1602/1934.

between inventions and models, leading to the necessity of putting each kind of innovation in the proper "box".

From a broader perspective, one additional element can help explain the immediate success of this approach. It should not be forgotten that patent law, at that time, did not mention "inventiveness" among the requirements for protection and that this omission continued until quite recently, when it was reformed in connection with the making of the European Patent system. In 1934, the law made it clear not only that examination and opposition proceedings were limited to novelty, but also that the Patent Office acted under an explicit prohibition against evaluating the technical or economic value of the invention.[16] Against this backdrop, drawing the distinction between inventions and utility models with regard to their higher or lower degree of originality seemed to be out of question, notwithstanding a common understanding that utility models were meant to cover minor innovations.

7.4.2 *Patents and Utility Models under the Law of 1940*

Implementing substantive examination and opposition procedures proved so difficult that, in a matter of years, the legislature decided to abandon the reform of 1934. The new law on patents of 1939 confirmed the authority of the Italian IP Office to examine patent applications with regards to their substance[17] but, at the same time, abolished the prior art search, which was needed to make substantive examination more than just a fiction. Additionally, it entirely displaced the Italian IP Office opposition proceeding and left third party challenges entirely in the hands of the judiciary.

When, in 1940, the legislature also reformed the law on utility models, it did not engage with the problem of governing their intersection with patents, which was left to the rule on alternative applications and to a transitional provision identical to the one already discussed with reference to the law of 1934.[18]

Not surprisingly, the theory affirming the existence of a qualitative difference between inventions and models continued to prevail.[19] The idea that models could be conceived as "smaller inventions" was considered, even by the case law, to be

16 Cf. Art. 27 R.D. 1602/1934. Cf. Jannoni Sebastianini 1936, 27 ff. and 35 ff., who repeatedly stresses the prohibition to extend the pre-grant examination or opposition to the technical or economic value of the invention.

17 Ubertazzi 1988, 558; contra Spolidoro 1981, 1088 ff.

18 Art. 14 law 1411/1940, which repeats verbatim Art. 138 R.D. 1602/1934.

19 Many consider the shift from the idea that utility models protect "petty inventions", i.e., innovations showing a lesser degree of originality than patentable inventions, to the conception of utility models as protecting a different kind of innovation in comparison to patents as a consequence of the abolition of the substantive examination of patents. See, e.g., Floridia 2000, 353.

equivocal or spurious[20] and was seldom followed by courts.[21] This stands to reason. On one hand, the *de facto* abolition of substantive examination for patent applications made the explanation of utility models as a cheaper alternative to patents untenable.[22] On the other hand, the rule on alternative applications and the transitional provision allowing transformation of patent applications into utility model applications continued to offer a relatively solid argument in favor of a subject matter–based distinction.

This, in turn, prompted additional efforts to draw a sufficiently clear distinction between the subject matter of patents and, respectively, of utility models. Early on, such distinction was found, essentially, in contrasting the invention of something new, on one hand, and the refinement of something already known, on the other hand. Then, in order to combine this view with the long-established patentability of inventions consisting of improvements to existing products, additional efforts were made to distinguish improvements that do not alter the nature of the goods, which were to be protected under the utility models regime, and improvements that are so substantial as to make the product a "new product", which would be entitled to a patent.[23]

In spite of these efforts, reliable criteria were badly needed, as inventors remained exposed to the risk of losing any protection theoretically available if they failed to select the appropriate right for their innovations at the time of the filing. Once granted, a patent could be invalidated if it claimed something that qualified as a utility model, and vice versa. It was a serious risk. Indeed, alleged infringers often relied on this argument to defend themselves, sometimes successfully. Not even filing alternative applications offered a safe harbor: the fact that the choice of the wrong "box" was due to a mistake by the examiner in selecting which application to prosecute had no relevance; judicial invalidation would follow all the same.[24]

To minimize risks,[25] patentees sometimes adopted the expedient of filing simultaneous independent applications (i.e., without qualifying them as "alternative"). However, this practice was opposed by the Patent Office, which considered it *contra legem*, and eventually disqualified by the Supreme Court in the early 1980s.[26]

7.4.3 *The 1987 Reform*

A major reform of the patent system occurred at the end of the 1970s, prompted by the obligations arising under the Strasbourg Convention, the European Patent

20 This wording may be found in *Successori v Sergio Verdini* (App. Bologna 1972). In a similar vein see A.C.F.A. *v Ruggiero Olivieri* (App. Milano February 1972)

21 For a rare example see *Rivest Polival v ditta Piero Brambilla* (App. Milano 1971).

22 *Cf.* Vanzetti 2008, 191.

23 *See* Greco and Vercellone 1968, 389 ff. A similar reasoning may arguably be applied to dependent (or derivative) inventions.

24 *Cf.* Floridia 2000, 354.

25 Including risks of professional liability for patent attorneys.

26 See *Bellco v Ministero Industria* (Cass. 7398/1983).

Convention (EPC), and the Patent Cooperation Treaty. At that time, Italy decided not to abolish utility models, even though they did not have an equivalent within the system established by the EPC. Under the EPC, only the rules on conversion of European patents/patent applications into national patents/patent applications, as well as the rules on priority and simultaneous protection, extended to utility models if provided for by national law.[27] The decision to maintain utility models in Italy was followed by a reform of their legal regime, which occurred in 1987 (by Law 60).

Generally, the reform bridged some of the gaps created by the lack of coordination between patent and utility models protection described above.

In 1979, the legislature had already taken advantage of Art. 140 EPC to introduce the possibility of transforming an application for a European patent refused by the EPO into an application for an Italian utility model.[28] With the 1987 reform, a specific provision was introduced to deal with national applications in a similar, although not identical way. As already mentioned, applicants were allowed under the 1940 law to simultaneously file a patent and a utility model application for the same innovation, which would be considered as alternatives by the Italian IP Office. However, if applicants missed this opportunity, they were not allowed to transform their original application to overcome a refusal of grant by the receiving office based on failure by the applicant to select the right "box" for their innovation. The 1987 reform changed this by entrusting the Italian IP Office with the task of inviting the applicant to modify its request, without impact on the filing date, if it wrongly claimed patent protection for a utility model or utility model protection for an invention.[29]

Additionally, the 1987 reform introduced the possibility of converting a revoked European patent[30] or an invalid Italian patent[31] into a utility model. Again, the rule had to be differentiated. With regards to European patents, conversion could only go in one direction: from a revoked European patent to an Italian utility model. Not so with regards to Italian grants. In their case, conversion of an invalid utility model into a patent was also provided for, although licensees or third parties who made investments to use the utility model after the lapse of its term of protection had the right to obtain a nonexclusive, free-of-charge, compulsory license for the extra years of exclusivity deriving from the longer term of protection applicable to patents.[32]

All in all, these rules appear more consistent with the idea that patents and utility models are distinguishable on the basis of their specific subject matter rather than the degree of originality that they require. Indeed, it may be argued that there is no

[27] Art. 140 EPC.

[28] Art. 6.2 DPR 32/1979.

[29] Art. 9.1 law 60/1987.

[30] Art. 6.2 DPR 32/1979 was amended to include the case of European patents targeted by a successful post-grant opposition.

[31] Art. 59 R.D. 1127/1939, as amended by Art. 7 law 60/1987.

[32] Art. 7 law 60/1987.

other reasonable explanation for allowing conversion of an invalid utility model into a patent, if not for the case, which appears rather theoretical, of a utility model wrongly granted for a method. The Italian Supreme Court has consistently upheld this approach.[33]

7.4.4 *Latest Developments*

Since their introduction, utility models have never attracted great attention from users of the patent system. As already mentioned, their allure as a cheap and easy-to-obtain protection tool in comparison to patents disappeared once it became clear, back in the 1930s, how difficult it was to establish substantive examination for full-fledged inventions as originally envisaged. Since then, utility models have been more a problem than a solution for applicants, considering the risks stemming from the unclear distinction between inventions and utility models. Once these risks were addressed by the transformation of applications and conversion of granted rights, utility models regained some of their attractiveness as a safety net for patentees who faced invalidity challenges from alleged infringers. This, in turn, prompted a revival of discussions regarding the distinction between utility models and patents.

Meanwhile, the abolition of utility models has regularly been discussed in Italy. At the end of the 1970s, when the last major reform of patent law occurred, utility models survived due to a lack of legislative authority of the government, which had been authorized by the Parliament to legislate only to the extent necessary to fulfill international obligations related to patents. Twenty-five years later, when the Industrial Property Code was enacted, history repeated itself. This time, doubts regarding the scope of legislative authority delegated to the government were coupled with uncertainties regarding potential developments at the EU level. Indeed, it appeared reasonable not to discontinue utility models while European institutions were discussing a harmonization directive that emphasized the relevance of this IP right for small and medium sized enterprises.

The project of EU harmonization faded away one year after the adoption of the IPC.[34] Nonetheless, interest in utility models was revitalized by a decree of the Ministry of economic development of October 3, 2007, giving effect to Art. 170.1 IPC, which outsourced to EPO's examining divisions the provision of search reports to be used by the Italian patent office to examine national patent applications. This measure was meant to support extension through the EPC of national applications more than to enhance the capacity of the Italian patent office to filter out inventions lacking novelty or inventiveness. Nonetheless, it had some impact on the number of

[33] See *Inoxa v Compagnucci* (Cass. 7110/2020); *Tecnosystem v Vecam-Co.* (Cass. 16949/2016); *Bosch v Candy* (Cass. 8510/2008). Also the lower courts follow the approach: see *Combustion and Energy v Sirena* (Trib. Torino 2022).

[34] See Chapter 20 (European attempts at harmonization of utility models).

applications for utility models, which were left untouched by this development and, therefore, continued to be examined only on the basis of information disclosed in the application itself or generally known. However, it soon became clear that negative search reports issued by EPO's examiners did not lead to refusals to grant when applicants provided reasonable counterarguments against such findings. This might be one of the reasons that the number of applications for utility models, which had been modestly rising in the second half of the 2000s, again turned downward a few years later.[35]

In view of the entry into force of the Agreement establishing the Unified Patent Court, legislative decree no. 18/2019 included applications for European patents with unitary effects which have been refused or withdrawn, as well as European patents with unitary effect that have been revoked, in the list of patent applications that can be transformed into applications for utility models.[36] Interestingly, the same decree left untouched Art. 76.3 IPC, which deals with conversion of invalid patents into utility models. Therefore, this provision continues to provide for the conversion of invalid patents into utility models generally, without making it explicit whether conversion can also apply to invalid Italian portions of European patents and to the effects in Italy of invalid European patents with unitary effect. The ability to convert invalid Italian portions of European patents into Italian utility models seems straightforward. However, one could ask if and how this could happen if the validity of the European patent is challenged before the Unified Patent Court. This question appears even more relevant during the transitional period established by Art. 83 UPCA, considering the concurrent competence of national courts and, therefore, the risk that different regimes will apply depending on where invalidity claims are raised – that is, before an Italian court or the UPC. Similarly, one could question the rationale of denying conversion if exclusivity with effect in Italy had been obtained through a European patent with, or without, unitary effect.

From a practical point of view, these questions lose some of their relevance if the patentee takes advantage of the abolition in 2023 (law 102) of a rule that was meant to avoid the cumulation of Italian and European patents for the same invention.[37] The

35 In 2023, 1,850 applications for utility models were filed; they were 2,464 in 2010 and 3,132 in 2000. Applications for patents have been stable: 9,453 in 2023, 9,663 in 2010, and 9,426 in 2000. Deposits of translations of granted EU patents have been increasing over the years: 23,568 in 2023 (but with a peak of over 40,000 in 2021), 26,089 in 2010, 17,966 in 2000. Statistics are available at https://statistiche.uibm.gov.it/; granted utility models can be accessed at www.uibm.gov.it/bancadati/Advanced_search/type_url?type = ut&cl = 1.

36 Art. 58.2 IPC. Revocation, in this context, refers to EPO decisions upholding post-grant oppositions.

37 Before its reform, Art. 59 IPC provided for a supremacy rule in favour of European patents in the event of cumulative protection. In particular, it established that

> 1. If an Italian patent and a European patent or a European patent with unitary effect valid in Italy have been granted for the same invention to the same inventor or successor in title with the same date of filing and priority date, the Italian patent, to the extent it

new text of Art. 59 IPC establishes that an Italian patent coexists with a European patent with unitary effect, or a European patent having effect in Italy, which has been granted for the same invention to the same patentee with the same date of filing or priority. Moreover, Art. 59.2 IPC declares that invalidation or revocation of the European patent does not affect the Italian patent.[38] These provisions make double patenting attractive. First, coexistence means that the patentee can pursue an infringement claim in Italy relying on the national patent to avoid the competence of the UPC. Second, the patentee can bring an infringement claim before an Italian court and, within the same proceeding, convert the patent into a utility model, notwithstanding the fact that the corresponding European patent with unitary effect or Italian portion of a European patent may have already been revoked or invalidated. Likely, many Italian inventors will take advantage of this opportunity, which comes at no cost when – as is often the case – their patenting strategy begins with the filing of a national application.

Going back to the questions whether European patents, with or without unitary effect, can be converted into Italian utility models and if the Unified Patent Court can do it, it might be observed that the EPC allows conversion of rejected European patent applications and European patents which have been successfully opposed into national utility models, if the applicable national law so provides.[39] Considering that the attribution of unitary effect presupposes that a European patent has already been granted, it follows that a refusal by the examination division leads to the same consequences irrespective of whether the applicant requested a traditional European patent or a European patent with unitary effect. In the case of revocation due to a successful opposition, on the contrary, the unitary effect has already been granted.[40] However, the lack of specific rules suggests that the regime is the same for all European patents: the patentee can file a request for conversion with the EPO, which, in turn, will forward it to the Italian IP office.[41] More complicated is the case of conversion of granted patents in other scenarios, that is, through an administrative

protects the same invention as the European patent, or the European patent with unitary effect, shall cease to have effect as of the date on which: a) the deadline for opposing the European patent or the European patent with unitary effect has lapsed without any opposition being filed; b) the opposition proceeding has definitively ended with the maintenance in effect of the European patent or of the European patent with unitary effect; c) the Italian patent has been issued, if that date is later than the date in letters a) or b). 2. The provisions of paragraph 1 remain valid even if the European patent or the European patent with unitary effect is subsequently cancelled or revoked. 3. As of the expiration of the deadlines indicated in paragraph 1, a person who has brought an action to protect an Italian patent may request a conversion of the same into a corresponding action to protect a European patent, or the European patent with unitary effect, without prejudice to the rights that result from the Italian patent for the earlier period.

[38] *Gemata v Bergi* (Cass. 2019/22984) reached the same conclusion based on the previous text of Art. 59 IPC. See Calabrese 2020, 576 ff., on implications of the entering into force of the UPC.

[39] Art. 140 EPC.

[40] Art. 4 EU Reg. 1257/2012.

[41] Art. 135–137 EPC and rule 155 of the Implementing Regulations.

or judiciary decision prompted by the patentee. Neither the EPC nor the UPCA deal with conversion of granted (and unrevoked) patents, leaving the matter to national laws. In the case of Italy, the IPC does provide for conversion of invalid patents generally, that is, without making distinctions between national or European patents, but in a specific setting: within judiciary proceedings in which validity of the patent has been challenged by the alleged infringer and through a decision having a negative content, where it affirms the invalidity of the patent, and a positive one, where it ascertains the fulfilment of the requirements for protection as a utility model.[42] Consequently, there seem to be no doubts that Italian portions of European patents can be converted by Italian courts, as already mentioned. However, it seems unlikely that the UPC could do the same, as it lacks competence to make a positive assessment concerning protection of the non-patentable invention as utility model and, in that case, to issue remedies against the infringer.[43] This leaves open to question whether the patentee could obtain conversion otherwise. A positive answer follows from the theory maintaining that – despite the wording of Art. 76 IPC – conversion happens ipso jure, in consequence of invalidation of a patent that refers to an innovation protectable as utility model.[44]

Lastly, it should be noted that law 102/2023 provides that, if an applicant files simultaneously with the Italian IP Office a patent application and a utility model application, to be considered alternatively, the (totally or partially negative) search report issued by the EPO concerning the main application must also be taken into account by the Italian IP Office when examining the auxiliary one. The legislative report indicates that this rule was not prompted by a desire to approximate further the regime of patents and utility models, but by the fact that the Office cannot avoid considering documents on the record. Be that as it may, the same reasoning seems to apply when the applicant files only for a patent and, after having received a negative search report from the EPO, decides to convert the application into a utility model. If this assumption is correct, then utility models can work as an easier-to-obtain IP right[45] in comparison to patents only if the applicant abstains from trying to obtain full patent protection to begin with.[46]

42 *See* Floridia 2000, 355.

43 *See* Art. 35 UPCA.

44 *Cf.* Ubertazzi 1988, 575.

45 But not quicker than patents: in both cases, grant follows within 180 days from publication of the application, which takes place after 18 months from filing (Art. 53 IPC). Utility models are also nowadays not substantially cheaper than patents. In case of e-filing, the filing fee is identical. Maintenance fees are due for patents from the fifth year on, on a yearly basis, while for utility models are due after five years and consist of a lump sum for the subsequent five years of protection. However, the total amount to be paid is not substantially different.

46 As opposition procedures are not available for (patents and) utility models, validity can be challenged by third parties only in court.

7.5 CONCLUSION

Despite repeated legislative interventions aimed at coordinating the Italian national patent system with the UPCA, a conundrum still exists.

So far, Italian courts have refused to base the distinction between patents and utility models on the degree of originality of innovations that can be protected under each regime. Their preferred "qualitative" approach implies that a patent can be invalidated if it claims protection for a utility model, and vice versa. However, neither the EPC nor the UPCA or other rules governing European patents with or without unitary effect provide for a similar ground of invalidation. Therefore, the UPC will not be in a position to invalidate a European patent on this basis, either with effect limited to the Italian portion of a traditional European patent or for all countries participating in the "unitary patent package". During the transition period, this might in turn lead to unintended consequences, such as differentiating the regime applicable to the same traditional European patent depending on the court that judges its validity, or to differentiate the regime applicable to European patents which have, or do not have, unitary effect. Also, as observed above, the execution of UPC decisions affirming the validity of European patents that protect – according to the "qualitative approach" – a utility model might raise difficult legal issues.[47]

Solutions to these issues are not easy to identify. At the end of the day, insistence of the Italian courts on the qualitative approach seems more to express a concern about granting protection to utility models devoid of any substantial merit than an attempt to restrict access to full patent protection for inventions impacting the configuration of a known object. However, translating this concern into practical rules that do not deprive utility models of any relevance, while being both compatible with the regime of European patents and consistent with domestic legislative texts, as they emerged over a century of not well-coordinated interventions, appears at the moment to be a problem without an entirely convincing solution.[48]

[47] *See* comment to *Tecnosystemi s.p.a. v Vecam-Co* (Cass. 16949/2016).

[48] Recent attempts include, at the extremes, protection for obvious utility models (Franzosi 2008, 165 ff.) and application to patents and utility models of the same requirements (Romandini 2011, 220 ff.); in between, a revival of the "quantitative" approach (Vanzetti 2008, 200 ff.).

8

Utility Model Protection in Poland

In Search of a Regulatory Framework Capable of Incentivizing Innovation

Rafał Sikorski

Poland has a relatively long tradition of providing utility model protection, a tradition that goes back to 1919. Polish law has been strongly influenced by German law where utility model protection originated in the second half of the nineteenth century.[1] This influence is still visible in the 2022 Explanatory Memorandum to the draft of the Industrial Property Law (Explanatory Memorandum).[2] The release of the draft of the new Industrial Property Law (draft IPL)[3] has spurred numerous debates about the need to modernize Polish utility model protection to make it more attractive for innovators. These local debates reflect the debates underway in many other countries, as well those at regional and international levels.

This chapter starts by providing historical perspective on the evolution of the Polish regulatory framework for the protection of utility models. Interestingly, the draft IPL takes us to legislative solutions already tested in the past. One might even say *nihil novi sub sole* (there is nothing new under the sun). In the next section, data about the functioning of the regime currently in force is presented. This is followed by a more general discussion, drawing on experience from other jurisdictions, of how various aspects of the regulatory framework might affect the ability of the system to promote innovation. Then, the current legislative framework will be presented against the backdrop of the solutions proposed in the draft IPL. Finally, the chapter will end with conclusory remarks.

[1] See Chapter 6 (Germany and Switzerland).

[2] Uzasadnienie projektu z dnia 25 kwietnia 2022 r. Prawo własności przemysłowej, available at https://legislacja.rcl.gov.pl/docs//2/12359055/12874004/12874005/dokument552323.pdf.

[3] Projekt z dnia 25 kwietnia 2022 r. Prawo własności przemysłowej, available at https://legislacja.rcl.gov.pl/docs//2/12359055/12874004/12874005/dokument552321.pdf.

8.1 HISTORICAL PERSPECTIVE

Utility models have been protected under Polish intellectual property law for over a hundred years. Early forms of utility model protection were introduced shortly after Poland regained its independence in 1919 in a *Decree on protection of designs and models*.[4] The 1919 Decree was repealed in 1924 by the *Law on inventions, utility models and trademarks*[5] and then subsequently in 1928 by a *Presidential decree on inventions, utility models and trademarks*.[6] The 1928 Presidential decree remained in force after the end of World War II and was the basis for utility model protection until 1962.

8.1.1 *German Origins and Utility Models Protection in the First Half of the Twentieth Century*

Polish utility model regulations were highly influenced by German and Japanese laws. Germany introduced utility model protection in 1891 to allow for protection of minor inventions by local innovators.[7] Japan followed suit and introduced a similar type of protection in 1905.[8] The new German law on utility models allowed for protection of minor inventions related to shape and construction of rather simple working tools and other useful objects. Since the right was aimed at protecting local innovators, it also adopted a concept of relative novelty – utility models met the novelty requirement if there were no prior publications of the model in Germany and the model was not used in Germany. Applications for utility model protection were not subject to substantive examination, they were only checked for formalities. German law required that models ensure some utility, thus setting the inventiveness bar rather low. The protection period was six years, divided into two three-year periods.

In its first five years after being established in 1919, the Polish Patent Office registered over 900 utility models. At that time, even though protection of patents was already available, no patent applications were examined due to organizational difficulties and the lack of personnel facing the newly established Patent Office.[9]

4 Dekret o ochronie wzorów rysunkowych i modeli, Dz.Pr.P.P. 1919 nr 13 poz. 138, available at https://isap.sejm.gov.pl/isap.nsf/DocDetails.xsp?id=WDU19190130138.

5 Ustawa z dnia 5 lutego 1924 r. o ochronie wynalazków, wzorów i znaków towarowych, Dz. U. 1924 nr 31, poz. 306, available at https://isap.sejm.gov.pl/isap.nsf/DocDetails.xsp?id=WDU19240310306.

6 Rozporządzenie Prezydenta Rzeczypospolitej z dnia 22 marca 1928 r. o ochronie wynalazków, wzorów i znaków towarowych, Dz.U. 1928 nr 39 poz. 384, available at https://isap.sejm.gov.pl/isap.nsf/DocDetails.xsp?id=wdu19280390384.

7 Gebrauchmustergesetz, 1 Juni 1891, RGBl s. 290. See Chapter 6 (Germany and Switzerland). See also Balicki (2020).

8 See Chapter 11 (Japan).

9 Balicki 2020.

Opting for registration of utility models rather than substantive examination allowed the Patent Office to overcome those difficulties.

The 1928 Presidential decree defined the characteristics of utility models' protection in Poland for the next 34 years. At that time the regulation of utility models was closely aligned with the protection of the so-called decorative or ornamental models – predecessor of design protection available today. The 1928 decree defined a model as an appearance of product reflected in its shape, drawings, colors, and materials.[10] The distinction between decorative (ornamental) models and utility models was based upon the purpose of the model. When that purpose was to provide for greater utility of the product, the model was a utility model, and when the purpose of a given model was to fulfill certain aesthetic functions, the model was a decorative (ornamental) model.[11]

The 1928 protection regime required a utility model to be novel. Novelty was not understood in absolute terms. It could be defeated through a publication of the essential features of the utility model in Poland or abroad or through its use or public exhibition in Poland.[12] The concept of novelty evolved over the years with the jurisprudence. First, strict identity of the later utility model with an earlier one was not required to defeat the novelty of the later utility model. It sufficed that the later utility model shared the same essential features with the earlier one.[13] Second, courts required that publications used to defeat novelty were publicly accessible. Thus, books or periodicals – available in bookstores or publicly accessible libraries – as well as patent descriptions could be used. Courts also required these publications to have been published in one of the European languages.[14] Finally, the concept of novelty evolved to include utility of the model. Utility meant that the product was easier or cheaper to produce or that it was more comfortable or capable of satisfying the needs of the user not previously recognized.[15]

Polish legislators were aware of the various organizational difficulties faced by the Polish Patent Office. Not only was there a limited number of patent attorneys, but the number of patent examiners was also limited. In fact, similar motivations were behind the adoption of the registration model in German law. Therefore, a full substantive examination of applications for protection was not an option. The Patent Office only examined the industrial application of the model. The protection was granted for a period of 10 years.

[10] Presidential Decree 1928 r, Art. 87 (1).
[11] Ibid., Art. 87 (2).
[12] Ibid.. Art. 90 (2).
[13] Balicki 2020.
[14] Balicki 2020.
[15] Balicki 2020.

8.1.2 *Utility Model Protection between 1962 and 2000*

Pre–World War II regulations on utility models were replaced first in 1962[16] and then later the 1962 Law on inventions was replaced by the new act in 1972.[17] Both acts mark a change of approach of the Polish legislator. Both acts concentrated on the protection of technical inventions.[18] Thus, whereas earlier regulations tied utility models with the predecessors of design rights, namely, decorative (ornamental) models, the 1962 and 1972 acts regulated both patent and utility model protection. This had consequences for utility models and resulted in patent law influencing the concepts used with respect to utility models.[19] Utility models were defined as novel and useful technical solutions related to the shape or structure of a durable object or an object of interconnected parts of a durable nature.[20]

The 1972 Law on inventions applied the concept of absolute novelty used with respect to patented inventions.[21] The absolute novelty requirement was not previously applied to utility models in Poland. In the 1928 regulation the concept of absolute novelty was rejected. Similarly, the 1962 Law on inventions provided that novelty could be defeated if there was prior publication of the model or its use in Poland.[22]

Unlike patents, there was no requirement of nonobviousness of the technical solution. In fact, no level of inventiveness was required at all. The 1972 Law did not demand that the technical solution be capable of industrial application. Only utility (usefulness) of the technical solution was required.[23] The concept of usefulness was applied with respect to patented inventions as well. It was applied in a very liberal way, thus it was sufficient for the applicant seeking protection to specify the area in which the product could be applied.

The 1972 Law on innovation contained an interesting procedure regarding the granting of utility model protection. Whereas patents were granted upon full examination, utility models were granted in a limited examination procedure. This limited examination model was an interesting combination of the two competing traditions in industrial property law – one of registering rights without having a substantive examination, as is the case in France, and the other where applications are subject to full substantive examination.[24] The limited examination model required examination of only a limited portion of the state of the art which comprised only of utility model rights and patents protected in Poland as well as

16 Ustawa z dnia 31 maja 1962 r. Prawo wynalazcze, Dz.U. 1962 nr 33, poz. 156.
17 Ustawa z dnia 19 października 1972 o wynalazczości, Dz.U. 1972 nr 43, poz. 272.
18 Grzybowski 1978, 9.
19 Grzybowski 1978, 51–53.
20 Art. 73 Law on inventions 1972.
21 Art. 78 Law on inventions 1972.
22 Art. 76 Law on inventions 1962.
23 Art. 77 Law on inventions 1972.
24 Szwaja 1978, 144–145.

of patent applications filed with the Polish Patent Office.[25] Thus, although the 1972 Law on Innovation applied the concept of absolute novelty, at the examination stage only Polish utility models and patents or applications for patent or utility model protection could be considered. Later, at the invalidation stage, utility models or inventions protected in other jurisdictions as well as applications for utility model or patent protection in other territories could be used to defeat novelty. Limited examination procedure certainly shortened the time required to obtain protection, while at the same time moved disputes over validity to the period following the grant of utility model protection.

8.2 RELATIVE SUCCESS OF UTILITY MODEL PROTECTION IN POLISH IP LAW

A recent OECD-sponsored study *Enhancing intellectual property use for a stronger innovation ecosystem in Poland*[26] provides data that might be helpful in explaining the relative popularity of the utility model protection in Poland. It shows that almost 70 percent of those taking part in an online survey conducted by OECD on IP use in Poland believe that utility models provide important protection for companies.[27]

That should not be surprising. The OECD study shows that a vast majority of Polish companies are small and even "micro" companies.[28] Given that utility models are generally regarded as suiting the interests of small and medium enterprises (SMEs), a large number of such enterprises creates a solid base of potential users of the utility model system.

Data published by the Polish Patent Office shows that the number of utility model applications has remained stable over the past decade. In 2022 – the last year for which the data is available – there were 673 utility model applications filed.[29] In the period from 2013 till 2021 that number varied from 759 to 1,151.[30] The number of utility model applications has remained relatively stable over the past 20 years.

Domestic applicants have always outnumbered foreign applicants. In 2022 – there were 63 foreign applicants.[31] In the period from 2013 to 2021 – there were between 37 and 79 utility model applications filed by foreign applicants per year. The number of foreign applicants has also remained relatively stable over the past 20 years, with a tendency to rise slightly.[32] In 2003 there were only 27 foreign applicants.

[25] Szwaja 1978, 146.
[26] Clayton et al. 2023.
[27] Clayton et al. 2023, 22.
[28] Clayton et al. 2023, 11.
[29] Polish Patent Office 2022, s. 60.
[30] Based on the data found in annual reports of the Polish Patent Office for years 2013–2022. The annual reports for years 2003–2022 are available at https://uprp.gov.pl/pl/publikacje/raport-roczny-uprp.
[31] Polish Patent Office 2022, 60.
[32] Based on the data found in annual reports of the Polish Patent Office for years 2013–2022.

The local character of utility model protection is further confirmed by the fact that rights are primarily obtained in a national procedure – in 2022 the national procedure was used in the case of 660 applications whereas the international Patent Cooperation Treaty (PCT) was used only 13 times.[33] In the period between 2018 and 2021, the PCT procedure was used in only 1.0–2.5 percent of cases.[34]

Data published by the Polish Patent Office reveals an interesting trend when broken down by the category of applicants. The 2022 Annual Report shows that publicly funded research and education institutions such as universities, the Polish Academy of Sciences and research centers accounted for 13 percent of domestic applicants.[35] In the top 10 of the applicants for the utility model rights, these publicly funded institutions had 5 representatives, whereas in the top 38 applicants there were 16 publicly funded institutions.[36] Natural persons accounted for 23 percent and business entities for 64 percent of domestic applicants.[37] The numbers for 2022 are similar to those from 2017 through 2021.[38]

Polish Patent Office reports also break down the data concerning applications by business entities. Here data is available only for patent and utility model applications jointly. The data for 2022 shows that among applicants that are business entities 60 percent employ less than 9 employees, whereas 13 percent employ between 10 and 49 employees.[39] This shows that over 70 percent of patent and utility model applicants are SMEs. These numbers are very similar to data available for the period from 2017 through 2021.

Data published by the Polish Patent Office is also broken down by field of technology. The majority of utility model applications cover civil engineering, handling, mechanical elements, and machines including electrical machines and apparatuses, consumer goods, medical equipment, and transport.[40] None or single applications are filed in such fields as telecommunications, digital communications, semiconductors, biotechnology, basic and foods chemistry.[41]

As of December 31, 2021, there were 3,529 utility models in force.[42] This number was relatively stable in the five-year period from 2017 through 2021.[43] The overall number of utility models however has steadily risen over the past 20 years. Shortly

[33] Polish Patent Office 2022, 91.
[34] Polish Patent Office 2022
[35] Polish Patent Office 2022, 95.
[36] Polish Patent Office 2022, 99–100.
[37] Polish Patent Office 2022, 95.
[38] Polish Patent Office 2022.
[39] Polish Patent Office 2022, 61.
[40] Polish Patent Office 2022, 92–93.
[41] Polish Patent Office 2022, 92–93.
[42] Polish Patent Office 2022, 100.
[43] Polish Patent Office 2022

before Poland joined the European Union in 2004, there were 1,978 utility model rights in force.[44]

Interesting conclusions can also be drawn when comparing the data for both patents and utility models. Whereas in 2022 there were 3,529 utility models in force, in the same year there were 16,243 national patents in force and over 94,156 European patents validated in Poland.[45] Whereas utility models are predominantly held by Polish applicants, the situation is different in the case of patents. European patents validated in Poland are generally held by foreign patentees, European patents validated in Poland by Polish applicants are only a small fraction of the overall number of European patents validated in Poland.[46]

Analysis of data concerning utility models in Poland confirms many of the assumptions usually made with respect to second-tier patent protection. First, utility model protection is predominantly used by national applicants, with foreign applicants constituting only a fraction of the overall number of applicants. Second, business entities constitute the largest group of applicants. Within that group, however, SMEs account for over 70 percent of the applicants. Individual applicants constitute the second-largest group of applicants. Third, publicly funded research and education institutions are also among the key groups who file for utility model protection. Their role in the field of "technical IP" becomes even more crucial when utility model applications are combined with applications for patents – then it reaches over 45 percent of the overall number of applications.

The third of the conclusions is probably the most surprising. It is even more puzzling when combined with the very low commercialization rate of the inventions and utility models coming from the publicly funded scientific and research sectors. The vast majority of protected inventions or utility models are neither licensed out nor practiced by these institutions themselves. Nor are these rights transferred to business entities. Though moving from invention to commercialization is always fraught with difficulties, in the case of IP owned by Polish educational and scientific institutions, the examples of successful commercialization are even harder to find.[47] This suggests that motivations behind obtaining IP rights by these institutions must be distorted in some way. One possible explanation is that both utility model and patent applications are used as indicators of academic achievement and are considered for assessment of academic activity and decisions on funding academic research.[48] Thus, to some extent at least, IP applications may substitute for publications in peer-reviewed journals.[49]

44 Polish Patent Office 2003.
45 Polish Patent Office 2022, 58.
46 Polish Patent Office 2022, 101–103.
47 Clayton et al. 2023, 18–19.
48 Clayton et al. 2023, 27.
49 Clayton et al. 2023

8.3 RATIONALE FOR UTILITY MODEL PROTECTION

The Explanatory Memorandum to the new draft Industrial Property Law explicitly states that the availability of utility model protection should incentivize investment in innovation.[50] This rationale for the protection of technical solutions, including utility models, has generally been accepted, including in Poland. The draft Industrial Property Law – in an attempt to make the system even more capable of providing incentives for technical innovation – simplifies the procedure for obtaining utility model protection. Instead of a full substantive examination it provides for a registration model, a change that is supposed to reduce the time necessary for obtaining the right from 24 months, which is the average time under the current legislation, to no more than 12 months.[51]

However, before analyzing specific rules on utility model protection – both those currently in force and those proposed in the draft legislation – it would first be interesting to look more generally at selected aspects of the regulatory framework that might influence the pro-innovation potential of utility model protection.

First, the criteria for granting utility model protection are crucial. On one hand, the bar for protection might be set very low. For example, it is possible – as is the case under Polish law – to require nothing but novelty of the utility model. But, IP legislators might also decide that at least some degree of inventiveness is required. That degree of inventiveness might be set at a low level. It is also possible, however, to demand the same degree of inventiveness as required under patent law. Generally, the higher the bar for inventiveness, the more difficult it is to obtain protection. With strict protectability criteria, obtaining utility model protection does not differ much from the traditional patent protection, consequently it becomes less attractive for SMEs.

It is also essential for the national legislators to frame the concept of novelty properly. When novelty is framed as absolute – obtaining protection is much more difficult.[52] SMEs, especially those operating locally, might not be aware of what has been disclosed to the public in other jurisdictions. If utility model protection is to provide an incentive for this group of applicants, then a limited concept of novelty would be preferable. The choice of a particular concept of novelty also influences the understanding of the concept of inventiveness.[53] If novelty is understood as absolute, then the concept of state-of-the-art covers anything that has been made available to the public irrespective of the territory in which it has been made available. For purposes of evaluating inventiveness, one always considers whether the particular invention is sufficiently distant from state-of-the-art. This assessment is made from the perspective of a person skilled in the art, that is a skilled practitioner

[50] Explanatory Memorandum (Poland), 22.

[51] Ibid.

[52] Dreyfuss and Benoliel 2022, 444.

[53] Dreyfuss and Benoliel 2022, 459–462.

in the relevant technology field. It is assumed that such a person is familiar with the state-of-the-art. Thus, the novelty concept influences the benchmark against which the inventiveness of a particular solution is assessed. Absolute novelty broadens the state-of-the-art and consequently raises the bar for the assessment of inventiveness.

Second, the definition of the subject matter protected is of paramount importance. The legislative choices with respect to the subject matter protected will determine the fields of technology in which utility model protection may provide incentives for innovation. The laws in various jurisdictions differ substantially in this respect. For example, some jurisdictions do not differentiate between patentable subject matter and the subject matter that is capable of protection as a utility model. Others limit protection to shapes and structures of products, excluding chemical substances, products containing biological material, or processes and new uses of known substances or devices.

The selection of protected subject matter must be very careful. When making that choice one should consider that the traditional purpose of utility model protection was to provide protection for minor technical improvements and adaptations of products, such as mechanical devices or apparatuses. Whereas patents may be used to protect breakthrough innovations, protection of utility models have always been envisaged as a means of protecting merely incremental innovation.[54]

It is not the purpose of this distinction to diminish in any way incremental innovation. Incremental innovation builds upon breakthrough inventions and enables the full exploitation of the potential of breakthrough innovation.[55] Minor adaptations are often required to enter new product markets, new market segments or new geographic markets.[56] They permit adaptation to changes in the legal and regulatory environment.[57] Frequently, they also enable an innovator to maintain market leadership by adopting customer requirements for new features, thereby helping to maintain or increase margin levels. Generally, incremental innovation is crucial for businesses to remain competitive in the market. The economics literature teaches that a successful innovator always relies on a mix of various types of innovation, consisting of more radical, sometimes breakthrough inventions, supplemented by lesser innovations that build upon earlier efforts.[58]

Incremental innovation also characterizes economies at a certain level of development. The economic literature describes three phases of development. Initially, economies aim at manufacturing products according to specifications provided by investors. Incremental innovation becomes possible once businesses have become

[54] Radauer et al. 2015, 12.
[55] Varadajan 2009, 21–29.
[56] Varadajan 2009
[57] Varadajan 2009
[58] Varadajan 2009

reliable producers. Finally, business entities in such catching-up economies turn to more radical and disruptive innovation.[59]

The micro- and macro-perspectives on incremental innovation shed some additional light on possible regulatory choices for utility model protection. On one hand, utility model protection seems to suit economies at certain levels of economic development. This explains the popularity of this type of protection in countries like South Korea and Japan through the 1970s. These economies, having achieved greater economic development, have moved from incremental innovation to more radical forms of innovation. That shift resulted in fewer applications for utility model protection as the business entities turned to more advanced forms of innovation for which patent protection is more suitable.[60] This might lead to a conclusion that after a certain point in time utility model protection might no longer be a desirable form of protection and could simply be abandoned. It is reasonable to claim that at a certain state of economic development patent protection of more advanced inventions would be sufficient, as it allows control over more radical and breakthrough inventions upon which incremental innovation is based.

One of the problems with second-tier patent protection in countries that are at a lower level of technological development is that once in place, protection must be available to nationals and entities from other countries as a result of national treatment clauses in international agreements such as the Paris Convention[61] and the TRIPS Agreement.[62] This opens utility model protection to foreign business entities and might allow them to "hijack" this IP right. This could, contrary to motivations behind the introduction of utility model protection, lead to even stronger barriers for effective competition by local business entities, for whom the system was designed in the first place.

Third, utility models are generally exclusive rights with the scope of protection being determined by the wording of the claims. The approach towards claim interpretation is one of the most contentious issues in patent law.[63] In some jurisdictions a more literal and strict interpretation of patent claims is the preferred option, while in others there is a tendency to interpret claims broadly.[64] Also, the approach towards equivalents varies significantly. Finally, the role of descriptions and drawings is perceived differently among jurisdictions.

With respect to utility model protection, similar problems need to be resolved. The solutions that will be adopted will likely influence freedom to operate by competitors. It seems that, given the nature of utility model innovation, namely its incremental character, that interpretation should be rather strict and literal. That

59 Krishnaswamy et al. 2015, 237–238.
60 See Chapters 11 (Japan) and 12 (Korea). See also Radauer et al. 2015, 21.
61 Paris Convention for the Protection of Industrial Property, Art. 2.
62 TRIPS Agreement, Art. 3.
63 du Vall 2017, s. 353–377.
64 du Vall 2017, 355.

does not exclude the use of utility model description or drawings. However, expanding the scope of the claims would not be justified for a utility model system. A lesser degree of inventiveness requires commensurate – in this case narrower – scope of protection.

Fourth, utility model protection is usually obtained faster than patent protection. Usually, it is also a cheaper form of protection. This is largely due to the fact that utility model applications are checked for formalities only, rather than subject to full substantive examination. The fact that patent offices do not examine utility model applications does not mean that there are no disputes over protection criteria. These are simply shifted in time, usually to the post-grant stage.

The registration system for utility models, though cheaper and faster than patent protection, comes with a significant and potentially anticompetitive downside. The ease of obtaining utility model protection might result in a significant number of rights that might create thickets, a phenomenon well-known in patent law[65] and at times also described with respect to other IP rights.[66] Thickets can be problematic, as they create uncertainty for competitors, especially in quickly evolving markets. Thickets make innovation riskier; they may discourage businesses from entering a market or force market exit in other cases. This problem will be further exacerbated when protectability criteria are set at a low level. Such thickets might also welcome abusive enforcement practices aimed at exploiting uncertainties surrounding validity and scope of protection in order to obtain excessive royalty payments.

8.4 CURRENT STATE OF UTILITY MODEL PROTECTION IN POLAND AND THE PLANNED REFORM

The modern Polish Industrial Property (IPL) Law was enacted in 2000.[67] The 2000 IPL was a comprehensive act that regulated virtually all types of industrial property rights including patents, utility models, industrial designs, geographical indications, trademarks, topographies of integrated circuits, and supplementary protection certificates. The IPL has been amended on numerous occasions. The most recent amendments to the chapter on utility models were adopted in 2019.[68] Currently, discussions are under way with respect to a draft of a new Industrial Property Law. The draft IPL envisages significant changes to the utility protection regime.

Set forth below, is an analysis of a number of selected aspects of the utility model regime currently in force, together with the proposals for amendment found in the

[65] Shapiro 2001, 119–122; Contreras 2018.

[66] See Copyright Trolling; Contreras 2018.

[67] Ustawa z dnia 30 czerwca 2000 r. Prawo własności przemysłowej, Dz.U. 2001, nr 49, poz. 508.

[68] Ustawa z dnia 20 lutego 2019 r. o zmianie ustawy Prawo własności przemysłowej, Dz.U. 2019, poz. 501.

draft IPL. These will include: the concept of the utility model, protectability criteria, and the procedure for the grant of utility model rights.

8.4.1 *Utility Model: Definition*

The current IPL defines utility models as solutions of a technical nature related to the shape or structure of a durable object or to an object which consists of functionally interconnected parts of a durable nature.[69] Since the technical solutions must always be related to a material three-dimensional object, the concept of utility models cannot cover processes or methods nor compositions of substances, mixtures, or liquids. Applicants have obtained protection for various shapes of windows, garden rakes, a hanger, a folding bike or a stroller, a container used in transportation, a car trailer allowing for easy maneuvering, and a multilevel highway intersection, among other things.[70]

The draft IPL simplifies the definition of the utility model and provides that a utility model is a solution of a technical nature.[71] The concept is not subject to the limitations imposed under the current IPL, thus the technical solution does not have to relate to the shape or structure of a durable object. Interestingly, there are a number of exclusions from protection. These cover objects made of biological material or containing such material, processes, chemical substances, and their mixtures, including pharmaceutical compositions, as well new uses.[72] All this suggests that a different drafting technique was used but the end result is generally the same. Though the definition of the concept of utility model is proposed to be simplified, it is unlikely to result in utility model protection being more appealing to new sectors of the industry, such as biotech, pharma or telecommunication or semiconductor sectors.

8.4.2 *Protectability Criteria: Novelty, Utility (Usefulness) and Industrial Application*

The IPL initially defined two criteria of protectability – novelty and utility (usefulness). These criteria were later amended in 2019. Whereas novelty remained, utility was replaced with capability for industrial application.[73] The draft IPL maintains both novelty and industrial application.[74]

[69] Art. 94 IPL.
[70] For examples see: www.pwrz.pl/rzecznik_patentowy/moje.html.
[71] Art. 111 draft IPL.
[72] Art. 112 draft IPL.
[73] Art. 94 IPL.
[74] Art. 111 draft IPL.

Polish law does not currently require any form of inventiveness for utility models. This omission makes Polish law different than that of many legal systems with utility model protection, which require at least some degree of inventiveness.

Prior to the 2019 amendments of the IPL, usefulness (utility) was one of the criteria for utility model protection. This concept was also part of the pre–World War II Polish IP legislation and was used to distinguish utility models and aesthetic models. In the 1928 Law the legislature demanded that the model "aims at achieving greater degree of utility" – this could be achieved by ensuring that manufacturing of the product is cheaper or safer, or that the product is more comfortable.[75] The same concept was used in 1962 when the Law on inventions was adopted and was repeated in 1972.[76] Though the utility requirement was interpreted in a liberal manner, the Patent Office denied protection in cases when utility was missing.[77]

Utility was also adopted as one of the protectability criteria for utility model protection in the IPL. According to Art. 94 IPL, a particular technical solution is regarded as useful if it enabled the achievement of an aim of practical significance for the manufacturing or use of the product. The wording of this provision, however, does not require greater utility, it merely requires utility. Therefore, the Patent Office checks for utility but is not required to compare two technical solutions and establish that one is in any way superior to the other. Thus, the utility requirement was practically devoid of any meaning.[78]

After amendments in 2019, the IPL no longer requires utility. Utility models, apart from being novel – must now be capable of industrial application. The same approach is taken in the draft IPL. Industrial application only requires that the technical solution be capable of being applied repeatedly while allowing achievement of the same result and without there being a need to resort to additional technical means or a different set of skills.[79] As such, industrial application does not introduce any requirements for inventiveness.

8.4.3 *Substantive Examination versus Mere Registration*

The IPL today requires that applications for utility model protection be filed with the Polish Patent Office. The Patent Office is responsible for the receipt and examination of applications. After 18 months from filing, the Patent Office announces that an application was filed in the Patent Office Bulletin.

The Patent Office conducts a full substantive examination of the applications to determine whether the requirements for obtaining utility model protection have been met. This examination substantially delays the grant of protection. At present,

75 Art. 87(2) Presidential Decree 1928.

76 Balicki 2020.

77 Balicki 2020.

78 Balicki 2020.

79 Ożegalska-Trybalska [2021]par. 32.

obtaining utility model protection takes 24 months on average.[80] The draft IPL envisages major amendments to the procedure for obtaining protection. If the draft IPL is passed, full substantive examination will be replaced by a registration procedure, thus shifting the analysis of the protectability criteria to post-grant opposition or invalidation proceedings. The Patent Office will no longer be required to publish information about the filing of applications 18 months after filing.

The draft IPL requires that, because there will be no substantive examination of the application during the registration procedure, the right holder – prior to filing a lawsuit or a motion for a preliminary injunction – must obtain a search report confirming the novelty and industrial application of the utility model.[81] That report will be attached to the lawsuit or the motion for the preliminary injunction.[82] Additionally, the draft IPL allows the Patent Office to conduct a substantive examination of a utility model application, but only when the application prima facie does not meet the protectability criteria.[83]

Certainly, replacing substantive examination with registration is a significant change, though one might also say that it would only result in adopting solutions well known in Polish intellectual property law. This change – so claim the drafters of the new IPL – would allow applicants to obtain protection in less than a year. That would in turn enable the achievement of the goals of the drafters of the new IPL, namely, to provide for more easily accessible intellectual property protection. Consequently, the drafters believe, easily accessible utility model protection would also result in more innovation and more rights being granted. It seems that the drafters were influenced by German law on utility models which also adopts the registration model for granting rights.

8.5 CONCLUSIONS

The protection of utility models has a long tradition in Poland, and it is unlikely to be abolished in the foreseeable future. Instead, discussions have centered around necessary reforms of the system. In many respects, the design of utility model protection in Poland resembles regulations in other jurisdictions – utility model protection can be obtained faster than patent protection. It is also cheaper than patent protection. Utility model protection is also easier to obtain since only novelty and industrial applicability are required. At the same time, it is shorter than patent protection and only lasts up to 10 years. Protectable subject matter is also limited, and the breadth of protection is likely to be narrower, as broad interpretation of claims is not an option with respect to utility models.

80 Explanatory Memorandum, 22.

81 This requirement is similar, for example, to that in France (Chapter 5) and Japan (Chapter 11).

82 Art. 477(2) draft IPL.

83 Art. 121(1) draft IPL.

At the same time there are concerns that utility model protection might be used for purposes that have little to do with innovation. One concern relates to use of the system by academic institutions. Utility model and patent grants are playing an important role in academic evaluations and are also considered when decisions to finance research are made. This leads to granting patents and utility models that might not be intended for commercialization, while diverting academic focus away from valuable research, the results of which would otherwise be published in peer-reviewed journals.

So far, utility model protection has been popular particularly with individual inventors and SMEs. Reform of utility model protection is likely to make the system even more attractive for SMEs. It remains to be seen whether changes in the law could lead to creation of thickets and possible abusive litigation by right holders. It also remains to be seen whether expected changes in the law would make the system more attractive for foreign filers. These concerns, however, might be overrated. Utility model protection is relatively narrow and design arounds are much easier. Therefore, utility models are less likely to be used abusively; rather, it is patents and copyrights that are more prone to such abusive use.

9

Key Performance Indicators for Utility Model Systems

An Application to Finland

Jussi T. S. Heikkilä[*]

The design and functioning of patent systems have been evaluated empirically for a long time[1] thanks to increasingly accessible patent data and statistics,[2] but much less is known about the functioning of utility model systems (or more generally second-tier patent systems)[3] and their interaction with patent systems. Both patents and utility models are protection methods for technical inventions, but the latter is often considered to be a flexible complement to the patent system that offers protection particularly for small and incremental inventions that have shorter lifecycles and for small and medium sized enterprises (SMEs) that have fewer resources to invest in patent protection.[4] Generally, there exists very little systematic empirical evidence on the benefits and positive impacts of national utility model systems, particularly in advanced economies.[5] Hence, the fundamental question remains whether societies are better off with or without utility model systems that bring flexibilities to the more harmonized patent systems.

The contribution of this chapter to the existing empirical literature utilizing utility model statistics,[6] is to apply the framework introduced by Heikkilä (2023a) to the analysis of the functioning of the Finnish utility model system. The focus is not

* The author thanks Hanna Aho and Pia Björkwall for helpful comments.

1 E.g., Hall and Harhoff 2012.

2 Griliches 1990.

3 Janis 1999; Radauer et al. 2019.

4 WIPO's definition: www.wipo.int/patents/en/topics/utility_models.html, Accessed 18 December 2023.

5 Kim et al. 2012; Johnson et al. 2015; Heikkilä 2018, 2023a, Suthersanen 2019. However, prior research indicates that utility models can be effective means for countries and companies in catching-up phase (e.g., Kim et al. 2012).

6 E.g., Cao 2015; Radauer et al. 2015; Prud'homme 2017a; Heikkilä and Lorenz 2018; Heikkilä and Verba 2018; Sun and Lei 2023. See also Chapter 2, summarizing empirical literature.

solely on economic impacts (e.g., innovation incentives and diffusion of innovations), but rather the aim is to provide a more holistic and comprehensive assessment which comprises dimensions such as the extent to which utility models bring flexibility and inclusiveness to the patent system and how the quality of utility models coevolves with that of patents. Finland is a European export-driven small open economy, so the external validity of the observations is limited but the findings are particularly interesting for countries with similar characteristics. It should be emphasized that the analysis is purely based on utility model and patent statistics and legal analyses of the evolution of the Finnish utility model system are beyond the scope.

The chapter is structured as follows. Section 9.1 describes the evaluation framework for the functioning of utility model systems. Section 9.2 describes the Finnish institutional context briefly and presents the empirical analysis and findings. Section 9.3 concludes.

9.1 KEY PERFORMANCE INDICATORS FOR UTILITY MODEL SYSTEMS

The World Trade Organization's (WTO) Agreement on Trade-Related Aspects of Intellectual Property Rights (TRIPS) sets the minimum standards for patent systems but not for utility model systems, which countries can design as they see fit.[7] Common rationales for a utility model system include ameliorating the defects of the national patent and design right systems and promotion of SMEs' innovation activity.[8] Thus, utility model systems cannot be evaluated without considering their interaction with the patent system. In principle, when an intellectual property (IP) office offers for applicants both patent and utility model protection, it provides a menu of options and applicants self-select – that is, make strategic choices between patents and utility models given their preferences. Therefore, there is sorting between patents and utility models (or other type of second-tier patents) by applicant and invention type.[9] It should be emphasized that in the European context one cannot ignore the interaction of utility model and other national IPR systems with the evolving European IPR institutions,[10] particularly European patents and registered Community designs (RCD).

As the chapters in this volume demonstrate, there are significant differences across utility model systems (and each country has its own mix of innovation policy instruments that interacts more or less with its national utility model system). Hence,

7 Janis 1999; Suthersanen 2006, 2019; Cahoy and Oswald 2021.
8 Suthersanen 2019.
9 Atal and Bar 2014; Heikkilä and Verba 2017; Heikkilä 2018.
10 Cf. Hall and Helmers 2019; Heikkilä and Peltoniemi 2023.

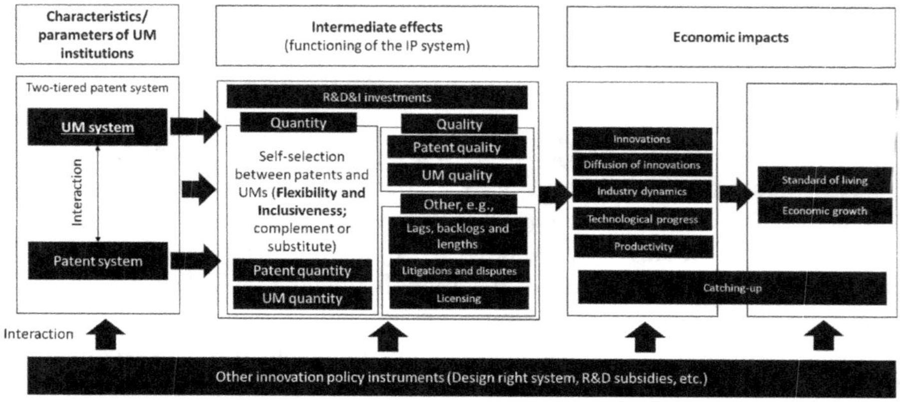

FIGURE 9.1 Framework for multidimensional analysis of utility model systems' performance
Source: Adapted from Heikkilä (2023a).

there is a need to conduct country-specific case studies that focus on specific institutional settings. Among others, Suthersanen (2006, 2019), Björkwall (2009), Prud'homme (2014, 2017a), Radauer et al. (2015, 2019) and Heikkilä and Verba (2018) have provided comparative analyses of selected national utility model systems. In addition, there are increasingly country-level statistical analyses of utility model and two-tiered patent systems.[11] To our knowledge, there are no studies that quantitatively analyze the interaction between the European Patent system (and registered Community designs) and European national utility model systems.

Recently, Heikkilä (2023a) reviewed the existing utility model literature and the information that 64 national IP offices provide about their national utility model systems on their websites and reported that shorter protection period is emphasized by approximately 60 percent of IP offices, the lower inventive step requirement by more than one third (approx. 38 percent) and the quicker and simpler process to obtain protection compared to patents by approximately 30 percent of IP offices. As there are no established performance measures for utility model systems, Heikkilä (2023a) suggested a systematic framework and "key performance indicators" (KPIs) for the holistic analysis of utility model systems. These are illustrated in Figure 9.1 and Table 9.1. Figure 9.1 distinguishes between intermediate effects and economic impacts. In the next section, we apply this framework to the Finnish utility model system and focus particularly on intermediate impacts and its coevolution with the Finnish patent system.

[11] E.g., Japan: Maskus and McDaniel 1999; Finland: Björkwall 2009; the Netherlands: Heikkilä 2017; South Korea: Kim et al. 2012; Germany: Bielig 2015; Australia: Johnson et al. 2015; China: Cao et al. 2015; Sun and Lei 2023; Kenya: Rutenberg and Mwangi 2017.

TABLE 9.1 *Objectives and selected indicators of utility model systems*

Objective	Key performance indicator
Innovation incentives	Number of UM filings Number of UM applicants Number of UM inventors Performance of firms using UMs R&D investments by firms using UMs Commercialization of UM-protected inventions
Diffusion of innovations	Number of published UM filings with descriptions of inventions Citations to UMs Licensing of UM-protected inventions
Rate and direction of technological change	Patent filings by IPC classes UM filings by IPC classes
Catching up	Resident UM filings Resident patent filings National R&D investments
Quicker protection	Registration/grant lags for inventions Backlog of pending patents
Inclusiveness	Patent and UM inventions overlap Patent and UM applicants overlap Patent and UM inventors overlap Number of UM filings by SMEs
International protection	Priority and non-priority UM filings
Quantity and quality of patents	Number of patent filings Share and absolute number of rejected patents Share and absolute number of granted patents Patent quality indicators

Adapted from Heikkilä (2023a). Achievement of objectives could be measured on different levels of aggregation, such as national, regional, industry or technology field (e.g., IPC), among others.

9.2 EMPIRICAL ANALYSIS OF THE FINNISH UTILITY MODEL SYSTEM

9.2.1 *Institutional Setting in Finland*

Finland is a developed small open economy and has been a member of the European Union (EU) since 1995. In 2022, Finland had a population of approximately 5.5 million and a gross domestic product of about 270 billion euros. Finland has been ranked among the most innovative countries in Europe[12] and the world[13] and Park's (2008) IPR index assigns a high score to Finland.

The Finnish utility model ("hyödyllisyysmalli") system is one of the "utility model-intensive" ones in which there are more than 100 utility model filings per year.[14] The system was established in 1992 shortly before Finland joined the EU in 1995 and the European Patent Convention (EPC) in 1996. The decision of Finland and Denmark (see Chapter 4) to establish national utility model systems in 1992 while other Nordic countries Sweden, Norway and Iceland chose not to, marked a divergence from the collaborative development of Nordic IPR institutions.[15]

In total there have been slightly more than 15,000 utility model applications in Finland by the end of 2022 and in 2023 there were slightly more than 2,000 utility models in force or pending in Finland.[16] Figure 9.2 shows the trends in utility model, patent and design right filings using data from the Finnish Patent and Registration Office (Patentti- ja rekisterihallitus, hereafter PRH), WIPO and EUIPO. The declining trend in utility model filings since the adoption of the system coincides with the decreasing utility model application trends in Germany and Denmark[17] as well as the declining trend in national design right filings. There is a negative correlation (−0.63) between the trend-like decline of utility model filings and increasing aggregate business sector R&D expenditure. The most visible impact in Finnish patent statistics is the drop related to the accession of Finland to the EPC in 1996 after which applicants could validate granted European patents in Finland instead of filing national patent applications at the PRH. Later, the introduction of the RCDs by EUIPO (OHIM at the time) in 2003 led to the collapse of Finnish design right filings.[18] However, it seems that these significant institutional changes had no radical immediate impact on the demand for Finnish utility models.

Important motivations for establishing the Finnish utility model system were that it would provide protection for inventions that do not satisfy patentability criteria and that cannot be protected with design rights as well as quick protection.[19] Furthermore, Radauer et al. report that "According to the Finnish Patent and Registration Office (PRH), the intention was to create a system for small innovations, i.e. one that would provide cheaper and faster protection than patents for

[12] European Commission 2023c.
[13] WIPO 2023c.
[14] Heikkilä 2023a.
[15] Laisi 2009. Björkwall (2009) provides a comparison between the Finnish, Danish and German utility model systems of the time.
[16] Patent Information Service of PRH lists 2,254 utility models as registered or pending as of 31 December 2023. See https://patenttitietopalvelu.prh.fi/fi/
[17] See Chapters 6 and 4. See also Bielig 2015; Radauer et al. 2015; Heikkilä 2023b.
[18] Heikkilä and Peltoniemi 2023.
[19] KTM 1986; Björkwall 2009.

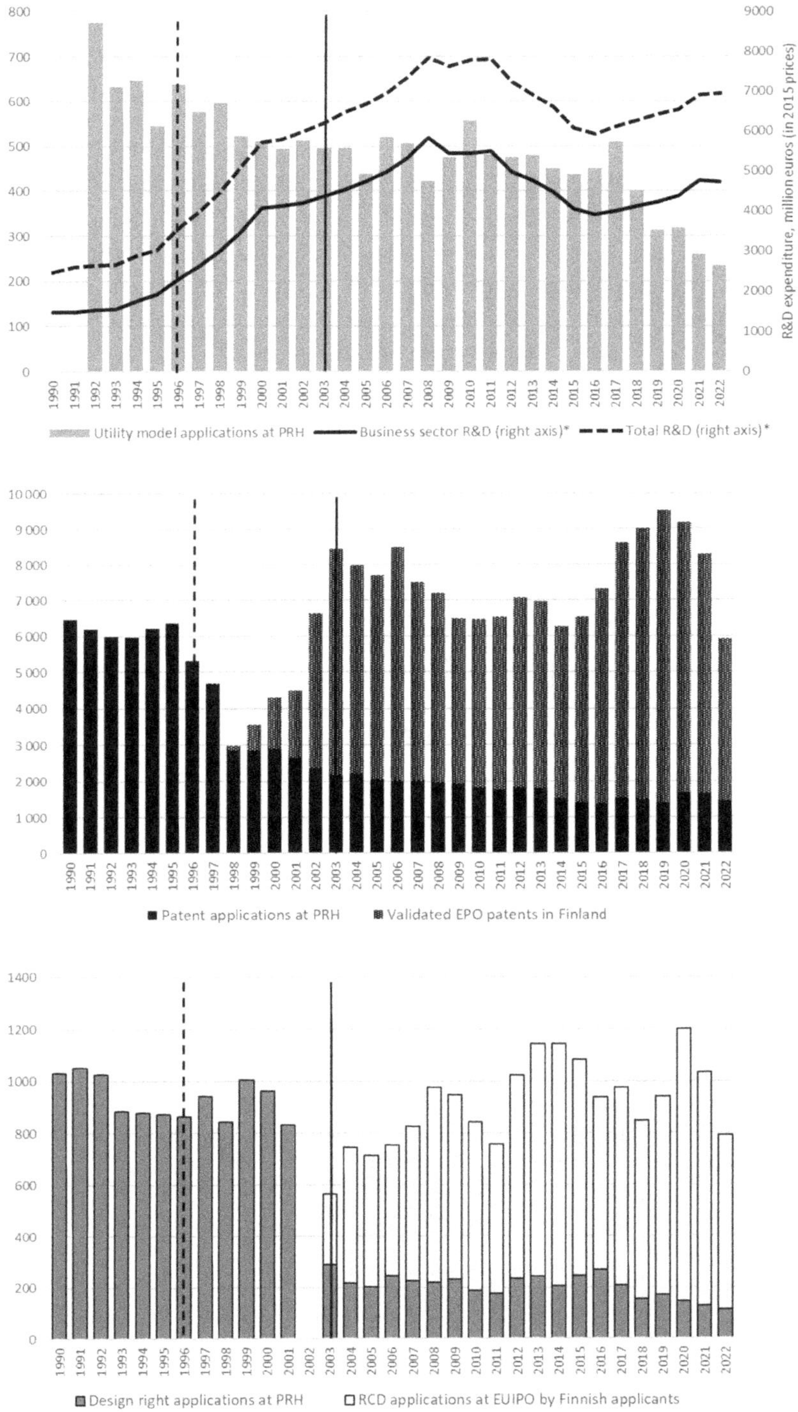

FIGURE 9.2 Evolution of utility model, patent and design right filings in Finland

simple objects."[20] Björkwall (2009) reports, based on a survey, that the Finnish respondents' most important reasons to apply for utility models were that its cheaper and quicker than the patent option. As of December 2023, PRH describes Finnish utility models on its website as follows: "Similar to a patent, a utility model is a way to obtain an exclusive right to an invention and prohibit others from exploiting the invention commercially. Utility models are quicker and cheaper to get than patents."[21]

Finland joined the European Patent Organisation (EPO) in 1996 after which patents in force have been increasingly those granted by the EPO instead of PRH. In 1997, the European Commission proposed a European community utility model (see discussion in Chapter 20). At the time, the EU had 15 member states of which 12 had some sort of utility model system and the proposal would have meant that Luxembourg, Sweden and the United Kingdom, which at the time did not have utility model systems, would have needed to introduce one into their domestic law. The proposal was abandoned in early 2000s and the EU has since expanded to 27 member states (after Brexit). Hence, as discussed in Chapter 20, the landscape of European utility model systems has remained unharmonized to date. Recently, Finland joined the Unitary Patent System and Unified Patent Court that began their operations in June 2023. Heikkilä and Peltoniemi (2023) provide a description of how the Finnish IPR service sector has evolved over the same period and particularly how this has impacted the business of Finnish patent attorneys. The key developments since 1980s include among others the following events:[22]

1983 The Association of Finnish Patent Attorneys expressed a wish to the Ministry of Trade and Industry to evaluate the need for the Finnish utility model system

1985 Utility model committee set up by the Ministry of Trade and Industry

1986 Utility model committee recommends establishing the Finnish utility model system

FIGURE 9.2 *(cont.)*
Sources: The sources of data are WIPO IP Statistics Data Center (design rights, information for 2002 missing), PRH, www.prh.fi/fi/patentit/tilastoja/eurooppapatentit.html and EUIPO, www.euipo.europa.eu/en/the-office/about-us/what-we-do/statistics. Finland joined the EPO on 1 March 1996 (scattered line) and unitary patent system on 1 June 2023. EUIPO (OHIM) introduced RCDs in 2003 (solid line). Statistical information on the Unitary Patent system is available online: www.epo.org/en/about-us/statistics/statistics-centre#/unitary-patent. By 31 December 2023, there were 16,482 registered unitary patents which are in force in Finland. *The source of R&D data is Statistics Finland, deflated using GDP deflator (in 2015 prices), interpolated for 1990, 1992, 1994 and 1996 https://data.worldbank.org/indicator/NY.GDP.DEFL.ZS?locations = FI.

[20] Radauer et al. 2015, 110.

[21] www.prh.fi/en/hyodyllisyysmallit.html, Accessed 18 December 2023. Similarly, a quick review of online marketing material of Finnish patent attorney firms indicates that "quick," "cost-effective" or "inexpensive" are common adjectives related to Finnish utility models.

[22] See KTM 1986; Björkwall 2009 and WIPO Lex for more details.

1991 Act on utility model rights 800/1991 and Decree on utility model rights 1419/1991
1992 Introduction of the Finnish utility model system
1994 The European Union Intellectual Property Office founded (formerly known as the Office for Harmonization in the Internal Market, OHIM, until 2016), WTO's TRIPS agreement signed
1995 Finland joins the EU
1996 Finland joins the EPC, European trademark system introduced
1997 European Commission proposes Community utility model
2003 European registered Community design system introduced
2006 Commission decides to halt the development of the community utility model
2011 The London agreement[23] enters into force in Finland
2023 Launch of the Unitary Patent System and Unified Patent Court[24]

Table 9.2 provides a comparison of selected key dimensions of the Finnish utility model systems and selected other interacting IPR institutions. It is important to highlight some peculiarities of the Finnish utility model system. There is no substantive examination of utility models at PRH but rather they are simply registered after formal examination (grant rate is close to 100 percent for those that are not withdrawn). Utility models are not granted for process inventions. There is inventive step requirement for Finnish patents but for utility models the requirement is lower: inventions must "differ distinctly from the prior art" to be eligible for utility model protection.[25] Utility models are granted for four years and can be renewed for an additional four years and two years so that the maximum term of protection is ten years (4+4+2). Since November 2011, as a consequence of the London agreement, there is no longer a need to translate Finnish patent applications filed in English to the Finnish language, but this does not apply to utility models, which still need to be filed in either Finnish or Swedish.

The most important trading partners of Finland include Sweden, Germany, the US, the Netherlands and China.[26] Historically, Russia has also been a significant import and export country for Finland. Of these countries, Sweden, Germany and the Netherlands are EU members states and Germany, China and Russia have utility model systems in place as of 2022. Particularly, the Finnish companies that have exported to these countries must have been at least to some extent aware of the functioning of the local utility model systems. Regarding the "stepping stone"

[23] No more requirement for Finnish translation of validated EPO patent specifications if the patent is granted in English or an English translation is supplied (still need to provide the claims in Finnish).
[24] See Chapter 17.
[25] Björkwall 2009.
[26] See Statistics Finland: International trade in goods and services, https://pxdata.stat.fi/PxWeb/pxweb/en/StatFin/StatFin__tpulk/statfin_tpulk_pxt_12gq.px/, Accessed 20 December 2023.

TABLE 9.2 *Selected characteristics of the Finnish utility model system and other interacting IPR institutions*

	Formal protection methods in Finland					
	Technical inventions				Designs	
	Finnish patents	**EPO patents (European patents)**	**Unitary patents**	**Finnish utility models**	**Finnish design rights**	**Registered Community design**
System introduced	1842	1977, Finland joined 1996	2023	1992	1971	2003
Regional scope	Finland	Validation possible in Finland and 38 other member states, one extension state and four validation states.	Finland and 16 other EU member states	Finland	Finland	Finland and 26 other EU member states
Official application languages	Finnish, Swedish or English	English, French and German		Finnish or Swedish	Finnish or Swedish	Any official language of the EU
Examination	Substantive examination	Substantive examination		Registration process	Registration process	Registration process
Novelty requirement	Global	Global		Global	Global	Global
Inventive step requirement	Inventive step	Inventive step (not obvious to a person skilled in the art)		Must differ distinctly from the prior art	Must have individual character	Must have individual character
Grant lag	Years	Years		Months	Months	Months
Maximum term of protection	20 years	20 years		10 years	25 years	25 years
In force in Finland	6,454*	50,014*	16,482**	2,254*	1,384*	296,912***

Information source is WIPO Lex (see also Björkwall 2009; Prud'homme 2014; Radauer et al. 2015); *Patents: PRH, 2022 information, www.prh.fi/en/patentit/Tilastoja/patentit.html; utility models: https://patenttitietopalvelu.prh.fi/fi/, Accessed 31 December 2023; Design rights: https://mallioikeustietopalvelu.prh.fi/, Accessed 31 December 2023; **www.epo.org/en/about-us/statistics/statistics-centre#/unitary-patent, Accessed 31 December 2023; ***WIPO IP Statistics Data Center, 2022 information.

hypothesis (companies using utility models learn and shift to use patents increasingly)[27] and from the perspective of IPR-related learning, it is interesting to analyze in which countries Finnish applicants apply for utility models beyond Finnish borders. According to the WIPO IP Statistics Data Center, the top foreign countries where Finnish applicants registered utility model applications from 1992 to 2021 were Germany (1,892), China (756), Austria (187), Russia (145) and Denmark (108).[28]

9.2.2 *Patent and Utility Model Statistics*

Since there are no explicit objectives set for the Finnish utility model system it has no specific KPIs. Therefore, the framework illustrated in Section 9.1 is applied to conduct a holistic analysis of the functioning of the Finnish utility model system. The interaction between the patent and utility model systems is analyzed using patent and utility model statistics. In particular, the coevolution of patent and utility model characteristics are compared, including the number of inventors, assigned IPC (International Patent Classification) classes, received citations, share of priority filings, patent and utility model family size (international filings) and structure, the use of utility models by industries and technology fields and grant/registration lags. The role of design rights (both national and RCDs) as complements and/or substitutes for utility models is left for future research.

The nature of this empirical analysis is purely descriptive. The statistical utility model and patent data comes from PRH, EPO (PATSTAT, Autumn 2023 version) and WIPO (IP Statistics Data Center).[29] PRH kindly provided information on the whole population of Finnish utility models and patent filings for the period 1992–2021. This includes information, among other things, about the use of professional representatives (patent attorneys).[30] There are slight differences between the data sources, but the presented trends are robust regardless of the chosen source.

9.2.3 *Findings*

9.2.3.1 Intermediate Impacts

9.2.3.1.1 QUANTITY AND QUALITY OF UTILITY MODELS AND PATENTS Figure 9.2 shows how the quantities of Finnish utility models and patents have evolved over time. Finland's accession to the EPC led to a sharp decrease in patent filings, but there was no similar drop in the case of utility models. Figure 9.3 distinguishes between resident and non-resident applicants. It illustrates how the utility model

[27] Kim et al. 2012.
[28] Heikkilä 2023b.
[29] PRH is gratefully acknowledged for providing the data.
[30] Cf. Heikkilä 2021; Heikkilä and Peltoniemi 2023.

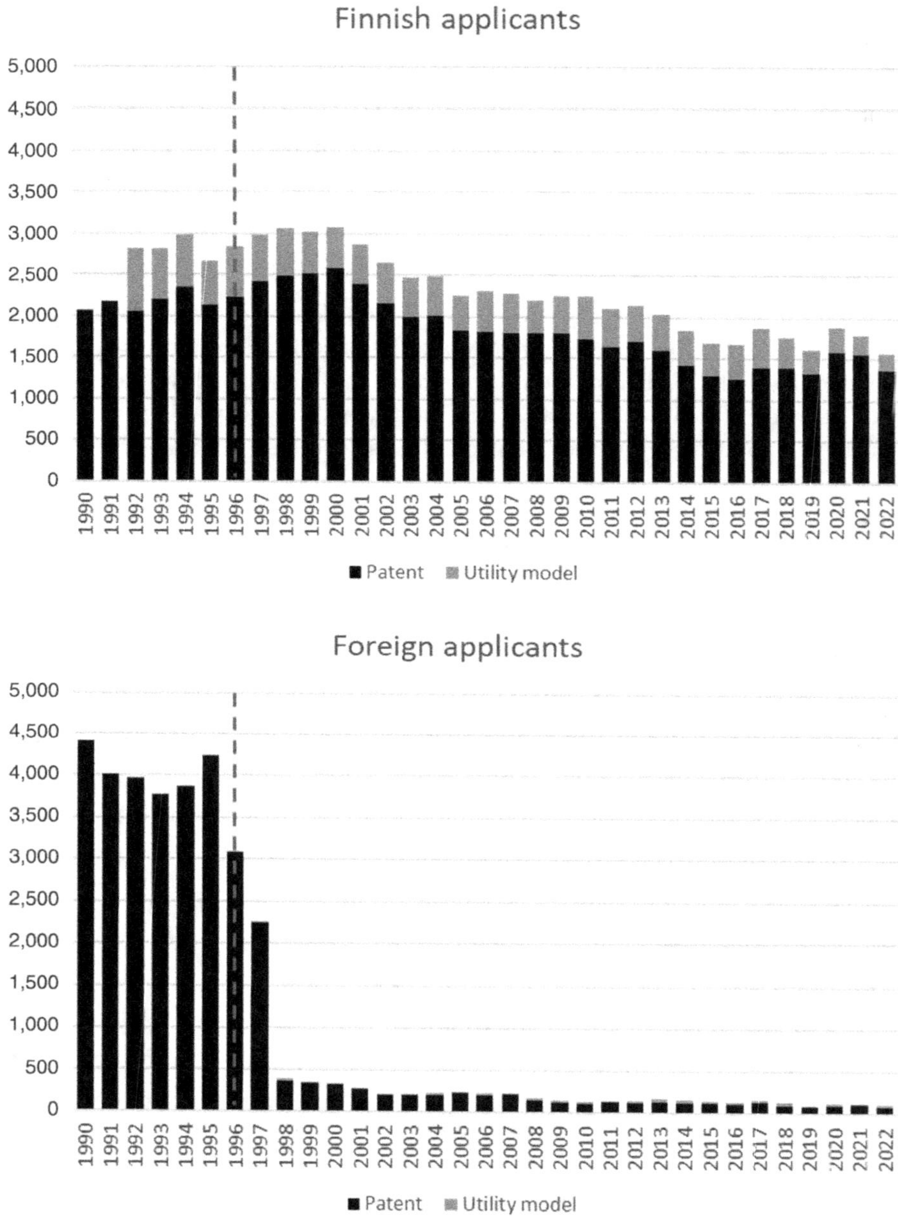

FIGURE 9.3 Patent and utility model applications by applicant origin at the Finnish patent office

Note: Dashed line indicates Finland's year of accession to the EPC.*Source*: PRH. utility models: www.prh.fi/en/hyodyllisyysmallit/Tilasto.html, patents: www.prh.fi/en/patentit/Tilastoja/patenttihakemusten_arkisto.html, Accessed 18 December 2023.

system increases particularly the filings by resident applicants whereas there were only a very small number of filings by non-residents. According to PRH, 675 (4.4 percent) utility model applications were filed by foreign applicants and the rest 14,509 (95.6 percent) were filed by Finnish applicants between 1992 and 2022. Figure 9.3 demonstrates how Finland's accession to the EPC led to collapse in Finnish patent filings by non-resident applicants at the PRH as they began to validate EPO patents in Finland instead. It seems that Finland's accession to the EPC did not have visible negative nor positive impacts on the utility model filings.

Diminishing demand for utility models may be a result of various factors. It may reflect a declining number of incremental inventions or the gradual learning process regarding the usefulness of utility models in innovation activity:[31] utility model holders and industries learn only gradually over time how effective utility models are in promoting their businesses and competitiveness and, for instance, excluding imitators from copying utility model-protected technical solutions. It may also reflect the recommendations by patent attorneys between patents and utility models. Heikkilä (2021) documented using PRH register data that a smaller share of utility model filings has a named professional representative (53.6 percent) compared to patents (69.9 percent) and that firms are more likely to have named representatives than individual applicants both for patents and utility models.

A patent family refers to all the patents and utility models that protect the same invention across countries and it consists of one or multiple priority filings and no or multiple subsequent filings.[32] Utility model protection is often sought for inventions where the idea is to obtain purely national protection.[33] Figure 9.4 illustrates how the share of priority filings has developed in patent and utility model filings over time. When Finland joined the EPO, the share of priority filings in the case of patents increased from some one-fourth to more than four-fifths. Concurrently, the number of national patent filings collapsed when particularly foreign firms quit filing national Finnish patents and instead used the EPO channel to obtain protection in Finland by validating EPO patents in Finland. This is consistent with the observations of Hall and Helmers (2019). Clearly, Finland's accession to the EPC had a major impact on patenting strategies of foreign applicants in Finland, whereas there seems to be no comparable impact on the utilization of utility models. Foreign applicants' demand for Finnish utility models has remained at a low level over the whole period.

The use of utility models as part of international patent filing strategies may reveal interesting patterns.[34] Figure 9.5 illustrates the evolution of patent family size (DOCDB) for both Finnish utility models and patents. Consistent with observations by Radauer et al. (2015), Heikkilä (2017), Heikkilä and Verba (2018), the patent

[31] Cf. Heikkilä and Peltoniemi 2019.

[32] Martínez 2011; de Rassenfosse et al. 2013; Heikkilä and Verba 2018.

[33] Heikkilä and Verba 2018.

[34] Heikkilä and Verba 2018.

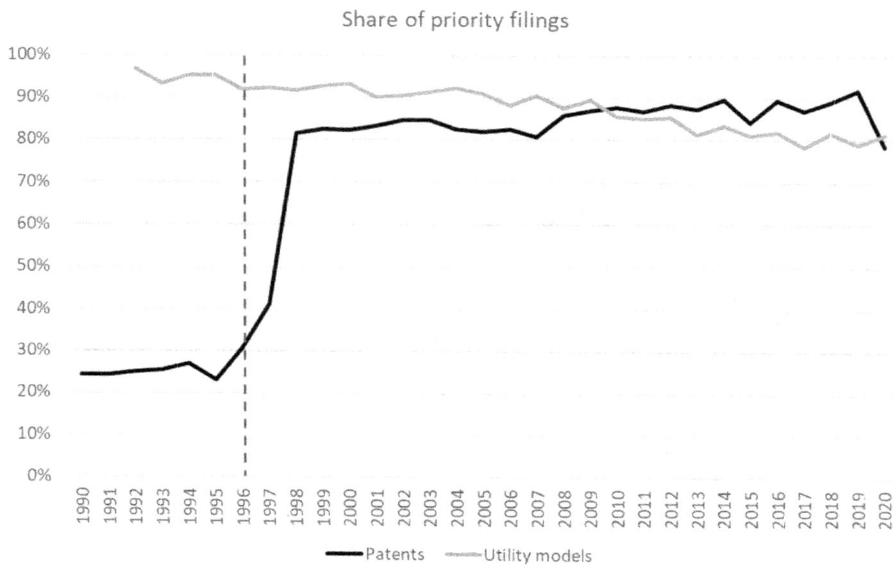

FIGURE 9.4 Patent families – share of priority filings
Source: PRH, Finnish patents and utility models.

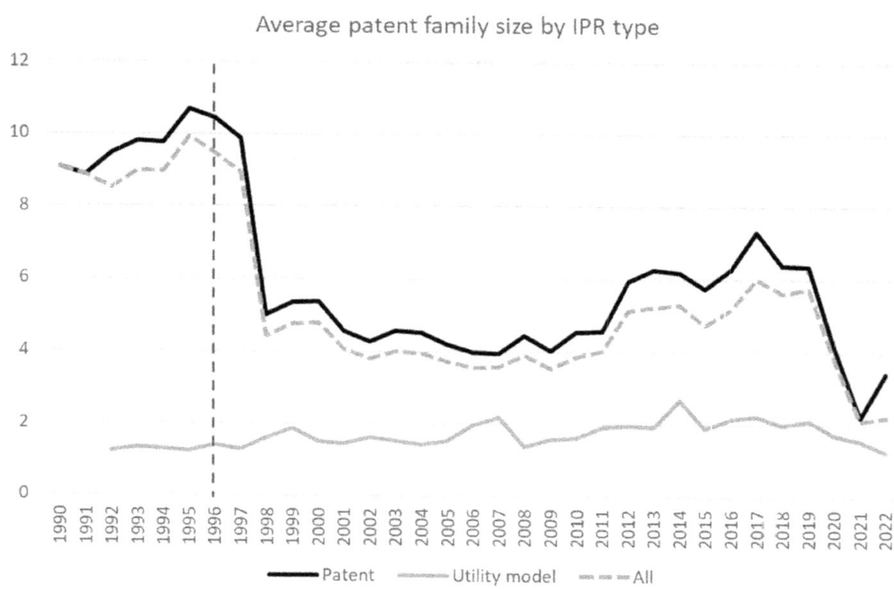

FIGURE 9.5 Patent families – average patent family size by filing year cohorts
Source: PATSTAT Online 2023 Autumn, Accessed 18 December 2023. Patent family refers to DOCDB patent family. The years are the years when the Finnish patent or utility model was filed as a member of the DOCDB patent family.

family size of utility models is systematically and significantly smaller compared to patents. As patent family size correlates with the value of the invention,[35] this can be interpreted as evidence that Finnish utility models are applied to protect less valuable inventions than Finnish patents, on average.

A singleton patent family is a peculiar patent family that has only one member – a single priority filing, be it eventually granted or not – and no subsequent related filings.[36] Hence, the number of utility models and patents that are singleton families reflects the number of inventions that would not otherwise be published in patent registers. Singleton patents and utility models have the minimum patent family size of 1 and, given that patent family size and value of the invention correlate, they presumably relate to the least valuable inventions for which the applicant has no value in extending the protection. In the absence of these singleton filings in patent registers there might be duplicative R&D (re-inventing the wheel) of these inventions.

Moreover, singleton patent families may also indicate a defensive publication strategy and production of registered and novelty-destroying prior art that prevents others from patenting the same technical invention ("pre-emptive patenting"). There were 14,626 utility models in the PATSTAT Online database (Autumn 2023 version), of which 83.5 percent (12,212) were singletons and approximately 16.5 percent (2,414) were members of patent families with at least two members. This indicates that Finnish utility models are indeed in the majority of cases related to less valuable inventions for which protection is sought solely in Finland and not in other countries. Of the non-singleton utility models there were 367 utility models (approximately 2 percent of all utility models) that are members of patent families[37] where there is also a Finnish patent filing. Of these 26 were filed on the same date, in 279 cases the patent application was filed before the utility model (the mean lag between patent and utility model filings was 617 days, with a median of 364) and in 62 cases a utility model was filed before a patent application (mean lag between utility model and patent filings was 354 days, with a median of 338.5 days). More detailed analysis of the patent families could reveal whether the cases correspond to using utility models for double-protection, as "fallback" options or as quick protection during the time when the patent is still pending.

Figure 9.6 shows that the average number of inventors (inventor team size) is systematically smaller in the case of utility models compared to patents. This is in line with earlier observations.[38] In approximately 75 percent of utility models there is only a single inventor while only approximately 40 percent of patents have only one named inventor.[39] The large number of sole inventors in utility models contrasts the

[35] E.g., Martínez 2011; Squicciarini et al. 2013; Heikkilä and Verba 2018.

[36] Martínez 2011; Heikkilä and Verba 2018.

[37] DOCDB, as of 27 December 2023.

[38] E.g., Heikkilä 2017; Heikkilä and Verba 2018.

[39] PATSTAT Online 2023 Autumn version.

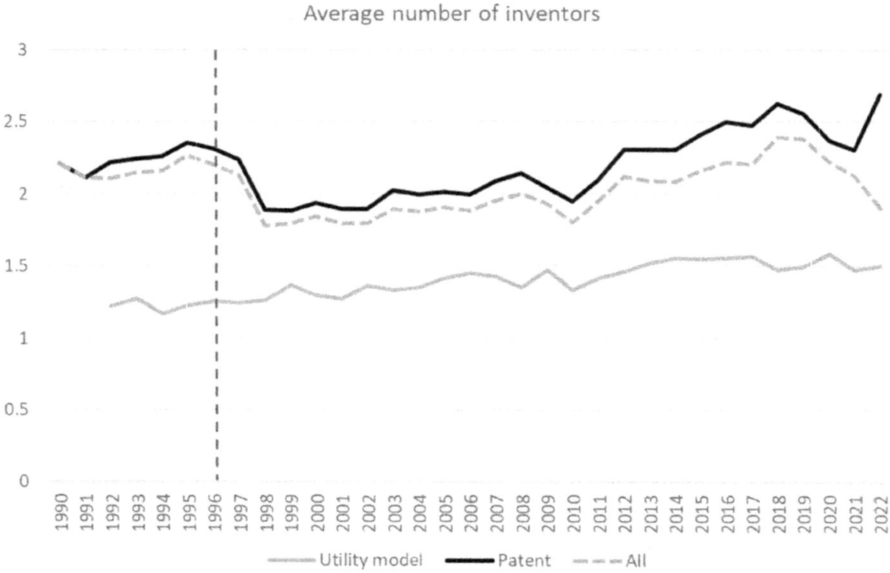

FIGURE 9.6 Quality of inventions – average inventor team sizes
Source: PATSTAT Online (2023 Autumn). Years refer to filing years. There is only a small number of patents (75) for which the number of inventors information is available for 2022.

more general trend that developing patentable inventions is increasingly international teamwork.[40] Nevertheless, the larger number of "lone inventors" in utility models compared to patents is consistent with the motivation of utility model systems as a particularly appropriate protection method for small inventors and for incremental inventions.[41]

Patent citations are the most common quality measure for patented inventions.[42] Figure 9.7 shows the evolution of average received citations for Finnish utility models and patents. Clearly, utility models have received only a limited number of citations: the average number of citations received by patent families (DOCDB) where Finnish utility models are members has hovered around 0.5 for most of the cohorts between 1992 and 2019. This illustrates that utility models seem to play only a minor role in cumulative innovation activity – very few inventions seem to be impacted by the technical content of Finnish utility models documents based on the "paper trail" of patent citations. Presumably, the fact that Finnish utility models are written in the Finnish or Swedish language further reduces the number of citations.

40 Cf. Kerr and Kerr 2018.

41 Radauer et al. 2019.

42 Jaffe and de Rassenfosse 2017.

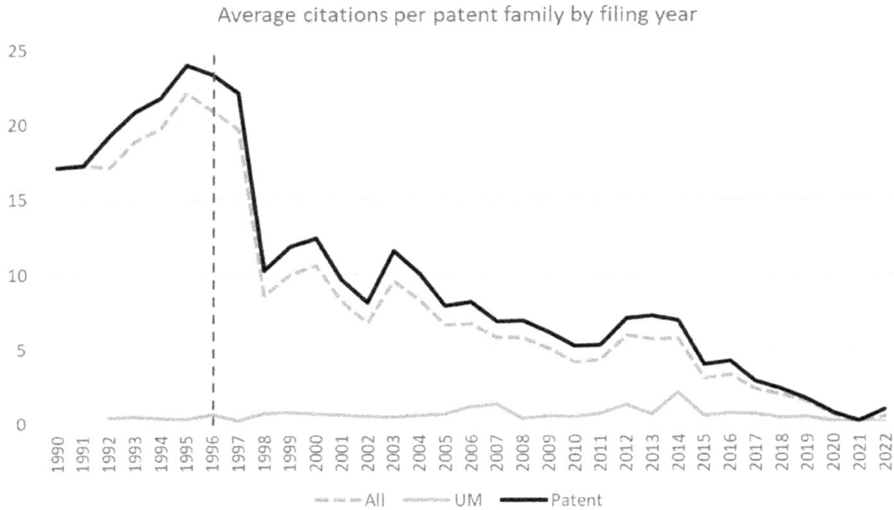

FIGURE 9.7 Quality of inventions – average received citations

Source: PATSTAT Online (2023 Autumn), Accessed 19 December 2023. The decreasing trend for citations is (partially) explained by the fact that more recently published patent documents have had less time to accumulate citations.

9.2.3.1.2 FLEXIBILITY AND INCLUSIVENESS Quick protection is an important reason for the existence of the Finnish utility model system[43] and Figure 9.8 illustrates the evolution of grant lags (time between filing and registration) for Finnish utility models and compares that to patents. Indeed, as also noted by the PRH, utility models provide quicker protection: The registration lag from filing to grant is several years in the case of Finnish patents but measured in months for utility models. For registered utility models the average grant lag between 1992 and 2021 was about five months (ca. 150 days) and Prud'homme (2014) reported that it was three months as of 2014.

The overlap between patent and utility model applicants and inventors sheds light on the extent to which a utility model system stimulates innovation activity by those applicants and inventors that do not file patent applications – that is, how inclusive the utility model system is. Heikkilä (2023b) made some back-of-the-envelope calculations using uncleaned Finnish patent and utility model applicant and inventor data from PATSTAT and reported that the patent registers have at maximum 40 percent (approx. 6,000) more unique applicants and 20 percent (approx. 6,500) more Finnish inventors than in the case if there was no utility model system. These rough estimates make the crucial simplifying assumption that there would be no substitution to patent filings in the absence of utility models and, thus, should be regarded as potential maxima. Another limitation is that the applicant and inventor data is not

[43] KTM 1986; Björkwall 2009; Radauer et al. 2015.

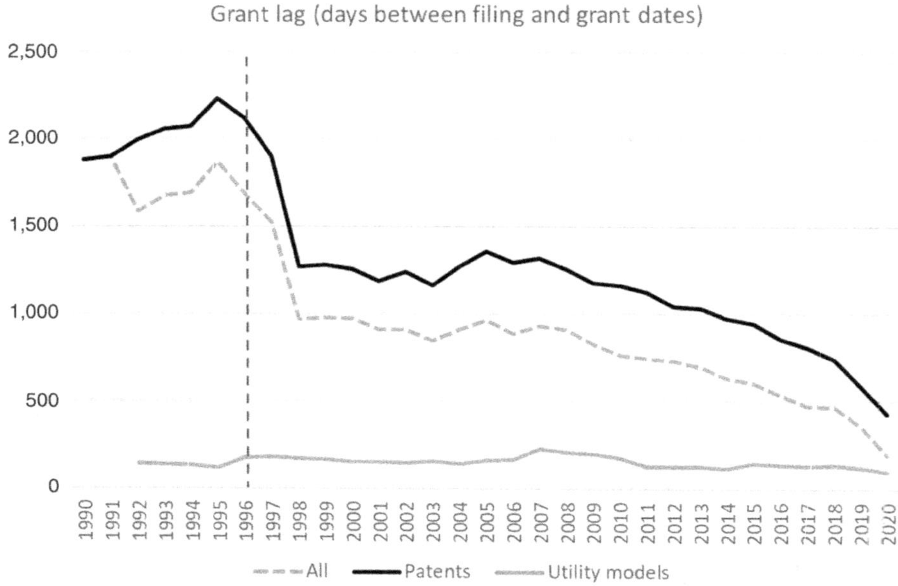

FIGURE 9.8 Grant lags of patents and registration lags of utility models
Source: PRH, situation as of December 2021. The "declining" pattern of the average grant lag of patents is partially explained by the fact that for more recent cohorts the share of pending patents is higher.

cleaned which leads to falsely distinguishing those applicants and inventors as "unique" where there is just some different format for the name or misspelling. Nonetheless, it seems that the utility model system has acted as an inclusive institution, and we observe more inventors and applicants in patent registers than we would in the absence of the utility model system. However, Heikkilä (2019) documented that the gender gap is larger and not decreasing in the context of the Finnish utility models compared to patents: over the period 1992–2013 the share of women among utility model inventors remained steadily at approximately 5 percent.

With the PRH and PATSTAT data, we cannot distinguish SMEs from large corporations. However, the Community Innovation Survey (CIS) contains questions regarding the use of IPR protection among Finnish companies. Figure 9.9 shows that the use of utility models as well as patents and design rights is positively correlated with firm size so that the larger a firm is the more likely it is to use IPR protection. Generally, the use of utility models is relatively rare as only approximately 2 percent of sampled respondent firms use them. The use of utility models is significantly less common compared to patents (approx. 8 percent) and approximately as common as the use of design rights. It should be noted, however, that the CIS questionnaire does not clarify in which countries companies have used patents, design rights and utility models so it is not entirely clear whether companies refer to Finnish utility models (patents, design rights) or utility models in other countries such as Germany or China.

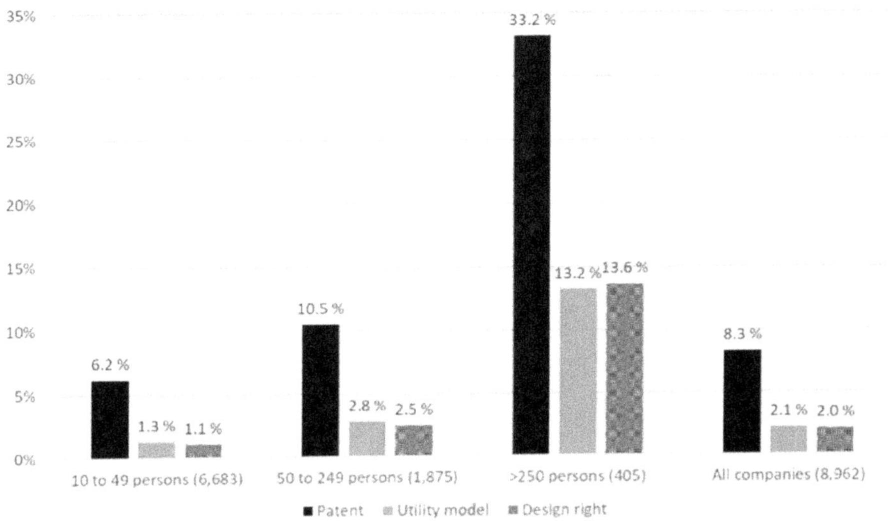

FIGURE 9.9 Share of firms using IPR protection by firm size
Source: Statistics Finland, Community Innovation Survey 2020, https://pxdata.stat.fi/PxWeb/pxweb/en/StatFin/StatFin__inn/statfin_inn_pxt_13k6.px/, Accessed 19 December 2023.

9.2.3.2 Economic Impacts: Rate and Direction of Innovation

The contribution of utility models to innovation incentives and R&D investments is challenging to investigate directly as we lack firm-level data. Like the patent system, the utility model system impacts industries and technology fields at different intensity. In other words, the utility model system may direct the rate and direction of technological progress towards those fields where it increases innovation incentives and promotes diffusion of innovations the most. Regarding the latter aspect, Figure 9.7 indicates that Finnish utility models are cited very seldom, so using this traditional metric we do not find significant impact ("a paper trail") on cumulative innovation and innovation diffusion. The language barriers are a potential reason for this as descriptions of utility models are written in Finnish or Swedish and the claims are available in Finnish and Swedish in public patent registers.

Table 9.3 shows the shares of Finnish innovative companies that have filed utility model or patent applications or registered design rights by industries with the highest utility-model-user intensity. Paper and machinery industries are clearly the most active users of utility models and, interestingly, in the furniture industry a larger share of firms uses utility models than patents and design rights. The Green Paper by the European Commission mentions that, "An industry-by-industry breakdown of utility model applications in the European Union shows that the industries most often concerned are mechanical engineering, electrical engineering, and precision

TABLE 9.3 *Industries where the largest share of Finnish innovative firms used utility models 2018–2020*

	Share of firms (%) with innovation activity applying IPR during the survey period 2018–2020		
	Utility model application	Patent application	Design right registration
C17 Manufacture of paper products	20.1	36.1	10.8
C28 Manufacture of machinery and equipment n.e.c.	13.6	50.3	8.4
C23 Manufacture of other non-metallic mineral products	11.4	14.6	2.5
C13 Manufacture of textiles	9.7	25	9.7
C31 Manufacture of furniture	7.7	4.7	2.3
C25 Manufacture of fabricated metal products, except machinery and equipment	7.5	8.4	3.3
C21 Manufacture of basic pharmaceutical products and pharmaceutical preparations	7.1	57.1	14.3
C32 Other manufacturing	6.9	10.1	18.7
C22 Manufacture of rubber and plastic products	6.3	17.3	12
C29 Manufacture of motor vehicles, trailers and semi-trailers	6	20	0
All firms with innovative activity	3.1	12.1	2.8

Source: Statistics Finland, Community Innovation Survey, https://pxdata.stat.fi/PxWeb/pxweb/en/StatFin/StatFin__inn/statfin_inn_pxt_13kx.px, Accessed 20 December 2023.

instruments and optics."[44] We observe from the Finnish patent and utility model register data that, indeed, there is different type of concentration between specific industries in the number of patent and utility model applications. It should be kept in mind that with utility models (in Finland) one cannot protect process inventions.[45]

With information about the international patent classes in which utility models are classified, it is possible to move from industry level to invention level in analyzing the use of utility models. Figure 9.10 shows the evolution of the average number of IPC classes for both patents and utility models. If the number of IPC classes is considered to be a proxy for the complexity of the invention so that more complex inventions are classified in more IPC classes, then Finnish utility models are clearly systematically "simpler" according to this measure compared to patents.

44 EC Green Paper 1995, p. 16.

45 Among the IPC-classes with the most utility model filings is A61H 33/06 that includes sauna heaters (saunas are an important part of Finnish culture) with 156 utility models filings cumulatively as of December 2023.

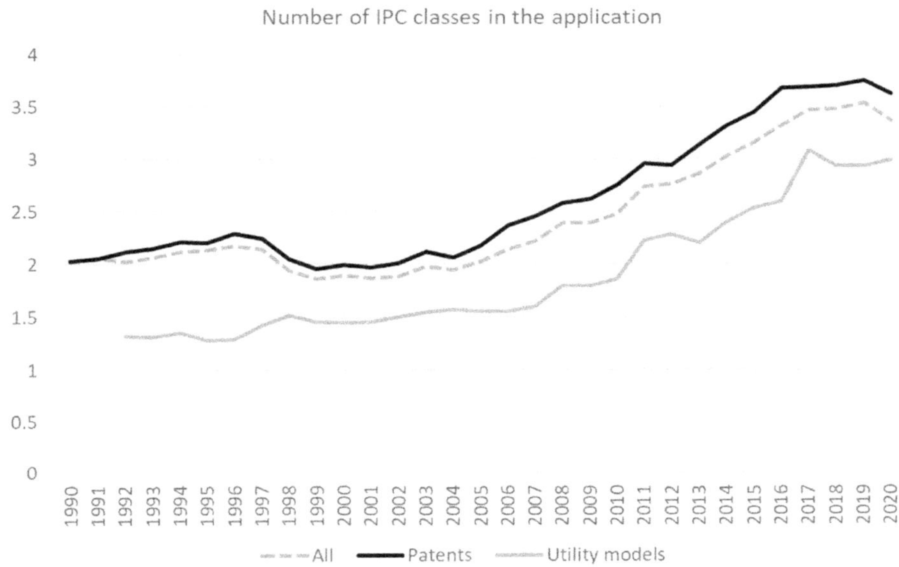

FIGURE 9.10 Number of IPC classes in Finnish patent and utility model applications
Source: PRH.

Due to field restrictions, utility models "direct" the technological change differently compared to patents if we judge on the basis of IPC classification of patent and utility model documents. In other words, they provide innovation incentives and promote the documentation of technical knowledge with different emphases across technology fields. As illustrated in Figure 9.10, the number of IPC classes in which patents and utility models are classified has increased over time: in 1992, patents were classified on average in 2 IPC classes and utility models in 1 whereas in 2020 utility models were classified on average in 3 while patents in 3.5 IPC classes. From 1992 (the introduction of the utility model system) until the end of 2021, the data indicates that patents were classified in 2.4 IPC classes on average whereas utility models had on average 1.8 IPC classes. The difference has remained roughly the same in absolute terms so that patents are classified on average in 0.5 more IPC classes. Also, utility models are more often classified in only one IPC class (slightly more than 50 percent of utility models) compared to patents (approx. one-third of patents).

The top 10 (first) 4-digit IPC classes with the highest number of utility models and patents are shown in Table 9.4.[46] In both cases these top 10 IPC classes account for approximately one-fourth of all first IPC classes. The fact that there is no overlap among top 10 IPC classes suggests that utility models promote innovation activity in

46 WIPO Statistics database provides information on IPC classes of patent filings but not of utility model filings. WIPO 2023d, Accessed 18 December 2023.

TABLE 9.4 *Top10 first (4-digit) IPC classes of Finnish patents and utility models 1992–2021*

Top10 (first) IPC classes with most UM filings		Utility models Obs.	%	Patents Obs.	UM/ patent ratio
1B65D	Containers for storage or transport of articles or materials, e.g. bags, barrels, bottles, boxes, cans, cartons, crates, drums, jars, tanks, hoppers, forwarding containers; accessories, closures, or fittings therefor; packaging elements; packages	493	3.76	2,640	0.187
2E04B	General building constructions; walls, e.g. partitions; roofs; floors; ceilings; insulation or other protection of buildings	481	3.67	1,222	0.394
3A01K	Animal husbandry; aviculture; apiculture; pisciculture; fishing; rearing or breeding animals, not otherwise provided for; new breeds of animals	339	2.59	568	0.597
4E06B	Fixed or movable closures for openings in buildings, vehicles, fences, or like enclosures, in general, e.g. doors, windows, bunds, gates	289	2.21	815	0.355
5A47B	Tables; desks; office furniture; cabinets; drawers; general details of furniture	286	2.18	356	0.803
6F24F	Air-conditioning; air-humidification; ventilation; use of air currents for screening	264	2.01	829	0.318
7A01G	Horticulture; cultivation of vegetables, flowers, rice, fruit, vines, hops or seaweed; forestry; watering	239	1.82	1,005	0.238
8A47C	Chairs; sofas; beds	231	1.76	357	0.647
9E04C	Structural elements; building materials	226	1.72	568	0.398
10E04F	Roof coverings; sky lights; gutters; roof working tools	205	1.56	340	0.603

Top10 (first) IPC classes with most patent filings		Patents Obs.	%	Utility models Obs.	UM/ patent ratio
1C07D	Heterocyclic compounds	2,477	4.4	14	0.006
2A61K	Preparations for medical, dental or toiletry purposes	1,913	3.4	35	0.018
3H04L	Transmission of digital information, e.g. telegraphic communication	1,579	2.8	14	0.009

Top10 (first) IPC classes with most patent filings		Patents Obs.	%	Utility models Obs.	UM/ patent ratio
4D21F	Paper-making machines; methods of producing paper thereon	1,404	2.49	167	0.119
5GO1N	Investigating or analysing materials by determining their chemical or physical properties	1,134	2.01	71	0.063
6HO4B	Transmission	1,082	1.92	8	0.007
7HO4W	Wireless Communication Networks	951	1.69	22	0.023
8D21C	Production of cellulose by removing non-cellulose substances from cellulose-containing materials; regeneration of pulping liquors; apparatus therefor	942	1.67	15	0.016
9HO4M	Telephonic communication	906	1.61	79	0.0987
10C07C	Acyclic or carbocyclic compounds	851	1.51	5	0.006

Source: PRH, covering the period 1992–2021.

other technology fields compared to patents. Moreover, among the top 10 IPC classes for patents there are very few utility model applications. While Finnish patents have been particularly utilized to protect inventions in chemical, medical, telecommunication and paper technology fields, the top IPC classes for utility models include inventions, for instance, in building and furniture technology fields.

9.2.4 *Limitations*

This analysis is mainly based on quantitative patent and utility model register data. Hence, there are several important limitations. First, the evolving motives of companies to use Finnish utility models have not been analyzed. For instance, without information on actual motives we cannot estimate the extent to which companies utilize the utility model system for defensive purposes (e.g., pre-emptive patenting and defensive publishing) or to what extent Finnish utility models owned by competitors limit their freedom to operate. Utility models and other second-tier patents in some countries have been criticized for the potential uncertainty that they create as rights that are granted without substantive examination at the patent office.[47] Replication of the survey by Björkwall (2009) could reveal interesting developments.

Second, there is no systematic evidence of the successful and unsuccessful commercialization of inventions protected by utility models, on the role of utility

[47] Cf. Johnson et al. 2015; Heikkilä 2017.

models in securing financing and we lack information on the licensing of utility models – although, anecdotal evidence and discussions with practitioners suggest that utility model licensing is rare.[48]

Third, this chapter does not analyze the impact of utility models on industry dynamics – that is, the level and interplay of innovation and competition across industries and technology fields. We lack data on the return on investments in utility model protection as well as whether the use of utility models is related to productivity development.[49] Also, analysis of utility model-related litigation and its impact on innovation activity was excluded from the analysis.[50]

Fourth, we lack data on renewal fee payments which could be used as an additional indicator for the value of utility models and the quality of the protected inventions. The more valuable invention and utility model protection are for a particular protected article, the longer the holder will pay renewal fees. In 2023, the registration fee was 250 euros (50 euro discount if filed online) for the first four years, 250 euros for the next four years and 200 euros for the last two years.[51] Registration costs are only a fraction of the professional patent attorney fees for drafting a utility model application which large Finnish patent attorney firms estimate on their websites to be approximately 5,000 euros – close to the fees related to drafting a patent application.

9.2.5 *Discussion*

In the Finnish context, it is remarkable that the demand for utility models has been steadily declining since the system was established in 1992. Finland became a member of the EU in 1995 and EPO in 1996 only a few years after the utility model system was introduced. The accession to the EPC led to immediate drop in national patent filings by foreign applicants,[52] as demonstrated more generally by Hall and Helmers (2019) when they substituted from national filings to EPO filings and national validations of granted European patents. This makes it challenging to identify and distinguish the impacts of the utility model system. Clearly, the average differences (e.g., grant lags, patent family size) between Finnish patents and utility models were much larger before Finland joined the EPO.

The declining trend in utility model filings follows the more general trend of the decreasing importance of national filings channels and shift to European filings

[48] But see Chapter 18 regarding the increasing declaration (and licensing) of utility models that are declared as essential to industry standards.

[49] Cf. Maskus and McDaniel 1999.

[50] IPR University Center provides summaries of Finnish patent and utility model disputes: Oikeustapaustietokanta (only in Finnish) https://ipruc.fi/tietopalvelut/oikeustapaustietokanta/, Accessed 18 December 2023.

[51] See www.prh.fi/en/hyodyllisyysmallit/hinnasto/hyodmaksut.html, Accessed 18 December 2023.

[52] Heikkilä and Peltoniemi 2023.

channels in the European context (Hall and Helmers 2019; Heikkilä and Peltoniemi 2023). Generally, the decreasing demand for utility model protections may indicate that the users of the utility model system have learned that the returns on registering utility models are relatively low and therefore not worth investing in. This pattern is similar to that of national design rights (cf. Figure 9.2). Alternatively, there might be lack of awareness of the possibilities and benefits of utility model protection. Here, the role of patent and IPR attorneys is crucial:[53] if they do not recommend filing utility models when applicants consult them regarding optimal IPR strategies, then naturally that has a negative impact on the demand for utility models, utility model awareness and accumulating experience of applicants regarding the effective use of utility models.

Table 9.5 summarizes observations applying and extending the KPI table introduced by Heikkilä (2023a, see Table 9.1). Clearly, a utility model system may provide flexibility and have multidimensional impacts on the functioning of the national patent system. Given the long-continued declining trends in utility model filings in Finland and in other advanced economies, it seems that the positive scenario of increasing utility model filings in the future is less probable than the negative scenario that the filings of Finnish utility models keep on declining – unless there are significant reforms. There are multiple factors that will impact the future of the Finnish utility model system. First, the role of professional patent attorneys is crucial as they are the ones that recommend – or don't – utility model filings for their clients and whether patents or utility models meet their needs better.[54] Second, harmonization of European utility model systems is an open question and seems not to be a priority as even the EU's IP action plan (European Commission 2020) does not mention utility models.[55] Third, a lot has changed since the Finnish utility model system was introduced in 1992 when also the commercial Internet was at its early stage. Digitalization has meant that the access to patent registers, including utility models, has democratized, and the related search costs of technical solutions have diminished significantly. In the era of artificial intelligence, what kind of exploration could the flexibility of utility model systems offer? Will we see more registered utility models where AI is a co-inventor?

9.3 CONCLUSIONS

This chapter provides a quantitative evaluation of the Finnish utility model system from its introduction in 1992 to early 2020s by applying the framework of Heikkilä (2023a) and relying on patent and utility model statistics from various sources. Its findings suggest that the Finnish utility model system has been used mainly by local

[53] Cf. Radauer et al. 2015; Heikkilä 2021.

[54] Cf. Radauer et al. 2015; Heikkilä and Peltoniemi 2023.

[55] See Chapter 20 re. European Harmonization.

TABLE 9.5 *Summary of findings, key performance indicators of the Finnish utility model system*

KPIs	Data sources	Finnish utility model system, selected observations
Innovation incentives		
Number of UM filings	PRH, WIPO, PATSTAT	Ca. 15,000 applications 1992–2023. Constant decreasing trend since the establishment of the system in 1992.
Number of UM applicants	PRH, WIPO, PATSTAT	Ca. 9,000 unique applicants (Heikkilä 2023b).
Number of UM inventors		Ca. 12,000 unique inventors (Heikkilä 2023b). Systematically smaller inventor team size in the case of UMs reflecting the fact that often individual inventors apply UMs.
Performance of firms using UMs	NA	
R&D investments by firms using UMs	NA	
Commercialization of UM-protected inventions	NA	Challenging to find examples and anecdotal evidence.
Diffusion of innovations		
Number of published UM filings with descriptions of inventions	PRH, WIPO, PATSTAT	Almost all UMs are registered (negligible rejection rate)*, so the number of invention descriptions is close to filed UMs. UMs are prior art that are published in Finnish and Swedish which may make them less accessible compared to Finnish patents.
Citations to UMs	PATSTAT	Very low number of citations to patent families with Finnish UMs.
Licensing of UM-protected inventions	NA	Challenging to find examples and anecdotal evidence.
Rate and direction of technological change		
Patent filings by IPC classes	PRH, WIPO, PATSTAT	Utility models are classified to systematically smaller number of IPC classes.
UM filings by IPC classes	PRH, PATSTAT	
Catching-up		
Resident UM filings	PRH, WIPO, PATSTAT	Majority of UM filing activity is by residents (ca. 95% over the period 1992–2022).
Resident patent filings	PRH, WIPO, PATSTAT	Foreign applicants (non-residents) shifted to use EPO channel for Finnish patents when Finland joined it in 1996.

KPIs	Data sources	Finnish utility model system, selected observations
National R&D investments	Statistics Finland	Negative correlation between the number of UM filings and business sector R&D expenditure.
Quicker protection		
Registration/grant lags for inventions	PRH, PATSTAT	The grant lag for UMs is a few months and multiple years for patents.
Backlog of pending patents	NA	(In principle, could be estimated from PRH and/or PATSTAT data)
Inclusiveness		
Patent and UM inventions overlap	PATSTAT	Ca. 2% of all UMs are members of (DOCDB) patent families with Finnish patents.
Patent and UM applicants overlap	PATSTAT	At maximum 40% (ca. 6,000) more unique applicants in patent registers due to UM system (with no Finnish patent filings, Heikkilä 2023b).
Patent and UM inventors overlap	PATSTAT	At maximum 20% (ca. 6,500) more Finnish inventors in patent registers due to UM system (with no Finnish patent filings, Heikkilä 2023b).
Number of UM filings by SMEs	Statistics Finland, Community Innovation Survey (CIS)	The propensity to file UMs increases with firm size (CIS: number of employees and Björkwall (2009) turnover).
International protection		
Priority and non-priority UM filings	PRH, PATSTAT	Majority of UMs are priority filings (>80%) and most priority filings are singletons (>80%, limited to protection in Finland).
Quantity and quality of patents		
Number of patent filings	PRH, WIPO, PATSTAT	Decreasing, shift to EPO. Cannot be explained by shift to UMs.
Share and absolute number of granted/rejected patents	PRH, PATSTAT	Close to 100% of UMs are registered* as there is no substantive examination.
Patent quality indicators	PRH, PATSTAT	UMs have systematically smaller team sizes, are members of smaller patent families and receive less citations.

Notes: utility model KPIs applied and extended from Heikkilä (2023a). *This refers to those utility model applications that are not withdrawn.

applicants and there is evidence that it has promoted flexibility and inclusiveness of the Finnish patent system. There are systematic differences between Finnish utility models and patents: (1) utility models are members of smaller patent families, (2) utility models have smaller inventor teams, (3) grant lags for utility models are significantly shorter than for patents and (4) both Finnish patents and utility models receive few citations, but utility models systematically receive less. Patent and utility model statistics indicate that Finland's accession to the EPC had much more significant impact on the patenting activity in Finland compared to the utility model system. The aforementioned average differences between Finnish patents and utility models were larger before Finland joined the EPC in 1996, which emphasizes the need to consider European integration and the evolution of European IPR institutions when evaluating utility model systems. Since, at the economy level, there is no positive association between Finnish utility model filings and R&D investments, more fine-grained industry or technology field-level analyses are needed to analyze the impact of the utility model system on innovation-based competition and industry dynamics. The role of professional patent attorneys in the demand for utility models as well as applicants' choices between utility models and patents is an interesting topic for future research.

10

Reinventing the Wheel

The Rise and Fall of the Australian Innovation Patent

Matthew Rimmer

In Australia, the credibility and legitimacy of second-tier systems for intellectual property has been the subject of ongoing debate and controversy.

In 2001, a patent attorney called John Keogh was issued an innovation patent by IP Australia for a 'circular transportation facilitation device'.[1] There were also patent claims relating to rubber wheels and tires. The field of the invention was a 'device for facilitating transport of goods and persons'.[2] The background explained that a 'circular transportation facilitation device' would be an improvement on walking, and on other devices, like 'skis, sleds, toboggans and the like'.[3] The application was accompanied by an illustration of a wheel (Figure 10.1).

There was also a perspective drawing of a cart incorporating 'a series of circular transportation facilitation devices in accordance with a preferred aspect of the present invention.'[4]

Keough said that he patented the wheel in order to establish that the innovation patent system was flawed because it did not need to be examined by the patent office. He explained his concerns:

> The patent office would be required to issue a patent for anything. All they're doing is putting a rubber stamp on it. The impetus came from the Federal Government. Their constituents claimed the cost of obtaining a patent was too high so the government decided to find a way to issue a patent more easily.[5]

Keogh noted that he had no immediate plans to patent fire, crop rotation, or other fundamental advances in civilization. John Keogh had previously written about the

[1] John Keogh (applicant), 'Circular Transportation Facilitation Device', Innovation Patent No. AU 2001100012 A4, Filing Date 24 May 2001.

[2] Ibid.

[3] Ibid.

[4] Ibid.

[5] Cochrane 2001a, 3.

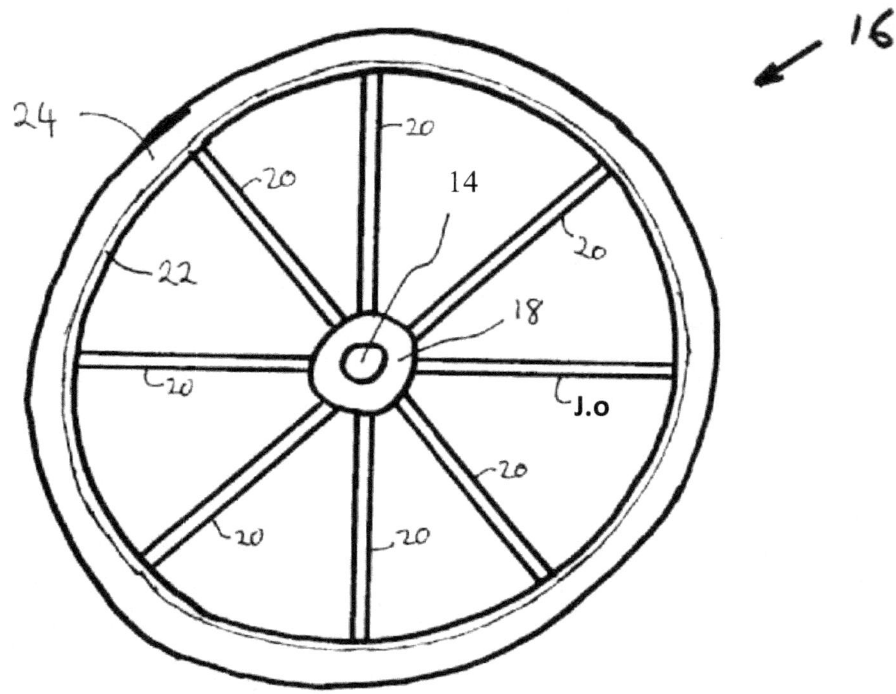

FIGURE 10.1 John Keogh, 'Circular Transportation Facilitation Device'

dangers of innovation patents, warning: 'These junk patents may bring the entire Australian patent system into disrepute'.[6]

The intervention received wide attention in the Australian media,[7] international news,[8] and even in august scientific magazines and journals, such as *New Scientist*.[9]

IP Australia were publicly outraged at the patent application. Commissioner of Patents Vivienne Thom commented that there was a danger of patent fraud. 'To obtain the patent for a wheel would require a false claim, which is a very serious matter and would certainly invalidate the patent as well as amounting to a misrepresentation on the part of the applicant and unprofessional conduct by any professional advisor.'[10] IP Australia later revoked the patent application. John Keogh won an Ig Nobel Prize for his efforts.[11] The prize ceremony stated: 'The Ig Nobel Prize

[6] Brennan and Keough 2000, 30. There was rebuttal in the letters to such an attack on the innovation patent. See Mischlewski 2000, 24.

[7] Cochrane 2001a, 3; Progress Press 2001, 9.

[8] See BBC 2001 (UK); CNN 2001 (US); Osgood 2001 (Canada); Christchurch Press 2001 (New Zealand).

[9] Knight 2001.

[10] CNN 2001.

[11] Business Times Singapore 2001; Radford 2001, 16; Scott 2001.

for Technology is awarded jointly to John Keogh of Hawthorn, Victoria, Australia, for patenting the wheel in the year 2001, and to the Australian Patent Office for granting him Innovation Patent #2001100012.'[12] Keogh hoped that the Ig Nobel Prize would result in a rethink of the innovation patent: 'I was amused and it just shows the silliness of it all that people around the world are giving us awards for silliness.'[13]

The intervention certainly follows in an Australian tradition of hoaxes,[14] fakes, and tall stories. Yet, this controversy cannot be dismissed as a mere joke. It highlights problems both with the operation of the innovation patent system, and the public perceptions of the legitimacy of the regime. The ignominious case of patenting the wheel has been re-invoked – as further scandals over innovation patents have emerged.[15]

This chapter charts the historical evolution of second-tier patent systems in Australia – looking at the establishment of the petty patent system, the rise and fall of the innovation patent, and the new focus of the Albanese Government upon breakthrough inventions. In terms of its methodology, this chapter provides a historical study of intellectual property reform in Australia.[16] It follows in the rich tradition of historical research in respect of intellectual property in the jurisdiction.[17] This chapter also uses socio-legal methodologies to highlight the gap between the aspirations for the innovation patent system, and the operation of the system in practice.[18] It also draws upon empirical research into intellectual property registration data.[19] This work is an investigation of litigation in respect of innovation patents – the so-called 'patent wars'.[20] As well as exploring intellectual property, the chapter also considers Australia's innovation policies – particularly in respect of small-to-medium enterprises[21] and lone inventors.[22] It highlights the tensions between the nationalistic vision of Australian policy-makers, and the larger forces of globalization.

[12] Flatow 2001.

[13] Cochrane 2001b, 4.

[14] In Australian literature, there has been a long tradition of hoaxes – see Heyward 1993; Jost et al. 1996; Manne 1996; Rimmer 2000; Carey 2003; Caterson 2006; Caterson 2009.

[15] The investigative journalists at the *Sydney Morning Herald* mentioned the controversy in a piece looking at the innovation patent applications of Jack Vaisman of the Advanced Medical Institute for sex treatments and therapies – Burke and McClymont 2009.

[16] Kenyon et al. 2009; Alexander 2020, 175–188.

[17] See for instance various historical studies of Australian intellectual property – Sherman and Bently 1999; Bently 2004; Bond 2016; Op Den Kamp and Hunter 2019; Scardamaglia 2020; Bellido and Bowrey 2022.

[18] Gallagher and Halbert 2021, 547–557.

[19] With its establishment of an economics unit, IP Australia has increasingly been focused on data analytics of its intellectual property data. See IP Australia 2023c.

[20] Allison et al. 2014; Cotter 2018.

[21] Hughes and Mina 2010.

[22] Lemley 2012.

This chapter is organized according to the chronology of the policy debate over second-tier innovation systems in Australia. Section 10.1 details the establishment of the petty patent system in Australia in the 1970s; the hopes of Australian policy-makers for this regime; and the reasons for its demise. Section 10.2 explores the institution of the innovation patent regime – the replacement for the petty patent system. Section 10.3 focuses upon filing and registration data on innovation patents. Section 10.4 charts litigation over innovation patents – particularly highlighting the decision of the High Court of Australia in *Aristocrat* v. *Commissioner of Patents*[23] on patentable subject matter, and the precedent on the threshold of an innovative step in *Dura-Post (Aust) Pty Ltd* v. *Delnorth Pty Ltd*.[24] Such disputes have highlighted both fundamental issues around patentable subject matter as well as the threshold required for an innovation patent. Section 10.5 focuses upon the reflections of the Advisory Council of Intellectual Property upon the innovation patent system and its relation to other intellectual property regimes. Section 10.6 looks at the work of the Productivity Commission in its analysis of Australia's intellectual property arrangements. Section 10.7 charts the work of IP Australia on the innovation patent – particularly in respect of the data on the innovation patent, and the economic impact of the regime. Section 10.8 looks at the abolition of the innovation patent regime – with the support of major parties in the Australian Parliament. Section 10.9 focuses on the new approach of the Albanese Government in promoting breakthrough innovation in key industries – rather than, so much, incremental innovation. The conclusion questions the future of utility models of patent protection – given the extinction of petty patents and innovation patents in Australia.

10.1 THE PETTY PATENT SYSTEM

At the outset, it is helpful to engage in archaeological historical examination of the political debate over the petty patent system in Australia in the 1970s.

There was a concern that Australia's standard patent system, and regime for designs protection, was ill-suited for small-to-medium enterprises and lone inventors in the 1960s and 1970s.[25] In 1973, the Franki Designs Law Review Committee produced reports on designs law, and utility models of patent protection.[26] The Committee preferred the language of 'petty patents' to that of 'utility models': 'The name "petty patent" appears to use to convey slightly more meaning on first sight and we think it is also a more appropriate name in view of the recommendations we have to make in respect to this form of protection.'[27] The Committee referred to previous consideration of the topic of petty patents in the United Kingdom.

[23] Aristocrat Technologies 2022.
[24] Dura-Post 2009.
[25] Christie and Moritz 2007, 119–141.
[26] Designs Law Review Committee 1973; Designs Law Review Committee 1974.
[27] Designs Law Review Committee 1974, 7.

The Committee undertook detailed research of the utility models adopted in Germany and Japan. The report noted the lack of harmonization: 'It appears clear from our investigations that the nature of the protection afforded by the various systems differs greatly and that there is no single recognized field for the operation of a petty patent system.'[28]

The Franki Designs Law Review Committee recommended the 'introduction in Australia of a system of petty patents to form part of the patent system'.[29] The Committee was satisfied that petty patents should 'cause the minimum of inconvenience to Australian industrial and manufacturing interests and we hope that, at least in the long term, the introduction of our recommended system might result in an improved patent system by encouraging applications for petty patents in respect of all inventions other than those for which a short term of protection and the limitation of a single claim would be inappropriate.'[30]

In 1979, the Australian government introduced the petty patent system to assist Australian small to medium business enterprises.[31] The government intended the system to provide a quicker and cheaper form of patent right for inventions with a short commercial life.

The Hon. Ian Macphee, Member for Balaclava and Minister for Productivity, introduced the *Patents Amendment Bill* 1979 (Cth).[32] Macphee was laudatory of the petty patent system:

> This measure is an extremely innovative development in the Australian patent system. The fundamental purpose of the new petty patent system is to encourage the commercial exploitation of inventions which now go largely unexploited or unprotected or both due to deficiencies in existing patent protection. In the past it has been too easily overlooked that the simple kind of inventions involved constitute a big proportion of patentable inventions. They encompass many areas, particularly in consumer-oriented products which collectively have considerable marketing potential. When the number of inventions involved and the extent of their potential use are considered it is clear that our failure in the past to provide adequate protection for such inventions seriously diminished the effectiveness of the patent system. A large part of the inventive effort of Australians has always been directed to such inventions. It follows that the patent system has not been utilising the product of that effort.[33]

Macphee concluded his speech recognizing the uniqueness of the Australian petty patent system: 'Because the particular petty patent system of this Bill is unique and has no counterpart in other industrial property legislation in the world, the

[28] Designs Law Review Committee 1974, 8.
[29] Designs Law Review Committee 1974, 8.
[30] Designs Law Review Committee 1974, 8–9.
[31] See Australian Patents Amendment Act 1979, § 17.
[32] Hon. Ian Macphee 1979, 183.
[33] Hon. Ian Macphee 1979.

introduction of the system is to a large degree experimental.'[34] He recognized that there could be a dissonance between the plans for the legislation, and the operation of the regime in practice: 'In view of its unique character, it is not possible to predict the exact effects which the system will achieve in practice, although its broad impact is clear enough.'[35] Macphee assured the Australian Parliament that 'the system will be continuously monitored with a view to making such alterations as from time to time appear necessary to ensure that the basic aim of assisting innovation and productivity in Australia is fulfilled.'[36]

From the Government, Liberal MP Gordon Dean (member for Herbert in Northern Queensland) discussed the legislative reforms in the House of Representatives of the Australian Parliament.[37] Dean discussed the merits of the petty patent system:

> By virtue of the short term of a petty patent monopoly the petty patent system introduced in the present Bill will accelerate the availability to industry of the information contained in petty patent documents. Moreover, experience with the present patent system suggests that the new petty patent system, by providing a form of protection adapted to assist the commercial exploitation of simple, consumer orientated inventions, has considerable potential for increasing the information available to industry about inventions conceived in Australia. For many years, the number of patent applications made by Australian inventors has remained static at about 4,000 applications a year. Approximately 3,000 of those applications are abandoned without maturing into a patent and without the documents being published. If the petty patent system encourages those applicants to obtain a petty patent, the resulting publication associated with the grant of the petty patent will make considerably more information available to Australian industry. The fact that the information concerns developments originating in Australia can be expected to give such publication added significance to industry.[38]

Dean concluded his speech, observing: 'Invention and technological change are essential elements in the continuing and increasing competitiveness of industry, and industry must learn about and make use of all relevant information, in particular that information available through the patents system.'[39] This speech on the petty patent system is underpinned by an Australian nationalism, and a desire to remain competitive with other nations in the Asia-Pacific, such as Japan: 'It is clear from the experience of countries, such as Japan, which have a very high usage of patent

[34] Hon. Ian Macphee 1979.
[35] Hon. Ian Macphee 1979.
[36] Hon. Ian Macphee 1979.
[37] Hon. Gordon Dean 1979, 446.
[38] Hon. Gordon Dean 1979.
[39] Hon. Gordon Dean 1979.

systems that the Australian patent system has the potential to play an increasingly important role in our future industrial development.'[40]

The Hon. Peter Shack also added his comments to the debate over the legislation.[41] Shack welcomed the legislation, noting that 'it is proposed to bring into operation an optional form of patent protection that has been devised specifically to assist small Australian industries and businesses and in doing so to encourage the inventive activity of Australians in fields that are particularly suited to commercial exploitation by small Australian enterprises'.[42] Shack supported the legislation as a means of economic modernization: 'I see the legislation as part of a process by this Government to upgrade Australia's industrial property laws through a process of reform which the Government believes ... will make those laws more responsive to the economic needs of the nation.'[43]

The representative of the Opposition Australian Labor Party, Chris Hurford (MP for Adelaide), expressed some early misgivings as to whether the petty patent regime would fulfil such high hopes.[44] Hurford outlined the purpose of the Bill:

> The purpose of this Bill is to bring into operation an optional form of patent protection by creating a new short-term patent to be known as a petty patent. In contrast, of course, with the standard patent, which has a 16-year term, the petty patent will have a minimum term of one year and, with suitable extensions, could have a term as long as six years. As I understand it, the aim of the new petty patents system is to encourage commercial exploitation of inventions which now go largely unexploited or unprotected because of deficiencies in the existing system. Also as I understand it, the existing law is based on a system of uniform, relatively long-term protection for inventions. The system provides certainty, but at the cost of delays and expense. This penalises particularly those inventions which have only one inventive characteristic and which, therefore, have short commercially exploitable lives. These involve mainly consumer oriented products such as household accessories, gadgets and so on.[45]

Hurford raised several reservations. First, Hurford questioned whether 'the new system [will] really give a much needed boost to inventive activity?'[46] He noted in particular that the Inventors Association was 'not convinced that that the proposed petty patents system will directly aid individual inventors but believes instead that it may be of value only to small manufacturers.'[47] Second, Hurford wonders 'whether we can be guaranteed that the new system achieves a proper balance between the

[40] Hon. Gordon Dean 1979.
[41] Hon. Peter Shack 1979, 451.
[42] Hon. Peter Shack 1979.
[43] Hon. Peter Shack 1979.
[44] Hon. Chris Hurford 1979, 449.
[45] Hon. Chris Hurford 1979.
[46] Hon. Chris Hurford 1979.
[47] Hon. Chris Hurford 1979.

need to stimulate inventive activity on the one hand and freedom of access to all publicly available technology on the other hand.'[48] Third, Hurford was sceptical of the claims that the petty patent system was unique: 'After all, many other countries have had, as I mentioned earlier, a two-tiered system for some time.'[49] He wondered 'why our legislation differs from the two-tiered systems elsewhere.'[50] (Such a concern is at the heart of this comparative collection.) Finally, Hurford questioned whether there was a need to give so much discretion to the Commissioner of Patents in the operation of the system. The member of Adelaide wondered 'if the legislation were much more detailed it could become a jungle such as the tax legislation has become a jungle.'[51] Such questions seem prophetic – not only in relation to the operation of the petty patent system, but in respect of its successor, the innovation patent system.

However, the petty patent system was not well used, as well documented by Sam Ricketson and Megan Richardson.[52] The textbook writers commented: 'Although it is clear that petty patents are potentially a very appropriate form of protection for particular kinds of inventions that can, by their nature, be brought to commercialization more rapidly than others, there has scarcely been an extensive usage of the regime.'[53] Ricketson and Richardson said of petty patents: 'Petty patents are essentially "quickie" patents intended for innovations that are more readily commercialized.'[54]

The Advisory Council on Industrial Property reviewed the operation of the petty patent system in 1995.[55] It recommended that there should be a new second tier patent system in Australia to fill gaps in the range of intellectual property regimes (including in between patent law, designs law, and copyright law).

Likewise, the Intellectual Property and Competition Review Committee – with Henry Ergas, Professor Jill McKeough, and John Stone – recommended that the petty patent system should be replaced with an innovation patent system.[56] In its advice, 'The Committee strongly supports the Advisory Council on Intellectual Property (ACIP) Review of Petty Patents recommendations on the innovation patent, and urges the Government to expeditiously progress the relevant changes to the *Patents Act*.'[57] The Intellectual Property and Competition Review Committee commented: 'We believe that the role of the innovation patent will be enhanced if the Committee's proposals for higher thresholds for the standard patent are

48 Hon. Chris Hurford 1979.
49 Hon. Chris Hurford 1979.
50 Hon. Chris Hurford 1979.
51 Hon. Chris Hurford 1979.
52 Ricketson and Richardson 1998, 763–765.
53 Ricketson and Richardson 1998, 764.
54 Ricketson and Richardson 1998, 695.
55 Advisory Council on Intellectual Property (Australia) 1995.
56 Intellectual Property and Competition Review Committee (Australia) 2000.
57 Intellectual Property and Competition Review Committee (Australia) 2000, 16.

implemented.'[58] The Intellectual Property and Competition Review Committee observed: 'The Petty Patent was supposed to particularly encourage SMEs to innovate and patent, but it is not widely used.'[59] The Intellectual Property and Competition Review Committee later noted that utility models of patent protection were popular in comparative jurisdictions: 'Many countries have a lesser patent (often called a 'utility' patent), which attempts to balance lower threshold tests with a lower level of protection (length and breadth) to encourage lower levels of innovation, particularly by small to medium enterprises.'[60]

Professor Jill McKeough has been an influential figure in intellectual property law reform in Australia.[61] She has been insistent that intellectual property should be redesigned to better promote competition policy.[62]

10.2 INNOVATION PATENT

In his 2000 second reading speech, the Hon. Warren Entsch – the parliamentary secretary to the Minister for Industry, Science, and Resources – explained the impetus for the *Patents Amendment (Innovation Patents) Bill* 2000 (Cth):

> The government has acted on these recommendations and devised a 'second-tier' patent system to better address the needs of business, particularly small to medium enterprises. The innovation patent will be relatively inexpensive, quick and easy to obtain. It will provide the same scope of protection as the standard patent; however, it will require a lower inventive threshold than that required for a standard or a petty patent. An innovation patent will have a maximum patent term of eight years, compared to a 20-year term for a standard patent.[63]

The Secretary said: 'A major factor contributing to the reduced cost of obtaining an innovation patent will be the grant of a patent without substantive examination – the time consuming and costly process during which an application is assessed against relevant statutory criteria.'[64] He noted: 'Substantive examination will only occur if directed by the Commissioner of Patents or requested by the patent owner or a third party.'[65] Entsch commented: 'However, to reduce the scope for unsubstantiated threats, the owner of an innovation patent may only take action to exercise their rights if their patent has been substantively examined.'[66]

58 Intellectual Property and Competition Review Committee (Australia) 2000, 16.
59 Intellectual Property and Competition Review Committee (Australia) 2000, 157.
60 Intellectual Property and Competition Review Committee (Australia) 2000, 157.
61 Bowrey 2021.
62 McKeough 2003.
63 Hon. Warren Entsch 2000.
64 Hon. Warren Entsch 2000.
65 Hon. Warren Entsch 2000.
66 Hon. Warren Entsch 2000.

Entsch added: 'Although innovation patents will be available for most of the types of invention currently covered by standard patents, they will not be available for plants and animals, or biological processes for the generation of plants and animals.'[67] He noted: 'This exclusion does not include microbiological processes and innovation patents will be available for processes such as cheese and wine making and the synthesis of industrial compounds using micro-organisms.'[68] Entsch observed: 'Over 48 other industrialised countries, including Japan and Germany, have already introduced second-tier patent systems.'[69] He contended: 'Overseas experience suggests that the innovation patent should provide better access to intellectual property rights and foster innovation by local enterprises.'[70]

The main opposition, the Australian Labor Party, supported the passage of the legislation. The Hon. Bob McMullan expressed his party's enthusiasm for the innovation patent regime:

> It is fundamental to being a successful, modern, industrial country that we have a contemporary, effective, strong body of intellectual property protection laws. This legislation is part of modernising that framework, and we support it... In essence, it goes to what is important about intellectual property in general historically and certainly in the 21st century successful economies are going to be based upon the successful development of ideas. There are many phases in that. What has now become 'the national innovation system' is a phrase that covers a multitude of sins. But I think there is now probably quite a well-developed concept of the cyclical nature of the process. We used to see it as more linear from invention to commercialisation and we now see it as a mutually reinforcing, more circular, process. The Wills report called it a virtuous circle.[71]

McMullan hoped that 'when subsequent reviews are done, they will say that Australia's international patent performance is at the international cutting edge, instead of just fair to middling, and that our research and development performance is improving.'[72] He trusted that the adoption of the innovation patent system would encourage further investment in Australian research and development:

> And when investors around the world look at where they might locate major research and development activity, they will be encouraged to believe that our intellectual property framework is so rigorous, so comprehensive and so contemporary that this will be the place in which they choose to make that investment, to create those jobs and to generate the ideas that could be the foundation for our successful 21st century economy.[73]

67 Hon. Warren Entsch 2000.
68 Hon. Warren Entsch 2000.
69 Hon. Warren Entsch 2000.
70 Hon. Warren Entsch 2000.
71 Hon. Bob McMullan 2000.
72 Hon. Bob McMullan 2000.
73 Hon. Bob McMullan 2000.

In retrospect, the Australian Labor Party could have been more circumspect about the adoption of the regime, and questioned whether the scheme was likely to achieve its objectives.

His colleague Dick Adams agreed that the patent regime had a significant role to play in innovation policy: 'The protection provided through the patent scheme has had a big part to play in this success and will encourage people to continue their research to develop new and innovative products, exploit new technology and promote the transfer of technology to Australia.'[74] Nonetheless, he was doubtful as to whether the Coalition Government had provided sufficient support for education, research, and science: 'It seems a great pity that so much can be achieved by Australians all over the nation, yet this government is not prepared to put decent amounts of funds into research and development, or create policies to do so.'[75] In his view, 'It cannot just be left to the business community to put up the wherewithal to develop ideas' because 'there are times when there is insufficient risk capital available for the private sector to invest.'[76]

In the Senate, Senator Kay Patterson of the Government noted: 'The *Patents Amendment (Innovation Patents) Bill* 2000 (Cth) is a key part of this process, building on the government's commitment to providing a patent system which better meets the needs of Australian business and ensuring that Australian intellectual property laws remain internationally competitive.'[77] She was pleased that the opposition was prepared to support the regime: 'As I said, I welcome the opposition's support of the bill, which will enable both large and small businesses to profit from their investments in innovation.'[78]

While these excerpts represent key contributions of politicians in the debate, it should be noted that there was some other commentary from politicians about the proposed new innovation patent system as well.

In 2001, the Australian Government replaced the petty patent system with the innovation patent regime as a lower tier patent to supplement the standard patent system. Essentially, this scheme offers protection for a maximum term of eight years in respect of inventions that display an innovative step. Substantive examination will only occur if directed by the Commissioner of Patents or requested by the patent owner or a third party or if there is an infringement suit.

There was significant discussion about the threshold for an innovation patent – namely, the requirement for an innovative step, as opposed to an inventive step in relation to a standard patent.

74 Hon. Dick Adams 2000.
75 Hon. Dick Adams 2000.
76 Hon. Dick Adams 2000.
77 Senator Kay Patterson 2000.
78 Senator Kay Patterson 2000.

10.3 FILING AND REGISTRATION DATA ON INNOVATION PATENTS

In its 2016 inquiry, the Productivity Commission reviewed the filing and registration data on innovation patents.[79] The Productivity Commission observed: 'In 2015, there were around 6500 active innovation patents in Australia (compared to over 130,000 standard patents).'[80] The Productivity Commission highlighted that the innovation patent system had a significantly lesser level of use: 'Between 2010 and 2015 the number of innovation patents granted each year ranged between 1300 and 1800 (compared to around 18,000 per year for standard patents).'[81] The Productivity Commission commented that most innovation patent applicants only used the system once: 'Parties that use the [Innovation Patent System] typically do so only once.'[82]

The Productivity Commission also charted the use of innovation patents across various technology fields: 'Most active innovation patents in 2015 were in the fields of civil engineering, furniture and games, IT methods for management, and electrical machinery, apparatus, and energy.'[83] They observed: 'Use of innovation patents relative to standard patents varies across technology fields.'[84] The Productivity Commission commented: 'Relative use of innovation patents is highest in the IT methods for management technology field, where they make up around 20 percent of total patents.'[85] Nonetheless, the Productivity Commission observed that there was little use of the innovation patent system in the life sciences: 'At the other end of the scale, innovation patents comprise less than 1 percent of total patents granted in chemistry-related technologies such as organic fine chemistry and biotechnology.'[86]

In a scathing review, the Productivity Commission questioned the social value of a number of innovation patents. It provided a gallery of absurd innovation patents in its policy analysis. The Productivity Commission highlighted a 'Heart rate path optimiser (2015101130)', which was 'A device for determining the heart rate of a user comprising, among other things, a sensor configured for providing heart rate signals.'[87] The Productivity Commission noted an innovation patent for 'A Bed for a Pet (2013100250)' which consisted of 'A mat and a frame that elevates the mat.'[88] The Productivity Commission also showcased the innovation patent for a 'Pizza Box Bib (2015100884)' which consisted of 'A pizza box where the lid includes a removable section, which when removed forms a recess that accommodates the neck of a

79 Productivity Commission (Australia) 2016, 243.
80 Productivity Commission (Australia) 2016, 243.
81 Productivity Commission (Australia) 2016, 243.
82 Productivity Commission (Australia) 2016, 243.
83 Productivity Commission (Australia) 2016, 243.
84 Productivity Commission (Australia) 2016, 243.
85 Productivity Commission (Australia) 2016, 243.
86 Productivity Commission (Australia) 2016, 243.
87 Productivity Commission (Australia) 2016, 246.
88 Productivity Commission (Australia) 2016, 246.

user.'[89] The Productivity Commission emphasized that 'Innovations are of greater social value where they advance technology and human knowledge, and generate knowledge spillovers in other areas of the economy.'[90]

The mass media also raised concerns about questionable innovation patents being granted for sex treatments and therapies.[91]

10.4 LITIGATION OVER INNOVATION PATENTS

It is a difficult exercise to engage in empirical research in respect of litigation involving innovation patents. There were a range of lawsuits, which emerged over the twenty years of the innovation patent. The Australian Legal Information Institute (AustLII) database brings up 120 documents related to the innovation patent from the Australian Patent Office database.[92] The AustLII database also contains a number of instances of litigation involving the innovation patent – raising issues about patent validity and patent infringement.

10.4.1 *Manner of Manufacture*

In Australia, the courts have traditionally taken a broad approach to patentable subject matter, drawing upon the *Statute of Monopolies*, and relying on the precedent of *National Research Development Corporation* v. *Commissioner of Patents* ("*NRDC*").[93]

Much like its counterparts in the Supreme Court of the United States and the Supreme Court of Canada, the High Court of Australia has been hearing a number of cases on the limits of patentable subject matter – which is discussed in terms of the terminology of 'manner of manufacture' in Australian law. Many of these cases have concerned standard patents. In *Grant* v. *Commissioner of Patents*, the Federal Court of Australia held that a method for protecting assets from unsecured creditors was not patentable because it was an abstract idea.[94] Most notably, in the *D'Arcy* v. *Myriad Genetics Inc.* case, the High Court of Australia rejected a patent application in respect of breast and ovarian cancer testing on the basis that it was 'an exorbitant monopoly' which sought to monopolise intellectual information.[95]

However, there has been an important case on patentable subject matter involving an innovation patent. In the 2022 case of *Aristocrat Technologies Australia Pty*

[89] Productivity Commission (Australia) 2016, 246.

[90] Productivity Commission (Australia) 2016, 246.

[91] Burke and McClymont 2009.

[92] The Australasian Legal Information Institute (AustLII) is a joint facility of UTS and UNSW Faculties of Law, which provides free online access to Australian legal information: www.austlii.edu.au/

[93] National Research Development Corporation 1959.

[94] *Grant* 2006.

[95] *D'Arcy* 2015. For commentary, see Rimmer 2017.

Ltd v. *Commissioner of Patents*, the High Court of Australia considered whether innovation patent applications for electronic gaming machines constituted a 'manner of manufacture.'[96]

The dispute had progressed through a number of decision-makers. The Commissioner of Patent's delegate had ruled that the innovation patents were not patentable subject matter because the substance of the invention was the game rules of gaming machines. The Federal Court of Australia allowed an appeal by Aristocrat, but the Full Court of the Federal Court of Australia allowed an appeal by the Commission of Patents. The High Court of Australia heard argument in July 2022.[97]

In the High Court of Australia, Kiefel CJ, Gageler and Keane JJ observed: 'In accordance with the approach in *Myriad*, it is necessary to characterise Aristocrat's claimed invention by reference to the terms of the specification having regard to the substance of the claim and in light of the common general knowledge.'[98] The judges found: 'In the absence of a claim to some variation of or adjustment to generic computer technology to give effect to, or accommodate the needs of, the new game, there is no reason to characterise the claimed invention as other than a claim for a new system or method of gaming: it is only in relation to the feature game that the invention is claimed to subsist.'[99]

The judges held: 'In the absence of such a finding, there is no basis for concluding that the claimed invention is patentable subject matter.'[100] The judges found: 'It is no more than an unpatentable game operated by a wholly conventional computer, using technology which has not been adapted in any way to accommodate the exigencies of the game or in any other way.'[101] The judges commented: 'Claim 1 of the 967 patent does not disclose any technical contribution to either computer or gaming technology outside the common general knowledge.'[102] The judges observed: 'At best, the claimed invention contains a new game which may enhance player enjoyment; but that cannot be said to amount to a technical contribution or to solve a technical problem in the field of computer or gaming technology.'[103]

The court also addressed an amicus curiae submission by the Institute of Patent and Trademark Attorneys of Australia. The judges noted: 'The IPTA also expressed concern that the approach of Middleton and Perram JJ would have "seismic" effects beyond the gaming industry, rendering unpatentable "swathes of inventions" that otherwise would have been, such as medical imaging and diagnostic machines,

96 Aristocrat Technologies 2022.
97 Aristocrat Technologies 2022.
98 Aristocrat Technologies 2022., 73.
99 Aristocrat Technologies 2022.
100 Aristocrat Technologies 2022, 76.
101 Aristocrat Technologies 2022.
102 Aristocrat Technologies 2022., 84.
103 Aristocrat Technologies 2022.

speed detection camera systems and biotechnology inventions such as COVID 19 diagnosis systems.'[104] The judges explained: 'It must be understood that a claimed invention for patentable subject matter does not become unpatentable because it is operated by generic computer technology.'[105]

The judges also heard arguments from the amicus curiae, the Fédération Internationale des Conseils en Propriété Intellectuelle, on patent-eligible subject matter under United States law. This amicus curiae warned that a narrow approach to patentable subject matter would have a chilling effect on innovation in Australia. The judges rejected their argument: 'Having regard to the reasons set out above, it can be seen that the FICPI's argument is unnecessarily alarmist.'[106] The judges noted: 'Since the relevant US statutory provision is different from the relevant terms of the Act, it will be readily apparent that the decisions in cases such as *Alice* have little significance for the outcome of this case.'[107] The judges observed: 'The foregoing reasons for holding that the appeal to this Court should be dismissed involve no reliance on the reasoning in *Alice*, or any other decision of the US courts.'[108] The judges commented: 'It is of little assistance to the application of Australian law to criticise the jurisprudence of a different legal system for reaching the same solution to a problem that Australian courts have reached.'[109]

Gordon, Edelman and Steward JJ dissented: 'In the 21st century, a law such as s 18 (1A) of the Patents Act that is designed to encourage invention and innovation should not lead to a different conclusion where physical cogs, reels, and motors are replaced by complex software and hardware that generate digital images.'[110] The judges commented 'Throughout this litigation, the Commissioner attempted to avoid such a curious result by re-characterising Aristocrat's claim as a mere scheme or abstract idea.'[111] The judges noted: 'The Commissioner could only achieve that characterisation by filleting from the claim essential and interdependent integers providing for the implementation of the game on the EGM.'[112] The judges argued: 'The integers stripped from the Commissioner's characterisation included components as basic as the display component of the player interface on which the images of symbols generated by the software and hardware appeared.'[113] The judges maintained that the appeal must be allowed because 'Claim 1 is a manner of manufacture within the meaning of s 6 of the *Statute of Monopolies*.'[114]

[104] Aristocrat Technologies 2022., 87.
[105] Aristocrat Technologies 2022.
[106] Aristocrat Technologies 2022., 92.
[107] Aristocrat Technologies 2022.
[108] Aristocrat Technologies 2022.
[109] Aristocrat Technologies 2022, 93.
[110] Aristocrat Technologies 2022, 97.
[111] Aristocrat Technologies 2022.
[112] Aristocrat Technologies 2022.
[113] Aristocrat Technologies 2022.
[114] Aristocrat Technologies 2022, 155.

In line with the *Judiciary Act*'s rules on split decisions, the appeal was dismissed with costs. However, the close 3-3 outcome highlights some strong philosophical differences in the court as to the limits and boundaries of patentable subject matter.

The ruling certainly received an animated response from Australian law firms – which sought to parse the decision.[115] The law profession was particularly concerned and worried about the lack of clarity and certainty around the boundaries of patentable subject matter.

10.4.2 *An Innovative Step*

The key precedent on the operation of the innovation patent system is the matter of *Dura-Post (Aust) Pty Ltd* v. *Delnorth Pty Ltd*.[116] The matter raised questions about manner of manufacture (the Australian language for patentable subject matter), and the threshold standard of an innovative step.

The case concerned three innovation patents for a 'Roadside Post'. The decision at first instance upheld infringement claims made by Delnorth Pty Ltd, and rejected Dura-Post's challenge to the validity of three patents (save in relation to claims 1 and 2 of each of Patents 2 and 3, which lacked an innovative step). Dura-Post mounted an appeal. The Full Court of the Federal Court considered questions of manner of manufacture, novelty, and innovative step.

Kenny and Stone JJ provided an overview of the innovation patent system. The judges rejected the contention that the patented invention was not a manner of manufacture. The judges found that there was no anticipation to require the lack of novelty conclusion for which Dura-Post argued. Kenny and Stone JJ held: 'In order for there to be a valid innovation patent, the invention disclosed in the patent must, amongst other things, involve an "innovative step".'[117] The judges added: 'In substance, s 7(4) deems an invention as claimed to involve an innovative step unless the invention does not differ from the relevant prior disclosure in a way that makes a substantial contribution to the working of the invention as claimed – in the sense of the device or process the subject of each claim.'[118] The judges found: 'On the basis of Mr Dowling's evidence, no relevant error is discernible in the primary judge's finding that each of these features made a substantial contribution to the working of the invention.'[119]

Monash Law School Professor Ann Monotti – who has sadly since passed away – wrote a detailed case note on the dispute, analysing its significance.[120] Monotti observed of the ruling on an innovative step: 'The result is probably quite a low

[115] See for instance, Cordiner et al. 2022; Gilchrist 2022; McKinley 2022; Rankine 2022.
[116] Dura-Post 2009.
[117] Dura-Post 2009, [49].
[118] Dura-Post 2009, [79].
[119] Dura-Post 2009, [85].
[120] Monotti 2010, 93–97.

threshold for protection.'[121] She commented that this position 'contrasts with the assessment of an inventive step, which requires a direct comparison to be made between the invention as claimed and the common general knowledge alone or in combination with prior art information.'[122]

10.4.3 *Prior Use and Prior Secret Use*

In the 2017 case of *Coretell Pty Ltd* v. *Australian Mud Company Pty Ltd*, the Full Court of the Federal Court of Australia considering innovation patents related to core sample orientation – which is commonly used in relation to geological survey operations and other drilling operations.[123] The Full Court of the Federal Court of Australia considered whether claims of innovation patents were fairly based on disclosure in a provisional application.[124] The Full Court of the Federal Court of Australia considered whether innovation patents were invalid on the basis of prior use or secret use. The judge found that field trials had been conducted in confidence.

10.4.4 *Infringement*

There was early litigation over the innovation patent in respect of micro-dot technology. DataDot Technology launched legal action in the Federal Court, claiming that a rival company, Alpha Microtech, infringed its innovation patent. DataDot developed an invention which sprays cars with more than 10,000 'micro-dots' to deter car thieves from breaking up stolen cars to rebuild them or sell their parts. Alpha offered a similar system, called the SmartDot security marking and identification system. The precedent of *Datadot Technology Ltd* v. *Alpha Microtech Pty Ltd* provided an early insight into the operation of the regime in respect of enforcement of innovation patents.[125]

In the 2011 case of *Seafood Innovations Pty Ltd* v. *Richard Bass Pty Ltd*, the Full Court of the Federal Court of Australia considered claims that innovation patents had been infringed.[126] The field of the invention of the innovation patents related to fish stunning apparatus. Setting aside the first instance decision, Bennett J held that the Bass devices infringed various claims of the two innovation patents. Bennett J noted: 'Bass submits that Seafood Innovations is not entitled to claim a monopoly for all fish stunning devices in which a fish moves unidirectionally from the front entrance to the rear exit, irrespective of the technical method for achieving that

[121] Monotti 2010, 96.
[122] Monotti 2010.
[123] Coretell 2017.
[124] Coretell 2017.
[125] Datadot Technology 2003.
[126] Seafood Innovations 2011.

result.'[127] Bennett J commented: 'However, there is no requirement that the means of achieving that result must be included in the claims, although there is a requirement for sufficient description of the invention, including the best method, in the specification (s 40(2)(a) of the Act).'[128]

10.4.5 *Remedies*

As Katrina Crooks has observed, there was judicial debate over the timing of damages for the infringement of innovation patents.[129]

In *Britax Childcare Pty Ltd* v. *Infa-Secure Pty Ltd*, there was litigation related to nine innovation patents and one standard patent owned by child safety seats.[130] Each of the innovation patents was divided out of Britax's earlier standard application. The court expressed some concern about some of the patents and claims being specifically draft to catch allegedly infringing Infa products. In the 2012 case of *Britax Childcare Pty Ltd* v. *Infa-Secure Pty Ltd (No 3)*, a judge in the Federal Court of Australia held that infringement of an innovation patent could run from the 'date of the patent'.[131]

In the 2017 case of *Coretell Pty Ltd* v. *Australian Mud Company Pty Ltd*, the Full Court of the Federal Court of Australia overturned the ruling in *Britax* on this point.[132] Justice Burley referred to the infringement provisions of the *Patents Act* 1990 (Cth), observing that they refer to infringement of 'a patent', inferring a granted patent.

In the 2020 case of *Quaker Chemical (Australasia) Pty Ltd* v. *Fuchs Lubricants (Australasia) Pty Ltd (No 2)*, there was dispute over the validity of an innovation patent related to a method for detecting high pressure fluid injection.[133] Fuchs argued that there was a lack of novelty. Fuchs argued that the innovation patent was invalid on the grounds of lack of utility, insufficiency, lack of clarity and lack of fair basis. Fuchs also raised concerns of secret use. The judge rejected these arguments, challenging the validity of the patents. The judge held that there was infringement of the patent. There was an argument for additional damages. The judge held that it was inappropriate to award additional damages: 'Although Fuchs made the supplies to Broadmeadow having regard to its commercial position vis-à-vis Quaker and to guard against losing market share in relation to other products as well, I do not consider its conduct as warranting additional damages.'[134]

[127] Seafood Innovations 2011.
[128] Seafood Innovations 2011.
[129] Crooks 2017.
[130] *Britax* 2012a.
[131] *Britax* 2012b.
[132] Coretell 2017.
[133] Quaker Chemical [2020].
[134] Quaker Chemical [2020], 853.

10.5 THE ADVISORY COUNCIL ON INTELLECTUAL PROPERTY

The Advisory Council on Intellectual Property was a specialist body established by the Federal Government to provide expert advice on intellectual property law reform (particularly in the areas of industrial property).[135] The organization included representatives from business and manufacturing, the legal and patent and trademark attorney professions, academia, and research.

There was also debate about the interrelationship between the innovation patent system and secondary forms of intellectual property – most notably plant breeders' rights.[136] The Advisory Council on Intellectual Property led by Professor Andrew Christie of the University of Melbourne investigated the interrelationship between plant breeder's rights and the innovation patent.[137]

An issues paper was released in 2002.[138] The Advisory Council on Intellectual Property sought comment on a number of questions. Is the current 'gap' in IP protection for inventions with a lower level of threshold, that involve plant and animal subject matter, seen as an existing or potential problem? Given the existence of the standard patent system and the PBR system, is there a need for those involved with plant and animal subject matter R&D in Australia to be able to protect their research with the innovation patent? What, if any, are the national benefits of excluding plant and animal subject matter from the innovation patent? What impact would the innovation patent have on non-IP-rights holders were it to include plant and animal subject matter? There were strong objections from the plant breeders' rights community who were concerned that the innovation patent system could provide competition and duplication for its system.

A final report was delivered in November 2004.[139] The Advisory Council on Intellectual Property observed: 'Where a proposal to restrict competition lacks clear benefits, the status quo should be maintained.'[140] The Advisory Council on Intellectual Property demurred from expanding the innovation patent system: 'As relatively little concern has been expressed over the innovation patent exclusion for animals and processes for their generation, ACIP considers that there is insufficient reason for change at this stage.'[141] The Advisory Council on Intellectual Property did contemplate that there was scope for a reconsideration of the issue in the future: 'However, in the future innovation patent protection may be needed due to an

[135] IP Australia 2023a.
[136] The *Plant Breeder's Rights Act* 1994 (Cth). For commentary on the regime, see Rimmer 2003.
[137] Advisory Council on Intellectual Property (Australia) 2002.
[138] Advisory Council on Intellectual Property (Australia) 2002.
[139] Advisory Council on Intellectual Property (Australia) 2004.
[140] Advisory Council on Intellectual Property (Australia) 2004, 2.
[141] Advisory Council on Intellectual Property (Australia) 2004, 2–3.

increase in the development of genetically modified organisms, which is a potentially more costly form of breeding.'[142]

There was also concern about overlap between the regime for industrial designs, and the innovation patent. There has been ongoing process of law reform in Australia in respect of the industrial designs system.[143] Nonetheless, the designs regime is still only used in a minor way compared to the heavy use of patents and trademarks.

The Advisory Council on Intellectual Property conducted a full-scale inquiry into innovation patents.[144] There was an issues paper.[145] There was an options paper.[146] There was a Final Report published in 2014, and revised in May 2015.[147] There was also an accompanying Verve Economics Report on the Economic Value of the Innovation Patent.[148]

Initially, in the 2014 version of the final report, the Advisory Council on Intellectual Property equivocated as to the fate of the innovation patent.[149] The organization argued that 'ACIP has been unable to obtain adequate empirical evidence as to whether the system does or does not stimulate innovation in Australian SMEs.'[150] Accordingly, 'ACIP is therefore unable to make a recommendation on whether to retain or abolish the innovation patent system.'[151] The Advisory Council on Intellectual Property did make some contingent law reform recommendations: 'If the government chooses to retain the system, then ACIP urges it to consider various recommendations in this report to enhance its effectiveness and to reduce some of the system's unintended consequences.'[152] In particular, the Advisory Council on Intellectual Property recommended raising the innovative step threshold; adoption of substantive examination; rules on the use of the term 'patent'; the operation of manner of manufacture for innovation patents; and the use of remedies for infringement of innovation patents.

In a May 2015, Corrigendum, the Advisory Council on Intellectual Property further revised its position on the innovation patent, calling for its abolition.[153] The Advisory Council on Intellectual Property took note of the economic analysis of IP Australia: 'A key finding in this research paper is that Australian SMEs are less likely to use the patent system after filing an innovation patent than a company that

[142] Advisory Council on Intellectual Property (Australia) 2004, 3.
[143] Designs Act 2003 (Cth); Designs Amendment (Advisory Council on Intellectual Property Response) Act 2021 (Cth); IP Australia 2021; IP Australia 2023b.
[144] Advisory Council on Intellectual Property (Australia) 2015.
[145] Advisory Council on Intellectual Property (Australia) 2011.
[146] Advisory Council on Intellectual Property (Australia) 2013.
[147] Advisory Council on Intellectual Property (Australia) 2015.
[148] Zeitsch 2013.
[149] Advisory Council on Intellectual Property (Australia) 2015.
[150] Advisory Council on Intellectual Property (Australia) 2015, 5.
[151] Advisory Council on Intellectual Property (Australia) 2015, 5.
[152] Advisory Council on Intellectual Property (Australia) 2015, 5.
[153] Advisory Council on Intellectual Property (Australia) 2015, 2.

has not previously filed an innovation patent.'[154] The Advisory Council on Intellectual Property concluded that 'innovative activity is not being stimulated among these groups by the innovation patent system.'[155] The Advisory Council on Intellectual Property observed: 'In light of the information made available by the IPGOD dataset and the analysis presented in this research paper, ACIP is now able to make an assessment of the innovation patent system's effectiveness in stimulating innovation among SMEs.'[156] The Advisory Council on Intellectual Property concluded: 'ACIP considers it likely that the innovation patent is not achieving this objective and the Government should therefore consider abolishing the system.'[157]

The Advisory Council on Intellectual Property was subsequently dissolved by the Abbott Government – as part of its effort to reduce 'red tape' in the operation of government. This decision meant that IP Australia has had to increasingly do its own 'in-house' law reform and public policy work, because of a lack of a specialist advisory body. Moreover, other generalist law reform bodies like the Productivity Commission and the Australian Law Reform Commission have had to take up major work in respect of intellectual property law reform. Parliamentary committees have often questioned whether they are best placed to deal with the technicalities of intellectual property law reform. It is doubtful that the abolition of the Advisory Council on Intellectual Property has led to any further efficiencies in the law reform process in Australia in relation to intellectual property.

10.6 THE PRODUCTIVITY COMMISSION

The Productivity Commission is a unique Australian policy body, which provides independent research advice to the Australian Government on economic and social issues affecting the welfare of Australians. The Productivity Commission is known for conducting extensive empirical research in respect of public policy issues. The Productivity Commission has been influential in driving law reform and public policy debate in Australia across a range of fields.

The Productivity Commission has been given a number of references over the years in respect of matters of intellectual property. The Productivity Commission has considered the interaction between intellectual property and trade policy.[158] The Productivity Commission has examined the operation of flexibilities in respect of compulsory licensing and crown use for the patent regime and industrial designs.[159]

[154] Advisory Council on Intellectual Property (Australia) 2015, 1.
[155] Advisory Council on Intellectual Property (Australia) 2015.
[156] Advisory Council on Intellectual Property (Australia) 2015, 2.
[157] Advisory Council on Intellectual Property (Australia) 2015.
[158] Productivity Commission (Australia) 2010.
[159] Productivity Commission (Australia) 2013.

The Productivity Commission has also engaged in a systematic evaluation of the entirety of Australia's intellectual property regime.[160]

The then Treasurer Joe Hockey asked the Productivity Commission to investigate Australia's intellectual property system – making specific reference to 'the findings and recommendations of the Advisory Council on Intellectual Property's Review of the Innovation Patent System'.[161]

A key issue in its inquiry into Australia's intellectual property arrangements was the question of the innovation patent regime. The Productivity Commission produced an issues paper and a discussion paper, and sought feedback from a wide array of stakeholders. There were submissions on the topic of an innovation patent from various interested parties.

The generic pharmaceutical company Alphapharm was an opponent of innovation patents, expressing concerns that such a regime could be exploited for the purposes of 'evergreening'.[162] In other words, the generic company was concerned that pharmaceutical drug companies would seek to extend the life of an initial patent, with further innovation patents. Alphapharm maintained that innovation patents should not be available for therapeutic goods: 'Immediately amend the *Patents Act* 1990, with retrospective effect, so that an innovation patent cannot contain a claim relating, concerning or associated with a therapeutic good.'[163]

While Apple had filed many innovation patents, Microsoft was by contrast a staunch opponent of innovation patents.[164] Microsoft commented: 'Microsoft agrees with a number of the Draft Report's conclusions and recommendations relating to various improvements to Australia's patent regime (including the proposed abolition of the innovation patent system and adoption of a more stringent standard for inventive step).'[165] Microsoft clearly took the strategic view that it had a much more sophisticated system of standard patents than many of its rivals and competitors, and could operate without a second-tier regime of innovation patents.

The key defender of innovation patents was the patent attorney profession. They mounted a rearguard action, calling for the maintenance or reform of the innovation patent system, instead of abolition of the system. Patent attorney and blogger Mark Summerfield bemoaned the push to terminate the innovation patent system, as an over-reaction by the Federal Government.[166] He argued that 'the overwhelming majority of those advocating to retain the system support reforms to mitigate

[160] Productivity Commission (Australia) 2016.
[161] Productivity Commission (Australia) 2016, v.
[162] Alphapharm 2015.
[163] Alphapharm 2015, 5.
[164] Microsoft 2016.
[165] Microsoft 2016, 5.
[166] Summerfield 2018.

some of the problems that have become apparent, and improve its effectiveness as a second-tier right that can support the needs of SMEs.'[167]

In its key points, the Productivity Commission commented: 'Australia's patent system grants exclusivity too readily, allowing a proliferation of low-quality patents, frustrating follow-on innovators and stymieing competition.'[168] The Productivity Commission observed: 'To raise patent quality, the Australian Government should increase the degree of invention required to receive a patent, abolish the failed innovation patent, reconfigure costly extensions of term for pharmaceutical patents, and better structure patent fees.'[169] In its overview, the Productivity Commission stressed that 'the "second-tier" patent experiment has failed.'[170] The Productivity Commission noted: 'Some participants have called for the IPS to be abolished; others have called for its reform.'[171]

The Productivity Commission questioned whether it was viable to reform the Innovation Patent regime, making reference to the film *Groundhog Day*, directed by Harold Ramis, and starring Bill Murray and Andie MacDowell:

> Were the [Innovation Patent System] to be reformed, there would be strong grounds to exclude obvious inventions by setting the innovative step at the same level as the inventive step for standard patents. It would also be necessary to address strategic behaviour, most likely by reintroducing a mandatory examination process, and limiting the period in which damages could apply. However, reforming the [Innovation Patent System] along these lines would see innovation patents resemble petty patents, and so represent a return to an approach already found to be lacking—tantamount to a policy 'Groundhog Day'.[172]

The Productivity Commission concluded: 'The community's interests, and the interests of SMEs, would be better served by abolishing innovation patents and directly tackling the IP issues of greatest concern to SMEs, such as patent infringement and enforcement costs.'[173]

In its analysis of Australia's intellectual property system, the Productivity Commission devoted a full chapter to the innovation patent system in its final report.[174] The Productivity Commission were critical of the operation of Australia's innovation patent system, questioning whether it was serving its original purpose. The Productivity Commission lamented: 'By failing to target socially valuable, additional innovations, the IPS can have unintended consequences.'[175] The Productivity Commission commented: 'Some participants linked the low innovative threshold

[167] Summerfield 2018.
[168] Productivity Commission (Australia) 2016, 2.
[169] Productivity Commission (Australia) 2016.
[170] Productivity Commission (Australia) 2016, 17.
[171] Productivity Commission (Australia) 2016.
[172] Productivity Commission (Australia) 2016.
[173] Productivity Commission (Australia) 2016.
[174] Productivity Commission (Australia) 2016.
[175] Productivity Commission (Australia) 2016, 252.

to a proliferation of obvious patents, legal uncertainties and patent thickets, which in turn raise barriers to entering markets and blunt competitive pressure, itself a driver of innovation.'[176] The Productivity Commission lamented: 'A multitude of low-value patents make it harder for an innovative firm to be sure it is not infringing someone else's patent.'[177]

Ultimately, the Productivity Commission supported the abolition of the innovation patent system:

> Abolishing the [innovation patent system] would deliver greater benefits for the community. It would simplify the overall patent system, reduce administrative and transaction costs, and remove the ability for patent holders to use the system strategically. To the extent that innovative and socially valuable ideas currently receive protection under the IPS, these would be expected to receive protection under the standard patent system. Innovations that would not pass the inventive step threshold under the standard patent system are more likely to impose net costs on the community, and should not receive protection.[178]

The Productivity Commission submitted its report to the Treasurer Scott Morrison – who was subsequently the next Conservative Coalition Prime Minister of Australia.

10.7 IP AUSTRALIA

In addition to the work of these other law reform bodies, IP Australia[179] has also undertaken its own empirical research into the operation of innovation patents.

The economics unit of IP Australia engaged in data analysis of Australia's innovation patent system. This study raised questions as to whether the scheme was operating as it was intended – namely, to support inventors and small-to-medium inventors. The report found as follows:

> The evidence shows that firms who file innovation patents are less likely to participate in the standard patent system afterwards. The great majority of Australian SMEs and private inventors appear to gain little benefit from the system. Three quarters of these applicants file one innovation patent and then never file another innovation or standard patent again.[180]

[176] Productivity Commission (Australia) 2016.
[177] Productivity Commission (Australia) 2016.
[178] Productivity Commission (Australia) 2016, 261.
[179] IP Australia is an Australian government agency which administers the registration of patents, trademarks, registered designs, and plant breeder's rights in Australia – www.ipaustralia.gov.au/ As well as being involved in IP administration, IP Australia plays a key part in law reform – particularly since the abolition of the Advisory Council on Intellectual Property.
[180] Johnson et al. 2015.

The research paper observed: 'Only 23 SMEs have become moderate users of the innovation patent system, filing at least 5 innovation patents, with at least one enforceable right, and entering the patent system via an application for an innovation patent.'[181] The research paper added: 'The average SME or private inventor files once and never again (74%) does not receive any enforceable right (83%), and lets their patent expire early because they see its value at less than the $110–$220 cost of renewal (78%).'[182] The research paper concluded: 'The low levels of repeated use by SMEs suggest that the innovation patent is not fulfilling its policy goal of providing an incentive for Australian SMEs to innovate, and the evidence shows a reduced likelihood of patenting after participating in the innovation patent system.'[183] The research paper maintained: 'Given the low private value of the system, it is likely that the system is a net cost to most of the SMEs that use it, and the system has imposed a regulatory burden of more than $100m since its introduction.'[184]

10.8 ABOLITION OF THE INNOVATION PATENT

As a result of these various investigations, the Australian Government decided to abolish the innovation patent. IP Australia observed that 'innovation patents were being used by large firms as a strategic tool to stifle competition'.[185] IP Australia was worried that 'low standards for innovation patents inhibit genuine innovation and competition'.[186] Moreover, IP Australia expressed concerns that 'innovation patents put Australian innovators at risk in overseas markets', because there was not necessarily matching protection in other jurisdictions.[187]

There was some resistance to this proposal for the abolition of the innovation patent. Professional organisations representing patent attorneys and trademarks mounted a desperate but ultimately futile political campaign to save the innovation patent, lobbying policy-makers to reconsider the issue.[188] Nonetheless, the Conservation Coalition that made up the Federal Government was unmoved, and proceeded with its plan to phase out the innovation patent.

181 >Johnson et al. 2015.
182 >Johnson et al. 2015.
183 >Johnson et al. 2015.
184 >Johnson et al. 2015.
185 IP Australia 2019.
186 IP Australia 2019.
187 IP Australia 2019.
188 'IPTA will continue to lobby to retain innovation patents. To do so effectively, however, requires more case studies from Australian SMEs demonstrating the benefits of the innovation patent system. For this reason, we ask members to continue to contribute to the momentum that has been building to retain the innovation patent system.' Shoebridge 2018; The Institute of Patent and Trade Mark Attorneys of Australia 2018.

Opposition Labor Senators argued that 'the evidence provided from a number of parties suggests a significant gap could emerge if the innovation patent is removed without alternative mechanisms being put in place to specifically assist small- and medium-sized enterprises (SMEs) to access the patent system and innovate.'[189]

The *Intellectual Property Laws Amendment (Productivity Commission Response Part 2 and Other Measures) Act* 2019 (Cth) has enabled the phase out of the innovation patent system. In her second reading speech, the Hon. Karen Andrews – the Minister for Industry, Science, and Technology – explained the decision.[190] She said: 'This second-tier patent was intended to incentivise small to medium-sized Australian businesses to invest in research when it was introduced in 2001.'[191] Andrews commented: 'However, in the 18 years since then, it has become clear that the second-tier patent has been more harmful than helpful for SMEs.'[192] She observed: 'There is widespread agreement among stakeholders that the system is not fit for purpose.'[193] Andrews noted: 'Some people argue that the second-tier patent should be reformed, but there is no agreement on a workable alternative.'[194] She pointed to the outcome of law reform reviews: 'Both the Productivity Commission and the former Advisory Council on Intellectual Property recommended that the innovation patent system be abolished'.[195] Andrews noted: 'Both found there is no evidence that the second-tier patent stimulates innovation or research in Australia.'[196] She stressed: 'What it does do, according to both bodies, is lead to uncertainty, confusion and a higher regulatory burden, particularly for our Australian SMEs.'[197] Andrews commented: 'The amendments ensure that existing rights, filed before commencement, are maintained and protected, ensuring a balanced phasing out.'[198]

The Australian Labor Party recognized that there were flaws with the regime. The Shadow Minister the Hon. Clare O'Neil – the member for Hotham – questioned whether the abolition of the innovation patent would be helpful for SMEs:

> The issue that Labor members of parliament raised in reaction to the bill is that the government was essentially proposing that we abolish this bill – that we take away something that exists specifically to assist small business – and not put anything in its place. We had a great problem with that. The reason for that is that the only alternative that would have left would be the standard patent systems. Standard patent systems are difficult: they're very complicated, it's very expensive to get one

[189] Sadler 2019.
[190] Hon. Karen Andrews MP 2020, 297.
[191] Hon. Karen Andrews MP 2020.
[192] Hon. Karen Andrews MP 2020.
[193] Hon. Karen Andrews MP 2020.
[194] Hon. Karen Andrews MP 2020.
[195] Hon. Karen Andrews MP 2020.
[196] Hon. Karen Andrews MP 2020.
[197] Hon. Karen Andrews MP 2020.
[198] Hon. Karen Andrews MP 2020.

> and it's administratively burdensome. That's fine when you can absorb all the expenses associated with that into a company which might have a whole legal department and might have its own intellectual property lawyer, but if you're running a small business with a couple of people on the books there is just no way you can put the effort into creating an application for something like that.[199]

O'Neil said that the Australian Labor Party had two proposals: 'The first was that we want to make sure that there's a proper, thorough statutory review done into the appropriateness of the IP system for small business, to make sure that we are thinking about these 2.2 million small businesses when we create a system and when we make legislative change.'[200] She also noted that the opposition party wanted there to be more time before the phase out of the innovation patent system: 'The second part of this was just giving small business a bit more time.'[201]

The Australian Labor Party's Graham Perrett worried: 'Removing the innovation patent scheme without any alternative mechanisms being put in place simply creates a significant and serious gap for small and medium businesses seeking support to access the patent system and to innovate.'[202]

The Australian Labor Party's Hon. Anika Wells MP expressed concerns that 'some law firms specialising in intellectual property are strategically using these very innovation patents as a way to increase uncertainty over the scope of rights for competitors and improve their own clients' bargaining position in patent disputes and to frustrate entry by competitors.'[203]

South Australian Senator Rex Patrick (of the Centre Alliance originally, and then later an independent) called for the retention of the innovation patent system.[204] He observed that SMEs would be hurt by the abolition of the regime. Likewise, Senator Malcolm Roberts of One Nation opposed the removal of the innovation patent system.[205]

Senator Matthew Canavan of the National Party, and a Minister in the Coalition Government closed the Senate discussion, observing: 'This bill will help ensure that Australia's intellectual property system remains fit for purpose into the future and balances the needs of innovators and users of technologies with those of the general public too.'[206]

The Australian Government has taken a further step in the process of phasing out the innovation patent which began in February 2020, with final applications accepted on 25 August 2021. There are no plans to reintroduce a second tier system

[199] Hon. Clare O'Neil MP 2020, 299.
[200] Hon. Clare O'Neil MP 2020.
[201] Hon. Clare O'Neil MP 2020.
[202] Hon. Graham Perrett MP 2020, 308.
[203] Hon. Anika Wells MP 2020, 305.
[204] Senator Rex Patrick 2019, 3092.
[205] Senator Malcolm Roberts 2019, 3099.
[206] Senator Matthew Canavan 2019, 3106.

of patents in Australia. The New Albanese Government of the Australian Labor Party has shown no enthusiasm for revisiting the question of innovation patents.

10.9 BREAKTHROUGH PATENTS

The new Albanese Government has a strong emphasis on the promotion of breakthrough inventions by Australian researchers in the private sector and the public sector. The Institute of Patent and Trademark Attorneys called for a reintroduction of a modified version of innovation patents.[207] However, the Australian Labor Party does not seem interested in revisiting the demise of the innovation patent system. Indeed, the Albanese Government is very much focused upon pioneering inventions – rather than incremental innovation.

The new Minister for Industry and Science, Ed Husic MP, gave a landmark address to the National Press Club, outlining the innovation policy of the new Albanese Government.[208]

Husic said that the Albanese Government was 'encouraging Australians to invest in new ideas and new businesses that could be our next big breakthrough.'[209] He highlighted in particular quantum technologies, robotics and sensing technologies, and clean energy generation and storage technologies. The Minister emphasized: 'Having coherent, national approaches to the development and uptake of key emerging technologies, are part of ensuring these technologies don't just deliver economic growth, but safeguard our national wellbeing.'[210]

Husic did note the Government's commitment to small to medium enterprises: 'For this manufacturing base to be sustained, we must provide more opportunities for Australian businesses to develop and market their products within Australia and overseas.'[211] He highlighted the Buy Australia plan, a significant procurement reform program. Husic said that this programme 'aims to level the playing field for SMEs, regional and Indigenous-owned businesses, and support the creation of new jobs.'[212] It is a different policy lever to support small to medium enterprises (as opposed to say a second-tier patent system).

In conclusion, Husic stressed: 'Our government is laying the foundation for Australia's future prosperity and wellbeing: a nation that makes things here and trades them with the world.'[213] He maintained: 'The decisions we are making today are all in pursuit of a vibrant future for science, industry and manufacturing in

[207] Sadler 2022.
[208] The Hon. Ed Husic MP 2022.
[209] The Hon. Ed Husic MP 2022.
[210] The Hon. Ed Husic MP 2022.
[211] The Hon. Ed Husic MP 2022.
[212] The Hon. Ed Husic MP 2022.
[213] The Hon. Ed Husic MP 2022.

Australia.'[214] Noting 'We come up with big ideas', Husic observed that 'as a country we must cultivate the courage to follow them through.'[215] Husic commented: 'We must make these investments in our human capital, in these big ideas, and in our technological potential, work together.'[216] He emphasized: 'The Albanese Government has faith in Australian know-how; faith in our people; faith in our ability to build things here.'[217]

10.10 CONCLUSION

Starting with the case of study of the innovation patent application for reinventing the wheel, this chapter has sought to chart the rise and fall of the innovation patent system in Australia. This historical study has certainly highlighted how perennial these debates have been around on second-tier patent systems in Australia. It has highlighted the initial enthusiasm and exuberance of policy-makers for the adoption of a second-tier utility patent system in Australia – with first the petty patent system, and then the innovation patent system. This chapter has also highlighted the dysfunction of the innovation patent system. The lack of proper substantive examination raised questions about the legitimacy and credibility of the system – most notably, with the innovation patent granted for a wheel. There has been debate about the limits of patentable subject matter for innovation patents – particularly in light of the *Myriad* dispute. There remain profound philosophical differences amongst judges as to how to define the limits and boundaries of patentable subject matter. There has also been angst about the threshold requirement for an innovative step under an innovation patent. There has been a concern about the abuse of innovation patents in infringement proceedings – with worries about the rise of patent trolls and gamesmanship amongst patent applications. The Productivity Commission, the Advisory Council on Intellectual Property, and IP Australia have all undertaken incisive reviews into the operation of the innovation patent regime, highlighting malfunctions in the system. This chapter has reviewed the efforts of law reform bodies to overhaul and eventually abolish the innovation patent system. It has observed that the new Albanese Government has focused on breakthrough innovation – rather than incremental innovation. The Australian story of the innovation patent is a cautionary tale for other jurisdictions in setting up and running a second-tier patent system. The disappearance of the petty patent system and the extinction of the innovation patent regime in Australia raises questions on whether utility models of patent protection will survive elsewhere around the world.

[214] The Hon. Ed Husic MP 2022.
[215] The Hon. Ed Husic MP 2022.
[216] The Hon. Ed Husic MP 2022.
[217] The Hon. Ed Husic MP 2022.

11

China's Utility Model Patent Legal System

Past, Present, and Future

*Yu Yang**

It is widely acknowledged in the world today that the fundamental goal of the patent system is to encourage invention and creation, promote technological achievement, international technological exchange, and economic development by recognizing and protecting the intellectual achievements of inventors. In this respect, China[1] is no exception. Patents have been playing an important role in stimulating technological innovation in the process of China's modern development. Especially noteworthy, the number of patents has exploded in the past decade.[2]

Although the initial establishment of China's intellectual property system started relatively late, this transplanted legal system has maintained rapid development in recent years. The fast-growing increase in the number of granted patents is one of the typical signs of this rapid development process. In general, the sharp increase in the number of patent grants reflects the fast-reviving progress of China's contemporary science and technology to a certain extent, but it should not be forgotten that the number of granted patents is merely one of the oft-used indicators of innovation ability.[3] In contrast, the quality of granted patents, invention patents in particular, is usually the best indicator of technological advancement. Unfortunately, the recent explosion in the number of patents in China has been accompanied by the emergence of low-quality patents, seriously eroding the legislative purpose of the patent system.[4] Such low-quality

* The writing of this chapter was supported by the 2023 Dongfang Yingcai Jihua Bajian Project.

1 In this chapter, China refers to the mainland of the People's Republic of China.

2 See WIPO 2022a, 7, in which China ranked first again both in terms of worldwide patent applications and worldwide utility model applications.

3 According to the latest statistics and rankings released by the World Intellectual Property Organization, China still is not in the top-tier category in terms of global innovation power. *See* WIPO 2022b, 22 ("China moves up to 11th place").

4 This type of detrimental effect has caught wide attention and research at home and abroad. *E. g.*, *see* Liang 2014. ("As the number of patent applications and grants has grown rapidly, the quality of patents has not. A large number of patent applications pouring into the patent

patents are closely linked to patents in the category of utility model patents. Naturally, many take a dim view of this patent sphere with relatively low quality, or even no quality at all, that is, so-called "junk patents".[5] These institutional and practical deficiencies suggest a pressing need for systemic improvement. As a result, China has steadily taken measures to improve the quality of its issued patents.[6]

Since April 1, 1985, when China's first Patent Law[7] came into effect, China has established a legal protection system for utility models. At present, after four revisions of the Patent Law, China's utility model patent legal system has also been improved to a certain extent. However, among the authorized utility model patents, those that fully meet the necessary conditions of novelty and inventive step have not yet dominated. Of course, this phenomenon is not unique only in China. Historically and globally, utility model patents have been dubbed "petty patents" essentially on account of their limited scope, lower requirement for inventiveness, lack of stringent substantive examination, uncertainty of validity, and shorter term.

The purpose of this chapter is to illuminate the ongoing optimization of the Chinese utility model patent system in the context of the development of China's overall patent system. Accordingly, Section 11.1 traces the emergence of China's Patent System, including the Chinese utility model patent-based subsystem. Section 11.2 centers on the basic contours of the Chinese utility model patent system. Section 11.3 then summarizes existing deficiencies of the Chinese utility model patent system and future development trends. It concludes with a discussion of potential implications of proposed revisions to the Chinese utility model patent system.

11.1 FOUNDATION AND FORMATION OF CHINA'S UTILITY MODEL PATENT SYSTEM

11.1.1 *Inception of China's Modern Intellectual Property System*

At the beginning of the founding of the People's Republic of China in 1949, an intellectual property protection system involving the protection of patents,

examination department are not directly translated in the explosive growth of industrial innovation."); Prud'homme 2015b, 619–625 ("[t]he intellectual-property component of China's technological catch-up strategy has been geared towards, first, focusing on quantity of outputs and then eventually shifting towards ensuring the quality of outputs. Disconcertingly, in recent years, this strategy has created negative impacts on patent quality and thus may have hampered innovation in China.")

5 See infra Section 11.3.1.

6 *See e.g.*, Feng 2009, 54 (noting that the third amendment's "adoption of the standard of absolute novelty shows that the Patent Law of China has raised the requirements of quality of patent").

7 *See* Patent Law (1984). In addition, a series of translated multi-tiered legal documents are available on WIPO's website. WIPO 2024.

trademarks, and copyrights was implemented. However, from 1957 to 1979, these early intellectual property protection institutions disappeared. As one Western observer noted:

> China's traditional failure to protect what the nonsocialist world refers to as industrial or intellectual property was evidence of Marxist hostility to the concept of private property, and particularly to monopolistic private control of socially useful inventions. In China, all inventions and technology were, for practical purposes, the property of the state.[8]

Initially, the formal establishment of modern intellectual property laws in the PRC after its reopening in the late 1970s was mainly encouraged by the United States.[9] Thus, to a certain degree, "[t]he history of intellectual property laws in China is a history of legal transplants."[10] Article VI of the Agreement on Trade Relations between the United States of America and the People's Republic of China,[11] *inter alia*, epitomized this kind of international push. Specifically with regard to China's patent law, the initial general characteristics of the patent law enacted in 1984 after China's reopening resembled U.S. patent law.[12] Nevertheless, on the other hand, China had self-motivated drivers, such as invigorating its domestic economy after weathering prior hardship, to formulate a modern legal system of intellectual property rights as well. For instance, as pointed out on the *PEOPLE'S DAILY* (Overseas Edition, January 20, 1992) by Wu Yi, then-deputy minister of Ministry of Foreign Economic Relations and Trade (MOFERT) and head of the Chinese Delegation at the negotiations:

> To enhance the level of protection of IPRs of China, not only meets the need of further reform and opening to the outside world [and] the need of developing science and technology, but [also] meets the need of speeding up the construction of modernization of China.[13]

Thus, on the whole, the process of transplanting a western legal system of intellectual property rights to China was not a purely coercive process driven by foreign countries, like the ones in the Qing dynasty.[14] Rather, it was a process of amalgamation embodying both "push" and "pull" factors.[15]

8 *See* Theroux 1980, 228.
9 The United States took a series of such bilateral measures to exert similar institutional push for similar effects in the 1980s. E.g., *see* Wilson 1988, 447.
10 *See* Yu 2016, 20.
11 *See* Agreement on Trade Relations (1979).
12 *See* Winter 1987, 330 ("China enacted a new patent law in 1984 that is quite similar to the system in the United States and other market economy countries").
13 *See* Dexi 1993, 288.
14 *See e.g.*, Hart 1907, 630.
15 *See* Yu et al. 2022, 1553.

11.1.2 *Basic Statutory Rationale for the Chinese Utility Model Patent Legal System*

As noted in Chapter 1, there is no legally binding provision in the TRIPS Agreement[16] relating to Utility Model Patents. In addition, there are no articles in the Paris Convention embodying minimum substantive standards for the protection of utility model patents, except for some articles regarding international priority and national treatment.[17] As a result, utility model patent regulations were left to each jurisdiction's discretionary needs and priorities.

China initially introduced a utility model patent system in its 1984 Patent Law. In essence, the initial establishment of the Chinese utility model patent legal system was on a substratum of a hybrid of realistic needs. Even today, the fundamentally unchanged utility model patent system's lower inventiveness threshold legally permits technical followers rather than pioneers to seek protection for their minor or incremental inventions that would not otherwise be protected under the framework of patent law. Admittedly, there were pros and cons of whether to incorporate a utility model patent legal mechanism into the unprecedented patent law in the history of the PRC at the time. After taking stock of all sorts of relevant factors and weighing potential benefits and costs, China finally decided to include it in the patent law.[18]

In view of the generally low inventiveness threshold for Chinese utility model patents, this type of patent does not require substantive examination. The lack of examination has the benefit of alleviating the heavy workload of the Patent Office, a benefit shared by foreign Patent Offices with utility model patent systems.[19] At the early stage of China's patent system, the vast majority of patents were issued to foreigners, while the registration of utility models was primarily of benefit to domestic innovators.[20] Given that, by and large, China at the time lagged far behind the most technically innovative countries, there seemed to be no wonder why the vast majority of invention patents, particularly those representing technical breakthroughs, were issued to foreigners and in contrast utility models, without necessitating substantive examinations and typically focusing on mere incremental innovation, were much

[16] *See* TRIPs Agreement.

[17] *See* Chapter 1, Section 1.2.3.

[18] *See* Kay 1985, 361 (noting the comment made by Huang Kunyi which provided the only official explanation for the final decision to include utility models, i.e., "Considering there are more small and medium sized enterprises in our country and a rather low industrial standard of technology, we will use the form of the utility model patent to stimulate the initiative and enthusiasm of the masses."). Similar views are confirmed by a successor of Mr. Huang Kunyi, i.e., Mr Gao Lulin. *See* Gao 2019, 193, 194.

[19] *See* Naumann 1958, 801 ("... the Patent Office had to examine a large number of patent applications that would not have been filed if there had been a utility model patent law.")

[20] *See* Pager 2007, 803.

more accessible and attractive to domestic innovators with relatively lower innovation capabilities.

Judging from the metric of incremental innovation, there has been a clear demarcation line between normal applicants and abnormal applicants for Chinese utility model patents. The normal purpose of Chinese utility model patents is to enable applicants to profit from valuable incremental innovations. Thus, industries that attach importance to incremental innovations, such as food, transportation, domestic articles, and basic electronics, are the main normal users of Chinese utility model patents.[21]

For instance, in the field of refrigeration and air-conditioning, frequently seen technical inventions and creations are small-scale incremental improvements made on the basis of existing technologies. These small improvements may not meet the requirements of inventiveness for invention patents, but they can meet those requirements for Chinese utility model patents. Meanwhile, the costs of Chinese utility model patent applications and reviews are much lower than those of invention patents because there is no substantive examination process.[22]

Unlike normal Chinese utility model patent applicants, the main purpose of abnormal Chinese utility model patent applications deviates from the legislative purpose of the patent law and includes goals such as seeking occupational performance credits and promotions through Chinese utility model patent filings, rather than promoting incremental innovation. Squarely in response to these abnormal Chinese utility model patent applications and their concomitant detrimental effects, follow-up amendments to the Chinese utility model patent legal system have been gradually developed and enforced.

11.1.3 *Follow-Up Amendments to Chinese Utility Model Patent Legal System*

After the establishment of the Chinese utility model patent legal system, there was growing awareness of deficiencies that necessitated amendments to the system. As a result, Chinese utility model patent-related institutional revisions on different levels were implemented. These fall into two categories. One category consists of revisions embodied in a series of patent law amendments (including subsequent implementation rules) and the other includes revisions that wholly or partially touched upon Chinese utility model patent-related issues in multi-level patent-related official documents.

11.1.3.1 Patent Law Amendments

The 1992 Patent Law extended the term of Chinese utility model patents from five years to ten years and thus, in so doing, greatly enhanced the legal protection of

[21] *See* Yang 2014, 411.
[22] *See* Xue 2020, 1.

Chinese utility model patents. In the 2008 revision of the Patent Law, an absolute novelty standard was implemented for both utility model and invention patents,[23] which substantially raised the standard for a utility model patent. Procedurally, the same applicant was allowed to apply for a utility model patent and an invention patent for the same invention at the same time, and a utility model patent could make up for the lack of temporary protection measures during the pendency of an invention patent application. Subsequently, in the revision of the Detailed Rules for the Implementation of Chinese Patent Law in 2010, the scope of preliminary examination of utility model patent applications was further expanded, and the examination of manifest novelty defects and manifest practicality defects was added,[24] so as to improve the quality of utility model patents. These amendments embody the most important Chinese utility model patent-related institutional overhauls, but more detailed operating rules aimed specifically at implementing and supplementing those overhauls were dispersed among a host of multi-level patent-related official documents discussed below.

11.1.3.2 Multi-level Patent-Related Official Documents

Given the widely perceived low quality of a large number of granted Chinese utility model patents, relevant governmental bodies like the China National Intellectual Property Administration (CNIPA),[25] envisioned an array of regulatory rules aimed at decreasing or gradually eliminating the issuance of low-quality patents.

In this regard, the SIPO for the first time released a specific administrative regulation: Several Provisions of the State Intellectual Property Office on Regulating Patent Application Activities[26] in 2007 seeking to inhibit abnormal patent application activities.[27] Put another way, this regulation provided an unprecedented official definition on what shall be regarded as "abnormal patent application activities". According to Article 3, activities that fall within the ambit of either of the two specifically listed scenarios qualify as "abnormal patent application activities". One is "the same entity or individual submits multiple patent applications of evidently similar content or instigates any other person to submit multiple patent applications of evidently similar content"; the other is "the same entity or individual submits multiple patent applications involving evidently plagiarized existing

[23] *See* Patent Law (2008, art. 9, 22).

[24] *See* Detailed Rules (2010, art. 44).

[25] This new English name was adopted on August 28, 2018. *See* The State Council of the People's Republic of China, 2018. For the purpose of precision, this article uses the new English name for all the events and documents released after the Notice and the previous name, State Intellectual Property Office (hereinafter SIPO), for earlier events and documents.

[26] *See* Order No. 45 (2007).

[27] *See* Order No. 45 (2007, art. 3).

technologies or designs or instigates any other person to submit multiple patent applications involving evidently plagiarized existing technologies or designs."

Before the administrative adjustment in 2013, the preliminary examination system for utility model patent applications implemented in China did not allow the use of search methods, which inevitably caused "examination of obvious substantive defects" in the utility model patent examination process to be de facto useless in the actual examination process. The administrative adjustment in 2013 fixed this institutional loophole by stipulating that:

> Where a utility model may involve an abnormal application, such as the obvious copying of prior art or the repeated submission of an application for a patent whose content is apparently identical in substance, the examiners shall, on the basis of the comparative documents retrieved or information obtained through other means, examine whether the application for a utility model patent is obviously lacking in novelty.[28]

Subsequently, the SIPO issued the Decision of the State Intellectual Property Office on Amending the Several Provisions on Regulating Patent Application Activities (2017)[29] and the amended Article 3[30] of the previously released Several Provisions of the State Intellectual Property Office on Regulating Patent Application Activities in 2007 expanded coverage of the definition of "abnormal patent application activities".

Even with these reforms, the view of many in the government was that abnormal patent applications were neither sufficiently under control nor completely eliminated. Thus, in 2021 the CNIPA published the Notice by the China National Intellectual Property Administration of Further Strictly Regulating Patent Application Activities.[31] This is the first time that the CNIPA institutionally underscored the necessity of "eliminating abnormal patent application activities not intended for protecting

[28] *See* Order No. 67 (2013, part I).

[29] *See* Order No. 75 (2017).

[30] *See* Order No. 75 (2017, part I).

> In item (1), "or instigates any other person to submit multiple patent applications of evidently similar content" is deleted.
>
> In item (2), "or instigates any other person to submit multiple patent applications involving evidently plagiarized existing technologies or designs" is deleted.
>
> One item is added as item (3):
>
> "(3) The same entity or individual submits multiple patent applications in which different materials, ingredients, proportions and components, among others, are simply replaced by each other or re-combined."
>
> One item is added as item (4):
>
> "(5) The same entity or individual submits multiple patent applications for the product's shape, pattern or color randomly generated by computer technologies."
>
> Item (3) is renumbered as item (6) and amended to read:
>
> "(6) help any other person to submit or the patent agency submits patent applications as set forth in items (1) to (5) of this article."

[31] *See* Notice by the China National Intellectual Property Administration (2021d).

innovation" and thereby eliminating previous undesirable effects of "seriously disturbing administrative order, injuring the public interest, interfering with enterprise innovation, wasting public resources, and undermining the patent system" for the sake of "strictly implementing the requirements for high-quality development, further regulating patent application activities, improving the quality of patent applications". Soon after this Notice, the CNIPA formally released the Measures for Regulating Patent Application Activities,[32] which is addressed in the next section.

11.2 MAIN FEATURES OF EXISTING CHINESE UTILITY MODEL PATENT LEGAL SYSTEM

11.2.1 *Protection Standards for Utility Models*

The substantive standard for issuing Chinese utility model patents is one of the key components in the Chinese utility model patent legal system and one of the most controversial as well. To a great extent, the quality of Chinese utility model patents is contingent on a set of substantive standards. As shown above, many subsequent multi-level Chinese utility model patent-based institutional improvements also surround this key component.

The current protection standards are enshrined in article 22 of the 2020 Patent Law which states that a "utility model for which a patent is to be granted shall be novel, inventive and practically applicable". Particularly with regard to the standard of inventiveness, a salient distinction between invention patents and utility model patents is stressed, that is:

> Inventiveness means that, as compared with the technology existing before the date of application the invention has prominent substantive features and represents a notable progress and that the utility model patent has substantive features and represents progress.

In addition, there are detailed operating guidelines in the Guidelines for Patent Examination[33] issued by the CNIPA. Some of the proposed revisions are discussed in Section 3.2.

11.2.2 *Basic Process for Obtaining a Utility Model Patent*

The application process for utility model patents today is largely electronic via the China Patent Electronic Application Network.[34] Normally, the process comprises nine steps:

[32] *See* Announcement No. 411 (2021).
[33] *See* Order No. 78 (2023).
[34] *See* China Patent Electronic Application Network 2024.

1. Going through the e-application for user registration
2. Preparing to create the electronic application documents
3. Making electronic application documents
4. Checking the documents before submission
5. Signing with a digital certificate
6. Submitting documents and receiving receipt
7. Receiving electronic notification of application
8. Submitting supporting documents
9. Checking the website for post-application information

Specifically with respect to step 8, a brief explanation is in order:

> For the relevant documents that should be submitted in the original form according to the Patent Law and its rules for implementation and the Patent Examination Guidelines, the applicant may submit only the electronically scanned original documents; If the electronically scanned documents cannot be submitted due to actual limitations, the original documents can be submitted. In the former case, the examiner may, if necessary, require the applicant to submit the original within a specified time limit.[35]

11.2.3 *Chinese Utility Model Patent to Invention Patent Conversion Mechanism*

Under the patent law, a utility model patent can be converted into an invention patent provided that some legally defined requirements are met. Article 9 of the patent law embodies the essential requirement in this regard:

> Only one patent right can be granted for the same invention. However, where the same applicant applies for both a utility model patent and an invention patent for the same invention on the same day, and the patent right for utility model obtained earlier has not been terminated, and the applicant has declared to renounce the patent right for utility model, a patent right for invention may be granted.[36]

Generally speaking, the reasons which would motivate the holder of a utility model patent to convert it to an invention patent essentially depend on commercial strategy. To be more specific, for an invention related to a product that can be put on the market quickly and that can easily be imitated, if its market life is expected to be relatively short, a utility model patent is often applied for, so as to achieve the purpose of obtaining the patent right protection as quickly as possible. On the contrary, an invention patent is usually applied for if more stringent inventiveness standard can also be met.

[35] *See* China Patent Electronic Application Network 2024.
[36] *See* Patent Law 2020.

For an invention related to a product with both anticipated short-term and long-term market benefits, the applicant will often consider applying for both an invention patent and a utility model patent, if possible. In this way, the utility model patent application can be authorized earlier and protection will be available more quickly. Then, after the invention patent is granted, the protection can continue to be extended via the invention patent.

11.2.4 *Validity-Challenging Procedure for an Authorized Utility Model Patent*

A utility model patent is prima facie valid until proven otherwise. There are two viable ways of challenging an authorized utility model patent's validity in China. The first one is the administrative reexamination procedure governed by the Patent Reexamination and Invalidation Department of the CNIPA.[37] Examples of these challenges are publicly available on the website of this department.[38]

The second way is through the civil judicial procedure by competent courts. There are many adjudicated legal cases in which the validity of asserted utility model patents has been challenged. At least some of them are available online. The case *Bai Wanqing v. Chengdu* has been categorized as a guiding case (指导案例) by the Judicial Committee of the Supreme People's Court.[39] In this case, on the basis of the specifications of the patent involved and the evidence provided by Bai Wanqing, the court found that it was difficult for technicians in the field to determine the specific scope or definition of "high magnetic inductivity" as claimed, nor could they accurately determine the protection scope of the claims and make a substantive comparison for infringement between the asserted patent and the alleged infringing product. Therefore, the Supreme People's Court upheld the lower court's determination that Bai Wanqing failed to produce evidence to prove that the alleged infringing product fell within the scope of the claims.

11.2.5 *Judicial Protection Mechanism for Utility Model Patents*

The ultimate institutional avenue for assessing the substantive standards of patentability for utility model patents is the judiciary. In order to be in line with Article 62.5 of the TRIPS Agreement, which stipulates that administrative decisions in any proceeding for the acquisition and maintenance of intellectual property rights must be subject to judicial review, the 2000 Patent Law removed the prior finality of the Reexamination Board's decision on the validity of the patent right for utility models and designs.

[37] As regards an official introduction to this department, including history, main responsibilities, organization, examination system, examination procedure, and a number of latest statistics, see CNIPA 2021a.

[38] *See* CNIPA 2024.

[39] See Bai Wanqing (2015).

Today, the judicial assessment of utility model patents has been playing an increasingly important role. In this specific context, a recently noteworthy case finally adjudicated by the Guangdong High People's Court, *Gree v. Aux*,[40] set a new national record in terms of the amount of damages (40 million RMB) arising from an alleged Chinese utility model patent infringement. According to a judge in this court, "this is the largest intellectual property case ever awarded by a court in the field of home appliances."[41]

11.3 DEFICIENCIES AND DEVELOPMENT TRENDS OF CHINESE UTILITY MODEL PATENT LEGAL SYSTEM

China's current utility model patent legal system has pros and cons. On one hand, it has advantages such as "the rapid protection of short-lived innovations".[42] On the other hand, deficiencies have long been identified, particularly over the past decade, which have resulted in national attention and corresponding multi-level official institutional revisions to the law.

11.3.1 *Main Deficiencies of the Chinese Utility Model Patent Legal System*

There are two principal types of deficiencies in China's current utility model patent legal system. One of these deficiencies is shared by utility model patent systems around the globe: the existence of a large quantity of UMPs with low quality.[43] The other type of deficiency, which is a series of domestic subsidy-related and tax-related industrial policies mostly misused by domestic enterprises, is more indigenous[44] in nature. Even so, in practice, these two kinds of deficiencies seem to be inseparable from each other.

11.3.1.1 Utility Model Patent-Based Intrinsic Deficiencies

Chinese utility model patent-based controversies are due in part to the long-debated proliferation of "junk patents" or, at a minimum, "questionable patents". The definition

[40] *See* Case No. 390, First Instance (Guangdong High People's Ct. 2017); Case No. 1132, Second Instance (Guangdong High People's Ct. 2018).

[41] *See* Chen 2020, 85–89.

[42] *See* Naumann 1958, 803.

[43] *See* Naumann 1958, 814 ("... there are already far-too many patents, whose level of invention is not very high").

[44] China has increasingly realized the undesirably detrimental effects of crafting and implementing those subsidy-related and tax-related industrial policies in recent years. As a result, some corrective measures have been implemented. For instance, the CNIPA released the Notice on Continuously Strictly Regulating Patent Application Behavior so as to gradually reduce all kinds of financial support for patent grants by at least 25 percentage points per year until all are eliminated by 2025. The ultimate objective of this Notice is to further eliminate the adverse effects of evaluation indicators and patent subsidy policies, place greater emphasis on high-quality development, and correct the tendency to blindly pursue quantity. See Xinhua News Agency 2022.

of "questionable patent" is subject to different opinions. According to Tian Lipu, former director of CNIPA, there is an essential difference between "questionable patents" and "junk patents".[45] The terminology of "questionable patent" refers to a patent whose scope of protection is too broad or the patent right per se does not comply with the relevant provisions of the Patent law even after the patent is granted. The terminology of "junk patents" refers to patents that do not contain any innovative content. These so-called "junk patents" are concentrated in two areas: utility model and design.[46]

These "abnormal" patents have triggered serious concerns at home and abroad. About a decade ago, many observers of China's patent system equated "junk patents" with "utility model patents".[47] This observation echoed the corresponding public sentiments concerning the often-reported "low-quality" status of utility model patents. Yet there may be only a small difference between patents that claim a trifling technical improvement and patents that have no innovative content. Consequently, to some degree, as long as the Chinese utility model patent legal system exists in its current form, the issuance of Chinese utility model patents on low-quality inventions may be inevitable.

11.3.1.2 Chinese Utility Model Patent Filing Trends and Responses

According to WIPO, in 2021, China received 1.59 million patent applications, more than twice as many as the United States.[48] Moreover, as regards utility model patents, the vast majority of applications worldwide are filed by Chinese applicants.[49] As indicated by WIPO, there were 2,852,219 Chinese utility model patent applications in 2021 with 99.76 percent filed by domestic applicants (2,845,318 domestic applications).[50] Moreover, even though the working rate of Chinese utility model patents, as measured by the CNIPA, has been increasing steadily over the past

[45] Observers argued that "patent subsidies incentivize applicants to file opportunistic applications for inventions of low patentability or low value that would have not been filed without those subsides. Thus they claim that most filings in this China patent boom are so-called 'junk inventions'." *see* Lei et al. 2013, 2.

[46] *See* Legal Daily 2005.

[47] *See e.g.*, Prud'homme 2012 ("particularly observers of China's patent system, appear to only consider invention patents as of good quality, whereas all non-invention patents (or utility models in particular), are 'junk' (low quality)".). See also Moga 2012, 8 (noting that "the Chinese utility model patent – which, in 2011, represented 35.8% of the 1,633,347 patent applications filed in China – is contrary to the national innovation initiatives and threatens the health and growth of Chinese business that it was intended to help."). In contrast, other sharply opposite views regard China's utility model patents as treasure rather than trash. *See e.g.*, Lui 2014, 253 (stressing that China's utility model patents are "absolutely not trash at all. On the contrary, they, in fact, are definitely treasure.").

[48] *See* World Intellectual Property Organization 2022a, 9.

[49] *See* Yu 2017, 51–58.

[50] *See* CNIPA 2022b.

five years, nearly 40 percent of granted Chinese utility model patents have not been practically used via effective working.[51]

Commentators have theorized that the underlying cause of these filing trends, especially in the past 10 years, is attributable, at least in part, to domestic subsidy-related and tax-related industrial policies that incentivized the filing of patent applications. These policies had been initially formulated to encourage domestic innovation but were misused by many domestic enterprises that pursued an "innovation by numbers" strategy designed to maximize patent filings without regard to the quality of the underlying inventions.[52]

11.3.2 *Development Trends in the Chinese Utility Model Patent Legal System*

Long vexed by the institutional issues described above, China has been exploring a range of reforms to the Chinese utility model patent legal system. Reform proposals have been made both by academics and legal practitioners, some of which are briefly summarized below.[53]

11.3.2.1 Domestic Model Patent-Related Reform Proposals

Some scholars have proposed a range of modifications to the Chinese utility model patent legal system to avoid its worst abuses. For example, three Chinese scholars have recently argued that:

> A more rational Chinese utility model patent institution should follow the path of Japan and South Korea and take the initiative to considerably reduce the institutional dependence when nearing or entering the phase of high-income countries. Therefore, the government should weaken the incentive policy for the number of utility model patents, take the initiative to adjust the examination system for utility model patents, steer the market to decrease the use of Chinese utility model patent institution timely, and enhance the contribution of the patent system to economic growth.[54]

A somewhat more radical view is that the Chinese utility model patent legal system should be completely abolished instead of being partially revised. One commentator adopting this position has noted that:

> Without public examination of utility model patents, the public cannot raise objections to patented technologies. Once a utility model patent is granted, it becomes a deadly tool for some big companies to beat small ones. Invalidation

[51] *See* China Patent Survey Report 2021, 33.

[52] *See* Li and Zheng 2016, 60–73.

[53] *See e.g.*, Zhu 2015 (proposing a four-dimensional revamping scheme for improving Chinese utility model patents' quality).

[54] *See* Mao et al. 2018.

and litigation cost a lot of money for small companies, and they can't afford to have a bunch of patents thrown at them.[55]

In response to this view, the CNIPA officially responded:

> For more than 30 years, the Chinese utility model patent system has played an important and positive role in stimulating innovation enthusiasm, promoting technology transformation and protecting innovation achievements. As for the problem that 'there is no public examination of the patent for utility model and the public cannot raise objections to the patented technology' mentioned by you, the following measures can be taken under the current institutional framework: First, for the authorized utility model patents, any entity or individual that considers that the grant of the patent right does not comply with the relevant provisions of the Patent Law may file a request for invalidation; Second, in order to make up for the deficiency that the application for a utility model patent has not been substantively examined, paragraph 2 of Article 61 of the Patent Law provides that, where a patent infringement dispute involves a utility model patent, the people's court or the administrative department for patent affairs may require the patentee or an interested party to produce an evaluation report on the patent right made by the CNIPA; Third, in a patent infringement dispute, if the accused infringer has evidence to prove that the technology applied is prior art, he may file a defense against prior art in accordance with Article 62 of the Patent Law.[56]

Given such indications by CNIPA, it is unlikely that the Chinese utility model patent system will be abolished in the near future. Rather, the key question is how to reform it so as to eliminate its worst abuses.

Recently, the patent community in China was called upon to consider ways that the Chinese utility model patent legal system could be modified to eliminate its worst abuses. In the past decade, in response to this badly needed answer for this key question, numerous suggestions have been offered from various perspectives.

11.3.2.2 Further Proposals for Chinese Utility Model Patent-Focused Institutional Overhauls

Chinese utility model patent reform measures are currently going on in China, especially on the national level. The most significant of these is focused on raising the level of innovation quality embodied in utility model patents by requiring that utility model patent applications be substantively examined for inventiveness. In reality, the arguments for adding a substantive examination mechanism for evaluating inventiveness of utility model patents are not new. Such arguments have previously been made by academia and even some high-level government

[55] The State Council of the People's Republic of China 2021a.

[56] The State Council of the People's Republic of China 2021a

officials.[57] These earlier actions laid the groundwork for the CNIPA to officially identify in 2021 the necessity of "eliminating abnormal patent application activities not intended for protecting innovation" for the sake of "strictly implementing the requirements for high-quality development, further regulating patent application activities, improving the quality of patent applications" in its above-mentioned Notice.[58] As of this writing, two noteworthy Chinese utility model patent-centered national initiatives are being advanced aimed at raising the level of innovation quality embodied in utility model patents.

First, in 2021, the CNIPA released a Notice on Soliciting Public Opinions on the Draft Revision of the Guidelines for Patent Examination (Draft for Comment)[59] which addressed the level of inventiveness in the process of preliminary examination of utility model patent applications. The relevant sentence in the Notice reads:

> Based on the information available to the examiner regarding the prior art, the examiner may examine whether the application for a utility model patent lacks obvious inventiveness.

The incorporation of this new factor of "obvious inventiveness" into the Guidelines for Patent Examination is intended to reduce the number of low-quality Chinese utility model patents that are issued.

The second initiative is the Promotion Plan for In-depth Implementation of the Opinions on Strengthening the Protection of Intellectual Property Rights[60] (hereinafter the Promotion Plan). This is the latest comprehensive national administrative plan aimed at effectively promoting the recent top-level IP strategy co-issued by General Office of the CPC Central Committee and The State Council.[61] The Promotion Plan covers a wide range of IP-based affairs, including 114 items of national emphasis, including one relating to utility model patents. The 26th item of the Promotion Plan reads:

> To push forward the reform of the utility model patent institution and introduce an examination mechanism for screening utility model patent applications that obviously lack inventiveness. (To be completed by the end of December 2025)

Again, this statement reiterates the Chinese government's desire to reduce the number of low-quality patents, including Chinese utility model patents, that are being issued.

57 *See e.g.*, Chen 2013 (arguing that "adding a substantive examination mechanism for evaluating inventiveness when appropriate").

58 *See* CNIPA 2021a.

59 *See* CNIPA 2021b. In addition, on October 31, 2022, the CNIPA issued the Notice on Soliciting Public Opinions on the Draft Revision of the Guidelines for Patent Examination (Draft Again for Comment). CNIPA 2022a.

60 *See* CNIPA 2022c.

61 *See* The State Council of the People's Republic of China 2019.

The core concern in implementing this reform will thus be defining an appropriate level of non-obviousness for screening utility model patent applications. In doing so, policy makers should be cautious against introducing an excessively high level of inventiveness, which could blur the line between invention patents and utility model patents and thus render the utility model patent legal system meaningless.

To date, the Detailed Rules for the Implementation of the Patent Law of the People's Republic of China has recently been amended at the end of 2023 and has just come into effect on January 20, 2024.[62] Article 50 of this set of amended Rules explicitly stipulates the above-mentioned enhanced non-obviousness screening standard for utility model patent applications. In addition, to be in tandem with the implementation of the amended Detailed Rules for the Implementation of the Patent Law, Guidelines for Patent Examination was amended at a synchronized pace, which has just come into effect on January 20, 2024 as well.[63] According to the newly amended Guidelines, "examiners can examine whether a utility model patent application obviously lacks inventiveness based on the information they have obtained about the prior art."[64]

Even so, it is likely that the final achievement of this socially desirable optimal level of inventiveness will necessitate a continuum of adjustments. As a result, the real implementation effects of the above-mentioned reforms remain to be seen in the coming years.

Although it is impossible to second-guess all future Chinese utility model patent-based institutional reforms, there is no doubt that China will make this legal institution better-suited to its increasingly stressed innovation-related development landscape for the sake of achieving the ultimate strategic objective enshrined in *An Outline for Building a Powerful Intellectual Property Nation (2021–2035)*.[65] That is, Chinese utility model patent-based institutional refinements might be regarded as a means of "achieving a high level of scientific and technological self-reliance, stepping into the forefront of innovative countries".[66]

11.4 CONCLUSION

China originally introduced the Chinese utility model patent system in response to external pressures on its intellectual property system. Then, in an effort to bolster domestic innovative activity, it introduced a series of incentives and subsidies that resulted in overuse of the Chinese utility model patent system, yielding a large number of low-quality utility model patents for which it has received both domestic and international criticism. In an effort to reform this system, China has introduced

62 *See* Detailed Rules (2023).
63 *See* Order No.78 (2023).
64 *See* Order No. 78 (2023, 70).
65 *See* The State Council of the People's Republic of China 2021b.
66 *See* The State Council of the People's Republic of China 2022.

new procedural requirements to its utility model patent legal system, including, most importantly, a substantive examination to determine whether an application obviously lacks inventiveness. While the precise definition of this threshold is yet to be developed, policy makers should seek to maintain at least some difference between utility model patents, which serve valuable social goals, and ordinary patents, which are subject to a higher standard of inventiveness. Hopefully, these essentially self-driven ongoing technology-enhancing initiatives may benefit not only China but also contribute to a globally virtuous cycle of technological competition.[67]

[67] Coincidentally, China's ongoing inventiveness-enhancing moves towards further optimization of the Chinese utility model patent system echoed some notable foreign proposals for desirable improvements to the Chinese utility model patent system, especially from technically advanced countries or regions. E.g., the EU put forward a specific suggestion on improving the Chinese utility model patent registration mechanism by introducing a higher threshold as regards the inventive step. See European Commission 2023b, 19.

12

Utility Models in Japan

Masabumi Suzuki

Japan introduced its utility model system in 1905, twenty years after the introduction of the patent system in 1885. Although the utility model system has been maintained to this day, the content and use of the system have changed considerably over the past century.

In rough summary, Japan's utility model system played a major role in the development of Japanese industrial technology until the 1970s. That is, until the 1970s, the number of applications for utility model registrations exceeded that for patents. However, with the improvement of the Japanese industry's technological capabilities and other factors, patent applications began to outnumber utility model applications around 1980, and the number of utility model applications declined sharply from 1985 onward. In response, the utility model system was extensively revised in 1993, including the abolition of substantive examinations, with the aim of making the system more attractive by ensuring that the system provides early protection for technologies with short life cycles. However, this revision caused problems, such as the loss of stability of rights, and the number of utility model applications has continued to decline to the present day. The recent utilization of the utility model system in Japan is about 5,000 applications/registrations per year.

This chapter first provides an overview of the current utility model system in Japan. Second, the historical background of the system is reviewed. Third, the recent use of the utility model system is presented. Fourth, an evaluation and some proposals for the revision of the utility model system in Japan will be presented.

12.1 OUTLINE OF THE CURRENT UTILITY MODEL SYSTEM IN JAPAN

12.1.1 *Overview*

The current utility model system in Japan can be summarized as follows. Supplementary explanations will be provided in the next section.

- The subject of protection is a "device," which relates to the shape, structure, or combination of articles.[1] Here, "device" means "the creation of technical ideas utilizing the laws of nature."[2]
- The substantive requirements for utility model rights are novelty, inventive step (it must not be "extremely easy to devise"), and industrial applicability.[3] In addition, the first-to-file principle is adopted.[4]
- The examination by the Japan Patent Office (JPO) is conducted on the formal aspects of the application only, and not on its substantive aspects.
- The right holder may enforce the right only after obtaining a Utility Model Technical Opinion from the JPO and warning the alleged infringer by presenting the Opinion.[5] Upon the request for a Utility Model Technical Opinion, the JPO examiner conducts a substantive examination of each claim and evaluates the validity of the utility model right.[6]
- Term of protection is 10 years from filing date.[7]
- Criminal penalties may be imposed for infringement of utility model rights.[8]
- Conversion is possible among applications for utility model registrations, patents, and industrial design registrations.[9]
- The invalidation trial system is available to dispute the validity of a patent or utility model.
- Utility model registrations are published in the Gazette published by the JPO.[10] The information in the Gazette can be accessed online by anyone from the Japan Platform for Patent Information (J-PlatPat) provided by the National Center for Industrial Property Information and Training (INPIT).[11]

12.1.2 *Subject of Protection*

A "device," the subject of protection of utility model rights, is defined as "the creation of technical ideas utilizing the laws of nature."[12] In contrast, an "invention,"

1 Articles 1 and 3(1) of the Utility Model Act (hereinafter, the "Act"). An English translation of the Act is available at www.japaneselawtranslation.go.jp/en/laws/view/4259.

2 Article 2(1) of the Act.

3 Article 3 of the Act.

4 Article 7 of the Act.

5 Article 29*bis* of the Act.

6 Article 12 of the Act.

7 Article 15 of the Act.

8 Article 56 of the Act.

9 Article 10 of the Act, Article 46 of the Patent Act, and Article 13 of the Industrial Design Act.

10 Article 14(3) of the Act.

11 www.j-platpat.inpit.go.jp/s0000/ja.

12 Article 2(1) of the Act.

which is the subject of patent protection, is defined as "the highly advanced creation of technical ideas utilizing the laws of nature."[13]

Utility model rights are granted for "a device which relates to the shape, structure, or combination of articles."[14] Therefore, a technical idea relating to an article that does not have a certain form (such as a composition of matter) or an idea relating to a method does not fall under the scope of protection. A part of an article, that is, a component part of an article that is not treated as an independent article, is also considered an article.

12.1.3 *Application Procedures and Costs*

The utility model application procedure is shown in Figure 12.1.

The cost of the application is as follows.[15]

- application fee: JPY 14,000
- registration fee per year: JPY 2,100 + number of claims × 100
- patent attorney's fee (estimate): JPY 150,000 – 250,000

12.1.4 *"Basic Requirements" and Registration*

When an application for a utility model registration is filed, the JPO examines whether the application meets the "basic requirements," but not any substantive requirements, and if the basic requirements are met, the utility model is registered.[16] The JPO may order an amendment to an application that does not meet the basic requirements.[17] If no amendment is made within the time specified in the amendment order, the JPO may dismiss the application.[18]

The basic requirement means that the application does not fall under the following categories:[19]

- The application is not for a device that can be subject to protection, that is, a device relating to the shape, structure, or combination of articles.
- Violation of public order and morals
- Violation of formal description requirements for claims
- Violation of the requirement of unity provided in Article 6 of the Act
- Material inadequacy in the description, etc.

[13] Article 2(1)(i) of the Patent Act.

[14] Article 3 of the Act. For the concepts of "article," "shape," "structure," and "combination," see part X, chapter 1, "2. Judgment on the Basic Requirements" of the JPO's "Examination Guidelines for Patent and Utility Model" available at www.jpo.go.jp/e/system/laws/rule/guideline/patent/tukujitu_kijun/index.html.

[15] US$1 ≈ JPY 150, as of November 2023.

[16] Article 14(2) of the Act.

[17] Article 6*bis* of the Act.

[18] Article 2*ter* of the Act.

[19] Article 6*bis* of the Act.

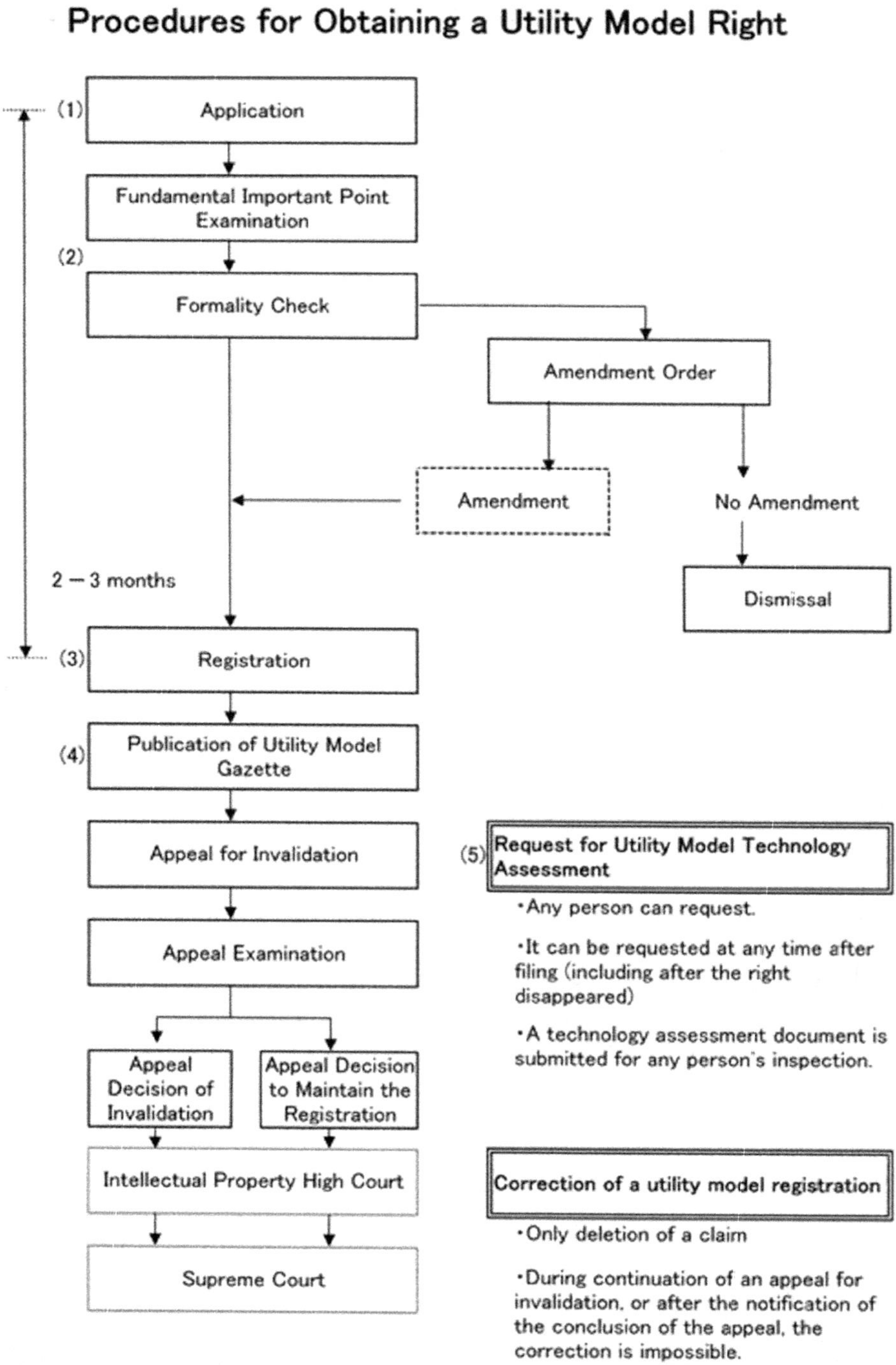

FIGURE 12.1 Procedures for obtaining a Japanese utility model right

12.1.5 *Substantive Requirements and Technical Opinion by the JPO*

Substantive requirements for utility model rights include novelty, inventive step, and industrial applicability of the filed device relating to the shape, structure, or combination of articles.[20] In addition, the application must be the first to be filed for the same device (first-to-file principle).[21]

Of these, the inventive step requirement is provided as meaning that a person skilled in the art cannot "very easily" devise from publicly known devices.[22] In contrast, the inventive step requirement for patents is provided as meaning that the filed invention is simply not "easy to invent" from prior arts.[23]

The JPO does not examine these substantive requirements as a matter of course at the time of filing the application. After filing an application, any person may request the Commissioner of the Patent Office for a Utility Model Technical Opinion, and upon such request, the examiner will evaluate whether or not the claimed device meets the substantive requirements.[24]

It is understood that the Utility Model Technical Opinion by the JPO does not, by itself, have any determinative legal effect on the validity of the right.[25]

12.1.6 *Conversion of Application*

Applications for utility model registration, patents, and industrial design registration may be converted into one another, provided that a request for the conversion is made within a certain period of time.[26] The holder of a utility model right may also file a patent application based on their utility model registration for a period not exceeding three years from the filing date of the utility model registration.[27] In such a case, the patent application will be deemed to have been filed at the time of filing of the application for utility model registration. In addition, the utility model right must be waived at the time of filing the patent application.

[20] Article 3 of the Act.

[21] Articles 7 and 3*bis* of the Act.

[22] Article 3(2) of the Act.

[23] Article 29(2) of the Patent Act. See Section 12.4 for a critical view of the actual implementation of these requirements.

[24] Article 12 of the Act.

[25] See the decision of the Tokyo District Court of December 7, 1999, 1999 (Gyo U) 216.

[26] Article 10 of the Act, Article 46 of the Patent Act, and Article 13 of the Industrial Design Act. For example, an application for utility model registration may be converted to a patent application within three years after the application. A patent application may be converted to an application for utility model registration until the earlier of either three months from the date on which the certified copy of the examiner's initial decision rejecting the patent application is served, or nine years and six months after the filing date of the patent application.

[27] Article 46*bis* of the Patent Act.

12.1.7 *Utility Model Rights and Infringement*

Once a utility model is registered, a utility model right arises.[28] A utility model right is an exclusive right to work a registered utility model in the course of business.[29] Here, "working" means the act of manufacturing, using, assigning, leasing, exporting, importing, or offering for assignment or lease an article pertaining to a device.[30]

A utility model right expires after 10 years from filing date.

For infringement of a utility model right, the right holder may claim civil remedies such as injunction[31] and compensation for damages.[32] There are special provisions concerning the presumption of the amount of damages in the Act.[33]

The holder of utility model rights may not exercise their right against an infringer until they give a warning by presenting the technical opinion report pertaining to their registered utility model.[34]

Criminal penalties (imprisonment with work for a term not exceeding five years and/or a fine not exceeding 5 million yen) may be provided for infringement of utility model rights.[35]

12.1.8 *Procedure for Invalidation*

Any person may file a request with the JPO for a trial to invalidate a granted utility model. At the trial, a panel consisting of three (or five in exceptional cases) administrative judges examines the validity of the utility model registration and invalidates it when the panel finds a violation of basic or substantive requirements or any other reason.[36] A party dissatisfied with the decision by the panel may appeal to the Intellectual Property High Court.

In addition, in a lawsuit concerning infringement of a utility model right, the alleged infringer may assert that the utility model registration has grounds for invalidation and prevent the alleged infringer from exercising their rights.[37]

[28] Article 14(1) of the Act.
[29] Article 16 of the Act.
[30] Article 2(3) of the Act.
[31] Article 27 of the Act.
[32] Article 709 of the Civil Code.
[33] Article 29 of the Act.
[34] Article 29*bis* of the Act.
[35] Article 56 of the Act.
[36] Article 37 of the Act.
[37] Article 30 of the Act and Article 104*ter* of the Patent Act.

12.1.9 *License*

The holder of a utility model right may grant a nonexclusive or exclusive license.[38] The licensee of an exclusive license registered with the JPO may seek an injunction or compensation for damages from an infringer.[39]

12.2 HISTORICAL DEVELOPMENT OF JAPANESE INTELLECTUAL PROPERTY LAW AND THE UTILITY MODEL ACT

12.2.1 *Establishment of Intellectual Property System*

In 1867, Japan underwent a political revolution known as the Meiji Restoration, shifting from its previous system of rule by feudal lords of the samurai class to a modern system of governance. The Meiji government aimed to gain an equal footing with Western countries in diplomacy, commerce, and other areas, and rapidly developed various systems for a modern nation. This included the establishment of an intellectual property system. Specifically, the copyright system (Publication Ordinance) of 1869, the trademark system (Trademark Ordinance) of 1884, the patent system (Monopoly Patent Ordinance) of 1885, and the design system (Design Ordinance) of 1888 were established in succession. Then, the Constitution of the Empire of Japan was promulgated in 1889, the Diet was established in 1890, and in 1899, after deliberation by the Imperial Diet, the various ordinances were enacted as laws (the Patent Act, Design Act, Trademark Act, and Copyright Act). In the same year, 1899, Japan became a signatory to the Paris Convention for the Protection of Industrial Property Rights and the Berne Convention for the Protection of Copyright.

12.2.2 *Introduction of the Utility Model System*

In 1905, about 20 years after the introduction of the patent system, the utility model system was introduced in Japan by the Utility Model Act. The reasons for the introduction of the utility model system were as follows:[40]

> First, the need to protect "new practical devices" and "light inventions"[41] that did not fall under the definition of inventions covered by the patent system was recognized. This recognition was fueled by an awareness that the level of technology in Japan's domestic industry was still inferior to that of Europe and the U.S.,

[38] Articles 18 and 19 of the Act.

[39] Article 27 of the Act and Article 709 of the Civil Code.

[40] JPO 1984, vol. 1, 192–194. The footnotes to the following quote are not in the original, but added by the author.

[41] In the Diet deliberations on the Utility Model Act, these expressions were used by the proponents of the bill. See JPO 1984, vol. 1, 193–194.

that the establishment of a patent system would further increase the number of applications by foreigners, and that the system at that time did not provide protection for "utility model-like new devices that fall somewhere between inventions and designs".

Second, the introduction of the Utility Model Protection Law in Germany in 1891 had a significant impact on Japan.[42]

12.2.3 *Changes in the Utility Model System*

12.2.3.1 First Utility Model Act

The essence of the Utility Model Act of 1905 may be summarized as follows.

First, the scope of protection was defined as "a practical new device relating to the shape, structure, or combination of industrial articles." As discussed above, the current Utility Model Act protects "devices relating to the shape, structure or combination of articles," and there are differences in the inclusion of "practical" and "industrial" in the definition. We will see later that the 1921 Act introduced the concept of "type."

Second, novelty was a requirement for registration. Specifically, novelty was recognized if the invention was not identical or similar to a device that, at the time of application, was in public use in Japan or described in a public publication concerning the same or similar goods. The original Utility Model Act, like the original Patent Act, did not provide for an inventive step requirement, and, in effect, the inventive step requirement was examined within the novelty requirement, since a device that was "similar" to a publicly known device was not considered to satisfy the novelty requirement.

Third, the first-to-file principle was adopted, whereby the first to file an application for the same device could obtain a registration.

Fourth, a substantive examination system was established. In other words, an examiner of the Patent Office examines all applications for novelty, first application, non-applicability of grounds for non-registration (violation of public order and morals, etc.), and the like.

Fifth, a system of conversion of applications was established. Specifically, it became possible to convert an application for a patent or a design registration into an application for a utility model registration. However, at this point in time, the system did not permit conversion of an application for a utility model registration into an application for a patent (the latter was permitted under the 1959 Law).

[42] After the Meiji Restoration, it was the German legal system that had the most significant influence on the modernization of the Japanese legal system. The field of intellectual property law was no exception, with the Patent Act and other legal systems modeled after the German system.

Sixth, the utility model right was considered to be an exclusive right to manufacture, sell, disseminate, or use the registered article. The term of protection was three years from registration, but could be extended for another three years upon request, for a total of six years.

Seventh, the invalidation trial system was established as a procedure to dispute the validity of utility model registrations. The JPO examined the validity of a registration based on a petition, and those who were dissatisfied with the decision of the JPO (trial decision) could appeal to a court. This mechanism basically remains the same today.

12.2.3.2 Until the 1921 Amendment

Subsequently, in the 1909 amendment, the Utility Model Act was amended to limit the effect of the utility model right to acts "in the course of business." The Industrial Design Act was also amended to the same effect at the same time. In 1916, the Utility Model Act was also amended to extend the duration of the utility model right by an additional four years. This allowed protection for up to ten years, instead of the previous term of six years (three years, and three years by extension). The reasons for this extension were that the previous six-year term was not sufficient to obtain profits from the market through products protected by the utility model right, and that the term of protection was too short compared to patent rights (the maximum term of protection at that time was twenty-five years) and industrial design rights (ten years at that time).[43]

In 1921, another amendment was made. In this amendment, first, the scope of protection of the utility model system was changed to "a practical type" relating to the shape, structure, or combination of articles. This change was made because of criticism that the conventional "device" was not substantially different from "invention," which was the subject of patent protection.[44] Here, "type" is a term modeled after "Muster" in German law. In the Diet debate on the amendment, the representative of the government explained that "type" meant the external form of an article.[45] In other words, a type was understood to be the specific form of an article.

Second, the 1921 amendment set the term of protection for utility model rights at ten years. The previous system allowed the term to be extended for up to ten years, but the new system provided uniform protection for a period of ten years.

Third, a compulsory licensing system was introduced. Under this system, where a holder of a utility model right was required to work a registered utility model or registered design of another person in order to work the utility model, and the other person refused to license the utility model or registered design right without

[43] JPO 1984, vol. 1, 316.
[44] JPO 1984, vol. 1, 431.
[45] Ibid.

justifiable reason, the holder could compel the other right holder to license the latter's right through a trial before the JPO.[46]

To mention the Paris Convention, the 1911 revision (Washington Act of 1911) clearly included the utility model in Article 2 of the National Treatment Principle. At this time, only Germany and Japan had a utility model system.[47] Furthermore, the Paris Convention Revision of 1925 (Hague Act of 1925) placed a definition of industrial property in Article 1, in which utility models were specifically mentioned. On the other hand, Article 2 on national treatment stopped enumerating individual industrial property (including utility models) and replaced it with the general term "industrial property."

12.2.3.3 Enactment of the 1959 Act (Current Law)

Japan suffered a devastating blow in World War II. After the war ended in 1945, the country began to rebuild, and in the process, a review of the industrial property system was conducted. In 1950, the "System Revision Study and Deliberation Office" was established within the JPO, and in 1951, an advisory council was established to study the revision of the industrial property system. As a result, the four industrial property laws (the Patent Act, Utility Model Act, Industrial Design Act, and Trademark Act) were enacted as entirely new laws in 1959, and these laws went into effect in 1960. These 1959 laws remain the current laws, although they have undergone many amendments since then.

The main changes in the 1959 Utility Model Act are, first, that the subject of protection was modified from "type" (since the 1921 Act) to "device" as a technical idea, returning to the concept of the original Act.

Second, a new inventive step requirement was established. As mentioned above, an inventive step was previously evaluated in the examination of the novelty requirement, but in 1959 this was made an independent requirement (similar amendments were made to the Patent Act).

Third, the conversion of an application for a utility model registration to an application for a patent or a design registration was permitted in addition to the previously permitted conversion of an application for a patent or a design registration to an application for a utility model registration.

In the process of reviewing the system in the 1950s, the abolition of the utility model system was also discussed. The main rationale advanced for abolition was the overlap with the patent system. The significance of the utility model system had long been debated. In addition, in the discussion for the 1959 revision, the scope of protection of the utility model system was going to be revised from the traditional

46 The compulsory licensing system exists in the current Act in a more expanded manner. See Articles 21–23 of the Act.

47 Ricketson 2015, 422.

"type" to "device" as a technical idea, and its character as a protection system for technical ideas similar to the patent system became clearer again. The question was raised as to whether the coexistence of the patent system and the utility model system was necessary.

However, the government argued for maintaining the utility model system, pointing out that the utility model system had been actively used, especially by small and medium-sized enterprises (SMEs), contributing to industrial development, and that if the utility model system were abolished, many of the subjects of the system would be incorporated into the patent system, which would mean a decline in the level of patented inventions. The argument was also made that the abolition of the utility model system would lead to the protection of technical ideas that would not be suitable for strong protection under the patent system, which would be contrary to the original purpose of the patent system.[48]

Regarding the significance of the utility model system at the time of the enactment of the 1959 Act, for example, a contemporaneous commentary by two renowned scholars explains:[49]

> In general, the Utility Model Act plays an extremely insufficient role in terms of a country's policy for technological development or in terms of its function as a market regulation, and even the necessity of its existence is questionable.
>
> However, despite such a nature of the Utility Model Act, it is clear that, both in reality and historically, Japan's utility model registration system has been used extensively and has fulfilled a significant function. In other words, the protection provided by the Utility Model Act in Japan is much stronger than the protection under the equivalent law in Germany, the mother country of utility model law, and since the enforcement of this Act in 1905, the number of applications for registration under this system has far exceeded that of patent applications. Needless to say, this fact clearly shows that the utility model registration system, which was originally not necessary to exist, is actually indispensable and plays an important role under Japan's industrial structure. This is a clear indication of the peculiarities inherent in the process of technological development, and thus in the industrial structure of Japan.
>
> The rapid expansion of the use of this system is testimony to the extremely low level of technology in Japan at the time, and the fact that most new technologies were either for light consumer goods, or for producer goods that were very low-level. The role of the Utility Model Act was further strengthened after World War I, albeit in a different aspect. Here, the imbalance in the industrial structure had to be adjusted in response to the fact that Japan's industries had established production of producer goods on the one hand and created small and medium-sized enterprises (SMEs) on the other. The coexistence of the Patent Act and the Utility Model Act became necessary as a system to deal with the dual structure of technology that emerged,

[48] JPO 1984, vol. 2, 285.

[49] Kaneko and Someya 1960, 456–457.

and the Utility Model Act began to function as a special market regulation for competition among SMEs, as a way to prevent collusion in the fierce competition among SMEs.

> In the postwar period, Japan's technology developed rapidly, mainly through the introduction of advanced technologies from Western countries. The division into a small number of large industrial sectors with a high level of technology (the so-called basic production goods and raw materials production sector and the general assembly industry sector) and small and medium-sized industrial sectors with a low level of technology (the so-called nondurable light consumer goods production sector and the secondary processed products production sector) became more extreme and the technology gap widened during the rapid development of technologies. And the qualitative development of so-called technological innovation was almost exclusively concentrated in the former.
>
> The Utility Model Act ... is forced to further strengthen its character as a market regulation against competition among SMEs with a low degree of technology, and, since the Patent Act is intended to protect only higher technology, the Utility Model Act is required to protect lower technology. ... Therefore, it is necessary to satisfy both aspects: on the one hand, to strengthen the character of the Utility Model Act as a market regulation, and on the other hand, to create a link between the subject matter of patents and the subject matter of utility model registrations, that is, to replace the distinction between the two by a quantitative rather than a qualitative one, so that they can interact with each other. In order to achieve this, the imbalance in the legal system and difficulties in the examination process caused by the lack of a clear distinction between the subject matter of the patent and utility model systems must be accepted.

12.2.3.4 1993 Law Amendment and Subsequent Amendments

Utility model applications in Japan have declined sharply since the late 1980s. Therefore, in the 1990s, a major review of the utility model system was conducted, and the Act was revised in 1993. First, the substantive examination was abolished and the system shifted to a nonexamination registration system. Second, the term of protection was shortened to six years from the filing date. The purpose of this amendment was to clarify the division of roles between the patent system and the utility model system as systems for the protection of technical ideas, and to simplify the latter into a system that provides early protection for technologies with short life cycles. Another reason for abolishing the substantive examination was to reduce the burden of patent and utility model examinations, which at the time were being delayed considerably.[50]

However, even after the 1993 revision of the Act, the number of applications for utility model registrations continued to decline, and the annual number of applications, which peaked at over 200,000 (in 1987), fell to less than 10,000 in 2000.

[50] Yoshifuji 1998, 702–703.

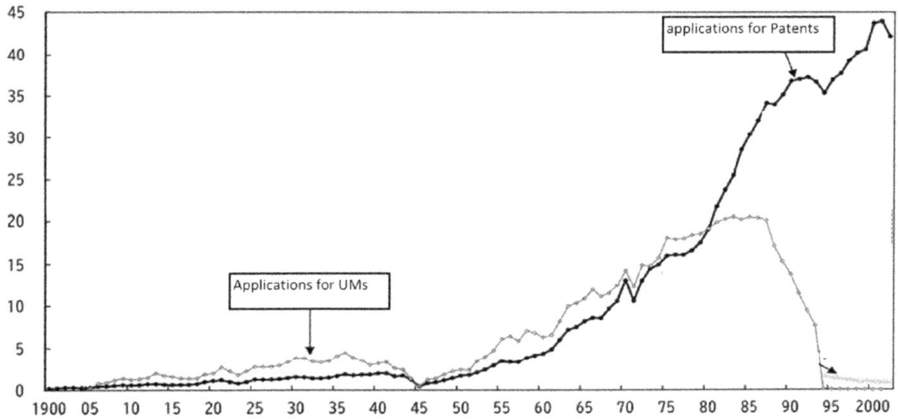

FIGURE 12.2 Applications for Japanese patents and utility models
Based on Advisory Council for the Japan Patent Office 2004, 8.

In 2005, in an effort to make the utility model system more attractive, the term of protection was extended (from six to ten years from the filing date) and a mechanism allowing patent applications based on utility model registrations was introduced.[51] However, the number of applications and registrations has been still on the decline, standing at around 5,000 per year in recent years (see below).

12.3 STATUS AND USE OF THE UTILITY MODEL SYSTEM

12.3.1 *Trends in Applications and Registrations*

Figure 12.2 shows trends in applications for utility model registrations and patents up to the year 2000. The number of applications for both types increased significantly during the period from around 1955 to 1973 which is called the "high-growth" period of the Japanese economy. Until around 1980, the number of applications for utility model registration was higher than that for patents. Thus, the utility model system was actively used until that time.

However, after around 1980, patent applications continued to increase significantly, while applications for utility model registrations remained almost flat and declined sharply from the late 1980s onward. This is believed to be due to the rise in the level of technology in Japan.

Recent trends in applications and registrations are shown in Figure 12.3 and Table 12.1.[52]

[51] Article 46*bis* of the Patent Act. See Section 12.1.6.

[52] The data are from the statistics available from the JPO website at www.jpo.go.jp/e/resources/statistics/index.html.

TABLE 12.1 *Utility models in Japan (2011–2022)*

	Utility models		Patents	
Year	Applications	Registrations	Applications	Registrations
2022	4,513	4,615	289,530	201,420
2021	5,239	5,499	289,200	184,372
2020	6,018	5,518	288,472	179,383
2019	5,241	5,033	307,969	179,910
2018	5,388	5,303	313,567	194,525
2017	6,106	6,024	318,481	199,577
2016	6,480	6,297	318,381	203,087
2015	6,860	6,695	318,721	189,358
2014	7,095	7,017	325,989	227,142
2013	7,622	7,363	328,436	277,079
2012	8,112	8,054	342,796	274,791
2011	7,984	7,595	342,610	238,323

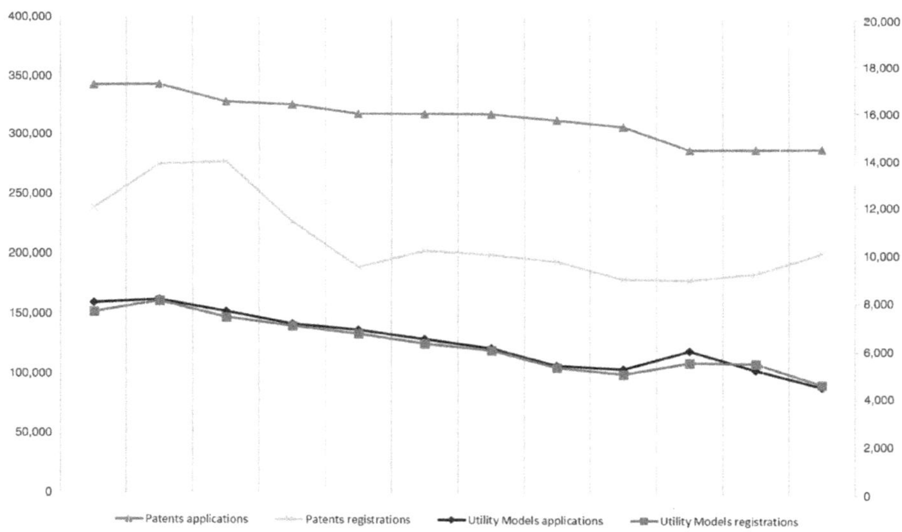

FIGURE 12.3 Applications and registrations for utility models (in units in the right axis) and patents (in units in the left axis) from 2011 to 2022

12.3.2 *Sectors Utilizing the System*

According to a list by the JPO,[53] the largest numbers of utility model applications in 2021 were made for furniture and household goods, transportation or packaging items, clothing, and medical or veterinary items.

[53] See JPO 2023, 22–24.

12.4 RECENT DISCUSSIONS ON THE SYSTEM

A research committee established by the Japan Patent Attorneys Association in 2021 has identified the following problems with the current utility model system in Japan.[54]

- It is difficult to exercise the rights. Because the rights are registered without substantive examination, the rights are not stable, and there is a restriction that rights can be exercised only after a warning is given by presenting a Utility Model Technical Opinion, making the system difficult for users to utilize.
- The scope of protection is too narrow and does not adequately respond to recent technological trends.
- With respect to the inventive step requirement, although the Act adopts a standard of being not "very easy to devise," distinguishing it from the inventive step requirement under the Patent Act, there is no substantive difference in the actual examination by the JPO.
- In recent years, the examination of patent applications in Japan has become more expeditious and the accelerated examination mechanisms are also available, making the advantages of early grant of rights in the utility model system relatively small.

Therefore, the committee recommended reform of the utility model system. Specifically, the proposed amendments include the following:

- Expand the scope of protection. The limitation that a device must relate to the shape, structure, or combination of articles should be abolished, and general devices (technological ideas) should be eligible for protection.
- Substantive examinations should be introduced as a mandatory or optional system.
- With regard to the inventive step requirement, the examination guidelines should be revised in order to appropriately implement the statutory language that it is not "very easy to devise."
- Shorten the term of rights protection.

A prominent scholar has also proposed a reform to make the utility model system more user-friendly for individual inventors and small high-tech companies, including by expanding the scope of protection, simplifying disclosure and claim forms, simplifying examination, and granting statutory nonexclusive licenses to third parties who agree to cross-license in the future.[55]

Despite the above recommendations, at this point, there is no explicit indication that the JPO will review the utility model system, and for the time being the status quo is likely to continue.

[54] First Team of the 2021 Committee on Patents 2022, 5.

[55] Takenaka 2021b.

13

Utility Models in Korea

Sang Jo Jong

13.1 HISTORY OF UTILITY MODEL PROTECTION IN KOREA

Just after the liberation of Korea from Japanese colonial rule, the US Military Government enacted the Patent Act in 1946, which contained statutory provisions on utility models as well as patent protection. However, due to the Korean War and social unrest, utility model applications under the Patent Act of 1946 were extremely insignificant. The National Reconstruction Supreme Council, which was established as a result of General Park Chung-hee's coup, enacted the Utility Model Act on December 31, 1961, while planning the first 5-year economic development plan.

Until the mid-1980s, Korea's economy developed rapidly with an average annual GDP growth rate of 9.5 percent, which depended mostly on highly educated workers with Korean companies learning Western technologies and improving them to suit domestic manufacturing conditions. Naturally, companies and technicians with low technological standards preferred utility model protection to patents.

Rapid economic developments in Korea[1] have caused substantial changes in both the country's general economic structure and the role of IP law. In the mid-1980s, Korea experienced numerous labor disputes and such rapid wage increases that its economic structure had to shift from labor-intensive industries to technology-intensive ones. And with its aggregate R&D/GDP ratio increasing to more than 2.5 percent, indigenous R&D capabilities of Korea began to grow markedly.[2] In 1986, all the relevant statutes regarding intellectual property rights were amended to significantly strengthen their protection. Since then, while the number of patent applications increased rapidly, the growth rate of utility model filings began to decline. In order to facilitate utility model registration, in 1999 the Korean government introduced a non-examination advance registration system by amending the

[1] The GDP per capita of Korea increased from US$158 in 1960 to US$2,834 in 1986, when intellectual property laws were amended. The World Bank 2024.

[2] Kim et al. 2012, 372.

Utility Model Act. The introduction of the advance registration system increased the number of utility model applications slightly, but after the abolition of the advance registration system in 2006, the trend of decreasing utility model applications accelerated.

13.2 STATUTORY RATIONALE

The Utility Model Act is designed to contribute to industrial development by protecting and encouraging the creation of practical devices and promoting the utilization thereof to promote the development of technology. The statutory rationale of utility model protection is exactly the same as that of patent protection with the only difference that the subject matter is a utility model device or a patentable invention.[3] Utility model devices are usually small inventions, that is, inventions that are one level lower than patented inventions. Until the mid-1980s, during the course of learning and improving Western technologies, domestic companies made some small inventions, that is, utility model devices which have been subject to legal protection under the Utility Model Act. The absence of utility model protection might have reduced incentives for domestic companies to engage in incremental innovations. In this sense, utility model protection allows developing economies to build up their indigenous innovative capacities. The statutory rationale for utility model protection is well supported by the statistical data showing that foreign applicants who filed the most utility model applications in Korea were Taiwanese companies in the 2000s and Chinese companies in the 2010s.

13.3 SUBJECT MATTER

A utility model right is granted for a device related to the shape or structure of an article or a combination of shape and structure of an article which is industrially practicable, novel, and nonobvious. Unlike the German Utility Model Act (see Chapter 6), the Korean statute protects only devices that are embodied in a specific form. Accordingly, a gaseous or liquid substance without a fixed shape, a new animal breed, a new plant, or a computer program as such is not subject to utility model protection in Korea. Likewise, a method that is not embodied in a specific form (such as a manufacturing method, usage method, or processing method) is also beyond protection. A manufacturing method may be described in the claims for utility model registration, and the utility model registration is not invalidated by the description of such a manufacturing method. However, it is not possible to claim the nonobviousness of a utility model based only on the manufacturing method described in the utility model claims.[4]

[3] The Utility Model Act, Section 1; the Patent Act, Section 1.

[4] Patent Ct., 2003He0915.

13.4 SUBSTANTIVE REQUIREMENTS

To obtain a utility model registration, a device must be industrially practicable, novel, and nonobvious, which is equivalent to the requirement for patent registration.[5] The only difference is that the nonobviousness of utility model devices may be lower than that of patentable inventions. Although the level of nonobviousness is described differently under the statutory provisions, neither examiners nor judges know how to distinguish the level of nonobviousness of utility model devices from that of patentable inventions.

During the course of examining the novelty of a utility model device, patented or patentable inventions are also considered as prior art. Likewise, utility model devices act as prior art against patent applications. The Patent Act denies patentability of an invention if the invention is identical to a device described in the specification or drawings initially accompanying an application for registration of a utility model when the utility model application has been filed before the filing date of the patent application at issue.[6] In addition, when an invention for which a patent application is filed is identical to a device for which an application for registration of a utility model is filed, only the applicant who filed first is entitled to a registration. If they are filed on the same date, only the person agreed upon both by the patent applicant and the utility model applicant may obtain registration.[7] In any event, the number of utility model applications has recently decreased so much that utility models are rarely cited in patent applications and such first-to-file disputes today are rare.

13.5 PROCEDURE

The basic process for obtaining a utility model is the same as for patents. Utility model devices have a relatively short lifespan in the market. Due to the long examination period of 37 months in Korea, utility model applications began to decline in the mid-1990s. Looking at the patent examination period in foreign countries at that time, it took 19 months in the US, 24 months in Japan, and 24 months in Europe.[8] The government introduced an advance registration or quick registration system to protect utility models or small inventions at an early stage and promote commercialization of technologies by small and medium-sized companies. According to the advance registration system that took effect on July 1, 1999, the Korean Intellectual Property Office only examines whether an application for utility model registration has formal and basic details. If there is a utility model registration application, anyone can request a technical evaluation of the filed utility model

[5] The Utility Model Act, Section 4; the Patent Act, Section 29.
[6] The Patent Act, Section 29(4).
[7] The Patent Act, Section 36(3).
[8] Chang 2017, 109.

device to the Commissioner of the Korean Intellectual Property Office.[9] The examiner at the Korean Intellectual Property Office examines whether or not the substantive requirements like novelty and nonobviousness for utility model registration are met as a result of technology evaluation, and then makes a decision to maintain or cancel the utility model registration.[10] In order for a utility model right holder or an exclusive licensee to assert or exercise their rights against an infringer, they must present a certified copy of the decision to maintain their utility model registration and give a warning to the alleged infringer.[11]

In the 2000s, the Korean Intellectual Property Office drastically increased the number of examiners and outsourced prior art searches to shorten the examination period by a third, taking 12.2 months as of 2021.[12] As the examination and processing period was dramatically shortened and the problem of misuse and abuse of utility model registration was raised, the previous examination-and-registration system was restored in 2006. Although the introduction of the advance registration system led to an increase in utility model applications in the short term, the number of applications started to decrease again from the fifth year after its introduction. After the abolition of the advance registration system, the number of applications began to decrease even more rapidly. Now there are debates as to whether the utility model system is still necessary or useful in Korea as there is no practical benefit to distinguish it from a patent in terms of registration requirements or examination period.[13] Since the government uses patent applications as the standard for research fund execution and evaluation, universities and public research institutes also prefer patent applications to utility model applications.[14]

The application fee for utility model registration is $16 (20,000 Korean Won) for online applications and $23 (30,000 Won) for paper applications. For applications written in a foreign language, the online application fee is $25 (32,000 Won) and the written application fee is $33 (42,000 Won). The utility model registration fee starts with $10 (12,000 Won) annually from the time of registration until the third year and increases to $20 (25,000 Won) annually from the fourth to sixth years, and $46 (600,000 Won) from the seventh to ninth years and $123 (160,000 Won) thereafter.[15] The cost of a patent attorney is typically less than $1,000 per case, so individual inventors can apply for utility model registration without much financial burden. That is why there are still some utility model applications.

It is also possible for a patent application (or its particular claims) to be converted to a utility model application. If a patent application for an invention is rejected by

9 The Utility Model Act, Section 21.
10 The Utility Model Act, Section 25.
11 The Utility Model Act, Section 44.
12 Korean Intellectual Property Office 2022, 38.
13 Park and Noe 2013, 226.
14 Chang 2017, 124.
15 Korean Intellectual Property Office 2023.

an examiner for failing the inventive step requirement and is then converted to a utility model application, registration may be obtained. An applicant for a patent may convert their patent application into an application for utility model registration within the extent of the descriptions in the specification or drawings initially attached to the patent application. A converted application may not be made, however, when 3 months have elapsed since a certified copy of the initial decision of rejection was served in connection with the patent application.[16] A conversion application in the opposite direction is also possible. In other words, a utility model applicant can convert their initial application into a patent application within the scope of the descriptions in the initial specification or drawings.[17] Once registration is done, a conversion is not allowed from a patent to utility model registration, nor from a utility model to a patent registration.

13.6 REGISTRATION

Until the 1980s, the number of utility model registrations in Korea outnumbered that of patents. Patent applications and registration increased more rapidly than utility model applications beginning in the mid-1980s. The number of patent applications exceeded that of utility models in 1989 and the number of patent registrations did in 1991, as shown in Figure 13.1. When the advance registration system disappeared in 2006, the number of utility model applications and registration began to decrease sharply. The number of utility model registration was merely 1817 in 2021, which is equivalent to just 1.2 percent of patent registration.[18]

Looking at the details of registration, it is worth noting that foreign utility model registrations are negligible compared to domestic ones. Out of the 413,229 utility models issued in 22 years from 2000 through 2021 in Korea, only 10,272 came from abroad, which is little more than 2 percent of the total. In case of patent registration, 23 percent were issued to foreign patentees in the same period. The rights to register varies significantly from country to country. While applicants from the United States, Japan, and Germany obtained an overwhelmingly large share of patent registrations, applicants from China and Taiwan obtained far more utility model registration than applicants from other countries.

While patents are used mostly by corporations, utility models are used more by individual applicants. For example, there were 145,882 patents issued in 2021, of which 85 percent were issued to corporations. In contrast, there were only 1,817 utility models issued in 2021, of which 50 percent were issued to individuals.

16 The Utility Model Act, Section 10.

17 The Patent Act, Section 53.

18 The Korea Intellectual Property Office Statistics. www.kipo.go.kr/en/HtmlApp?c=97000&catmenu=ek07_03_01.

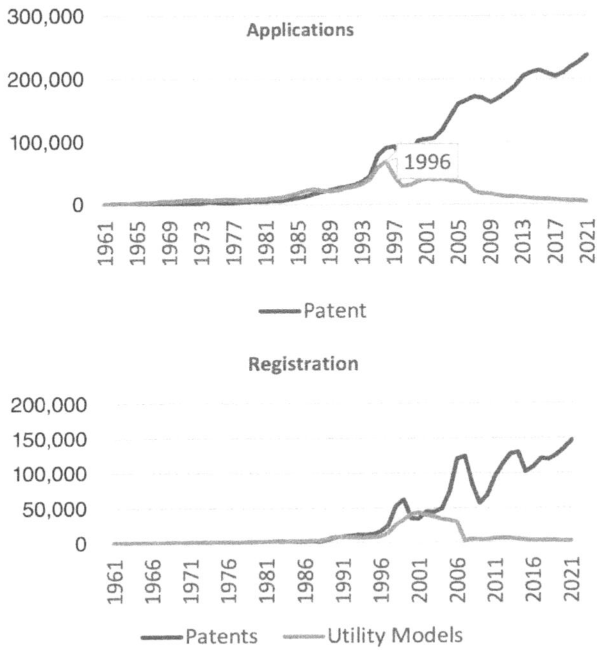

FIGURE 13.1 Korean patent versus utility model applications and registrations

13.7 INVALIDATION

The elements of inventive step are central in both infringement and invalidation actions, which are separated under a two-tier system in Korea. While infringement actions are brought to judicial courts, invalidation actions have to go through the IP Tribunal first. Like the Patent Act, the Utility Model Act of Korea only negates the effects of a utility model right through an invalidation trial at the IP Tribunal.[19] An appeal against the decision of the IP Tribunal must be filed with the Patent Court of Korea. Since the Patent Court is a court of appeal, it takes appeals not just from the IP Tribunal but also from the decisions of judicial courts on patent infringement.

The two-tier system has often led to time-consuming and high-cost dispute resolution processes.[20] For example, the courts have allowed the "publicly known or worked invention/device" defense even in infringement actions. Thus, even before the IP Tribunal's decision to invalidate a patent has become final and conclusive, judicial courts that tried infringement lawsuit have made findings as to whether there are grounds for invalidation. Reflecting on the lower courts' findings

[19] The Utility Model Act, Section 31.

[20] Supreme Ct., 99Hu2150.

and decisions, the Supreme Court eventually held that, even before an IP Tribunal's decision to invalidate a patented invention is confirmed, if it is clear that the patent will be invalidated due to the lack of an inventive step, a claim for injunction against infringement or a claim for damages based on the patent right constitutes an abuse of right.[21] The same theory of abuse will certainly apply to utility model infringements even if there is no decision by the IP Tribunal on validity.

13.8 INFRINGEMENT

In case of infringement, remedies such as injunctions and damages are available to the owner of utility models, just as they are to the owner of a patent. Whereas injunctions are an equitable remedy in the United States, injunctions are automatically granted by courts in Korea when utility model infringement has been found. As an exception, the court may decline to grant an injunction when the owner of a utility model is found to have abused its rights. For example, when a utility model device clearly lacks novelty or nonobviousness, the courts can find that its owner has committed an abuse of rights by bringing a lawsuit to seek an injunction. Accordingly, the court will often deny an injunction in such cases.

Even if there is an infringement that has been proved with enough evidence, it has been difficult to prove the actual amount of damage caused by the infringement. Accordingly, the Utility Model Act provides that Section 128 of the Patent Act shall apply mutatis mutandis to the protection of the owners of utility model rights.[22] Several methods of calculating damages are suggested in Section 128 of the Patent Act: "Damage based on the amount of sales," "damage based on the infringer's profit," "damage equivalent to royalties," or "amount of damage subject to the discretion of the court." At the court of first instance, plaintiffs have claimed "damage based on the infringer's profit" in 66 percent of cases, and "damage equivalent to the royalties" in only 12.9 percent of cases. Despite the plaintiff's preference for "amount of damage based on the infringer's profit," the highest proportion (61.3 percent) of judicial decisions were made on the basis of the "amount of damage subject to the discretion of the court."[23] In relying on its discretion to calculate the amount of damages, courts usually take into account the infringer's sales, the infringer's profit, reasonable royalties or any other available factors. The court's preference for its discretion is understood as enabling the court to determine the most appropriate level of damages.

The amount of damages not only becomes an important variable in the value of intellectual property rights, but also significantly affects technological innovation in the long run. The level of damages awarded in courts of Korea is so low that there

[21] Supreme Ct., 2010Da95390.
[22] The Utility Model Act, Section 30.
[23] Choi 2016, 248.

have been concerns that Korean intellectual property rights may be undervalued. With the low number of utility model registrations over the past decade, there are few litigations concerning utility model infringement. In 2021, there were 2,500 claims filed at the IP Tribunal, but only 43 concerned utility models. In the same year, while there were 853 cases alleging invalidity of patent rights and confirmation of the scope of rights at the IP Tribunal, only 23 utility model cases were filed.

14

Utility Models in Brazil

Luca Schirru and Maikon Oliveira

This chapter describes the issuance and litigation of Utility Models in Brazil. Although considered "Patents" in Brazil, utility models have a different treatment from Patents of Invention, having some specificities such as those related to the requirements for protection and the term of duration. This chapter will provide an overview of the Brazilian Patent System by outlining the scope of protection and requirements to obtain a utility model Patent in comparison with patents on invention, and by commenting on the enforcement of these rights in the judicial and administrative spheres.

14.1 THE BRAZILIAN LEGAL FRAMEWORK ON UTILITY MODELS

Regarding the international context, although Brazil is not a party to a few IP international treaties like the WIPO Copyright Treaty (WCT) and the WIPO Performances and Phonograms Treaty (WPPT), it is a signatory to most of the main IP-related treaties including the Patent Cooperation Treaty (PCT),[1] the Berne Convention,[2] the Agreement on Trade-Related Aspects of Intellectual Property (TRIPS),[3] and the Paris Convention,[4] among others.

Internally, the origins of the patent laws in Brazil can be traced to the year 1809 with an Order (*Alvará*) granting 14 years' "exclusive privilege" to inventors.[5] The first Brazilian Constitution of 1824 also provided that inventors would have

1 Patent Cooperation Treaty 2001.

2 Berne Convention for the Protection of Literary and Artistic Works 1886.

3 Agreement on Trade-Related Aspects of Intellectual Property Rights 1994.

4 Paris Convention for the Protection of Industrial Property 1979.

5 For more on this Order, see Abrantes 2014. For a comprehensive historical analysis of the patents system in Brazil, see Malavota 2011. See also, Brazil, House of Representatives 2013. Brazil 1809.

property rights in their productions or discoveries during a limited period of time.[6] When it comes to Utility Models, although there are documented sources indicating their official recognition in Brazil during the twentieth century,[7] art. 1 of Law 3.129/1882 already contained a definition that bears resemblance to what is recognized as a utility model today:

> Art. 1[. . .] § 1 The following constitute an invention or discovery for the purposes of this law: 1- The invention of new industrial products; 2 -The invention of new means or the new application of known means to obtain an industrial product or result; 3- The improvement of an already privileged invention, if it makes the manufacture of the product or use of the privileged invention easier, or if it increases its usefulness.[8]

Currently, the Brazilian legal framework on IP includes multiple federal laws related to copyright,[9] integrated circuit topographies,[10] plant varieties,[11] and, central for the purposes of this chapter, industrial property.[12] The Brazilian Law on Industrial Property (LPI) addresses issues related to patents (both patents of inventions and utility models),[13] industrial designs,[14] trademarks,[15] geographical indications,[16] unfair competition (which may also encompass issues related to slogans, and other advertising signs, consumer confusion, and trade secrets),[17] and crimes against industrial property.[18] It also provides some regulatory aspects on licensing, and the administrative procedure carried out by the Brazilian Industrial Property Office (INPI).

The interpretation and content of all federal laws mentioned above must be in accordance with the Brazilian Federal Constitution of 1988, which also expressly

6 Brazil 1824: "Art. 179. A inviolabilidade dos Direitos Civis, e Politicos dos Cidadãos Brazileiros, que tem por base a liberdade, a segurança individual, e a propriedade, é garantida pela Constituição do Imperio, pela maneira seguinte. [. . .] XXVI. Os inventores terão a propriedade das suas descobertas, ou das suas producções. A Lei lhes assegurará um privilegio exclusivo temporario, ou lhes remunerará em resarcimento da perda, que hajam de soffrer pela vulgarisação."

7 See Gama et al. 2016. See also, Richards 2010.

8 Even before 1882, there were legal texts providing definitions that may be similar to what are considered Utility Models today, as it is the case of the Law from August 28, 1830, that granted privileges related to inventions and provided in its art. 2 that "Anyone who improves a discovery or invention has the right of discoverer or inventor in the improvement." Brazil 1830.

9 Brazil 1998a; Brazil 1998b.

10 Brazil 2007.

11 Brazil 1997.

12 Brazil 1996.

13 Brazil 1996, arts 6–93.

14 Brazil 1996, arts 94–121.

15 Brazil 1996, arts 122–175.

16 Brazil 1996, arts 176–182.

17 Brazil 1996, art. 195.

18 Brazil 1996, arts 183–195.

addresses Intellectual Property Rights, mainly in art. 5, XXVII, XXVIII and XXIX.[19] In Brazil, the right to property is a fundamental right (art. 5, XXII, CF88). However, this right is not an absolute one, since "property shall observe its social function" (art. 5, XXIII, CF88).[20] Several authors have argued that there is no legitimate property without it being tied to its social function,[21] agreeing with the idea that "[...] property endowed with a social function, which is not fulfilling it, will no longer be the object of legal protection."[22]

To exercise such a right according to its social function can be understood under a more objective lens, as it is seen in the case of rural property under art. 186 of the Brazilian Federal Constitution, as to which cumulative factors must be considered in order to assess whether the social function is met.[23] Nevertheless, the "social function" of property, and therefore intellectual property, is more than complying with a list of factors.[24] Regarding IP rights, limitations and exceptions (L&Es) can help to define the social function of property,[25] reaffirming that the property right is not absolute and must consider the social interest.[26] It becomes clear from the reading of the text of art. 5, XXIX of the Brazilian Federal Constitution that the granting

[19] Brazil 1988.

[20] Brazil 1988: "Article 5. All persons are equal before the law, without any distinction whatsoever, Brazilians and foreigners residing in the country being ensured of inviolability of the right to life, to liberty, to equality, to security and to property, on the following terms: [...] XXVII – the exclusive right of use, publication or reproduction of works rests upon their authors and is transmissible to their heirs for the time the law shall establish; XXVIII – under the terms of the law, the following are ensured: a) protection of individual participation in collective works and of reproduction of the human image and voice, sports activities included; b) the right to authors, interpreters, and respective unions and associations to monitor the economic exploitation of the works which they create or in which they participate; XXIX – the law shall ensure the authors of industrial inventions of a temporary privilege for their use, as well as protection of industrial creations, property of trademarks, names of companies and other distinctive signs, viewing the social interest and the technological and economic development of the country."

[21] Tepedino and Schreiber 2005, 111–112: "É evidente que a função social também varia de acordo com o estatuto proprietário em questão, mas o texto constitucional não deixa dúvidas de que toda propriedade tem, ou deve ter, função social."

[22] Grau 1990, 316: "[...] a propriedade dotada de função social, que não esteja a cumpri-la, já não será mais objeto de proteção jurídica."

[23] Brazil 1988: "Article 186. The social function is met when the rural property complies simultaneously with, according to the criteria and standards prescribed by law, the following requirements: I – rational and adequate use; II – adequate use of available natural resources and preservation of the environment; III – compliance with the provisions that regulate labour relations; IV – exploitation that favours the well-being of the owners and labourers."

[24] For further information on this matter, we recommend the following works by Brazilian authors: Fachin 1995; Souza 2021; Tepedino and Schreiber 2005.

[25] Souza 2006, 282: "A efetivação da função social tem como objetivo principal a limitação da utilização social dos bens intelectuais pelo titular, em razão de diversos interesses da coletividade."

[26] Tepedino and Schreiber 2005, 111–112: "A pluralidade de manifestações do fenômeno proprietário não afasta, contudo, a necessidade de conformação do seu exercício aos interesses sociais relevantes. É evidente que a função social também varia de acordo com o estatuto proprietário em questão, mas o texto constitucional não deixa dúvidas de que toda propriedade tem, ou deve ter, função social."

of IP rights (including those related to utility models) is subject to consideration of the social interest and the technological and economic development of Brazil.[27]

The next section will address how Patents of Invention and Utility Models are regulated under federal law, that is, the LPI, in Brazil.

14.2 PATENTS ON INVENTION AND UTILITY MODELS

Today, the LPI provides two types of patents: Patents on Invention and Utility Models. Patents on inventions are granted to those inventions "that meet the requirements of novelty, inventive step, and industrial application," [28] whereas a utility model is an "object of practical use, or part thereof, susceptible to industrial application, which includes a new form or arrangement, involving an inventive act resulting in a functional improvement to the use or manufacture."[29] Table 14.1 summarizes the principal requirements for patents on inventions and utility models in Brazil.

While the LPI formally treats "novelty" and "industrial application" in the same way,[30] the same cannot be said for the "inventive act/step." Art. 13 of the LPI clarifies the scope of "inventive step" requirement for patents on invention: "An invention is endowed with an inventive step provided that, to a technician versed in the subject, it is not derived in an evident or obvious way from the state of the art." Regarding utility models, art. 14 provides that a "utility model is endowed with an inventive act provided that, to a technician versed in the subject, it is not derived in a common or ordinary way from the state of the art."

The Utility Model Patent Examination Guidelines provided by the Brazilian Patent Office (INPI) (2012, p. 5) establish that an inventive act is characterized by the presence of an unusual difference between an already existing object in the state of the art and the new invention. In other words, the difference must not be ordinary for a person skilled in the art. The inventive act presupposes a lower degree of inventiveness:

> An inventive act is considered to exist when the modification introduced to an object results in a functional improvement in its use or manufacture, facilitating human activity, or improving its efficiency. The inventive act is of the same nature as the inventive activity, but with a lower degree of inventiveness.[31]

[27] Brazil 1988, art. 5, XXIX.

[28] Brazil 1996, art. 8.

[29] Brazil, art. 9.

[30] Brazil 1996, arts 11; 15: "11. An invention and a utility model are considered to be new if they are not part of the state of the art. [. . .] 15. An invention and a utility model are not considered susceptible of industrial application when they can be used or produced in any kind of industry."

[31] Independent translation. Original text available at INPI 2002: "Considera-se que existe ato inventivo quando a modificação introduzida num objeto resulta em melhoria funcional de seu uso ou fabricação, facilitando a atividade humana, ou melhorando sua eficiência. O ato inventivo é da mesma natureza que a atividade inventiva, mas com menor grau de inventividade."

TABLE 14.1 *Requirements for Patent Protection in Brazil (patent on invention and utility model)*

Technical requirements	Formal requirements
Novelty: Everything that is not included in the state of the art is considered new, that is, made available to the general public up to 12 months before the filing of the patent application	**Descriptive Sufficiency:** The text of the Patent Application must describe the protected article or process in such a way that it can be reproduced by a person skilled in the art.
Inventive step (Patent on Invention): innovative characteristic that do not result in an evident or obvious advance over the state of the art.	**Formatting:** The text of the Patent Application must be formatted in compliance with current regulations established by the INPI
Inventive act (Utility Model): innovative characteristic that does not result in a common or vulgar advance over the state of the art.	**Unit of Invention:** the text of the Patent Application must correspond to a single invention or a group of interrelated inventions in order to comprise a single inventive concept
Industrial application: characteristic that allows the patented article or process to be used or produced in some type of industry.	**Payment of Fees:** The Patent Application must be accompanied by the fees necessary for its acceptance, in accordance with the regulations established by the INPI
Legal clearance: the innovation cannot be framed within the legal prohibitions provided for by the LPI	

Source: Oliveira 2020, 15.[32]

According to Barbosa, identifying the inventive act in utility models is a more complex endeavor than that concerning the inventive step in patents on invention:[33]

[32] Independent translation. Original at Oliveira 2020, 15: "Requisitos Técnicos: Novidade: É considerado novo tudo aquilo não compreendido no estado da técnica, isto é, disponibilizado ao conhecimento do público em geral até 12 meses antes do depósito do Pedido de Patente. Atividade Inventiva (Patente de Invenção): característica inovadora que não decorra de maneira evidente ou óbvia do estado da técnica. Ato inventivo (Modelo de Utilidade): característica inovadora que não decorra de maneira comum ou vulgar do estado da técnica. Aplicação industrial: característica que permita com o que o objeto ou processo patenteado possa ser utilizado ou produzido em qualquer tipo de indústria. Desimpedimento legal: a inovação não pode estar enquadrada nas proibições legais previstas pela LPI. Requerimentos formais: Suficiência Descritiva: O texto do Pedido de Patente deverá estar descrito de tal forma que seja hábil sua reprodução por um técnico no assunto. Formatação: O texto do Pedido de Patente deverá estar formatado de modo a cumprir com a normativa vigente instituida pelo INPI. Unidade de Invenção: o texto do Pedido de Patente deverá corresponder a uma única invenção ou a um grupo de invenções interrelacionadas de maneira a compreenderem um único conceito inventivo. Pagamento de Taxas: O Pedido de Patente deverá ser instruído das taxas necessárias ao seu aceite, de acordo com a normativa instituída pelo INPI."

[33] Barbosa 2010, 1717.

It is difficult, however, to discern the difference between the "evident or obvious consequence of the state of the art", typical of Patent of Inventions, and the "ordinary result of the state of the art", typical of models. Is the subjective parameter the relevant one? Would the person skilled in the art, necessary judge of the inventive step, be replaced by a layman in the case of the inventive act? What is the fine line between an invention that is evident or obvious and one that is common or vulgar? Because it is in this seamless limit that the Utility Model in its new version should exist.[34]

Despite the differences between utility models and patents on invention under Brazilian Law, there is the possibility of the conversion (usually referred to as "change of nature") of a Utility Model to a Patent on Invention and vice-versa.[35] Arts. 35, II and 36 illustrate scenarios in which such change of nature may occur:

Art. 35. Upon technical examination, a search report and an opinion will be prepared related to: [...]

II - adjustment of the application to the nature of the protection claimed;
III - reformulation division of the application; or
IV - technical requirements.

Article 36. When the office action is for the non-patentability, or inadequacy of the application to the nature of protection claimed, or formulates any requirement, the applicant shall be notified to respond within 90 (ninety) days.

Paragraph 1. Upon failure to meet the requirement, the application shall be definitively dismissed.

Paragraph 2. In case the requirement is responded, even though not met, or its formulation is reconsidered and independently of arguments being filed regarding the patentability or suitability, the examination shall continue.

Finally, another difference between Patents on Inventions and Utility Models is their term or duration: "[a]n invention patent shall remain in force for a period of 20 (twenty) years, and a utility model patent for a period of 15 (fifteen) years from the date of filing."[36]

34 Independent translation. Original text available at Barbosa 2010, 1717: "Fica difícil, porém, de discernir a diferença entre a "decorrência evidente ou óbvia do estado da arte", própria das patentes de invenção, e a "decorrência comum ou vulgar do estado da técnica", própria dos modelos. Será o parâmetro subjetivo o relevante? O técnico no assunto, juiz necessário da atividade inventiva, seria substituído por um leigo no caso do ato inventivo? Qual o tênue limite entre o invento que seja evidente ou óbvio e aquele que seja comum ou vulgar? Pois que é neste inconsútil limite que deverá existir o Modelo de Utilidade na sua nova versão."

35 This and the other legal acts concerning the filing and obtaining of a patent are carried out before the Brazilian Patent Office (INPI), as described in the next section.

36 Brazil 1996, art. 40. Until 2021, art. 40 of the Brazilian Industrial Property Law had a sole paragraph providing that "The term shall not be less than 10 (ten) years for an invention patent and 7 (seven) years for a utility model patent, beginning on the date of granting, unless the INPI has been prevented from examining the merits of the application by a proven pending

14.3 ADMINISTRATIVE PROCEDURE BEFORE THE INPI

In Brazil, Patents, and therefore Utility Models, are granted by the Brazilian Patent Office (INPI). Created in 1970,[37] the INPI is the federal authority responsible for administering Industrial Property in Brazil, and for making enactments "on the advisability of signing, ratifying and denouncing conventions, treaties, covenants and agreements on industrial property."[38] In addition to analyzing applications and granting patents, the INPI is also responsible for registering trademarks, industrial designs, software,[39] geographical indications, integrated circuit topography, and technology transfer agreements.[40]

When it comes to utility model filings in Brazil, data from January and February 2022 show that 98% of the applicants are Brazilian residents, which is a very different scenario when we compare to Patents on Inventions during the same period (USA 31%, Brazil 17%, Germany 7%, China 7%, Japan 6%, Switzerland 5%, UK 4%, and France 4%).[41] With regard to the nature of the applicants, 64% of the utility model applicants for January/February 2022 were Individuals, 20% were small businesses, and individual entrepreneurs (MEI) and medium or large size companies represented 13% of the applicants.[42] In terms of overall applications, and comparing the applications filled for patents on invention and utility models it is clear that, in Brazil, patent on invention applications are substantially higher than those for utility models. These results are illustrated in Figure 14.1.

Reducing the time between filling a patent application and having it granted has been one of the priorities of the INPI, mainly for patents on invention, which may have contributed to the growth of Decisions on patents on invention between 2018 and 2020, as shown in Figure 14.1.[43] As of October–December 2022, the average time for a technical decision once the Request for Examination is filed is 2.6 years for utility models.[44] Compared to patents on invention, it is difficult to compare the pendency time of utility models and patents on invention because the pendency of patents on invention varies according to the nature of the invention. While the average time for a

judicial dispute or for reasons of force majeure." However, in May 2021, the Supreme Court extinguished the sole paragraph on the basis that it was unconstitutional (Brazil, ADI 5529). Brazil, Supreme Court, Unconstitutionality Action (ADI) n. 5529 (Action n. 4000796-72.2016.1.00.0000). https://portal.stf.jus.br/processos/detalhe.asp?incidente=4984195.

37 Brazil 1970, art. 1.

38 Brazil 1970, art. 2.

39 Despite the possibility of registering a software before the INPI, software (source and object code) is protected under copyright and, therefore, registration is not mandatory.

40 More information can be found in the INPI's website: www.gov.br/inpi/pt-br.

41 INPI 2022a.

42 INPI 2022a.

43 More information can be found at: www.gov.br/inpi/pt-br/servicos/patentes/plano-de-combate-ao-backlog.

44 INPI 2022b.

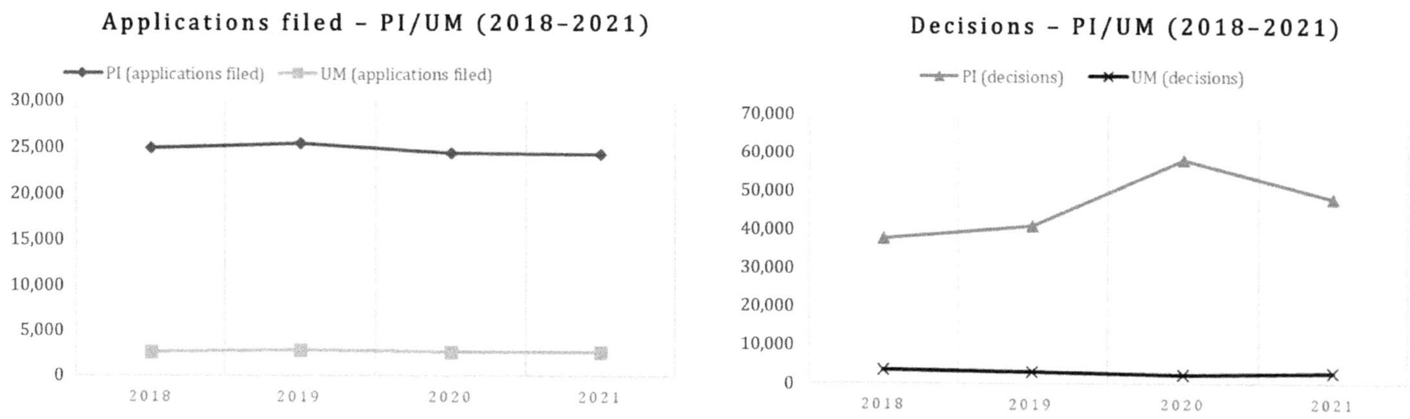

FIGURE 14.1 Patent on invention and utility model applications and decisions (2018–2021)
Source: The authors (2023) based on official data from INPI available at: www.gov.br/inpi/pt-br/central-de-conteudo/estatisticas/arquivos/publicacoes/boletim-mensal-de-propriedade-industrial-marco-de-2022.pdf

technical decision for inventions in the field of cosmetics is 2.1 years, the time for biopharmaceuticals is 5.4 years, once the Request for Examination is filed.[45]

Today, the complete administrative procedure to obtain a patent for a utility model can be carried out online via the "e-INPI" and "e-Patentes" systems.[46] Briefly stated, the user must sign in to the system, gather all relevant documentation regarding the utility model, the inventor, the applicant, the invention, pay the necessary official taxes, fill out forms and file the application online.[47] The application must be filed according to art. 19 of the LPI and "shall contain: I. the request; II. the specifications; III. the claims; IV. drawings, if applicable; V. the abstract; and VI. proof of payment of the filing fee."[48]

Once it is filed, the user can keep track of the application online and must respond to any office actions and any further requests for additional information/documentation.[49] On the INPI side,

> the Institute will carry out a preliminary formal examination of the application and, if there is full compliance with art. 19, the protocol will take place. In the event of formal failure to comply with art. 19, but the application provides data referring to the object, the applicant and the inventor, the INPI will formulate an office action to be fulfilled within 30 days, under penalty of having the application dismissed. Once the application is filed, it will be kept confidential for a period of 18 months from the filing date. It should be noted that the applicant must request the examination of the application within 36 months from the date of filing, under penalty of having the application dismissed, however, the INPI can only start the examination after 60 days from the publication of the Application.[50]

According to art. 34 of the LPI, "[a]fter the examination has been requested, [a set of documents listed art. 34] must be submitted within a period of 60 (sixty) days, whenever requested, under penalty of having the application dismissed." The technical examination will encompass the preparation of a search report and an opinion by the INPI regarding: "I. patentability of the application; II. appropriateness of the application given the nature claimed; III. reformulation or division of the application; or IV. technical requirements."[51]

In case INPI finds the "non-patentability of the application or the incompatibility of the application to the nature claimed, or makes some demand, the applicant shall be notified to submit comments within a period of 90 (ninety) days."[52] In case the

45 INPI 2022b.

46 The INPI's searchable database for utility models is available at: https://busca.inpi.gov.br/pePI/jsp/patentes/PatenteSearchBasico.jsp.

47 INPI 2023a.

48 Brazil 1996, art. 19; Oliveira 2020.

49 INPI 2023a.

50 Oliveira 2020; Brazil 1996.

51 Brazil 1996, art. 35.

52 Brazil 1996, art. 36.

applicant does not respond to the request from the INPI, the application will be dismissed, and if there is any response, the examination will continue.[53] Finally, according to art. 37, "[o]nce the examination has been concluded, a decision shall be handed down, either approving or rejecting the patent application."

It should be noted that additional costs to those paid at the time of the patent application filing may arise from, for example, compliance with Office Actions, the issuance of the Patent Certificate, and the payment of annuities.[54] In accordance with art 9 of Law n. 5648/70,[55] all the official information provided in the online system is also published in the INPI's official gazette.[56]

14.4 ENFORCING UTILITY MODELS IN BRAZIL

Enforcing exclusive rights in Utility Models is possible both in the administrative and judicial (civil and criminal) systems in Brazil, and the choice of one does not exclude the other.[57]

14.4.1 *Administrative Procedure*

According to art. 51 of the LPI, and within six months of the date of the grant of a patent, it is possible to file an Administrative Nullity Proceeding ("ANP") on grounds that the patent (either patent on invention or utility model) is not compliant with the requirements provided in the law and administrative regulations (e.g., legal and formal requirements, specifications, and claims).[58] The "procedure may be initiated ex officio or at the request of any person with legitimate interest."[59] Once the ANP is initiated, the titleholder may submit comments after sixty days of its publication,[60] which will be followed by an Opinion of the INPI.[61] Then, both the applicant and the titleholder will have an additional sixty days to submit their final comments.[62] The final step of the administrative procedure is the analysis of the case

[53] Brazil 1996, art. 36.
[54] INPI 2023a.
[55] INPI 2023a.
[56] Available at: revistas.inpi.gov.br/rpi/.
[57] Brazil 1996, art. 207: "207. Independently of the criminal action, the aggrieved party may bring any civil suits he considers as appropriate pursuant to the Civil Procedure Code."
[58] Brazil 1996, art. 50.
[59] Brazil 1996, art. 51.
[60] Brazil 1996, art. 52.
[61] Brazil 1996, art. 53.
[62] Brazil 1996, art. 53.

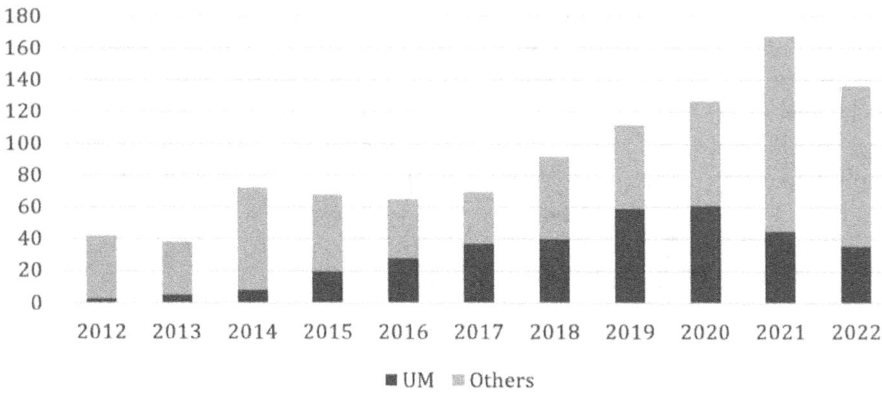

FIGURE 14.2 Total Administrative Nullity Proceedings (ANPs) (2012–2020)
Source: The authors (2023) and INPI 2023b, 132–133.

by the president of INPI.[63] Figure 14.2 shows an overview of the number of ANPs filed per year between the years 2012 and 2022.

Focusing on the acts of the utility model division, Figure 14.3 shows the INPI decisions nullifying the patent and those in which the patent was maintained (even with a restriction, which is called "partial nullity"). From the data below, it is clear that the majority of the decisions issued by the utility model Division on ANPs reject the ANP and uphold the utility model.

According to data made available by the INPI for the period between 2012 and 2022, an average of 1–2 percent of the total decisions for approval[64] (for patents on invention and utility models) are subject to an ANP.[65] When analyzed by market sector, the highest number of cases of ANPs appear in the "Division of Patents of Agriculture and Engineering Elements" ("Divisão de Patentes de Agricultura e Elementos de Engenharia") with 2.35 percent of the decisions being followed by ANPs and the Division of Utility Models Patents ("Divisão de Patentes de Modelo de Utilidade"), with 2.97 percent.

The nullity of a patent can also be judicially requested while the patent is in force, and must be filed before the Federal Court with the participation of the INPI (even

63 Brazil 1996, art. 54.

64 It is important to clarify that, according to art. 38 of the LPI, the patent will be granted if, after the decision for the approval, the applicant proves that the necessary official fees were paid within the legal term.

65 INPI 2023b, 26.

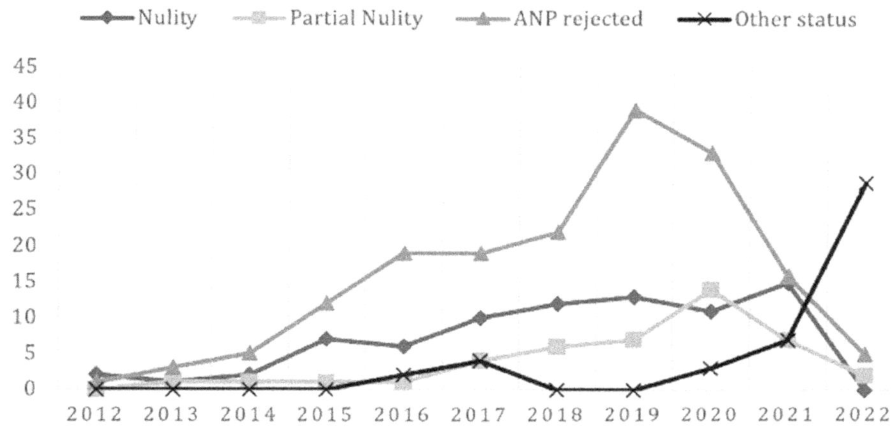

FIGURE 14.3 Decisions/status of ANPs filed at the utility model division (2012–2022)
Source: The authors (2023) and INPI 2023b, 228–229.

if it is not the plaintiff).[66] Once the Court decision is final, the INPI will make it public in its official gazette and the parties informed about it.[67]

14.4.2 *Judicial Procedure*

To better understand the current number of legal actions involving patents on invention and utility models, both in the Criminal and Civil spheres, we used a private third-party software "*webseek*" owned by LDSoft.[68] This software uses the existing data in the INPI database with the possibility of applying different filters in the searches.

For this particular purpose, we searched for all the patents and applications with decisions tagged with codes 15.23 ("*notice of legal action concerning the application*") and 22.15 ("*notice of legal action concerning the patent*") for the last thirty years (between January 1, 1993, and January 1, 2023). The results are provided in Figure 14.4.

While the above figures provide insight into the volume of legal proceedings involving patent on invention and utility models, it should be clarified that they may not reflect the exact and total number of cases discussing patents in Brazilian courts. These statistics likely only account for cases where details about the judicialization were formally documented in the administrative records of the INPI.

66 Brazil 1996, arts 56, 57.
67 Brazil 1996, art. 57 (2).
68 LDSoft, n.d. www.ldsoft.com.br/webseek/.

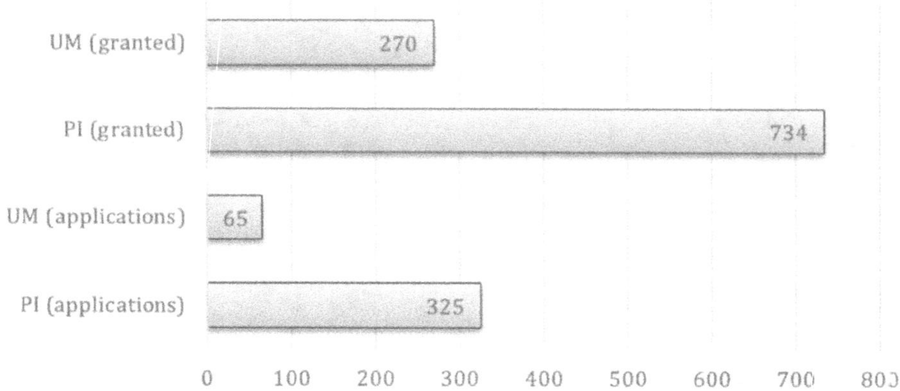

FIGURE 14.4 Notices of legal action for patents on invention and utility models (1993–2023)
Source: The authors (2024) with information from the INPI database on the number of patents and applications with decisions tagged with codes 15.23 and 22.15.

When it comes to criminal actions, the Brazilian legal framework is quite peculiar, since industrial property crimes are not listed in the Criminal Code anymore but are included in the LPI. Nevertheless, "[c]riminal action and the preliminary proceedings of search and seizure, in crimes against industrial property, shall be governed by the Criminal Procedure Code, with the modifications set forth in the Articles of this Chapter [of the LPI]."[69] Moreover, in Brazil, the procedure concerning crimes against patents usually starts with the filing of a criminal complaint by the offended, often the rightsholder, and not by initiative of the State, which can be represented by the Public Prosecutor's Office.[70]

Subject to fines, search and seizure,[71] destruction of the infringing products,[72] and even imprisonment (the penalty varies from one month to one year depending on the crime committed),[73] there are several acts like manufacturing, exporting, importing, or supplying patented products without authorization that are considered as crimes against patents in Brazil.[74] Imprisonment time can be extended when the infringer is or was a representative, agent, partner, employee, or licensee of the

69 Brazil 1996, art. 200.
70 Brazil 1996, art. 199.
71 See, e.g., Brazil 1996, arts 201, 202, 203 and 204.
72 See Brazil 1996, art. 202.
73 It should be noted that these penalties may be increased according to art. 196 of the LPI: "196. The penalties of imprisonment for the crimes set forth in Chapters I, II and III of this Title shall be increased by one-third to one-half if: I. the offending party is, or was, the representative, mandatory, agent, partner or employee of the patentholder or titleholder of the registration or of his licensee; or II. the mark that has been altered, reproduced or imitated is famous, well known, or is a certification or collective mark."
74 Brazil 1996, arts 183–186.

patentee.[75] Similarly, fines could be majored in certain cases.[76] Additionally, there are unfair competition crimes that are closely related to patents. We provide a summary of these crimes in Annex I.

In addition to criminal procedures, holders of patent on invention and utility model can also file civil infringement lawsuits. If successful, these suits can result in the payment of compensation, which is "determined by the benefits that the injured party would have gained had the violation not occurred."[77] When it comes to the calculation of "lost profits," the LPI provides multiple criteria, from which the most beneficial to the injured party can be applied, these being: (i) "the benefits that the injured party would have obtained if there were no infringement";[78] (ii) "the benefits obtained by the infringing party"[79] and (iii) "the remuneration that the infringer would have paid to the rightsholder for a licensee that would allow it to lawfully use the asset."[80]

[75] Brazil 1996, art. 196.
[76] Brazil 1996, art. 197, sole paragraph.
[77] Brazil 1996, arts 207–208.
[78] Independent translation. Brazil 1996, art. 210, I.
[79] Independent translation. Brazil 1996, art. 210, II.
[80] Independent translation. Brazil 1996, art. 210, III.

Appendix I

Crimes against patents	Legal Basis	Penalty
Manufacture "a product that is the object of an invention or utility model patent, without authorization from the titleholder";	Art. 183, I of the LPI	Imprisonment (3m–1y) or fine
Export "sells, displays or offers for sale, has in stock, conceals or receives, with a view to use for economic purposes, a product manufactured in violation of an invention or utility model patent [. . .]."	Art. 184, I of the LPI	Imprisonment (1m–3m) or fine
Import "a product that is the object of an invention or utility model patent, or obtained by a means or process patented in this country, for the purposes set forth in the preceding Item, and that has not been placed on the foreign market directly by the patentholder or with his consent."	Art. 184, II of the LPI	
Supply "a component of a patented product, or material or equipment to execute a patented process, provided that the final application of the component, material or equipment leads necessarily to the exploitation of the object of the patent."	Art. 185 of the LPI	
Crimes of unfair competition (potentially connected with patents)	**Legal Basis**	**Penalty**
Employ "fraudulent means to divert the customers of another person to his or another party's advantage."	Art. 195, III of the LPI	Imprisonment (3m–1y) or fine
Sell, display or offer "for sale a product declaring that it is object of a patent that has been filed or granted, or of an industrial design that has been registered, when it has not, or mentioning it in an advertisement or a commercial paper as being filed or patented, or registered, when it has not."	Art. 195, XIII of the LPI	
Divulge, exploit, or utilize "without authorization, results of tests or other undisclosed data whose preparation involves considerable effort and that were submitted to government agencies as a condition for obtaining approval to commercialize products."	Art. 195, XIV of the LPI	

15

Utility Models in Kenya

Isaac Rutenberg

15.1 CONTEXTUALIZING THE KENYAN UMC

From independence in 1963 until 1990, patents in Kenya were extensions of patents filed and granted in the United Kingdom. From 1990 until 2001, patent and UMC (utility model certificate) applications in Kenya were filed under The Industrial Property Act, Cap. 509, which commenced on February 2, 1990. The same law created the Kenya Industrial Property Office (KIPO, now known as the Kenya Industrial Property Institute, KIPI), which, unusually for African patent offices, includes an examiner corps for carrying out substantive patent examination. Applications are currently filed under the Industrial Property Act of 2001 ("IPA2001"), which repealed Cap. 509 and was passed in response to the requirement for modernization under TRIPS. In practical terms, however, the Industrial Property Act of 2001 is similar in most respects to Cap. 509, and changed little for the procedures applied to applications for patents and UMCs.

To obtain exclusionary rights in Kenya for inventions, applicants have numerous options. The legal framework includes the option to file national applications directly at KIPI, and the applicant may file the application as either a patent or UMC. In both cases, the applicant may also elect to file the application as a "provisional" or "final" specification – in the case of the former, a final specification must be filed within 12 months from the filing of the provisional application, and must claim priority to the provisional application, which automatically expires at the end of that period.

Alternatively, applicants can enter the national phase in Kenya after filing an application through the Patent Cooperation Treaty (PCT). Applications can enter the national phase either as patent or UMC applications. Local applicants can access the PCT either through KIPI, as a Receiving Office, or by filing directly through the International Bureau. PCT applications can claim priority to Kenyan national applications, whether such applications are for patents or UMCs.

As a third option, protection can be obtained through the regional system, the African Regional Intellectual Property Organization (ARIPO), for which Kenya is a founding member and a signatory of the Harare Protocol on Patents and Industrial Designs. ARIPO receives, processes, and grants or rejects applications independently of the national patent offices for its various member states. Both patent and UMC applications are possible through the ARIPO route. After ARIPO receives, examines, and decides to grant a patent or UMC, it notifies the member state national offices that have been designated by the applicant, and gives such offices a period of time to object to the grant of the patent or UMC.[1] If no objection is raised, the application proceeds to grant, and the granted patent or UMC has the effect of a patent or UMC granted by the national office.

The IPA2001 takes a very favourable position toward encouraging innovation, in particular by allowing UMCs that grant patent-like protection for inventions that do not meet the threshold of inventive step. The law goes even further, providing a form of intellectual property referred to as "technovations", which are designed specifically to reward innovation and innovative thinking by employees of companies. A "technovation" is defined as

> a solution to a specific problem in the field of technology, proposed by an employee of an enterprise in Kenya for use by that enterprise, and which relates to the activities of the enterprise but which, on the date of the proposal, has not been used or actively considered for use by that enterprise.

This definition means that, in contrast to patents and UMCs, technovations require neither global nor national-level novelty, but rather merely require company-level novelty (i.e., the technology is novel within the company in which the employee works). An employee may suggest to their employer a technology that they developed or that was found from another source. If the company had not yet used or considered using the technology, and certain other requirements are met,[2] the employee is then entitled to receive a Technovation Certificate from the company. The employee may, then, also be entitled to receive remuneration from the company. The origin of technovations is a model law developed by WIPO in 1980, and that model law was adopted almost verbatim by Kenya.[3] Technovations appear to exist, however, only in the laws of Kenya and Uganda.[4]

1 Objections can be raised, for example, if the application violates national law in terms of subject matter eligibility, or on grounds that the patent or UMC would go against "public order".

2 For example, Section 95 of the IPA2001 also requires that the duties of the employee should not be making and proposing technovations – i.e., the employee should not be regularly tasked with innovating for the company.

3 WIPO 1980.

4 WIPO LEX database.

15.2 NOTABLE ASPECTS OF THE LEGAL FRAMEWORK FOR UMCS IN KENYA

The legal framework for UMCs in Kenya consists of a mere three sections in the IPA2001; more detail was not necessary, as the legislative drafters applied many of the provisions of patents mutatis mutandis. The UMC therefore resembles patents, with the same bundle of rights and mechanisms of enforcement, but with key distinctions. The three sections, then, specify the differences between UMCs and patents, and are described below.

The substantive requirements for a UMC are novelty and industrial applicability; inventive step is not required, as it is in patents. Substantive examination by KIPI is a requirement for patents, and was originally also carried out for UMC applications. A major change occurred in 2014 when KIPI ceased to perform substantive examination of UMC applications after an applicant claimed that the IPA2001 did not authorize that procedure.[5] The validity of this claim has been reviewed and refuted, although KIPI did not resume examination, and all applications since 2014 remain unexamined. Without a substantive examination process, UMCs are now granted roughly 18 months after the filing date (assuming all fees are paid). This also means there is not (or should not be) a presumption of validity in any litigation involving a UMC granted after 2014.

The term of a UMC was, under the original IPA2001, 10 years as measured from the date of grant of the UMC. Considering that patent terms were 20 years measured from the filing date, and that substantive examination and grant procedures for patents could take numerous years, the effective term of UMCs could be relatively similar to that of patents. This was changed in a 2007 amendment to the IPA2001, and UMC term is now 10 years from the filing date.

In another key distinction, potentially inconsistent language in the IPA2001 raises questions about eligible subject matter. Section 82 of the IPA2001 lists sections of the patent law that "shall not apply" to UMCs, but does not include Sections 21 and 26, which collectively address subject matter eligibility. Section 21 provides that "inventions" are patentable, including both products and processes, while a subsequent subsection as well as Section 26 list non-patentable subject matter (discoveries, scientific theories, etc.). This framework seems to imply that the subject matter available for UMCs is the same as the subject matter available for patents. This interpretation is either conflicting with, or perhaps modified by, the express definition of "utility model", which is provided in Section 2 of the IPA2001:

> "utility model" means any form, configuration or disposition of element of some appliance, utensil, tool, electrical and electronic circuitry, instrument, handicraft mechanism or other object or any part of the same allowing a better or different functioning, use, or manufacture of the subject matter or that gives some utility,

[5] Author's personal communication with KIPI.

> advantage, environmental benefit, saving or technical effect not available in Kenya before and includes micro-organisms or other selfreplicable [*sic*] material, products of genetic resources, herbal as well as nutritional formulations which give new effects.

This express definition seems to exclude processes (among other things allowed for patents) from eligibility for protection by UMCs. Nevertheless, as noted above, Section 21(2), relating to patent subject matter, applies to UMCs, mutatis mutandis, and specifies that inventions can be either products or processes. No judicial decisions and no guidance from the Office of the Registrar at KIPI have clarified this apparent contradiction.[6]

Under the IPA2001, infringement and legal proceedings pertaining to revocation or invalidation are the same for UMCs and for patents. Notably, for both patents and UMCs, Section 103 of the IPA2001 provides that revocation and invalidation may be litigated on grounds of lack of novelty,[7] lack of sufficient written description, subject matter ineligibility, lack of disclosure of the best mode, or material misrepresentation in the filing documents, but may not be based on the grounds that there is a lack of inventive step.

15.3 TRENDS IN THE ACQUISITION AND USE OF KENYAN UMCS

As a fully fledged form of intellectual property right, a variety of tactics are possible for users of UMC systems. As discussed throughout this volume, in some countries, the utility model and patent systems are integrated, or are intended to operate in a complementary fashion. One or more of a variety of factors may lead to this situation: applications may be easily converted from UMCs to patents (and vice versa), or it may be possible to hive off a UMC from a patent application; there is no prohibition against obtaining a patent and UMC for the same invention; one system covers classes of inventions that are not eligible for protection in the other system, etc. In Germany, for example, UMCs are used primarily by patent applicants in a strategic manner, particularly since the (unexamined) UMC can be filed based on an existing patent application, and will proceed to grant substantially more quickly than the (examined) patent application (see Chapter 6). An applicant might obtain a UMC in order to signal to the market their claim of ownership to a particular technology, and to quickly initiate legal proceedings without waiting for the examination process.

In contrast, the UMC and patent systems exist in Kenya largely as substitutes for one another. Although conversion between patent and UMC applications is possible under Section 83 of the IPA2001, rather than a strategy for using the systems in

6 But see note 15, and associated text for a discussion of a case that addresses invalidity of a UMC.

7 See note 15. The cited case involved a claim of invalidity over a lack of novelty, among other defects.

a complementary manner, it typically is the result of a substantive rejection during examination of a patent application. It may also occur where the applicant decides not to wait through the process of substantive examination, or would prefer to forgo examination fees and to pay the lower annual fees of a granted UMC as compared with the granted patent.[8] Although there is no prohibition under the IPA2001 against simultaneously holding a patent and UMC for the same invention, it is not common in practice.

The first application for a UMC in Kenya was filed in 1993 by the International Centre for Insect Physiology and Ecology (ICIPE), an international research institution with strong ties to the region. Growth in the number of applications remained slow for some time, and by 2011, only about 240 applications were on file, with 60 of those having been granted as UMCs.[9] As noted above, KIPI ceased substantive examination of UMC applications in 2014. Without the gate-keeping function of examination, the number of granted UMCs increased after 2014.

The applicants for UMCs in Kenya are predominantly local (i.e., the applicant has a Kenyan address).[10] In UMCs granted through 2016, applicant identity was reported as follows: 87% local filers, 1% foreign filers, and 12% unknown.[11] This trend remains consistent: for the 210 UMCs granted in the period 2020–2023, 200 (95%) have local applicants and 10 (5%) have foreign applicants.[12] Interestingly, comparing the same periods for patents, the proportion of local applicants has dramatically increased. Whereas 168 of the 725 patents (23%) granted through 2016 had local applicants, local applicants accounted for 65 of the 162 patents (40%) granted in the period 2020–2023. This may represent an increase in the level of innovation, and/or an increase in the use of the patent system by local innovators.

The identities of UMC applicants have evolved over time. Out of the 210 UMCs granted within the period 2020–2023, 84 (40%) list a company as the applicant, 22 (10%) list a university, and one (<1%) lists a government entity.[13] The remaining 103 UMCs (49%) list an individual (or several individuals) as the applicant. These

8 Fees are provided in the Industrial Property Regulations 2002, Second Schedule. For example, an application fee for a patent is 3,000 KES, but for a UMC is only 1,000 KES. Annual fees for patents range from 2,000 KES in the first year to 50,000 KES in the 20th year. Annual fees for UMCs range from 1,000 KES in the first year to 5,500 KES in the final (10th) year. An examination fee of 5,000 KES applies only to patent applications.

9 A small number of the remaining 180 applications were granted after 2011, but most were abandoned at the application stage.

10 The data in this paragraph are reported for national-route applications filed directly at KIPI or national phase applications filed through the PCT. ARIPO-route applications are not considered.

11 See Rutenberg 2017, 212. For the 12 "unknown" applicants, no data was present in the dataset received from KIPI, but presumably all 12 applications have local applicants. A "local" applicant is one in which the official KIPI record lists a Kenyan address.

12 Data obtained directly from KIPI.

13 In the data provided by KIPI, "companies" are assumed for any applicant name that includes "Limited", "LTD", "store", "trust", "pharmaceuticals," or other obviously commercial terms.

percentages indicate strong growth in filings in the corporate sector – for all granted UMCs until 2016, only 20% listed a corporate applicant.[14] This suggests that the innovation ecosystem in Kenya is increasingly favouring innovation in the private sector (or, at least, that the private sector is increasingly using the UMC system).

Litigation involving UMCs is rare, and most of it proceeds in the Intellectual Property Tribunal (IPT). In one case before the IPT,[15] the UMC at issue was directed to "a computer implemented banking system" consisting of components that are enumerated and described, and the system "is utilized for payment processing between conventional and business banking channels."[16] In response to the accusation of infringement of the UMC, one of the defendants argued that "the invention does not relate to an art, process, use, machine, manufacture, or composition of matter", as well as arguing that the protected invention lacked industrial utility, lacked a complete written description, and lacked novelty, among other arguments. Interestingly, in view of the discussion above regarding allowable subject matter for UMC protection, the defendant did not argue that the UMC was invalid for claiming unprotectable subject matter (i.e., a process). The IPT also did not address whether UMCs may claim processes, but instead held the UMC invalid for being directed to a "mere method of doing business" which is "not capable of protection as provided under section 23(3)(b) of the industrial property Act." The IPT also held that the invention lacked a "technical effect," and on this point cited, as informative, precedent in the Supreme Court of the United States.[17]

In a second case before the IPT,[18] the defendant was accused of infringing seven separate UMCs (all owned by the plaintiff) drawn to various household fixtures. The case was dismissed as the IPT concluded that there was insufficient objective evidence on record to support the accusation of infringement. The case is therefore notable for setting a minimum evidentiary standard in cases of UMC infringement.

15.4 TRENDS IN THE ACQUISITION OF UMCS AT ARIPO

The Harare Protocol, which implements the patent system at ARIPO, entered into force in 1984, and the first patent applications were filed at ARIPO that same year.[19] Although the Harare Protocol also provides for utility models, the first UMC application serial numbers date from 2001. It is unclear whether there were no

[14] Rutenberg 2017, 212.

[15] In re Request for Relief by Alex Muigai Muchiri and Itesyl Technologies (IPT 2021).

[16] Quoted material is from the abstract of UMC 315, as restated in the IPT judgment. The text of the claims of the UMC are not recited in the judgment.

[17] *Mayo Collaborative Services* v. *Prometheus Laboratories, Inc.*, 566 U.S. 66 (2021).

[18] *Zaidat Limited* v. *Fenesi Management Limited and Fenesi Limited* (IPT 2020).

[19] See Section 15.1 for a description of the process and territorial effects applicable to ARIPO patents and UMCs.

utility model applications before 2001, or whether ARIPO was not at that time assigning serial numbers that identify them as such.

Although ARIPO receives and processes a large number of patents compared with the national patent offices of member states, it receives a relatively low number of utility models. Data were obtained for filings between 2001 until the beginning of 2023.[20] During that period, 224 utility model applications were received and assigned filing numbers. In contrast, by the end of 2021, over 13,000 patent application serial numbers had been assigned at ARIPO. The pool of patent and UMC applicants at ARIPO is diverse inasmuch as it represents a large number of countries – both within and external to the regional membership. This includes applications originating from countries without Utility Models, such as the United States. It is not surprising, then, that the more popular filing option is the patent route.

15.5 CONCLUSION

The Kenyan legal framework for UMCs provides a cheaper, faster alternative to patents. The UMC is also attractive as it is available to inventions that are merely novel, and would not necessarily satisfy the inventive step requirement for patents. These advantages are balanced by the shorter term and unexamined nature of the UMC, which may make a granted UMC less valuable to applicants seeking longer, more certain protection. In general, UMCs are primarily used by local applicants, and are a valuable legal instrument for delivering patent-style rights to local innovators.

[20] Data obtained from Patentscope, a service of the World Intellectual Property Organization. In a Patentscope search of all patents filed in ARIPO, 52 records have serial numbers that begin with "AP/U" (as opposed to "AP/P", indicating a patent application). The most recent entry has a filing date in February 2023, and a serial number of 224. Assuming that serial numbers are sequential for all filed applications, this indicates that at least 172 UMC applications are not included in the records of Patentscope.

16

The Debate over Second-Tier Patent Protection in the United States*

Jorge L. Contreras and Mark D. Janis

Unlike most of the other jurisdictions discussed in this book, the United States (US) does not currently have, nor did it ever have, a utility model or other system of second-tier patent protection. This being said, discussion and debate over the institution of such a system in the US has been ongoing for more than a century. In this chapter, we discuss the history and current status of this debate, as well as alternative approaches that US agencies and legislators have taken to address the needs and concerns of small and medium-sized inventors.

16.1 CURRENT FORMS OF INVENTION PROTECTION IN THE US

16.1.1 *Utility Patents*

Like most countries, the US grants patent protection for inventions that meet statutory requirements for patentable subject matter, utility, novelty, and nonobviousness,[1] as these requirements have been interpreted by the US Patent and Trademark Office (USPTO) and the courts over the years. These patents are formally referred to as "utility patents" (to distinguish them from design patents and plant patents, discussed below), though they are often referred to simply as "patents".[2]

Applications for patent protection are examined by the USPTO and involve repeated interactions between the examiner and the applicant. The average prosecution time (the period from filing through final disposition) for US patents is

* The authors acknowledge research assistance provided by Daniel Berger at the University of Utah S.J. Quinney College of Law and Jacob Boesch, Karen Kukla, Maame Yaa Norman, and Sydney Schnur at the Indiana University Maurer School of Law (Bloomington).

[1] 35 U.S.C. §§ 101, 102, 103.

[2] Burk and Lemley 2009, 8–9.

slightly more than two years, increasing to slightly less than four years for applications that include a request for continued examination, more than five years for continuation applications and nearly eight years for divisional applications.[3]

The cost of obtaining a patent in the US includes both governmental filing fees as well as attorney and search fees. Patent application filing and issuance fees range from approximately $1,000 to $2,000.[4] The amount of attorney fees varies based on the complexity of the invention, with one estimate of fees ranging from $5,000 to $7,000 for an "extremely simple" invention to more than $16,000 for "software, automated systems, business methods" patents.[5] The same commentator estimates search costs of $1,000 to $3,000 per application.

Applicants in the US are also given the opportunity to file a "provisional" patent application, which may contain less information than a full patent application.[6] If the applicant wishes to proceed with a full patent application, it must file a patent application corresponding to the provisional application within 12 months.[7] The option to file a provisional patent application reduces the cost of the initial filing and gives the applicant the ability to limit its further costs if it elects not to move forward with the application.

16.1.2 *Design Patents*

In addition to utility patents, the US Patent Act allows for the registration and protection of industrial designs.[8] Like applications for utility patents, applications for design patents are examined by the USPTO, though design patents are granted for terms of 15 years from the date of grant, rather than 20 years from the date of application. The major distinction between design and utility patents is in their subject matter. Whereas utility patents are directed toward "any new and useful process, machine, manufacture, or composition of matter, or any new and useful improvement thereof",[9] design patents are directed toward "any new, original and ornamental design for an article of manufacture."[10] Thus, while a patentable invention must perform a useful function, a patentable design must possess an "ornamental" visual appearance, meaning an appearance that is not dictated by function.[11] It must also meet other criteria, including the requirement of nonobviousness, to be protectable.[12] Moreover, US design patents resemble copyrights in the scope of their

3 U.S. Patent & Trademark Off. 2023d.
4 U.S. Patent & Trademark Off. 2023e.
5 Quinn 2015.
6 35 U.S.C. § 111.
7 35 U.S.C. § 119.
8 35 U.S.C. §§ 171–173.
9 35 U.S.C. § 101.
10 35 U.S.C. § 171(a).
11 See Du Mont and Janis 2012, 264.
12 35 U.S.C. § 171(b).

protection, as copyright law also seeks to account for functional features in assessing visual similarity of protected and accused designs.[13]

The US system for design protection was originally proposed in 1841 as a registration system similar to the copyright-based system created by the UK Design Registration Act of 1839 (see Section 3.1 in Chapter 3). As noted in Section 3.1 of Chapter 3, the UK design protection system was bifurcated shortly thereafter, with ornamental designs continuing to be protected under a registration-based system pursuant to the Ornamental Designs Act of 1842, and designs "having reference to some purpose or utility" being subjected to a patent-like pre-grant examination system under the 1843 Utility Designs Act. For these useful designs, the 1843 Act sought to overcome the many impediments and weaknesses of the then-prevailing UK patent system.

No comparable bifurcation occurred in the United States. When the US Congress enacted patent protection for "any new and original design for a manufacture" (Act of August 29, 1842, ch. 263 § 3, 5 Stat. 543), this new design patent scheme addressed ornamental designs that were not already eligible for patent protection. And, as noted above, the US design patent system as ultimately enacted included a pre-grant examination procedure and fee schedule resembling that of the utility patent system. Thus, the United States wound up with examination-based systems for both ornamental designs and inventions, and did not enact an additional examination-based system for useful designs, as the United Kingdom did in its 1843 legislation.

16.1.3 *Specialty Protection Regimes*

Two specific types of functional designs – semiconductor chip layouts and marine vessel hulls – may be protected in the US under domain-specific statutory regimes that were seemingly enacted to fill the gaps between utility patent protection for functional inventions, on one hand, and design patent and copyright protection for ornamental designs, on the other.

The Semiconductor Chip Protection Act of 1984[14] protects the physical three-dimensional layout of a semiconductor chip's circuitry from copying. While the logical circuit design of a semiconductor chip may be protectable by utility patents, the physical layout of that circuit design can usually be accomplished in multiple ways, just as the software embodiment of a patentable algorithm may be coded in many different ways. But while software has been interpreted to constitute a "work of authorship" under the Copyright Act, a chip design, with fewer creative authorial elements characteristics, may be less amenable to copyright protection. As a result, the SCPA creates a sui generis protection scheme for semiconductor chip layouts – largely to protect them from "slavish" copying.[15]

[13] See Du Mont and Janis 2013, 843.
[14] 17 U.S.C. §§ 901–914.
[15] See Kasch 1992.

The Vessel Hull Design Protection Act of 1998[16] gives a 10-year period of protection to the designs of marine vessel hulls and decks that are registered with the US. Copyright Office. To be eligible for protection, the design must be used in "a useful article which makes the article attractive or distinctive in appearance to the purchasing or using public"[17] – thereby combining the features of innovations protectable by utility patents (functionality) and design patents and copyrights (ornamentality).

While still on the books, both the Semiconductor Chip Protection Act and the Vessel Hull Design Protection Act are seldom used and of largely historical interest.[18]

16.1.4 *Plant Protection*

Before 1980, new plant varieties were not considered to be eligible for protection by US utility patents.[19] As a result, two earlier protection regimes were established to protect new plant varieties in the US: Plant Patent Act of 1930[20] and the Plant Variety Protection Act of 1970 (PVPA).[21]

In 1930, the Plant Patent Act established a special "plant patent" form of protection for "any distinct and new variety of plant" that is invented through asexual reproduction (i.e., produced by grafting). In effect, plant patents are similar to other utility patents, save for the specific subject matter of their coverage.

Forty years later, the PVPA introduced a certificate protection scheme for "any novel variety of sexually reproduced plant" (i.e., produced by selective breeding). For most plants, protection under a PVPA certificate lasts for 20 years from the certificate's issuance (25 years in the case of a tree or vine). Unlike the Plant Patent Act, the PVPA requires that a protected plant variety be both uniform and stable.[22] In addition, the PVPA contains compulsory licensing provisions for plant varieties that the Department of Agriculture finds necessary to address food supply in the US,[23] an explicit research exemption,[24] and a provision that allows farmers to save and replant seed on their own farms.[25]

16.1.5 *Copyright for Functional Items*

The US Copyright Act extends copyright protection to all works of authorship, including visual works in two and three dimensions. Though in its earliest forms copyright in visual works existed only in works of "fine art" and did not extend to

16 17 U.S.C. §§ 1301–1332.
17 17 U.S.C. § 1301(a)(1).
18 See Kasch 1992; Olson 2007.
19 *Diamond* v. *Chakrabarty*, 447 U.S. 303, 311 (1980).
20 35 U.S.C. § 161.
21 7 U.S.C. ch. 57.
22 7 U.S.C. § 2402(a).
23 7 U.S.C. § 2404.
24 7 U.S.C. § 2544.
25 7 U.S.C. § 2543.

industrial products or designs, this changed with the Copyright Act of 1909, which expanded the scope of copyrightable subject matter to all works of authorship, including industrial designs.[26] With the recognition under the 1976 Copyright Act of copyright in computer software, it became clear that entire categories of functional works could become the subjects of copyright protection.

Yet, even today, copyright only extends to the ornamental and nonfunctional features of useful objects. Thus, sub-patentable innovations that serve a useful function, but which fall short of utility patent protection, remain unprotectable in the US, except in the special categories noted above.

16.2 THE DEBATE OVER SUB-PATENT PROTECTION IN THE US

Despite the assortment of special-purpose statutes described above, the US does not have a general system for the protection of functional innovations that fall below the threshold for utility patent protection. This absence, and the discrepancy between US law and that of many other large economies including Germany, France, China, Japan, and South Korea has led to ongoing discussion of a utility model or other sub-patent innovation system in the US.

16.2.1 *Critiques of the US Patent System for Sub-patentable Innovation*

Many of the proposals for utility model protection in the US arise from critiques of the utility patent system. One of the principal critiques of the utility patent system is that it is too slow, burdensome, and expensive to meet the needs of individuals and small and medium entities (which we refer to collectively as SMEs).[27] That is, SMEs may lack the funds or other resources to prosecute a utility patent application to completion. Moreover, competitive pressures may make the years-long wait for the issuance of a patent impractical for SMEs (e.g., if a competing business engages in infringement, it may drive the inventor out of business before a patent is issued). The low-cost and rapid availability of utility models may be seen as a remedy for these issues.[28]

A second critique is that the criteria for patentability are too stringent, thereby failing to protect worthy and socially beneficial innovations. This critique has become particularly intense following the US courts' tightening of criteria for both patentable subject matter under Section 101 of the Patent Act (rendering many

[26] Act of March 4, 1909, ch. 320, § 4, 35 Stat. 1075, 1076. See Du Mont and Janis 2013, 851.

[27] See Janis 1999, 151; Robinson 2014.

[28] This sentiment is reflected in the comments of a U.S. Senator at a recent hearing on patent issues. After noting that many of her constituents are individuals with single patents, often relating to the automotive industry, she asked the witness, "What about the two-tier system like Germany has? Where you can get the petty patent, or the smaller patent, or the gold-plated patent ..." U.S. Senate Judiciary Committee, Subcomm. on Intellectual Property, Hearings – Protecting Real Innovations by Improving Patent Quality, June 22, 2021 (question by Sen. Marsha Blackburn (R-TN) posed to Prof. Jorge Contreras).

innovations relating to software and medical diagnostics unpatentable)[29] and enablement and written description under Section 112 (rendering some biological innovations with large numbers of possible structures, such as antibodies, unpatentable).[30] The gist of this critique is generally that patentability thresholds should be lowered so that more innovations become eligible for utility patent protection.

A final avenue of critique, pioneered by Jerry Reichman, seemingly accepts the existing contours of utility patent law, but argues that innovations that fail to meet the criteria for utility patent protection may still be deserving of some form of legal protection.[31] Reichman observes that these "small scale innovations" are particularly vulnerable to appropriation because they are often readily discerned from products distributed on the open market and thus difficult to keep secret. As a result, this type of innovation may be discouraged, even though it may have significant social value, particularly on a cumulative basis.

16.2.2 *Academic Proposals regarding a US Sub-patent Innovation System*

Though there have been occasional legislative proposals in the US to implement a utility model or other sub-patent protection system,[32] none has, to our knowledge, ever gained serious momentum. Nevertheless, a number of proposals for sub-patent innovation protection systems have been made in the academic literature.

16.2.2.1 Traditional Utility Models

Some commentators, largely responding to SME cost and access concerns, have suggested that the US adopt a utility model system akin to that found in Germany and other countries.[33] Arguing for the adoption of a utility model system in the US, Karl Jorda reasons that "individual inventors, entrepreneurs, startups and small entities would welcome a lower-cost alternative to a utility patent."[34]

16.2.2.2 Research-Promoting Innovation Patents

Responding to the stringency of current utility patent requirements, Dmitry Karshtedt proposed the creation of a "research patent" that would provide a limited set of enforcement rights to the inventors of "upstream" innovations that do not yet fully meet the thresholds for utility patent protection (primarily utility, enablement and eligible subject matter).[35] Sean Seymore proposes the creation of a slightly different "research patent" that overcomes the need for chemical discoveries to have

[29] Karshtedt 2015; Lefsin et al. 2018.
[30] Karshtedt 2015; Lemley and Sherkow 2023.
[31] Reichman 2000.
[32] E.g., the Article Protection Act of 1995 proposed in the U.S. House of Representatives, which would have established a three-year term of protection for certain sub-patentable innovations. Jorda 2007, 3.
[33] Brack 2009; Jorda 2007.
[34] Jorda 2007, 3.
[35] Karshtedt 2015, 1015–1017.

a known utility.[36] Both of these proposals are directed toward the incentivization of scientific research through the granting of sub-patent rights when utility patent protection is not otherwise available.

16.2.2.3 Relaxed Examination Standards

Ann Bartow has taken a different tack, proposing a second-tier "origination patent" system that includes most of the requirements of the current utility patent system, but eliminates nonobviousness as a ground for invalidation (though leaving nonobviousness in place as a requirement for issuance).[37] Origination patents would have terms of only three to five years and have an accelerated examination pathway of no more than one year. The mechanism would, in theory, permit innovators to obtain quick, short-duration rights for minor innovations (she mentions toothbrushes and hairbrushes), while at the same time "strengthening the obviousness inventiveness requirement of traditional patents by diverting less innovative but currently patentable inventions into second tier protection, in a manner that benefits society and offers advantages to the second tier patentee."[38]

16.2.2.4 Further Domain-Specific Protection

The domain-specific protections afforded under US law for sub-patentable innovations such as vessel hulls, semiconductor layouts and plant varieties have been widely criticized and are not used heavily.[39] Nevertheless, scholars concerned about innovation in particular industries have proposed a variety of additional domain-specific protection schemes for technologies including software,[40] DNA sequences[41] and environmental technologies.[42]

16.2.2.5 Liability Rule Frameworks

Jerry Reichman, critical of the continued expansion of exclusive property-like rights to sub-patentable innovations, argues against the definition of new domains for patent-like protection.[43] Yet recognizing that the lack of protection for "small scale innovations" results in reduced incentives for the creation of these socially valuable innovations, Reichman proposes a "liability rule" scheme whereby the creators of sub-patentable innovations would be entitled to compensation for the use of those innovations, but do not have the right to exclude others from using them.[44]

36 Seymore 2021.
37 Bartow 2000.
38 Bartow 2000, 13.
39 Burk and Lemley 2009, 98–100.
40 Long 2004, 546 n. 194 (collecting and summarizing proposals).
41 Holman and Munzer 2000.
42 Derzlm 1996.
43 Reichman 2000.
44 Reichman 2000. See also Rutschman and Reichman 2023.

In a similar gesture toward liability rules, Toshiko Takenaka has proposed a novel "inclusive patent" system that would entitle any user of a covered innovation to obtain a compulsory license from third party holders of blocking patents.[45] Though Takenaka's inclusive patent would be granted without substantive examination, its scope appears to be comparable to that of a utility patent.

16.2.2.6 Rational Ignorance and Registration Systems

Other authors have looked critically at the US patent examination system and its frequent failure to screen out "bad" patents.[46] Assessing this situation, Mark Lemley famously, and counterintuitively, concluded in 2001 that "the PTO doesn't do a very detailed job of examining patents, but we probably don't want it to. It is 'rationally ignorant' of the objective validity of patents, in economics lingo, because it is too costly for the PTO to discover those facts."[47] That is, the cursory examination given to patents may be warranted, as most patents are never licensed or asserted, and the validity of valuable patents can be tested in litigation. F. Scott Kieff took this reasoning a step further in 2003, arguing that the most efficient patent system would require only registration, with no substantive examination at all, leaving any determination of validity to post-issuance litigation and thereby removing any presumption of validity for issued patents.[48]

Neither Lemley nor Kieff explores, nor even mentions, the registration-based systems used for utility models in many countries. Nevertheless, the persistence of scholarly ruminations about registration-based systems for patents suggests that such systems may have salience even in the US. This being said, registration-based systems have obvious drawbacks, particularly for SMEs, by allowing the unrestricted creation, exploitation and enforcement of tentative rights in an environment where litigation is costly and lengthy. As the Supreme Court observed in *Lear* v. *Atkins*, issued but invalid patents pose a threat the market by encumbering "the important public interest in permitting full and free competition in the use of ideas which are in reality a part of the public domain."[49]

16.2.3 *Potential Features of a US Utility Model System*

As discussed in the other chapters of this book, utility model systems differ from patent systems in significant ways. The table below presents some of the potential differences that a utility model system in the US might have from the existing utility patent system. As in other countries, these differences would be directed at

45 Takenaka 2021a.

46 Lemley 2001, 1495–1496 (collecting sources).

47 Lemley 2001, 1497.

48 Kieff 2003, 70–72.

49 *Lear, Inc.* v. *Atkins*, 395 U.S. 653 (1969). See also Contreras 2021, 8–9 (enumerating market risks arising from the circulation of "bad" patents).

TABLE 16.1 *Comparison of principal features of US utility patents, design patents and hypothetical utility models*

Feature	Utility patent	Design patent	Utility model (hypothetical)
Examination	Yes	Yes	No or abbreviated
Nonobviousness requirement	Yes	Yes	No (novelty only or novelty plus some "soft" nonobviousness requirement)
Term	20 years from date of application	15 years from date of grant	Shorter (e.g., 10 years from date of application)
Presumption of validity	Yes	Yes	No

making it easier and less costly for individuals and small businesses to obtain a low level of protection for sub-patentable innovations. Table 16.1 summarizes how these distinctions might play out were the US to adopt a utility model system.

16.3 REFLECTIONS ON THE FUTURE OF UTILITY MODELS UNDER US LAW

In 1999, one of us (Janis) examined the history and then-existing practice of second-tier patent regimes outside the US (incorporating within that label utility models and a variety of subsidiary patent regimes), and argued that the US should not create a utility model system.[50] As of the time of this writing – nearly a quarter century later – much has changed in US patent law and policy, and in approaches to second tier patents around the globe. And, still, a good deal has remained the same. A fresh look is warranted at the issues likely to arise if the US were to contemplate introducing a utility model system today.

We have divided the discussion into three parts. First, we consider the doctrinal issues concerning the grant of utility model rights, focusing on the nonobviousness doctrine. Second, we consider how the existence of a utility model system might change the patent enforcement landscape in the US. Finally, we address a few key questions about the politics and political economy of utility model rights.

16.3.1 *Obtaining Utility Models: The Soft Nonobviousness Problem*

Utility model skeptics and proponents alike surely would agree that the critical issue in designing protectability rules for a utility model system concerns nonobviousness – specifically, whether to incorporate the invention patent standard, dispense with a nonobviousness requirement altogether, or fashion a new doctrine that is less

50 Janis 1999.

stringent than the invention patent standard but that performs a similar function of tuning the system's ex ante incentives on a case-by-case basis with greater sensitivity than is feasible through the use of loss-of-right provisions alone.

For invention patents, nonobviousness[51] remains the "ultimate condition of patentability"[52] and the most important hurdle to patentability for most types of subject matter[53] from a practical perspective, and from a theoretical perspective as a tool for fine-tuning ex ante patent incentives. Given the high stakes surrounding nonobviousness determinations, it is not surprising that the contours of nonobviousness doctrine in US patent law remain in ferment.

The Supreme Court's 2007 decision in *KSR* v. *Teleflex*[54] has not eliminated debates over fundamental aspects of the nonobviousness inquiry. The Court in *KSR* warned against the use of "rigid" approaches to the teaching/suggestion/motivation element of the nonobviousness calculus but stopped short of eliminating or replacing that element.[55] Unsurprisingly given *KSR*'s ambiguities, some commentators have characterized the decision as a watershed, while others have viewed it as considerably less momentous. What *KSR* has perhaps most clearly shown is that nonobviousness is likely to be the subject of perpetual cycling between strict and relaxed applications, perhaps reflecting deep divides among judges about the ultimate economic function of the patent grant.[56]

In addition, the US invention patent system has undergone a major process shift in the past decade: many nonobviousness determinations today arise from *inter partes review* (IPR) proceedings conducted in the first instance by the Patent Trial and Appeal Board (PTAB) of the USPTO, rather than in district court litigation. The long-term ramifications of this shift for patentability doctrines such as nonobviousness are yet to be worked out.

What might we expect if the US were to implement a utility model system? First, we would expect to see statutory language that is configured to leave much of the development of the second-tier nonobviousness standard (whatever that might be) to the courts and the PTAB. This is a familiar pattern in US patent legislation.[57] Nonetheless, it suggests that the validity of hypothetical US utility model rights would be subject to an initial period of instability and uncertainty as the jurisprudence of second-tier nonobviousness developed. Compounding the problem, if the frequency

[51] 35 U.S.C. § 103.

[52] Witherspoon 1980.

[53] For some types of software and biotechnology inventions, eligibility may have eclipsed obviousness in importance in recent decades.

[54] *KSR Intern. Co.* v. *Teleflex Inc.*, 550 U.S. 398 (2007).

[55] Ibid. at 415.

[56] Holte and Sichelman 2019.

[57] See, e.g., *Graham* v. *John Deere & Co.*, 383 U.S. 1, 16 (1966) (explaining that when Congress added the obviousness provision to the patent statute, the provision was intended to partially codify existing judicial practice and allow space for further judicially developed tests to be worked out).

of litigation (and post-grant administrative challenges) is considerably lower than for utility patents, as seems possible, then the period of instability may be protracted.[58] Moreover, constructions of Section 103 in utility patent law proceeded against the backdrop of a century of common law development. Constructions of a second-tier nonobviousness provision would proceed in a vacuum, comparatively speaking.

Second, we would expect that the standard for second-tier nonobviousness would be defined relative to the invention patent standard. This may set in motion an uneasy push-and-pull between the invention patent and utility model regimes, the consequences of which might not be foreseeable. At a minimum, it would suggest that changes in the invention patent nonobviousness jurisprudence necessarily would trigger corresponding changes in the utility model jurisprudence. It might also suggest the analogous phenomenon in reverse: decisions that modify the second-tier nonobviousness standard could have knock-on effects on the invention patent obviousness standard. One possible outcome is that equilibrium is never reached; instead we might see cycles of movement as one standard shoves the other and vice versa. Alternatively, if decisionmakers find it all but impossible to establish a uniform conceptual space between the invention patent nonobviousness standard and its second-tier counterpart, they might eventually give up the task, with the result that one comes to resemble the other.[59] Scholars who are already concerned that the invention patent nonobviousness standard is too generous may find it eroded still further. Or, conversely, those who believe that second-tier patents would fill a gap in intellectual property rights by providing some protection for innovations that do not quite rise to the level of invention patents may be disappointed to discover that second-tier nonobviousness is not materially different from invention patent nonobviousness, subverting the primary goal of having second-tier protection.

16.3.2 *Enforcing Utility Models: Utility Model Thickets?*

According to the now-familiar anti-commons argument popularized by Heller and Eisenberg in the 1990s[60] and carried forward by many other scholars, in technology areas where patent rights are abundant and their ownership is fragmented, technological innovation may be inefficiently underused due to the high costs of assembling commercially viable clusters of patent rights. Many scholars have used the

[58] Design patent law or plant patent law may furnish appropriate analogs, but in those regimes applications are examined ex parte for nonobviousness, which leads to the development of some norms and practices at the USPTO. That would be absent for utility models if those applications are not examined ex parte.

[59] Not everyone is daunted by the difficulty of distinguishing between nonobviousness and soft nonobviousness. See Kennedy 2015 (arguing for the addition of a “partial obviousness” criterion to utility patent law).

[60] Heller 1998, 621; Heller and Eisenberg 1998, 698–701.

metaphor of "patent thickets" to describe a type of anti-commons problem or the conditions that might give rise to an anti-commons.[61]

The patent thicket/anti-commons argument is relevant for utility models because the very nature of utility model protection suggests the potential for congestion of rights. The introduction of utility model protection would increase the sheer aggregate number of exclusive rights, and individual utility models are likely to be narrow in scope, suggesting the prospect of highly fragmented ownership.[62]

But rights congestion arising from the presence of numerous separately owned utility models is only one of the conditions that might give rise to a thicket of rights and an anti-commons problem. The other has to do with the technological resource to which a particular cluster of utility models attaches. For example, how likely is it that a cluster of utility models would cover inputs that a third party might need to incorporate in manufacturing a complex product? How probable is it that third parties would confront the need to investigate and work around utility model rights in order to enter a market? We suspect that there is no general answer to these questions.

Even where the conditions appear favorable for the development of an anti-commons, it does not invariably follow that this is problematic – that is, it is not clear that the problem of inefficient underutilization necessarily (or even frequently) results when an anti-commons exists. Transaction-cost-reducing mechanisms such as patent pooling arrangements or group commitments to grant licenses on specified (e.g., FRAND) terms, as is seen with heavily patented technical standards, may be brought to bear.[63] Third parties may simply choose to infringe and rely on the high cost of enforcement to discourage rights-holders from suing.[64]

A word may be in order here about technological prospects. Early fears about anti-commons emergence focused on the patenting of gene fragments uncovered in genome mapping projects (or used as research tools in those projects). Prompted in part by these fears, the PTO and courts deployed the utility requirement[65] to curtail patent grants (and thus technological prospecting) in genomics.

Most discussions of utility model protection appear to assume that these events have little to do with utility model systems. To be sure, it is probably safe to predict that the usual subject matter of utility model protection would be modest (sub-patentable) but commercially desirable modifications to mechanical devices. But, in theory, utility models could become an avenue for attempts to secure protection for subject matter such as research tools, medical diagnostic methods, business methods, or the like. This may suggest the need for carefully crafted utility and eligibility rules for utility models, and might in turn suggest that the utility model

61 Egan and Teece 2015.

62 Janis 1999.

63 See Chapter 18 (discussing FRAND licensing commitments applied to utility models that are declared essential to certain standards).

64 For discussions of these and other mechanisms, see Eisenberg 2008; Teece 2017.

65 In re Fisher, 421 F.3d 1365 (Fed. Cir. 2005).

scheme could become a new front for litigation over those rules, akin to the wars over subject matter eligibility that have typified recent US invention patent law.

16.3.3 *Who Would Benefit from a US Utility Model System?*

We now turn from doctrine and theory to pragmatic political questions. Who would most benefit from the creation of a utility model system in the US? What does that tell us about whether creating such a system would advance US patent policy goals?

16.3.3.1 SMEs?

Perhaps the most common argument voiced in support of the creation of utility model systems is that it would offer SMEs a reduced-cost alternative to invention patents (see Section 16.2.1). These assertions indulge several important assumptions: first, that SMEs are a significant source of socially valuable innovation; second, that much of this innovation may be of the sub-patentable variety (chiefly because it may be deemed obvious in view of the prior art under applicable invention patent standards); and, third, that the sheer cost of obtaining and enforcing invention patent rights reduces the level of R&D investment that SMEs might otherwise command, or thwarts SMEs entirely from inventing and disclosing their inventions. Accepting *arguendo* the first two assumptions, we are left with questions about whether creating a utility model system in the US would address the problem of cost. It would not surprise us if the cost issue were a focal point of any future debate in Congress about whether to create a utility model system.

Of course, if the cost of invention patent protection is the crucial problem, attacking it directly may be more efficient than creating a new form of intellectual property right and all the administrative infrastructure that would be required to support it. Indeed, within the past two decades, the US has put in place mechanisms designed to facilitate access to the existing utility patent system, and we expect that US utility model skeptics would argue that these mechanisms could be refined (and are being refined) on an ongoing basis at relatively low administrative costs.

One such mechanism is fee discounts for SMEs. For example, effective in 2013, the PTO established a "micro-entity" status available to applicants who meet the small entity requirement,[66] have a gross income falling below a specified cap, and who have not filed more than five patent applications.[67] Micro entities receive an 80 percent reduction in government filing fees.[68]

In addition, under current UPSTO rules,[69] any applicant may request deferral of an application for up to three years from the earliest date of filing. The USPTO will

[66] 37 CFR 1.27.
[67] 37 CFR 1.29.
[68] U.S. Patent & Trademark Off. 2023b.
[69] 37 CFR 1.103(d).

not grant such a deferral request until all required fees (including search and examination fees) have been paid and the application is complete. In an effort to make the patent system more accessible to small and medium enterprises (SMEs), in 2023 USPTO proposed a "Track Three Pilot Program" that would permit qualifying "micro entity" applicants to delay payment of search and examination fees for 30 months from the earliest filing date claimed.[70] This fee deferral, if adopted, would permit SME applicants to "test the waters" regarding the viability of the market for the products subject to their patent applications before incurring the more substantial costs of examination.[71]

To reduce another major source of cost of obtaining patents – attorney fees – the USPTO has partnered with law schools, bar organizations, and other nonprofits to create a nationwide network of patent hubs that seek to match SMEs with patent lawyers who provide pro bono patent application services.[72] In addition, several law schools now offer patent-related pro bono clinical services to qualifying SMEs, including the preparation and prosecution of patent applications.[73]

These efforts, of course, do not address the costs associated with enforcing patent rights – costs that are surely prohibitive for many SMEs. And there is no sign that those costs are easing. While the US introduced expanded forms of administrative patent validity challenges through the America Invents Act,[74] it is not evident that those mechanisms have reduced the overall cost of resolving disputes over validity, even though administrative challenges are now frequently used. Moreover, although Congress passed legislation in 2020 establishing a small claims tribunal for copyright disputes,[75] no analogous patent small claims court exists in the US, although interest in exploring the feasibility of such a court continues.[76]

This being said, an appreciable number of patent infringement suits in the US are brought by attorneys on a contingency fee basis, in which they receive payment only if the patentee receives a damages award or the case is settled with a payment.[77] Moreover, the use of third party litigation financing by patent litigants has also increased in recent years,[78] a development that, in theory, could make the assertion of patents by SMEs more accessible.

70 U.S. Patent & Trademark Off., Request for Comments on a Proposed Track Three Pilot Program with a Pre-Examination Search Option, 88 Fed. Reg. 34,136 (May 26, 2023).

71 See ibid. ("The USPTO recognizes that under-resourced applicants may need a low-cost option with minimal requirements to allow them additional time for commercialization efforts and to ascertain the value of their inventions.")

72 U.S. Patent & Trademark Off. 2023c.

73 U.S. Patent & Trademark Off. 2023a (describing the USPTO's program for certifying law school clinics).

74 See 35 U.S.C. §§ 311–319 (inter partes review); 35 U.S.C. §§ 321–329 (post-grant review).

75 U.S. Copyright Off. 2023 (noting the creation of the Copyright Claims Board); Copyright Alternative in Small-Claims Enforcement Act (CASE Act) of 2020, Pub. L. No. 116-260, Title II, § 212.

76 See Administrative Conf. of the U.S. (ACUS) 2023; U.S. Patent and Trademark Off. 2022.

77 Schwartz 2012.

78 Wild 2023.

Utility model skeptics might point out that utility model systems as historically implemented have seemed to contemplate that utility models would be enforced in the same way as invention patents – through existing civil litigation channels (both in the courts and at the International Trade Commission, an independent executive agency that has played an increasingly prominent role in patent litigation but whose authority over sub-patentable innovation protection would need to be addressed via its own governing statute). Indeed, many discussions about utility models may assume that utility models will rarely be the subject of enforcement actions. But the cost of enforcement should not be overlooked, and it may weigh heavily in debates in the US, where the notoriously high cost of civil discovery and the American rule against attorney-fee-shifting may present policymakers with a cost/benefit analysis for utility models that differs significantly from that of other parts of the globe.

16.3.3.2 Non-practicing Entities?

Proponents of utility model systems should also be prepared to deal with the argument that a US utility model system would create a new fertile environment for litigation on the part of non-practicing entities (NPEs). NPE interest in utility models would seem virtually inevitable. Indeed, NPEs are sometimes characterized as market intermediaries who facilitate the enforcement of patent rights by carrying out enforcement actions more efficiently than individual rightsholders might be capable of doing, and this surely describes the circumstances of the prototypical SME utility model owner. Add to that the prospect that utility models would be issued with limited or no pre-grant substantive examination, and one may wonder whether NPEs might perceive utility models as an irresistible new vehicle for litigation.[79] Indeed, as shown in Chapter 16, a significant number of the few enforcement actions involving standards-essential utility models have been brought by NPEs.

At minimum, then, it would seem that any modern legislative proposal for utility models in the US would need to contend with the specter of NPE litigation. Contemporary patent jurisprudence provides some relevant insights. Discussions about the availability of permanent injunctive relief for NPEs in *eBay*,[80] about retaining an objective element in the test for willful infringement to guard against aggressive NPE assertions,[81] about the good faith belief in invalidity as a defense against indirect infringement allegations (especially those made by NPEs),[82] and about NPE forum shopping[83] may all be germane to the design of a utility model system for the US.

[79] There are mitigating considerations: utility models are likely to be of very limited scope and would have a short duration. But it seems to us a tricky path for utility model proponents to tread, saying on one hand that utility models would confer significant private value on their SME holders, but on the other hand that utility models would not be of such value as to attract NPEs.

[80] *eBay Inc.* v. *MercExchange, L.L.C.*, 547 U.S. 388 (2006).

[81] *Halo Elecs., Inc.* v. *Pulse Elecs., Inc.*, 579 U.S. 93 (2016).

[82] *Commil USA, LLC* v. *Cisco Sys., Inc.*, 575 U.S. 632 (2015).

[83] *TC Heartland LLC* v. *Kraft Foods Group Brands LLC*, 581 U.S. 258 (2017).

16.3.3.3 The Usual Suspects?

The debate over passage of the America Invents Act revealed a critical fissure in US patent politics between interests associated with the pharmaceutical/life sciences industry and those associated with the software/tech industry. We wonder whether a proposal to bring utility model protection to the US would trigger a similar clash, with the software industry opposing utility model protection and the pharmaceutical industry favoring it.

One reason that the pharmaceutical industry might support utility model protection is that the industry may see utility model protection as an avenue for capturing the value of a wide range of sub-patentable innovation that is incidental to drug development. Suppose, for example, that a pharmaceutical company holding a soon-to-expire invention patent on a pioneer drug sought utility model protection on novel (but obvious) dosage formulations, packaging, or the like. Some might regard this as a new form of evergreening,[84] suggesting that the arrival of utility model protection might add to what is already one of the most contentious debates in contemporary patent law.

In the law of invention patents, the typical doctrinal response to concerns about evergreening is to strengthen the nonobviousness doctrine,[85] or, relatedly, the obviousness-type double patenting doctrine,[86] which is "intended to prevent a patentee from obtaining a time-wise extension of patent for the same invention or an obvious modification thereof."[87] If utility model protection were introduced, we may begin to see litigation over the complexities of patent-to-utility model obviousness-type double patenting. More importantly, we might see calls for boosting the utility model nonobviousness standard. But this would in turn presumably make it harder for SMEs to obtain utility model protection, and thus would seem to undermine a key argument for introducing utility model protection in the first place.

16.4 CONCLUSION

The US is one of the few major patent-granting jurisdictions that lacks a utility model or other sub-patent innovation protection regime. While a number of domain-specific protection regimes have arisen over the years to fill this gap for

[84] But *cf.* Lietzan 2019, 805 (questioning the use of the terminology).

[85] Or for applying inherent anticipation vigorously. *Scherer Corp.* v. *Geneva Pharms.*, 339 F.3d 1373 (Fed. Cir. 2003) (ruling that the disclosure of a compound inherently disclosed metabolites of the compound).

[86] See, e.g., In re Cellect, 81 F.4th 1216 (Fed. Cir. 2023) (ruling that the expiration date for purposes of an obviousness-type double patenting analysis where a patent has received patent term adjustment for PTO delays is the date that includes the patent term adjustment).

[87] In re Lonardo, 119 F.3d 960, 965 (Fed. Cir. 1997).

specialized technologies such as semiconductor topographies and vessel hulls, a broad, generalized sub-patent protection regime has never been established or meaningfully considered.

Part of the intuitive aversion to sub-patent systems in the US may arise from the canonical American myth of the "lone genius" inventor exemplified (largely inaccurately, from a historical standpoint) by folk heroes such as Thomas Edison, Robert Fulton, Eli Whitney and the Wright Brothers.[88] Patents, according to the myth, should reward "extraordinary inventions", with more ordinary innovations accepted only grudgingly. During the mid twentieth century, this perception even seemed to find favor among some Supreme Court justices. As Justice Douglas wrote in 1950:

> It is not enough that an article is new and useful. The Constitution never sanctioned the patenting of gadgets. Patents serve a higher end – the advancement of science. An invention need not be as startling as an atomic bomb to be patentable. But it has to be of such quality and distinction that masters of the scientific field in which it falls will recognize it as an advance.[89]

Against this backdrop, it is not surprising that the US has not adopted a formal regime of sub-patent protection. Yet in its absence, scholars and the USPTO have proposed a range of mechanisms that could address perceived cost and access issues with the invention patent system. Any such proposals, if implemented, would invariably result in conflicts with, and potential alteration of, the invention patent system in ways whose benefits are far from clear. As such, it does not appear that a utility model or similar system is likely to emerge in the US in the foreseeable future.

88 Lemley 2012.

89 *Great Atlantic & Pac. Tea Co.* v. *Supermarket Equip. Corp.*, 340 U.S. 147 (1950) (Douglas, J., concurring).

PART II

Utility Models in Action

17

The Unitary Patent System and Utility Models

Lisa van Dongen, Timo Minssen and Tine Sommer*

Since the Unified Patent Court (UPC) and the UP system officially entered into force on 1 June 2023, European patent law is experiencing a procedural and substantial regime shift. Before, only the prosecution of European Patents (EP) at the European Patent Office (EPO) was harmonised through a centralised procedure granting a "bundle of patents," designating various Member States. The post-grant litigation of European Patents, however, was exclusively dealt with by national law. This changed with the introduction of European patents with unitary effect, which are litigated within the UPC system. These exciting developments correspond with a trend of increasing harmonisation in the European Intellectual Property (IP) arena through various EU legal acts, which pertain to a broad range of other rights such as supplementary protection certificates (SPCs), regulatory exclusivities, trade secrets, trademarks, industrial designs and copyrights.

However, as the process leading up to the necessary national ratification of the Unified Patent Court Agreement (UPCA) has demonstrated, the speed, scope and degree of the much-coveted harmonisation is not straightforward, and there is still a patchwork of various interacting rights and national peculiarities that need to be carefully considered. Consequently, the UP system and alternative forms of protection do not only offer new promises and opportunities, but also persisting uncertainties, legal lacunae and perils that need to be navigated by all relevant stakeholders.

In that context, it is important to recall that patents do not offer the only pathway to protect technical solutions to technical problems through negative exclusionary rights for a limited period of time. Unless Inventors choose to keep their inventions secret or to rely on regulatory exclusivities, some jurisdictions still offer UM

* Minssen's research for this chapter was supported by a Novo Nordisk Foundation Grant for a scientifically independent International Collaborative Bioscience Innovation & Law Programme (Inter-CeBIL programme – grant no. NNF23SA0087056).

protection for (minor) inventions, also called "small patents," "utility patents," "innovation patents," "second-tier patents" and "short-term patents." In this chapter, we refer to this form of protection as utility models, or in short: UMs. Generally, the European Commission and IP offices stress that UMs are shorter, simpler, faster and cheaper protection methods compared to patents, but there are differences in how these features are implemented.[1] The differences between UMs and patents result in multidimensional sorting as economic agents choose within the IP menu in accordance with the specific differences in characteristics and outcomes of patents and UMs.[2] Strategic choices are complicated by the fact that various European and international jurisdictions display very different approaches with regard to UMs, that is, in terms of availability, procedure, scope, enforceability and how requirements are interpreted.[3] It is further important to note that UMs are also not *directly* covered by the UP system, and since earlier attempts towards a harmonised EU system for UMs have failed,[4] national rules and disparities remain applicable, despite their kinship to patents.

But how will the UPC interact with and affect the system for UM protection in Europe and vice-versa? This is an important question. It relates to both procedural dynamics and substantial effects in prosecution and litigation, which will, in turn, influence the stakeholder's choices and the different IP strategies that these may pursue. Within the patent context, stakeholders will have to consider, amongst other things, which forum to seek for litigation and, more specifically, if it would be better to "opt out" from the UPC system and, if having done so, when to withdraw from the "opt out."[5] On top of all this, they will have to consider if UMs should be part of their IP and innovation strategy, be it as a sole form of protection that is sought for a given jurisdiction from the start, or whether and when patent (applications) should be converted into UMs or branched off. This chapter attempts to shed some light on these issues, which are as relevant as they are elusive.

Specifically, it focuses on the delicate interplay between the new European Unitary Patent (UP) system and utility model (UM) protection. To set the stage and provide the necessary background, Section 17.1 will start out with a brief recap and overview of the relationship between the EU, the European Patent Convention (EPC),[6] and the UPCA. Section 17.2 will then elaborate on the differences among relevant jurisdictions with regard to the availability of UPs and UMs. This section will also deliver a brief description of the basic formal relationship between the EPC, the UPCA, the EU, UMs, the European Patent Office (EPO) and national

1 Heikkilä 2023a; Utility Models and European harmonisation is discussed in more detail in Chapter 20.
2 Ibid.
3 For further details, see Björkwall 2009, 309; Ruse-Khan 2012.
4 COM (95) 370; COM (97) 691; COM 1999, 309; 26 July 2001; SEC 2001, 1307.
5 Minssen and Lundqvist 2014, 340–357.
6 European Patent Convention 1973.

granting authorities. Next, Sections 17.3–17.5 will explore how the changes brought about by the introduction of the UPC and UP into the existing patent-UM landscape may affect business strategies involving patents and UMs of businesses operating in Europe. Section 17.3 first examines the division of judicial competences now that the UPC has become operational, and Section 17.4 then scrutinizes the relationship between domestic courts and UPC divisions. This is followed by Section 17.5 which will start by digging deeper into the general reasons and strategic considerations that stakeholders might have for converting patents into UMs or for branching them off, and then considers the specific issues of how double patenting and the BOUM ("branched-off utility models") strategies might be affected post-UPC, as well as the cost of a UP. This provides the basis for Section 17.6, vis-á-vis strategic choices, followed by concluding remarks pointing towards unresolved issues and areas for future research in Section 17.7.

17.1 THE EU, THE EPC AND THE UPCA

From a patent law perspective, it is noteworthy that today's *EU patent with unitary effect* has been in the making since 1976.[7] Ever since the Treaty of Rome[8] entered into force in 1958, a project to establish an EU patent as a unitary right has been discussed. The EU Commission has published communications and reports and proposed several drafts for legislation for an EU patent.[9] Until 2023, the impact of EU law on patent law has been largely negligible.

The Treaty of Rome was silent on IPR issues, and simply stated in Article 295 (now Article 345 of the TFEU)[10] that it in no way prejudiced the rules of Member States governing the system of property ownership. However, the protection of IPRs was included in the original Treaty structure in a more indirect way. Article 36 of the Treaty (now Article 36 of the TFEU) did allow Member States to restrict the free movement of goods (one of the four major freedoms established by the Treaty of Rome) on specific grounds, which included "the protection of industrial and commercial property." Nevertheless, the European Court of Justice (now Court of Justice of the European Union, CJEU) did not allow all restrictions on free movement rights to be justified by national IP rights, and already in its early case law it was distinguishing between the *existence* of a right (Article 345) and the *exercise* of a right, therefore interpreting Article 36 as covering only the "*specific subject matter*" of the right.[11] Accordingly, the CJEU interpreted the provision as a requirement of non-discrimination in the granting and protection of IPRs in the

[7] European Patent Convention (76/76/EEC); and L/401/1 30 December 1989 (89/695/EØF).
[8] Rome Treaty 1957.
[9] COM 2000, 412; COM 2010, 790; COM 2011, 215.
[10] Lisbon Treaty 2016.
[11] Pila 2022, 538–539.

Community.[12] It developed the doctrine of regional exhaustion of rights by the lawful placing of a product on the market in the Community.[13] Without direct treaty authority, the CJEU thus managed to develop a set of rules on patent law on the way to a non-discriminatory trade law.

The furthest point so far, at the treaty level, is Article 118 of the TFEU adopted by the Lisbon Treaty in 2009. It states that the European Parliament and the Council shall provide measures for the creation of European IP rights to provide uniform protection throughout the Union. In addition to this, Article 262 of the TFEU provides for conferral of jurisdiction on the Court of Justice of the European Union in disputes relating to IP rights. So far, uniform protection has been established for trademarks and designs.[14] Somehow patent protection slipped through the net, probably to some degree due to the entering into force of the 1973 European Patent Convention (EPC 1973).[15] Due to the EPC, which established the European Patent Organisation (EPOrg) in 1973, EPs reside outside the EU, and the number of contracting states to the EPC has increased during the years. Today, it has 39 members.[16] All EU Member States are also members of the EPOrg and, since a UP will start out as an application for an EP, the EPO will continue as an important player in the European patent landscape.

In a way, the EPC was a compromise, as the political landscape at the time of the adoption of the EPC did not allow for a unitary European Community Patent. Consequently, it was decided to follow a different pathway. According to its preamble, the EPC is a special agreement within the meaning of Article 19 of the Paris Convention[17] and a regional patent treaty pursuant to Article 45 of the Patent Cooperation Treaty (PCT).[18] Therefore, Article 1 of the EPC establishes a substantive and procedural European law for the grant of EPs as a "system of law, common to the Contracting States, for the grant of patents for invention" and it allows applicants either to obtain a bundle of patents designating various contracting states or to designate a single contracting state only.[19]

As for UMs, the EU Commission's endeavours to establish uniform UM protection have failed.[20] In March 2000, the Commission suspended its proposal due to

[12] Dashwood et al. 2011, 499ff.; and joint cases C-56/64 and 58/64 Établissements Consten S.à. R.L. and *Grundig-Verkaufs-GmbH* v *Commission of the European Economic Community*; and case C-15/74 *Centrafarm BV and Adriaan de Peijper* v *Sterling Drug Inc.*; Sommer et al. 2023.

[13] Case C-15/74 *Centrafarm* v *Sterling Drug*. See Cook 2010, 35; Pila 2022, 537ff.

[14] Regulation 2017/1001 on the European Union trade mark; and regulation 6/2002 on Community designs (the latter is currently under review for amendment, see COM 2022/666 final; and COM 2022/667 final).

[15] European Patent Convention 1973.

[16] European Patent Office 2023b.

[17] Paris Convention 1967.

[18] Patent Cooperation Treaty 1970.

[19] See Singer and Stauder 2003, Articles 1 and 3.

[20] COM 1995, 370; COM 1997, 691; COM 1999, 309; SEC 2001, 1307. The process has been discussed in: Beier et al. 1994; Kern 1994b. Finally in its communication COM 2005, 462, the

difficulties in reaching consensus on its substance among Member States, and utility protection was abandoned in favour of unified patent protection.

By 1 June 2023 – 50 years after the foundation of the EPC and 65 years after the first attempt to adopt an EU patent – the "unitary patent package" entered into force and introduced a new concept, namely a "European patent with unitary effect" (UP), and the UPC emerged as the new patent judiciary for enforcement of EP with and without such unitary effect.[21] The unitary patent package consists of the UPCA,[22] the Unitary Patent Regulation (UPReg)[23] and the Translations Regulation (UPTReg).[24] The road to unitary patent protection was enabled in 2012 by enhanced cooperation, which is used when the EU as a whole cannot achieve the goals of cooperation in a particular field within a reasonable period. The outcome of this lack of coherence has been a rather atypical sort of EU harmonisation combining EU regulations, an international agreement – the UPCA – on the judiciary (in principle, the UPCA is placed outside the scope of the CJEU) with a granting authority – the EPO – disconnected from the EU. For contrast, the EU trademark and EU design right are genuine EU rights, granted by the EU Intellectual Property Office (EUIPO) and reviewed by its boards of appeal and the General Court and, on points of law, the CJEU.[25]

The "new" UPs must be registered by the EPO and will be effective in the 18 Member States which take part in the enhanced cooperation in the creation of unitary patent protection enacted by UPReg and which have ratified the UPCA. Both the EP and UP are granted by the EPO under the rules of the EPC, and there are no changes to the pre-grant phase or the EPC's substantive patent law in this regard. Only after the granting, the patent holder can request unitary effect, meaning uniform patent protection in 18 EU Member States.[26]

Article 3(1) of the UPReg states that a European patent granted with the same set of claims in respect of all the participating Member States shall benefit from unitary effect in all participating Member States; and in Article 4, that the unitary patent is effective on the date of publication in the European Patent Bulletin; implying that the participating Member States shall ensure that a European patent is deemed not to have taken effect as a national patent in their territory on the date of publication; and in Article 5(2) that the scope of that right and its limitations shall be uniform in all participating Member States in which the patent has unitary effect.

Commission has redrawn the proposal for utility model harmonisation. See Chapter 20 (European Harmonisation).

21 Geiger et al. 2018; Schovsbo et al. 2015, 271–274; Van Dongen 2023, 359.

22 UPCA 2013.

23 UPReg 2012.

24 UPTReg 2012.

25 Article 58a of the Statute of the Court of Justice of the European Union.

26 The UPReg, Article 9(1)(g) requires the applicant to request for unitary effect no later than one month after the grant of a European patent is published. See further European Patent Office 2022, B II, point 46.

As it follows from Article 3(b) of the UPCA, the agreement also applies to SPCs. According to Article 30, a SPC shall confer the same rights as conferred by the patent and shall be subject to the same limitations and the same obligations. In two 2023 proposals for regulations on unitary supplementary certificates for medicinal products and for plant protection products, the EUIPO was named as the central examination authority, and its opinion would be binding upon the national offices of the designated Member State which remains the granting authority. Because UPs are granted by the EPO, combined with the fact that the EP, UP and SPCs are closely linked, this may add to the confusion in the patent landscape.[27] This confusion may increase when considering UMs, for which some of the Member States that are part of the unitary patent area also provide protection in their national systems. This will be further explored in the next section.

17.2 PROTECTING UMS IN (SOME) EU MEMBER STATES AND THE TENTATIVE BEGINNING OF THE UPC ARRANGEMENT

This section starts out by providing a brief overview of the differences among relevant jurisdictions with regard to their participation in the UPC, and the availability of UPs and UMs. Next follows a brief description of the basic formal relationship between the EPO, UPs and UMs, as well as the interplay between the EPO, UMs and national granting authorities.

17.2.1 *An Overview*

As mentioned above, only 18 EU Member States are currently taking part in the UPC arrangement.[28] Only 11 UPC participating EU Member States provide for UM protection: Austria, Bulgaria, Denmark, Estonia, Finland, France, Germany, Italy, Portugal, Romania and Slovenia; whereas Greece, Hungary, Ireland and Slovakia are Member States that have signed but not yet ratified the UPCA, and UM protection can be obtained in these Member States. Also, Croatia, Poland and Spain are EU Member States with UM protection, but these Member States are not participating in the UPCA. Due to the gap and diversity in the EU Member States towards the UP and the UPC as such, and since all EU Member States

[27] In 2023, the Commission has adopted proposals on *unitary* supplementary certificates for medicinal products and plant protection products, COM (2023) 231 and (2023) 223. In its proposal for a regulation on compulsory licensing for crises management (COM 2023(224)), Article 2, UMs are included in the scope of the Regulation and thus subject to a Union compulsory license of IP rights that are necessary for the supply of crisis-relevant products to the Member States in the context of a Union crisis or emergency mechanism.

[28] Austria, Belgium, Bulgaria, Denmark, Estonia, Finland, France, Germany, Italy, Lithuania, Luxembourg, Latvia, Malta, Netherlands, Portugal, Sweden and Slovenia.

(including those with UM protection) are also Members of the EPO, the future UM landscape is rather blurred.

These numbers are summarised in Table 17.1.

TABLE 17.1 *European States and participation in European patent institutions*

Organisation/system	Number of Member States	Number of Member States with UM protection
European Union	27	18
Unified Patent Court Agreement (initial Signatory State)	24	15
Unitary Patent Area (completed ratification UPCA)	18	11
Non-participating Member States	3	3
European Patent Organisation	39	22

For inventors residing and/or operating in those EU Member States not yet part of the unitary patent area who can only obtain a EP, they may only opt for protection in the form of a bundle of national patents within and/or outside of the unitary patent area.

Despite the lack of coherence in the EU as to UM harmonisation and patent law harmonisation, some EU Member States, namely Germany, Spain, Italy, France and Poland are in the top 20 offices regarding the number of received UM applications, indicating a salience in the field of UM protection.[29] Thus, one cannot neglect the relevance of UM protection in the EU Member States.

17.2.2 *The EPC, the UPReg, the UPCA and How They Relate to UMs*

The EPOrg and the EU are two separate organisations, and so far EU legislation on substantive patent law has been minimal. However, the adoption of the first – and so far, the only – act on patentable subject matter in the EU, Directive 98/44/EC on biotechnological inventions (Biotech Directive),[30] has had an impact on the EPC. Its provisions on patentable subject matter were inserted into the Implementing Regulation of the EPC.[31] However, in the aftermath it was made clear that although the wording of the provisions is formulated similarly at different regulatory levels, their interpretations at the different levels are legally independent of each other.[32]

[29] WIPO 2023c, table A54.

[30] Biotech Directive.

[31] Implementing Regulations 2022, Chapter V, Rule 27–29.

[32] Case C-34/10 *Brüstle* v *Greenpeace*; Implementing Regulations Rule 28(c); Sommer 2013, 188; Sommer et al. 2023, 187–202.

The vulnerable point in European patent law is the increasingly mixed competences of the EPO and EU – now further confused by UPReg and the UPC. The UPReg is virtually deprived of substantive patent law,[33] whereas the UPCA's Chapter V forms the basis for future UPC jurisprudence.[34] Furthermore, the UPC must apply Union law and respect its primacy, as well as cooperate with the CJEU in accordance with Article 267 of the TFEU. Since EU law is almost silent on substantive patent law, it is hard to picture future CJEU involvement on a frequent scale concerning substantive patent law. Altogether, the CJEU's involvement seems rather limited, and the current frame is aimed at preventing the CJEU from becoming an appeal court for revocation and infringement while, at the same time, preserving its grip on Union law primacy. In other words, the UPC is a pretty isolated specialised court in European patent law. In this context, the UPC is likely to become a central policymaker in the future EU patent system despite its transnational character, as will be considered further in Section 17.5.[35]

Presently, the centre stage of the European patent system is taken by the EPO and its Boards of Appeal as developers of substantive patent law. The EPO has considerable autonomy towards granting, but subsequently limited judicial control. It is therefore possible to narrow down this section to focus on the EPO/EPC and UPC/UPCA. The EP (39 contracting states) and the UP (18 EU Member States) are both granted by the EPO under the rules of the EPC.

The EPC is the legal source for the pre-grant and granting procedure, only as such on patents and not on UMs. In other words, the unitary patent system and UMs are not clearly related, especially since the latter is not an EU or EPC harmonised right and falls outside the scope and competence of the UPC as such. However, as the EPC preamble clearly refers to the Paris Convention and PCT, it cannot contravene the provisions thereof. Article 1, subsection 2 of the Paris Convention states that the protection of industrial property has as its object patents, UMs and more. Therefore, in countries where UM protection is available, the general principles of the Paris Convention, such as national treatment and the right of priority, are also applicable to UMs. If an international patent application under the

[33] Included only in Article 6 and Article 8 on the exhaustion of rights and licenses of right.

[34] For completeness, the first provision of Chapter V, Article 24(1), refers to other sources of law, stating that "[i]n full compliance with Article 20 [on the primacy of EU law], when hearing a case brought before it under [the UPCA], the [UPC] shall base its decisions on: (a) Union law, including [the UPReg] and [UPTReg]; (b) [the UPCA]; (c) the EPC; (d) other international agreements applicable to patents and binding on all the Contracting Member States; and (e) national law." In addition, Article 5(3) of the UPReg conveys that "[t]he acts against which the [unitary] patent provides protection [. . .] and the applicable limitations shall be those defined by the law applied to European patents with unitary effect in the participating Member State whose national law is applicable to the European patent with unitary effect as an object of property in accordance with Article 7."

[35] Schovsbo et al. 2015, 272.

PCT is filed, UMs are available at the national level in designated countries that have a UM system. Article 43 of the PCT provides the legal basis for an international applicant to obtain a UM instead of or in addition to a patent (in accordance with national law), cf. Article 4(3) and R 4.1 (b)(iii) of the PCT.

Further, despite the EPC being patent-centred, UMs are no stranger to the convention. Article 140 of the EPC (Part VIII Impact on national law), stipulates that Articles 66, 124, 135, 137 and 139 of the EPC shall apply to UMs and utility certificates (the latter is a French instrument (see Chapter 5), and to applications for UMs and utility certificates registered or deposited in the Contracting States whose laws make provision for such models or certificates.[36] This interface of patent applications and UM applications motivates us to consider whether decisions by the UPC may impact UM protection and prosecution in the Member States.

17.2.3 *The EPO, UMs and National Granting Authorities*

Article 140 of the EPC provides the basis for a European patent application to be converted into a national UM application while maintaining its priority claim, cf. Articles 66 and 135. It further follows from Article 87, subparagraph 1, of the EPC, that the right of priority according to the Paris Convention applies to UMs and utility certificates.[37] Pursuant to Article 124 of the EPC, the applicant on request of the EPO must inform the office of all states in which it has filed UMs and the reference number of these applications.[38] Articles 135 and 137 of the EPC allow the application to be converted into a national UM or certificate without any additional national formal requirements.

Article 140 of the EPC is only directed towards patent applications to be converted into national UM applications by a request from the applicant. By the time the patent is granted and published – with or without a further request for unitary effect according to Article 9 (1)(g) of the UPReg – it is no longer relevant.

The UPC has not been given jurisdiction over UM protection, and once a patent application has been converted into a national UM application, all future aspects concerning the UM application are left to the autonomy of the national patent authority. Nevertheless, we cannot disregard that the UPC can have a potential impact on, for example, EPO patent families which have a UM registered as well.

[36] By virtue of Article 140, the other provisions apply to utility models and certificates covering, respectively, equivalence, information on prior art, request for conversion of a European patent to a national patent (or utility model or certificate), the formal requirements for conversion, and priority.

[37] Suominen et al. 2023, 152; Singer and Stauder 2003, 573–574, 567.

[38] Ibid.388: “Article 124 requires an applicant to mention all states, i.e., not only contracting states, in which they have filed corresponding *patent* applications.” Singer and Stauder 2003, 572: “There is no obligation to supply information on the filing of *utility model* applications in non-Contracting States, such as Japan.”

Thus, UPC case law might (indirectly) affect UM claim interpretation or undermine their validity given their potential overlap or connection to an EP or a UP.

17.3 DIVISION OF JUDICIAL COMPETENCES POST-UPC

As alluded to before, the UP and the UPC only form an extra layer in the existing patent landscape; they do not replace any type of patent or court.[39] However, this new patent and court are not created to form an isolated system either, which results in an interesting patchwork of jurisdiction in Europe. Moreover, it will both affect existing judicial relationships and create new ones. Directly or indirectly, such shifts may, in turn, bring about change in legal doctrine and who drives it for a given territory. It is improbable that these changes will be without some impact on business strategies involving patents and UMs of businesses operating in Europe. What the next part of this chapter contributes is a first exploration into some of the avenues that may effect change now that the UPC has become operational, starting with the division of jurisdiction.

17.3.1 *Jurisdiction on Non-national Patents*

What the creation of this new system means for the division of judicial competence on patents in Europe is as follows. According to the UPCA, the UPC will have exclusive competence on actions for revocation and enforcement of both classical EPs and UPs, as well as SPCs.[40] That is, after the expiration of the transitional period. The UPCA provides for a transitional regime for certain categories of patents during the first seven years (subject to a potential extension) of entry into force of the UPCA.[41] Until this regime lapses, disputes involving EPs and SPCs may also still be brought before national courts, resulting in shared competence between the UPC and national courts for such rights.

However, the UPCA also provides the option to formally opt out of the UPC's jurisdiction.[42] EPs and SPCs for which their proprietors have made use of the possibility to opt-out of the UPC's jurisdiction, remain the sole prerogative of the competent national courts within the territories in which they are valid even after the expiration of the transitional period. This point will not be pursued further, but it bears mentioning that the new UPC will thus essentially be competing with

[39] Van Dongen 2023, 359.

[40] UPCA 2013, Articles 3(a), (c) and 32(1)(a)–(f).

[41] As part of the transitional regime there is, however, the possibility for proprietors of European patents to opt out of the UPC's jurisdiction by means of notification to the Registry within seven years after the date the UPCA went into force, unless an action has been brought before the UPC concerning that patent before the proprietor's opt-out notification. Ibid Article 83. UPCA (2013), Article 83(1) and (5).

[42] UPCA 2013, Article 83(3), (4).

domestic courts for the favour of patentees. The system will only succeed, if patentees are willing to use the system, either by obtaining a UP or by choosing not to opt out for their EP. Another important caveat here is that the UPC's decisions will not have the same territorial effect for UPs and EPs and SPCs without unitary effect. As already mentioned in Section 17.1, in the UPReg and UPCA, it is stated that the UPC's decisions on unitary patents shall have effect for the whole of the "unitary territory,"[43] whereas for EPs, the UPC's decisions will cover only "the territory of those Contracting Member States for which the European patent has effect."[44] It is certainly a positive development that the need to conduct parallel litigation in Europe for the same dispute is mitigated. This also seems to limit the pre-UPC possibilities for parties to commence in forum shopping, without completely foreclosing such opportunities.[45] Nevertheless, it should be noted that this also has its (potential) repercussions for, amongst other things, litigation costs, invalidation for the entire unitary patent area, being able to only focus on markets of consequence, the ability to recover from being enjoined and the attractiveness of designating European countries for a EP outside of the unitary patent area.

17.3.2 *Jurisdiction on National Patents and UMs*

What has been discussed in the previous subsection does not apply to the last category of patents in Europe, namely national patents, nor does it apply to UMs. Both remain national rights within the exclusive competence of the relevant domestic courts. It is worth reiterating that, in contrast with national patents, the relationship of the UPC with UMs has not been formally addressed. The UPC has not been given jurisdiction on either national right but, again, UMs are not even mentioned in the instruments of the Unitary Patent Package (including the Rules of Procedure of the Unified Patent Court "RoP"). In fact, this omission is notable, as the failed instrument for a Community Patent did contain a provision declaring certain provisions applicable to UMs, as well.[46] However, the absence of references to such rights in the Unitary Patent Package does not mean that UMs will not be affected by

[43] UPReg, Article 5(2).

[44] UPCA 2013, Article 34.

[45] The UPCA contains limitations on where a case may be brought based on where the infringement took place and the defendants are based, with München as the fallback jurisdiction. For disputes with cross-border elements, e.g., the infringement took place in multiple states and/or the alleged infringer is based in multiple states, this does mean room remains within those perimeters for the rights holder to choose where to bring their claims. However, for certain counterclaims by the defendant, additional limitations exist for where those may be brought. Consequently, room for forum shopping persists, but a lot of different elements affect the margin in a given case.

[46] The Community Patent Convention stated in Article 84(1) that "Articles 37 [on national prior rights], 80 [prohibiting double patenting] and 81 [on exhaustion] shall apply to utility models and utility certificates and to applications for utility models and utility certificates in the Contracting States whose laws make provision for such models or certificates." To reiterate,

the UPC's decisions due to their potential connections with patents (e.g., double patenting, branched-off UMs).

As pointed out above, another complicating factor in this respect is the patchwork of different types of legal instruments that may (indirectly) apply in a given case, particularly when combined with the varying national scope limitations on UMs. The influence of a particular instrument depends on, amongst other things: (a) whether a country is a member to a particular organisation and (b) the nationally determined scope of a UM. This has its implications for which granting and judicial bodies have some authority in the matter, and to what extent. The most dominant form of a UM appears to be a cheaper and more attainable patent, but there are variations between states such as in the patentability requirements and exclusions of subject matter.

A good example to explore this with is the EU's Biotech Directive.[47] Since an EU directive is not directly applicable, EU Member States had to transpose its mandatory provisions, and their courts (and the UPC[48]) must ensure that national law is interpreted and applied in compliance with this instrument. If we take a look at what this would mean for Germany and Italy, the Biotech Directive is relevant for their national patenting of biotechnological inventions, but both preclude UMs on that category of subject matter.[49] Consequently, there should logically not be any influence from the Biotech Directive upon their national UMs as far as their exclusion goes. This might be different for EU Member States which have chosen not to exclude biotechnological inventions from the subject matter of UMs, such as France and Denmark. In France, the patentability requirements and eligible subject matter are the same for UMs as for patents (see Chapter 5). What applies to patents in terms of biotechnological inventions, would thus generally be understood similarly for UMs. There are repercussions to the relevance of the Biotech Directive, such as some role for the CJEU as to what this instrument requires and inhibits within the Member States.

Another exclusion of note from the coverage of UMs is processes and methods (in general). This exclusion is adopted in, for example, Germany, Italy, Czechia and Denmark, whereas countries such as France and Austria allow it. This has ramifications for any potential overlap allowed between patents and UMs.[50] Under the EPO, the protection afforded by a process patent also covers the direct resulting product, as long as the product itself is also patentable and meets the requirements. Particularly, there is a whole range of inventions for which the line between process and product has arguably blurred, for example, product-by-process claims. Additionally, as

such a provision did not make it into the UPCA, nor into the other instruments part of the unitary patent package.

47 Biotech Directive.

48 UPCA 2013, Article 24(1)(a).

49 Sec. 1(2) and (3) German Utility Model Act; Barbieri 2017, 1; Suthersanen 2019, 3.

50 Prud'homme 2014, 26.

explained on the EPO's website, "[f]or many inventions, claims in more than one category are needed for full protection."[51] Decisions by the EPO's bodies, including the Boards of Appeal, on the interpretation of concepts (also) relevant to process and use claims, as well as their validity, also have their bearing on UMs when subject to the same requirements and exclusions as patents in a given territory. As noted in Section 2.3, the EPC even contains some mandatory law applicable to UMs.[52]

Importantly, these examples predate the UPC becoming operational and the creation of the UP. It underscores that UMs and patents were already subject to a fragmented field of legal instruments and authorities even before the addition of the unitary patent and UPC. The chosen construct, of the EPO as the granting authority and the UPC as the main judicial authority, with the latter bound by EU law and thus the CJEU's decisions, alongside (and interacting with) pre-existing systems of granting and adjudicating pre-UPC categories of patent rights (including national rights), adds to that. Again, it is difficult to predict how this will affect the proprietors of patents and UMs. It is arguable that it will not necessarily make navigating this field post-UPC that much harder for aspiring proprietors of UMs within their home jurisdictions. It may get more complicated when there is a cross-border element or there is a connection between UMs and certain categories of patents. The introduction of the UPC and UP have certainly made the legal fragmentation more complex.

To explore this, the following section will look at how the UPC will operate vis-á-vis other authorities, and the implications thereof for, amongst other things, (new) occupants of this already fragmented field. This section will first lay some of the groundwork to reflect upon connections between patents and UMs post-UPC, starting with a procedural perspective on the relationship between domestic courts and the UPC.

17.4 THE RELATIONSHIP BETWEEN DOMESTIC COURTS AND UPC DIVISIONS

The relationship between the domestic courts in the EU and the UPC divisions heeds some further consideration given the partial overlap of competence and, more importantly, the exclusive competence of both courts over separate rights with potentially connected subject matter. More specifically, a brief closer look at their potential feedback loop is warranted. To this end, we will mostly leave UMs and patents aside for a moment to consider some of the practical aspects of the (indirect) working relationship between these different judicial bodies on a more abstract level. This is important to show the potential influence of the UPC, even on matters not directly within the UPC's jurisdiction. Hence, Section 17.4.1 will focus on

[51] European Patent Office 2024.

[52] European Patent Convention (1973), Articles 140, 66, 124, 135, 137 and 139.

staying the proceedings and judicial dialogue, and Section 17.4.2 will contemplate the driving force of these courts to develop legal doctrine.

17.4.1 *The Working Relationship*

First, there is the possibility for both types of courts to stay their proceedings to await and consider the other's decision. The RoP offers a number of grounds upon which a UPC division may decide to stay its proceedings, some of which are mandatory or subject to additional requirements.[53] When it comes to proceedings on actions involving the same patent, SPC, or a related UM playing out before national authorities (including national courts), the RoP specify that the UPC *may* stay the proceedings.[54] The UPC has been awarded discretion in this respect and is not required to await the decisions of national courts to avoid any potential conflict in its decisions. However, in reference to opposition or limitation proceedings on a patent before a national court, the rule in question adds "where a decision in such proceedings may be expected to be given rapidly."[55] This signals that if there is doubt about the speediness of such a decision, the UPC should actually refrain from staying the proceedings. The importance placed on expedient proceedings is also stressed in the Preamble of the RoP: "[. . .] proceedings *shall* be conducted in a way which will normally allow the final oral hearing on the issues of infringement and validity at first instance to take place within one year whilst recognising that complex actions may require more time[. . .]."[56] Evidently, this limits the UPC's discretion in favour of preserving the speed of their own procedure.

Another aspect relevant here is that no official forum for dialogue appears to have been provided between national courts and UPC divisions that would allow for potential mitigation or avoidance of potential conflicts in judgments or misapplication of national law. The UPC is set to apply national law of the participating EU Member States, as the UP will be governed by the law of the Member State where the applicant had its residence or principal place of business or, if inapplicable, had a place of business, on the date of filing.[57] Therefore, at the time of writing, each unitary patent is governed by the national law of one out of 18 EU Member States currently part of the unitary patent area. However, which UPC division has competence to hear a case depends on the type of claims brought by parties,[58] as well as on

[53] Rules of Procedure (2022), Rule 295(a)-(l).

[54] Ibid. Rule 295(a) and (b). There are some mandatory exceptions to this, such as in case of the death of a party (stay mandatory until a successor has been determined) or insolvency (stay the proceedings up to three months, or sooner if, e.g., a decision has been made on the continuance or abandonment of the proceedings by the relevant/someone with authority to do so). Ibid. Rules 310(1) and 311(1).

[55] Rules of Procedure, Rule 295(a).

[56] Ibid. Preamble, recital 7. Emphasis (Italic) added by the authors.

[57] UPReg, Article 7(1)(a) and (b), respectively.

[58] UPCA, Article 32(1)(a)-(i).

where the infringement occurred within the unitary territory or where defendants have their residence or (principal) place of business.[59] This means that a UPC division in Italy – where the infringement took place or the defendant resides – may have to decide a dispute on a unitary patent governed by Belgian law – the place of residence or business of the proprietor. What is more, there may be connected proceedings in a normal domestic court at the same time.

While there are certainly some mitigating factors (which will be considered below), there is some concern about the consistency and accuracy of the interpretation and application of all the different sets of national laws by judges not always familiar with them, particularly in the early days of the UPC. Moreover, the UPC judges will have to navigate the development of doctrine and (potentially connected) judgments in normal domestic courts and the EPOrg's Board of Appeals, as well as to observe EU law.[60] A forum for dialogue on national law – especially in the early years of the UPC's operation – may have been useful to ensure uniformity and legal certainty and avoid potential conflicts between the UPC's and domestic judgments. This is especially true considering that UPC divisions may have to apply national law foreign to them. Still, there are annual conferences which provide for a more informal forum at which judges can exchange insights.[61] Such forums were already popular pre-UPC, so these may continue to aid judges with the laws of different jurisdictions in this respect. Furthermore, many UPC judges are likely to maintain a domestic judicial position part time until the case load picks up enough to require their UPC appointment to be fulfilled full time, which may not ever occur for some divisions. Such judges will thus continue to be involved in the development of domestic case law and generally be more aware of local pending

59 Ibid Article 33(1)(a) and (b).

60 With regard to EU law, the UPC is under the same obligations as "normal" domestic courts of EU Member States, meaning the UPC is compelled to apply EU law and consult the CJEU through the preliminary reference procedure on questions concerning EU law. This procedure has its general limits, but more particularly in the patent law context because of the holes in EU legislation in patent law. As mentioned previously, EU patent law is at this stage quite limited, meaning preliminary questions referred to the CJEU by the UPC are likely to centre more on areas more firmly situated within the EU's competences, such as competition law (including the SEP context) and fundamental rights. There are, however, some examples of EU patent law over which the CJEU will retain its authority as the prime judicial interpreter. First, there is *lex generalis* applicable to patents, namely the IP Enforcement Directive. Then there is the *lex specialis* on biotechnological inventions, the Biotech Directive. Those two remain the main sources of EU patent law, next to the newer UPReg and the UPTReg. Additionally, there are some other instruments containing exceptions relevant to patent law, such as the SPC Regulation and the Veterinary Medicinal Products Directive. That means that all the CJEU's (pre-existing) case law based on these instruments combined with those exceptions applies to the patent context. However, there is also the emphasis on speed of the UPC's own proceedings to consider, and the CJEU's preliminary reference procedure is notorious for creating a delay. It remains to be seen how active a role the CJEU will play here.

61 One example of such a conference is the annual WIPO Intellectual Property Judges Forum in Geneva, Switzerland. Additionally, there are IP-oriented conferences which are often frequented by national judges, too.

cases. Another apt mitigating factor is that all of the UPC divisions have a multinational composition, meaning that each division will represent a perspective broader than a single national judicial experience. Other than such informal avenues, the UPC and "normal" domestic courts may be expected to talk to each other largely through their judgments.

17.4.2 *Driving the Doctrine*

Presumably, it will take some time for the new UPC and domestic courts to sort out their working relationship. It will also be interesting to see how the feedback loop develops and evolves between the national courts and the UPC, given the division of jurisdiction over different categories of patents, SPCs and UMs. However, this is further complicated as key matters for patent enforcement are spread out over several instruments of varied origin and impact. As noted in Section 17.3.2, some EU or international instruments may also be applicable to some extent to national UMs. National law, the UPReg (an EU regulation) and the UPCA (an intergovernmental treaty) all – in varying degrees – contain some substantive patent law, in addition to the EPC's provisions on matters such as inventiveness, sufficiency of disclosure and equivalence.

The rights conferred by the unitary patent and exceptions were dealt with in earlier drafts of the UPReg (Articles 6–8) but were ultimately moved to the UPCA.[62] According to the UPReg, national law determines the scope of protection in terms of the acts against which the UP protects, the limitations of the right and the exceptions available.[63] However, the UPCA also contains provisions which set forth acts of direct and indirect infringement, thereby creating two competing sources of law on the same matter. This is yet another example of the created confusion emanating from the chosen manner for introducing this new layer for a new patent and court system. As the UP is supposed to be governed by the law of a single Member State throughout the unitary patent area by virtue of an EU regulation, combined with the consideration that the UPC is bound by EU law, national law should presumably have priority here.[64] This invites the interpretation that, at least on this specific matter, the UPCA should be understood as the boundary within which to interpret and apply national law. This also seems likely considering the objective behind this

[62] Kaisi 2014, 172–173. One key factor driving this decision was that no agreement could be reached on the involvement of the CJEU. By moving certain provisions to a document outside of the CJEU's competence, proponents sought to isolate the Unified Patent Court from the CJEU's influence. The success and implications of this move will not be explored further here.

[63] UPCA 2013, Article 5(3). It says: "The acts against which the patent provides protection referred to in paragraph 1 and the applicable limitations shall be those defined by the law applied to European patents with unitary effect in the participating Member State whose national law is applicable to the European patent with unitary effect as an object of property in accordance with Article 7."

[64] Van Dongen 2023, 377.

project is to further European harmonisation towards an EU patent system. If this interpretation is correct, this emphasis on national law bestows a bigger role on domestic courts in driving the doctrine, both nationally and for the UPC to apply. Naturally, national courts are the judicial authorities on the interpretation and application of their respective national legal systems. However, the exact reliance on, and weight given to, these transnational instruments, particularly in relation to national law, is another aspect that will become clearer over time through the UPC's case law.

Regardless of the ultimate interaction and priority between these sources of patent law, some thought needs to be given to the impact that the decisions of UPC divisions will have in general. If the system proves successful, the UPC divisions will undoubtedly help develop the national system further and help evolve judicial doctrine, particularly states' local or regional divisions. What is more, this will inevitably lead to national patent systems moving closer to each other. Furthermore, the UPC will be capable of gaining a lot of experience within its field of specialisation in a short period of time thanks to the combined effect of its mandate and territorial reach, and the potential counterbalancing influence it may have as a result on the EPOrg's strong executive and administrative arms.[65] There is some reasonable expectation that the UPC, created by an intergovernmental treaty between some EU Member States and an even smaller portion of EPOrg members, will have greater ramifications for the EPC system. Due to the UPC's competence to review the validity of rights granted by the EPO for a larger geographical area, this court may interfere with the EPO on granting matters. This means that the UPC's decisions may quickly gain a lot of weight in the European patent arena, irrespective of which law it applies. The broader reach of the UPC's decisions makes for a stronger impact on the stability of both national and European patent law, as well as related areas of law. That also has its downside, as the broader reach of the UPC's decisions may increase the impact of conflicting decisions on the same or overlapping subject matter by the UPC and national courts, and misinterpretation and/or misapplication of national law by UPC divisions. Naturally, conflicting decisions issued by judges from different states occurred frequently pre-UPC, but these judges only decide for their respective territory;[66] the UPC's decision will have effect for the combined territory of states designated for a EP within the unitary patent area, be it a portion or the entirety of this area. This means the consequences thereof are more serious across the board, not just for the parties to the dispute, but also for specific third-party interests or the public interest

65 For more on the latter point, see, for instance, Schovsbo et al. 2015, 271; Van Dongen 2023, 378–379.

66 Except, of course, in cases involving, e.g., cross-border injunctions in interlocutory proceedings.

at large or, on a more abstract level, the stability and consistency of national or regional legal systems.

With regard to the latter, patent disputes are generally not isolated from other areas of law. Obvious examples of such areas are civil procedure, domestic contract law, and competition law, but also the different UM systems provided for by some of the participating countries. Naturally, the UPC cannot directly rule on UMs since such rights have not been placed within its jurisdiction. However, as discussed in this and the previous subsection, the potential of the UPC's (indirect) influence in Europe should not be underestimated. As will be discussed in the coming sections, there are strategies which were used by companies prior to the UPC that involved both patents and UMs, for example, branched-off UMs. Moreover, the UPReg has allowed for the possibility of double patenting in states where the law permits this. If disputes involving patents using such strategies make it before the UPC, the UPC's decisions could directly affect national rights and indirectly impact national legal doctrines in this particular field. This will be explored further in the next section.

17.5 CONVERTING, DOUBLE PATENTING AND BRANCHING OFF (BOUM)

Again, while it is not possible within the scope of this research and the instruments at our disposal to say something more meaningful about the exact impact and likelihood, it is possible to observe where the new system may limit or enhance the potential of pre-UPC strategies combining different types of patent rights. The analyses in the next subsection will thus first focus on pre-existing conversion and BOUM strategies, followed by a subsection on the room for double patenting and branched-off UMs strategies post-UPC, and last, by a third subsection which briefly considers the costs of a UP, particularly given territorial limitations.

17.5.1 *Reasons for Converting Patents into UMs or for Branching Them Off (Pre-UPC)*

In addition to offering the possibility of seeking UM protection from the start, many countries allow the conversion of a patent application into a UM application. If a patent application has a very low chance of being granted, for example, due to prior art that is close to the claimed invention, converting the patent application into a UM might offer an attractive option. However, in some countries there is a time limit for doing so.[67] If a patent application is refused, some countries allow the

[67] See European Commission's IP Helpdesk 2024.

patent application to be converted into a UM within a certain period after the refusal.[68]

Moreover, in some countries, such as Germany and Denmark,[69] UMs can be branched off (also called "split off") from a pending international, European or national patent application by claiming the filing date or priority date of the first filing. A branch-off is possible in Germany, for example, until up to two months after granting a patent or withdrawing or rejecting the patent application.[70]

In light of these procedural options, several – often interrelated – factors may make UMs an attractive strategic option for small and medium-sized entities (SMEs), as well as larger institutions or companies.[71] For example, UMs usually have a faster registration process compared to the lengthy patent prosecution procedures. This can be a huge advantage in fast-paced industries, such as software or telecommunications, where swift market approval and product adoption is critical. By converting a patent into a UM or branching it off as a separate UM, inventors can expedite the registration process and secure faster protection for their inventions.[72] In terms of strategic timing, a German branched-off UM is also well suited to stop infringement activities during grant proceedings in Germany.[73]

Moreover, cost-effectiveness is an important consideration for many stakeholders, and in particular for SMEs. UMs are generally less expensive to register and to maintain compared to national and European patents.[74] Obtaining UM protection instead of a patent may be the preferred option when a patent is not generating – or expected to generate – any more substantial revenue. This is particularly relevant when the cost of maintaining a patent outweighs its economic benefits. The same reasoning applies to branch-offs: a German branched-off UM, for example, is an alternative to a costly divisional application.[75]

The limited lifespan of UMs, which typically ranges from 6 to 10 years, can also entail strategic benefits, for example, in fast-paced technologies with shorter

68 Ibid.

69 § 12 the Danish Consolidate Utility Model Act (*Branching-Off*). The Danish Ministerial Order on examination, Section 13: "A patent application for Denmark may be used in whole or in parts as a basis for the utility model application relating to the same creation for up to ten years from the date of filing the patent application or from the date which is deemed to be the date of filing. A patent application for Denmark shall mean: A European patent application designating Denmark and a European patent application converted into a Danish patent application as well as an international application proceeded with in Denmark and finally a Danish patent application."

70 Wittmann 2024. Concerning the procedure in Germany, see German Patent and Trademark Office (2021).

71 Radauer et al. 2019.

72 Heikkilä and Lorenz 2018.

73 Wittmann 2024. In 2023 the Danish Maritime and Commercial High Court ruled that the DKPTO is not obligated to consider ex officio the risk of double patenting for UMs, cf. U 2023.2178 SHR.

74 Heikkilä and Verba 2018, 694 ff.

75 Wittmann 2024.

commercial lifespans. In some fast-moving and highly dynamic industries, such as in software, energy storage or telecommunications, converting a patent into a UM or branching it off as a UM allows the inventor to align the duration of protection with the expected commercial viability of the invention. In such cases the cost-benefit ratio of UM protection is more beneficial and attractive in comparison to patents, which typically have a longer lifespan, usually 20 years from the filing date.

Furthermore, regional considerations and IP strategies will also be considered by inventors. Seeking UM protection can be particularly beneficial when aiming to expand the protection of an invention in a specific market, while seeking to reduce the costs and time that would need to be spent when filing separate patent applications in multiple jurisdictions.[76] Even under the new UP system, patent laws and regulations will continue to differ across various jurisdictions. For example, an inventor might prefer UM protection for the aforementioned reasons, but also hold patents in countries without any available UM protection, such as the United Kingdom or Sweden. If that patentee prefers to protect the invention as a UM in another country where UMs are recognised, such as Germany, converting the patent into a UM or branching it off as a UM can provide a cost-effective local protection in that jurisdiction.

Last, but not least, the scope of protection is another important consideration that might motivate stakeholders to pursue UM protection instead of – or in addition to – patents. In many innovative technologies, UMs typically provide narrower protection compared to patents. By converting the patent into a UM or branching it off as a UM, inventors can obtain additional protection for those specific features or improvements of an invention that are not covered by the existing patent claims.[77] Provided that such features are not automatically excluded from UM protection, which can be the case in some areas of health and life science inventions, such strategies can be particularly useful when there are incremental improvements or variations with a considerable commercial value that may not meet the more restrictive novelty or inventive step thresholds for a patent.

Before the UPC system became operational, the possibility to simultaneously apply for and convert a UM, a national patent, and/or a EP – now with or without unitary effect – was thus already widely available. There is nothing to suggest that such opportunities would cease post-UPC. Indeed, the expected dominance of German law for governing UPs would make this very likely to subsist as a common business strategy, as their system for branched-off UMs appears to be thriving.[78] This will be further explored in the next section, focusing predominantly on the possibility for double patenting post-UPC.

[76] Cahoy and Oswald 2021, 525–526, and 578.
[77] Janis 1999, 156ff. See also Prud'homme 2017a.
[78] Montañá 2023; Neuhaus et al. 2023; Van Dongen (2024).

17.5.2 *National Examples of Double Patenting within the Unitary Patent Area*

The UPReg specifically addresses the possibility of double patenting. Article 4, second paragraph, requires that

> [t]he participating Member States shall take the necessary measures to ensure that, where the unitary effect of a European patent has been registered and extends to their territory, that European patent is deemed not to have taken effect as a national patent in their territory on the date of publication of the mention of the grant in the European Patent Bulletin.

This is similarly stressed in Recital 8, last sentence, of the UPReg for national patents when an EP is granted. Put simply, it inhibits double patenting. Since the possibility of the simultaneous protection by a UM is not mentioned, this possibility may arguably depend on the existence of a national law preclusion.

However, this prohibition on double patenting is undercut by Recital 26 of the same instrument, which provides that this does not affect "the right of the participating Member States to grant national patents and should not replace the participating Member States' laws on patents." This suggests that, if a state allows for double patenting (e.g., the same matter protected by both a national patent and a EP), this should remain possible. This interpretation, that Recital 26 allows for double patenting, is one settled upon by important patent jurisdictions in Europe such as Germany, France and Italy, which have all amended their laws to this effect *after* the adoption of the UPReg. Their systems are discussed elsewhere in this volume in more detail, but it is useful to mention these specific changes briefly to consider their implications for the UPC-context.

Specifically, Germany technically allowed for some form of double patenting previously, as it was possible to maintain a national patent and EP on the same invention in Germany.[79] However, Article II, section 8, of the German Act on International Patent Conventions ("Gesetz über internationale Patentübereinkommen"[80]) undercut the usefulness of maintaining the national patent. It provided that a defendant against which the patent was asserted in court proceedings could object to its effect because it was already covered in Germany by a EP. As for France, before 2018, a French patent would lose its effect upon conclusion of opposition proceedings or after the expiration of the period to initiate such proceedings.[81] The same was true in Italy. All three countries have amended their respective patent laws to allow for some form of double patenting, but there is a striking difference in the Italian approach.

First, the undercutting German provision has been amended in 2017 – so after the UPReg was adopted – for the "no-effect" limitation to only apply to a EP valid in

79 Mertzlufft-Paufler and Yip 2022.

80 Old Gesetz über internationale Patentübereinkommen, Teil II Nr. 32, Artikel II(8).

81 According to the old Articles L. 614-13 and L. 614-14 of the French Intellectual Property Code.

Germany for which its proprietor has successfully opted out of the UPC's jurisdiction.[82] Put differently, it means that defendants would no longer be able to challenge the national patent's effect when it is covered by a corresponding UP or EP valid in Germany falling within the UPC's jurisdiction. France has essentially done the same in response to the UPReg with their 2018 amendment.[83] A French national patent will only lose its effect if it concerns a corresponding EP valid in France for which the proprietor has chosen to opt-out of the jurisdiction of the UPC. The result is that there is a possibility for double patenting in cases where there is a clear separation of jurisdiction between the "normal" German/French domestic courts and UPC divisions.

Interestingly, the same applies to the Italian national patent, but without a very important caveat: it has been reported by several sources that the Italian version does not limit this possibility for double patenting in case of EPs in Italy to those instances of a successful opt-out.[84] This means that non-opted-out European patents could co-exist with Italian national patents, resulting in a shared competence between UPC divisions and "normal" Italian domestic courts on – albeit it being different types of – patents with the same subject matter. It would seem that, so far, the Italian legislator has not yet provided any mechanisms or limitations for the domestic courts in case of parallel proceedings on the same subject matter before the UPC.

Whether businesses will make use of these new avenues for double patenting that some states have created in response to the UPCA remains to be seen. Businesses will presumably continue to base their patenting and UM strategies in Europe on, inter alia, which markets are most important to them, the costs of applying for and maintaining such rights in a given jurisdiction, and where enforcement mechanisms are most attainable and effective. Over the years, this has led to a shift in focus from applications for national patents at national patent offices to designating the states of choice through an application at the EPO. Now, businesses can opt to apply at the EPO for a UP instead, meaning that, if granted, the UP is valid in all states part of the unitary patent area. For businesses, the potential of combining an EP or UP with a national patent (or UM) within the same territory will hinge on whether the national right would likely form a substantial asset on top.

17.5.3 *The Cost of the Unitary Patent Area: A Boost for Other Rights?*

It is prudent to explore next when a UP might be an attractive alternative to pre-existing options, and under what circumstances it may make national patents or UMs more advantageous for (aspiring) right holders, be it as a supplement or an

[82] New Gesetz über internationale Patentübereinkommen, Teil II Nr. 32, Artikel II, §8(1).

[83] Franceschelli and Trabucco 2023; Maureau 2023.

[84] Article 59 of the Italian Intellectual Property Code. Ercoli 2023; Franceschelli and Trabucco 2023; Marchesoni 2023.

alternative. Cost is one of the key factors for deciding whether or not to apply for a UP instead of opting for pre-existing patenting or UM strategies. Cost-saving and procedural streamlining were important factors for the uptick in applications for the EP at the expense of national patents. Lower cost and ease are also cited by proponents of UMs, irrespective of whether this is demonstrated to be the case in practice.[85] One of the key objectives stressed in favour of the UP is also cost-saving. A closer look at the cost of opting for a UP is thus warranted. This section will briefly explore this issue based on the application and renewal costs of a UP, and relevant territorial limitations.

Generally, applying for a UP and maintaining it is less costly than applying for a EP designating all states that are part of the unitary patent area. According to the EPO's website, the annual fees for the entire area "[correspond] to the combined renewal fees due in the four countries where European patents were most often validated in 2015, when the fee level was agreed by the Select Committee."[86] Consequently, the UP could make for a cost-effective option should a business be interested in obtaining a patent in those particular four states or, alternatively, if interested in a selection of countries within the unitary patent area that would amount to the same total of renewal fees or surpass it. However, if this is not the case, the UP may cost more than the traditional routes. Notably, even if a business were interested in obtaining protection in those four states that are part of the unitary patent area or, alternatively, if interested in a selection of countries within the unitary patent area that would amount to the same total of renewal fees or surpass it, the cost of obtaining a UP may be infeasible for many businesses.

For some businesses, it may be more cost-effective to opt for a more selective approach in designating states for a EP or national rights, or a combination thereof. This is especially true when additional rights would have to be obtained by a business for jurisdictions of note outside of the unitary patent area. As discussed in Section 17.2.1, there are currently six EU Member States which are not yet part of the unitary patent area. That means that businesses from those states would automatically lose out on the possibility to have a UP covering their home state. The same is true for businesses originating from the other 12 states which are part of the EPO, but not members of the EU. Obtaining additional protection outside of the unitary patent area would amount to an additional set of costs, on top of those for the UP.

This may be a more potent issue than just the omission of the home state, as one key patent jurisdiction in Europe is not part of the unitary patent area as a result of BREXIT, namely the United Kingdom. If there is need and/or value in obtaining a patent in the United Kingdom, this must be done separately from the application for a UP, or via its designation in an application for a EP. As a result, obtaining a UP

[85] Radauer et al. 2019, 771; Suthersanen 2019.
[86] European Patent Organisation 2024.

may prove to be too costly for a lot of businesses, even without factoring in other aspects such as the risk of invalidation for a larger territory or, conversely, the rewards of enforcement in this larger territory.

This may affect business strategies towards patents and UMs, both within and outside this area, but this is not a given. For many businesses, the UP may simply be too costly or not attractive for other reasons. They will presumably continue to rely on pre-UPC strategies encompassing EPs, national patents or UMs, or a combination thereof (e.g., BOUM). The only additional considerations for such companies are whether or not to make use of the more recent room for double patenting created in some jurisdictions, and whether opting out of the UPC's jurisdiction is a relevant and desirable option (and if/when to opt back in).

Businesses for which a UP is worthwhile and feasible would need to determine whether additional protection outside of the unitary patent area is necessary and cost-effective. Because obtaining a UP is already quite pricy, for those jurisdictions important to a company's business falling outside of this territory, a UM may be an interesting alternative if it provides for equivalent protection to patents. However, if a business can afford a UP and a jurisdiction outside of the unitary patent area really is an important market, this may still move a business to apply for a patent instead. Yet, there may still be companies which may abandon any efforts towards additional protection in Europe outside of the unitary patent area. It remains, for example, to be seen whether the United Kingdom is able to retain its notable importance in the European patent area, that is, what number of applicants for UPs will make a separate application for this jurisdiction, or whether this will affect whether aspiring patentees will choose a UP over an EP.

Be that as it may, many more questions on the potential relationship of the UPC with UMs remain open. The next section will discuss some of the implications of the more important factors that we have considered so far, along with the limits of what can be concluded and some more food for thought. More specifically, it considers all the previously discussed factors and other grounds bearing on the decision on whether or not to opt out of the UPC system, before circling back to when UMs are a good alternative or addition to the IP strategy.

17.6 DISCUSSION OF FINDINGS AND STAKEHOLDER CHOICES

Patent protection has always been at the top of the agenda in the EU to achieve a fully harmonised IP system, whereas an EU-wide approach to UM protection became a subordinated goal. Now, with the UPC having become operational on 1 June 2023, European patent law has been subject to a regime-change involving a new transnational institution and an unusual combination of EU and transnational law outside the scope of traditional EU harmonisation. Yet, as we have explored in the previous sections, the chosen route towards a harmonised patent in the EU is not without its complications for the European patent arena, nor for UMs. A lot of literature has already been dedicated to such complications on different aspects and types of patents, but the implications for UMs are generally overlooked. How this long-awaited achievement will impact UMs remains to be seen, but the establishment of the UPC and UPs necessitates reflections on UM protection as such. On this background, we have asked if the troublesome way to a transnational regime has left the protection of UMs behind. Based on our explorations in the previous sections, this section will highlight some of the implications for inventors and companies.

To reiterate, our starting point is that UM protection is a national matter only, but for several reasons it can be linked to either an EP, SPC (European, EU or otherwise) or to a UP. As we have discussed in Section 17.2, the unitary patent area (18 Member States) overlaps with UM systems in 11 EU Member States. The granting of EPs and UPs are subject to EPO's authority, and the granting of UMs and national patents are subject to national authority. In a current Commission proposal on a Regulation on SPC's it is suggested that the (new) unitary SPC's are to be granted by the national authorities with the EUIPO as the central examination authority.[87] Thus, stakeholders will then have to involve three different authorities to protect and arrange for a broader IP portfolio, let alone consider the territorial implications and the interplay of different types and sources of law that may have their bearing on (parts of) their portfolio.

Then there is the matter of authorities in the post-granting phase. It is mostly the establishment of the UPC as a transnational patent court which we expect to have an impact on the future UM landscape in Europe. If a UP is declared void by the UPC, such a ruling may have spill-over effects on (connected) UMs in one or more of the 11 UPC participating Member States with UM systems. What is more is that the decision may have an impact on the non-participating UPC Member States who have UM protection as well. Domestic courts within those jurisdictions are not in any way bound to follow the UPC's decisions relevant to disputes pertaining to their own jurisdiction, particularly when it comes to national rights such as UMs. There is the additional aspect of meaningful legislative differences in their national UM model to patents that may warrant a different approach or outcome, even if the normal domestic court considers the UPC's findings. However, as we have argued, there are several reasons not to underestimate the UPC's authority and territorial reach. If the UPC succeeds, its harmonising force is likely to affect EU Member States currently not part of the unitary patent area. That may not be on the forefront for all companies when planning their IP strategies, but the decision of whether or not to choose a route which would lead to the involvement of the UPC has to be made early on in most cases.

That said, when considering the uncertainties and risks associated with interpreting Article 83 of the UPCA and its subsections (1), (3) and (4) on opting out, it is challenging to determine the best course of action. This concerns in particular the

[87] COM 2023, 231; 2023, 223.

benefits and risks of opting out. Each option has its own strengths, weaknesses, opportunities and threats. The suitability of each approach must be evaluated on a case-by-case basis, taking into account the invention, patent claims and business strategy.[88] And this will also have to include the consideration of opting for UM protection, i.e., either from the start, by conversion or by "branching off."

When it comes to the "opt-out" question for European patents, two basic criteria should be carefully considered when making strategic decisions for relevant portfolios. First, the strength of the patent(s) and their enforceability in infringement and invalidation proceedings should be evaluated. Second, estimating the importance of the patent(s) to the relevant business and technology is also crucial. In general, the larger the patent portfolio, the more difficult it becomes to find a clear solution to minimize risks. The strategies that need to be employed become more complex.[89] It is crucial to remain in control and anticipate potential actions by licensees, infringers or as a claimant. Additionally, future filing strategies should be anticipated, tailored and diversified. In specific cases concerning EP applications, this may involve considering the use of divisionals or branching off UM protection in different systems. If available, UM protection can be useful for establishing priority for future patent applications.[90]

If the patent claims are strong and enforceable, it might generally be advisable not to opt out, convert claims into UM or branch off during the transitional period to take full advantage of the benefits and choices offered by the new system. The higher the likelihood that an important and strong patent will be upheld within the UPC system, the less reason there is to pay significant opt-out fees and risk competitors initiating national proceedings, which would eliminate the option to "withdraw the opt-out" under Article 83(4) of the UPCA and proceed at the UPC. However, if a patent is very important but includes claims that are at high risk of not surviving a central challenge within the UPC system, opting out, converting it into a UM or branching off certain claims as UMs to defend them on a country-by-country basis may make sense. In other words, opting out or UM protection could be helpful to avoid the risk of the patent being invalidated in one proceeding across Europe.[91] If a patent is not very relevant, however, spending money on a substantial opt-out fee might not make any sense. Patent holders should consider letting it expire, or converting it into a UM, which is also cheaper to maintain.[92]

17.7 CONCLUDING REMARKS AND OPEN QUESTIONS

Given the pre-UPC fragmentation of the law and institutions for patents and UMs, the attempt towards harmonisation in the former field is, on its face, progress. Since the latter was not included, this raised the question how the UPC will interact with

88 Minssen and Lundqvist 2014.
89 Minssen and Lundqvist 2014.
90 Minssen and Lundqvist 2014.
91 Minssen and Lundqvist 2014.
92 Minssen and Lundqvist 2014.

and affect the system for UM protection in Europe and vice versa. The progress towards establishing a unified patent system in the EU has (almost) achieved its first objectives, but what the impact on UM protection and their strategic use will be remains to be seen. As our chapter has demonstrated, the direct consequences and wider implications of the latest UPC and UP developments raise numerous questions, not only about the interplay between the patent system and UM protection, but also on the role of UMs in today's innovation systems and their underlying rationales as such. Given this backdrop, it is pertinent to question whether the arduous journey towards harmonising IPR in the EU has overlooked the protection of UMs.

In this chapter, we have outlined some of the forthcoming considerations that the IP system is likely to confront with regards to UMs in Europe. The fragmentation in European patent law and UMs is exacerbated by the introduction of the UPC and UP, an odd repercussion for an (at least partially successful) attempt at harmonisation. In the coming years, it will be important to monitor the implications of this and, if necessary, to mitigate them. However, too little is currently known to make recommendations on this. In fact, it is clear that much more research is necessary on both the value of legal harmonisation in the IP space in general,[93] and on the benefits and drawbacks of European UMs in a highly competitive global economy, in particular.[94] Ultimately, this also entails the question whether the distinct European national frameworks for UM protection should be harmonised and introduced into the legislative system of all EU Member States by EU legislation, or if the European IP and innovation landscape would be best served and "harmonised" simply by getting rid of UM protection. Both may simplify matters, both may make them worse. The empirical research on the value of UMs is not unequivocal. Moreover, there are EU Member States in which the system is quite widely used, and taking away rights – particularly types of property rights – is tricky, to say the least.

Unfortunately, tackling this provocative question would also mean that we would have to confront an elusive and technology-specific "elephant in the room," which is still extraordinarily difficult to study: the strategic use of trade secrets as an alternative. There is always the consideration that, if some form of protection is not offered, businesses may resort to secrecy instead. Not all types of UMs would lend themselves to reliance on secrecy, such as those on improvements in the shape of a product. Such improvements may generally be unearthed by third parties without relative difficulty upon studying the product. Yet, in those jurisdictions where the UM takes on a more patent-like nature with the same eligible subject matter, this may indeed be a concern. Would we lose out on knowledge, on innovative progress, should we abandon UMs? If so, is it concerning *enough* to provide for UM protection? We are convinced that unpacking, analysing and understanding these intricate dynamics will be one of the more important research tasks of the future.

93 Cahoy and Oswald 2021, 525–526, and 578.
94 Suthersanen 2019.

18

Treatment of Utility Models as Standards-Essential Patents*

Jorge L. Contreras and Magnus Buggenhagen

Utility models (UM) are not patents, yet in some cases they may be treated like patents. One such case is the declaration of UM as "essential" to industry standards such as Wi-Fi and 5G, and the attendant licensing of these UM to the manufacturers of standardized products on terms that are "fair, reasonable and nondiscriminatory" (FRAND) under the rules of the relevant standards-development organization (SDO). This chapter explores the prevalence and implications of declaring and licensing UMs as standards-essential patents.

18.1 STANDARDS-ESSENTIAL PATENTS AND UTILITY MODELS

18.1.1 *FRAND Licensing Commitments*

Some technical standards, particularly in the telecommunications and computing sectors, can be covered by hundreds or thousands of patents.[1] Accordingly, SDOs often require their participants to disclose patents believed to be "essential" to the implementation of a standard (standards-essential patents, or SEPs) to other participants in the SDO prior to approval of the standard. This obligation is intended to allow SDO members to work around or avoid any patent that could unduly impair the broad adoption of the standard.[2] SDO participants that fail to disclose SEPs when so required by an SDO's policies can be found to have breached the SDO's policy or to have engaged in deceptive or anticompetitive conduct.[3]

* Portions of this chapter are adapted from Jorge L. Contreras and Magnus Buggenhagen, *Standards Essential Utility Models*, 64 *Jurimetrics J.* 1 (2024).

1 Baron and Pohlmann 2018.

2 National Research Council 2013, 73.

3 U.S. Dept. Justice & Federal Trade Comm'n, 2007, 43–45.

Furthermore, in order to promote broad adoption and use of their standards, most SDOs also require that participants license their SEPs to the manufacturers of standardized products ("implementers") on terms that are either royalty free or bear royalties that are "fair, reasonable and non-discriminatory" (FRAND).[4] This obligation is intended to assure implementers that they will be able to incorporate widely adopted standards into their products without the threat of being sued by the holders of SEPs.

18.1.2 *Essentiality*

A SEP holder's obligations to disclose and grant licenses generally applies only to patents that are "essential" to the implementation of the standard. That is, a product implementing the standard will necessarily infringe the claims of the patent.[5] Despite the importance of the concept of essentiality to the value of patents covering standardized products, the essentiality of a particular patent to a particular standard is usually determined unilaterally by the patent holder without external verification.[6] Yet this decision is often made with incomplete information at a time when the patent in question may still be in prosecution and the standard is not yet finalized.[7] As such, the declaration of a patent as a SEP often constitutes a best guess by the SEP holder as to the likely essentiality of an issued patent, or a patent application, to a draft or published standard.

Not surprisingly, given the potential royalty revenue that may be earned from SEPs, and the potential liability that can arise under the antitrust and competition laws from the *failure* to disclose SEPs in compliance with an SDO's policies, SDO participants have often erred on the side of over-declaration of SEPs in relation to many standards.[8] For this reason, the essentiality of declared SEPs to particular standards is frequently challenged in litigation, with the result that some patents asserted against products implementing standards as to which they were declared essential are found to be neither essential to the standard nor infringed by the product implementing the standard.[9]

4 *See* Lemley 2002.

5 There are a few different variations of the "essentiality" definition, including some that are based on the "technical" essentiality of the patent in question (whether any product implementing the standard will infringe as a technical matter) versus "commercial" essentiality (whether any commercially viable product will infringe). *See* Contreras 2017b.

6 Contreras 2017b.

7 Contreras 2017b.

8 For example, in one frequently cited series of studies, only 28%, 29% and 50% of patent families declared "essential" to the 2G, 3G and 4G wireless telecommunications standards, respectively, were assessed by an independent reviewer to be essential to the implementation of those standards. Contreras 2017b, 224–225.

9 *See* Lemley and Simcoe 2019.

18.1.3 *Injunctive Relief and SEPs*

One of the typical remedies available to a patent holder upon proving infringement is a court-ordered injunction preventing the infringer from continuing to make or sell infringing products. The availability of injunctions when SEPs are infringed has been the subject of considerable debate, as the general availability of the injunction remedy can be seen to conflict with the SEP holder's commitment to grant licenses to all implementers of the standards covered by the SEPs.[10] As a result, the availability of injunctive relief when SEPs are infringed by an unlicensed implementer varies by country, and may depend on applicable competition law as well as a determination whether the infringing implementer is "willing" to accept a license on FRAND terms.[11]

18.1.4 *Utility Models as Standards-Essential*

In addition to patents, some SDO policies require SDO participants to disclose UMs as potentially essential to implement their standards. This requirement is made explicit, for example, in the *Guidelines for Implementation of the Common Patent Policy* of the International Telecommunications Union (ITU), International Organization for Standardization (ISO) and International Electrotechnical Committee (IEC), which defines a "patent" as including "those claims contained in and identified by patents, utility models and other similar statutory rights based on inventions (including applications for any of these)".[12] Other prominent SDOs, including the European Telecommunications Standards Institute (ETSI), the Internet Engineering Task Force (IETF) and the HDMI Forum, also expressly require the disclosure or licensing of UMs that are believed to be essential to a standard.[13]

While the policies of some SDOs expressly mention UMs, the policies of other SDOs, including ATSC[14] and JEDEC,[15] do not, and instead apply their disclosure and licensing requirements only to "patents". At these SDOs, it is not clear what

[10] *See* Baron et al. 2023; Contreras et al. 2019.

[11] *See* Contreras et al. 2019.

[12] Int'l Telecommunications Union, Int'l Org. for Standardization, Int'l Electrotechnical Comm., Guidelines for Implementation of the Common Patent Policy for ITU-T/ITU-R/ ISO/IEC (November 2, 2018) at 2.

[13] *See* Bekkers and Updegrove 2013, 54 (listing utility model requirements of major SDOs), Contreras et al. 2022 (noting "catch all" term that includes utility models in SDO disclosure policies).

[14] Advanced Television Systems Committee, Inc., Patent Policy – Document B/04 at § 11.b (December 13, 2007) ("'Essential Claim' means claims of all patents issued, and patent applications filed, under the laws of any country that are necessarily infringed by implementing the normative portion of a Specification Document").

[15] JEDEC, JEDEC Manual of Organization and Procedure § 8.2.1 (December 2022) (defining "Patent" as "All classes or types of patents other than design patents (including, without

effect the disclosure of a UM under the SDO's disclosure or licensing policies would have, and whether the FRAND or other licensing commitments of the SDO apply to UMs. Conversely, it is not clear whether an SDO participant's failure to disclose a UM would constitute a violation of such an SDO's disclosure policy or deceptive conduct that is otherwise actionable. The implications of this definitional gap are considered more fully in Section 18.3.1.

And while commentators have casually observed that UMs have infrequently been disclosed as essential to technical standards,[16] there has not, until this study, been an empirical assessment of the rate at which UMs are declared to be essential. With the caveat that, just as with patents, a declaration to an SDO that a UM is believed to be essential to the implementation of particular standard is not an assurance that the UM will ultimately be found to be essential, this chapter refers to such declared UMs as "standards-essential utility models" (SEUMs).

18.2 FINDINGS: STANDARDS-ESSENTIAL UTILITY MODELS

18.2.1 *Methodology*

This study utilized data on UM filings around the world provided by the World Intellectual Property Organization (WIPO)[17] as well as the IPLytics platform (now a part of Lexis-Nexis).[18] As an official United Nations organization, WIPO makes available filing data from the patent offices of its 193 member states.[19] The IPLytics database includes patent and UM filing data from 98 national and regional patent offices.[20] IPLytics also contains SEP declarations made at 35 different SDOs and 11 patent pools, including disambiguated information regarding SEP declarants, as well as information (sourced from Darts IP) concerning SEPs that have been litigated.[21] These databases were queried between March and May 2023. Separately, detailed information regarding litigated SEUMs was sourced from Darts IP.

limitation, originals, divisions, continuations, continuations-in-part, extensions or reissues), and applications for these classes or types of patents throughout the world.")

16 *See, e.g.* Bekkers and Updegrove 2013, 54.

17 WIPO 2023d.

18 https://platform.iplytics.com

19 WIPO 2023e (updated as of February 2023 at time of search).

20 IPLytics, IPlytics Platform Data Sources 5. Most countries that issue UMs do not provide for the multiple continuations and divisional applications that are available for patents, further limiting the set of related UMs that might be viewed as belonging to the same "family". Accordingly, it is not apt to refer to UMs filed in different jurisdictions as belonging to the same "family" in the same manner as patents.

21 The IPLytics database, which we utilized in this study, does not distinguish between litigation in judicial proceedings and validity challenges at patent offices and other administrative tribunals.

18.2.2 *Findings: Standards Essential Utility Models (SEUMs)*

18.2.2.1 Technical Content of SEUMs

As discussed elsewhere in the volume, UMs may cover anything from very simple mechanical designs to complex technological systems. In the case of SEUMs, the technical complexity of claimed inventions tends toward the more complex, given that most standardization activity in which patents and UM are filed occurs in the information and communications technology (ICT) sector in which products are largely electronic and software-based. As a result, the technical descriptions and claims contained in most SEUM documents are largely indistinguishable from those contained in patent documents.

18.2.2.2 SEUM Declarations

In considering SEUMs, it is important to recall that a single UM (like a single patent) may be declared as potentially essential to different standards and different versions of the same standard.[22] Thus, when considering standards-essential patents (SEPs), from 1990 to 2022, approximately 5.9 million individual SEP declarations have been made across all SDOs tracked by IPLytics, covering approximately 500,000 unique patents (counted by declaration year). The number of SEUMs is far lower. During the same period, approximately 7,700 SEUM declarations corresponding to 947 unique UMs were identified, representing approximately 0.2 percent of all SEP declarations.

Figure 18.1 shows total SEUMs by year of UM issuance and year of first declaration. Declarations can be made years after a patent is issued (e.g., in response to a "call for patents" made when a draft standard is submitted to the SDO for approval[23]), explaining why declarations appear to be weighted toward later years. Yet as shown in Figure 18.1, there does not appear to be a discernable trend in SEUM declarations over time, either increasing or decreasing.

18.2.2.3 Geographic Distribution of SEUMs

A total of 946 SEUMs were declared across a total of fourteen jurisdictions between 1990 and 2022.[24] Data regarding each jurisdiction in which SEUMs were declared during this period, compared to overall UM filings and SEP declarations in these jurisdictions, is contained in Supplemental Data Table 2.

[22] Moreover, some SDOs (such as IEEE, responsible for the pervasive Wi-Fi standards) do not require the declaration of specific SEPs but instead permit participants to make "blanket" commitments to license all patents/UM that they hold on specified (i.e., FRAND or royalty-free) terms. These patents/UMs, while potentially numerous, are not included in these data.

[23] See Contreras et al. 2022.

[24] Excludes five apparently spurious/erroneous UM declarations arising from what appear to be errors in declaration documents filed with the ATSC SDO.

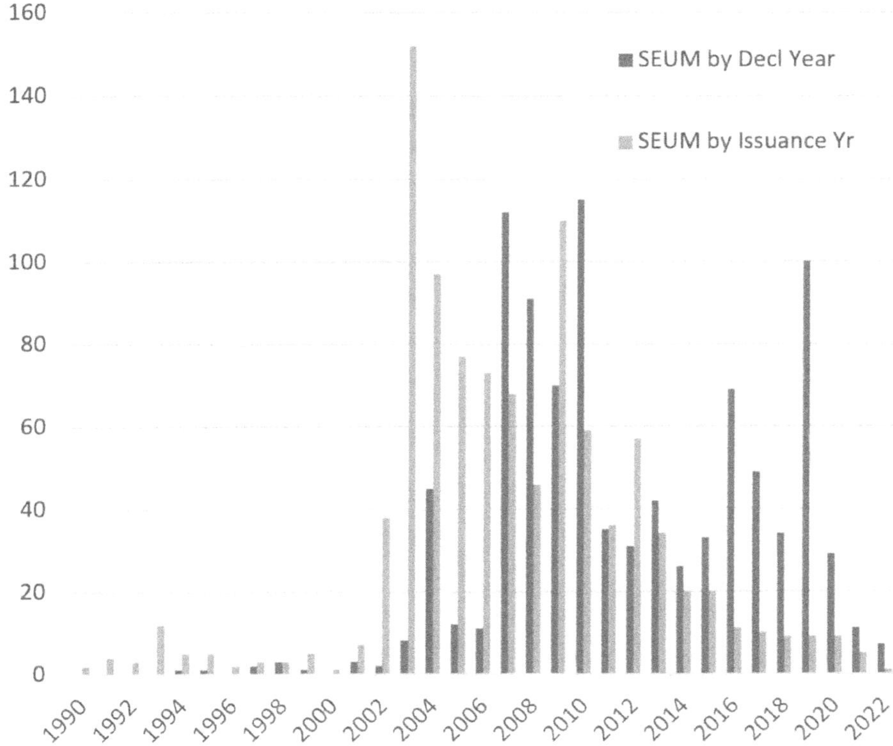

FIGURE 18.1 SEUM filings by year

Figure 18.2 illustrates the distribution of SEUMs among jurisdictions, which varies significantly both from that of all UMs generally and that of all SEP declarations. First, the number of SEUMs is considerably lower than the total number of declared SEPs in those jurisdictions.[25] SEUMs make up the highest portion of SEPs in Germany (4.26 percent) and Taiwan (2.05 percent). This percentage approaches zero in most other jurisdictions, with six or fewer SEUMs declared in all but the top five jurisdictions.[26]

Perhaps the most notable divergence among filing rates of SEUMs, SEPs and UMs within a jurisdiction can be seen in China, which has by far the greatest number of UMs worldwide (97.6 percent). While patents issued by China have been declared as SEPs more than patents issued by any other country in this study,[27] the total number of Chinese SEPs exceeds that of Japan and Korea by only a factor

[25] Note that total SEP figures include SEUMs.

[26] While UMs filed in different jurisdictions may be, and likely are, related to the same or similar inventions, they are not readily identified as belonging to the same "family" in the same manner as patents.

[27] Data from countries, such as the US, that lack UM systems is not included. From 1990 to 2022, 102,663 U.S. patents were declared as SEPs.

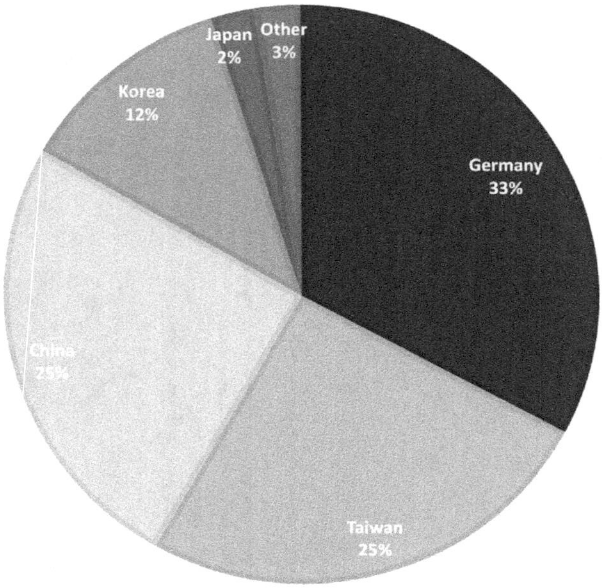

FIGURE 18.2 Share of SEUM declarations by jurisdiction, 1990–2022

of two. Of Chinese SEPs, only 237 are SEUMs (0.32 percent), placing China behind both Germany and Taiwan in terms of SEUM declarations and behind Germany, Taiwan, Ukraine and France in terms of the percentage of UMs that are declared as SEUMs. Moreover, given China's huge number of UMs (nearly 20 million), the percentage declared as SEUMs is vanishingly small. These results reinforce the notion that the Chinese UM system is largely oriented toward local manufacturing of simple products and not toward the type of sophisticated international technology development that occurs within SDOs. Nevertheless, Chinese UMs are still declared as SEUMs more than UMs from any countries other than Germany and Taiwan. Thus, even though representing a small percentage of China's overall UM volume, the number of Chinese SEUMs is significant.

18.2.2.4 SEUM Declarants

Unlike ordinary UMs, which have applicants from a broad cross-section of industries and geographies, the majority of SEUM declarations have been made by a single firm: US-based Interdigital, which held 613 of a total 985 declared SEUMs (61 percent) from 1990 to 2022. Figure 18.3 shows the number of declared SEUMs held by declarants of ten or more SEUM during this period (with full data in Supplemental Data Table 3).

As shown in Figure 18.3, InterDigital, based in the US, has been the most prolific declarant of SEUMs by a wide margin. Yet InterDigital's SEUM filing and declaration program is of largely historical interest. Representatives of InterDigital note

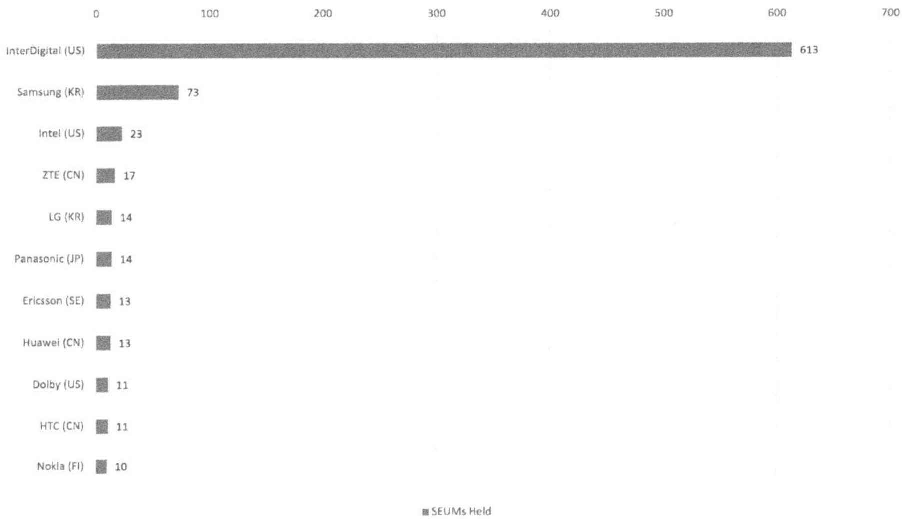

FIGURE 18.3 Top SEUM declarants, 1990–2022

that the company filed numerous UMs between March 2001 and January 2012, with the volume decreasing substantially beginning in 2009.[28] As of July 2023, InterDigital claims that it holds no active UMs.[29]

In addition to InterDigital, the top eleven SEUM filers include two other US firms, Intel and Dolby Laboratories, despite the fact that the US does not itself have a UM system. This observation suggests that firms such as these operate strategically across borders, irrespective of the rights offered by their home jurisdictions.[30] The other top SEUM holders originate from Korea (Samsung and LG), China (ZTE, Huawei), Taiwan (HTC), Japan (Panasonic), Sweden (Ericsson) and Finland (Nokia). Each of these jurisdictions has a UM system.

Below the top eleven firms, 123 additional firms from a range of countries held between 1 and 7 SEUMs each, with a total of 173 SEUMs among them. This "long tail" suggests that, other than InterDigital during the early 2000s and, possibly, some of the other top SEUM filers, firms involved in standardization have not developed a concerted strategy of filing UMs or declaring SEUMs at SDOs, resulting in SEUM declarations that are for the most part sporadic and nonpurposive.

While the absolute number of SEUM declarations made by individual firms may allow conclusions to be drawn about firm strategy, additional insight can be gained by comparing SEUM declarations with SEP declarations made by these firms. Accordingly, Figure 18.4 compares the SEUM declarations made by the top

[28] Email correspondence between the author and Jim Harlan, InterDigital, July 25, 2023 (on file with the author).

[29] Ibid.

[30] *See* Cahoy and Oswald (2021) and Chapter 19 regarding firm strategy concerning UM filing.

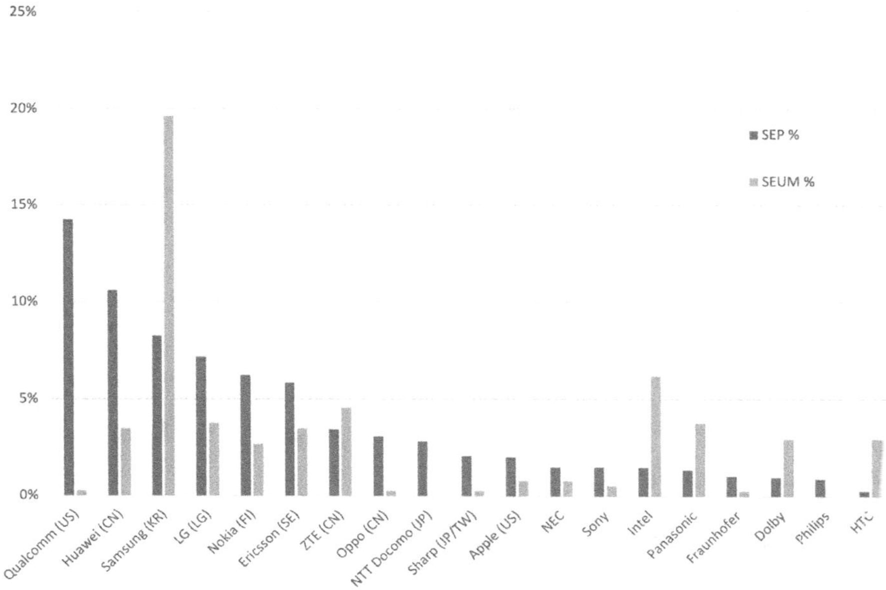

FIGURE 18.4 Comparison of SEP and SEUM declaration shares by Top SEUM declarants (excluding InterDigital), 1990–2022

SEUM declarants (excluding, for purposes of presentation, InterDigital[31]) with SEP declarations by those firms and other "top" SEP declarants, in each case based on the percentage that such firms' declarations represent of all SEUM and SEP declarations.

Interestingly, there appears to be little correspondence between the percentage of SEP and SEUM declarations made by any given firm. Most striking is InterDigital (omitted from Figure 18.1 to delineate the shares of other firms more clearly), which declared 613 of 985 SEUMs (62 percent) but only 21,404 of 502,717 SEPs (4.3 percent). As shown in Figure 18.1, Samsung, Intel, Panasonic, Dolby and HTC follow a similar pattern, accounting for a much larger share of SEUM than SEP declarations. In contrast, firms such as Qualcomm, Huawei, LG, Nokia, Ericsson, Oppo, NTT Docomo, Sharp and Apple were responsible for a much larger share of SEP than SEUM declarations.

18.2.2.5 Jurisdictional Choices by SEUM Declarants

The jurisdictions in which SEUMs are issued does not correspond to the national origin of their declarants, nor follow any discernable pattern at all. Table 18.1 shows

[31] InterDigital is excluded from Figure 18.3 to avoid its graphical "swamping out" the distinctions among other SEUM declarants.

TABLE 18.1 *Jurisdictions of SEUMs filed by top filers, 1990–2022*

	InterDigital	Samsung	Intel	ZTE	LG	Total
Taiwan	228					228
China	201		9			210
Germany	105	66	13	9	9	202
Korea	79	6			5	90
Japan		1				1
France			1			1
Denmark				5		5
Hungary				2		2
Finland				1		1
Total	613	73	23	17	14	740

the countries in which declared SEUMs have been issued for the top five SEUM holders.

Perhaps the only general conclusion that can be drawn from Table 18.1 is that most large holders of SEUMs declared German SEUMs. Despite China's significant share of all global UMs, only InterDigital and, to a lesser degree, Intel, have declared SEUMs issued in China.

Curiously, ZTE, a large Chinese handset manufacturer, has declared no SEUMs issued in China, but is the declarant of the only SEUMs issued by three smaller European jurisdictions (Denmark, Hungary and Finland). While Finland, the headquarters of Nokia, can potentially be explained for this reason, there is no obvious explanation for ZTE's interest in Denmark or Hungary, and, again, this declaration pattern must be attributable to ZTE's unique business objectives and strategies.

In short, these data reveal a highly idiosyncratic pattern of SEUM declaration across firms, which is likely driven by individual firm strategies.[32]

18.2.2.6 SEUMs and SDOs

SEUMs have been declared across a variety of SDOs. Table 18.2 shows the SDOs at which SEUMs have been declared from 1999 to 2022 across the top five UM filing jurisdictions.

Not surprisingly, the "xG" series of wireless telecommunications standards developed under the aegis of ETSI, which are documented as having the largest number of SEP declarations,[33] also have the most SEUMs declared against them. Yet several other SDOs also have declared SEUMs. ATSC, ITU-T and JEDEC

[32] Such idiosyncratic UM strategies were also observed by Cahoy and Oswald with respect to the automotive industry and its pursuit of UM. See Cahoy and Oswald 2021, 568.

[33] *See* Baron and Pohlmann 2018.

TABLE 18.2 *SDOs in which SEUMs are declared, 1999–2022*

SDO	China	Germany	Japan	Korea	Taiwan
ANSI	1				1
ARIB		1	2	1	
ATSC	7	22	4	7	7
Blu-Ray		1			
ETSI	220	281	13	111	226
IEC	1				
IEEE		1			
IETF			1	1	1
ISO		3			
ITU-T	1	9	1	1	2
JEDEC	7	6	1	2	4
OMA		1			
SMPTE				1	
WPC		1			

include declared SEUMs from each of the top 5 SEUM jurisdictions, while nine other SDOs have a handful of SEUM declarations.

Moreover, individual firms choose which SDOs to participate in based on their own product offerings and research programs. Thus, firms primarily engaged in wireless telecommunications and heavily involved in standardization at ETSI would not necessarily participate in JEDEC, which focuses on semiconductor memory devices.

18.2.3 *SEUMs in the Judicial System*

SEPs can give their owners significant leverage in the negotiation of licensing agreements, in part, because SEPs can be enforced in court against unlicensed implementers. Depending on the jurisdiction, a court may award a SEP holder that successfully enforces its SEP against an unlicensed implementer monetary damages and fee awards and may also enjoin the implementer from further manufacturing or selling standards-compliant products.[34] In recent years, there has been a significant amount of SEP- and FRAND-related litigation. One 2023 study commissioned by the European Commission identified more than 1,000 reported judicial decisions involving FRAND issues around the world between 2009 and 2021.[35] Another recent study found that in the US, disclosed SEPs are more than five times more likely than non-SEPs to be litigated.[36] Litigation of SEPs is thus a significant feature of the standards-setting environment.

[34] Contreras et al. 2019; Lemley and Simcoe 2019, 610.
[35] Baron et al. 2023, at 71, fig. 13.
[36] Bekkers et al. 2023, 7, table 4.

In addition to enforcement litigation, the validity of SEPs can be challenged in judicial and administrative proceedings around the world (e.g., oppositions at the European Patent Office and *inter partes* review proceedings at the US Patent Trials and Appeal Board). We are unaware of statistics regarding the total number of such challenges, though Lemley and Simcoe recently studied validity rates of SEPs challenged in US litigation.[37]

The frequency with which SEUMs are enforced or challenged in administrative proceedings (which, for the sake of convenience, we refer to as "litigated"), however, has not been studied. This section provides initial descriptive statistics concerning litigation and challenge of UMs and SEUMs.

18.2.3.1 Litigated Utility Models

From 2000 to 2022, we identified approximately 30,000 UMs that were the subject of judicial proceedings, including both administrative challenges and court litigation.[38] These figures do not include UMs that were subject to arbitration proceedings. As shown in Table 18.3, litigated UMs can be found across a wide range of jurisdictions, from large, developed economies to small and developing ones.

Consistent with its position as the leading jurisdiction in terms of overall UM filings, China is also the site of the greatest number of UMs subject to litigation (69.5 percent). This being said, this share is significantly lower than China's share of overall UM filings during this period (95.6 percent). As such, China appears to have a somewhat lower rate of litigation than other jurisdictions.

Other jurisdictions in which large numbers of UMs are filed (i.e., Germany, Japan, Russia, Korea) also lead the rankings for litigated UMs. Nevertheless, there is a "long tail" of jurisdictions in which UMs are litigated but relatively few UMs have been issued. For example, Finland, with 79 litigated UMs, ranks 13th in terms of litigated UMs, but only 23rd in terms of overall UM filing during the period. Moreover, some jurisdictions that rank fairly high in terms of UM issuance (e.g., Australia, France, Philippines) have very little UM litigation, and Thailand, Mexico and Hong Kong, which ranked 11th, 17th, 19th, respectively, in terms of UM issuances during the period, had no reported UM litigation during the period.

A wide range of parties have been involved in UM litigation, with no individual party holding more than 0.2 percent of total UMs subject to litigation (either as the

[37] Lemley and Simcoe 2019, 627 (finding that, in their sample of 49 U.S. cases, SEPs were found valid 83.7 percent of the time).

[38] The IPLytics database, which we utilized in this study, does not distinguish between litigation in judicial proceedings and validity challenges at patent offices and other administrative tribunals. Moreover, some jurisdictions whose sub-patent systems are referred to by names other than "utility models", such as the now-discontinued "registration patents" in the Netherlands, are not identified by IPLytics as UMs, even though such rights may have been subject to significant litigation activity.

TABLE 18.3 *Jurisdictions where utility models were litigated, 2000–2022*

Jurisdiction	Litigated UMs	Jurisdiction	Litigated UMs
China	21,018	Peru	22
Germany	2,589	Chile	21
Japan	1,377	Austria	14
Russia	1,292	Bulgaria	14
Taiwan	1,213	Colombia	13
Korea	911	Hungary	11
Brazil	512	Australia	6
Turkey	341	France	6
Czech Rep.	257	Philippines	4
Spain	249	Costa Rica	4
Italy	101	Estonia	4
Poland	97	Argentina	3
Finland	79	Romania	2
Denmark	36	Greece	1
Slovakia	36	Moldova	1
Ukraine	25	Portugal	1

plaintiff or defendant). Of the 20 firms holding the largest number of UMs subject to litigation from 2000 to 2022 (ranging from 22 to 63 UMs), 3 were Taiwanese and 17 were Chinese. Even among the top 50 holders of litigated UMs, the large majority were Chinese (including Segway, the former US manufacturer of personal mobility devices, now a Chinese-held firm), together with a handful of Taiwanese and Japanese firms.

18.2.3.2 Litigated SEUMs

Unlike UMs more generally, IPLytics identified only 13 SEUMs that were involved in judicial or administrative proceedings around the world between 2000 and 2022: six in China and seven in Germany (Table 18.4).

Despite the low number of litigated SEUMs, Table 18.4 makes possible a few observations. First, as noted above, SEUMs are technical in nature, often indistinguishable in their specifications and claims from patents. This being said, upon a cursory inspection, at least two of the three SEUMs declared with respect to JEDEC standards appear to relate more to physical connections among electronic components than the internal functionality of those components (a more typical approach for UM). The SEUMs declared with respect to ETSI standards, however, appear highly technical in nature and are of a nature similar to other SEPs declared at ETSI.

Second, the large majority of these cases (92 percent) involved administrative validity challenges to SEUMs. In China, these were brought in the Reexamination

TABLE 18.4 *Litigated SEUMs, 2000–2022*

Jurisdiction	Type of action	Owner	First declared	SDO	Standard	UM title
Germany	Admin. challenge	Samsung	2003	ETSI	2G 3G 4G 5G	Device for channel coding and multiplexing in a CDMA communication system in a CDMA communication system
Germany	Admin. challenge	Samsung	2003	ETSI	3G 4G 5G	Uplink transmitting device for mobile communication system, has rate matcher that bypasses information symbols and processes parts of first and second parity symbols according to given rate matching rule
China	Admin. challenge	InterDigital	2008	ETSI	3G	User equipment for high-speed shared control channels
Germany	Enforced and Admin. challenge	Netlist	2010	JEDEC	3DS LRDIMM	System that uses distributed bytewise buffers on a memory module
China	Admin. challenge	InterDigital	2011	ETSI	3G	User equipment of media access control multitasking/ de-multitasking and base station
China	Admin. challenge	Foxconn	2011	JEDEC	SO-006SODIMM	Opposite-linked connection assembly
Germany	Admin. challenge	ZTE	2011	ETSI	5G	Apparatus for generating and breaking down signaling of uninterrupted means
China	Admin. challenge	Foxconn	2013	JEDEC	SO-018	Card rim connector
Germany	Admin. challenge	Samsung	2015	ETSI	3G 4G 5G	Device for performing a handover in a mobile communication system
China	Admin. challenge	InterDigital	2016	ETSI	3G 4G 5G	Radio communication system for providing channel distribution information for supporting UL and DL channel
Germany	Enforced	Nokia	2016	ETSI	4G	Randomization of block-spread signals
China	Admin. challenge	InterDigital	2020	ETSI	2G 3G 4G	High speed down-stream chain circuit public channel subscriber equipment able to support mixed automatic repeated request
Germany	Enforced and Admin. challenge	IP Bridge	2020	ETSI	4G	Terminal device

and Invalidation Department of the China Patent Office, though three of the six challenges were appealed to the Chinese courts.

In Germany, these administrative challenges were brought at the Deutsches Patent und Markenamt (DPMA) (the German Patent and Trademark Office). Of the seven German SEUM cases identified, two involved both an administrative validity challenge at the DMPA and a judicial enforcement action (one in Düsseldorf and one in München), and one involved only an enforcement action (brought in München). All of the German administrative challenges appear to have been unsuccessful, as each of the challenged UMs is recorded as having expired at the natural end of its 10-year term (i.e., it was not prematurely canceled).

The three German enforcement actions were brought by IP Bridge, a patent assertion entity, and Netlist and Nokia, product-based companies that are active in patent enforcement.[39] Florian Mueller offers a first-hand report on the Netlist litigation, which involved prominent litigation counsel and sophisticated legal issues and was seemingly tied to related litigation in other jurisdictions.[40]

18.2.4 *Summary of Findings*

The principal findings of this study can be summarized as follows:

1. Some, but not all, SDOs expressly permit or require the disclosure and licensing of UMs that are potentially essential to their standards. The requirements of SDO policies that do not expressly mention UMs are ambiguous.
2. Nearly 1,000 UMs (SEUMs) have been declared as essential to broadly adopted industry standards at ETSI and other prominent SDOs in the ICT sector.
3. Firm strategies appear to differ dramatically in terms of SEUM declaration, ranging from intensive to virtually no SEUM activity, even among firms of similar size and market focus.
4. Though far less than other SEPs, SEUMs have been subject to litigation multiple times in China and Germany, and there appears to be no structural barrier to their litigation in other jurisdictions.

18.3 DISCUSSION

The findings of this study raise a number of implications for governmental policy, SDO operations and firm strategy, and also suggest numerous avenues for additional research.

39 *See* Stanford Law Sch., NPE Litigation Database, https://npe.law.stanford.edu (visited September 17, 2023) (classifying patent asserters).

40 Mueller 2018.

18.3.1 *SDO Policies and UMs: Is a UM a "Patent"?*

One of the key questions raised about UMs is whether they should be considered to be "patents" for purposes of SDO policy requirements. While UMs are clearly distinct from patents under international IP treaties and the laws of countries with UM systems, the distinction may be less clear when viewed from outside those countries.[41] And, as noted in the Introduction, some jurisdictions refer to UMs as petty patents, innovation patents or registration patents,[42] implying that, at least in a broad definitional sense, they constitute a form of patent.

As discussed in Section 18.1.4, while some SDOs, such as ETSI and IETF, expressly require the disclosure and licensing of SEUMs in their IPR policies, other SDOs do not expressly include UMs within the scope of their patent disclosure and licensing commitments. Yet, as shown in Table 18.2, firms have nonetheless disclosed SEUMs to SDOs, such as JEDEC and ATSC, that fail to include UMs within their definitions of "patents".

At these SDOs, the legal effect of such disclosures is not entirely clear. Would a UM declared as essential to a standard be treated in the same manner as a patent declared under that policy and thus be subject to the SDO's FRAND licensing requirements? Or would the UM disclosure be disregarded as noncompliant with a policy that only permitted the disclosure of patents, and thus lack any legal effect?

The converse question also arises: if an SDO policy does not explicitly require the disclosure of UMs, then what obligation, if any, does the holder of an SEUM have to disclose and/or license that UM to implementers of the standard? Technically speaking, if UMs are not subject to an SDO's FRAND licensing requirements, then an SEUM holder would be free to charge supra-FRAND royalties for its SEUMs, or to refuse to license them at all. Though one could argue that the nondisclosure or concealment of a UM would implicitly violate the spirit of the SDO's disclosure and licensing policies, or even applicable competition law.[43]

It is likely that the answers to these questions would depend on the specific understandings and intentions of the SDO members who drafted and approved the relevant policy,[44] and would thus be highly fact-specific (and vulnerable to differing recollections). In order to avoid these interpretive uncertainties, SDOs that have not expressly addressed the treatment of UMs under their disclosure and

[41] For example, in *In re Carlson*, 983 F.2d 1032, 1033 (Fed. Cir. 1992), the U.S. Court of Appeals for the Federal Circuit held that a German UM "constitutes an 'invention ... patented ... in ... a foreign country' within the meaning of 35 U.S.C. § 102(a) and thus may be considered prior art".

[42] See note 3, *supra*, and accompanying text.

[43] *See* Hesse and Marshall 2017 (describing legal enforcement actions against firms that withheld information about SEPs from SDO and other participants).

[44] *See* Contreras 2017c, 219–220 (discussing *Rambus* and Broadcom cases in which understandings of SDO participants have been recognized notwithstanding SDO policy language to the contrary).

licensing policies (as well as any governmental policies relating to SEPs) would do well to do so.

18.3.2 *Including SEUMs in SEP Databases*

While some UMs are currently included in SDO-maintained databases of SEPs, it is sometimes difficult to distinguish SEUMs from ordinary SEPs in the relevant database entries.[45] Understanding this distinction could be useful for SDO participants and standards implementers, however, given the shorter duration of UMs and their different use in litigation. SDOs could do more to clarify the type of rights that are listed in their databases by clearly identifying which disclosed rights are SEUMs versus SEPs.

In addition to SDOs, the European Commission recently proposed legislation that, among other things, would create a new official registry and database for SEPs issued in the European Union.[46] Though early drafts of the proposal included utility models within the scope of the proposed regulation,[47] the current proposal does not contemplate UMs,[48] thereby omitting these potentially important rights. The reasons for this change have not been disclosed publicly by the Commission.[49] As one of us has previously noted in written comments submitted to the Commission, it should revise its proposed regulation to include European UMs along with patents or, at a minimum, reduce ambiguity by indicating why UMs were excluded from the proposal.

18.3.3 *Enforcement of SEUMs*

The potential overlapping coverage of patent and UM protection and the malleable nature of UM claims (including the ability, in countries such as Germany and Italy, to alter them during the course of litigation),[50] have led to their tactical use in infringement litigation. This degree of uncertainty is not likely to improve the clarity or predictability of the standardization ecosystem, particularly if individual firms begin to increase their declaration of UMs as SEUMs. While it appears that little

[45] Some countries designate UM numbers distinctly from patent numbers, but this distinction is not always easy to identify, particularly with non-Western character sets.

[46] European Commission 2023c.

[47] Proposal for a Regulation of the European Parliament and of the Council on Standard Essential Patents (leaked draft, March 29, 2023), art. II(3) ("'patent' means patent or utility model"), Art. II(3) ("'patent' means patent or utility model").

[48] European Commission 2023c (definitions in Art. II refer only to patents).

[49] Mueller hypothesizes that two factors may have contributed to the change: a desire not to subject shorter-term UMs to the mandatory 9-month deliberation period introduced elsewhere in the Proposal, and the possible legal issues arising from an attempt by the EU to regulate UMs, which are not EU-harmonized rights (Mueller 2023).

[50] See Chapters 6 (Germany) and 7 (Italy).

short of national UM reform and/or harmonization can fully address these concerns (see Section 18.3.5), SDOs could eliminate at least some potential ambiguity by affirmatively including UMs within the scope of their disclosure and licensing requirements. Doing so would, at a minimum, reduce the likelihood that SEUMs could be used to obtain injunctions against the use of standards by implementers "willing" to obtain licenses of SEUMs on FRAND terms.

18.3.4 *Essentiality of SEUMs*

As discussed in Section 18.1.2, patents are defined as SEPs only if they are "essential" to the implementation of a standard, where essentiality exists if a product implementing the standard necessarily infringes the claims of the patent. The obligation to disclose SEPs (and, presumably, SEUMs) typically arises during development of a standard, prior to its approval and publication by the SDO. Yet UM claims may be more malleable after issuance than those of patents. This malleability raises questions concerning the potential essentiality of SEUMs, and the degree to which changes to claim scope can or should be taken into account when assessing the effect of FRAND commitments on UMs.

18.3.5 *SEUMs and FRAND Royalties*

If SEUMs are deemed to constitute SEPs under an SDO's disclosure and licensing policies, SEUMs raise distinct but related questions regarding the calculation of FRAND royalties. First, given that UMs are generally not given substantive examination by relevant patent offices, their terms are shorter than those of patents and in some jurisdictions they lack direct enforceability, an argument could be made that UMs are, on average, less "valuable" than patents. As such, an argument could be made that the "fair and reasonable" royalty payable with respect to a SEUM should be less than the "fair and reasonable" royalty payable with respect to a SEP. By extension, the value of (and the FRAND royalty payable with respect to) a portfolio that includes SEUMs should be less than the value of a similarly sized portfolio that includes only SEPs. If SEUMs are not distinguished from SEPs when portfolios are valued, then incentives will exist for opportunistic firms to "stuff" their portfolios with cheap and easy-to-obtain SEUMs of questionable validity and essentiality in order to increase the size (and putative value) of those portfolios.

The issue of SEUM valuation has implications not only for transactions between individual holders of SEUMs and potential infringers, but for *all* holders of SEPs (and SEUMs) that are declared to be essential with respect to a particular standard. For example, when SEPs and SEUMs are placed into a pool for collective licensing to implementers of a standard, the royalty received from implementers is often distributed among pool members in proportion to the number of patents that they have licensed to the pool. The share of such royalties allocable to SEUMs, however, should arguably be lower than the share allocable to SEPs.

The same issue arises in connection with the "top-down" calculation of FRAND royalties payable with respect to a standard. Top-down royalty calculation methodologies seek to determine the overall value of a standard to a product, to use that value to assess an aggregate royalty for SEPs covering the standard, and then allocate a portion of the aggregate royalty to each holder of SEPs based on the number (and possibly the value) of its SEPs.[51] Top-down FRAND royalty calculations, which have already been utilized in judicial decisions in the US, UK and Japan may take on even greater prominence under a recent European Union proposal to implement a top-down calculation methodology in official calculations of aggregate SEP royalties.[52]

If SEUMs are valued lower than other SEPs, then in such top-down royalty determinations, the presence of SEUMs should be a factor used in determining both the overall level of royalties payable with respect to a standard, as well as the share of such aggregate royalty that is allocated to different holders of SEPs and SEUMs.

18.3.6 *Harmonization*

Traditionally, UMs have existed largely as devices of national law with little harmonization among jurisdictions, even within closely knit regions such as the European Union. Yet the entry of UMs into the field of technical standardization, an inherently multinational arena, begs the question whether UM systems should be harmonized to a greater degree. That is, if UMs can effectively be utilized to expand individual firm portfolios of patents subject to FRAND licensing, then jurisdictions that make it easier to obtain UMs are likely to attract more UM filers, and perhaps to draw applicants away from their own, or other, patent systems (e.g., if a UM can be obtained for one fourth the cost of a patent, in one fourth the time, but yields a similar value, then UMs could quickly become preferred instruments in some markets). What's more, fast and cheap UMs could result in a "race to the bottom" among jurisdictions seeking to capitalize on the "numbers game" among SEP holders. These considerations should encourage policy makers to consider more closely aligning UM systems across borders.

18.3.7 *The Costs of Uncertainty Surrounding SEUMs*

As noted above, UMs involve substantial uncertainty, both as to their coverage and enforceability, as well as their status (or not) as SEPs. This uncertainty can be utilized opportunistically by actors within the standardization ecosystem. For example, depending on the relevant SDO policy in effect, the holders of UMs

[51] *See* Contreras 2017a, 692–696.

[52] Eur. Comm'n 2023.

may argue that UMs are excluded from the SDO's FRAND disclosure or licensing commitments, thus giving them free rein to conceal these UMs from SDOs and implementers and to charge supra-FRAND royalties for the use of these rights. Likewise, UMs may be used tactically to seek injunctive relief against implementers before SEPs are issued. On the other hand, implementers that wish to delay negotiation over FRAND licenses (i.e., "holding out") may raise the inherent uncertainty of UMs when negotiating such licenses. This uncertainty could thus destabilize the standardization system, imposing greater transactional costs on both UM holders and implementers, delaying the development of important new standards, imposing costs on consumers and depriving the market of new standardized products.

18.3.8 *SEUMs and Innovation*

UM systems were introduced in many jurisdictions to stimulate local innovation and industry via a low-cost pathway to intellectual property protection for modest or incremental designs not rising to the level of patentable invention. Yet our findings show that SEUMs are largely being filed and declared by major international firms with active patenting programs, and that these UMs often cover technologies that are, or could also be, covered by patents. To the extent that UMs are being used primarily to obtain duplicative coverage for the same technological innovations, or for tactical litigation advantage, they may not be achieving the goals for which they were originally designed. As a result, policy makers may wish to consider the findings of this study when evaluating the ongoing value of UM systems in their countries.

18.3.9 *Areas for Further Research*

There remains more to be studied with respect to UMs and the standardization ecosystem. One area for further research is an assessment of the "quality" of UMs that are declared as SEUMs, both in comparison to other UMs and to SEPs. The question of patent quality has attracted significant attention from scholars as well as governmental authorities in recent years, and numerous metrics for the measurement of patent quality have been developed (e.g., citation analysis). However, we are unaware of any significant study of UM quality or analysis on whether the same metrics applied to patents can be applied to UMs. Further research of these questions would help to establish the value of SEUMs that form a part of SEP portfolios and to establish FRAND royalty rates both for individual SEUMs, portfolios including both SEUMs and SEPs, and for top-down FRAND royalty determinations for entire standards.

It would also be useful to gain a better understanding of the business strategies that have led some firms to declare SEUMs in large quantities, while others have largely ignored them. Thus, just as Ford Motor Co. in the automotive sector has been observed by Cahoy and Oswald to have adopted a business strategy involving the acquisition (and possibly assertion) of UMs,[53] InterDigital, during the 2000s, appears to have adopted such an approach in the ICT sector, particularly around standards developed under the aegis of ETSI. Samsung, the second highest holder of SEUMs, appears to have adopted a similar strategy. A greater appreciation for firm strategy in relation to UMs could help policy makers to tailor their UM systems to the needs of the private sector.

Further research into SEUM assertion and litigation is also warranted. The litigation data that we reviewed could be supplemented with more detailed information regarding case outcomes, timing and tactics. Greater visibility into these issues could help policy makers to assess whether UMs are being (or could be) abused as litigation devices, and whether procedural safeguards should be put in place to avoid such abuse in the future.

18.4 CONCLUSION

UMs, once a "back water" of intellectual property scholarship,[54] may be more relevant to technology-intensive standards than previously thought. This study demonstrates that UMs are being declared essential to industry standards in significant numbers, at least by some firms. Given the relative ease, speed and cost-effectiveness of obtaining UMs, it is possible that this trend will continue. Yet UMs involve a degree of uncertainty, both as to their coverage and enforceability, as well as their status (or not) as SEPs. Such uncertainty imposes unnecessary costs on the standardization ecosystem and can be utilized opportunistically both by UM holders and implementers. Accordingly, policy makers and SDOs should thus consider clarifying, and more intensely harmonizing, their rules concerning UMs and SEUMs. Firms and courts should likewise consider the value of SEUMs when calculating FRAND royalties for portfolios and overall standards. Finally, these findings invite reconsideration of the role of UMs in the innovation ecosystem.

[53] Cahoy and Oswald 2021, 568.

[54] Janis 1999.

19

Navigating Incomplete Harmonization

Businesses and the Utility Model Environment

Daniel R. Cahoy and Lynda J. Oswald[*]

In a world of increasing harmonization of intellectual property rights, the "utility model" stands out as a stark outlier. This specialized form of a lesser innovation right is available in only about half of the world's intellectual property systems, and the scope of protection and rules for acquisition can vary widely among offering countries.

This disharmony is surprising as utility models fill a unique niche in the innovation ecosystem. Although a utility model has claims like a standard patent, utility models cover a narrower range of inventive activity, are subject to less governmental scrutiny, and have a significantly shorter life than standard patents. In most respects, utility models provide a simpler route to low-level protection for useful inventions. Intuitively, they should be attractive to a variety of actors, including small firms whose inventive activity does not rise to the level required for standard patents or large firms that wish to more completely blanket the landscape. The disparate embrace of utility models in the world's intellectual property systems, however, means that this option is often unavailable to actors who might benefit from it.

Despite the differential availability of national utility model rights we see no evidence of businesses or policymakers pushing to harmonize in this field. Rather, firms appear to adopt country-specific intellectual property strategies that leverage differential qualities in legal protection and maximize available efficiencies in a manner that would be otherwise unavailable in a fully standardized intellectual property environment.[1]

This chapter draws on empirical research that demonstrates that utility model protection can address differential capture or appropriability[2] needs for a firm's

[*] This chapter is drawn from Cahoy and Oswald, 2021, with permission.

[1] Frischtak 1993.

[2] Ceccagnoli 2009.

portfolio of inventions in terms of time and cost. We propose that a "zone of appropriability preference" exists when utility models and standard patents overlap, and this zone provides important opportunities to firms with global intellectual property portfolios. Using the European Patent Office's PATSTAT patent data and a novel experimental construct that tracks inventions that are pursued as a utility model instead of a standard patent, we demonstrate that firms appear to seek utility model protection when their overall appropriability needs differ by region. We make the case that a firm may choose standard patent protection in one region and utility model protection in another, even though standard patent protection is available in both settings.

Our analysis suggests that firms exploit utility model disharmony to their benefit, choosing utility models over standard patents in some countries or certain instances in order to better appropriate (i.e., obtain greater economic returns on) their innovations. This behavior, along with the relative indifference of policymakers, firms and commentators to the fractured utility model landscape, indicates that disharmony may provide an important means of addressing differential national and firm-level needs and preferences. In the end, the strategic advantages that utility models provide to firms along with the additional flexibility such systems give countries to tailor and optimize national intellectual property protection schemes raise the counterintuitive possibility that disharmony in this field of intellectual property law may in fact be the best policy.

19.1 GLOBAL IP STRATEGY AND THE CHALLENGE OF UTILITY MODEL DISHARMONY

Multinational firms have a strong interest in relatively uniform and predictable legal rules and regulations across countries. More consistency in legal regimes lowers transaction costs and creates efficiencies that can be leveraged as a firm extends its reach in new territories. In addition, because information can be so easily appropriated by competitors, it is extremely important to have the assurance of legal protection for inventive technologies and creative ideas before products and services are globally disseminated. Foreign direct investment also hinges on consistency in intellectual property protection.

However, intellectual property rights are national in character and may vary in availability or enforceability across countries. For that reason, governments have undertaken a purposeful effort to harmonize intellectual property through treaties and other international rights. As a result, a firm can expect to encounter a patent system that is generally nondiscriminatory in its protection,[3] a copyright system that protects computer programs[4] and a common system for registering trademarks in

[3] TRIPS 1994, art. 27.
[4] WIPO Copyright Treaty 1996, art. 4.

multiple jurisdictions.[5] Even rights that still have significant national differences in scope and nature, such as trade secrets, nonetheless carry an expectation that some level of protection will exist based on treaty obligations.[6] The convergence of intellectual property rules and norms across the world is a legal harmonization success story.

Utility models have been conspicuously absent from the harmonization conversation, despite the important niche they purportedly fill. Policymakers in many countries believe that intellectual property rights serve as an important incentive for small business investment,[7] but that obtaining patent rights is burdensome and expensive for small and medium-sized enterprises.[8] Moreover, development advocates and scholars argue that less-invention-intensive rights could serve a potentially important role for emerging economies.[9]

Despite these policy rationales arguing for utility model systems, harmonization efforts in this field have been very rare. There was, for example, discussion about regional harmonization of utility model systems in the European Union (EU) in the 1990s.[10] The effort eventually resulted in a formal proposal from the European Commission for a utility model "directive," but the effort stalled in the early 2000s when member states decided to instead focus on a standard European patent.[11]

Other countries have eliminated their utility model systems in recent years. For example, citing legal uncertainty and a lack of innovation enhancement, the Netherlands abolished its "short-term" patent system in 2008.[12] Belgium eliminated its "small patent" in 2009 for essentially the same reason.[13] The lost filings in both countries arguably were absorbed by the standard patent system.[14] Australia replaced its 1970s-era "petty patent" right with a new "innovation patent" in 2001, but eliminated the relatively new right just twenty years later,[15] fearing it conveyed few benefits to inventors and created risks of abuse.[16]

Efforts to implement new national utility model systems are even scarcer and typically unsuccessful. A Private Member bill to create such a system was introduced in New Zealand in 2018, but it was not supported by Government; a motion to pass the bill failed at the first reading.[17] In 2011, India issued a discussion paper inviting public commentary on the potential adoption of a utility model system. After

5 Madrid Agreement Concerning the International Registration of Marks 1891.
6 TRIPS 1994, art. 39.
7 Suthersanen 2006.
8 Suthersanen 2006.
9 Suthersanen 2006, 7 & 8; Kim et al. 2012; Prud'homme 2017b.
10 Königer 2009, 19.
11 Königer 2009.
12 Janis 1999, 11.
13 Janis 1999, 11–12; *see also* Radauer et al. 2015, 23–24.
14 Prud'homme 2014,11 n. 22; *see also* Radauer et al. 2015, 24–27.
15 *See* IP Australia 2023d.
16 Productivity Commission (Australia) 2016.
17 *See* Cox 2018.

evaluating extensive commentary on draft policies, the IPR Think Tank recommended adoption of such a system in its final report in 2015, but no further action has been taken.[18]

Thus, utility model systems are characterized by profound disharmony at the global level. Moreover, no overarching historical theme dictates whether a country has a utility model system. The developmental status of a country appears to be disconnected from this question, as utility model systems can be found in a selection of countries ranging from major developed economies[19] to least developed countries.[20]

One might assume that, if utility model systems convey advantages to society, efforts to expand their presence are justified and arguably should be the subject of international harmonization. Moreover, if there is a particular set of utility model attributes that are optimal, discordant systems should be brought in line. This has been the global approach in almost every other intellectual property context.

However, our study of the real-world use of utility model systems by firms suggests that a broad harmonization effort would be misplaced. Our findings suggest that the firms and individuals that rely on innovation incentives not only accept the discordant environment of utility models but may even embrace it as a means of achieving optimal protection under different conditions. Additionally, from a policy perspective, our findings further suggest that division creates diversity at the national level that may act as a laboratory for innovation stimulation.

In sum, our investigation of utility model use supports the general notion that harmonization is not always the answer; a nuanced and informed approach to modifying existing protection schemes is more important than is generally acknowledged.

19.2 EVIDENCE OF FIRM UTILITY MODEL USE AND STRATEGY

How do users of the intellectual property system respond to utility model regimes? Who is actually obtaining utility models, and what does that say about whether this form of intellectual property law protection is integrated into innovation markets or is an outlier? Recently available data on utility model use is the best starting point to better understand their impact.

[18] *See* IPR Think Tank 2015.

[19] Four countries – France, Germany, Italy and Japan – appear both on the United Nations' 2020 list of "major developed economies," *see* United Nations, Department of Economic and Social Affairs 2020, and on the WIPO list of countries with utility model systems, *see* WIPO 2023a.

[20] Four countries – Lao People's Democratic Republic, Mozambique, Uganda and the United Republic of Tanzania – appear on both the United Nations' list of least developed countries, United Nations, Dept. of Economic and Social Affairs 2020, and on the WIPO list of countries with utility model systems. WIPO 2023a.

19.2.1 *Overall Business Use of Utility Models*

It is difficult to identify which industries make use of utility model protection globally, because the covered subject matter can differ from country to country, skewing the results.[21] For example, a software invention protectable as a utility model in one country may be excluded in another. In addition, surprisingly few studies detail use of utility models by industry, as opposed to the countries targeted or the size of applicants. However, a recent review of several EU countries noted that the "mechanical engineering" sector was dominant across the board, followed closely by "electrical engineering."[22] Even more specifically, the study found the top industries linked to utility models in each country were all manufacturing related, but the order of each specific type can differ.[23]

19.2.2 *Existing Assessments of Utility Model Disharmony Impact on Firm Strategy*

Existing assessments on the impact of utility models disharmony on firm intellectual property strategy are limited.[24] A 2015 study conducted by the Technopolis Group, tendered by the European Commission (the "Technopolis Report"), involved a review of the literature and available evidence on the impact of utility models on European states as well as selected non-EU countries that offer the rights.[25] It found that legal uncertainty across systems was a key barrier to more widespread use of utility models by firms.[26] But more importantly for our purposes, the study noted that utility models were used as an auxiliary tool by practitioners to avoid perceived problems in the standard patent system rather than as a primary protection mechanism for "minor inventions by small inventors."[27] It concluded that the evidence on the impact of utility models to support innovation was ambiguous[28] and recommended against a move to harmonize utility models similar to standard patents.[29]

In a similar study funded by the European Commission and the Office for Harmonization of the Internal Market (OHIM), Prud'homme (2014) undertook a

[21] Richards 2010, tbl. II.

[22] Radauer et al. 2015, 65, 74, 83, 92, 102, 113.

[23] The study linked NACE (Nomenclature des Activités Économiques dans la Communauté Européenne) industry classifications to utility model filings and counted the top classifications in Germany, Austria, Denmark, Italy, Poland, Czech Republic, Spain, Finland and France from 1995–1999 and 2007–2011. See generally Radauer et al. 2015.

[24] *See* Radauer et al. 2015, 1. Examples of research addressing utility models at least in part include Maskus and McDaniel (1999); Kumar (2003); Thomä and Bizer (2013); Evenson and Westphal (1995); Kardam (2007); Johnson et al. (2015); Li (2012); Wang (2015).

[25] Radauer et al. 2015, 1 n.1.

[26] Radauer et al. 2015, 3–4.

[27] Radauer et al. 2015, 3.

[28] Radauer et al. 2015, 5.

[29] Radauer et al. 2015, 6.

more granular analysis by considering the legal details of different utility model systems to determine if a particular iteration has a more positive economic impact. He compared the systems of Austria, China, the Czech Republic, Finland, France, Germany and Italy in terms of qualities such as subject matter, duration, filing costs, examination form and nature, and the potential for double or parallel filing.[30] Prud'homme found that utility models are of some, but limited, use to developing countries.[31] Moreover, there are specific attributes of systems (e.g., electronic filing, subsidies or restricted subject matter) that are clearly more preferable from the perspective of the offering country.[32]

19.3 A NEW VIEW ON UTILITY MODELS: THE ZONE OF APPROPRIABILITY PREFERENCE

The existing literature permits few conclusions on the likely impact on innovation from utility model systems. Observers can reasonably disagree on whether this form of intellectual property serves as a complement to standard patents, a competitor, or simply a distinct right with no clear analogy in systems such as the United States. Without more, it is impossible to say anything definitive on the need for harmonization of utility model systems. A deeper dive into firm-level strategic choices for innovation protection is necessary.

19.3.1 *"Carve-outs" versus "Add-ons" and the "Zone of Appropriability Preferences"*

A common context for assessing whether utility model systems are advantageous is the understanding that they are "add-ons" to the standard patent system; that is, that utility models protect inventions that would not normally be covered by patents because they are not sufficient advances over existing technology.[33] The evaluation of the contribution of utility models to a country's innovative output necessarily considers whether this separate system actually encourages more inventive activity or simply pulls information out of the public domain to the detriment of the overall environment. The add-on opportunity is how the literature to date has viewed utility models.

However, we posit a novel possible explanation of how utility model systems are used: they provide an important choice to firms by serving as an alternative to standard patents. In some systems, such as China's, firms may have the option to file a utility model and standard patent application on the same invention; in those

30 Prud'homme 2017b, 14–16.
31 Prud'homme 2017b, 54.
32 Prud'homme 2017b, 56–57.
33 *See, e.g.*, Janis 1999, 178; Suthersanen 2006, 7.

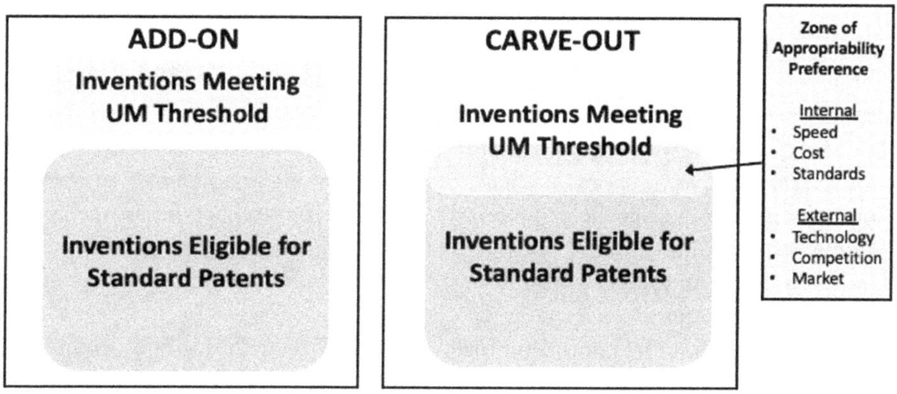

FIGURE 19.1 Role of utility models in a country's IP system

instances, the utility model rights could act less like an add-on regime, and more like a partial "carve-out." In other words, utility models in these systems pull some inventions away from standard patents. The carve-out is not simply a matter of failed attempts at full patenting, but rather a deliberate strategic choice by the applicant to opt for the second-tier right. Importantly, the extent to which a system facilitates a carve-out strategy is highly dependent on the various elements that define its utility model rights. This difference is essentially the result of disharmony.

Why would a firm ever choose a utility model when its invention is eligible for a stronger standard patent? In fact, there are advantages to the generic utility model that may be more important for certain inventions in particular locations. One such advantage is speed. Because utility models generally require no initial examination, they issue quickly, providing a firm with rights that it can assert and license. Additionally, given the possibility of protecting additional pieces or branches of a core invention, it may be possible to blanket a product with rights that essentially create a single-firm thicket that competitors find difficult to avoid. Finally, a firm's operations in a particular location with a particular legal system might be optimally protected by many utility models over a few standard patents.

We define the decision-making process of choosing utility models over standard patents (or vice versa) in those systems that treat utility models as carve-outs as operating in the "zone of appropriability preference" (see Figure 19.1). In this zone, inventors and firms have a choice between protection regimes – standard patents or utility models – and their choice represents a preference among qualities that differ between the two. For example, the choice for speed in securing a utility model over the longer protection period for a slower-to-issue standard patent represents such a preference. The existence of the zone allows a firm to extract optimal appropriability from invention rights and not waste resources on securing protection that is too powerful or too long.

19.3.2 *Data Supporting Optimal Appropriability Strategies*

There is support for the proposition that sufficient knowledge and legal flexibility exist to enable businesses to engage in invention appropriation preference strategies. The 2015 Technopolis Report concluded that in developed economies, utility models can be used "as an auxiliary tool to patenting for a range of specific purposes" and they can help "deal with certain country-specific issues …."[34] Moreover, according to the report's assessment of firm use, it appears that utility models "are utilised to a considerable extent to overcome specific challenges in the national patent systems …."[35]

Two studies explicitly connecting patents and utility models – one centered in Europe and one in China – also provide some empirical evidence of the zone of appropriability preference theory. Heikkilä and Verba (2018) considered connections between standard patent and utility model filings in the European Union. Using PATSTAT data, they collected one dataset comprising (1) patent and utility models families filed at any EU patent office offering utility model protection, and another (2) restricting such families to those claiming priority from an EU patent or utility model filed at any EU patent office offering utility model protection.[36]

Heikkilä and Verba found that utility model filings may be used as part of an international filing strategy, belying the idea that utility models only cover minor inventions worthy of protection in the domestic market.[37] However, they also found that inventions with patent priorities are of higher quality than those with utility model priorities.[38] Those quality differences between patent and utility model priorities are less important than other indicators of patent quality, such as citation count, patent family size and whether there is an associated Patent Cooperation Treaty (PCT) filing.[39] Heikkilä and Verba failed to find any clear indication of strategies to obtain quick rights related to utility model priorities.[40]

Cao et al. (2014) considered Chinese patent and utility model applications that served as priority for a U.S. patent application that was subsequently granted. Similar to our construct below, they assumed that any utility model application that was sufficiently inventive to serve as a basis for a U.S. patent must be inventive enough to also qualify for a Chinese patent.[41] Therefore, their study set considered patents of similar quality that are *by choice* filed as either patents or utility models in China. One important finding from Cao et al.'s work is that inventions filed as Chinese

34 Radauer et al. 2015, 1.
35 Radauer et al. 2015, 176–177.
36 Heikkilä and Verba 2018, 695.
37 Heikkilä and Verba 2018, 697.
38 Heikkilä and Verba 2018, 706.
39 Heikkilä and Verba 2018, 713.
40 Heikkilä and Verba 2018.
41 Cao et al. 2014, 4.

utility models have much shorter time lags between applications, indicating that the applicant desired speed in particular.[42] These patents are also less likely to have continuations filed at the U.S. Patent and Trademark Office or to be maintained during the patent term.[43] Again, this indicates that utility models are connected to inventions that do not require the full length of U.S patent rights. Applicants are exposing their appropriability interests and making more efficient use of them through the broader options in protection offered by China's system.

19.3.3 *Additional Litigation Evidence of Utility Model Use*

If firms indeed perceive utility models as a useful tool for optimally appropriating innovation, one would expect to see more substantive activity than simple rights accumulation. Effectively capturing innovation should include enforcement activities. Conversely, if utility models serve primarily as a weak credential for individuals and firms wishing to memorialize innovative activity, one might expect very little litigation and low rates of success when it does occur. Unfortunately, the lack of comprehensive global litigation data in the utility model arena makes it difficult to decide between real value or mere credential.

Fortunately, China, the most prominent utility model filing target, has now made available a significant amount of information.[44] Those data suggest that, despite the lower standards and lack of examination, utility model rights fare quite well in terms of enforcement success: they are enforced at a level at least as high as standard patents with better win rates for rights holders. Unofficial sources have reported this robust litigation activity for some time.[45] Bian (2018) conducted an empirical analysis of Chinese patent litigation using an official source, China Judgements Online. According to Bian's analysis of final judgments from 2014, owners of Chinese utility models constitute a greater share of the litigation landscape than standard patents (25% versus 13%), and are slightly more likely to be successful, with a win rate of 77% versus 72%.[46]

For purposes of our analysis, perhaps the most interesting statistic in Bian's article is the fact that foreign litigants make up 3.33% of the plaintiffs in the cases studied.[47] Although this is relatively low – and certainly much lower than the 28.44% foreign litigant share in standard patent cases – it is higher than the percentage of foreign utility model ownership (1.12%).[48] This indicates that foreign utility model owners litigate at a higher rate than domestic owners. In other words, foreign owners of

[42] Cao et al. 2014, 6.
[43] Cao et al. 2014, 7.
[44] China Judgements Online 2020.
[45] *See* Liu 2014, 243; Gajewski 2019.
[46] Bian 2018, 446–447.
[47] Bian 2018, 459.
[48] Bian 2018.

Chinese utility models seem to value their rights as real appropriation tools at least as much as, if not more than, domestic owners.

Of course, it is possible that the litigation numbers might reflect a selection bias rather than suggest that utility models are generally valuable (e.g., perhaps only the strongest or more straightforward utility models are asserted). However, this is no different than with standard patents; most are not enforced and those that are can be viewed as part of a specialized subset.[49] Based on this slice of the global litigation environment, utility models seem to have an enforceability potential that allows them to serve as a reasonable innovation investment incentive.

19.4 BUSINESS STRATEGY AND MOTIVATIONS FOR UTILITY MODEL FILINGS: A STUDY OF U.S. PATENT-TO-UTILITY MODEL PATHWAYS

With the Heikkilä and Verba (2018) and Cao et al. (2014) studies in mind, we endeavored to extend the analysis to better understand the patent-utility model strategy. Are patent-utility model pairs simply a subclass of substandard inventions that are crammed into the standard patent system in order to execute a broader rights grab? Or is there evidence that firms are attempting to optimize a differential appropriation strategy, in which utility models provide distinct advantages in place of or in addition to standard patents in certain countries or instances? To better assess the strategic opportunity in filing utility models, we carried out our own novel empirical analysis.

In a study presented in more detail in a separate paper,[50] we used PATSTAT data to focus on a particularly relevant stream of utility model rights that could provide a unique perspective on (1) how these rights impact innovation and (2) what firms appear to exploit system disharmony. Specifically, we considered inventions objectively viable as standard patents that are nonetheless filed as utility models in at least one country. Our presumption was that firms see a particular advantage in undertaking the time and expense of such filings, and this can reveal important information about the appropriability potential of certain systems.

We looked for indicators that would permit us to assess the validity of two hypotheses. First, we propose that this subset of utility model applicants is choosing this form of innovation protection in order to attain some local advantage. Again, because we presume the applicant could have filed only a standard patent, the choice to file a utility model evinces a strategy that accounts for the expense of filing for and possibly enforcing a lower form of intellectual property.

Additionally, we considered the possibility that firms filing a large number of utility models may simply be attempting to obtain every right possible in every location possible. This kind of strategy conflicts with the more purposeful strategy

49 *See* Chien 2016, 841–842.

50 Cahoy and Oswald 2021.

that acknowledges utility models are an advantage only in some countries for some technologies. We believe that firms are more likely to choose the latter, more specific strategy and that it is useful to distinguish between the two.

Our analysis bore out the hypothesis that firms chose to file utility models when a standard patent would be attainable to take advantage of country-specific conditions. Moreover, as to whether patent-to-utility model strategies are simply an attempt to accumulate more rights whatever the cost, we looked to the number of different utility model filings per U.S. patent application. If rights accumulation were the ultimate goal, we would expect to see a large percentage of the inventions filed in multiple countries.

However, the evidence suggests that broad rights accumulation is not the dominant strategy. In our study set, we found that most applicants file for a utility model in only one country. Overall, throughout the studied time period, 79.5% of the U.S. patent applications were filed in a second country as a utility model, and only 16% were filed in two additional countries as utility models (with the remaining percentage being filed in three to fourteen countries).

Additionally, we find that the top technologies underlying the utility models change by forum (see Figure 19.2). In China, we see "electrical machinery, apparatus, energy" at the top whereas Germany's filings are led by "computer technology." Similarly, digital communication draws a relatively high filing rate in Germany but not in China. Pharmaceuticals factor highly in Germany's filings but low in China, though this is likely due to the fact that, strictly speaking, chemicals and pharmaceuticals are not protected under China's utility model system.

Again, these data support the conclusion that, at least in some industrial sectors, firms are employing a forum-specific strategy rather than broad rights collection. We infer that firms are likely considering local industries and markets in seeking utility model protection.[51]

19.5 INSIGHTS ON NAVIGATING UTILITY MODEL DISHARMONY

Despite existing in disharmony, utility models are an important part of the global intellectual property system for innovators. Our analysis, as well as recent literature, suggests that firms value utility model rights and actually use them to protect truly inventive activity. Typically, a discordant intellectual property system that plays a contributing role in creating innovation incentives would be a target for harmonization, yet there is no evidence of significant lobbying by either firms or policymakers to harmonize global utility model law. This suggests that both groups of stakeholders find the disharmonious status quo satisfactory.

[51] *See* Moga 2012, 14–16.

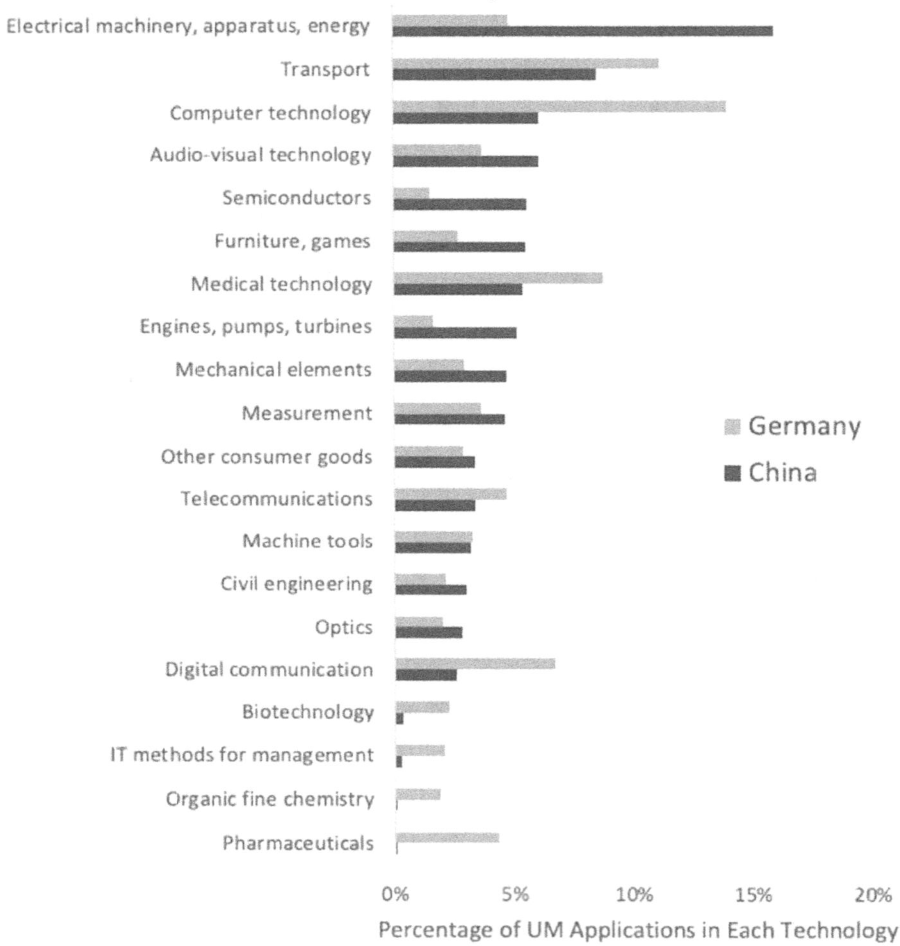

FIGURE 19.2 Share of U.S. patent-to-utility models in selected technologies (2000–2018)

Note: The technology fields in PATSTAT are based in the WIPO Statistics Database IPC8 Technology Concordance. *See* Schmoch 2008.

The results of our study help explain the lack of enthusiasm for harmonization by providing important evidence that firms can effectively navigate the disharmonious environment of utility model systems. Importantly, ours was the first work to assess utility model use in a context that suggests a purposeful strategy of optimal intellectual property protection rather than simple rights capture. Although additional research is necessary to determine whether disharmony is better for global innovation or a particular country's economic health, our proposed framework posits that, at the firm level, an innovator may consider the availability of utility models around the world and utilize the systems it finds advantageous in view of the overall economic, legal and political environment.

In particular, firms can optimize the differential appropriability of utility models to achieve protection efficiencies and accommodate national differences. Possible applications include employing utility models as an efficient antipiracy device in foreign locations, rather than a long-term, global competition exclusion tool as they would with traditional patents. Firms in fast-moving industries can put up roadblocks with utility models on their minor advances that are otherwise easy to copy. With cheap filing costs and no examination, ultimate enforceability may not be so important. In other cases, utility models may fill a gap that exists between what can be protected through design patents or other industrial design measures and what is worth protecting with traditional patents.[52] And, if there are differences in standard patent acquisition and enforcement rules between countries of interest, utility models may fill that gap as well.

At the national level, individual countries may well benefit from not being forced into a harmonized utility model system. They may use utility model systems to experiment with a combination of intellectual property protection elements that best optimize their desired economic or policy goals. They may adopt utility model systems to fill a specific national need, such as satisfying inventor rights or providing a defensive publication to preclude another's capture of an invention.[53] Some countries may even seek to align their systems with desired firms or economic outcomes and modify utility model attributes in accordance.[54]

Of course, even though disharmony may have some benefits for some firms or some countries, those benefits could be outweighed by anti-competitive negatives. For example, commentators have noted the potential to use easy-to-obtain utility models as a vehicle for trolling.[55] Given the efforts in the United States to curb abusive patent behavior, firms and policymakers may be loath to see another potential trolling vehicle arise in other systems. Additionally, the higher costs of navigating disparate systems may disadvantage smaller firms with global goals.

More broadly, our study and related analysis are the first to present the idea of utility models as an appropriability choice rather than a means of capturing otherwise unprotectable inventions; as such, our study may address a persistent problem in innovation system assessment. Namely, study after study has failed to find sufficient evidence for changing the status quo regarding utility model structures as a component of national or regional innovation systems. For example, the Technopolis Report stated that "it is not possible for us to conclusively say whether

[52] Where such a gap filler does not exist (as in the United States), it is possible that firms are relying on design patents to carry some of the weight (i.e., trying to use the nonfunctional right to overlap onto the functional).

[53] Radauer et al. 2015, 781.

[54] *See generally* Prud'homme 2017a.

[55] Moga 2012, 25; Productivity Commission (Australia) 2016, 17.

UM systems – or particular incarnations of those – actually support innovation."[56] A follow-up article by Radauer et al., discussing evidence since the study, doubled down on this conclusion.[57] Similarly, Prud'homme found that while utility model systems can be useful tools to stimulate innovation and technological diffusion in some developing countries, they "can grow to be of limited value in developed countries."[58] Other studies reach similar conclusions.[59]

Although one possibility may be that utility model systems fundamentally fail as innovation incentives, the zone of appropriability preference model suggests that innovators may be simply allocating the same inventions between different protection regimes. To be sure, optimal capture may have some positive impact on the incentive to innovate and one might still expect to see that in measures of innovative activity. The reason this does not show up in the studies is likely that this impact is far less significant than that which one would expect from bringing an entirely new group of innovators into the system.

Taken together, one can reasonably conclude that the invention appropriation advantages of utility models, lack of evidence of significant abuse in the existing systems and relatively small impact on the overall innovation activity of countries or regions produce general satisfaction with disharmony among both firms and policymakers. Reports suggest that the small portion of the intellectual property community that has an interest in utility models does not generally favor harmonization efforts.[60] Moreover, users of the global intellectual property system would probably be wary of reform that may not address known problems but instead end up eliminating the strategic advantages in pursuing utility model protection.[61] Considering all available information, including our study results, we believe that policymakers have a basis to determine that a TRIPS-like harmonization effort for utility models would be unhelpful and even potentially harmful.

Finally, one might ask if it is legitimate for there to be a policy contrast between utility models and standard patents. In other words, if disharmony is permitted for utility models, how can it be problematic for standard patents? However, the contrasting conditions underlying such an inquiry may not be as stark as many assume. In fact, there is actually some variation in standard patent rights across the world. In particular, enforcement systems can differ in aspects such as government prosecution, bifurcated validity and infringement proceedings, criminal liability and the availability of jury trials.[62] It is primarily the availability of basic protection that is

[56] Radauer et al. 2015, 5.
[57] Radauer et al. 2019, 782.
[58] Prud'homme 2014, 61.
[59] *See* Kim et al. 2012, 374; Productivity Commission (Australia) 2016, 17.
[60] *See* Radauer et al. 2015, 173–176.
[61] Radauer et al. 2015, 182.
[62] WIPO 2018, 13, tbl. S1.

harmonized through TRIPS[63] and other treaties such as the PCT.[64] More uniformity may be desired, but it may be impossible to fully harmonize every aspect of various domestic legal systems, even in a narrow area like invention rights. Firms naturally look to a means for accommodating the disparity. In this space, the utility model fills the gap and provides a buffer of disharmony that allows a more optimal capture of a given invention in a given country.

In the end, we believe that there is a basis for the counterintuitive proposition that disharmony can be the optimal intellectual property policy from a country-level perspective in some instances to maximize efficiency, exploit system differences and experiment with specific protection standards. Although such an approach conflicts with the historical and political drive toward harmonization, it is a flexibility that may be demanded by the complexities of global production and trade. If the status quo works, the harmonization journey may not be the best policy route.

19.6 CONCLUSION

Based on empirical evidence of the use of utility model systems coupled with the relative indifference on the part of policymakers and firms, we believe that there is support for the proposition that marginal disharmony can work in the context of utility models. In this particular intellectual property rights setting, disharmony may allow countries space for experimentation and tailoring to national policy objectives while not impeding effective management of global intellectual property portfolios at the firm level. Reasonable policymakers may conclude that uniformity in intellectual property protection is not necessarily the correct objective.

63 TRIPS 1994.
64 Patent Cooperation Treaty 1970.

PART III

The Future of Sub-patent Innovation Rights

20

Utility Models and the European Union

A Fresh Look at the Need for Harmonisation

Martin Stierle

20.1 THE SURPRISING LACK OF HARMONISATION

Intellectual property (IP) laws have experienced considerable harmonisation[1] within the European Union (EU) in the last decades. The success story of EU IP law began in the 1980s with Directive 89/104. Today, EU IP law covers trademarks,[2] designs,[3] geographical indications,[4] copyrights,[5] plant varieties[6] and trade secrets.[7] The EU even managed to achieve a certain degree of harmonisation in the field of patent law with Directive 98/44, and most recently Regulation 1257/2012 that introduced enhanced cooperation for the creation of unitary patent protection. Looking at the IP family, in comparison to its siblings, the utility model (UM) has been EU's "Cinderella" up until now. No directive or regulation deals specifically with UM protection.

The vacuum of EU law in the field of UMs is surprising for at least three reasons: Firstly, UM protection in the EU is nationally fragmented and porous.[8] Germany

[1] The terms "harmonisation" or "approximation" (see Part Three, Title VII, chapter 3 of the TFEU ("approximation of laws")) can be used in a narrow sense for legal acts aiming directly at the approximating of national laws but also in a wider sense including the creation of unitary IP rights. Cf. Kellerbauer 2019c, para. 2 f. (stating that the introduction of an EU IP right based on Art. 118 TFEU does not aim at the approximation of laws strictly speaking).

[2] See, e.g., Regulation 2017/1001.

[3] See, e.g., Regulation 6/2002.

[4] See, e.g., Regulation 2023/2411.

[5] See, e.g., Directive 2001/29.

[6] See, e.g., Regulation 2100/94.

[7] See, e.g., Directive Regulation 2016/943. Whether trade secrets are actually IP is unclear in the EU. See Ohly 2021 (arguing for trade secrets to be legal hybrids of unfair competition law and IP).

[8] Besides the country chapters of this book, an overview of UM protection within the Member States can be found at Radauer et al. 2015, 23 ff. The years of the introduction of UM systems in different countries is also mentioned in Kraßer 1995, 956 ff.

(since 1891),[9] Poland (since 1919)[10] and Spain (since 1929), for example, have provided UM protection for approximately a century. France introduced its first law on "*certificats d'utilité*" in January 1968.[11] Countries such as Hungary (since 1991), Denmark (since 1992),[12] Finland (since 1992),[13] Czechia (since 1992), Bulgaria (since 1993) and Austria (since 1994) all implemented UM protection in the final decade of the twentieth century. Belgium and the Netherlands had protected inventions for quite some time under a regime of so-called "short-term" patents but have no such system in place today. Other countries like Sweden and Luxembourg have never had a sub-patent protection regime.

Secondly, UM protection clearly varies within the EU Member States that afford protection to UMs.[14] There is no homogenous understanding as to many core features of UM protection, for example the eligible subject matter, the requirements for protection (e.g. novelty or inventive step) or the term of protection.[15] One of the reasons for these divergences is the lack of minimum standards for UM protection within the international framework. Copyright, trademark or patent law, for example, have received a certain degree of international harmonisation, at least via TRIPS, while UMs were only mentioned in the Paris Convention after the Revision Conference of Washington in 1911.[16] The policy space countries enjoy in designing their national UM systems is therefore quite broad.[17]

Thirdly, the lack of EU harmonisation is surprising, as UM systems are traditionally intended to offer protection for technological advancements at low costs and thus to address the particular needs of small and medium-sized enterprises (SMEs).[18] The European Commission (EC) has repeatedly emphasised the importance of SMEs for Europe's economy[19] and the need to boost their use of IP.[20] Nevertheless, the EU never implemented a regulation or directive on UM protection.

9 See Chapter 6.
10 See Chapter 8.
11 See Chapter 5.
12 See Chapter 4.
13 See Chapter 9.
14 This situation is mentioned in many publications: EC 1995, ii; Llewelyn 1997, 8; Gómez Segade 2008, 136.
15 Cf. the country chapters of this book. For an overview, Radauer et al. 2015, 2019.
16 See Gómez Segade 2008, 135 f. (mentioning that UMs might not fit in the "dominant US world view of the field of intellectual property"); Cahoy and Oswald 2021, 527 (mention that the scope of protection and rules for acquisition can vary widely among offering countries due to the lack of international harmonisation).
17 Grosse Ruse-Khan 2012, 7; 2013, 1; Radauer et al. 2015, 7.
18 EC 1997, 11, para. 28 and the recitals on 30; Boztosun 2010, 430; Radauer et al. 2015, 99; Suthersanen 2019, 11.
19 EC 2024 ("backbone of Europe's economy"; "key role in adding value in every sector of the economy"; "central to the EU's twin transitions to a sustainable and digital economy"; "essential to Europe's competitiveness").
20 EC 2020, 11.

This chapter will take a fresh look at the need for harmonisation of UM protection in the EU. It will first look back at EU harmonisation efforts in the past (Section 20.2), before demonstrating the need for EU harmonisation (Section 20.3). It will then describe and question the traditional arguments for UM protection (Section 20.4). Thereafter, the chapter will lay out the EU's policy options and analyse them critically (Section 20.5). It will become clear that there are no perfect solutions to address the need for harmonisation. The chapter will offer thoughts on a new conceptional starting point for further reform efforts (Section 20.6) before concluding (Section 20.7).

20.2 FAILED ATTEMPTS OF THE EC

The EC took serious steps towards unification and harmonisation of UM protection during the flourishing years of EU IP law in the 1990s. The EC authorised a study on the economic impact of UM protection with the German Ifo Institute for Economic Research[21] in the early 1990s. The Institute undertook a two-step survey in France, Italy, Spain and the UK questioning first patent attorneys and later industrial companies and independent inventors about their use and or desirability for UM protection in the European Community.[22] The EC interpreted the results as indicating that manufactures, inventors and patent lawyers advocated a unified system of UMs in the European Community.[23]

A potential European reform of UMs in the 1990s also attracted interest from the academic community. Although the director of the influential Max-Planck Institute (MPI), Friederich-Karl Beier, was in 1991 still sceptical about a unified European UM and more in favour of a mere approximation of the respective national laws through a Community Directive,[24] his opinion changed. In the first half of the 1990s, the MPI held various workshops and discussions with experts from academia and practice,[25] after which it proposed a Community UM and a full draft Regulation in 1994.[26]

All of these developments led to the EC's Green Paper on the Protection of Utility Models in the Single Market in July 1995.[27] The Commission introduced four different options.[28] Firstly, a directive approximating all national laws, secondly, a directive requiring the mutual recognition of national rights in other member states, thirdly, a Community UM, and fourthly, a combination of the options. The

[21] The Ifo Institute for Economic Research is a Munich-based think tank. It is known for its analyses of economic policy and is one of the most influential German research institutions.

[22] Weitzel 1994. See also Weitzel 1995.

[23] EC 1995, iv.

[24] Beier 1991, 166 f.

[25] See, e.g., the report by Kern 1994a.

[26] Max Planck Institute 1994.

[27] EC 1995.

[28] EC 1995, 43 ff.

Commission's Green Paper was in favour of the third option: the creation of a new UM right at the EC level.

However, the creation of a Community UM received very little support.[29] Firstly, some Member States did not see sufficient reason to introduce such a system, in particular the powerful UK,[30] which did not offer second-tier protection of inventions in its national laws.[31] Secondly, the language issue remained a barrier. To be a low-budget alternative to patents, the application process needs to be affordable. Therefore, translations in all official EU languages were not feasible for a pan-European UM application. Versions in just one or only a few privileged languages (e.g. English, French and German) would have been cheaper but particularly detrimental to the targeted user community of the system, namely SMEs outside of countries in which these languages were widely spoken.[32]

Consequently, the Commission proposed a directive approximating the legal arrangements for the protection of inventions by UMs on 12 December 1997.[33] After the Opinion of the Economic and Social Committee of 27 May 1998 and the Resolution of the European Parliament of 12 March 1999, the Commission presented an amended proposal for a directive on 28 June 1999.[34]

The work on the adoption of the proposal was suspended in March 2000.[35] The Commission prioritised the renewed efforts of a Community Patent Regulation (CPR), which resulted in a proposal in 2000.[36] Ultimately, not only did the CPR not materialise, but the Commission also withdrew the amended proposal for a UM directive in September 2005,[37] allegedly because it was unlikely to advance further in the legislative process as it could not overcome the opposition from a minority of Member States including the UK.[38]

In 2013, the EC intended to update its information and analysis on the economic effects of UMs.[39] It commissioned a study on the economic impact of UM legislation in selected Member States, the final report from which was published in 2015. The study suggested refraining from making a decision on a unitary UM at the European level for the moment, so as to investigate further possibilities and to

29 See, however, Kraßer 2000, 810 f. (arguing for centralised filing and granting by the EPO which could be offered by the EPO).

30 See, e.g., Llewelyn 1997 (commenting critically from a distinct UK perspective). See also Forrest 2004.

31 The UK, however, had a UM system until the beginning of the twentieth century with its Utility Designs Act 1843. See, Chapter 3 and Bently and Sherman 1997.

32 Weinmiller 1996, 150.

33 EC 1997. See Ravillard 2000.

34 EC 1999.

35 See, Gómez Segade 2008, 137.

36 EC 2000. Critical Gómez Segade 2008, 137 f.

37 EC 2005a.

38 Kardam 2007, 160; Gómez Segade 2008, 138. See also Loth 2001, para. 33 (pointing out that the different opinions on the required level of inventiveness for UM protection were pivotal).

39 Cf. Mercell 2014.

pursue a careful harmonisation process of national UM systems.[40] Since then, no further action has been taken.

Many things have changed since the main attempts were made to introduce an EU UM law in the 1990s. During these earlier discussions, the UK was one of the leading Member States opposing such measures. Since then, the UK has withdrawn from the EU, and with it one of the major opponents to the EU UM law.[41] Moreover, recent advances in the unification of the patent system have generated momentum for a re-evaluation of EU UM protection. Although the EU has not managed to set up an own patent system yet, the European patent with unitary effect and the Unified Patent Court (UPC) are built on initiatives within the EU and are based to a certain extent[42] on EU law.

20.3 TWO REASONS FOR THE HARMONISATION OF UM LAW

20.3.1 *The Existing EU IP Framework*

The first reason for EU harmonisation is linked to parts of the EU's secondary law.[43] Various legal acts refer to UMs in their scope of application. Given the heterogeneous nature of UM protection within the EU Member States, it is unclear under which conditions a legally protected subject matter is considered a UM and therewith falls in their scope.[44] For example, Regulation 608/2013 on customs enforcement of IP rights (Customs Regulation, IPCR) defines UMs as an IP right (Art. 2 (1) (k)). The Regulation sets out the conditions and procedures for action by the customs authorities regarding goods suspected of IP infringement. However, the Regulation does not define what a UM is or what conditions qualify a protected subject matter as such. As discussed earlier, the conditions for UM protection clearly varies within the EU Member States that afford protection to UMs.

The situation is similar for Directive 2004/48/EC (Enforcement Directive, IPED). The IPED does not mention UMs explicitly, but it does apply to any infringement of IP rights as provided for by EU law and/or by the national laws of

[40] Radauer et al. 2015, 6.

[41] See Radauer et al. 2019, 783 (arguing that the chances of a unitary UM system being adopted without the UK participating may be larger than in the past).

[42] Cf., Regulation 1257/2012 implementing enhanced cooperation in the area of the creation of unitary patent protection.

[43] The treaties between the EU member states are known in the EU as primary law. The body of law that is based on the primary law is known as secondary law, and includes, for example, regulations and directives.

[44] During the drafting of the proposals for UM directives in the 1990s, the Commission realised these uncertainties at least regarding the scope of the targeted directives. Therefore, Art. 1 of the proposals clarified the scope of this intended directive by referring directly to the names of the national rights in the respective national language, e.g. "*Gebrauchsmusterrecht*" for Austria and Germany and "*Certificat de utilité*" for France (see EC 1997, Art. 1).

the Member States (Art. 2 IPED) without defining what an IP right or UM is.[45] It is therefore unclear which kind of national sub-patent rights the Member States must protect with the full spectrum of measures, procedures and remedies enshrined in the IPED. Even an early draft of the EC's proposal for a regulation on standard essential patents included UMs within its scope.[46] It would have raised a similar uncertainty, though subsequent versions of the proposal removed UMs from its scope.

The lack of a common concept of UM creates not only issues for the application of the EU's secondary law but also for its interpretation. The aforementioned Customs Regulation and Enforcement Directive set certain standards for the enforcement of IP law. In the last decades, awareness has been growing that a one-size-fits-all approach is detrimental to an efficient IP framework. A more holistic approach is required taking into account the nature of the IP right, the context of the infringement and the proportionality of a remedy.[47] If the ECJ were to decide on the requirements to issue a preliminary injunction based on a UM under Art. 9(1)(a) of the IPED, it would be impossible to strike the right balance without having a common understanding of the protected subject matter the law intends to enforce. A holistic approach would need to differentiate based on the conditions for UM protection in the Member States. This distinction is crucial because the right balance significantly varies whether the subject matter is a trivial advancement, possibly even obvious to a person skilled in the art,[48] or if the national UM is essentially a full-fledged patent with just a shorter duration and no prior substantive examination before the grant.[49] One might argue that patentability requirements are neither harmonised by the EU, so these uncertainties are not specific to the UM rights but to the protection of inventions on a more general level within the EU. A significant distinction to patents is, however, that the conditions for patent protection are harmonised either through or as a consequence of the Strasbourg

[45] See also EC 2005b (mentioning utility models as one IP right covered by the scope of the Directive).

[46] EC 2023a, Art. 2(3) ("'patent' means patent or utility model"). See, however, EC 2023b, Art. 2 (does not mention UMs; definitions refer only to patents). See also Chapter 16, discussing standards-essential UMs.

[47] A prominent example is the discussion about proportionality and patent injunctions. In Germany, the quasi-automatic approach to permanent patent injunctions (see Stierle 2019 ("quasi-automatische Unterlassungsanspruch")) was changed by an amendment in 2021 introducing a proportionality defence. The amendment takes into account the effects of a potential injunction. For an overview of the new law see Stierle and Hofmann 2022 (referring in particular to third-party effects); Picht and Contreras 2023, 435 ff. (assessing the effects of the new defence in SEP cases).

[48] Poland, e.g., does not require any degree of inventiveness for UM protection. See Chapter 8 or Bury 2022, 40.

[49] See, e.g., Germany where the requirement of inventive step is interpreted similarly to the non-obviousness requirement in patent law, according to *Demonstrationsschrank*, FCJ 2006. Cf. Chapter 6.

and the Munich conventions.[50] Moreover, a general framework can be found in Article 27 ff. of the TRIPS Agreement that brings the national patent systems within the EU closer together than the UM systems.

One might think that an ECJ interpretation of the term "UM" or "IP" after a referral by a national court could have at least a similar effect. With its preliminary ruling in "Cofemel", for example, the Court set the requirements for copyright-protectable work due to the absence of a definition in the various legal acts of the EU.[51] However, the situation in copyright law is hardly comparable to UM law as various legal acts by the EU design a copyright framework with exploitation rights, limitations and exceptions, etc.[52] These legal acts as well as the respective decisions[53] give at least a certain guidance on a general understanding of copyright law as well as some key features of the copyright framework which hints towards an EU concept of "work". There is no secondary law of the EU addressing UM protection. Moreover, UMs are registration rights where legal clarity provided by a Directive or Regulation is more important than in the field of unregistered rights such as copyrights.[54]

20.3.2 *The Single Market*

The second reason for the introduction of an EU UM law refers to the concept of the EU single market and is based on the EU's primary law. The discussions which took place in the 1990s and the proposals of the EC have already featured these aspects.[55] The recitals of the two proposed directives outline the porous nature of the protection of UMs across the EU and the differences in the existing UM protection systems, which have the potential to obstruct the free movement of goods and distort competition within the internal market. The explanatory memorandum mentioned explicitly Art. 2,[56] Art. 3(c),[57] Art. 3(g)[58] and Art. 7a[59] of the old EC Treaty in this regard. According to the Commission, the fragmentation of protection forces right holders to avoid markets in which they cannot obtain an equivalent protection for their invention.[60] Moreover, the significant variations between national systems

50 Cf. Max Planck Institute 1987, 314 (mentioning this difference regarding the obstruction of the free movement of goods).
51 *Cofemel*, CJEU 2019, para. 26 ff.
52 See, e.g., Directive 2001/29/EC.
53 Cf. the references to prior decisions in *Cofemel*, CJEU 2019, para. 26 ff.
54 Art 5 (1) of the Berne Convention.
55 EC 1997, 30 f. and EC 1999, Recital 3 and 15 ("transparent, obstacle-free single market; "in order to safeguard the proper functioning of the single market and ensure that competition is not distorted").
56 Ibid., 8, para. 19.
57 Ibid., 6, para. 14.
58 Ibid., 8, para. 19.
59 Ibid., 6, para. 14.
60 Ibid., 7, para. 16.

make it even more difficult to obtain cross-border protection as an invention which qualifies for protection in one Member State may not qualify, at least not on the same terms, in another, according to the EC.[61] These aspects trigger a need for legal expert advice creating administrative difficulties and a major cost factor. The Commission pointed out that such a situation restricts innovative activity and distorts competition.[62] In 2008, Gómez Segade advanced that these risks are even stronger today than they were in the 1990s due to the subsequent EU enlargement increasing the degree of fragmentation and heterogeneity.[63]

In its reasoning more than 25 years ago, the Commission focused largely on the interests of potential right holders – an approach that stems from the IP zeitgeist of that period. However, not all the points the EC advanced are entirely convincing. There are doubts as to whether businesses would avoid the EU or specific Member States for the sole reason that their inventions would not be eligible for UM protection in these jurisdictions. Third parties can copy and sell their products in these countries regardless of whether the originator is present. Offering goods also in these national markets can be attractive for the originator if he can recoup his R&D costs through his business in a Member State that protects his technology as a UM anyways. A recent study even suggests that marginal disharmony in the field of UMs works reasonably well for those right holders who can effectively navigate such environments.[64] They are able to optimise the differential appropriability of these rights to achieve protection efficiencies and accommodate national differences, according to Cahoy and Oswald.[65]

A modern analysis of the effects of the status quo needs to integrate the perspective of the right holders' competitors. Today, this appears to be the major reason for UM harmonisation from a "single market perspective". The lack of harmonisation and therewith the lack of transparency creates disincentives to commercialise products also on the side of enterprises who do not hold any rights, or which hold rights in another Member State. A firm willing to offer goods within the internal market is at risk of running into UM infringement in one part of the single market while selling products legally in another part. This risk, along with the lack of transparency, currently poses the most significant potential threat to hinder the free movement of goods and to distort competition as companies might refrain from offering their goods and services in Member States where they are not entirely aware of the peculiarities of the national law on UMs.

61 Ibid., 6, para. 16 f.

62 Ibid., 7, para. 18.

63 Gómez Segade 2008, 138 (referring to the EU enlargement in 2004 and pointing out that the new Member States Romania and Bulgaria have UM protection systems; since then, also Croatia joined the EU).

64 Cahoy and Oswald 2021, 573 ff. and Chapter 18.

65 Cahoy and Oswald 2021, 574 and Chapter 18.

20.4 GENERAL REASONS FOR UM PROTECTION

We have seen now that the existing EU's secondary law on IP as well as the concept of the single market call for a harmonisation of UM protection on an EU level. Before looking into the EU's policy options, we want to get a clearer picture of the general reasons for UM protection as these aspects will have an impact on the analysis of the policy options for harmonisation.

Traditionally, governments, institutional actors, practice and scholarship indicate three main reasons to establish or maintain a UM system. Notably, all three refer somehow to the patent system ("cheaper", "faster" and "lower"), which makes them "relative grounds" for UM protection. Therefore, the justification for UM systems is also a "relative justification" as it bears a strong tie to its "big brother" – the patent system. It will become clear that the main task of a UM system is to perform a gap-filling function, which intends to overcome certain shortcomings of this brother system.[66] It will also become apparent that the traditional arguments for UM protection are to a certain extent ambiguous and the justification of UM protection is therefore rather weak.

20.4.1 *Cheaper*

UM systems are intended to lower the cost barriers for the IP protection of technical inventions,[67] and come in the form of "registration rights".[68] UMs do not have to pass a full-blown substantive examination before protection is granted.[69] This is different than the majority of patent systems in the EU and the European Patent Convention (EPC) where an office investigates substantive patentability requirements before registering the right. Hence, IP offices can offer UM protection for less than patent protection. As mentioned in the beginning, UM protection is therefore supposed to be particularly attractive for SMEs which have a relatively small budget for IP protection in comparison to larger enterprises.[70]

The potential savings for an SME to obtain UM protection instead of patent protection might be less than expected. The office fees for UM protection are indeed lower than the fees for patent protection in many countries. However, some SMEs, in particular micro entities, can achieve patent protection with discounts in

[66] See, e.g., Bently and Sherman 1997, 277; Reichman 1998, 48-2; Boztosun 2010, 431. Heikkilä and Verba 2018 claim that data on UM needs to be taken into account when analysing patent families. The same is true for a thorough investigation of the patent system as such which also requires to factor in the effects of an accompanying UM system.

[67] For the cost barrier to obtaining patents, see Holgersson 2013.

[68] Radauer et al. 2019, 777. But see Cummings 2010, 301 (stating that some countries have implemented systems of substantive examination similar to standard patent systems).

[69] Gómez Segade 2008, 135.

[70] EC 1995, 15.

various jurisdictions.[71] Furthermore, the overall costs for UM protection are primarily driven by patent attorney fees for drafting claims and specifications, which are comparable to those within the patent system.[72] Finally, it is more likely that the UM will be challenged than a patent for the same invention during its lifetime as the office does not perform a full-blown substantive examination of UM applications. Therefore, the enforcement costs of UMs can be even higher than the enforcement costs within a patent system.[73] Taking this into account, UMs may not provide SMEs access to effective IP protection that is substantially cheaper.

20.4.2 *Faster*

As there is no requirement for a substantive examination, a UM system offers protection faster than a patent system.[74] Patents are generally granted years after the application, whereas UMs will be registered within months or even weeks. In Germany, one of the countries prominent for its UM system,[75] the registration procedure to obtain UM protection is completed after 4.2 months on average while the patent granting procedure takes usually 2.5–3 years.[76]

Given the speed of registration, UMs are sometimes used as measures to protect an invention that is subject to a patent application while the application is still pending. A patent application does not provide a right to an injunction in many jurisdictions[77] while a UM does.[78] Therefore, companies may "branch-off" UMs from prior patent applications as permitted in some Member States. An applicant is allowed to claim the filing and, if applicable, priority date of a previously submitted patent application for a subsequent UM application provided the latter application concerns the same invention.[79]

However, fast IP protection is in numerous cases not very attractive. UMs are published upon registration as a quid pro quo for protection. Therewith, the invention leaves the sphere of secrecy more rapidly than it would under the 18-month

[71] See, e.g., the new fee system for European patent applications effective from 1 April 2024.

[72] Janis 1999, 180; Radauer et al. 2019, 782 f. See also Takenaka 2021a, 622 (arguing that official fees are low, but costs for preparing claims and specifications high for individual inventors).

[73] Cf. Janis 1999, 182 (arguing that the costs and complexity of IP enforcement are the most significant obstacles to SMEs' access to the patent system).

[74] Some IP offices proactively advertise national UM protection as fast protection. See, e.g., DPMA 2020 ("Utility models are 'fast IP rights'".).

[75] Cf. Bently and Sherman 1997, 266 (mentioning that the German UM system is widely regarded as the prototype for second tier protection); Kardam 2007, 156 (calling it the mother of all UM laws).

[76] See Chapter 6. See also Heikkilä and Lorenz 2018, 3.2.

[77] See, e.g., Austria, Denmark or Germany.

[78] See Art. 9 (1) (a) Directive 2004/48/EC applicable to all IP rights.

[79] See, e.g., Chapters 4 (Denmark) and 6 (Germany). See also Radauer 2015, 32 ff. (for Germany), 51 (for Austria), 62 (for Denmark), 90 (for Czech Republic), for 110 (Finland). Branching-off is not possible in France, though (Radauer 2015, 120).

publication delay for patent applications. Thereafter, competitors can use the information as a springboard for subsequent developments, which might not make UM protection very attractive for applicants. We can observe similar reluctance to opt for fast protection with patents. Patent applicants requiring faster search or examination can ask the European Patent Office (EPO) to have their applications processed under the programme for accelerated prosecution of European patent applications (PACE).[80] However, data indicate that very few applicants are interested in such fast-track proceedings,[81] allegedly due to the secrecy inherent in a slower examination.[82]

Even if access to speedy IP protection is necessary while a patent application is prosecuted, patent internal measures might be just as feasible as a separate UM registration and allow for a more coherent policy approach.[83] Art. 67 (2) of the EPC, for example, requires the Contracting States to ensure at least that the applicant can claim compensation reasonable in the circumstances from any person who has used the invention after the date of publication of the application. However, the Contracting States are free in granting earlier or stronger protection,[84] for example enshrining a UM-style right to an injunction in their national laws.[85]

20.4.3 *Lower*

Traditionally, UM systems offer protection for incremental innovation while the patent system is supposed to protect more substantial improvements over the state of the art. In many jurisdictions, the requirements for UM protection are lower than the prerequisites for patent protection, in particular the level of required

80 See EPO 2015a; EPO 2015b.

81 See also Hilty and Batista 2023, 829.

82 There are also other strategic considerations of applications that weigh against the use of a fast-track, e.g. the lifetime of a pending application becomes shorter and therefore the time to file divisional applications is reduced or the fact that a long patent prosecution is beneficial for the applicant who has not yet actually reduced the invention to practice.

83 Cf. Königer 2017 (pointing out that the advantages for the inventor could be reached by small changes to patent law if wanted).

84 Cf. Art. 67 (2) EPC (enshrining that a Contracting State may prescribe that a European patent application shall not confer the same protection as a granted patent but not that it cannot).

85 For the situation in the Contracting States, see, e.g., Art. 132 (1) of the Italian Code of Industrial Property allowing for precautionary protection if the application has been made available to the public or with respect to the persons to whom the notification of the application was given. For the UK, see [2022] EWHC 959 (Ch), para. 16 ff. according to which the High Court has jurisdiction prior to grant of the patent to issue an interim injunction, although it did not grant such relief in the specific case (damages were considerate to be an adequate remedy if the claimant were to ultimately prevail). However, the majority of Contracting States do not offer the possibility to issue preliminary injunctions based on patent applications. For an overview, see EPO 2023, 99 ff. For Germany, as one example, see Sec. 1 (1) (3) of the German Law on International Patent Treaties and *RRMS-Therapie*, RCD, 2022. See also Bouvier-Ravon and Hoppe 2024, 7 for the situation under the UPCA.

inventiveness.[86] At the same time, UM protection is weaker and shorter[87] than patent protection as the idea is to provide a moderate IP right for the corresponding level of innovation.

However, it is often unclear precisely how to distinguish between low and high standards of inventiveness. In its groundbreaking decision "Demonstrationsschrank", the German Federal Court of Justice pointed out that this is hardly possible in practice.[88] Moreover, granting UM protection below the non-obviousness standard of patent law offers IP protection for subject matter that is theoretically obvious to the person skilled in the art. This result amounts to a break in the general understanding of IP law and cannot be justified against the background of the constitutionally protected freedom of action of third parties, according to the German Federal Court of Justice.[89] The Court therefore held that the required threshold for inventiveness in UM law can only be the same as in patent law. Other countries followed suit.[90] These judicial concerns cast doubt on the viability of the lower standard of inventiveness in UM law from a legal perspective.

From public policy perspective, it is debatable whether monopoly rights should be granted for trivial achievements, particularly in times of IP thickets. The German Federal Court of Justice addressed this point from a purely legal perspective when referring to the third-party freedoms protected by fundamental rights. But one can also raise this argument from an economic perspective, as it has been done in the scholarship on UM protection.[91] Enterprises already have problems to identify the relevant patent rights during a freedom-to-operate (FTO) analysis when they seek to avoid IP infringement and hold-up. The efforts of firms must be substantially stronger when grain-sized innovation receives protection since trivial achievements are harder to trace. Moreover, in the case of UMs, the rights were not examined by the patent offices. Hence, the competitors are forced to investigate the validity of the claims.[92] This is particularly problematic for SMEs, the alleged core user of the UM

86 See, e.g., Chapter 4 (noting that Danish patent law requires that inventions differ essentially from the state of the art while UM law requires only that inventions differ distinctly) or Chapter 8 (describing that Polish UM law has no requirement of inventiveness).

87 See the examples in Suthersanen 2019, 5.

88 *Demonstrationsschrank*, FCJ 2006, para. 19. See also Hüttermann and Storz 2006, 3180 (pointing out that it was unclear before the decision as to how the different standard for UM protection would even make a difference in practice) and Chapter 4 (pointing out that it can be difficult to measure the exact content of the required degree of inventiveness in Danish UM law (differ distinctly from the state of the art) in comparison to Danish patent law (differ essentially)).

89 *Demonstrationsschrank*, FCJ 2006, para. 20 ("Systembruch"). See also Meier-Beck 2007, 915 (arguing that this cannot be the legislator's intention).

90 See, e.g., Teleskopausleger (Austria). For a discussion of the case, see Adocker 2011.

91 See, e.g., the application of the theory of anticommons property to UM protection by Janis 1999, 200 ff. or the discussion of his prominent "green tulip" problem by Reichman 2000, 1756 ff.

92 Königer 2017, 75.

system. Many authors have therefore unmasked the notion of UMs as small patents for small inventors as a myth.[93] There is a particular concern that large firms flood a promising area of technology with an array of UMs,[94] particularly since major international enterprises appear to be the core users of many national UM systems.[95]

The overall economic impact of sub-patent protection within the EU appears therefore unclear and potentially negligible. Economic scholarship has found that UMs favour growth in developing countries when the capacity to conduct innovation research does not exist.[96] A minor innovation can be a learning device and thus a stepping stone for developing patentable inventions later.[97] UMs are considered particularly useful in times of "catching up"[98] but there is no conclusive evidence regarding their positive impact in developed and highly developed countries or economic unions. As discussed at length in Chapter 10, the impact of UMs in a highly developed country has been studied deeply and at different points in time in Australia where a UM-like system was established in 2001. However, after a short span of protection lasting about 20 years, the Australian government began the process of phasing the system out as it did not achieve its intended objectives. It is therefore very unclear whether there is a need to incentivise incremental innovation with the prospect of an inclusive right such as a UM.

20.5 THE POLICY OPTIONS

If the EU wants to become more proactive in the field of UM, there are multiple policy options to consider. The following gives an overview of the legally binding options based on regulations and directives. The overview leaves out the possibilities of enhanced cooperation (Art. 20 TEU)[99] and common European approaches beyond EU law.[100] A sound policy option needs to accomplish a difficult task: On the one hand, it must address the two major reasons that require an EU harmonisation of UM protection (see Section 20.3). On the other hand, it has to take into account that the justification for UM protection in general is rather weak (see Section 20.4).

[93] Janis 1999, 179, 186; Forrest 2004, 216; Königer 2017, 75. Terminology after Radeauer et al. 2019.

[94] Janis 1999, 187; Forrest 2004, 220.

[95] See Chapter 2.

[96] Kim et al. 2012, 358; Radauer et al. 2015, 20. See also, Chapter 22, describing UMs as "development tools" and Suthersanen 2006 for an assessment of UM protection in developing countries.

[97] Kim et al. 2012, 358; Radauer et al. 2015, 20.

[98] Kardam 2007, 173. See also Prud'homme 2017a (demonstrating that there is also a tendency within UM systems to apply lower standards in times an economy is "catching up" and higher, more patent-style standards once the economy is more developed).

[99] See, e.g., Regulation 1257/2012 implementing enhanced cooperation in the area of the creation of unitary patent protection.

[100] See, e.g., the European Patent Organisation and the EPC.

20.5.1 *The Instruments*

In general, the EU has several different options for becoming more proactive in the field of EU IP law. The binding legal acts available to unify UM protection or to approximate the respective national laws are regulations and directives.[101] A regulation is binding in its entirety and directly applicable in all Member States (Art. 288(2) of the Treaty on the Functioning of the European Union (TFEU)). A directive is binding as well but only as to the result to be achieved. Hence, national authorities have the discretion to choose the form and methods (Art. 288 (3) TFEU) and, as a general rule,[102] direct effect does not apply. In sum, it is for the Member States to adjust their laws and to give effect to the directive.

We must distinguish between maximum or full harmonisation on one hand and minimum harmonisation on the other when referring to the level of approximation the EU intends to achieve with a directive.[103] A directive can regulate a particular area exhaustively and preclude Member States from deviating from defined standards (maximum or full harmonisation). In the case of minimum harmonisation, the EU sets minimum standards and allows Member States to maintain or provide for more stringent national laws.

20.5.2 *The Competences*

The EU has no competences by right as they are all voluntarily conferred on it by its Member States (principle of conferral, Art. 5(1) of the Treaty on European Union (TEU)). It can only act within these competences defined by the Member States in the Treaties (Art. 5(2) TEU). Competences not conferred upon the EU in the Treaties remain with the Member States (Art. 4 (1), 5 (2) TEU).

We need to distinguish between the competencies to establish an EU IP right and the competencies to harmonise national laws on IP. Art. 118 TFEU empowers the EU to introduce an EU UM system,[104] and allows measures to be established for the creation of European IP rights to provide uniform protection throughout the EU and for the setting up of centralised EU-wide authorisation, coordination and supervision arrangements.[105] Art. 118 TFEU does not constitute "competition rules"

[101] For an overview of the legal acts of the EU, see Art. 288 TFEU.

[102] In special cases, Directives can have a direct effect if they are unconditional and sufficiently precise and the Member State has failed to implement it in domestic law by the end of the period prescribed or where the Member State failed to implement it correctly. See *Dominguez*, ECJ, 2012, para. 33 with further references.

[103] For an overview, see Kellerbauer 2019a, para. 4.

[104] Kellerbauer 2019b, para. 7; Wichard 2022, para. 3.

[105] For example, the reform of the Community trademark was based on Art. 118 TFEU. See Regulation 2015/2424. As a general rule, Art. 114 TFEU is not a suitable legal basis in such cases where a co-existing legal regime of EU law that supplements national law without harmonising

for the purpose of Art. 3(1)(b) TFEU but it does fall within the "internal market" area in which the EU has shared competences under Art. 4(2)(a) TFEU.[106] Accordingly, pursuant to Art. 5(3) TEU, the principle of subsidiarity applies where EU legislature makes use of Art. 118 TFEU.[107] In practice, however, the importance of this principle is limited since it will be difficult for Member States to achieve the creation of IP rights, including an EU UM right, which benefits from EU-wide protection without EU intervention.[108] Hence, Art. 118 TFEU would serve as a basis to create an EU UM system by a Regulation.

An EU directive which does not establish uniform IP protection by the EU but merely intends to approximate national IP laws cannot be based on Art. 118 TFEU.[109] However, Art. 114 TFEU does provide a general competence for harmonisation measures "which have as their object the establishment and functioning of the internal market". To limit the danger of an unduly wide interpretation that would lead to an open-ended form of EU power, the European Court of Justice (ECJ) requires for the substantive conditions to be fulfilled that the measures have the genuine objective of improving the conditions for the establishment and functioning of an internal market. They should address disparities between the legal systems of the Member States that significantly obstruct fundamental freedoms and thus have a direct effect on the functioning of the internal market.[110] The current situation has the potential to obstruct the free movement of goods and distort competition within the internal market, as discussed above. This gives the EU the competence to harmonise national UM regimes based on Art. 114 TFEU. The principle of subsidiarity also applies[111] in the framework of Art. 114 TFEU but its importance is again limited in practice. If the substantive condition in the interpretation of ECJ is fulfilled, Member States will regularly struggle to prevent any negative impact on the international market without the action of the EU.[112]

or replacing it is introduced. See, both with further references: Kellerbauer 2019a, para. 28; Korte 2022, para. 24.

[106] *Kingdom of Spain and Italian Republic* v *Council*, ECJ, 2013, para. 16; *Kingdom of Spain* v *EP and Council*, ECJ, 2015, para. 40; Kellerbauer 2019b, para. 2.

[107] Kellerbauer 2019b, para. 10.

[108] Kellerbauer 2019b; Stieper 2022, para. 28; Wichard 2022, para. 12.

[109] Khan 2015, para. 6; Bings 2018, para. 3; Stieper 2022, para. 21; Wichard 2022, para. 3.

[110] The Queen, on the application of *Vodafone Ltd and Others* v *Secretary of State for Business, Enterprise and Regulatory Reform*, ECJ, 2010, para. 32; *Philip Morris Brands SARL and Others* v *Secretary of State for Health*, ECJ, 2016, para. 58.

[111] See The Queen, on the application of *Alliance for Natural Health and Nutri-Link Ltd* v *Secretary of State for Health and The Queen*, on the application of *National Association of Health Stores and Health Food Manufacturers Ltd* v *Secretary of State for Health and National Assembly for Wales*, ECJ, 2005, para. 103; Kellerbauer 2019a, para. 37, 40.

[112] Kellerbauer 2019a, para. 40.

20.5.3 *UM Regulation*

20.5.3.1 Policy Option 1: EU UM Right

The first policy option is to adopt a regulation based on Art. 118 TFEU and to introduce an EU UM right providing for unified protection similar to the Community/EU trademark or the Community design. As mentioned in Section 20.2, this was the policy option the EC originally favoured in its green paper 1995. The registration would be administered by the European Union Intellectual Property Office (EUIPO). The EUIPO's lack of expertise in assessing technical subject matter would be insignificant. UMs are registration rights, so the EUIPO's task would be to perform a formality check prior to registration while EU UM courts could assess the substantive requirements for protection during infringement proceedings. The unification of UMs would ensure protection in all Member States of the EU but, at the same time, an objection against this EU right in any Member State could defeat or invalidate the right in its entirety. The regulation would provide a full-fledged and autonomous system including provisions on protected subject matter, infringement and enforcement. This new regime would not touch the national UM systems which could continue to exist in parallel if desired.

An EU right would solve the problem for inventors of the fragmented and porous nature of UM protection within the EU. Nonetheless, the fragmented protection provided by national UMs and the divergent national laws would persist, leading third-party businesses to encounter substantial expenses when conducting an FTO for the single market in order to mitigate the risk of infringing a parallel national right in one of the Member States. It is unclear whether such an EU system would lead at least de facto to a certain harmonisation of national systems in the long run.

Users seeking EU-wide protection will save costs with a pan-European right. Nevertheless, the costs for the EU and users to establish such a system, to maintain it and to make use of it cannot be underestimated. For example, the language issue mentioned above, which was a determining factor in the discussions of the 1990s, has still not entirely been solved. Today's translation software dramatically reduces the administrative costs in comparison to the situation 30 years ago, but the EU has increased significantly in size (i.e. the number of Member States, and thus languages) since then. Also, overall administrative costs would increase to the extent that Member States retain their national UM systems and administration while the EU must invest in setting up and running a pan-European administrative structure.

In general, having an IP system that spans multiple countries and languages could not be anything but expensive. Thus, whether such a structure can provide an IP right for SMEs at low costs is doubtful. If such protection is indeed desired, it appears rather obvious that it should be offered "in the basement" via national UM rights with low administration costs while the more expensive European "*bel étage*" is reserved for substantial innovation examined by an office and protected by patents.[113]

The other two substantial arguments against an EU UM are linked to the general justification of UM protection. First, as outlined above, the arguments and justifications for a UM protection system in a highly developed economic union lack strength. There is no conclusive evidence that a pan-European UM system would have a positive impact on the EU's public welfare. It would be an experiment. One might argue that a regulation would be the right way to carry out such an experiment. In a more general context, Martin Husovec has advanced that if the EU legislator intends to experiment with new IP rights, it should use regulations instead of directives.[114] He made the point that if the EU has to repeal such an instrument once it has failed to deliver on its promises, it automatically ceases to exist also on the national level.[115] The EU legislator is not required to clean up and coordinate a removal in the national laws.[116] Although IP policy is less dynamic in reality than in theory,[117] Husovec's point appears correct in the field of copyright law where rights come into existence without registration.[118] However, setting up a new EU registration system, hiring staff for an EU office, and teaching users on a pan-European level how to make use of new structures is far more costly and time consuming than a national experiment, making it also rather unlikely, not only for political reasons, that the EU would eventually repeal such a right. Hence, without a strong justification for UM protection, the EU should refrain from introducing an EU UM system – even if intended as a mere experiment.

The second substantial argument against an EU UM system arises from the framework of the system. Even if one sees the need for EU UM protection, it is unclear how one should design it. As noted above, UM systems are supposed to perform a gap-filling function. However, national patent laws are not harmonised, so the gaps to be filled are of different sizes and are based in different locations depending on the Member State. It is impossible to suggest a one-size-fits-all auxiliary tool in this constellation where the main system is multifaceted.[119]

[113] See, for this distinction within a two-track system, Beier 1991, 166.

[114] Husovec 2020, 2.

[115] Husovec 2020.

[116] Husovec 2020.

[117] See also Husovec 2020 (mentioning that the legislator almost never goes back to question its old choices).

[118] Ibid., 1 used examples from the copyright sphere, e.g. high publishers' rights, data producers' rights, sport events organisers' rights, databank protection.

[119] Gómez Segade 2008, 136.

20.5.4 *UM Directive*

The other policy options would address national laws with a directive and would be based on Art. 114 TFEU. The directive could be combined with the first option (EU UM right) described above, similar to the situation in EU trademark or design law. Also, the following options could be combined.

20.5.4.1 Policy Option 2: Negative Full Harmonisation

There are two types of full harmonisation here. The first is negative full harmonisation, whereby EU law approximates national laws by pre-empting the field of UM protection.[120] Member States with a UM protection system would be required to abolish it as negative full harmonisation leaves no leeway for the national systems. This would create full transparency within the internal market, in particular for businesses that intend to operate across all geographical areas but are currently afraid of overlooking a national UM right in one Member State. Negative full harmonisation would also eliminate all costs related to the establishment, maintenance and usage of the UM system.

Pre-empting national IP rights means interfering with Art. 17(2) of the EU Charter of Fundamental Rights (CFR).[121] Nevertheless, this interference is easily in line with the Charter if it does not concern inventions that already exist as Art. 17 does not embrace any kind of institutional guarantee for IP rights which the legislator cannot touch.[122] Even if a "core property" were to exist that places certain forms of property outside of the legislator's reach, it appears to be obvious that UM rights which have never been protected in some Member States would be considered to fall outside this scope.

Although Art. 17 CFR does not prohibit negative harmonisation, the legal and political threshold for such a measure is very high. According to the literature, negative harmonisation of IP rights is not necessary to overcome issues concerning the single market.[123] The European legislator is required to demonstrate that the national solution harms and should be avoided,[124] which might be possible given the considerable differences in national UM protection and the potential effects for the internal market. Most notably, however, negative harmonisation would imply that UM protection as such is expendable. Although the arguments for UM protection appear to be rather weak, it is also not possible to conclusively say that UM systems generate negative net effects. Therefore, the EU cannot pre-empt or impose to repeal such national systems.

[120] Max Planck Institute 1994, 703.
[121] Husovec 2020, 3.1.
[122] Husovec 2020, 3.2 and 3.3.
[123] Stieper 2022, 28; Wichard 2022, 12.
[124] Husovec 2020, 2.

20.5.4.2 Policy Option 3: Positive Full Harmonisation

The second type of full harmonisation is positive harmonisation. A directive would describe and impose a full-fledged UM protection system in Member States under their national laws. All Member States would be required to implement exactly the same system enshrined in this directive. The EC intended to go down this road during the harmonisation efforts in the second half of the 1990s, after the initial idea to create a Community UM right had received strong headwind.

The approximation of national laws could be combined with a mutual recognition of national UM rights by the Member States, as already mentioned in the EC's Green Paper of 1995.[125] It would require the Member States to amend their own legislation to allow the applicant to request that his domestic UM is valid in another Member State and has similar effects there. However, this broader alignment would be hard to sell to the Member States as the registration of a national authority would go beyond the principle of territoriality with its effect in other Member States of the EU.

If the EU were to opt for a positive full harmonisation, national IP rights would still exist. The likelihood of continued porous protection would be reduced since inventors could apply cross-border for UM protection with similar national rights in all Member States. However, Option 3 would require the EU to take a positive stance on UM protection as per Option 1. As already discussed, the foundation for such a broad recommendation is rather weak.

20.5.4.3 Policy Option 4: Positive Minimum Harmonisation

Minimum harmonisation, in contrast, would not impose a specific system but rather set a minimum standard for the protection of UM that Member States could not fall below, for example requirements for protection or a minimum scope of protection provided by national UMs. The national law would need to implement these standards, but the individual Member States would have some leeway to exceed the terms of the directive in a defined direction.

The analysis of Option 4 is similar to that of Option 3. The major difference is that Option 4 gives Member States flexibility to react to national particulars with legislative choices. At the same time, however, this possibility might lead to the continuation of heterogeneous UM protection within the EU at least to a certain extent.

20.5.4.4 Policy Options 5 and 6: Opt-In Harmonisation (Minimum or Full)

A final policy option is opt-in harmonisation, whereby a Member State can freely decide whether it wants to maintain a UM system or not. However, should the

[125] EC 1995, 48.

Member State opt to protect UMs, the EU obliges the national system to conform to standards stipulated in the directive. The directive could have either a maximum/ full or minimum harmonisation character meaning it could impose a specific framework that the Member State needs to implement (Policy Option 5) or merely define the key cornerstones of a UM system as minimum standards (Policy Option 6).[126] The main benefit of introducing opt-in harmonisation is to clarify the concept of a UM, especially with regard to existing secondary law of the EU, for example the IPCR and the IPED. As far as we are aware of, such an opt-in concept was not discussed by the EC during the 1990s.

Opt-in harmonisation does not force the EU to make a final decision on the establishment or maintenance of a UM protection system. It is for the Member States to make their own legislative choice. Given the inconclusive arguments for a UM protection system and its gap-filling function as an auxiliary tool to mainly non-harmonised patent systems, the national systems might be in the best situation to take such a decision.

If a Member State offers UM protection, users will be aware of the legal framework as it is the case in all Member States protecting UMs (Option 5) or at least they will be familiar with its key features which have to be the same (Option 6). An opt-in harmonisation would reduce, to some extent, the uncertainty deriving from the heterogeneous protection schemes currently existing in the EU. However, the general fragmentation and porous nature of protection with its detrimental effects on the single market would continue to exist. Furthermore, the EU would be required to set a proper, convincing and full-fledged blueprint for the design of national UM systems in the directive. As already mentioned above, this is hardly feasible given the gap-filling function of UM systems and the unharmonised area of patent law.

20.5.5 *Recommendations*

None of the policy options described above are entirely satisfying. All options except for the opt-in harmonisation would require a final stance by the EU on whether UM protection is positive or negative for the Member States. It is recommended that the Union refrains from such a decision as the general foundation of UM protection is ambiguous. There is no convincing argument for the introduction of a UM protection system in well-developed countries but there is also no conclusive argument that Member States should refrain from such protection. Moreover, designing a universal UM framework means filling gaps in the conspicuously heterogeneous national patent systems. Logically, before harmonising the UM framework, one would need to harmonise the patent system, but such an endeavour is not realistic at the moment.

If at all, harmonisation should address the different national laws by an opt-in harmonisation. This would leave the more general decision as to whether a national

[126] Radauer et al. 2015, 183.

system requires a sub-patent protection system to the respective Member State. An opt-in solution would clarify the concept of UM for the application and interpretation of the other EU's secondary law on IP, for example the Enforcement Directive. However, this option will not entirely resolve the existing problems of businesses working across boarders within the single market. These entities would still be required to inquire whether a certain invention is protected by a national UM in all Member States relevant for their business to avoid the risk of hold-ups. It will, however, implement one single standard for the UM framework of the national laws.

The overall analysis suggests that the EU is not well advised in implementing any of the outlined policy options. At the same time, the status quo is unsatisfactory and calls for an EU harmonisation, as pointed out in Section 20.3. Hence, further research is required to formulate compelling solutions.

20.6 A NEW CONCEPTIONAL STARTING POINT

20.6.1 *Two Assumptions for Further Research*

Further research on the harmonisation of UMs within the EU should be based on two assumptions. Firstly, future efforts at harmonisation should embrace an outside-the-box thinking and consider a new understanding of the concept of UMs. As discussed above, one of the main reasons why UM protection within the EU is diverse is the lack of international harmonisation. At the same time, this vacuum offers a tremendous policy space to reflect on the understanding of UMs when defining a suitable UM policy for the EU.

Secondly, further research should not only aim at optimal policy options but also consider second-best solutions. The analysis above suggests that perfect results are not in sight as certain optimal conditions are incompatible. For example, not taking any stance on the design of UM laws and overcoming the heterogeneous forms of protection within the EU appears impossible.

20.6.2 *UMs as Remuneration Rights and Opt-In Harmonisation*

Given the unsatisfying policy options available, a valuable starting point for new research on the EU harmonisation of UM law might be a critical reflection on the basic concept of UMs. Legal entitlements can be protected with a liability rule instead of a property rule, as recognised by Guido Calabresi and Melamed in their seminal contribution on the methods of protection.[127] A liability rule does not prevent the use of an entitlement by a third party, but the right holder can ask for

[127] Calabresi and Melamed 1972.

a remuneration as a compensation.[128] Such mechanisms are particularly recognised in EU copyright law.[129]

In the following, we will touch upon the idea of a system that enshrines a liability rule and understands UMs as remuneration rights. "Take-and-pay" approaches for UM law have not been discussed to a noticeable extent in Europe.[130] This lack of research does not come as a surprise as the existing UM protection systems of the Member States work with property rules. The US scholarship, however, has examined the protection of UMs by a remuneration right.[131] The primary intention of these scholars is the reduction of barriers to markets[132] – an idea that works particularly well also in the EU where a single market is subject to heterogenous forms of UM protection with the respective negative effects on competition.

We will include this new conceptional starting point in the framework of the most promising policy options outlined above: an opt-in harmonisation. The decision on the protection of UMs will still be left for the Member States. Nevertheless, if a Member State protects sub-patentable inventions, it would have to implement a liability rule. Hence, the EU is not required to decide on whether Member States can or must protect UMs but, as a second-best solution, the directive will decide on the "how". Therefore, the act would leave no national leeway when defining the effects of UMs (full harmonisation) while other features of the UM system could be subject to a mere minimum harmonisation.

20.6.3 *Addressing the Two Reasons for EU Harmonisation*

Above, we pointed out two reasons for the need for EU harmonisation of UM law. One of them related to the existing IP framework in EU law and the lack of a common understanding of a UM right when interpreting and applying this law (see Section 20.3.1). An opt-in harmonisation of UM protection would solve this issue as it would give a clear definition of the concept of an UM.[133]

The second reason for EU harmonisation concerned the adverse impact of the diverse UM frameworks on the single market (see Section 20.3.2). Businesses are at risk to infringe national UMs if they aim to operate in multiple countries of the EU without conducting a proper and expensive FTO in each and every relevant Member State. Their concern to be caught in a hold-up has a detrimental effect on the free movement of goods and bears the potential to obstruct competition in

[128] Calabresi and Melamed 1972, 1092.

[129] See, e.g., Art. 5 (2) (a), (b) and (e) Directive 2001/29/EC.

[130] But see Takenaka 2021c (proposing a royalty-free statutory license for the German UM system as long as the licensee grants cross licenses).

[131] See Reichman 1994; Janis 1999, 215; Reichman 2000, 1776; Reichman and Rutschman 2024.

[132] See Reichman 2000, 1746; Reichman and Rutschman 2024, § II (including n. 25), and §§ IV.B. and C.

[133] At the same time, the proposed directive would need to clarify that UMs are not subject to the property rule enshrined in parts of the existing EU acts, e.g. Art. 9 and 11 IPED.

the internal market. The opt-in options discussed above (Policy Options 5 and 6) were able to address this issue only to a limited extend.

Obviously, the proposed concept of a remuneration right does not solve the existing problem for the single market entirely either. It does not overcome the fragmentation or porous UM protection within the EU. However, a liability approach will mitigate its effects as the extent of the negative effects are directly linked to the concept of UMs as exclusive rights. Remuneration in case an entity infringes an overlooked national UM in one part of the internal market creates fewer negative effects than a full-fledged exclusive right entitling preliminary and permanent injunctions and the risk of hold-up.[134] An understanding of UMs as remuneration rights has the potential to accommodate the interests of businesses better than a property rule regime. This is particularly true for SMEs which do not have the financial means to conduct EU-wide FTOs.

20.6.4 *Accounting for the Conceptional Differences with Patents*

Although the EU would be able to refrain from a general decision of UM protection, this proposal requires the Union to be convinced about the advantages of a liability rule over a property regime in UM law. A decision on the form of protection is less far-reaching than imposing a decision on the general existence of a UM protection system, particularly when choosing with liability rules an "intermediate form" of protection. Nevertheless, it is the potential trouble spot of this approach. Further research will need to examine the actual effects of such a concept for the European systems. At least to some extent, this research will be able to rely on the existing US literature.[135]

Already now, it appears to be clear, that a liability rule will account better for the conceptional differences of patents and UMs. The prevailing consensus is that UMs are less robust than patents, with a lower threshold for protection, with a mere registration requirement, and with a pure gap-filling function to perform. It is therefore striking that UM holders are entitled to the same remedies as patent holders in the existing national laws and the EU framework.[136]

UM protection systems appear to be one of the most appropriate systems of industrial property protection to work with a liability rule. In general, property rules have one main advantage over liability regimes: It is the form of entitlement which

[134] Cf. the US scholarship (arguing that liability rules avoid legal barriers for market entry by UMs): Reichman 2000, 1746; Reichman and Rutschman 2024, § II. (including footnote 25), IV.B. and C.

[135] Reichman 1994; Janis 1999, 215; Reichman 2000, 1776; Reichman and Rutschman 2024.

[136] For the national laws, see the chapters on the different countries in this book. For the EU approach, cf. Art 2(1) IPED ("measures, procedures and remedies provided for by this Directive shall apply [...] to any infringement of intellectual property rights") which includes UMs in the scope of its application.

gives rise to the least amount of state intervention after the grant of a right.[137] It is for the parties to agree on a price for the usage of the protected subject matter while liability rules require some organ of the state to determine a value.[138] Hence, one could fear that shifting the existing property rule approach to a liability regime would increase the involvement of the judiciary in UM disputes. However, unlike most patent systems worldwide, the existing sub-patent protection systems work without pre-grant examination. These protection mechanisms are already court-intense in their design. The validity of the entitlement has not been examined by an IP office. The structure of the system leaves it for the *post*-registration phase and therewith for the courts to assess the protectability of the subject matter if a dispute arises.

20.6.5 *Fulfilling the Auxiliary Function and Curing the Patent System*

One concern of the Member States might be whether UMs as mere remuneration rights will still be able to fulfil their intended auxiliary function. UM protection systems are devised to cure gaps in the patent protection ("cheaper", "faster", "lower"). However, as briefly discussed above in Sections 20.4.1 and 20.4.2, the Member States have sufficient leeway to improve their national patent system if needed to provide for cheaper and faster protection. For example, if a Member State wants to offer cheaper access to IP protection to accommodate the needs of SMEs, it can offer fee discounts for such patent applicants. Moreover, if a Member State wants to offer faster protection for technical inventions by a property rule, e.g. already during patent prosecution, it could offer patent applicants access to interim injunctions if a preliminary assessment of the court deems the subject-matter patentable. Hence, Member States will need to internalise some of the auxiliary functions ("cheaper", "faster" protection) performed by their existing national UM systems in their patent systems if they think that a property rule is required.

As a core result of such a directive, the Member States will not be able to offer a full exclusive right for inventions which do not fulfil the requirements of patent protection ("lower" protection). The national systems will need to accept the imposed remuneration approach if they opt for a UM protection system. It is unclear whether this could be a major concern for Member States. It is difficult to imagine cases in which compensation as protection is not sufficient to protect sub-patentable inventions that do not fulfil the requirements of patentability. This idea aligns with the broader consensus that stronger rights come with more stringent requirements. It is well-recognised in copyright law where neighbouring rights tend to protect less original subject matter with a more limited set of rights.

[137] Calabresi and Melamed 1972, 1092.
[138] Calabresi and Melamed 1972.

20.6.6 *The Structure for Remuneration*

There are two ways in which the proposed directive could implement a structure for remuneration. The directive might foresee the establishment of a collection society. Such bodies relieve the burden on individuals to enforce their own rights within the realm of copyright law.[139] UMs are registered rights which facilitate the collective management of royalties. However, setting up and running such organisations entail high administrative costs.

As an alternative, the directive could enshrine a compensation claim of the right holder against the user of a UM. The burden of enforcement of such an individual claim would lie on the right holder. Therefore, we recommend that the directive works with incentives that users inform the right holder about their exploitation of the UM ("notify-and-use"). This could be achieved by an obligation of the user to inform the right holder prior to the use or shortly thereafter. If not informed, the right holder will be entitled to claim double compensation.

20.7 CONCLUSION

In the last decades, the EU made tremendous efforts to approximate national IP laws and introduce unitary EU IP rights. Nevertheless, the realm of UM law has remained untouched, despite the various attempts of the EC during the 1990s. The UM protection in the EU is currently fragmented and porous since some Member States have UM protection systems in place while others do not. The existing systems also lack any homogenous understanding as to many core features of UM protection. The lack of harmonisation is surprising as UM systems are traditionally intended to offer protection for SMEs and the EC has repeatedly emphasised their importance for the European economy.

The concept of the single market and the existing EU IP framework call for a harmonisation on an EU level. The current situation builds obstacles to the free movement of goods and has the potential to distort competition due to the risk of hold-ups for businesses, particularly SMEs, which are supposed to be the core beneficiaries of UM systems. Moreover, the lack of a common understanding of UMs leads to problems in the interpretation and application of the EU's secondary laws that refer to UMs without defining their concept.

The EU can harmonise UM protection either by a regulation or a directive based on Art. 114 or 118 TFEU. However, none of the policy options at hand are entirely convincing. Most of the options would require the EU to take a final decision on the

[139] For the benefits of such a collective management, see Nérisson 2017, 75. Most recently, Reichman and Rutschman have proposed collective management of royalties if the US were to implement a sub-patentable innovation system. See Reichman and Rutschman 2024, Part III. C. 3 and Chapter 16 (United States).

existence of a national or EU UM protection system. Such a step cannot be recommended as the arguments for UM protection are to a certain extent ambiguous. UM systems perform a gap-filler function to overcome shortcomings of the patent system and most of the gaps could be dealt with by amending patent legislations instead of maintaining a sub-patent protection system. Moreover, there appears to be no conclusive evidence that the protection of inventions under lower standards than the patent system is contributing to public welfare in highly developed economies. At the same time, one can also not argue convincingly for the abolishment of UM protection systems. There is no proof that the social costs of UM systems offset their positive effects in the Member States. The best option appears to be an opt-in harmonisation of national UM systems which avoids a decision on the general existence of UM laws by the EU. However, it would not solve the negative effects of the fragmented and porous UM protection within the EU entirely. Moreover, it would require the EU to design a full-fledged gap-filling system in a constellation where the patent system as the main system is varying from Member State to Member State.

This dilemma leads to two assumptions: Further research should reconsider the basic concept of UMs when reflecting on EU harmonisation. Thereby, it should also consider second-best solutions. A new conceptional starting point might be an opt-in harmonisation of national UM systems requiring the Member States to shift from a property rule regime to a liability rule if they want to implement or maintain an UM protection system. This approach would address both reasons for an EU harmonisation. Particularly, a mere remuneration for UM usage by third parties would reduce the negative effects of the fragmented and porous UM protection in the single market. The Member States would be required to fill the existing gaps in their patent system with patent-inherent means. Although the EU would not be forced to take a final decision on the existence of UMs in the EU, it would impose a compulsory remuneration scheme. Further research will need to investigate whether the EU should feel comfortable in doing so.

21

Heterogeneities in Utility Model Accessibility

Quantitative and Qualitative Insights

Dan Prud'homme

Utility model patents and similar second-tier rights, collectively referred to as "utility models" for simplicity, are an important yet understudied class of intellectual property (IP) assets.[1] As discussed throughout this volume, these rights can offer quicker protection than conventional patents, thereby enabling better appropriability of shorter life-cycle innovations;[2] protect incremental inventions incapable of meeting the higher standards for conventional patents;[3] and more readily facilitate learning about how and why to use IP than the conventional patent system allows.[4] The main mechanism behind these benefits lies in the greater *accessibility* of utility models compared to conventional patents – namely the formal institutional regime that makes utility models easier, cheaper, and quicker to obtain from the government.[5]

However, despite these purported benefits, there is scant comparative research examining *the impacts of heterogeneities in the accessibility of utility models over time and around the world*. These impacts may include, for example, differences in firms' decisions to apply for utility models depending on the accessibility of the regime governing the rights, as well as lawmakers' decisions to amend the regimes governing the rights due to concerns that they offer too much accessibility and therefore undermine utility model "quality."[6] Examining these issues in further detail is important for several reasons. It can inform lawmakers about how to maximize utility model accessibility, which should enable wider adoption of the rights. Further research in this space can also maximize state revenues from utility model filing fees. It can also help lawmakers by identifying when too much

1 Janis 1999; Suthersanen 2006, 2019; Suthersanen and Dutfield 2007; Prud'homme 2014, 2017a.
2 Prud'homme 2014; Radauer et al. 2015, 2019; Heikkilä and Lorenz 2018; Heikkilä 2023a; Heikkilä and Verba 2018.
3 Suthersanen 2006, 2019; Prud'homme and von Zedtwitz 2018; Cahoy and Oswald 2021.
4 Lee and Kim 2010; Kim et al. 2012.
5 Prud'homme 2017b
6 Prud'homme 2017a, b

accessibility can incentivize too many low-quality utility models and thus hamper innovation.[7]

The purpose of this chapter is to evaluate the impacts of heterogeneities in the accessibility of utility models over time and in different economies (i.e., countries and regions) around the world. I do this by, first, briefly conceptualizing the core components of utility model accessibility: the height of the requirements governing the rights, the strictness of the requirements' administration, and associated direct fees. Then, I summarize work in progress of mine that quantitatively analyzes how differences in the accessibility of utility models over time across a sample of 25 economies impacts the frequency of filing utility models.[8] Then, drawing directly on other prior research of mine, I provide a more granular, qualitative analysis for a subset of these economies that highlights differences in the accessibility of utility model regimes and their reforms in response to utility model quality concerns.[9]

My research offers a few important lessons. First, there is evidence of an inverted U-curve between utility model regime accessibility and utility model usage: a moderate amount of accessibility may lead to more filings than a lot or a little accessibility – at least over time and multiple economies, ceteris paribus. Second, firms may substitute other means of appropriability for utility models when a utility model regime is less accessible and conventional patent regimes offer stronger rights. Third, utility model regimes may be made less accessible over time to limit quality problems with the rights, although the exact parameters of these reforms must be decided on an economy-by-economy basis.

21.1 ACCESSIBILITY OF UTILITY MODEL REGIMES

The accessibility of an IP right is determined by how difficult it is to obtain from the government and to maintain as valid.[10] This accessibility dimension of an IP legal regime joins, of course, the distinct set of rules establishing the length and breadth of IP rights, as well as the mechanisms for their enforcement – referred to in shorthand by the economics and management literature as the "strength" of IP institutions.[11] The comparative accessibility of utility model regimes make utility models easier, cheaper, and quicker to obtain from the government than conventional

[7] Prud'homme and Zhang 2019.

[8] Some of the text here is reproduced from Prud'homme, 2024 (a working paper), with permission.

[9] Some of the text here is reproduced from Prud'homme, 2016a, with permission.

[10] Lemley 2001; Prud'homme 2017a,b.

[11] Ginarte and Park 1997; Park 2008; Prud'homme 2019; Prud'homme et al. 2021; Prud'homme and Tong 2023. In Park 2008, e.g., patent breadth is represented by patentable subject matter; enforcement mechanisms available (e.g., preliminary injunctions, contributory infringement, burden of proof reversal); restrictions on usage or lack thereof (e.g., working requirements, compulsory licensing, revocation of patents); and a patent's length is measured by its duration from grant date considering patent-term restoration or lack thereof.

patents.[12] Utility model regimes' accessibility is determined by several components: the height of the legal requirements governing the rights, strictness with which the rights' requirements are administered, and direct fees.

21.1.1 *Height of Legal Requirements Governing the Rights*

There are several subcomponents of the height of the legal requirements for utility models. The first is novelty. The strictest novelty threshold is absolute novelty, the next most restrictive threshold is relative novelty, and the least stringent threshold is local novelty. When novelty standards for utility models and conventional patents differ within economies, they are sometimes lower for utility models but still exist or, in some cases, are completely nonexistent in law.[13]

The next subcomponent is the legal requirements for inventive step. Inventive step for conventional patents is usually thought of as the "nonobviousness" of an invention to a person skilled in the relevant prior art, but exact definitions for utility models differ among economies.[14] Moreover, some economies' utility model systems have no inventive step requirements, while others have inventive step requirements but they are lower than for conventional patents, and some economies have the same inventive step requirements for both utility models and conventional patents.[15]

Yet other requirements can fit underneath the height umbrella. These include, for example, standards for sufficiency of disclosure and establishing industrial applicability of the invention. These may vary somewhat among economies.[16]

21.1.2 *Strictness of Requirements' Administration*

There are several subcomponents of the strictness of how requirements for utility models are administered. The first is the examination process. Generally, there are two types of utility model patent examinations: a Preliminary Examination and Substantive Examination. Preliminary Examinations often only check formalities, for example, the clarity and completeness of claims and descriptions in the utility model application. However, in some cases, they may include a limited assessment of some substantive aspects of the application. In contrast, Substantive Examinations are more in-depth, assessing the extent to which the utility model application satisfies the legal requirements for novelty, inventive step, industrial applicability, patentable subject matter, among other standards (e.g., sufficiency of disclosure). In some economies, a Search Report – an assessment of the prior art most directly related to a patent application – is used in addition to a Preliminary Examination or as part of a Substantive Examination. This report can be mandatory and considered as a basis to

[12] Prud'homme 2017b.
[13] Prud'homme 2014,2017a,b; Suthersanen 2006; Suthersanen and Dutfield 2007.
[14] Prud'homme 2014, 2017a,b.
[15] Prud'homme 2014, 2017a,b.
[16] Prud'homme 2014, 2017a,b.

not grant the utility model, mandatory but not considered as a basis for not granting the right, or simply available upon request to the applicant and/or other interested parties and kept only for their own purposes. Although some economies only require Preliminary Examinations for utility models while requiring Substantive Examinations for conventional patents, others require Substantive Examinations for both types of rights.[17]

The second subcomponent is observations and related mechanisms. Economies have widely varying mechanisms to challenge the granting and validity of utility models. These can include an opposition mechanism, under which, during a certain period of time, third parties submit evidence to support the decision not to grant the utility model in the first place (pre-grant) or invalidate the right (post-grant). Although not always opposition mechanisms stricto sensu, various related mechanisms exist in different economies. Some economies have third party observation mechanisms under which third parties can submit information related to the patentability of a utility model, typically after publication but before grant; and this information may be "considered" to varying degrees, including not at all, by the patent office as a basis for not granting the utility model. Some economies have reexamination mechanisms, which can be ex parte or inter partes. Some economies have administrative revocation and invalidation mechanisms, which may or may not have time limits on when invalidation cases can be brought. Some economies have a combination of several of these mechanisms. Such mechanisms are similarly structured for utility models and conventional patents in some economies, although sometimes they are different for utility models, or do not exist at all.[18]

21.1.3 *Direct Fees*

The official government fees associated with satisfying the aforementioned requirements and obtaining and maintaining a valid utility model are another important aspect of the accessibility of utility model regimes. Utility models around the world usually have substantially lower costs to obtain and maintain than conventional patents owing to their lower and less strict legal requirements.[19]

21.2 QUANTITATIVE ANALYSIS OF IMPACT OF UTILITY MODEL REGIME ACCESSIBILITY ON UTILITY MODEL USAGE

In this section, I draw directly on work in progress of mine that examines the impact of utility model regime accessibility on utility model usage.[20] On one hand, I conceptualize IP institutions that are too accessible (in other words, too lax) as

[17] Prud'homme 2014, 2017a,b.
[18] Prud'homme 2014, 2017a,b.
[19] Prud'homme 2014.
[20] Prud'homme 2024.

disincentivizing firms from using those institutions. Here, insufficiently high institutional requirements will attract IP filings of low economic value, while insufficiently strict institutional requirements will create excessive uncertainty about the legal value of those IP filings. Eventually, this will create a vicious cycle whereby, on average, the IP right obtained is of such low economic and legal value that it is not worth the costs, including transaction costs, to obtain and maintain it in the first place. On the other hand, I conceptualize IP institutions that are insufficiently accessible as disincentivizing firms from using those institutions. Here, more restrictive institutional requirements will raise the costs, including transaction costs, of obtaining and maintaining the IP right beyond its economic and legal value.[21] In short – holding the breadth and length of IP offered by the state, and the associated direct fees, constant – while institutional requirements must be high and strict enough to make IP net beneficial to applicants, those that are excessive will make IP net costly. I therefore predict (H1): *The accessibility of utility model regimes will have an inverted U-shaped relationship with utility model filings.*

I formulate another prediction as well. Prior economic research indicates that firms may substitute conventional patents for utility models over time.[22] However, this research does not examine how the institutional requirements governing utility models vs. conventional patents may play into this decision-making. Building upon my aforementioned hypothesis, I propose that utility model regimes that are insufficiently accessible (i.e., too restrictive) may incentivize firms to consider filing conventional patents instead. This is because conventional patent regimes can offer much greater appropriability length and breadth, and more feasible enforcement, for the inventions they protect when compared to the protections afforded by utility model regimes. For example, the duration of protection for utility models is only a fraction of that afforded by conventional patents, and utility models may only protect a more restricted set of product subject matter and often exclude processes entirely.[23] As such, when conventional patent regimes offer especially strong protection and utility model regimes are relatively inaccessible, the former should be even more attractive substitutes for the latter. I therefore predict (H2): *There will be fewer utility model filings in economies with both less accessible utility model regimes and conventional patent regimes that offer stronger rights.*

I test these two hypotheses on a sample of 25 economies with utility model regimes or equivalents. These economies include Argentina, Austria, Brazil, Bulgaria, China, Colombia, Costa Rica, the Czech Republic, Ecuador, Germany, Guatemala, Italy, Japan, Mexico, Panama, Peru, Philippines, Poland, Russia, Spain, Taiwan, Thailand, Turkey, Ukraine, and South Korea. These economies were

[21] van Pottelsberghe de la Potterie 2011; de Saint-Georges and van Pottelsberghe de la Potterie 2013.

[22] Lee and Kim 2010; Kim et al. 2012.

[23] Prud'homme 2014, 2017a,b.

selected because they are major sources of economic activity in their respective regions, collectively account for the vast majority (99 percent) of utility model filings around the world,[24] and the laws governing their utility models (in English or their native languages) over time could be relatively confidently located.

The *dependent variable* for both hypotheses is the annual filings of utility models in each country in the sample (*UMs*). Utility model grants were also separately analyzed, and similar findings were reached. This data was collected from WIPO's IP Indicators database and from the official websites of the national IP offices. Since data prior to 1980 is highly spotty, as is newer data for some economies, I limited the sample to 1980–2014. This time period, nearly 40 years, is reasonable to evaluate the hypotheses. Also, most of the utility model institutions outside of Europe in my sample were first introduced in 1980 or later anyway.

Independent variable: For the first hypothesis, my independent variable is an index measuring the accessibility of utility model regimes in the sampled economies (*UM Accessibility Index*). The basis for the index is the laws, which I analyzed with support from a team of research assistants, governing utility models for each of the 25 economies in the sample from 1980 to 2014. Copies of the laws for each economy were obtained either from the official government websites of their IP offices or from the WIPO Lex Database. To construct my index from these laws, I build on the methodology developed and validated by Prud'homme (2017a). However, I simplify my index somewhat to minimize error in the scoring process – as interpreting the laws of some of the 25 economies across these sub-indicators was sometimes overly difficult due to their lack of clarity. Table 21.1 outlines the indicators and sub-indicators used. The index is reverse coded, such that higher scores reflect a less accessible utility model regime.

For hypothesis 2, the independent variable is the interaction between my *UM Accessibility Index* and Park's (2008) Patent Strength Index (*Park Patent Index*), data for which is available until 2015. The Park Patent Index proxies patent length and breadth from conventional patent regimes around the world.

I included several *control variables*. I constructed an index of the length (maximum duration of rights) and breadth (patentable subject matter) of the utility model regimes per country in the sample (*UM Length & Breadth Index*) from the same set of laws used for the *UM Accessibility Index*. A dummy variable was included to control for effects from utility model regimes being in place before the time period I analyzed, namely prior to 1980 (*Old UM Regime*). I further controlled for the *Park Patent Index*, *GDP*, *population*, *total factor productivity*, *conventional patent filings*, and *economy fixed effects* and *year fixed effects*.

In terms of estimation methods, for H1, following the methods in Haans et al. (2016), the independent variable was squared to estimate the inverted-curvilinear relationship. For H2, curvilinear estimates with moderation effects (Haans et al.

[24] See, e.g., WIPO 2023d.

TABLE 21.1 *Indicators for UM accessibility index*[a]

Indicator	Sub-indicators	Sub-indicator scoring	Sub-indicator weighting	Highest score possible
1. *Novelty*	1. Absolute novelty	3	2	6
	2. Relative novelty	2	2	
	3. Local novelty	1	2	
	4. None	0	2	
2. *Inventive step*	Requirement (of any kind) for utility models or not	3 or 0	1.75	5.25
3. *Examination*	1. Patentability of subject matter examined (in any way) or not	3 or 1	0.1	3
	2. Industrial applicability examined (in any way) or not	3 or 0	0.15	
	3. Novelty examined (in any way) or not	3	0.3	
	4. Inventive step examined (in any way) or not	3	0.45	
4. *Opposition and related mechanisms*	1. Pre-grant mechanism (of any kind) or not	3 or 0	0.4	3
	2. Post-grant mechanism (of any kind) or not	3 or 0	0.6	

[a] *Source*: Prud'homme 2024.

2016) were used. In both estimations, the RHS variables were log-transformed and lagged by one year to avoid simultaneity with the dependent variable.

Figures 21.1 and 21.2 visually represent the results for H1 and H2, respectively. These figures and the full set of regression results, available upon request, provide robust, statistically significant support for both hypotheses.

21.3 QUALITATIVE ANALYSIS OF IMPACT OF UTILITY MODEL REGIME ACCESSIBILITY ON UTILITY MODEL QUALITY

In this section, I draw directly on prior work of mine to provide a qualitative comparative analysis of accessibility dimensions of the utility model regimes in a subset of economies studied in the prior section.[25] I focus on Austria, China, the Czech Republic, Finland, France, Germany, and Italy, but also briefly consider Belgium and the Netherlands. I organize the analysis within the three-part categorization of utility model regime accessibility set forth earlier. When apparent,

[25] Some of the text here is reproduced from Prud'homme 2016a, with permission.

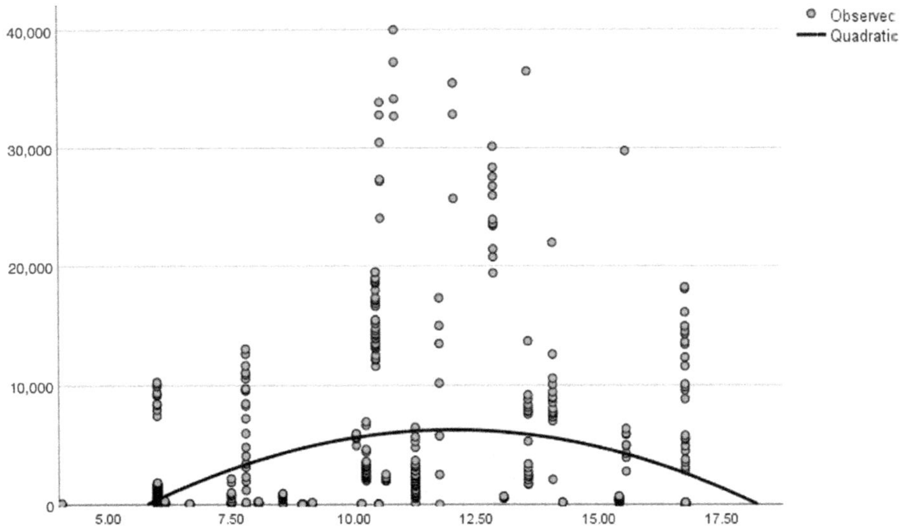

FIGURE 21.1 Impact of UM regime accessibility on UM filings around the world
Source: Prud'homme 2024. Sample of 25 economies from 1980 to 2014. Y axis = UM filings, X axis = UM Accessibility Index. Y axis observations over 40,000 (for China) removed from figure simply to allow easier visual interpretation; all results hold strong with and without these outliers.

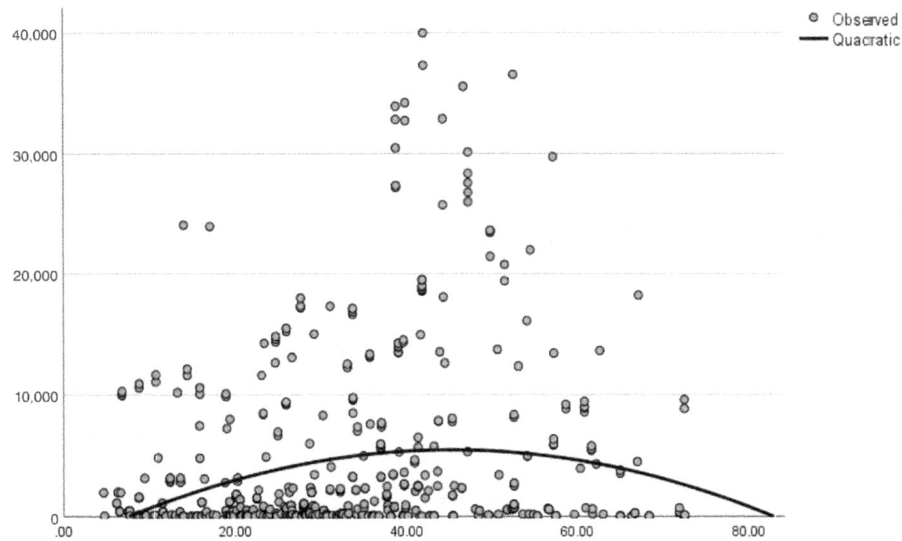

FIGURE 21.2 Joint impact of UM regime accessibility and conventional patent regime strength on UM filings around the world
Source: Prud'homme 2024. Sample of 25 economies from 1980 to 2014. Y axis = UM filings, X axis = UM Accessibility Index X Park Patent Index. Y axis observations over 40,000 (for China) removed from figure simply to allow easier visual interpretation; all results hold strong with and without these outliers.

I emphasize situations where officials in the patent/utility model offices of these economies suspected that the accessibility of their utility model regimes was creating "quality" concerns and reformed their regimes in response. By "quality" of an IP right I broadly mean how well it is drafted, a definition often favored by IP attorneys; the extent to which it meets the legal standards for being granted, a definition often favored by legal scholars; and its technological and/or commercial worth, a definition often favored by economists.[26] As explained by Prud'homme and Zhang, the quality of all types of patents, utility models included, is important because:

> First, an economy rife with low-quality patents is dangerously self-reinforcing because in such an environment rational firms seek more low-quality patents rather than higher-quality patents ... In other words, poor patent quality creates path-dependency on inventions that do not significantly contribute to innovation. Second, poor patent quality generates uncertainty, which leads to lower incentives to innovate, which stifles technological development, entrepreneurship, employment, and ultimately growth and consumer welfare ... Third, poor patent quality can increase barriers to entry, i.e., more patents blocking freedom-to-operate (FTO), and raise IP-related transaction costs. These barriers and costs are faced when merely identifying the rights in order to maintain FTO; otherwise navigating licensing of the rights; proactively invalidating the rights to maintain FTO; invalidating the rights as a defense in (frivolous or other) infringement disputes; otherwise defending against the rights, if they are difficult to invalidate, in infringement litigation; and defending against the rights if used as a basis for invalidity cases.[27]

21.3.1 *Height of Legal Requirements Governing the Rights*

Among the economies studied, only Germany has relative novelty for utility models, whereas the other economies currently have an absolute novelty standard for utility models.[28] While Germany has maintained its novelty standard for some time now, the absolute novelty standard is inferably viewed by the other economies as useful to ensure utility model quality in an increasingly interconnected world.[29]

Some economies have the same *inventive step requirement for utility models* as for conventional patents. Evidence is mixed, however, as to if this is optimal for balancing utility model quality with incentives to seek utility models in the first place. The experience of Germany offers a natural experiment highlighting this trade-off. A 2006 decision from the German Supreme Court changed the prior way of interpreting inventive step for utility models as lower than for conventional patents to require that the inventive step requirement be the same for both

[26] Prud'homme and Zhang 2019, 53.

[27] Prud'homme and Zhang 2019, 54.

[28] DPMA 2014; Article 3, Austrian Utility Model Law (2009); Article 22, Patent Law of China (2008); Article 4, Czech Republic Utility Model Law (2006); Intellectual Property Code of France (2014), Article L611–11; Societa Italiana Brevetti, Intellectual Property Consultants, 2014.

[29] Prud'homme 2016a.

rights.[30] While perhaps encouraging higher-quality utility models according to some scholar's conceptualization of the term, this decision was criticized by a range of experts based on legal grounds.[31] Also, the decision has been scrutinized on economic grounds given it appears to have discouraged filing of utility models by German entities at a time when filing for such rights could be helpful to improve their competitiveness.[32]

The other economies studied have varying approaches to inventive step requirements for utility models relative to conventional patents. France has consistently maintained the same inventive step requirement for utility certificates and conventional patents.[33] In 2006, the Austrian Supreme Court ruled that the inventive step threshold for utility models, conversely to what the German court ruled the same year, should continue to be lower for utility models than conventional patents; however, in practice, the inventive step for the two rights is assessed similarly.[34] China,[35] Finland,[36] and Italy[37] have lower inventive step thresholds in statute for utility models than conventional patents. The Czech Republic has lower inventive step thresholds in statute for utility models than conventional patents, although in practice the inventive step requirement is basically the same.[38]

Different economies use varying *methods to determine inventiveness* of utility models. China is unique among the economies studied as it has written examination guidelines recommending narrowing prior art to one or two pieces, as well as narrowing the number of technical fields considered, when assessing the inventive step of utility models in "normal" cases.[39] However, in practice, the patent offices in the Czech Republic[40] and Finland[41] also usually use no more than one or two pieces of prior art to determine the validity of a utility model – although there are no

30 Decision of the Demonstrationsschrank, German Federal Supreme Court, X ZB 27/05, June 20, 2006. The German Utility Model Law (2013) stipulates utility models must have inventive step, but it does not provide a definition for inventiveness. In Article 4 of the German Patent Law (2013), inventiveness for patents is determined as being "not obvious to a person skilled in the art from the state of the art."

31 Written correspondence from Dr. Johannes Holzer, DPMA, June 2014.

32 Ibid.

33 Article L611–14 of the Intellectual Property Code of France (2014).

34 Decision of the Austrian Supreme Court, No. 4 Ob 3/06d, July 12, 2006; Written correspondence from Dr. Johannes Werner, APO, June 24, 2014. Note: the Austrian Utility Model Law (2009) and Austrian Patent Act (1994) treat inventiveness for utility models and invention patents in the same manner as the corresponding German laws do.

35 Article 22 of the Patent Law of China (2008).

36 Article 2 of the Finnish Utility Model Act (2013); Article 2 in the Finnish Patents Act (2013).

37 Italian Industrial Property Code (2012), Article 82.1; Article 48 of the Italian Code of Industrial Property (2012); Written correspondence from Loredana Guglielmetti, IPTO, August 2014.

38 Article 1 of Czech Republic's Utility Model Law (2006); Article 6 of the Czech Republic's Patent Act (2007); Consultations with Šimon Bednář, IPO CZ, May 21, 2014 roundtable.

39 Part IV, chapter 6, Section 4(2), Patent Examination Guidelines of China (2013); Part IV, chapter 6, Section 4(1), Patent Examination Guidelines of China (2013).

40 Consultations with Šimon Bednář, IPO CZ, May 21, 2014 roundtable.

41 Written correspondence from Hanna Aho, PRH, June 2014.

written rules requiring this and, like in China, there is flexibility to use more pieces of prior art as necessary. Austria, Germany, and Italy have no such restrictions in practice or otherwise. Inventiveness of utility models in Italy and utility certificates in France is determined by the courts through a proceeding removed from the purview of the patent office in which external technical experts can be involved.[42]

21.3.2 *Strictness of Requirements' Administration*

Requiring a *Search Report* prior to granting a utility model, even if not considered as a basis for not granting the application but simply presented alongside it, can be a useful method for ensuring the quality of utility models. This approach is mandatory in Austria.[43] The costs of such a procedure to patent examiners or externally contracted agents can be included in the fees for filing the utility model. Some offices studied offer Search Reports or a type of report listing prior art relevant to utility model applications prior to publication of the application upon the applicants' request and for a fee. They also offer such reports to any entity at any time after a utility model is granted for a fee, and such reports are available to the public. This appears to provide the requestor improved certainty regarding the quality of the utility model.

All economies studied consider several formalities in their *Preliminary Examinations* of utility models. These include the clarity and completeness of claims and descriptions. In some economies, Preliminary Examinations also examine more substantive elements. Finland requires an assessment of industrial applicability of utility models in the Preliminary Examination stage.[44] China[45] and the Czech Republic[46] require assessing if utility models "obviously" lack industrial applicability. Preliminary Examinations of utility model applications in Austria,[47] the Czech Republic,[48] China,[49] Finland,[50] France,[51] and Italy[52] assess the patentability of subject matter therein in some form, in terms of obvious nonconformity or otherwise. Meanwhile, the only substantive element examined in the Preliminary Examination of a utility model in Germany is if the invention in the application has a technical background.[53]

42 Prud'homme 2016a.

43 Article 19 of Austria Utility Model Law (2009); Consultations with Dr. Johannes Werner, APO, May 21, 2014 roundtable.

44 Written correspondence from Hanna Aho, PRH, September 17, 2014.

45 Article 44, Implementation Regulations of Patent Law of China (2010).

46 Article 11 (4) of the Utility Model Law of the Czech Republic (2006).

47 Presentation by Dr. Johannes Werner, APO, May 21, 2014 roundtable.

48 Article 11 (1) of the Utility Model Law of the Czech Republic (2006).

49 Article 44, Implementation Regulations of Patent Law of China (2010).

50 Written correspondence from Hanna Aho, PRH, September 17, 2014.

51 Cabinent Beau de Lomenie 2014.

52 Article 170 of the Italian Industrial Property Code (2012).

53 Article 8 (1) of the German Utility Model Law (2013); Written correspondence from Dr. Johannes Holzer, DPMA, October 31, 2014.

China is unique among the economies studied as the country's National Intellectual Property Administration (CNIPA)'s Preliminary Examination for utility models assesses if the invention in the application "obviously" lacks novelty[54] and, as of very recently, inventiveness.[55] These requirements appear useful to ensure the quality of utility models.[56]

None of the economies studied require a full *Substantive Examination* for utility models. The lack of this requirement is said to enable utility models to be granted much quicker and cheaper than conventional patents which undergo such an examination. (This being said, multiple economies around the world do require substantive examinations for utility models.[57]) Moreover, in the cases of the Netherlands and Belgium, lack of a substantive examination – or at least examination of novelty via a Search Report – appears to have created significant uncertainty in the equivalent of utility model regimes there by incentivizing the filing of low-quality rights. In fact, partially because of this, these economies ultimately abolished their utility models regimes in 2008 and 2009, respectively.[58]

The economies studied adopt different approaches to *third party observation mechanisms*. A third-party observation mechanism is used for utility certificates in France.[59] Third parties in Italy can submit petitions on utility models during the examination procedure, although they are not considered part of a formal third party mechanism nor do they serve as a basis for the Italian patent office to not grant a utility model.[60] In Austria, while there is no formal mechanism to collect third party observations, if third parties provide the Austrian Patent Office with their observations they will be considered prior to the publication of the Search Report.[61] These mechanisms can help ensure quality utility models are granted.

54 Article 44, Implementation Regulations of Patent Law of China (2010); SIPO's Decision on Amending the Patent Examination Guidelines (September 16, 2013). This includes determining if "abnormal" utility model applications – such as applications that obviously copy prior art or are repeatedly filed with substantially identical content to another application – indeed obviously lack novelty.

55 Part I, chapter 2, Section 11, CNIPA's Patent Examination Guidelines (December 21, 2023).

56 China, in particular, also offers "Patent Evaluation Reports," which are primarily intended to help courts to decide whether to stay a utility model infringement proceeding until the administrative decision on validity is issued by the patent office. However, this report should not be confused with a Search Report, Preliminary Examination, or Substantive Examination, nor does it constitute an administrative decision from the patent office (Prud'homme 2014, 2016b).

57 For example, according to DIPP (2011), the Andean Community, Argentina, Brazil, Bulgaria, Chile, Guatemala, Indonesia, Malaysia, Mexico, Philippines, Poland, Portugal, South Korea, Thailand, and Vietnam require Substantive Examinations before grating utility models.

58 Written correspondence from D. J. de Groot, Director of the Netherlands Patent Office, August 22, 2014.

59 Article L612–13 3° Industrial Property Code of France (2014).

60 Written correspondence from Loredana Guglielmetti, IPTO, September 17, 2014. Note: The Italian Industrial Property Code (2012) only establishes specific rules for third party observations before granting of trademarks and plant varieties, not for invention patents or for utility models.

61 Written correspondence from Dr. Johannes Werner, APO, September 15, 2014.

The economies studied institute different utility model *invalidation procedures*. Some invalidation cases go directly to courts without involvement of patent offices, as in France and Italy. In the other economies studied, their patent offices serve as at least a first instance reviewer in a procedure that can then be appealed to the courts. As it is not straightforward to determine from available evidence, it is beyond the scope of this article to assess which of these two approaches are better for utility model quality.

21.3.3 *Direct Fees*

Relatively low *official fees* are another classic component of the utility model regime, at least costs lower than those associated with conventional patents. This differential reflects the often less-substantive nature of the examination process for utility models when compared to conventional patents. Also, the lower costs are meant to be one mechanism to enable small-scale inventors, who typically have limited money to protect their inventions, to obtain IP protection. Among the economies studied in this chapter, the nonsubsidized/otherwise preferentially reduced official costs associated with utility models are the lowest in the Czech Republic. This is one main reason cited by the Czech IP Office for the attractiveness of the utility model system to inventors in that economy.[62]

Some economies offer *special reductions and subsidization of official filing fees and other expenses* associated with utility models. This does not necessarily create problems for utility model quality. For example, available evidence shows that subsidies for intellectual property rights in Italy – which, when distributed by provincial and local level entities, can go to utility models – do not appear to significantly hurt patent quality; however, they also do not appear to do much to improve patent quality.[63] However, in the case of China, some provincial/municipal and local subsidies and state-provided financial awards for utility models appear to have led to a surge in low-quality utility models.[64] In reaction to this, China's CNIPA has continued to work with IP bureaus and other departments across the country to modify and restrict such incentive schemes.[65] The more significant size and widespread use of state-provided monetary patent incentives in China vs. in European economies, amongst other factors, likely explains the especially negative utility model quality in China.[66]

[62] Written correspondence from Šimon Bednář, IPO CZ, May 2014.

[63] Xu and Munari 2016.

[64] Prud'homme 2012, 2014, 2015a,b, 2016a,b, 2017a,b, 2025; Long and Wang 2016; Prud'homme and Zhang 2019.

[65] Prud'homme 2012, 2014, 2015a,b, 2016a,b, 2017a,b, 2025; Long and Wang 2016; Prud'homme and Zhang 2019.

[66] Prud'homme 2016b.

In summary, utility model regimes need not be homogeneously accessible. However, sometimes, regimes that are too accessible need to be reformed to safeguard against significant utility model quality problems. This is illustrated by China's experiences with significant state financial incentives for utility model fees alongside low and not strictly administered requirements for obtaining utility models, which stimulated low-quality utility models. The importance of carefully calibrating utility model regimes to safeguard the quality of corresponding rights is also illustrated by the low and not strictly administered requirements for obtaining the equivalent of utility models in Belgium and the Netherlands, which contributed to the abolishment of the regimes governing those rights altogether. In short, utility model regimes may be made less accessible over time to limit quality problems with the rights, although the exact parameters of these reforms need to be decided on an economy-by-economy basis.

21.4 CONCLUSIONS

This chapter examined the impacts of heterogeneities of utility model accessibility over time and around the world. I provided evidence of an inverted U-curve between utility model regime accessibility and utility model usage. I also showed that firms may substitute other means of appropriability for utility models when a utility model regime is less accessible and conventional patent regimes offer stronger rights. Lastly, I showed that utility model regimes may be made less accessible over time to limit quality problems with the rights, although the exact parameters of these reforms must be decided on an economy-by-economy basis.

22

Utility Models and Innovation in Low-Income Economies

Uma Suthersanen

> Poor countries may find [IPRs] useful provided they are accommodated to suit local palates. The Commission suggests that the appropriate diet for each developing country needs to be decided on the basis of what is best for its development, and that the international community and governments in all countries should take decisions with that in mind.
>
> —Sir Hugh Laddie

This chapter explores the following theoretical extrapolations which are grounded from previous research findings in this area.[1] Based on the historical and existing literature review, it appears that utility model (UM) law has been defined and rationalized in various ways. And yet, UM laws can subsist as an independent (sui generis) regime within the IP pantheon of rights, untethered to international rules or global norms (save for procedural rules such as priority rules). As the law has pluralistic justificatory bases, and absent strict international rules, policy makers are free to choose existing rationales and/or expand the justifications for UM laws which best suit the local conditions. National UM laws can be sculpted to suit *any* local socio-economic interest or need.

Can UM law therefore be harnessed to plug existing gaps in protection for innovative practices outside the capitalist economy, including indigenous, traditional and/or community-based innovative practices? This endogenous growth approach would perhaps allow some countries to be guided by the diverse economy school of thought – whereby all types of innovations, initiatives and investments (including non-capitalist yet valued practices) can be nurtured through tailored property rights, or non-property-related remuneration schemes.

[1] Cummings 2010, 303; Prud'homme 2017a; Suthersanen 2019. For older studies in this area: Janis 1999; Suthersanen 2001, 2006; Suthersanen and Dutfield 2007.

22.1 THE UNEASY DISCOURSE: PATENTS, HYBRIDS AND INNOVATION

The quote at the start of this chapter derives from a 2002 report which analysed the capacity of intellectual property rules [IPRs] to develop in such a manner as to take greater account of the interests of developing countries and poor people.[2] One recommendation was that lawmakers in developing countries should introduce a system of utility models to foster "domestic innovation" as well as incremental innovation. The Report acknowledged the fact that parties in many low-income developing countries filed very few patent applications despite the presence of innovative activity; the problem was assigned to the defects within patent law namely high transaction costs in terms of fees, examination and grant timelines, high thresholds and overall institutional complexity.[3]

The "patent defects" argument is the traditional basis for three further interrelated rationales for UM systems: (i) a flexible hybrid right to ameliorate patent law defects, (ii) an IPR tool for small inventors/small and medium-sized enterprises (SMEs) to prevent free riding/imitative copying in important small and local industries, (iii) an IPR that acts as a spur to enhanced levels of innovation and technological catch-up and/or for improving the environment of developing countries.[4] Juma sets out a further justification for UMs in that they "may become a source of data on innovative activity and experience in technological management".[5]

The "patents promote innovation" refrain runs strongly in many other discourses on extending protection to new types of subject matter. Take, for instance, the 2021 Australian decision on the patentability of AI-generated inventions where the first tribunal determined that the meaning of "inventor" (and thus patent protection) should be extended to AI systems. Why? Because the policy objective of the Australian Patents Act 1990 was to promote

> technological innovation and the publication and dissemination of such innovation by rewarding it, irrespective of whether the innovation is made by a human or not.[6]

This line of reasoning (especially in relation to a no-examination and low-threshold UM system) leads to further assumptions as to how a comprehensive and extensive IPRs-framework benefits local economies: it encourages local innovations within indigenous cottage industries, it prevents the free-riding of minor or

[2] UK Report of the Commission on Intellectual Property Rights 2002, vi. The genesis of this report was the UK Government's optimistic White Paper – see *Eliminating World Poverty: Making Globalisation Work for the Poor*, Stationery Office 2000, 98.

[3] Ibid., 134–136.

[4] Janis 1999; Heikkilä 2023a.

[5] Juma 1989, 231–232.

[6] *Thaler* v. *Commissioner of Patents* (2021) FCA 879 at [124], relying on s2A of the Australian Patents Act (Cth) 1990. The decision was subsequently reversed by the Australian Federal Court in *Commissioner of Patents* v. *Thaler*, [2022] FCAFC 62.

cumulative innovations, and it improves the legal and investment environment of developing countries, which in turn boosts local R&D needed to turn inventions into marketable innovations.[7]

Two queries come immediately to mind. First, is there empirical evidence that existing UM systems encourage the innovation practice and environment? We deal with this in Section 22.2. However, a secondary query which is dealt with immediately below is: if lower patent thresholds can boost minor or cumulative innovation, why not just adopt lower patent thresholds?

22.1.1 *Cumulative and Incremental Innovation: Lower Thresholds and Policy Limits*

Innovation as a concept lies on a spectrum ranging from Arrow's sweeping conception (innovation is the production of information) to Schumpeter's broad definition.[8] Irrespective of the development and technological stage of the country or the company concerned – a lot of "innovation" is incremental and cumulative. This is equally true of both industrial and cultural innovation.[9] One of the key implications of that is the creation of new works requires access to and use of pre-existing data and works. So, lowering thresholds within patent (and even design) laws would be a useful policy if it extends to reward cumulative or minor innovation in ways that do not impose high transaction costs on follow-on innovations.

But such low thresholds, whilst benefitting the innovators of today, may hinder the innovation of tomorrow. Good policy dictates that all innovations cannot be categorized as legally patentable inventions. Moreover, if patent protection is structured in such a manner as to unduly require the sacrifice of scarce resources, any societal benefits and economic rent accruing from patent law would be dissipated. These arguments also explain (i) the high levels of novelty and inventiveness (theoretically) required, (ii) the range of limitations and exclusions in national IP laws to ensure that commonplace, obvious or mere workshop inventions and works are not protected,[10] and (iii) the lack of global consensus as to the eligibility of

[7] Radauer et al. 2019.

[8] Arrow 1962; Schumpeter 1934, 66.

[9] Scotchmer 1999; Cohen and Lemley 2001, 5 (the software industry "is characterized by rapid sequential innovation"); also Merges and Nelson 1990, 880–881, citing examples in the toy and consumer product industry. Part of this argument derives from Dutfield and Suthersanen 2004.

[10] In relation to commonplace works or functional features or basic building blocks of creativity, IP law has devised a myriad of doctrines including the idea-expression principle, the functionality doctrines within copyright, design and trademark laws, and abstract subject matter. See, e.g., the United States Copyright Act – 17 USC § 102(b); for the international position, note Article 9(2) of the TRIPS Agreement and Article 2 of WIPO Copyright Treaty.

patentable subject matter such as computer programs, methods, genetic materials or inventions contrary to "morality and *ordre public*"?[11]

Instead of lowering eligibility thresholds, the other historical solution is to either introduce a liability-rule-based system such as a statute-based tort or misappropriation law, or a hybrid property rights system. We will consider these next.

22.1.2 *Revised Rationale for UMs*

As I suggested above, the "IPRs promote innovation" mantra is not new and runs throughout the IP literature; and one can detect its influence when the discourse shifts to justifying new hybrid IPR systems in different contexts including fashion, design and plant variety rights.[12] And indeed, historically, local Procrustean solutions were the ideal means to overcome patent law defects. The solutions could accommodate "forbidden" subject matter, bypass inconvenient policy rules and remove procedural thresholds such as examination or even registration. Existing laws can be re-purposed and extended; or new sui generis rights can be created which emulate existing rights and rationales. Or liability-rule-based systems can be employed to introduce new tort actions.[13] These systems could operate in place of patents or copyright, or could alternatively operate in parallel, so that patents and copyright could then be used only for those inventions and creative works displaying a demonstrably high inventive step or level of creativity. In this manner, all sorts of new subject matter can be accommodated within any national IPR framework as ostensibly new sui generis regimes (or liability rule systems) can subsist.

The policy criticisms against such hybrid rights are varied. But they can be reduced to a single contention: by constructing a loose hybrid misappropriation or property regime, the traditional IPR system is in danger of being captured by the wrong parties and of being ignored by the "chosen" stakeholders. In the case of UMs, the targeted party usually includes local SMEs or the sole, indigenous innovator. On the other hand, hybrid rights may well be the best way to do so due to the inherent flexibilities in such systems; note such flexibilities within IP law in relation to non-creative databases, test data exclusivity, plant variety and plant patent rights, AI-derived and computer-generated works, and geographical indications.[14]

So perhaps a better rationale for hybrid rights is that property rights may be a necessary allocation to underwrite/support risk-laden, investment-driven knowledge

[11] Saw 2016. For attempts to align the US position with that of the European Patent Office, see Lefstin et al. 2018. For the international and European position, see Article 27(2) of TRIPS Agreement and Article 53(a) European Patent Convention.

[12] Reichman 1994; Suthersanen 2013.

[13] Reichman 2000, 1771 et seq; Cornish 1993, 54–55.

[14] Bonadio and Goold 2023: the various chapters in the book rationalise these subject matters (and more) on a broad basis – a thing of value should/will become property, irrespective of consequentialist reasoning.

activities and results. This chapter employs this revised rationale to explain why UMs can play a role in a country's local innovative system. As Cahoy and Oswald argue, UMs are "purely economic rights and are offered in countries at very different levels of development".[15]

22.1.3 *UMs as Development Tools*

A final consideration is in relation to the many studies which have emphasized the role of UMs as a catch-up and developmental tool in different contexts.[16] Thus, Maskus and McDaniel report that technology diffusion through UM applications had had a positive impact on Japan's post-war productivity growth. Importantly, UM applications had an indirect impact on patent applications. They opine that this perhaps reflects a more fundamental industrial invention, through their stimulation of follow-on utility model applications, which were quickly diffused into commercial use.[17]

A more recent empirical study by Kim et al. affirms this general conclusion in a more concise manner. According to them, UM protection allows developing economies to build up their "indigenous innovative capacities".[18] Moreover, within such developing economies, the study found that UMs contributed specifically to technologically lagging firms.

> Once firms become more technologically advanced, their performance is driven less by utility model innovations and more by patentable innovations. These results thus indicate that different types of intellectual property rights are more appropriate for countries at different stages of economic development. [...] Incremental, adaptive R&D leads to innovations that qualify for such utility model protection and provides a foundation upon which to eventually produce patentable innovations.[19]

This finding appears to lend credence to one of the rationales of UM in that it can enhance the capacity of SMEs/sole innovators to produce (future) patentable inventions – this is discussed further in Section 22.2.2.

Kim et al. conclude that developing countries need to construct the sort of IPR framework which is appropriate for their economic and development level; and that UM protection "can be an important factor affecting the production of patentable innovations *only* in middle-to-low income countries". (emphasis added).[20] A more recent 2020 study for the Asian Development Bank confirms this – at least from the

[15] Cahoy and Oswald 2021, 548. See also Chapter 18.
[16] Prud'homme 2017a; Juma 1989, 231–232; Maskus and McDaniel 1999; Boztosun 2010.
[17] Maskus and McDaniel 1999.
[18] Kim et al. 2012.
[19] Kim et al. 2012, 359.
[20] Kim et al. 2012, 367.

Korean perspective. Depending on the development stage of a firm (or country), the innovation policy should shift between the different forms of IPRs: early stages of development were associated with UMs while catch-up stages required trademark and design, and the globalization stage required patents.[21] Other studies have also alluded to the holistic IPR framework by noting that technologically strong and developed economies distrust an "easy" system and switch to the more rigorous patent regime, as their concerns shift to market-based competitiveness, the need to attract foreign direct investment, and the use of the utility model system by foreign companies (as in Australia and Japan[22]).

The lesson for developing countries is to seriously consider introducing UMs into their IPR framework. But a lot of initial discourses must be had. And such countries should be realistic and view IPRs as mere tools for economic advancement that contribute to the enrichment of society. If it does not do this, then dump the policy.

What of developed nations? The reasoning appears to be linked again to the economic and innovative environment of the country in question. The 2013 Australian economic review confirmed that the economic effect of UMs decreases with the rise of technological capacity in industries (see Chapter 9 on the Australian system); however, the report also concluded that the continued use of UMs in Japan, Germany, France and Italy (see Chapters 11, 6, 5 and 7, respectively) suggests that these instruments may have a role in innovation and economic growth even in developed economies.[23]

22.2 MAPPING A SUI GENERIS UM SYSTEM

The proliferation and diversity of UM laws globally is intriguing. There is no harmonized legal understanding nor pattern to UM protection under international law, with the different agreements being silent as to the nature and extent of the second-tier patent/UM right.[24] However, despite the recalcitrance of substantive international law to engage with UMs, these rights are recognized within the

[21] Lee et al. 2019, 2, 31–32.

[22] There is much literature on this: Odagiri et al. 2010, 1–28; Kardam 2007; Kim et al. 2012.

[23] Zeitsch 2013.

[24] Suthersanen 2019; Cahoy and Oswald 2021, 527; Bodenhausen 1969, 29. For legislative ambivalence, see Art. 2 Patent Cooperation Treaty (references to applications covers patents for inventions, inventors' certificates of addition, and utility certificates of addition); Art. 2 Agreement for the International Patent Classification 1971 (the IPC refers to patents for invention, inventors' certificates, utility models and utility certificates); Art. 1(2), Paris Convention for the Protection of Industrial Property of 20 March 1883 (1967, Stockholm revision); Arts 1(2) and 2(1), TRIPS Agreement, Annex 1C of the WTO Agreement, 15 April 1994 (The TRIPS Agreement, in incorporating salient Paris Convention provisions, extends the WTO-based IP umbrella to UMs; but the Agreement fails to establish any other international benchmark for this IP right).

intellectual property chapters of free trade agreements[25] or as investment assets under international investment agreements.[26] More than 100 countries have laws referencing second-tier patent protection resembling UM protection in some form or another.[27] Heikkilä's analysis shows the following regional percentages of countries with a two-tiered patent system: 58% of EPO member states, 45% of ARIPO members and 60% of ASEAN members.[28]

The studies show that developing economies can have mixed results due to changing national policies: on the one hand, UM and patent laws are transplanted from other more mature legal regimes, and then countries are faced with the task of transforming such laws to meet evolving local needs of the recipient country. Thus, patent regimes have been weakened in certain countries in order to shift low-income economies into the middle-income stages.[29] As one study concluded, national IPR policy should be holistically implemented in relation to how the IPR ecosystem works with the different development stages. Thus, in relation to Korean firms, the finding was that national policies should cater for different levels and different forms of IPRs for different development stages: from UMs at an earlier stage to designs in export-oriented sectors or trademarks in domestic market-oriented sectors, and finally to patents at the later development stages.[30]

Using existing laws as a base template, developing countries are thus free to formulate or reject UM protection as they see fit. And should a country introduce such a regime, it can emulate existing regimes or build a bespoke system which is exclusively adapted to local socio-economic conditions and infrastructure subject to mutual reciprocity rules.[31]

22.2.1 *Narrow, Short and Non-registered?*[32]

The next step would be to consider the undesirable consequences of introducing a UM right which is too broad in terms of eligible subject matter, duration and scope

[25] EU – CARIFORUM European Partnership Agreement and the Japan-Indonesia Economic Partnership Agreement; see generally Grosse Ruse-Khan 2012.

[26] Germany – Pakistan Bilateral Investment Agreement 2009; Japan-Indonesia Economic Partnership Agreement 2007; German Model Bilateral Investment Treaty 2005. See Grosse Ruse-Khan 2015, 14–15; Liberti 2010.

[27] WIPO 2023d.

[28] Heikkilä 2023a, 2.

[29] Prud'homme 2017a cites many empirical studies; of note is that by Maskus and Penubarti 1995.

[30] Lee et al. 2019, 2, 31–32. See also Chapter 12 (Korea).

[31] Paris Convention, Arts 4(E)(1), 4(E)(2), Art. 5A, Arts. 5D and 11. It should be noted that Paris Union countries cannot discriminate against a foreign rights holders in terms of recognition and enforcement of such utility models pursuant to the generally applicable national treatment obligation. Reciprocal national treatment will also apply for select international principles including the right of priority, the importation and forfeiture clauses, and the compulsory licensing arrangements.

[32] This section is based on a longer discussion published as: Suthersanen 2019, 2–24.

of protection. Such concerns can include: excessive protection of innovations leading to an increase in wasteful claims and litigation; increased rent-seeking behaviour re-directing funding away from innovation or marketing to obtaining more rights via UM; over-utilization by foreign companies accompanied by under-utilization by local firms, leading to an increased outward flow of royalties and licensing fees; using UM system to cordon off research areas.

I would suggest, however, that the most fundamental questions to determine are:

Subject matter: Developing countries, in particular, should be cautious in broadening protection to cover all types of innovations – irrespective of whether they are minor and low-cost innovations, or whether they involve complex and cutting edge technologies such as biological and pharmaceutical products.[33] Previous experiences show that a generous UM regime will attract larger market players who use the UM regime as a means of circumventing the more stringent criteria under the patent system, and overuse the system in ways that make it hard for SMEs to compete.[34] Conversely, some of the UM laws are confined to protecting three-dimensional functional or technical designs and innovations, the term of protection is to a short 3–5 year duration, a local novelty threshold is adopted, and the scope of protection is limited to five or fewer claims.

Patent-type registration: Another consideration is whether developing countries should adopt a registration-based system? Especially one which emulates existing patent regimes, and its accompanying procedural formalities and costs? For example, the Australian Government's report noted that one of the illusory benefits of the "innovation patent" regime was that the upfront and maintenance costs for innovation and standard patents were similar.[35] From the German perspective, it is apparent that imposing identical application structures on both standard patents and UMs (i.e. claims, description and drawings) results in incurring the same costs in the form of the trained patent agent. "The idea that a utility model application needs less care and competence than a patent application can have fatal consequences especially for sole inventors".[36] And surely a quick, automatic right would solve the needs of SMEs to obtain quick injunctive relief again copying?

[33] Thus, the draft EU utility model proposal excluded biological or pharmaceutical inventions on two grounds: such subject matter calls for lengthy preparation before being placed on the market and should therefore be given patent protection that lasts longer than UM protection; and that these sectors are complex areas in which property rights involving no examination as to novelty or inventive step are out of place.

[34] See Chapter 10 (Australia).

[35] Productivity Commission (Australia) 2016, 248–258.

[36] Königer 2017.

Hybrid design/UK right: An alternative way to protect cumulative or minor innovation would be to introduce a hybrid IPR fashioned on both industrial design and UM principle – such as the United Kingdom-type unregistered design right which extends to protecting functional shapes.[37] Historically, this is rather similar to first second-tier patent systems in the world. Both the British and German laws incorporated elements that would ordinarily constitute functional or utilitarian designs or objectives with spatial forms.[38]

22.2.2 *For Whom? Local Industries and SMEs*

Who are the ultimate beneficiaries of UM laws? It may be that this will be dependent on the innovative capacity of each country, which in turn will depend on the industrial sector in focus. As this author and others have previously highlighted, a key argument for UMs is the ability of such second-tier laws to prevent free-riding and imitative copying. This is more so in relation to certain types of product sectors which are concerned, not so much with revolutionary technological breakthroughs, but more so with incremental or improvement innovation. And that it is quite likely that individuals or SMEs have a large presence in such industries where minor innovation is the norm, and unfair copying is rife.

Prud'homme, for example, notes several studies showing how UMs have had a significant effect on the labour productivity in China, with some benefit accruing directly to individual inventors and SMEs.[39] Similar reasons were also offered by the European Commission when it initially proposed the (unsuccessful) draft UM directive. In addition to highlighting certain local European industries in need of further protection, the Commission had highlighted the failure of patent law to protect minor innovations from SMEs.[40] The contrary narrative stems from Australia where a 2015 report noted that it was "unable to obtain adequate empirical evidence as to whether the system does or does not stimulate innovation" in Australian SMEs; a year later, the Australian Government's Productivity report concluded that the UM system had failed to be a strategic tool to help SMEs.[41] More recent surveys note that it is the larger firms with more resources and IPR know-how who have utilized UMs as complementary instruments.[42]

[37] Ss. 213 et seq., United Kingdom Copyright, Designs and Patents Act 1988. The UK sui generis unregistered design right protects functional three-dimensional shapes, using much lower criteria. See also Chapter 3 (UK).

[38] The 1843 UK Utility Designs Act; 1891 German Act on Utility Models. Bently and Sherman 1997; Janis 1999, 156; Suthersanen 2006; Königer 2017.

[39] Prud'homme 2017a, citing several empirical studies from 2002 to 2011. See also Chapter 17.

[40] European Commission 1995.

[41] Australian Government's Advisory Council on Intellectual Property 2015, 28; Johnson et al. 2015; Australian Government Productivity Commission 2016.

[42] For sceptics of the SME/sole innovator argument, see Radauer et al. 2019.

There are grumbles even under the much-lauded German UM system, with one commentator going as far as to suggest – as I do above – why not just change patent law and thus render UMs redundant?

> Since the utility model is not examined by the Patent Office, the competitors are forced to examine the validity of the claims. These costs can be especially high for small and medium-sized companies (SMEs) which are not used to such examinations and need more advice. Thus, in many cases, SMEs are not the beneficiaries of the fact that the utility model is not examined, but the victims.[43]

22.3 VALUING "REAL INNOVATION" IN DEVELOPING COUNTRIES: SDGS AND THE "DIVERSE ECONOMIES" PARADIGM

IPRs ostensibly exist to benefit society. But this does not tell us much about the ends they are meant to serve nor how these ends ought to be achieved. Much of the literature and discourse revolve around the elusive and almost undefinable concept of "innovation" (or *minor* innovation).

"Innovative" countries which have national utility model regimes include Japan, China, Republic of Korea and Germany.[44] Conversely, other top "innovative" countries which have not embraced a national utility model regime, and which may or may not have similar economic histories or current innovative practices, include Switzerland, the United States, the United Kingdom, Singapore, Sweden and Canada.[45]

22.3.1 *Registrations Reflect Local Context*

A recurring challenge is to resolve the conflicting picture that emerges from various empirical studies: some countries respond to the existence of a UM system, whilst others barely use it. The discourse in Section 22.2 reflects particularly pertinent considerations when we look at the global statistics issued by WIPO from 2019 to 2023.

With the major exceptions of China, Germany, Japan, Korea, Russia and Ukraine, UMs have not been well exploited in many of these countries. The standard patent protection system has been used more extensively and – apart from China – only a handful of UMs have been filed in those countries offering UM

43 Königer 2017.

44 For instance, the Global Innovation Index (GII) Database compiled by WIPO for 2023 rank these countries as follows: Germany (8), Korea (10), China (12), Japan (13).

45 As classified by the GII Database 2023: Switzerland (1), Sweden (2), the United States (3), the United Kingdom (4), Singapore (5) and Canada (15).

protection.[46] Heikkilä's work shows that for each of the 40 years preceding 2020, UM filings at the patent offices of China, Japan, the Republic of Korea and Germany accounted for about 90 per cent or more of all global utility model filings.[47] If we focus solely at the global filings in 2023, we get an impressive figure of 3 million plus filings for UMs as opposed to 3.5 million for patents, and 1.5 million for industrial designs.[48] But 2.95 million filings originated in a single country – China. The second top country in terms of filing is Germany recording a very modest filing number at 9469.[49]

If we turn to look at other regions, the registration figures remain low. For example, the 2022 ASEAN region statistics show the following approximations:[50]

Indonesia – 3,200
Thailand – 3,700
Malaysia – 200 plus
Cambodia – 13 (in 2018 registrations)
Philippines – 1,800 plus
Vietnam – 340

It is also difficult to reconcile the development ethos with the low registration rate in some African states which come under the Harare Protocol.[51] On the one hand, the UM system is treated as being a success in Kenya since (i) there has been a continuous increase in the UM application rate annually, and (ii) more than 90 per cent of UM applications were made by local entities. However, the actual numbers remain low: prior to 2015 when substantive examination was carried out on UMs, the success rate was as follows: out of 450 UM applications, 85 were registered (18.8 per cent success rate).[52]

However, what do these statistics reveal other than registration is not a preferred mode by sole or small entitles? Do the registration figures for China indicate high innovative capacity or is it due to China's distinctive national innovation policy which embraces, *inter alia,* innovation parks, IPRs pledge loans, compulsory

[46] Harrison 2023, 128. Harrison interestingly correlates the growth of UM systems in Central and Eastern European countries from the fall of the Soviet Union and the establishment of the market economy. And it may be that many of the former Soviet Bloc countries felt the need to implement a low-cost IPR for the encouragement and protection of local industry. But Harrison notes that the Eastern European systems were set up with the help of the German Patent and Trade Mark Office.

[47] Heikkilä 2023a.

[48] WIPO IP Facts and Figures, www.wipo.int/en/ipfactsandfigures/patents

[49] www3.wipo.int/ipstats/key-search/search-result?type = KEY&key = 231

[50] WIPO IP Statistics.

[51] Harare Protocol on Patents and Industrial Designs within the Framework of the. African Regional Intellectual Property Organization (1982).

[52] Mboya 2018.

licences and talent plans?[53] And to what extent do registration statistics indicate the local innovative environment or show that UM systems encourage domestic innovation?

22.3.2 *Determining "Local Innovation"*

Many economists, by focussing on Schumpeter's narrow usage of innovation, see innovation as something which introduces new technology to the market.[54] This tends to view innovation as something inextricably linked to patent systems, and usually as extractive and capitalist commodities – discussed further in Section 22.3.3.

However, as Scherer points out, innovation does occur in cultural spheres such as music performance and composition, film making and book writing.[55] Innovation must be understood in the broader Schumpeterian sense: the usage of information in the creation of scientific and cultural goods. A correlated view is that most innovations, as opposed to groundbreaking and dramatic inventions, are routine and primarily devoted to product improvement or enhanced user-friendliness or searches for new uses for those products.[56]

In sum, innovation is a complex process intertwined with factors such as the strength of the knowledge base, institutional arrangements, qualifications of the labour force, openness of the economy and an overall ability to take on board improvements achieved in other countries or sectors.[57]

It may be more helpful to treat IP systems holistically and also as public policy regulatory institutions. Institutions that evolve over time and operate in diverse ways according to the local innovation and economic contexts. Therefore, the same UM system may be appropriate and functional in one context (e.g. under China's national innovation policy) but inappropriate and dysfunctional in another (e.g. the Australian example). It can be difficult to predict how well such an institution transplanted to a completely different cultural, political or economic milieu will work in practice. And history offers some clear and important indicators. Take the case of Germany where UMs were introduced when the changing economic and industrial policies and landscape generated a perfect incubator for the newly coherent and unified industrial property policy, in the German free trade area in the late

[53] "Talent plans" (offering financial rewards, housing benefits, etc. to overseas Chinese expats) – see Shao 2014. See also Chapter 10 (China).

[54] Note Merges' very narrow perspective: "An innovation is the 'debugged' and functional version of the invention: the version first offered for sale". Merges 1988, 807, 845 *cf* 851. See also Nelson and Winter 1982, 263.

[55] Scherer 2001, 12.

[56] Baumol 2002, 22.

[57] Dutfield and Suthersanen 2004.

nineteenth century. And with Germany industrialising rapidly, the anti-monopoly and anti-patent movements were collapsing.

22.3.3 *Observing and Valuing "Real Innovation": Diverse Economies: An Inventory of Local Entrepreneurship*

Part of the problem with any UM study is, I believe, the approach which accepts the categorization of UMs as "industrial property" under the Paris Convention. This leads to the logical extension of perceiving UMs as a subaltern second-tier regime, as an off-shoot of the "parent first-tier" patent regime, and as being a registered right. This is curious when one argument for UMs is the "flexibility" inherent in international IP and the flexibility that most nations presume when designing bespoke utility model laws.[58] It is arguable that the true test of the flexibility of UM systems would be to escape the strict IP typology and if UMs can be re-fashioned so as to protect "local innovation" in a broader and more meaningful fashion. The optimal way forward would be to (i) identify with precision the innovation culture within the country, thus optimizing the entire IPR framework needed, (ii) identify which cottage or fledgling industries are to be encouraged, thus tailoring the subject matter of protection to such industries, and (iii) map the different stages of development within that country for those specific industries.

I suggest that this sort of analysis, which will differ according to different economic and technological contexts, may be undertaken within the diverse economies framework. This theoretical framework has been labelled as a Marxist approach though a more gentle description may be that the diverse economies framework invites us to consider the heterogeneity of economic practices which produce knowledge and endeavours (including innovation).[59]

Developing countries should cast a wide net to inventorize, capture and valorize all sorts of innovative activities, which are not necessarily produced as surplus, through locally grounded enterprises including cooperative, ecological, communal, non-profit and tribal enterprises. Such a diverse economies inventory may work to identify why, despite local innovative practices, there is so little interest in registration systems. Examples of diverse enterprises include:

> tenant farmers in India who are in feudal-like relationships but manage up to one-fifth of India's land holdings; or self-employed farmers in Kenya that make up almost 500 million small farm households worldwide;[60]

[58] Janis 1999; Suthersanen 2006; Boztosun 2010; Grosse Ruse-Khan 2012; WIPO's Database on Flexibilities in the Intellectual Property System considers utility models as a type of flexibility, available at www.wipo.int/ipdevelopment/en/agenda/flexibilities/database.html

[59] The examples and discussion are based primarily on Cameron 2021, 26–39; St Martin 2021, 271–282.

[60] Cameron 2021, 27–28.

> the Mondragon Corporation representing 250 companies in the Basque region of Spain who engage in participatory cooperative activities to produce "innovative" products across finance, industrial, retail and knowledge sectors;[61] and
>
> the Trent Market Garden/Flint Corn Community projects which are mixed student, Aboriginal cultural knowledge, and Indigenous seed saving supply and educational initiatives.[62]

If we focus on IPRs and local innovation, a good example is the Sri Lankan cosmetics industry which incorporates traditional knowledge. According to findings, such industries are hesitant to use the patent system due to fear of (i) disclosure of valuable information to competitors, (ii) delays in the registration process which affects the short product life-cycle, (iii) lack of novelty and inventive step. And thus the authors suggest that UMs may be very appropriate for Sri Lanka at this stage.[63]

More engagingly for our purposes, the diverse economies outlook asks policy makers to re-think and re-frame the "type" of sole innovators/SMEs that work and live in specific contexts. Are we expecting them to be the capitalist entrepreneur at the heart of the economic process: the heroic, charismatic, special people, with high levels of vigour, persistence and self-esteem, rational Western white males? Or can we expand our vision to include, say, SME owners who have limited cash flows and an unsympathetic bank manager?

> Small and medium-sized enterprise (SME) owners often "just about manage" [...]in the global South, this is especially so. [...] Many fail, and enthusiasts for entrepreneurialism pay too little attention to the costs of this failure in financial terms (leading to debt poverty, perhaps homelessness) and in terms of mental health issues, internalization of feelings of being a "loser" who made "bad choices" in the enterprise culture, family breakups, and homelessness.[64]

In this reality, SME owners may have very limited time, cash, energy and resources, it is odd, therefore, to believe that a *registered* system, with complex forms calling for legal services, would be the pathway to economic success in developing countries. Moreover, a truly local and small business is usually embedded within the local communities – staying through good times and bad, having a reputation to maintain, and using their surplus profits to support local services, groups, pubs and cafes, etc.[65]

And yet, I have not found any UM law which emphasizes the "IPRs for local businesses" link or threshold.[66] Or else, one finds this link within national innovation

[61] https://innovative-thinking.mondragon-corporation.com/?idioma = en#seccion-pcolaborativos
[62] Lyne and Madden 2021, 78–79.
[63] Hewage and Sampath 2015, 107.
[64] North 2021, 98–105.
[65] North 2021, 102–103.
[66] Harrison 2023, 128.

policies such as the Chinese policy – which has led to more enthusiastic local participation. This re-assessment of "local innovation" can also vary widely despite the category of "developing countries". The starting assumption is that the latter term refers to a country with comparatively low economic output, the World Bank uses "developing countries" as a convenient nomenclature for "low and middle income countries", and bases its categorization on the gross national income (GNI). The UNDP Human Development Index looks at several factors in order to classify countries according to its "level of human development", whilst the UN itself uses "developed regions, and developing regions, and Least Developed Countries" and the IMF employs "advanced economies, emerging and developing economies". Therefore, Malawi and Mexico are developing countries but their respective GNIs are disparate: US$250 v US$9,860. This, in turn, does not explain other "developing" considerations, for example a developed country may still be an IP net importer nation.

22.3.4 *Linking Innovation and UMs to SDGs*

A final suggestion is that developing countries seriously consider tying UM legislation with SDGs, expressly in the statute or with a national innovation policy paper. "Innovation is not an end in and of itself: innovation is an instrumental good".[67] Or as the WIPO policy paper on the SDGs states:

> [w]e need innovation to help us rethink how to overcome poverty, hunger and premature mortality, how to combat climate change and preserve our natural world, how to optimize the use of artificial intelligence, and how to shape the future of work.[68]

The value scheme under SDG9 can be linked, in a similar manner as advocated under the diverse economies theory, to the types of innovative and entrepreneurial activities which are of importance in the Global South (but not necessarily in the US or EU): build resilient infrastructure, promote inclusive and sustainable industrialization and foster innovation.

We leave the final note to Noto La Diega, Cifrodelli and Dermawan who advocate this perspective in the new technological field of AI-generated inventions. The question is whether developing countries should adopt the US/EU perspective of what constitutes patentable innovation, or do such countries adopt SDG9 values since they "constitute an incentive for the promotion of sustainable industrialisation and the upgrade of technological capabilities".[69] Thus,

[67] Noto La Diega et al. 2024, 538, 565–567. Similarly, it has been noted that "[s]ustainable innovation deems welfare an intrinsic value and income generation an instrumental value" – António Abreu 2021, 257.

[68] WIPO 2021, 1.

[69] Noto La Diega et al. 2024, 565; McDave and Hackman-Aidoo 2021 (advocating for stronger IPRs in light of industrial development in Africa.)

> [t]o simply "export" the rationale for rejecting AI inventorship to the Global South should be regarded as a form of "patent colonialism". Based on a deeper understanding of the wider industrial and socio-economic context, governments in the Global South should be able to use the patent system as both an industrial policy tool and a means for sustainability, and this may well include the acceptance of AI systems as inventors.[70]

70 Noto La Diega et al. 2024, 567.

Bibliography

BOOKS, ARTICLES AND ONLINE MATERIALS

Abrantes, A. 'Brasil e o Alvará de 1809: uma ideia fora do lugar?' *Notícias em Patentes*, August 3, 2014. http://patentescomentarios.blogspot.com/2014/08/brasil-e-lei-de-patentes-de-1830-uma.html.

Abreu, António. 2021. *Innovation Ecosystems: A Sustainability Perspective*. Basel: MDPI.

Administrative Conf. of the U.S. (ACUS). 2023. 'Report on Patent Small Claims'. Retrieved December 6, 2023. www.acus.gov/report/report-patent-small-claims.

Adocker, Thomas. 2011. 'Österreichischer Oberster Patent- und Markensenat trifft Grundsatzentscheidung zum Verhältnis zwischen der Erfindungshöhe eines Patents und eines Gebrauchsmusters'. *GRUR International* 60(8/9): 673–676.

Alexander, Isabella. 2020. 'The Challenges of Intellectual Property Legal History Research', in Graeme Austin, Andrew Christie, Andrew Christie, and Megan Richardson, eds., *Across Intellectual Property: Essays in Honour of Sam Ricketson*. Cambridge: Cambridge University Press.

Allison, John, Mark Lemley, and David Schwartz. 2014. 'Understanding the Realities of Modern Patent Litigation'. *Texas Law Review* 92: 1769–1801.

Anon. 1840. 'Copyright of Designs'. *London Journal of Arts and Sciences* 16: 95.

1843a. 'An Act to Amend the Law Relating to the Copyright of Designs'. *London Journal of the Arts, Sciences and Manufactures and Repertory of Patent Inventions* 23: 143–147.

1843b. 'Copyright of Designs: The New Act'. *Mechanics' Magazine* 39(1047): 164.

1843c. 'List of Designs for Articles of Utility Registered under 5 & 6 Vict Cap 65'. *Mechanics' Magazine* 39(1051): 254.

1843d. 'New Copyright of Designs Act'. *London Journal of the Arts, Sciences and Manufactures and Repertory of Patent Inventions* 23: 228.

1843e. 'List of Registrations Effected under the Act for Protecting New and Original Designs for Articles of Utility'. *London Journal of the Arts, Sciences and Manufactures and Repertory of Patent Inventions* 23: 310.

1844. 'Police'. *The Times*, November 6 : 8.

1845. 'Police Courts: Guildhall'. *The Morning Advertiser*, March 24: 4.

1846a. 'A Terrible Army'. *Daily News*, April 27: 7.

1846b. 'Registration of Designs and the Registrar'. *Patent Journal and Inventors' Magazine* 1 (17): 248, 297–299.
1847a. 'Case of Alleged Infringement of Registered Design'. *Mechanics' Magazine* 46(1236): 383.
1847b. 'Copyright Designs as Distinguished from Patentable Inventions.' *Aris's Birmingham Gazette*. September 6: 3.
1847c. 'Patents v. Registration'. *Patent Journal and Inventors' Magazine* 2(43): 705.
1847d. 'The Aldermen and the Registration Act'. *Patent Journal and Inventors' Magazine* 2 (47): 772.
1847e. 'The Degrees of Protection Available to the Inventor under the Patent Laws and Non-Ornamental Designs Act, Relatively Considered'. *London Journal of the Arts, Sciences and Manufactures and Repertory of Patent Inventions* 30: 367–368.
1848a. 'Infringement of Registration'. *Patent Journal and Inventors' Magazine* 4(92): 335.
1848b. 'Reviews'. *Jurist* (Part II) 11: 275.
1849a. *The Builder*, 7(338): 359.
1849b. 'Ventilating Bricks'. *The Practical Mechanic's Journal* 2(18): 142.
1850a. 'Cheapening Patents'. *The Builder* 8(373): 151.
1850b. 'Extension of Copyright in Design – Provisional Registration – Patent Reform'. *Journal of Design* 4: 103.
1850c. 'Law of Copyright of Designs Amendment Act'. *Practical Mechanic's Journal* 3(31): 159.
1850d. 'Patent Agency and Its Professors' (a letter from a patentee). *London Journal of the Arts, Sciences and Manufactures and Repertory of Patent Inventions* 36: 321–324.
1850e. *Morning Chronicle*, October 24: 5 (Editorial).
1850f. 'Patent Law Reform'. *Patent Journal and Inventors' Magazine* 9: 180.
1850g. 'The Registration Act'. *Patent Journal and Inventors' Magazine* 9: 122.
1850h. 'The Registration Acts'. *Patent Journal and Inventors' Magazine* 9: 144–145.
1850i. 'The Existing Patent Laws, Their Defects and Remedies'. *The Engineer and Machinist: A Journal of Mechanical and Manipulative Arts* No 1: 2.
1851a. 'Invasion of the Rights of Inventors'. *The Engineer and Machinist: A Journal of Mechanical and Manipulative Art* 21: 259.
1851b. 'Patent Law Reform'. *Morning Advertiser*, January 8: 3.
1851c. 'The Prospects of the Bar'. *Law Magazine* 15: 276–280.
1851d. 'Review of Spence'. *The Practical Mechanics Journal* 4(41): 110.
1852. 'Multum in Parvo'. *Norwich Mercury*, October 2: 4.
1854. 'The City of London Corporation Inquiry'. *Law Review & Quarterly Journal of British & Foreign Jurisprudence* 19(2): 389.
1856. 'William Clarkson'. *Illustrated London News*, November 1: 11.
1858a. 'Insolvent Debtors'. *London Gazette*, April 20: 1981; April 27: 2091.
1858b. 'The Patent Law and Patent Office'. *Mechanics' Magazine* 68: 486,
1859a. 'Insolvent Debtors Court, Failure of Messrs Knight and Lacey'. *London Courier and Evening Gazette*, October 5, 1859: 4.
1859a. 'Editorial'. *Illustrated London News*, January 15: 6–7.
1864. 'Peregrine Bingham Esq.' *Illustrated London News*, November 12: 23.
1866. 'Memoir of William Johnson'. *Annual Report of the Institution of Civil Engineers*, reprinted in *Lancaster Gazette*, November 10: 10.
1868. *London Gazette*, November 13: 5903.
1875. 'Obituary. Thomas Webster, Q.C., F.R.S.'. *Journal of the Society of Arts* 23: 665–666.
1884. 'Copyright of Designs'. *Official Journal of the Patent Office* 91: 1086.

1891. 'Designs'. *The Illustrated Official Journal* (Patents). July 8, 131: 567.

1904. 'Death of Mr. George Shaw: A Remarkable Career'. *Birmingham Daily Mail.* August 15: 2.

Arrow, Kenneth. 1962. 'Economic Welfare and the Allocation of Resources for Invention', in National Bureau of Economic Research, *The Rate and Direction of Inventive Activity.* Princeton, NJ: Princeton University Press.

Atal, V. and Bar, T. 2014. 'Patent Quality and a Two-Tiered Patent System'. *Journal of Industrial Economics* 62(3): 503–540.

Auerbach, Sascha. 2021. *Armed with Swords & Scales: Law, Culture and Local Courtrooms in London, 1860–1913*. Cambridge: Cambridge University Press.

Balicki, Marcin. 2020a. Sto lat w cieniu patent – ochrona wzorów użytkowych w Polsce, w: Alicja Adamczak, 100 lat ochrony własności przemysłowej w Polsce. Księga jubileuszowa Urzędu Patentowego Rzeczypospolitej Polskiej, Wolters Kluwer.

2020b. Wzór już nie-użyteczny? Nowelizacja definicji wzoru użytkowego ustawą z 16.10.2019 r. o zmianie ustawy – Prawo własności przemysłowej, ZNUJ. PPWI 2020/2/10-24, LEX.

Barbieri, Massimo. August 19, 2017. Utility Models in the Italian Patent System. https://ssrn.com/abstract=3022432 or http://dx.doi.org/10.2139/ssrn.3022432. Last revised in 2022.

Barbosa, Denis Borges. 2020. *Tratado da Propriedade Intelectual: Patentes.* 2nd ed. Rio de Janeiro: Lumen Juris.Baron, Justus, Arque-Castells, P., Leonard, A., Pohlmann, T., and Sergheraert, E. 2023. Empirical Assessment of Potential Challenges in SEP Licensing, Report Commissioned by the Eur. Comm'n Directorate-General for Internal Market, Industry, Entrepreneurship and SMEs, GROW/2021/MVP/0010 (GROW/2021/MVP/0010). Directorate-General for Internal Market, Industry, Entrepreneurship and SMEs.

Baron, Justus, and Tim Pohlmann. 2018. 'Mapping Standards to Patents Using Declarations of Standard-Essential Patents'. *Journal of Economics & Management Strategy*, 27: 504–534.

Barthes, Roland 1977a. 'Rhetoric of the Image' in Stephen Heath (trans. and ed.), *Image, Music, Text.* London: Fontana.

1977b. 'The Photographic Message' in Stephen Heath (trans. and ed.), *Image, Music, Text.* London: Fontana.

Bartow, Ann. 2000. 'Separating Marketing Innovation from Actual Invention: A Proposal for a New, Improved, Lighter, and Better-Tasting Form of Patent Protection'. *Journal of Small & Emerging Business Law* 4(1): 1–26.

Baumbauer, Derek. 2024. 'Everything You Want: The Paradox of Customized Intellectual Property Regimes.' *Berkeley Technology Law Journal* 39: 205–274.

Baumol, William. 2002. *The Free-Market Innovation Machine.* Princeton, NJ: Princeton University Press.

BBC. 2001. 'Lawyer Moves to Patent Wheel', *BBC*, July 2, http://news.bbc.co.uk/2/hi/asia-pacific/1418165.stm

Beier, Friedrich-Karl. 1991. 'The Future of Intellectual Property in Europe. Thoughts on the Development of Patent, Utility Model and Industrial Design Law'. *International Review of Intellectual Property and Competition Law* 22(2): 157–177.

Beier, Friedrich-Karl, R. Krasser, K. Haertel, and T. Bodewig. 1994. 'Proposal of the Max Planck Institute for a European Utility Model – Explanatory Report'. *International Review of Intellectual Property and Competition Law* 25(5): 700–735.

Bellido, Jose, and Kathy Bowrey. 2022. *Adventures in Childhood Intellectual Property, Imagination and the Business of Play*. Cambridge: Cambridge University Press.

Bekkers, Rudi, and Updegrove, Andrew. 2013. *IPR Policies and Practices of a Representative Group of Standards-Setting Organizations Worldwide*. Washington, DC: National Research Council. https://rbekkers.ieis.tue.nl/nas/Bekkers_Updegrove_NAS2013_updated_report.pdf

Bekkers, Rudi, C. Catalini, A. Martinelli, Cesare Righi, and Tim Simcoe. 2023. 'Disclosure Rules and Declared Essential Patents'. *Research Policy* 52: 104618.

Bentley, David. 1998. *English Criminal Justice in the Nineteenth Century*. London: The Hambledon Press.

Bently, Lionel. 2004. 'Copyright and the Victorian Internet: Telegraphic Property Laws in Colonial Australia'. *Loyola Los Angeles Law Review* 38: 71–176.

2018. 'The Design-Copyright Conflict in the United Kingdom: A History', in E. Derclaye, ed., *The Copyright-Designs Interface*. Cambridge: Cambridge University Press, ch 6 171–225.

Bently, Lionel, and Brad Sherman. 1997. 'The United Kingdom's Forgotten Utility Model: The Utility Designs Act 1843'. *Intellectual Property Quarterly* 25(3): 265–278.

Bian, Renjun. 2018. 'Patent Litigation in China: Challenging Conventional Wisdom'. *Berkeley Technology Law Journal* 33(2): 413–486.

Bianchin, S. 2021. Utility Model – The Underestimated Property Right. *Intelligent Asset Management*, October 21. www.iam-media.com/global-guide/innovation-invention-yearbook/2022/article/utility-model-the-underestimated-property-right

Bielig, A. 2015. 'Intellectual Property and Economic Development in Germany: Empirical Evidence for 1999–2009'. *European Journal of Law and Economics* 39: 607–622.

Billing, Sidney, and Alexander Prince. 1845. *The Law and Practice of Patents and Registration of Designs*. London: Benning & Co.

Bings, Sophie. 2018. 'Art. 118 AEUV', in Rudolg Streinz, ed., *EUV/AEUV. Vertrag über die Europäische Union. Vertrag über die Arbeitsweise der Europäischen Union. Charta der Grundrechte der Europäischen Union*. 3rd ed. Munich: C. H. Beck.

Björkwall, Pia. 2009. *Nyttighetsmodeller: Ett ändamålsenligt innovationsskydd?* Doctoral dissertation, Svenska handelshögskolan, Helsinki.

Bodenhausen G. H. C. 1969. *Guide to the Application of the Paris Convention for the Protection of Industrial Property, as revised at Stockholm in 1967*. Geneva: WIPO.

Bonadio, Enrico, and Patrick Goold, eds. 2023. *The Cambridge Handbook of Investment-Driven Intellectual Property*. Cambridge: Cambridge University Press.

Bond, Catherine. 2016. *Anzac: The Landing, the Legend, the Law*. Melbourne: Australian Scholarly Publishing.

Boschert, Tyler J. 2014. 'Would Utility Models Improve American Innovation – Evidence from Brazil, Germany, and the United States'. *Colorado Technology Law Journal* 12: 133.

Bostosun, N. Ayse Odman. 2010. 'Exploring the Utility of Utility Models for Fostering Innovation'. *Journal of Intellectual Property Rights* 15: 429.

Bottomley, Sean. 2014a. *The British Patent System and the Industrial Revolution, 1700–1852: From Privilege to Property*. Cambridge: Cambridge University Press.

2014b. 'Patenting in England, Scotland and Ireland during the Industrial Revolution, 1700–1852'. *Explorations in Economic History* 54: 48–63.

2019. 'Patents, Invention and Democracy in Britain and the United States to 1852'. *Jahrbuch für Wirtschaftsgeschichte* 60(1): 9–30.

Bouvier-Ravon, Sandrine, and Daniel Hoppe. 2024. 'Injunctive Relief Based on Published European Patent Applications'. *European Patent Litigation in Practice* 1(1): 5–10.

Bowen, J. H. 1843. 'Notice Issued by the Registrar: Copyright of Designs for Articles of Utility'. *Repertory of Patent Inventions* 2: 251.

Bowrey, Kathy, ed. 2021. *Feminist Perspectives on Law, Law Schools and Law Reform: Essays in Honour of Professor Jill McKeough*. Sydney: Federation Press.
Boztosun, N. Ayse Odman. 2010. 'Exploring the Utility of Utility Models for Fostering Innovation'. *Journal of Intellectual Property Rights* 15: 429–439.
Brack, Hans-Peter. 2009. 'Utility Models and Their Comparison with Patents and Implications for the US Intellectual Property Law System'. *Boston College Intellectual Property and Technology Forum* 2009: 1–15.
Brennan, David, and John Keough. 2000. 'Patenting the Wheel', *The Australian Financial Review*, December 20.
Brewster, David. 1850. 'Address to British Association for the Advancement of Science', in 'The British Association', *The Scotsman*, August 3: 5.
British Electrical Allied Manufacturers Association. 1916. BT 209/486.
British Science Guild. 1928. *Report on the Reform of British Patent System*. London: British Science Guild.
Burk, Dan L., and Mark A. Lemley. 2009. *The Patent Crisis and How the Courts Can Solve It*. Chicago: University of Chicago Press.
Burke, Kelly, and Kate McClymont. 2009. 'This Is Patent Nonsense', *The Sydney Morning Herald*, May 23. www.smh.com.au/national/this-is-patent-nonsense-20090522-bia2.html
Bury, Marek. 2022. 'Protection of Utility Models in Poland: A Brief History and Perspective for the Future'. *Law and Business* 2(1): 35–47.
Business Times Singapore. 2001. 'Achievements Nobel and Otherwise', *Business Times Singapore*, October 10.
Cabinent Beau de Lomenie. 2014. 'The French Patent System'. www.bdl-ip.com/
Cahoy, Daniel R., and Lynda J. Oswald. 2021. 'Is Legal Harmonization Always Better? The Counter-Case of Utility Models'. *American Business Law Journal* 58(3): 525–578.
Calabrese, Bernardo. 2020. 'Preminenza del brevetto europeo e autonomia del brevetto italiano'. *Giurisprudenza commerciale* 2020(3): II, 574–593.
Calabresi, Guido, and A. Douglas Melamed. 1972. 'Property Rules, Liability Rules, and Inalienability: One View of the Cathedral'. *Harvard Law Review* 85(6): 1089–1128.
Cameron, J. 2021. 'Framing Essay: The Diversity of Enterprise', in Gibson-Graham and K. Dombroski, eds., *The Handbook of Diverse Economies*. Cheltenham: Edward Elgar.
Campin, Frederick W. 1851. 'Patent Law Reform', *Morning Advertiser*, June 5, p. 2 (letter).
Cao, Siwei. 2015. *Patent System, Firm Patenting Strategy and Technology Progress*. PhD Thesis, University of California, Berkeley.
Cao, Siwei, Zhen Lei, and Brian Wright. 2014. 'Speed vs. Length of Patent Protection Evidence from Innovations Patented in U.S and China'. https://are.berkeley.edu/sites/default/files/job-candidates/pdfs/SiweiCao_WP101214.pdf
Carey, Peter. 2003. *My Life as a Fake*. New York: Knopf.
Carpmael, William. 1832. *The Law of Patents for Inventions, Familiarly Explained*. London: G. Wightman.
1846. *Registration of Designs in Order to Secure Copyright*. 3rd ed. London: Mackintosh.
Caterson, Simon. 2006. *Hoax!: A Short History of Fakes, Frauds and Imposters*, Melbourne: Hardie Grant Books.
2009. *Hoax Nation: Australian Fakes and Frauds from Plato to Norma Khouri*. Melbourne: Arcade Publications.
Ceccagnoli, Marco. 2009. 'Appropriability, Preemption, and Firm Performance'. *Strategic Management Journal* 30(1): 81–98.
Chang, Jinkyu. 2017. 'Study on the Management of Utility Model System'. *The Journal of Intellectual Property* 12(4): 103–134.

Chartered Institute of Patent Agents. 1996. 'Designs and Copyright Committee of CIPA Response'. *Journal of the Chartered Institute of Patent Agents* 25: 897.

Chen, Ruifang. 1983. 'The Utility Model System and Its Benefits for China'. *International Review of Intellectual Property and Competition Law* 14: 493.

Chen, Yong. 2013. 'On the Examination of Inventiveness for UMPs'. *Intellectual Property* 2013 (8): 73–76.

Chen, Zhongshan. 2020. 'Standards for Determining Obstruction of Proof and Malicious Infringement'. *The People's Judicature* 2020(8): 84–89.

Chien, Colleen V. 2016. 'Opening the Patent System: Diffusionary Levers in Patent Law'. *Southern California Law Review* 89(4): 793–862.

Choi, Jisun. 2016. 'Statistical Analysis and Its Implications on the Relative Rate of Utilization of Influencing Factors for Each Provision of Article 128 of the Patent Act When Calculating the Amount of Damages for Patent Infringement'. *Review of Law and Economics* 13(2): 248.

Christchurch Press. 2001. 'Wheel Reinvented', *The Christchurch Press*, July 7.

Christie, Andrew, and Sarah Moritz. 2007. 'Australia', in Uma Suthersanen, Graham Dutfield, and Kit Boey Chow, eds., *Innovation without Patents: Harnessing the Creative Spirit in a Diverse World*. Cheltenham:Edward Elgar, 119–141.

Church, Oliver, Estelle Derclaye, and Gilles Stupfler. 2021. 'Design Litigation in the EU Member States: Are Overlaps with Other Intellectual Property Rights and Unfair Competition Problematic and Are SMEs Benefitting from the EU Design Legal Framework?' *European Law Review* 2021(1): 37–60.

Civis. 1845. 'The Last Registration Decision: Woolley v. Warner & Sons'. *Mechanics' Magazine* 42 (1130): 238.

Claeys, Gregory. 2000. 'Political Economy and Popular Education: Thomas Hodgskin and the London Mechanics Institute', in Michael T. Davis, ed., *Radicalism and Revolution in Britain, 1775–1848*. Basingstoke: Macmillan.

Clayton, Tony, Antoine Dechezleprêtre, Hélène Dernis et al. 2023. OECD Study Enhancing Intellectual Property Use for a Stronger Innovation Ecosystem in Poland, OECD. www.oecd-ilibrary.org/docserver/42e389fa-en.pdf?expires = 1707515390&id = id&accname = guest&checksum = 4A38802C1A36771BD2B813A58C4C0EEE

CNN. 2001. 'Man Seeks Square Deal, Patents Wheel', *CNN*, July 2, https://edition.cnn.com/2001/WORLD/asiapcf/auspac/07/02/australia.wheel/

Cochrane, Nathan. 2001a. 'Melbourne Man Tries to Patent the Wheel', *The Age*, July 2.

2001b. 'Patently Theatre in the Round', *The Age*, October 9.

Cocks, Raymond. 1983. *Foundations of the Modern Bar*. London: Sweet & Maxwell.

Cohen Julie, E., and Mark A. Lemley. 2001. 'Patent Scope and Innovation in the Software Industry'. *California Law Review* 89: 1–57.

Cook, Trevor. 2010. *EU Intellectual Property Law*. Oxford: Oxford University Press.

Contreras, Jorge L. 2017a. 'Aggregated Royalties for Top-Down FRAND Determinations: Revisiting 'Joint Negotiation'. *Antitrust Bulletin* 62(4): 690–709.

2017b. 'Essentiality and Standards-Essential Patents', in J. L. Contreras, ed., *Cambridge Handbook of Technical Standardization Law: Competition, Antitrust, and Patents*. Cambridge: Cambridge University Press, 209.

2017c. 'From Private Ordering to Public Law: The Legal Framework Governing Standards-Essential Patents'. *Harvard Journal of Law & Technology* 30: 211.

2018. 'The Anticommons at Twenty: Concerns for Research Continue'. *Science* 361: 335.

2021. 'Patent Reality Checks: Eliminating Patents on Fake, Impossible and Other Inoperative Inventions'. *Journal of the Patent and Trademark Office Society* 102: 2.

Contreras, Jorge L., Cotter, Thomas J., Jong, S. J. et al. 2019. 'The Effect of FRAND Commitments on Patent Remedies', in C. B. Biddle, J. L. Contreras, B. J. Love, and N. V. Siebrasse, eds., *Patent Remedies and Complex Products: Toward a Global Consensus*. Cambridge: Cambridge University Press, 160–201.

Contreras, Jorge L., Djavaherian, Dave, Higgins, C., Jurata, J., and Luken, E., eds. 2022. *Guide to Patent Policies of Standards Development Organizations*. 2nd ed. Chicago: ABA Publishing.

Copinger, Walter A. 1870. *The Law of Copyright in Works of Literature and Art*. London: Stevens & Haynes.

1893. *The Law of Copyright in Works of Literature and Art: Including that of the Drama, Music, Engraving, Sculpture, Painting, Photography, and Designs*. 3rd ed. London: Stevens & Haynes.

Copyright Trolling – skala zjawiska i propozycje rozwiązań, March 10, 2016. https://centrumcyfrowe.pl/czytelnia/copyright-trolling-skala-zjawiska-i-propozycje-rozwiazan/

Cordiner, Tom, et al. 2022. 'Aristocrat Technologies Australia Pty Ltd v Commissioner of Patents', *CommBar Matters*, October 4. https://commbarmatters.com.au/2022/10/04/aristocrat-technologies-australia-pty-ltd-v-commissioner-of-patents/

Cornish W. R. 1993. 'The International Relations of Intellectual Property'. *Cambridge Law Journal* 52(1): 6–63.

Cotter, Thomas F. 2018. *Patent Wars: How Patents Impact Our Daily Lives*. Oxford: Oxford University Press.

Cox, Sarah. 2018. Same-Same but Different: Will the Fate of Second-Tier Patents Be the Same on Both Sides of the Tasman?. www.lexology.com/library/detail.aspx?g = 2b414420-b4e8-4ecd-842d-4a42b018d33a

Craig, Archibald. 1879. *Patents, Trade Marks and Designs*. London: The Bazaar Office.

Crary, Jonathan. 1990. *Techniques of the Observer: On Vision and Modernity in the Nineteenth Century*. Cambridge, MA: MIT.

Crooks, Katrina. 2017. 'Excesses of Innovation Patent Damages Pulled Back', *Mondaq Business Briefing*, April 29.

Cummings, Peter A. 2010. 'From Germany to Australia: Opportunity for a Second Tier Patent System in the United States'. *Michigan State Journal of International Law* 18(2): 297–322.

Cunninghame, H. 1894. *English Patent Practice*. London: Clowes.

Daniels, Edward Morton. 1884. *A Complete Treatise upon the New Law of Patents, Designs and Trade Marks*. London: Stevens & Haynes.

Dashwood, Alan, Michael Dougan, Barry Rodger, Eleanor Spaventa, and Derrick Wyatt. 2011. *Wyatt and Dashwood's European Union Law*. New York: Bloomsbury Publishing.

Davis, Jennifer. 1984 'A Poor Man's System of Justice'. *Historical Journal* 22: 309.

Derzlm, Natalie M. 1996. 'Using Intellectual Property Law and Regulatory Processes to Foster the Innovation and Diffusion of Environmental Technologies'. *Harvard Environmental Law Review* 20: 3.

Dexi, Qiao. 1993. 'A Survey of Intellectual Property Issues in China-U.S. Trade Negotiations under the Special 301 Provisions'. *Pacific Rim Law & Policy Journal* 2: 259, 288.

Di Cataldo, Vincenzo. 2012. *I brevetti per invenzione e per modello di utilità. I disegni e modelli*. Milano: Giuffrè.

Dickens, Charles. 1850. 'Poor Man's Tale of a Patent'. *Household Words* 2: 73–75.

Van Dongen, Lisa. 2023. 'Proportionality and Flexibilities in Final Injunctive Relief', in Alain Strowel et al. eds., *The Unitary Patent Package and Unified Patent Court: Problems, Possible Improvements and Alternatives*. Milan: Ledizioni, 357–387.

2024. Flexibilities in European Patent Enforcement: Law, Practice and Aspiration.

Dreyfuss, Rochelle C., and Daniel Benoliel. 2022. 'Technological Self-Sufficiency and the Role of Novelty Traps'. *Vanderbilt Journal of Entertainment and Technology Law* 24: 441.

Du Mont, Jason J., and Mark D. Janis. 2012. 'Functionality in Design Protection Systems'. *Journal of Intellectual Property Law* 19: 261–302.

2013. 'The Origins of American Design Patent Protection'. *Indiana Law Journal* 88(3): 837–880.

Dutfield, Graham, and Uma Suthersanen. 2004. 'The Innovation Dilemma: Intellectual Property and the Historical Legacy of Cumulative Creativity'. *Intellectual Property Quarterly* 4: 379–421.

Dutton, Harold. 1984. *The Patent System and Inventive Activity during the Industrial Revolution*. Manchester: Manchester University Press.

Edmunds, Lewis. 1890. *The Law and Practice of Letters Patent for Inventions*. London: Stevens & Haynes.

1895. *The Law of Copyright in Designs: Together with the Practice relating to Proceedings in the Courts and in the Patent Office*. London: Sweet & Maxwell.

Egan, Edward J., and David J. Teece. 2015. 'Untangling the Patent Thicket Literature, Tusher Center for the Management of Intellectual Capital Working Paper #7.'

Eisenberg, Rebecca S. 2008. 'Noncompliance, Nonconformist, Nonproblem? Rethinking the Anticommons in Biomedical Research'. *Houston Law Review* 45: 1059.

van Engelen, D. 2004. Beware the Wolf: Questions about the Dutch Registration Patent System. *Patent World, 2003/2004*.

Ercoli, Laura. 2023. 'What's New in the Law Revising Italy's Industrial Property Code'. *Società Italiana Brevetti*, July 26 2023. www.sib.it/en/flash-news/law-revising-italys-industrial-property-code-definitively-approved/

Espacenet. 2024. Patent Documents. https://worldwide.espacenet.com/patent/

Evenson, Robert E., and Larry E. Westphal. 1995. 'Technological Change and Technology Strategy', in Jere Behrman and T. Srinivasan, eds., *Handbook of Development Economics 3a*. Amsterdam: Elsevier. https://econpapers.repec.org/bookchap/eeedevhes/3.htm

Fachin, Luiz E. 1995. 'O estatuto civil da clausura real'. *Revista de Informação Legislativa* 32 (128).

Fazzini, Marco. 2019. 'Sub art. 82 IPC', in Luigi Carlo Ubertazzi, ed., *Commentario breve alle leggi su proprietà intellettuale e concorrenza*. Milano: Wolters Kluwer-CEDAM.

Feng, Xiaoqing. 2009. 'The Interaction between Enhancing the Capacity for Independent Innovation and Patent Protection: A Perspective on the Third Amendment to the Patent Law of the P.R. China'. *Pittsburgh Journal of Technology Law & Policy* 9: 1–130.

Flatow, Ira. 2001. 'Analysis: Ig Nobel Awards for 2001', Talk of the Nation: Science Friday, *NPR*, November 23.

Flexnor, Helen Hudson. 2014. *The London Mechanics' Institution: Social and Cultural Foundation, 1823–1830*. PhD Thesis, University College London.

Floridia, Giorgio. 2000. *Marchi, invenzioni e modelli*. Milano: Giuffrè.

Forrest, Heather Ann. 2004. 'Utility Model: Widening the Economic Divide between 'Legacy' and 'New' EU Member State'. *International Business Lawyer* 32(5): 216–221.

Franceschelli, Maria Luigia, and Giovanni Trabucco. 2023. 'Italy: Major Changes to Intellectual Property Code Come into Force'. *Hogan Lovells Engage*, August 23, 2023. www.engage.hoganlovells.com/knowledgeservices/news/italy-major-changes-to-intellectual-property-code-come-into-force/

Franzosi, Mario. 2008. 'Invenzione e modello di utilità. La Convenzione di Monaco comporta il rifiuto della distinzione qualitativa'. *Rivista di diritto industriale* 2008: I, 159.

Frischtak, Claudio R. 1993. 'Harmonization versus Differentiation in Intellectual Property Right Regimes', in Mitchel B. Wallerstein, Mary E. Mogee, and Robin A. Schoen, eds., *Global Dimensions of Intellectual Property Rights in Science and Technology*. Washington, DC: National Academies Press.

Frost, Robert. 1891. *A Treatise on the Law and Practice regarding Letters Patent for Inventions*. London: Stevens and Haynes.

Fulton, David. 1894. *A Practical Treatise on Patents, Trade Marks and Designs*. London: Jordan & Sons.

1902. *The Law and Practice Relating to Patents, Trade Marks and Designs*, 2nd ed. London: Jordan & Sons.

Gajewski, Daniel. 2019. 'Utility Model Examination in China is Quietly Changing'. *IPWatchdog*. www.ipwatchdog.com/2019/07/28/utility-model-examination-china-quietly-changing/id=111451/

Gallagher, William T., and Debora Halbert. 2021. 'Intellectual Property Law and Sociolegal Studies', in Irene Calboli and Maria Lilla Montagnani, eds., *Handbook of Intellectual Property Research: Lenses, Methods, and Perspectives*. Oxford: Oxford University Press.

Gama, Sonia Cristina Sequeira, Edimilson Junqueira Braga, and Ricardo Carvalho Rodrigues. 2016. 'A Patente de Modelo de Utilidade como ferramenta de estímulo ao desenvolvimento tecnológico nacional'. *Cad. Prospec.* 9(4).

Gao, Lulin. 2019. 'Forty Years of Patent in China', in Liu Chuntian, ed., *Forty Years of Intellectual Property in China*. Intellectual Property Publishing House.

Geiger, Christophe, Craig Allen Nard, and Xavier Seuba. 2018. *Intellectual Property and the Judiciary*. Cheltenham: Edward Elgar.

Germain Maureau. 2023. 'Double Protection between French and European Patents, What's New with the UPC', June 23, 2023. https://germainmaureau.com/en/2023/06/double-protection-between-french-and-european-patents-whats-new-with-the-upc/

Gervais, Daniel. 2008. *The TRIPS Agreement: Drafting History and Analysis*. 3rd ed. London: Sweet & Maxwell.

Ghiron, Mario. 1929. *Corso di diritto industriale*. Roma: Società Editrice del «Foro Italiano».

Gilchrist, Sue, et al. 2022. 'High Court Gamble Does Not Pay Out for Computer-Implemented Inventions in Australia', Herbert Smith Freehills, August 24. www.herbertsmithfreehills.com/latest-thinking/high-court-gamble-does-not-pay-out-for-computer-implemented-inventions-in-australia

Ginarte, Juan, and Walter Park. 1997. 'Determinants of Patent Rights: A Cross-National Study'. *Research Policy* 26: 283–301.

Gisclard, T., and Py, E. 2022. 'France', in J. L. Contreras and M. Husovec, eds., *Injunctions in Patent Law: Trans-atlantic Dialogues on Flexibility and Tailoring*. Cambridge: Cambridge University Press, 124–141.

Godson, Richard. 1823. *A Practical Treatise on the Law of Patents for Invention and of Copyright*. London: J. Butterworth.

Gómez Segade, Jose Antonio. 2008. 'Utility Models – Lost in Translation'. *International Review of Intellectual Property and Competition Law* 39(2): 135–139.

Gooday, Graeme, and Steven Wilf. 2020. *Patent Cultures: Diversity and Harmonization in Historical Perspective*. Cambridge: Cambridge University Press.

Grafton, G. F. 1846. 'To the Editor'. *Patent Journal and Inventors' Magazine* 1: 71.

Grau, Eros R. 1990. *A Ordem Econômica na Constituição de 1988 (Interpretação e Crítica)*. São Paulo: Revista dos Tribunais.

Greco, Paolo, and Vercellone, Paolo. 1968. *Le invenzioni e i modelli industriali*. Torino: UTET.

Griliches, Z. 1990. 'Patent Statistics as Economic Indicators: A Survey'. *Journal of Economic Literature* 28: 1661–1707.

Grosse Ruse-Khan, Henning. 2012. *Utility Model Protection in Pakistan as an Option to Incentivise Minor and Incremental Innovation*. Geneva: WIPO.

2013. 'The International Legal Framework for the Protection of Utility Models'. *The WIPO Journal* 4: 175–190.

Grzybowski, Stanisław. 1978. Prawo wynalazcze – pojęcie i systematyka, w: Stefan Grzybowski, Andrzej Koppf, Prawo wynalazcze. Zagadnienia wybrane, Państwowe Wydawnictwo Naukowe.

G.S. 1850. 'On Copyright in Design' by T. Turner' (review). *The Jurist* 13 (Part II): 270.

Haans, Richard, Pieters, Constant, and Zi-lin He. 2016. 'Thinking about U: Theorizing and Testing U- and Inverted U-Shaped Relationships in Strategy Research'. *Strategic Management Journal* 37: 1177–1195.

Hall, Bronwyn, and Harhoff, Dietmar. 2012. 'Recent Research on the Economics of Patents'. *Annual Review of Economics* 4(1): 541–565.

Hall, Bronwyn, and Helmers, Christian. 2019. 'The Impact of International Patent Systems: Evidence from Accession to the European Patent Convention'. *Research Policy* 48(9): 103810.

Hanly, Conor. 2006. 'The Decline of Civil Jury Trial in Nineteenth-Century England'. *Journal of Legal History* 26(3): 253.

Harrison R. 2023. 'Patents and Utility Models', in N. Wilkof, S. Basheer, and I. Calboli, eds., *Overlapping Intellectual Property Rights*. Oxford: Oxford University Press.

Hart, Albert Bushnell. 1907. 'American Ideals of International Relations'. *American Journal of International Law* 1(3): 624–635.

Hatfield, H. 1912. 'Utility Model Patents' (March 23, 1912), BT 209/479.

Hausser, Erich. 1987. 'Utility Models: The Experience of the Federal Republic of Germany'. *Industrial Property* 1987: 314.

Hay, Douglas, and Francis Snyder. 1989. 'Using the Criminal Law, 1750–1850: Policing, Private Prosecution, and the State', in Douglas Hay and Francis Snyder, eds., *Policing and Prosecution in Britain 1750–1850*, Ch. 1.

Heller, Michael A. 1998. 'The Tragedy of the Anticommons: Property in the Transition from Marx to Markets' *Harvard Law Review* 111: 621.

Heller, Michael A., and Rebecca Eisenberg. 1998. 'Can Patents Deter Innovation? The Anticommons in Biomedical Research'. *Science* 280: 698.

Heikkilä, Jussi. 2017. 'The Relationship between Patent and Second Tier Patent Protection: The Case of the Dutch Short-Term Patent System Abolition'. https://ssrn.com/abstract=2958107

2018. *Empirical Analyses of European Intellectual Property Rights Institutions*. Doctoral Dissertation, Jyväskylä University School of Business and Economics.

2019. 'IPR Gender Gaps: A First Look at Utility Model, Design Right and Trademark Filings'. *Scientometrics* 118(3): 869–883.

2021. 'The Demand for IPR Services: To Use or Not to Use a Professional Representative'. *International Journal of Intellectual Property Management* 11(3): 316–324.

2023a. 'Key Performance Indicators for Utility Model Systems'. *World Patent Information* 74: Article 102222.

2023b. Yli 30 vuotta suomalaista hyödyllisyysmallijärjestelmää, osa 1. *IPRinfo*, 5/2023.

Heikkilä, Jussi, and Annika Lorenz. 2018. 'Need for Speed? Exploring the Relative Importance of Patents and Utility Models among German Firms'. *Economics of Innovation and New Technology* 27(1): 80–105.

Heikkilä, J., and M. Peltoniemi. 2023. 'The Changing Work of IPR Attorneys: 30 Years of Institutional Transitions'. *Technological Forecasting and Social Change* 197: Article 122853.

2019. 'Great Expectations: Learning the Boundaries of Design Rights'. *Research Policy* 48(9): Article 103795.

Heikkilä, Jussi, and Michael Verba. 2017. 'Do Two-Tiered Patent Systems Induce Sorting? Evidence from European Countries'. Paper presented at the EPIP 2017 Conference, September 4–6, 2017, Bordeaux.

2018. 'The Role of Utility Models in Patent Filing Strategies: Evidence from European Countries'. *Scientometrics* 116: 689.

Heng, Genevieve, Martin Husovec, and Jorge L. Contreras. 2024. *Patentomania: The Cost of Embedding Patents in Social Policies*, University of Utah College of Law Research Paper No. 581 (January 30, 2024).

Hesse, Renata B., and Frances Marshall. 2017. 'U.S. Antitrust Aspects of FRAND Disputes', in Jorge L. Contreras ed., *Cambridge Handbook of Technical Standardization Law: Competition, Antitrust, and Patents*. Cambridge: Cambridge University Press, 263.

Hewage, P., and N. Sampath. 2015. Promoting a Second-Tier Protection Regime for Innovation of Small and Medium-Sized Enterprises in South Asia: The Case of Sri Lanka. MIPLC Studies No. 26. Nomos: Baden Baden.

Heyward, Michael. 1993. *The Ern Malley Affair.* Brisbane: University of Queensland Press.

Hilty, Reto M., and Pedro Henrique D. Batista. 2023. 'Potential and Limits of Patent Law to Address Climate Change'. *GRUR International* 72(9): 821–839.

Hindmarch, William Mathewson. 1846. *A Treatise of the Law Relating to Patent Privileges*. London: Stevens.

1851. *Observations on the Defects of the Patent Laws of this Country: With Suggestions for the Reform of Them*. London: W. M. Benning & Co.

Hodgskin, Thomas. 1859. Letter, 'The Times and Lord Brougham. Falsehood and Mendicancy'. *Morning Advertiser*, January 14, p. 3.

Holgersson, Marcus. 2013. 'Patent Management in Entrepreneurial SMEs: A Literature Review and an Empirical Study of Innovation Appropriation, Patent Propensity, and Motives'. *R&D Management* 43(1): 21–36.

Holman, Molly A., and Stephen R. Munzer. 2000. 'Intellectual Property Rights in Genes and Gene Fragments: A Registration Solution for Expressed Sequence Tags'. *Iowa Law Review* 83: 735.

Holte, Ryan T., and Ted Sichelman. 2019. 'Cycles of Obviousness'. *Iowa Law Review* 105: 107.

Hughes, Alan, and Andrea Mina. 2010. 'The Impact of the Patent System on SMEs', Centre for Business Research, University of Cambridge, Working Paper. No. 411.

Husovec, Martin. 2020. 'The Fundamental Right to Property and the Protection of Investment: How Difficult Is It to Repeal New Intellectual Property Rights?', in Christophe Geiger, ed., *Research Handbook on Intellectual Property and Investment Law*. Cheltenham: Edward Elgar, 385–405.

Hüttermann, Aloys, and Ulrich Storz. 2006. 'Die BGH-Entscheidung "Demonstrationsschrank" – eine Revolution im gewerblichen Rechtsschutz?' *Neue Juristische Wochenschrift* 59: 3178–3180.

Institute of Patent and Trade Mark Attorneys of Australia, 'Save the Innovation Patent Campaign', December 10, 2018. https://ipta.org.au/news/save-the-innovation-patent-campaign/

IPR Think Tank. 2015. IPR Policy. www.keionline.org/wp-content/uploads/national-ipr-policy.pdf

Isay, Hermann. 1932. 'Gebrauchsmuster', in Stringham 1935, Ch. 5, translated from *Patentgesetz und Gesetz betreffend den Schutz von Gebrauchsmustern*. 6th ed. Berlin: Franz Vahlen.

Jaffe, A., and de Rassenfosse, G. 2017. 'Patent Citation Data in Social Science Research: Overview and Best Practices'. *Journal of the Association for Information Science and Technology* 68(6): 1360–1374.

Janis, Mark D. 1999. 'Second Tier Patent Protection'. *Harvard International Law Journal* 40: 151–219.

Jannoni Sebastianini, Alfredo. 1936. *La tutela delle privative industriali e dei marchi di fabbrica e di commercio*. Padova: CEDAM.

Johnson, Matthew, Adam Bialowas, Peta Nicholson, Benjamin Mitra-Kahn, Bradley Man, and Sasan Bakhtiari. 2015. The Economic Impact of Innovation Patents. IP Australia Economic Research Paper 05, www.wipo.int/edocs/mdocs/mdocs/en/wipo_a_64_side_event_1/wipo_a_64_side_event_1_australia1.pdf.

Johnson, Phillip. 2017, 'The Report of the Parker Committee on Patent Law 1916'. *Queen Mary Journal of Intellectual Property* 7(2): 156–190.

Jorda, Karl F. 2007. 'Utility Models: The Panacea for Our Broken Patent System'. *Germeshausen Center Newsletter* Winter/Spring 2007: 1–3.

Jost, John, Gianna Totaro, and Christine Tyshing, eds. 1996. *The Demidenko File*. Melbourne: Penguin Books.

Juma C. 1989. *The Gene Hunters: Biotechnology and the Scramble for Seeds*. Princeton, NJ: Princeton University Press.

Kaisi, Avgi. 2014. 'Finally a Single European Right for the EU? An Analysis of the Substantive Provisions of the European Patent with Unitary Effect'. *European Intellectual Property Review* 36(3): 170.

Kaneko, Hajime, and Yoshinobu Someya. 1960. *Industrial Property Law*.

Kardam, K. S. 2007. Utility Model – A Tool for Economic and Technological Development: A Case Study of Japan. https://ipindia.gov.in/writereaddata/images/pdf/finalreport_april2007.pdf

Karshtedt, Dmitry. 2015. 'The Completeness Requirement in Patent Law'. *Boston College Law Review* 56: 949–1029.

Kasch, Steven P. 1992. 'The Semiconductor Chip Protection Act: Past, Present, and Future'. *Berkeley Technology Law Journal* 7(1): 71–105.

Kay, David Ben. 1985. 'The Patent Law of the People's Republic of China in Perspective'. *UCLA Law Review* 33: 331.

Kellerbauer, Manuel. 2019a. 'Article 114 TFEU', in Manuel Kellerbauer, Marcus Klamert, and Jonathan Tomkin, eds., *Commentary on the EU Treaties and the Charter of Fundamental Rights*. Oxford: Oxford University Press.

2019b. 'TFEU, Introduction to Part Three: Title VII, Chapter 3', in Manuel Kellerbauer, Marcus Klamert, and Jonathan Tomkin, eds., *Commentary on the EU Treaties and the Charter of Fundamental Rights*. Oxford: Oxford University Press.

Kennedy, Christopher C. 2015. 'Rethinking Obviousness'. *Wisconsin Law Review* 2015: 665.

Kenyon, Andrew, Megan Richardson, and Sam Ricketson, eds. 2009. *Landmarks in Australian Intellectual Property Law*. Cambridge: Cambridge University Press.

Kern, Michael. 1994a. 'Bericht über das Ringberg-Symposium "Europäisches Gebrauchsmusterrecht" des Max-Planck-Instituts vom 7. bis 12.11.1993'. *GRUR International*: 549–586.

1994b. 'Towards a European Utility Model Law'. *International Review of Intellectual Property and Competition Law* 25(5): 627–647.

Kerr, S., and W. Kerr. 2018. 'Global Collaborative Patents'. *The Economic Journal* 128(612): F235–F272.

Khan, Daniel-Erasmus. 2015. 'Article 118 TFEU', in Rudolf Geiger, Daniel-Erasmus Khan, and Markus Kotzur, eds., *European Union Treaties. Treaty on European Union, Treaty on the Function of the European Union. A Commentary*. Munich and Oxford: C. H. Beck and Oxford University Press.

Kieff, F. Scott. 2003. 'The Case for Registering Patents and the Law and Economics of Present Patent-Obtaining Rules'. *Boston College Law Review* 45(1): 55–124.

Kilpatrick Townsend. 2022. *Utility Models: Economical, Efficient, and Enforceable Patent Protection*. www.jdsupra.com/legalnews/utility-models-economical-efficient-and-4367830/

Kim, Yee Kyoung, Keun Lee, Walter G. Park, and Kineung Choo. 2012. 'Appropriate Intellectual Property Protection and Economic Growth in Countries at Different Levels of Development'. *Research Policy* 41(2): 358–375.

King, Peter. 2006. *Crime and Law in England 1750–1840*. Cambridge: Cambridge University Press.

Knight, Will. 2001. 'Wheel Patented in Australia', *New Scientist*, July 3, www.newscientist .com/article/dn965-wheel-patented-in-australia/

Königer, Karsten. 2009. 'Registration Without Examination: The Utility Model – A Useful Model?', in Wolrad Prinz zu Waldack und Pyrmont, Martin Adelman, Robert Brauneis, Josef Drexl, and Ralph Nack, eds., *Patents and Technological Progress in a Globalized World: Liber Amicorum Joseph Straus*. Berlin: Springer.

2017. 'The 125th Anniversary of the German Utility Model: A Reason to Celebrate?' *Journal of Intellectual Property Law & Practice* 12(2): 75.

Korte, Stefan. 2022. 'Art. 114 AEUV', in Christian Calliess and Matthias Ruffert, eds., *EUV/AEUV. Das Verfassungsrecht der Europäischen Union mit Europäischer Grundrechtecharta. Kommentar*. 6th ed. Munich: C. H. Beck.

Kraßer, Rudolf. 1995. 'Developments in Utility Model Law'. *International Review of Intellectual Property and Competition Law* 26(6): 950–963.

2000. 'Harmonization of Utility Model Law in Europe'. *International Review of Intellectual Property and Competition Law* 31(7/8): 797–812.

Kretschmer, Friedrich. 1987. 'Statutory Changes in German Industrial Property'. *International Review of Industrial Property and Copyright* 18: 767.

Krishnaswamy, K. N., M. H. Bala Subrahmanya, and M. Mathirajan. 2015. 'Technological Innovation Induced Growth of Engineering Industry SMEs: Case Studies in Bangalore'. *Asian Journal of Innovation and Policy* 4(2): 217–241.

KTM. 1986. 'Utility model committee's report' (original in Finnish: Hyödyllisyysmallitoimikunnan mietintö). KTM Komiteamietintöjä (1986: 48), The Ministry of Trade and Industry.

Kumar, Nagesh. 2003. 'Intellectual Property Rights, Technology and Economic Development: Experiences of Asian Countries'. *Economic & Political Weekly* 38(3): 209–226.

Ladas, Stephen. 1975. *Patents, Trademarks and Related Rights: National and International Protection*. Boston, MA:Harvard University Press.

Laisi, H. 2009. 75 vuotta teollisoikeudellista yhdistystoimintaa Suomessa. Oy Nordprint Ab.

LDSOFT. 2022. www.ldsoft.com.br/webseek/

Lee, Keun, and Yee Kyoung Kim. 2010. 'IPR and Technological Catch-Up in Korea', in H. Odagiri, A. Goto, A. Sunami, and R. Nelson, eds., *Intellectual Property Rights, Development, and Catch-Up: An International Comparative Study*. Oxford: Oxford University Press, 133–162.

Lee, K., R. Kang, and D. Park. 2019. 'Diverse Forms of Intellectual Property Rights, Innovations, and Firm Performance at Different Stages of Development: Findings from the Firm-Level Study in the Republic of Korea, 1970s–2010s', in *Background Paper for Asian Development Outlook 2020: What Drives Innovation in Asia?*

Lefsin, Jeffrey A., Peter S. Menell, and David O. Taylor. 2018. 'Final Report of the Berkeley Center for Law & Technology Section 101 Workshop: Addressing Patent Eligibility Challenges'. *Berkeley Technology Law Journal* 33(2): 551–605.

Legal Daily. 2005. '"Questionable Patent" Does Not Equal "Junk Patent"'. *Legal Daily*, December 28: 006.

Lei, Zhen, Zhen Sun, and Brian Wright. 2013. 'Patent Subsidy and Patent Filing in China'. https://funginstitute.berkeley.edu/wp-content/uploads/2013/12/patent_subsidy_Zhen.pdf.

Lemley, Mark A. 2001. 'Rational Ignorance at the Patent Office'. *Northwestern University Law Review* 95(4): 1495.

2002. 'Intellectual Property Rights and Standard-Setting Organizations'. *California Law Review* 90: 1989.

2012. 'The Myth of the Sole Inventor'. *Michigan Law Review* 110: 709–760.

Lemley, Mark A., and Timothy Simcoe. 2019. 'How Essential Are Standard-Essential Patents?'. Cornell Law Review 104: 607.

Lemley, Mark A., and Jacob S. Sherkow. 2023. 'The Antibody Patent Paradox'. *Yale Law Journal* 132(4): 994–1054.

Li, Wei. 2012. 'Analysis of Impact of Different Types of Patents on Technological Advancement in China'. *African Journal of Business Management* 6(10): 3623–3639.

Li, Wenjing, and Zheng Manni. 2016. 'Substantive Innovation or Strategic Innovation? The Impact of Macro-Industrial Policy on Micro-Enterprise Innovation'. *Economic Research Journal* 51(4): 60–73.

Liang, Zhiwen. 2014. 'Patent Quality Controlled by Judiciary'. *The Jurist* 144(3): 61–73.

Liberti, L. 2010. 'Intellectual Property Rights in International Investment Agreements: An Overview', in *OECD* Working Papers on International Investment 2010/01. OECD Publishing, http://dx.doi.org/10.1787/5kmfq1njzl35-en

Liesegang, Roland. 1992. 'German Utility Models after the 1990 Reform Act'. *Annual of the Intellectual Property Law Association Quarterly Journal* 20: 1.

Lietzan, Erika. 2019. 'The "Evergreening" Metaphor in Intellectual Property Scholarship.' *Akron Law Review* 53: 805.

Liu, Binqiang. 2014. 'China Utility Model Patent: Trash or Treasure – A Data-Based Analysis'. *IDEA: The IP Law Review* 54(2): 225–253.

Liverpool Financial Reform Association. 1851. *The Law for the Protection and Encouragement of Invention, (Financial Reform Tract No 22) in The Tracts of the Liverpool Financial Reform Association*. London: Standard of Freedom.

Llewellyn, Margaret. 1996. *Utility Models/Second Tier Protection: A Report on the Proposals of the European Commission*. London: Intellectual Property Institute.

1997. 'Is There a Need for a European Utility Model? A View from the United Kingdom'. *Annales De La Faculté De Droit d'Istanbul* 31(17): 1–26.

Lobban, Michael. 2002. 'The Strange Life of the English Civil Jury, 1837–1914', in John Cairns and Grant McLeod, eds., *'The Dearest Birthright of the People of England: The Jury in the History of the Common Law*. London: Bloomsbury.

Long, Cheryl Xiaoning, and Jun Wang. 2016. 'Evaluating Patent Promotion Policies in China: Consequences for Patent Quantity and Quality', in D an Prud'homme, and Hefa Song, eds., *Economic Impacts of Intellectual Property-Conditioned Government Incentives*. Springer, 235–257.

Long, Clarissa. 2004. 'Information Costs in Patent and Copyright'. *Virginia Law Review* 90: 465.

Loth, Hans-Friedrich. 2001. 'Vorb', *Gebrauchsmustergesetz*. Munich: C. H. Beck.

Lui, Binqiang. 2014. 'China Utility Model Patent: Trash or Treasure – A Data-Based Analysis'. *IDEA: The Intellectual Property Law Review* 54(2): 225–254.

Lyne I., and A. Madden. 2021. 'Enterprising New Worlds: Social Enterprise and the Value of Repair', in Gibson-Graham and K. Dombroski, eds., *The Handbook of Diverse Economies*. Cheltenham: Edward Elgar.

MacLeod, Christine. 1988. *Inventing the Industrial Revolution: The English Patent System, 1660–1800*. Cambridge: Cambridge University Press.

MacLeod, Roy. 1994. 'Science for Imperial Efficiency and Social Change: Reflections on the British Science Guild, 1905–36'. *Public Understanding of Science* 3: 155–193.

Madsen, Palle Bo. 2020. *Immaterialret*. Copenhagen: Jurist- og Økonomforbundets Forlag.

Malavota, Leandro M. 2011. *A construção do sistema de patentes no Brasil: um olhar histórico*. Rio de Janeiro: Lumen Juris.

Manne, Robert, 1996. *The Culture of Forgetting: Helen Demidenko and the Holocaust*. Melbourne: Text Publishing Company.

Mao, Hao, Yin Zhifeng, and Zhang Jin. 2018. 'Could China's Innovation Get Rid of the Trap of Utility Model Patent System'. *China Industrial Economics* 2018(3): 98–115.

Mao, Y., and Thomas, T. (June 23, 2022). Utility Models: Economical, Efficient, and Enforceable Patent Protection. *JD Supra*. www.jdsupra.com/legalnews/utility-models-economical-efficient-and-4367830/

Marchesoni, Evelina. 2023. 'The Reform of the Italian IP Code'. *Bird & Bird*, November 8, 2023 www.twobirds.com/en/patenthub/shared/insights/2023/italy/the-reform-of-the-italian-ip-code

Martínez, C. 2011. 'Patent Families: When Do Different Definitions Really Matter?' *Scientometrics* 86: 39–63.

Maskus, Keith E., and Christine McDaniel. 1999. 'Impacts of the Japanese Patent System on Productivity Growth'. *Japan and the World Economy* 11: 557–574.

Maskus, Keith, and M. Penubarti. 1995. 'How Trade-Related Are Intellectual Property Rights?' *Journal of Internal Economics* 39: 227–248.

Mathely, P. 1974. Le droit français des brevets d'invention, JNA.

Max Planck Institute. 1987. 'Harmonization of Industrial Property and Copyright Law in the European Community. Report of a Symposium held by the Max Planck Institute for Foreign and International Patent, Copyright, and Competition Law, at Ringberg Castle near Tegernsee'. *International Review of Intellectual Property and Competition Law* 18 (3): 303–337.

1994. 'Proposal of the Max Planck Institute for a European Utility Model. Explanatory Report'. *International Review of Intellectual Property and Competition Law* 25(5): 700–735.

Mboya, R. A. 2018. 'Utilization of Industrial Designs and Utility Models in Africa: A Case Study of Kenya'. WIPO-WTO Colloquium Papers, 2018 Africa Edition.

McDave, K. E., and A. Hackman-Aidoo. 2021. 'Africa and SDG 9: Toward a Framework for Development through Intellectual Property'. *US-China Law Review* 18: 12–29.

McKeough, Jill. 2003. 'Is Intellectual Property Different, or Are All Unhappy Monopolists Similar?' *University of New South Wales Law Journal* 26(1): 289–295.

McKinley, Daniel. 2022. 'Winner takes all! | Commissioner of Patents Succeeds over Gaming Machine Company and sets new precedent for Patent Eligibility of Computer Implemented Inventions', *Gestalt*, www.gestalt.law/insights/winner-takes-all-commissioner-of-patents-succeeds-over-gaming-machine-company-and-sets-new-precedent-for-patent-eligibility-of-computer-implemented-inventions

Meier-Beck, Peter. 2007. 'Die Rechtsprechung des Bundesgerichtshofs zum Patent- und Gebrauchsmusterrecht im Jahr 2006'. *GRUR* 109(11): 913–920.

Merges Robert P. 1988. 'Commercial Success and Patent Standards: Economic Perspectives on Innovation'. *California Law Review* 76(4): 803–876.

Merges Robert P., and R. Nelson. 1990. 'On the Complex Economics of Patent Scope'. *Columbia Law Review* 90: 839–916.

Mertzlufft-Paufler, Cornelius, and Matthew Yip. 2022. 'Double Patenting in Germany and the UPC'. *Maucher Jenkins*, April 8, 2022. www.maucherjenkins.com/commentary/double-patenting-germany-upc

Mes, Peter. 2013. Kommentar Patentgesetz/Gebrauchsmustergesetz, 5. Aufl., 2020, § 1 GebrMG, Rn. 13; Wenzel GRUR, 140.

2020. Kommentar Patentgesetz/Gebrauchsmustergesetz, 5. Aufl., 2020, § 5 GebrMG, Rn. 6.

Mingardi, Alberto. 2021. *Classical Liberalism and the Industrial Working Class*. Abingdon: Routledge.

Minssen, Timo, and Björn Lundqvist. 2014. 'The "Opt Out" and "Opt In" Provisions in the Unified Patent Court Agreement – Impact and Strategies for European Patent Portfolios'. *Nordiskt Immateriellt Rättsskydd* 83(4): 340–357.

Mischlewski, Darryl. 2000. 'Letter Patent Need for Such Protection', *Australian Financial Review*, December 28.

Mitchell, W. J. T. 1984. *Picture Theory: Essays on Verbal and Visual Representation*. Chicago: University of Chicago Press.

1986. *Iconology: Image, Text, Ideology*. Chicago: University of Chicago Press.

Moga, Thomas T. 2012. 'China's Utility Model Patent System: Innovation Driver or Deterrent'. *U.S. Chamber of Commerce*. www.uschamber.com/assets/archived/images/legacy/reports/1211_china_patent_paper.pdf

Monotti, Ann. 2010. 'Innovation Patents: The Concept of a Manner of New Manufacture and Assessment of Innovative Step: *Dura-Post (Aust) Pty Ltd* v *Delnorth Pty Ltd*'. *European Intellectual Property Review* 32: 93–97.

Montañá, Miquel. 'The UPC Is Dead. Long Live the UMC!' *Kluwer Patent Blog*, December 11, 2023 https://patentblog.kluweriplaw.com/2023/12/11/the-upc-is-dead-long-live-the-umc/.

Mott, Kelsey Martin. 1963. 'The Concept of Small Patent in European Legal Systems and Equivalent Protection under United States Law'. *Virginia Law Review* 49(2): 232.

Mueller, Florian. 2018. 'When Defending against Standard-Essential Patents, Beware of Standard-Essential Utility Models'. *FOSS Patents*. December 7. www.fosspatents.com/2018/12/when-defending-against-standard. html

2023. Standard-Essential Utility Models Are Major Loophole in Proposed EU SEP Regulation, Presumably Because of Fundamental Rights Issues: Structural Problems. September 9. *FOSS Patents*. www.foss patents.com/2023/09/standard-essential-utility-models-are.html

Murdoch, H. H. 1867. *Information Respecting British and Foreign Patents and the Registration of Designs*. London: published by the author.

Murfitt, Stephen Edward. 2017. *The English Patent System and Early Railway Technology 1800–1852*. PhD Thesis, University of York.

Musker, David. 2014. 'Design Crime. Back to the Future or Forward to the Past?' *Journal of Intellectual Property Law and Practice* 9(12): 976–985.

Nævnenes Hus. 2024. Case Law from the Board of Appeal for Patents and Trademarks. https://apv.naevneneshus.dk

National Research Council. 2013. *Patent Challenges for Standard-Setting in the Global Economy*, K. Maskus and S. A. Merrill, eds., Washington, DC: National Academies Press.

Naumann, H. 1958. 'Utility Model Patent Protection'. *Journal of the Patent Office Society* 40 (11): 800–814.

Nelson, R., and S. Winter. 1982. *An Evolutionary Theory of Economic Change*. Cambridge, MA: Belknap Press.

Nérisson, Sylvie. 2017. 'Remaining Scopes for Collective Management of Copyright in the Online World', in Kung-Chung Liu and Reto M. Hilty, eds., *Remuneration of Copyright Owners: Regulatory Challenges of New Business Models*. Berlin: Springer, 71–83.

Neuhaus, Stephan, David Por, and Mark Ridgway. 'What Does the UPC Mean for Patent Litigation?' *Allen & Overy publications*, May 31, 2023. www.allenovery.com/en-gb/global/news-and-insights/publications/what-does-the-upc-mean-for-patent-litigation

Newton, Alfred Vincent. 1879. *Patent Law and Practice: Showing the Mode of Obtaining and Opposing Grants, Disclaimers, Confirmations, and Extensions of Patents: With a Chapter on Patent Agents*. London: Trubner & Co.

Norman, John Paxton. 1851. *The Law and Practice of the Copyright, Registration and Provisional Registration of Designs*. London: S. Sweet.

North, P. 2021. 'Independent and Small Businesses: Diversity amongst the 99 Per cent of Business', in Gibson-Graham and K. Dombroski, eds., *The Handbook of Diverse Economies*. Cheltenham: Edward Elgar.

Noto La Diega, Guido, et al. 2024. 'Sustainable Patent Governance of Artificial Intelligence. Recalibrating the European Patent System to Foster Innovation (SDG 9)', in Matthew Rimmer, Caroline B. Ncube and Bita Amani, eds., *Elgar Companion on Intellectual Property and the Sustainable Development Goals*. Cheltenham: Edward Elgar.

Odagiri, A. H., A. Sunami Goto, and R. Nelson. 2010. 'Introduction', in H. Odagiri, A. Goto, A. Sunami, and R. Nelson, eds., *Intellectual Property Rights, Development, and Catch-Up – An International Comparative Study*. Oxford: Oxford University Press, 1–28.

Ohly, Ansgar. 2021. 'Jurisdiction and Choice of Law in Trade Secrets Cases: The EU Perspective', in Sharon K. Sandeen, Christoph Rademacher, and Ansgar Ohly, eds., *Research Handbook on Information Law and Governance*. Cheltenham: Edward Elgar, 234–258.

Oldham, James. 1987. 'Special Juries in England: Nineteenth Century Usage and Reform'. *Journal of Legal History* 8(2): 148.

Oliveira, Maikon A. B. 2020. 'Guia para proteção de inovação por obtenção de Carta Patente'. Master Thesis (Universidade Federal do Paraná. Programa de Pós-Graduação em Propriedade Intelectual e Transferência de Tecnologia para Inovação – PROFNIT).

Olson, Bradley J. 2007. 'The Amendments to the Vessel Hull Design Protection Act of 1998: A New Tool for the Boating Industry'. *Journal of Maritime Law and Commerce* 38(2): 177–190.

Op Den Kamp, Claudy, and Dan Hunter, eds. 2019. *A History of Intellectual Property in 50 Objects*. Cambridge: Cambridge University Press.

Osgood, Charles. 2001. 'To Protest New Patent Law, Patent Lawyer John Keogh Was Granted a Patent for a "Circular Transportation Facilitation Device," A Wheel', *CBC News*, July 3.

Osterrieth, Albert. 1912. 'Discussion of the German Patent Law and Patent Procedure', in Stringham, ed., 1935, ch 3.

Ożegalska-Trybalska, Justyna. [2021] 'Commentary to art. 94 IPL' in Łukasz Żelechowski, ed., Prawo własności przemysłowej.

Østerborg, Lise. 1983. 'Indledende Bemærkninger til Indførelse af Brugsmodelbeskyttelse i Danmark'. *Nordiskt Immateriellt Rättsskydd* 1984: 18–24.

Pager, Sean A. 2007. 'Patents on a Shoestring: Making Patent Protection Work for Developing Countries'. *Georgia State University Law Review* 23(4): 755–808.

Park, Jong R., and Sang O. Noe. 2013. 'Reexamination of the Effectiveness of Utility Model System in Korea'. *Law & Policy* 19: 201.

Park, Walter. 2008. 'International Patent Protection: 1960–2005'. *Research Policy* 37(4): 761–766.

Patent Law Firm Wittmann. 2024. German Utility Model. www.wh-ip.com/germany/german_utility_model.html

Pemberton, Gretchen A., and Mariano Soni, Jr. 1992. 'Mexico's 1991 Industrial Property Law'. *Cornell International Law Journal* 25(1): 103–130.

Picht, Peter Georg, and Anna-Lena Karczewski. 2022. 'Germany', in Jorge L. Contreras, and Martin Husovec, eds., *Injunctions in Patent Law : Trans-atlantic Dialogues on Flexibility and Tailoring*. New York: Cambridge University Press.

Picht, Peter, and Jorge L. Contreras. 2023. 'Proportionality Defenses in FRAND Cases: a Comparative Assessment of the Revised German Patent Injunction Rules and U.S. Case Law'. *GRUR International* 72(5): 435–450.

Pila, Justine. 2022. *Seville's EU Intellectual Property Law and Policy*. Cheltenham: Edward Elgar.

Polden, Patrick. 1999. *A History of the County Court, 1846–1971*. Cambridge: Cambridge University Press.

2010. 'The Legal Profession', in W. Cornish, Anderson, R. Cocks, M. Lobban, P. Polden, and K. Smith, eds., *Oxford History of the Laws of England, Vol XI, English Legal System*. Oxford: Oxford University Press.

van Pottelsberghe de la Potterie, Bruno. 2011. 'The Quality Factor in Patent Systems'. *Industrial and Corporate Change* 20: 1755–1793.

Progress Press. 2001. 'Expert Proves Patents Plan Is Wheely Silly', *Progress Press*, November 6.

Prud'homme, Dan. 2012. 'Dulling the Cutting Edge: How Patent-Related Policies and Practices Hamper Innovation in China'. *European Union Chamber of Commerce in China*. https://mpra.ub.uni-muenchen.de/43299/1/MPRA_paper_43299.pdf

2014. 'Creating a "Model" Utility Model Patent System: A Comparative Analysis of the Utility Model Patent Systems in Europe and China'. IP Key Working Paper for China's State Intellectual Property Office.

2015a. '"Soft Spots" in China's Utility Model Patent System: Perceptions, Assessment and Reform'. *European Intellectual Property Review* 37: 305–310.

2015b. ‘China’s Shifting Patent Landscape and State-Led Patenting Strategy’. *Journal of Intellectual Property Law & Practice* 10: 619–625 (corrected in 2016, 11(4): 315).

2016a. ‘Constructing Utility Model Patent Systems: Lessons from Europe and China’. *European Intellectual Property Review* 38: 437–444.

2016b. ‘IP-Conditioned Government Incentives in China and the EU: A Comparative Analysis of Strategies and Impacts on Patent Quality’, in Dan Prud’homme and Hefa Song, eds., *Economic Impacts of Intellectual Property-Conditioned Government Incentives*. Springer, 13–74.

2017a. ‘Utility Model Patent Regime “Strength” and Technological Development: Experiences of China and Other East Asian Latecomers’. *China Economic Review* 42: 50–73.

2017b. ‘Utility Model Patent Regimes and Innovation in China and Beyond’, in Yahong Li, ed., *Patents and Innovation in Mainland China and Hong Kong: Two Systems in One Country Compared*. Cambridge: Cambridge University Press.

2019. ‘Re-conceptualizing Intellectual Property Regimes in International Business Research: Foreign-Friendliness Paradoxes Facing MNCs in China’. *Journal of World Business* 52(4): 399–419.

2024. ‘The Impact of IPR Institutions’ Accessibility on Their Usage around the World: A Panel Study’. FIU College of Business Working Paper.

2025. ‘Alternative Responses to Patent Anti-commons: State Financing of Latecomer Patenting’, in Walter Park, ed., *Handbook of Intellectual Property and Innovation*. Oxford: Oxford University Press.

Prud’homme, Dan, and Tony Tong. 2023. ‘Rethinking Firm-Specific Advantages from Intellectual Property Rights: Boundary Conditions for MNEs’. *Journal of International Business Studies* 2023(1): 91–109

Prud’homme, Dan, and Max von Zedtwitz. 2018. ‘The Changing Face of Innovation in China’. *MIT Sloan Management Review* 59: 24–32.

Prud’homme, Dan, and Taolue Zhang. 2019. *China’s Intellectual Property Regime for Innovation*. Springer.

Prud’homme, Dan, Tony Tong, and Nianchen Han. 2021. ‘A Stakeholder-Based View of the Evolution of Intellectual Property Institutions’. *Journal of International Business Studies* 52: 773–802.

Quinn, Gene. 2015. ‘The Cost of Obtaining a Patent in the US’. *IPWatchdog*. Retrieved December 3, 2023, https://ipwatchdog.com/2015/04/04/the-cost-of-obtaining-a-patent-in-the-us/id = 56485/#.

Radauer, Alfred, Christina Rosemberg, Oliver Cassagneau-Francis, and Heinz Goddar, 2015. Study on the economic impact of the utility model legislation in selected Member States. Final Report, A study tendered by the European Commission – DG Internal Market and Services in 2013, MARKT/2013/065/D2/ST/OP.

Radauer, Alfred, Christina Rosemberg Montes, Oliver Cassagneau-Francis, Heinz Goddar, and C. Haarmann 2019. ‘The Myth of the “Small Patent for the Small Inventor” – Strategic Motives to Use Second-Tier Patent Systems (Utility Models) in Selected European Countries’. *Journal of Intellectual Property Law & Practice* 14(10): 771–783.

Radford, Tim. 2001. ‘Giants of the Improbable Claim their Due Reward’, *The Guardian*, October 5.

Rankine, Andrew. 2022. ‘What the High Court Decision in Aristocrat Means for Patent Owners’, Spruson, September 16, www.spruson.com/patents/what-the-high-court-decision-in-aristocrat-means-for-patent-owners/

de Rassenfosse, G., H. Dernis, D. Guellec, L. Picci, and B. van Pottelsberghe de la Potterie. 2013. 'The Worldwide Count of Priority Patents: A New Indicator of Inventive Activity'. *Research Policy*, 42(3): 720–737.

Ravillard, Patrick. 2000. 'The Proposal for a EU Directive on Utility Models'. *International Intellectual Property Law & Policy* 4: 36-1–36-13.

Reichman, Jerome H. 1994. 'Legal Hybrids between the Patent and Copyright Paradigms'. *Columbia Law Review* 94(8): 2432–2558.

1998. 'Industrial Designs and Utility Models under the European Communities' Proposed Initiatives: A Critical Appraisal'. *International Intellectual Property Law & Policy* 2: 48-1–48-46.

2000. 'Of Green Tulips and Legal Kudzu: Repacking Rights in Subpatentable Innovation'. *Vanderbilt Law Review* 6(6): 1743–1798.

Reichman, Jerome H., and Ana Santos Rutschman. 2023. 'The Case for a Liability Rule to Stimulate Investment in Sub-patentable Innovation', in Margaret Chon, Graeme B. Dinwoodie, Susy Frankel, Barbara Lauriat, and Jens Schovsbo, eds., *Improving Intellectual Property: A Global Project*. Cheltenham: Edward Elgar, 88–94.

2024. 'Protecting Sub-patentable Innovation: The Case for Codified Liability Rules'. *UC Davis Law Review* 57: 2027–2075.

Richards, John. 2010. 'Utility Model Protection throughout the World'. https://ipo.org/wp-content/uploads/2013/03/Utility_Model_protection.pdf

Ricketson, Sam. 2015. *The Paris Convention for the Protection of Industrial Property*. Oxford: Oxford University Press.

Ricketson, Sam, and Megan Richardson. 1998. *Intellectual Property: Cases, Materials and Commentary*. 2nd ed. Sydney: Butterworths.

Rimmer, Matthew. 2000. 'The Demidenko Affair: Copyright Law, Plagiarism and Ridicule'. *Media and Arts Law Review* 5(3): 159–176.

2003. 'Franklin Barley: Patent Law and Plant Breeders' Rights'. *Murdoch University Electronic Journal of Law* 10(4), QUT ePrints: https://eprints.qut.edu.au/85372/.

2017. 'An Exorbitant Monopoly: The High Court of Australia, Myriad Genetics, and Gene Patents', in Duncan Matthews and Herbert Zech, eds., *Research Handbook on Intellectual Property and the Life Sciences*. Cheltenham: Edward Elgar, 56–103.

Robertson, Joseph. 1846. 'Editorial Note to W.E. Staite, "The Law of Patents"'. *Mechanics' Magazine* 45: 174–176.

Robinson, W. Keith. 2014. 'Protecting American Innovators by Combating the Decline of Patents Granted to Small Entities'. *St. John's Law Review* 88: 379–432.

Romandini, Roberto. 2011. 'La distinzione tra brevetti e modelli di utilità: una diversa interpretazione della disciplina positiva'. *Rivista di diritto industriale* 2011: I, 200–225.

Roth, Elsebeth, and Niels Holm Svendsen. 1992. 'Lov om Brugsmodeller m.v.' *Ugeskrift for Retsvæsen* 1992B.223.

Ruse-Khan, Henning Grosse. 2012. 'The International Legal Framework for the Protection of Utility Models'. *Max Planck Institute for Intellectual Property & Competition Law Research Paper* 12(10): n/a. http://dx.doi.org/10.2139/ssrn.2160229

2015. *Utility Model Protection in Pakistan – An Option for Incentivising Incremental Innovation*, WIPO-commissioned report, www.ip.mpg.de/fileadmin/ipmpg/content/forschung_aktuell/05_utility_model_protection/wipo_study_on_utility_model_protection_in_pakistan.pdf

Rutenberg, Isaac, and Lilian Makanga. 2016. 'Utility Model Protection in Kenya: The Case for Substantive Examination'. *African Journal of Information and Communication (AJIC)* 19: 19–37.

Rutenberg, Isaac, and Jacqueline Mwangi. 2017. Do Patents and Utility Model Certificates Encourage Innovation in Kenya? *Journal of Intellectual Property Law & Practice* 12(3): 206–215.

Sadler, Denham. 2019. 'Government to Abolish Innovation Patents', *InnovationAus.com*, September 9, www.innovationaus.com/govt-to-abolish-innovation-patents-2/

2022. 'Calls for New Innovation Patents After Old Scheme Abolished', InnovationAus. Com, May 25, www.innovationaus.com/calls-for-new-innovation-patents-after-old-scheme-abolished/

de Saint-Georges, Matthis, and Bruno van Pottelsberghe de la Potterie. 2013. 'A Quality Index for Patent Systems'. *Research Policy* 42: 704–719.

Sander, Lorena. 2023. Intellectual Property and Innovation: What Can UNDP Learn from the Music World? (Part 1). May 3, www.undp.org/acceleratorlabs/blog/intellectual-property-and-innovation-what-can-undp-learn-music-world-part-1-0

Saw, C. L. 2016. 'Whither Gene Patenting and the Patenting of Diagnostic Methods Post-Mayo and Myriad: The Need for Certainty in Navigating the High Seas of Policy'. *Law Innovation & Technology* 8: 207–246.

Scardamaglia, Amanda. 2020. *Printed on Stone: The Lithographs of Charles Troedel*, Melbourne: Melbourne Books.

Scherer F. M. 2001. 'The Innovation Lottery', in Rochelle Cooper Dreyfuss, Diane Leenheer Zimmerman, and Harry First, eds., *Expanding the Boundaries of Intellectual Property: Innovation Policy for the Knowledge Society*. Oxford: Oxford University Press.

Schmoch, Ulrich. 2008. Concept of a Technology Classification for Country Comparison: Final Report to the World Intellectual Property Organization (WIPO). www.wipo.int/export/sites/www/ipstats/en/docs/wipo_ipc_technology.pdf

Schovsbo, Jens. 2006. 'Ny Dansk Lov om Brugsmodeller: En Oversigt' *Nordiskt Immateriellt Rättsskydd* 5: 489–493.

Schovsbo, Jens, Thomas Riis, and Clement Salung Petersen. 2015. 'The Unified Patent Court: Pros and Cons of Specialization – Is There a Light at the End of the Tunnel (Vision)?' *International Review of Intellecutal Property and Competition Law* 46(3): 271–274.

Schovsbo, Jens, Morten Rosenmeier, and Clement Salung Petersen. 2024. *Immaterialret*. Copenhagen: Djøf Forlag.

Schumpeter J. 1934. *The Theory of Economic Development*. Cambridge: Harvard University Press.

Schwartz, David L. 2012. 'The Rise of Contingent Fee Representation in Patent Litigation'. *Alabama Law Review* 64(2): 335.

Scotchmer, S. 1999. 'Cumulative Innovation in Theory and Practice'. GSPP Working Paper 240, University of Berkeley Working Paper Series.

Scott, Ian. 2001. 'Honouring the IgNobel', *ABC Science*, October 8, www.abc.net.au/science/articles/2001/10/08/384876.htm

Segade, Jose. 2008. 'Utility Models – Lost in Translation'. *International Review of Industrial Property and Copyright Law* 39(2): 135–139.

Seymore, Sean B. 2021. 'The Research Patent'. *Vanderbilt Law Review* 74(1): 143–186.

Shao, K. 2014. 'The Cores and Contexts of Chinas 21st-Century National Innovation System', in K. Shao and Feng Xiaoqing, eds., *Innovation and Intellectual Property in China: Strategies, Contexts and Challenges*. Cheltenham: Edward Elgar.

Shapiro, Carl. 2001. 'Navigating the Patent Thicket', in Adam B. Jaffe, Josh Lerner, and Scott Stern, eds., *Innovation Policy and Economy*. Cambridge, MA: MIT Press.

Sharma, Gutam and Hemant Kumar. 2018. Exploring the Possibility of Utility Model Protection in India. *J. Intel. Prop. Rights* 23: 119.

Sheikh, Sajid. 2022. Exploring the Possibility of Utility Model Protection in India. *Scholars Intl. J. of Law, Crime and Justice*. 5: 53.

Sherman, Brad, and Lionel Bently. 1999. *The Making of Modern Intellectual Property Law: The British Experience, 1760–1911*. Cambridge: Cambridge University Press.

Shoebridge, Grant. 2018. 'Innovation Patents; Safe for Now', The Institute of Patent and Trade Mark Attorneys of Australia, April 5, https://ipta.org.au/news/innovation-patents-safe-now/

Singer, J. (2022, December 30). How long does U.S. patent and trademark prosecution take? (2022 edition). *J.D. Supra*. www.jdsupra.com/legalnews/how-long-does-u-s-patent-and-trademark-8285966/

Singer, Margarete, and Dieter Stauder. 2003. *The European Patent Convention, A Commentary: Volume 1*. Thomson/Sweet & Maxwell.

Smith, Harry. 1969. 'The Resurgent County Court in Victorian Britain'. *American Journal of Legal History* 13(2): 126.

Societa Italiana Brevetti Intellectual Property Consultants, 2014. 'Utility Models'. www.sib.it/en/areas-of-practice/inventions/utility-models.html

Sommer, Tine. 2013. *Can Law Make Life (too) Simple? From Gene Patents to the Patenting of Environmentally Sound Technologies*. Copenhagen: Djøf Forlag.

Sommer, Tine, Victor Fasmer Henum, Nicolaj Bording, Nicolai Lindgreen, and Jens Schovsbo. 2023. 'Den Fælles Patentdomstol – Et Regimeskifte i Europa!' *EU-ret & Menneskeret* 30(4): 187–202.

Souza, Allan R. 2006. A Função Social Dos Direitos Autorais: Uma Interpretação Civil-Constitucional dos limites da proteção jurídica. Brasil: 1988–2005. Campos dos Goytacazes: Ed. Faculdade de Direito de Campos.

2021. 'Copyright, Human Rights, and the Social Function of Property in Brazil', in Jonathan Griffiths, and Tuomas Mylly, eds., *Global Intellectual Property Protection and New Constitutionalism: Hedging Exclusive Rights*. Online ed., Oxford: Oxford Academic. https://doi.org/10.1093/oso/9780198863168.003.0013

Spence, William. 1847a. *A Treatise on the Principles Relating to the Specification of a Patent for Invention*. London: Stevens and Norton.

1847b. *Copyright of Designs, as Distinguished from Patentable Invention*. London: Stevens and Norton.

1851. *Patentable Inventions and Scientific Evidence*. London: V. & R. Stevens, and G.S. Norton.

Spolidoro, Marco S. 1981. 'Domanda di brevetto per invenzione e per modello di utilità'. *Rivista trimestrale di diritto e procedura civile* 1981: I, 1081–1108.

Squicciarini, M., H. Dernis, and C. Criscuolo. 2013. Measuring Patent Quality: Indicators of Technological and Economic Value. OECD Science, Technology and Industry Working Papers, 2013/03, OECD Publishing.

St Martin, K. 2021. 'Framing Essay: The Diversity of Property', in Gibson-Graham and K. Dombroski, eds., *The Handbook of Diverse Economies*. Cheltenham: Edward Elgar.

Stieper, Malte. 2022. 'Art. 118 AEUV', in Eberhard Grabitz, Meinhard Hilf, and Martin Nettesheim, eds., *Das Recht der Europäischen Union. Band I. EUV/AEUV. May 2022, 76th EL*. Munich: C. H. Beck.

Stierle, Martin. 2019. 'Der quasi-automatische Unterlassungsanspruch im deutschen Patentrecht'. *GRUR* 121(8/9): 873–885.

Stierle, Martin, and Franz Hofmann. 2022. 'The Latest Amendment to the German Law on Patent Injunctions: The New Statutory Disproportionality Exception and Third-Party Interests'. *GRUR International* 71(12): 1123–1137.

Stringham, Emerson. 1935. *Patents and Gebrauchsmuster in International Law*. Madison: Pacot Publications.
Summerfield, Mark. 2018. 'A Brief History of the Australian Innovation Patent'. *Patentology*, July 10, https://blog.patentology.com.au/2018/07/a-brief-history-of-australian.html
Sun, Z., and Lei, C. 2023. Strategic Use of the Second-Tier Patent System for Short Life-Cycle Technologies – Evidence from Parallel Filings in China, https://ssrn.com/abstract = 4652908
Suominen, Kaisa, Nina Ferara, Peter de Lange, and Andrew John Rudge. 2023. *Visser's Annotated European Patent Convention*. Kluwer Law International.
Suthersanen, Uma. 2001. 'Incremental Inventions in Europe: A Legal and Economic Appraisal of Second Tier Patents'. *Journal of Business Law* 2001: 319–343.
2006. 'Utility Models and Innovation in Developing Countries'. *UNCTAD-ICTSD Project on IPRs and Sustainable Development*.
2013. 'Function, Art and Fashion: Do We Need the EU Design Law?', in C. Geiger, ed., *Constructing European Intellectual Property*. Cheltenham: Edward Elgar.
2019. 'Utility Models: Do They Really Serve National Innovation Strategies?', in J. Drexl and A. Sanders, eds., *Innovation Society and Intellectual Property*. Cheltenham: Edward Elgar.
Suthersanen, Uma, and G. Dutfield. 2007. 'Utility Models and Other Alternatives to Patents', in U. Suthersanen, G. Dutfield, and K. B. Chow, eds., *Innovation without Patents: Harnessing the Creative Spirit in a Diverse World*. Cheltenham: Edward Elgar.
Suthersanen, Uma, G. Dutfield, and K. B. Chow, eds. 2007. *Innovation without Patents: Harnessing the Creative Spirit in a Diverse World*. Cheltenham: Edward Elgar.
Svendsen, Niels Holm. 1993. 'Lov om Brugsmodeller m.v.' *Nordiskt Immateriellt Rättsskydd* 1993(2): 237–250.
Swamy, R. N. 2022. *Utility Models as a Second –Tier Patent System: Is It Worth Implementing in India?* https://papers.ssrn.com/sol3/papers.cfm?abstract_id = 4091118
Szwaja, Janusz. 1978. Powstanie i ustanie praw wyłącznych, w: Stefan Grzybowski, Andrzej Koppf, Prawo wynalazcze. Zagadnienia wybrane, Państwowe Wydawnictwo Naukowe.
Takenaka, Toshiko. 2021a. 'Inclusive Patents for Open Innovation'. *Texas Intellectual Property Law Journal* 29(2): 187–234.
2021b. The Role of the New Utility Model System in the Innovation Model of Industry 4.0, *Intell. Prop. L. Pol'y Stud. No*. 58, 1.
2021c. 'Breathing New Life into the German Utility Model System in the Industry 4.0 Era'. *GRUR International* 121(9): 621–632.
Teece, David J. 2017. 'The "Tragedy of the Anticommons" Fallacy: A Law and Economics Analysis of Patent Thickets and FRAND Licensing'. *Berkley Technology Law Journal* 32: 1489.
Temple Franks, W. 1912. 'Patents and Designs Act, 1907' (October 1, 1912) in BT 209/480.
Tepedino, Gustavo, and Anderson Schreiber. 2005. 'A garantia da propriedade no direito brasileiro'. *Revista da Faculdade de Direito de Campos* 6(6): 101, 111–112.
Terrell, Thomas. 1884. *The Law and Practice Regarding Letters Patent for Inventions*. London: Henry Sweet.
Theroux, Eugene A. 1980. 'Technology Sales to China: New Laws and Old Problems'. *Journal of International Law and Economics* 14(2): 185–252.
Thomã, Jörge, and Kilian Bizer. 2013. 'To Protect or Not to Protect? Modes of Appropriability in the Small Enterprise Sector'. *Research Policy* 42(1): 35–49.
Timbs, John. 1868. *The Yearbook of Facts in Science and Art*. London: Lockwood & Co.
Turner, Richard. 2019. 'Utility Models'. *Journal of the Chartered Institute of Patent Agents* 45 (9): 12–15.
Turner, Thomas. 1849. *On Copyright in Design in Arts and Manufacture*. London: Elsworth.
1850. *Counsel to Inventors of Improvements in the Useful Arts*. London: Elsworth.

1851. *The Law of Patents and Registration of Invention and Designs in Manufacture*. London: Crockford.

Ubertazzi, Luigi C. 1988. 'Armonizzazione della normativa in materia di brevetti per modelli e disegni industriali con le disposizioni dell'Accordo dell'Aja del 6 novembre 1925, e successive revisioni, ratificate con l. 24 ottobre 1980, n. 744'. *Le Nuove leggi civili commentate* 1988(4): 561–583.

du Vall, Michał. 2017. *Prawo patentowe*. Wolters Kluwer.

Van Zyl Smit, D. 1985. 'Professional Patent Agents and the Development of the English Patent System'. *International Journal of Sociology of Law* 13: 79.

Vanzetti, Adriano. 2008. 'Note sui modelli di utilità e invenzioni'. *Rivista di diritto industriale* 2008: I, 189–206.

Varadarajan, Rajan. 2009. 'Fortune at the Bottom of the Innovation Pyramid: The Strategic Logic of Incremental Innovations'. *Business Horizons* 52: 21–29.

Vindicator. 1835. *London Journal of Arts and Sciences* 6: 304.

Vossius, Volker, and Ulrich Christian Hallman. 1985. *Industrial Property Laws of the Federal Republic of Germany*. 2nd ed. Munich: Wila Verlag für *Wirtschaftswerbung Wilhelm Lampl*, 129–168.

Wang, Runhua. 2015. 'A Defense of Utility Models: The Case in China'. *Yonsei Journal of International Studies* 7: 212–237.

Ward, Cornelius. 1850. 'The Law of Patents' (letter). *Morning Chronicle* October 28, 6.

Webster, Thomas. 1851. *The Subject-Matter of Letters Patent for Inventions and Registration of Designs* (with Statutes and Cases). 3rd ed. London: Elsworth.

1852. *The New Patent Law: Its History, Objects and Provisions*. London: Elsworth.

1853. *On Property in Designs and Inventions in the Arts and Manufactures*. London: Chapman & Hall.

Weinmiller, Jürgen. 1996. 'Europäisches Weiterbenutzungsrecht statt Europäisierung des Gebrauchsmusterrechts'. *Mitteilungen der deutschen Patentanwälte* 87(6): 150–151.

Weitzel, Günter. 1994. Pilotstudie – Die wirtschaftliche Bedeutung des Gebrauchsmusterschutzes in der Europäischen Union.

1995. 'Die wirtschaftliche Bedeutung des Gebrauchsmusterschutzes im Europäischen Binnenmarkt'. *ifo Schnelldienst* 48(16): 9–17.

Weston, Walter. 1983. 'Registered Inventions'. *Journal of the Chartered Institute of Patent Agents* 13: 370.

Whitworth, Robert. 1848. *Equity Precedents*. London: William Benning & Co.

Wichard, Johannes Christian. 2022. 'Art. 118 AEUV', in Christian Calliess and Matthias Ruffert, eds., *EUV/AEUV. Das Verfassungsrecht der Europäischen Union mit Europäischer Grundrechtecharta. Kommentar*. 6th ed. Munich: C.H. Beck.

Wild, Joff. 2023. 'Patent Litigation Finance Works: No Wonder Some Want It Curtailed'. *Intelligent Asset Management*, February 9.

Wilkof, Neil, Shamnad Basheer, and Irene Calboli. 2023. *Overlapping Intellectual Property Rights*. 2nd ed. Oxford: Oxford University Press.

Wilson, David I. 1988. 'A Trade Policy Goal for the 1990s: Improving the Adequacy and Effectiveness of Intellectual Property Protection in Foreign Countries'. *Transnational Lawyer* 1(2): 421–448.

Winter, Harvey J. 1987. 'The Role of the United States Government in Improving International Intellectual Property Protection'. *The Journal of Law and Technology* 2(1): 325–332.

Witherspoon, John F., ed. 1980. *Nonobviousness – The Ultimate Condition of Patentability*. Washington, DC: Bureau of National Affairs.

Xinhua News Agency. 2022. 'China National Intellectual Property Administration: All Kinds of Financial Support For Patent Grants Will Be Canceled By 2025'. *Xinhua News Agency*, January 27, 2022. www.gov.cn/xinwen/2022-01/27/content_5670755.htm

Xu, Liang, and Federico Munari. 2016. 'The Impact of Public Support for SMEs' Patenting Activity: Empirical Evidence from Italy', in Dan Prud'homme and Hefa Song, eds., *Economic Impacts of Intellectual Property-Conditioned Government Incentives*. Springer, 101–131.

Xue, Mingjun, and Meng Xianyu. 2020. 'To Play the Role of Utility Model System and Enhance the Competitiveness of Innovators'. *Technology Wind* 2020(3): 1.

S.Y. 1844a. 'The Copyright of Designs, and Some Recent Magisterial Decisions'. *Mechanics' Magazine* 41 (1110): 329.

1844b. 'The Registration of Useful Designs'. *Mechanics' Magazine* 41 (1111): 357.

Yang, Yieyie. 2014. 'Reforming the Utility Model System in China: Time to Limit Utility Model Patents' Scope of Protection and Improve the Quality of Chinese Utility Model Patents'. *AIPLA Quarterly Journal* 42: 393.

Yoshifuji, Kosaku. 1998.Outline of the Patent Act (13th ed. revised by Kenichi Kumagai).

Yu, Feifeng. 2017. 'Drawbacks of Patent Law and Counter Measures'. *Journal of Nanjing University of Science and Technology* 30(1): 51–58.

Yu, Peter K. 2016. 'The Transplant and Transformation of Intellectual Property Laws in China', in Nari Lee et al. eds., *Governance of Intellectual Property Rights in China and Europe*. Cheltenham: Edward Elgar.

Yu, Peter K., Jorge L. Contreras, and Yu Yang. 2022. 'Transplanting Anti-Suit Injunctions'. *American University Law Review* 71(4): 1537–1618.

Zeitsch, J. 2013. *The Economic Value of the Australian Innovation Patent: The Australian Innovation Patent Survey*. Canberra: Verve Economics.

Zhang, Huiyan. 2022. 'Characteristics of Litigated Patents in Weak Intellectual Property Rights Regimes: Evidence from China'.

Zhu, Guangyu. 2015. 'On the Way to Improve the Quality of Utility Model Patents'. *Intellectual Property* 2015(7): 86–90.

REGULATORY AND LEGISLATIVE MATERIALS

Australia

Adams, Hon. Dick. 2000. 'Second Reading Speech on the *Patents Amendment (Innovation Patents) Bill* 2000 (Cth)', Hansard, House of Representatives, Australian Parliament, August 31, 2000, 19921. https://parlinfo.aph.gov.au/parlInfo/search/display/display.w3p;query=Id%3A%22chamber%2Fhansardr%2F2000-08-31%2F0145%22

Advisory Council on Intellectual Property (Australia). 1995. *Review of the Petty Patent System: A Report to Senator the Hon. Chris Schacht, Minister for Small Business, Customs and Construction*. Canberra: The Advisory Council on Intellectual Property, August.

2002. *Consideration of Excluding Plant and Animal Subject Matter from Innovation Patent: Issues Paper*. Canberra: Advisory Council on Intellectual Property.

2004. *Should Plant and Animal Subject Matter Be Excluded from Protection by the Innovation Patent?* Canberra: Advisory Council on Intellectual Property.

2011. Review of the Innovation Patent System: Issues Paper. Canberra: Advisory Council on Intellectual Property.

2013. Review of the Innovation Patent System: Options Paper. Canberra: Advisory Council on Intellectual Property, 2013.

2015. Review of the Innovation Patent System: Final Report. Canberra: Advisory Council on Intellectual Property, 2014, revised, May.

Alphapharm, 'Submission to the Productivity Commission on Intellectual Property Arrangements', November 30, 2015. www.pc.gov.au/__data/assets/pdf_file/0005/195080/sub093-intellectual-property.pdf

Andrews MP, Hon. Karen. 2020. 'Second Reading Speech on the *Intellectual Property Laws Amendment (Productivity Commission Response Part 2 and Other Measures) Act* 2019 (Cth)', Hansard, House of Representatives, February 5, 2020. https://parlinfo.aph.gov.au/parlInfo/search/display/display.w3p;query = Id%3A%22chamber%2Fhansardr%2F43b57ed0-16b8-4818-a5ea-01bcab23df0b%2F0209%22

Australian Patents Amendment Act 1979 (Cth). http://classic.austlii.edu.au/au/legis/cth/num_act/paa1979189/s17.html

Canavan, Senator Matthew. 2019. 'Second Reading Speech on the *Intellectual Property Laws Amendment (Productivity Commission Response Part 2 and Other Measures) Act* 2019 (Cth)', Hansard, Senate, Australian Parliament, October 16, 2019, 3106.

Dean, Hon. Gordon. 1979. 'Second Reading Speech on the *Patents Amendment Bill* 1979 (Cth)', Hansards, House of Representatives, Australian Parliament, February 28, 1979, 446. https://parlinfo.aph.gov.au/parlInfo/search/display/display.w3p;query = Id%3A%22hansard80%2Fhansardr80%2F1979-02-28%2F0049%22

Designs Law Review Committee. 1973. *Report on the Law Relating to Designs, First Term of Reference*. Canberra: Australian Government, 1973. https://catalogue.nla.gov.au/catalog/2728834

1974. *Report Relating to Utility Models, Second Term of Reference*. Canberra: Australian Government, 1973/1974. https://catalogue.nla.gov.au/catalog/2729094

Entsch, Hon. Warren. 'Second Reading Speech on the *Patents Amendment (Innovation Patents) Bill* 2000 (Cth)', Hansard, House of Representatives, Australian Parliament, June 29, 2000, 18583. https://parlinfo.aph.gov.au/parlInfo/search/display/display.w3p;query = Id%3A%22chamber%2Fhansardr%2F2000–06-29%2F0049%22

Hurford, Hon. Chris. 'Second Reading Speech on the *Patents Amendment Act* 1979 (Cth)', Hansard, House of Representatives, Australian Parliament, February 28, 1979, 449. https://parlinfo.aph.gov.au/parlInfo/search/display/display.w3p;query = Id%3A%22hansard80%2Fhansardr80%2F1979–02-28%2F0050%22

Husic MP, Hon. Ed. 'National Press Club Address: Building the Economy for the Future', National Press Club, November 29, 2022. www.minister.industry.gov.au/ministers/husic/speeches/national-press-club-address-building-economy-future

Intellectual Property and Competition Review Committee (Australia). 2000. *Review of Intellectual Property Legislation under the Competition Principles Agreement*. Canberra: Australian Government.

IP Australia. 2019. 'Innovation Patent Fact Sheet'. www.ipaustralia.gov.au/sites/default/files/innovation_patent_fact_sheet_2019.pdf (web page now archived)

2021. 'Case Study – Designs Reform Project', IP Australia: Annual Report, 2020–2021. www.transparency.gov.au/annual-reports/ip-australia/reporting-year/2020-21-21

2023a. 'ACIP IP Review Archive'. www.ipaustralia.gov.au/about-us/public-consultations/acip-review-archive

2023b. 'Enhancing Australian Design Protection'. https://consultation.ipaustralia.gov.au/policy/enhancing-australian-design-protection/

2023c. 'Data, Research and Reports'. www.ipaustralia.gov.au/tools-and-research/professional-resources/data-research-and-reports

2023d. 'Innovartion Patents'. www.ipaustralia.gov.au/patents/how-to-apply-for-a-standard-patent/innovation-patents

Macphee, Hon. Ian. 'Second Reading Speech on the *Patents Amendment Bill* 1979 (Cth)', Hansard, House of Representatives, Australian Parliament, February 21, 1979, 183. https://parlinfo.aph.gov.au/parlInfo/search/display/display.w3p;query = Id%3A%22hansard80%2Fhansardr80%2F1979-02-21%2F0063%22

McMullan, Hon. Bob. 'Second Reading Speech on the *Patents Amendment (Innovation Patents) Bill* 2000 (Cth)', Hansard, House of Representatives, Australian Parliament, August 31, 2000, 19915., https://parlinfo.aph.gov.au/parlInfo/search/display/display.w3p;query = Id%3A%22chamber%2Fhansardr%2F2000–08-31%2F0143%22

Microsoft, 'A Submission to the Productivity Commission on Intellectual Property Arrangements', June 3, 2016. www.pc.gov.au/__data/assets/pdf_file/0006/201102/subdr420-intellectual-property.pdf

O'Neil MP, Hon. Clare. 'Second Reading Speech on the *Intellectual Property Laws Amendment (Productivity Commission Response Part 2 and Other Measures) Act* 2019 (Cth)', Hansard, House of Representatives, February 5, 2020, 299.

Patrick, Senator Rex. 'Second Reading Speech on the *Intellectual Property Laws Amendment (Productivity Commission Response Part 2 and Other Measures) Act* 2019 (Cth)', Hansard, Senate, Australian Parliament, October 16, 2019, 3092.

Patterson, Senator Kay. 'Second Reading Speech on the *Patents Amendment (Innovation Patents) Bill* 2000 (Cth)', Hansard, Senate, Australian Parliament, November 2, 2000, 18960. https://parlinfo.aph.gov.au/parlInfo/search/display/display.w3p;query = Id%3A%22chamber%2Fhansards%2F2000–11-02%2F0067%22

Perrett MP, Hon. Graham. 'Second Reading Speech on the Intellectual Property Laws Amendment (Productivity Commission Response Part 2 and Other Measures) Act 2019 (Cth)', Hansard, House of Representatives, Australian Parliament, February 5, 2020, 308.

Productivity Commission (Australia). 2010. Bilateral and Regional Trade Agreements. Melbourne: Productivity Commission. www.pc.gov.au/inquiries/completed/trade-agreements/report

2013. *Compulsory Licensing of Patents*. Melbourne: Productivity Commission, 2013. www.pc.gov.au/inquiries/completed/patents/report

2016. *Intellectual Property Arrangements*, Inquiry Report No. 78. Canberra and Melbourne: Productivity Commission. www.pc.gov.au/inquiries/completed/intellectual-property#report

Roberts, Senator Malcolm. 'Second Reading Speech on the *Intellectual Property Laws Amendment (Productivity Commission Response Part 2 and Other Measures) Act* 2019 (Cth)', Hansard, Senate, Australian Parliament, October 16, 2019, 3099.

Shack, Hon. Peter. 'Second Reading Speech on the *Patents Amendment Act* 1979 (Cth)', Hansard, House of Representatives, Australian Parliament, February 28, 1979, 451, https://parlinfo.aph.gov.au/parlInfo/search/display/display.w3p;query = Id%3A%22hansard80%2Fhansardr80%2F1979–02-28%2F0051%22

Wells MP, Hon. Anika. 'Second Reading Speech on the *Intellectual Property Laws Amendment (Productivity Commission Response Part 2 and Other Measures) Act* 2019 (Cth)', Hansard, House of Representatives, Australian Parliament, February 5, 2020, 305.

Brazil

Brazil. Order from April 28, 1809. Coleção de Leis do Império do Brasil – 1809, Vol. 1. www2.camara.leg.br/legin/fed/alvara/anterioresa1824/alvara-40051-28-abril-1809-571629-publicacaooriginal-94774-pe.html

Political Constitution of the Empire of Brazil. March 25, 1824. www.planalto.gov.br/ccivil_03/constituicao/constituicao24.htm

Brazil. House of Representatives. 2013. 'A revisão da Lei de patentes : inovação em prol da competitividade nacional' Pedro Paranaguá (coord.). Dep. Newton Lima (Rel.). Laurez Cerqueira; Graziela Zucoloto; André de Mello e Souza; César Costa Alves de Mattos; Fábio Luis Mendes; Mauricio Jorge Arcoverde de Freitas. Brasília : Câmara dos Deputados, Edições Câmara. www2.camara.leg.br/a-camara/estruturaadm/altosestudos/seminarios/lancamento-patentes-9-10-13/a-revisao-da-lei-de-patentes

Instituto Nacional da Propriedade Industrial [INPI]. n.d. Instituto Nacional da Propriedade Industrial. www.gov.br/inpi/pt-br

n.d. Pesquisa em Propriedade Industrial. https://busca.inpi.gov.br/pePI/jsp/patentes/PatenteSearchBasico.jsp

2002. DIRPA, Diretrizes de Exame de Patentes, v.01.00. www.gov.br/inpi/pt-br/assuntos/arquivos-dirpa/resolucao64_2013_diretrizesoriginaisdepatentes.pdf

2012. DIRPA, Diretriz de Exame de Patentes de Modelo de Utilidade. www.gov.br/inpi/pt-br/servicos/patentes/consultas-publicas/arquivos/diretriz_de_mu_versao_2_original.pdf

2019. Plano de Combate ao Backlog. www.gov.br/inpi/pt-br/servicos/patentes/plano-de-combate-ao-backlog

2022a. Boletim mensal de propriedade industrial: estatísticas preliminares. www.gov.br/inpi/pt-br/central-de-conteudo/estatisticas/arquivos/publicacoes/boletim-mensal-de-propriedade-industrial-marco-de-2022.pdf

2022b. Indicadores (Tempo de Decisão Técnica e Número de Decisões). www.gov.br/inpi/pt-br/servicos/patentes/relatorios-gerenciais/tempodecisao_out-dez_2022.pdf

2022c. Coordenação Técnica de Recursos e Processos Administrativos de Nulidade em Patentes (COREP), Coordenação-Geral de Recursos e Processos Administrativos de Nulidade (CGREC). 2023b. Relatório COREP/CGREC – INPI: 2012–2022. Ed. 3. www.gov.br/inpi/pt-br/servicos/recursos-e-nulidades/relatorio-corep-2012-2022-corrigido.pdf

2023a. Solicitar patente de modelo de utilidade. www.gov.br/pt-br/servicos/solicitar-patente-de-modelo-de-utilidade

China

Agreement on Trade Relations between the United States and the People's Republic of China, China-U.S., July 7, 1979, 31 U.S.T. 4652.

China National Intellectual Property Administration [CNIPA], Notice No. 328 Concerning the Amendment of the Guidelines for Patent Examination, September 23, 2019. www.cnipa.gov.cn/art/2019/9/25/art_74_27623.html

2020. Announcement No. 391 on Amending the Guidelines for Patent Examination, December 11, 2020. www.cnipa.gov.cn/art/2020/12/14/art_74_155606.html

2021a. Announcement No. 411 on the Measures for Regulating Patent Application Activities, March 11, 2021. www.cnipa.gov.cn/art/2021/3/12/art_74_157677.html

2021b. 'Patent Reexamination and Invalidation Department of the Patent Office'. https://english.cnipa.gov.cn/module/download/downfile.jsp?classid = 0&showname = 2021-PATENT%20REEXAMINATION%20AND%20INVALIDATION%20DEPARTMENT%20OF%20THE%20PATENT%20OFFICE,CNIPA.pdf&filename = 90841f90246b474f975a39981500689e.pdf

2021c. 'Notice on Soliciting Public Opinions on the Draft Revision of the Guidelines for Patent Examination (Draft for Comment)', August 3, 2021. www.cnipa.gov.cn/art/2021/8/3/art_75_166474.html

2021d. 'Notice of Further Strictly Regulating Patent Application Activities', January 27, 2021. www.gov.cn/zhengce/zhengceku/2021-01/27/content_5583088.htm
2022a. 'Notice on Soliciting Public Opinions on the Draft Revision of the Guidelines for Patent Examination (Draft Again for Comment)', October 31, 2022. www.cnipa.gov.cn/art/2022/10/31/art_75_180016.html
2022b. 'Statistical Table of Three Kinds of Patent Applications at Home and Abroad'. www.cnipa.gov.cn/art/2022/7/28/art_88_172404.html
2022c. 'Promotion Plan for In-Depth Implementation of the Opinions on Strengthening the Protection of Intellectual Property Rights', October 28, 2022. www.cnipa.gov.cn/art/2022/10/28/art_545_179970.html
2024. 'Case Center'. www.cnipa.gov.cn/col/col2632/index.html
China Patent Electronic Application Network. 2024. http://cponline.cnipa.gov.cn
China Patent Survey Report. 2021.
Detailed Rules for the Implementation of the Patent Law of the People's Republic of China (2010).
Detailed Rules for the Implementation of the Patent Law of the People's Republic of China (2023). www.cnipa.gov.cn/art/2023/12/21/art_3316_189344.html
Patent Law of the People's Republic of China (1984).
Patent Law of the People's Republic of China (as amended on December 27, 2008).
Patent Law of the People's Republic of China (as amended on October 17, 2020).
The State Council of the People's Republic of China. 2018. 'Notice on the Official Launch of the New English Translated Name of the National Intellectual Property Administration', August 28, 2018. www.gov.cn/zhengce/zhengceku/2018-12/31/content_5443904.htm
2019. 'The General Office of the CPC Central Committee and the State Council Issued the Opinions on Strengthening the Protection of Intellectual Property Rights', November 24, 2019. www.gov.cn/zhengce/2019-11/24/content_5455070.htm
2021. 'The CNIPA Responded to a Netizen's Comment on the Proposal to Abolish the Chinese Utility Model Patent System and Improve the Preferential Examination System', May 26, 2021. www.gov.cn/hudong/2021-05/26/content_5611056.htm
2021. 'An Outline for Building a Powerful Intellectual Property Nation (2021-2035)', September 22, 2021. www.gov.cn/zhengce/2021-09/22/content_5638714.htm
2022. 'Xi Jinping: The Report to the 20th National Congress of the Communist Party of China', October 25, 2022. www.gov.cn/xinwen/2022-10/25/content_5721685.htm
State Intellectual Property Office. 2007. Order No. 45 – Several Provisions of the State Intellectual Property Office on Regulating Patent Application Activities, October 1, 2007.
2009. Order No. 67 – Decision of the State Intellectual Property Office on Amending the Guidelines for Patent Examination, September 16, 2013. www.cnipa.gov.cn/art/2013/11/6/art_99_28226.html
2017. Order No. 75 – Decision of the State Intellectual Property Office on Amending the Several Provisions on Regulating Patent Application Activities, April 1, 2017. www.gov.cn/gongbao/content/2017/content_5222952.htm
2023. Order No. 78 – Guidelines for Patent Examination, December 21, 2023. www.cnipa.gov.cn/art/2023/12/21/art_99_189202.html

Denmark

Consolidated Danish Patents Law Act No. 90 of 29 January 2019.
Consolidated Danish Utility Models Act No. 91 of 29 January 2019.

Courts of Denmark. 2024. Case law from the Maritime and Commercial High Court. https://domstol.dk/om-os/english/

Danish Patent and Trademark Office (DKPTO). 2024a. Utility Models Database. https://onlineweb.dkpto.dk/pvsonline/Patent

2024b. Årsstatistik. www.dkpto.dk/Media/638217241817850080/Årsstatistik%202023.pdf

Dansk Brugsmodel Tidende. 2024. Registered Utility Models. https://tidender2.dkpto.dk/

L 49 Forslag til lov om brugsmodeller af 9. november 2005.

Lovforslag nr. L 119 af 20. november 1991, L 49 Forslag til lov om brugsmodeller af 9. November 2005.

Ministerial Order No. 1605 of 8 December 2006, On the Examination and Other Processing of Utility Models Applications and Registered Utility Models.

The Utility Model Act No. 130 of 26 February 1992 and the Consolidated Act No. 367 of 9 June 1998, as amended by Act No. 1431 of 21 December 2005 and Act No. 538 of 8 June 2006.European Union

Administrative Committee. 2022. Rules of Procedure of the Unified Patent Court of 1 September 2022.

Agreement on a Unified Patent Court (2013/C 175/01) of 19 February 2013.

Agreement on Trade-Related Aspects of Intellectual Property Rights (TRIPS) of 15 April 1994.

Code de la Propriété Intellectuelle (French Intellectual Property Code/IPC) of 1 July 1992, last amended May 22, 2020.

COM (1995) 370 of 19 July 1995. The Protection of Utility Models in the Single Market.

(1997) 691 of 12 December 1997 and 28 June 1999. Proposal for a European Parliament and Council Directive appromixating the legal arrangements for the protection of inventions by utility model.

(1999) 309 of 29 August 2000. Amended propsal for a European Parliament and Council Directive approximating the legal arrangements for the protection of inventions by utility model.

(2000) 412 of 28 November 2000. Proposal for a Council Regulation on the Community Patent.

(2005) 462 of 27 September 2005. Outcome of the screening of legislative proposals pending before the Legislator.

(2010) 790 of 7 September 2010. Amending annexes VII, X and XI to Regulation (EC) No. 1774/2002 of the European Parliament and of the Council laying down health rules concerning animal by-products not intended for human consumption.

(2011) 215 of 13. April 2011. Regulation of the European Parliament and of the Council.

COM/2022/666 final. Proposal for a Regulation of the European Parliament and of the Council amending Council Regulation (EC) No. 6/2002 on Community designs and repealing Commission Regulation (EC) No. 2246/2002.

COM/2022/667 final. Proposal for a Directive of the European Parliament and of the Council on the legal protection of designs (recast).

COM (2023) 231 and 223 of 27 April 2023. Regulation of the European Parliament and of the Council on the Supplementary Protection Certificate for Medicinal Products.

(2023) 224. Proposal for a Regulation of the European Parliament and of the Council on compulsory licensing for crisis management and amending Regulation (EC) 816/2006.

Convention for the European Patent for the Common market (*Community Patent Convention*). (76/76/EEC), OJ L17/1. 1976.

Convention on the Grant of European Patents (*European Patent Convention*). 1973. 17th edition 2020.
Council Regulation (EC) No. 6/2002 of 12 December 2001 on Community Designs.
Council Regulation (EU) No. 1260/2012 of 17 December 2012 implementing enhanced cooperation in the area of the creation of unitary patent protection with regard to applicable translation arrangements (UPTReg).
Directive 98/44/EC of the European Parliament and of the Council of 6 July 1998 on the legal protection of biotechnological inventions (Biotech Directive).
Directive 2001/82/EC of the European Parliament and of the Council of 6 November 2001 on the Community code relating to veterinary medicinal products.
Directive 2004/48/EC of the European Parliament and of the Council of 21 April 2004 on the enforcement of intellectual property rights (IP Enforcement Directive).
European Commission. 1995. The Protection of Utility Models in the Single Market. Green Paper COM(95), 370 final. Brussels,July 19,1995.
1997. Proposal for a European Parliament and Council Directive Approximating the Legal Arrangements for the Protection of Inventions by Utility Models. COM(97) 691 final, December 12, 1997.
1999. Amended Proposal for a European Parliament and Council Directive Approximating the Legal Arrangements for the Protection of Inventions by Utility Models. COM(1999) 309 final, June 28, 1999.
2000. Proposal for a Council Regulation on the Community Patent. COM(2000) 412 final, August 1, 2000.
2005a. Communication from the Commission to the Council and the European Parliament. Outcome of the Screening of Legislative Proposals Pending before the Legislator. COM(2005) 462 final, September 27, 2005.
2005b. Statement by the Commission concerning Article 2 of Directive 2004/48/EC of the European Parliament and of the Council on the Enforcement of Intellectual Property Rights (2005/295/EC) April 13, 2005.
2020. Communication from the Commission to the European Parliament, the Council, the European Economic and Social Committee and the Committee of the Region. Making the Most of the EU's Innovative Potential. An Intellectual Property Action Plan to Support the EU's Recovery and Resilience. COM(2020) 760 final, November 25, 2020.
2023a. European Innovation Scoreboard.
2023b. 'Commission Staff Working Document: Report on the Protection and Enforcement of Intellectual Property Rights in Third Countries.' May 17, 2023. https://circabc.europa.eu/rest/download/7099aeeo-c68f-42c5-ae30–5350a879a30e
2023c. Proposal for a Regulation of the European Parliament and of the Council on Standard Essential Patents and Amending Regulation (EU)2017/1001, COM(2023) 232, April 27, 2023.
2024. Entrepreneurship and Small and Medium-Sized Enterprises (SMEs). https://single-market-economy.ec.europa.eu/smes_en
European Commission's IP Helpdesk. 2024. Utility Model. https://intellectual-property-helpdesk.ec.europa.eu/ip-management-and-resources/utility-model_en
European Patent Office. 2015a. Notice from the European Patent Office Dated 30 November 2015 Concerning the Programme for Accelerated Prosecution of European Patent Applications ("PACE"). OJ EPO 2015, A93.
2015b. Notice from the European Patent Office Dated 30 November 2015 Concerning Ways to Expedite the European Grant Procedure. OJ EPO 2015, A94.

2022. Unitary Patent Guide. 2nd ed., April 2022. www.epo.org/en/legal/guide-up
2023a. Member States of the European Patent Organisation. www.epo.org/about-us/organisation/member-states.html
2023b. National Law Relating to the EPC. European Patent Applications and Patents: Law and Practice of the EPC Contracting States, Extension and Validation States, 22nd ed., July 2023.
2024. 3.1 Categories. www.epo.org/en/legal/guidelines-epc/2023/f_iv_3_1.html
European Patent Organisation. 2024. Cost of a Unitary Patent. www.epo.org/en/applying/european/unitary/unitary-patent/cost
Implementing Regulations to the Convention on the Grant of European Patents of 5 October 1973, last amended by decision of the Administrative Council of the European Patent Organisation of 13 October 2022.
Mercell. 2014. Study on the Economic Impact of the Utility Model Legislation in Selected Member States. January 24, 2014. www.mercell.com/en/tender/40184664/study-on-the-economic-impact-of-the-utility-model-legislation-in-selected-member-states-tender.aspx
Protocol (No 3) on the Statute of the Court of Justice of the European Union, Annexed to the Treaty on the European Union and the Treaty on the Functioning of the European Union.
Regulation (EC) No. 469/2009 of the European Parliament and of the Council of 6 May 2009 Concerning the Supplementary Protection Certificate for Medicinal Products.
Regulation (EU) No. 1257/2012 of the European Parliament and of the Council of 17 December 2012 Implementing Enhanced Cooperation in the Area of the Creation of Unitary Patent Protection (Unitary Patent Regulation/UPReg).
Regulation (EU) 2017/1001 of the European Parliament and of the Council of 14 June 2017 on the European Union trade mark.
SEC (2001) 1307. Summary Report of Replies to the Questionnaire on the Impact of the Community Utility Model with a View to Updating the Green Paper on Protection by the Utility Model in the Internal Market.
Treaty Establishing the European Economic Community (Rome Treaty). 1957. Document 11957E/TXT.
Treaty on the Functioning of the European Union (Treaty of Lisbon), 2016/C 202/01.

Germany

Deutsche Patent and Trademark Office (DPMA). 2014. 'Utility Models FAQ', http://dpma.de/english/utility_models/faq/index.html
2017. 'Utility Models: An Information Brochure on Utility Model Protection'.
2020. 'Utility Models', October 20, 2020. www.dpma.de/english/utility_models/index.html
2021. 'Splitting Off a Utility Model from a Patent Application', March 5, 2021. www.dpma.de/english/utility_models/application/splitting_off/index.html
2024a. 125 Jahre Gebrauchsmusterschutz. www.dpma.de/service/presse/wissenswertes/schutzrechte/125_jahre/index.html
2024b. Aktuelle Statistiken: Gebrauchsmuster. www.dpma.de/dpma/veroeffentlichungen/statistiken/gebrauchsmuster/index.html
2024c. Questions around Utility Models. www.dpma.de/english/utility_models/faq/index.html
2024d. Questions around Patents. www.dpma.de/english/patents/faq/index.html
2024e. Utility Models. www.dpma.de/english/services/forms/utility_models/index.html

2024f. Fees for Utility Model Protection. www.dpma.de/english/services/fees/utilitymodels/index.html

Gebrauchsmustergesetz. May 5, 1936 (German Utility Model Act).

Gesetz zu dem Übereinkommen vom 27. November 1963 zur Vereinheitlichung gewisser Begriffe des materiellen Rechts der Erfindungspatente, dem Vertrag vom 19. Juni 1970 über die internationale Zusammenarbeit auf dem Gebiet des Patentwesens und dem Übereinkommen vom 5. Oktober 1973 über die Erteilung europäischer Patente (Gesetz über internationale Patentübereinkommen) Bundesgesetzblatt 1976 II Nr. 32, p. 649.

German Model Bilateral Investment Treaty 2005.

Germany – Pakistan Bilateral Investment Agreement 2009.

India

DIPP, 2011. 'Discussion Paper on Utility Models', Department of Industrial Policy & Promotion, Government of India. http://dipp.nic.in/english/Discuss_paper/Utility_Models_13May2011.pdf

International

Berne Convention for the Protection of Literary and Artistic Works, 1886.

General Agreement on Tariffs and Trade: Multilateral Trade Negotiations Final Act Embodying the Result of the Uruguay Round of Multilateral Trade Negotiations, April 15, 1994, D.O.S. 95–33, 33 I.L.M. 1125, 1197.

Harare Protocol on Patents and Industrial Designs within the Framework of the African Regional Intellectual Property Organization 1982.

Madrid Agreement Concerning the International Registration of Marks, April 14, 1891, as revised July 14, 1967, 828 U.N.T.S. 389; Protocol Relating to the Madrid Agreement Concerning the International Registration of Marks, June 28, 1989, as amended on November 12, 2007, 28 Indus. Prop. L. & Treaties 3-007, 001 (July–August 1989).

North American Free Trade Agreement (NAFTA), December 17, 1992, 32 I.L.M. 289 (preamble to chapter 10); 32 I.L.M. 605

Paris Convention for the Protection of Industrial Property, art. 1, ¶ 2, July 14, 1967, 21 U.S.T. 1583, 828 U.N.T.S. 305

Patent Cooperation Treaty, June 19, 1970, 28 U.S.T. 7645, 1160 U.N.T.S. 231.

TRIPS: Agreement on Trade-Related Aspects of Intellectual Property Rights, April 15, 1994, Marrakesh Agreement Establishing the World Trade Organization, Annex 1C, 1869 U.N.T.S. 299, 33 I.L.M. 1197.

United Nations, Department of Economic and Social Affairs. 2020a. 'World Economic Situation and Prospect'. www.un.org/development/desa/dpad/publication/world-economic-situation-and-prospects-2020/

2020b. 'Economic Analysis, LDCs at a Glance'. www.un.org/development/desa/dpad/least-developed-country-category/ldcs-at-a-glance.html

United Nations Conference on Trade and Development (UNCTAD). 2023. Revisiting Development Innovations in Least Developed Countries: A Practical Review of Selected Intellectual Property Rights Measures.

2024. Harnessing Intellectual Property Rights for Innovation, Development and Economic Transformation in Least Developed Countries. January 2024.

United States-Mexico-Canada Agreement (USMCA) December 10, 2019. 134 Stat. 11.

WIPO Copyright Treaty, December 20, 1996. S. Treaty Doc. No. 105-17 (1997); 2186 U.N.T.S. 121; 36 I.L.M. 65 (1997).

World Intellectual Property Organization (WIPO). 1980. WIPO Model Law for Developing Countries on Inventions: Examination and Registration of Contracts, Inventors' Certificates, Technovations, Transfer of Technology Patents. WIPO Publication 841, vol. 2.

2018. World Intellectual Property Indicators. Geneva: WIPO.

2021. Innovation Driving Human Progress. WIPO and the Sustainable Development Goals. Geneva: WIPO.

2022a. World Intellectual Property Indicators 2022. www.wipo.int/edocs/pubdocs/en/wipo-pub-941-2022-en-world-intellectual-property-indicators-2022.pdf

2022b. 'Global Innovation Index 2022: What Is the Future of Innovation Driven Growth?' www.wipo.int/edocs/pubdocs/en/wipo-pub-2000-2022-en-main-report-global-innovation-index-2022-15th-edition.pdf

2023a. World Intellectual Property Indicators 2023. www.wipo.int/edocs/pubdocs/en/wipo-pub-941-2023-en-world-intellectual-property-indicators-2023.pdf

2023b. Utility Models. www.wipo.int/patents/en/topics/utility_models.html

2023c. Global Innovation Index: Innovation in the Face of Uncertainty. World Intellectual Property Organization.

2023d. WIPO IP Statistics Data Centre. www3.wipo.int/ipstats/index.htm?tab = utility

2023e. Member States. www.wipo.int/members/en/

2024a. WIPO Lex. www.wipo.int/wipolex/en/index.html

2024b. WIPO Patentscope. www.wipo.int/patentscope/en/

2024c. Annual WIPO Intellectual Property Judges Forum (November, Geneva).

World Bank. 2023. GDP (current US$).

2024. 'GDP Per Capita (Current US$) – Korea, Rep.' https://data.worldbank.org/indicator/NY.GDP.PCAP.CD?locations = KR

Italy

Decree of the President of the Republic 8 January 1979, No. 32 on European and Community Patents.

Decree of the President of the Republic 22 June 1979, No. 338, Revision of the Legislation on Patents.

Law 30 August 1868, No. 4578 on Industrial Designs and Models.

Law 23 May 1977, No. 265 on the Duration of Patents for Utility Models and Ornamental Models and Designs.

Law 14 February 1987, No. 60 Harmonizing Laws on Patents for Models and Industrial Designs with the Hague Agreement of November 6, 1925.

Legislative Decree 2 February 2001, No. 95 Implementing Directive 98/71/CE on the Legal Protection of Designs and Models.

Legislative Decree 10 February 2005, No. 30, Industrial Property Code (IPC).

Regulation (EU) No. 1257/2012 of 17 December 2012 Implementing Enhanced Cooperation in the Area of the Creation of Unitary Patent Protection,

Royal Decree 13 September 1934, No. 1602 on Industrial Patents and Trademarks.

Royal Decree 29 June 1939, No. 1127 on Patents for Industrial Inventions.

Royal Decree of 25 August 1940, No. 1411 on Industrial Models.

Japan

Advisory Council for the Japan Patent Office. 2004. Report. www.jpo.go.jp/resources/shingikai/sangyo-kouzou/shousai/jitsuyou-wg/document/h16houkokusho/utility_model_wg.pdf

First Team of the 2021 Committee on Patents. 2022. Examination of a New System for Utility Models, Patent, vol. 75, no. 9.

Japan-Indonesia Economic Partnership Agreement 2007.

Japan Patent Office (JPO). 1984. One Hundred Year History of the Industrial Property System.

2023. Report. www.jpo.go.jp/resources/report/nenji/2023/document/index/0202.pdf

Korea

Korean Intellectual Property Office. 2022. 'Industrial Property Annual Report.'

2023. 'Fee Information'. www.patent.go.kr/smart/jsp/ka/menu/fee/main/FeeMain01.do

2024. 'Statistics'. www.kipo.go.kr/en/HtmlApp?c = 97000&catmenu = ek07_03_01

Poland

Explanatory Memorandum to the draft of the [Polish] Industrial Property Law. https://legislacja.rcl.gov.pl/docs//2/12359055/12874004/12874005/dokument552323.pdf

Patent Office of the Republic of Poland (Polish Patent Office). 2003. Annual Report. https://uprp.gov.pl/pl/publikacje/raport-roczny-uprp

2022. Annual Report.

United Kingdom

UK Board of Trade

BT 1/379. Report of Registrar of Designs to the Board of Trade respecting the origin, nature and tendency of the Designs Copyright Act (Letters to Board of Trade (November 3, 1841).

BT/1/413. 'The Prince Memorial' (June 29, 1843).

BT 45/1.

BT 45/2.

BT 45/3.

BT 45/4.

BT 45/5.

BT 45/6.

BT 45/7.

BT 45/9.

BT 45/10.

BT 45/12.

BT 45/14.

BT 50/21/16596.

BT 50/157/173011.

BT 51/9/16596.

BT 51/64/173011.

BT 209/283.
BT 209/282 BT 209/288 (Minutes of Meetings of Sargant Committee).
BT 209/479.
BT209/480.
BT 209/485 (Lord Parker's Committee).
BT 209/486 (Recommendations of the British Electrical Allied Manufacturers Association 1916).

UK Parliamentary Papers

Board of Trade, *Report of the Departmental Committee on Industrial Designs* (Cmnd. 1808) (1962) ('Johnston Committee').
The British Patent System. Report of the Committee to Examine the Patent System and Patent Law (Cmnd. 4407) (1970–71) ('Banks Committee').
Green Paper, *Intellectual Property and Innovation* (Cmnd 9117) (1983) ('Nicholson Committee').
Reform of the Law relating to Copyright, Designs and Performers' Protection (Cmnd. 8302) (1981).
Report of the Committee on the Signet and Privy Seal Offices: with minutes of evidence and appendix (1849) (C 1099) 22 PP 453 ('Report on Signet (1849)').
Report of the Departmental Committee on the Patents and Designs Act and the Practice of the Patent Office (Cmd. 3829) (1931) ('Sargant Committee').
Report and minutes of evidence taken before the Select Committee of the House of Lords appointed to consider Bill intituled "An act further to amend the Law touching letters Patent for Inventions" and also the Bill intituled "An Act for the further amendment of the Law touching Letters Patent for Inventions" (1851) (HC Papers 486) 18 PP 255 ('SCPB 1851')
'Report of the Proceedings of the Design Office' in *First Report of the Department of Science and Art* (1854) 28 PP 269, 463, App. N.
Report from the Select Committee on Letters Patent; together with the proceedings of the committee, minutes of evidence, appendix, and index (1872) (HC Papers 193), 11 PP.
Report from the Select Committee on the Law Relative to Patents for Inventions (1829) (HC Papers 332), 3 PP 415. ('SCLPI (1829)').
Report from the Select Committee on Pawnbrokers 1870 Together with Proceedings of the Committee, Minutes of Evidence and Appendix. 377. (1870) 8 PP.
Select Committee on Metropolis Police Offices 1837, (1837) 12 PP.
Select Committee on Metropolis Police Offices, Report, Minutes of Evidence, Appendix, Index 1838, (1838) 15 PP.
Select Committee of House of Lords to consider Bill, intituled, Act to extend provisions of Designs Act, 1850, and to give Protection from Piracy to Persons exhibiting new Inventions in Exhibition of Works of Industry of all Nations in 1851 (1851) (HC Papers 145) 18 PP 671. ('SCPI 1851').

Other UK Agency Materials

Department of Trade and Industry, *Intellectual Property and Innovation* (Cmnd. 9712) (1986).
Report of the Commission on Intellectual Property Rights. 2002. *Integrating Intellectual Property Rights and Development Policy*. London: Stationery Office.
Report on International Development. 2000. *Eliminating World Poverty: Making Globalisation Work for the Poor*. London: Stationery Office, Cm 5006.

Reports of Proceedings before Houses of Parliament

Hansard (HS), Vol. 278, col 349–50 (April 16, 1883) (Second reading of Patents, Designs and Trade Marks Bill).

UK Legislation

An Act for the Encouragement of the Arts of designing and printing Linens, Cottons, Calicoes and Muslins by Vesting the Properties thereof in the Designers, Printers and Proprietors for a Limited Time, 27 Geo. 3, c.23 (1787).

An Act for Amending and making perpetual an Act for the Encouragement of the Arts of designing and printing Linens, Cottons, Calicoes and Muslins by Vesting the Properties thereof in the Designers, Printers and Proprietors for a Limited Time, 34 Geo. 3, c. 23 (1794).

An Act to Secure to Proprietors of Designs for Articles of Manufacture the Copyright of such Designs for a Limited Time, 2 Vict., c.17 (1839).

An Act for regulating the Metropolitan Police Court, 2 & 3 Vict., c.71 (1839).

An Act to consolidate and amend the Laws relating to the Copyright of Designs for ornamenting Articles of Manufacture, 5 & 6 Vict., c.100 (1842) ('ODA').

An Act to consolidate amend the Laws relating to the Copyright of Designs, 6 & 7 Vict., c. 65 (1843) ('The UDA').

An Act for the More Easy Recovery of Small Debts, 9 & 10 Vict., c. 95 (1846) ('The County Courts Act').

An Act to facilitate the performance of the duties of Justices of the Peace out of Sessions within England and Wales, with respect to Persons charged with Indictable Offences 11 & 12 Vict., c. 42 (1848).

An Act to regulate certain Offices in the Petty Bag in the High Court of Chancery, etc., 11 & 12 Vict., c.94 (1848).

An Act to extend and amend the Acts relating to Copyright of Designs, 13 & 14 Vict., c. 104 (1850), ('Designs Act 1850').

An Act to Extend the Provision of the Designs Act, 1850, and to give Protection from Piracy to Persons exhibiting new Inventions in the Exhibition of the Works of Industry of All Nations in 1851, 14 Vict., c. 8 ('Protection of Inventors Act 1851').

An Act for Extending the Term of the Provisional Registration for Inventions under the Protections of Inventions Act, 15 & 16 Vict., c. 6 (1851).

An Act for amending the Law for granting Patents of Inventions, 15 & 16 Vict., c. 83 ('Patent Law (Amendment) Act 1852').

An Act to amend the act of the fifth and sixth years of Her present Majesty, to consolidate and amend the laws relating to the Copyright of Designs for ornamenting Articles of Manufacture, 21 & 22 Vict. c. 70 (1858) ('Copyright of Designs Act, 1858').

Patents Designs and Trade Marks Act, 46 & 47 Vict. c.57 (1883) ('PDTMA').

Patents Designs and Trade Marks Act, 51 & 52 Vict., c.30 (1888) (PDTMA 1888)

Patent Office (UK). 1884. Designs Rules. *Official Journal of the Patent Office*, January 4, 1884 1: 79.

Patents and Designs Act 1919.

Registered Designs Act 1949.

United States

U.S. Copyright Off. 2023. 'Copyright Small Claims and the Copyright Claims Board', December 6, 2023. www.copyright.gov/about/small-claims/.

U.S. Dept. Justice, & Federal Trade Comm'n. 2007. 'Antitrust Enforcement and Intellectual Property Rights: Innovation and Competition'.

U.S. Patent & Trademark Off. 2023a. 'Law School Clinic Certification Program'. December 6, 2023. www.uspto.gov/learning-and-resources/ip-policy/public-information-about-practitioners/law-school-clinic-1.

2023b. 'Micro Entity Status'. December 6, 2023. www.uspto.gov/patents/laws/micro-entity-status.

2023c. 'Patent Pro Bono Program: Free Patent Legal Assistance'. December 6, 2023. www.uspto.gov/patents/basics/using-legal-services/pro-bono/patent-pro-bono-program.

2023d. 'Patents Pendency Data October 2023', December 3, 2023. www.uspto.gov/dashboard/patents/pendency.html.

2023e. 'USPTO Fee Schedule'. December 3, 2023, www.uspto.gov/learning-and-resources/fees-and-payment/uspto-fee-schedule#Patent%20Fees.

U.S. Patent and Trademark Off. 2022. Small Claims Patent Court Study (Request for Comments). 87 Fed. Reg. 26183.

CASES

Australia

Aristocrat Technologies Australia Pty Ltd v. Commissioner of Patents [2022] Hearing (10 July, 2022), www.hcourt.gov.au/cases/case_s40-2022

Britax Childcare Pty Ltd v. Infa-Secure Pty Ltd [2012a] FCA 467 (May 9).

Britax Childcare Pty Ltd v. Infa-Secure Pty Ltd (No 3) [2012b] FCA 1019.

Coretell Pty Ltd v. Australian Mud Company Pty Ltd [2017] FCAFC 54.

D'Arcy v. Myriad Genetics Inc. (2015) 258 CLR 334.

Datadot Technology Ltd v. Alpha Microtech Pty Ltd [2003] FCA 962 (August 5, 2003).

Dura-Post (Aust) Pty Ltd v. Delnorth Pty Ltd (2009) 177 FCR 239

Grant v. Commissioner of Patents (2006) 154 FCR 62.

National Research Development Corporation v. Commissioner of Patents ('NRDC') (1959) 102 CLR 252.

Quaker Chemical (Australasia) Pty Ltd v. Fuchs Lubricants (Australasia) Pty Ltd (No 2) [2020] FCA 306.

Seafood Innovations Pty Ltd v. Richard Bass Pty Ltd [2011] FCAFC 83.

Thaler v. Commissioner of Patents (2021) FCA 879 at [124], relying on s2A of the Australian Patents Act (Cth) 1990. The decision was subsequently reversed by the Australian Federal Court in Commissioner of Patents v. Thaler, [2022] FCAFC 62.

Austria

Teleskopfausleger, Austrian Patent Office, Supreme Patent and Trademark Senate, Austria, decision of December 22, 2010, OGM 1/10.

Brazil

Brazil. Supreme Court, Unconstitutionality Action n. 5529 (Action n. 4000796-72.2016.1.00.0000. https://portal.stf.jus.br/processos/detalhe.asp?incidente=4984195

China

Gree v. Aux [案号：一审：（2017）粤73民初390号；二审：（2018）粤民终1132号] Case No. 390, First Instance (Guangdong High People's Ct. 2017), Case No. 1132, Second Instance (Guangdong High People's Ct. 2018) (China).
Bai Wanqing v. Chengdu Hard-to-Find Goods Marketing Service Center and Other Disputes Over Patent Infringement of Utility Models [指导案例55号：柏万清诉成都难寻物品营销服务中心等侵害实用新型专利权纠纷案（最高人民法院审判委员会讨论通过2015年11月19日发布）"] Sup. People's Ct. Guiding Case No. 55, November 19, 2015 (China).

European Union

Case C-15/74 Centrafarm BV and Adriaan de Peijper v. Sterling Drug Inc. (1974) ECR 1974 01147.
Case C-34/10 Brüstle v. Greenpeace [2011] ECR I-9849.
Cofemel – Sociedade de Vestuário SA v. G-Star Raw CV, European Court of Justice, decision of September 12, 2019, C-683/17.
Dominguez v. Centre informatique du Centre Ouest Atlantique, Préfet de la région Centre, European Court of Justice (ECJ), decision of January 24, 2012, C-282/10.
Joint cases C-56/64 and 58/64 Établissements Consten S.à.R.L. and Grundig-Verkaufs-GmbH v. Commission of the European Economic Community (1966) ECR 1966 00429.
Kingdom of Spain and Italian Republic v. Council of the European Union, European Court of Justice (ECJ), decision of April 16, 2013, joined cases C-274/11 and C-295/11.
Kingdom of Spain v. European Parliament and Council of the European Union, European Court of Justice (ECJ), decision of May 5, 2015, C-146/13.
Philip Morris Brands SARL and Others v. Secretary of State for Health, European Court of Justice (ECJ), decision of May 4, 2016, C-547/14.
The Queen, on the application of Alliance for Natural Health and Nutri-Link Ltd v. Secretary of State for Health and The Queen, on the application of National Association of Health Stores and Health Food Manufacturers Ltd v. Secretary of State for Health and National Assembly for Wales, European Court of Justice (ECJ), decision of July 12, 2005, joined cases C-154/04 and C-155/04.
The Queen, on the application of Vodafone Ltd and Others v. Secretary of State for Business, Enterprise and Regulatory Reform, European Court of Justice (ECJ), decision of June 8, 2010, C-58/08.
S.H.D. 6. januar 2023 i 1.-instanssag BS-25766/2021-SHR.

Germany

Demonstrationsschrank, Federal Court of Justice (FCJ), Germany, decision of June 20, 2006, X ZB 27/05.
RRMS-Therapie, Regional Court Dusseldorf (RCD), decision of September 1, 2022, 4a O 27/22.

Italy

App. Milano 22 October 1971, Rivest Polival s.d.f. c. ditta Piero Brambilla.
App. Bologna 1 February 1972, Successori Italo-Svizzera Macchine Agricole v. Sergio Verdini.

App. Milano 4 February 1972, A.C.F.A. Accessori Calzature Fibbie e Affini s.a.s. c. Ruggiero Olivieri e figli, Dolomite s.a.s., Gianni Munari e Marico Cagnoli e v. Calzaturificio San Marco.

Cass. 15 December 1983, No. 7398, Bellco s.p.a. v. Ministero Industria Commercio e Artigianato.

Cass. 2 April 2008, No. 8510, Candy v. BSH Bosch und Siemens Haugeräte.

Cass. 11 September 2009, No. 19688, Gipron Giuseppe Pronzati s.p.a. v. Masters s.r.l. et al.

Cass. 10 August 2016, No. 16949, Tecnosystem s.p.a. v. Vecam-Co. s.p.a. and VECAMCO s.r.l.

Cass. 16 September 2019, No. 22984, Gemata s.p.a. v. Bergi s.p.a.

Cass. 12 March 2012, No. 7110, Inoxa v. Compagnucci Rossano, Compagnucci Holding s.p.a. in liquidazione and Compagnucci s.p.a.

Trib. Torino 3 March 2022 (order), Combustion and Energy s.r.l., C&E Group s.r.l. v. Sirena s.p.a. and Obsta.

Kenya

In re Request for Relief by Alex Muigai Muchiri and Itesyl Technologies against Cooperative Bank Of Kenya Limited, Proptech Kenya and Ezen Partners Limited (Industrial Properties Tribunal) IPT Case Number E002 (2021).

Zaidat Limited v. Fenesi Management Limited and Fenesi Limited (Industrial Properties Tribunal) IPT Case No. 86, 88, 89, 90, 91, 92 and 93 (2020).

Korea

Patent Ct., 2004, 2003He0915 (S. Kor.)

Sup. Ct., April 12, 2002, 99Hu2150 (S. Kor.)

Sup. Ct. January 19, 2012, 2010Da95390 (S. Kor.)

United Kingdom

Barker v. Millingen, (1845) *Evening Standard*, July 22, p. 5; *The Times*, July 23, p. 7 (Vice-Chancellor).

Bentley v. Carver (December 4–5, 1844) *London Journal of Arts and Sciences* 25: 414 (nisi prius, Westminster, Tindal CJ with special jury).

Bentley v. Fleming (1844) *London Journal of Arts and Sciences* 25:199 (nisi prius, Liverpool Assizes, Cresswell J.); *London Journal of Arts and Sciences* 25:412, 1 C.B. 479, 135 E.R. 627(Common Pleas).

Besley v. Gallie (December 29, 1848) *The Times*, December 30, p. 7; *Morning Advertiser*, December 30, p. 4; *The Era*, December 31, p. 5; *The Times*, January 4, 1849, p. 5 (letter); *The Sun*, January 4, 1849, p. 1 (letter); (Bow St Police Court).

R v. Bessell (1851) 16 Queen's Bench Reports 810, 117 E.R. 109; 17 *Law Times* 104; *Morning Herald*, April 28, p. 6 (Queen's Bench).

Bessell v. Wilson (1852–1853) *Morning Chronicle*, July 9, 1852, p. 8; *The Times*, July 9, 1852, p. 8 (nisi prius); (November 3, 1852) (rule nisi); (January 19, 1853); (1853) 1 El & Bl 489; 118 E.R. 518; 20 *Law Times* 233; 17 *Justice of the Peace* 567; *The Times*, January 20, 1853, p. 7 (Queen's Bench).

Biddell v. Rogers and De Costa (October 1, 1852) *The Times*, October 2, p. 8; *Morning Herald*, October 2, p. 7; *The Globe*, October 2, p. 4; *Daily News*, October 2, p. 3 (Guildhall Police Court).

Boswell v. Denton (September 13, 1845) *The Times*, September 15, p. 8; *London Journal and Pioneer*, September 20, p. 6; *Repertory of Patent Inventions* 6: 265 (Guildhall Police Court).

Brown v. Wigram (1850) London Evening Standard, December 6, p. 4; Shipping and Mercantile Gazette, December 6 (Court of Exchequer).

Burkin v. Pratt, Hurst & Co. (1893) 12 RPC 371.

Burnett v. Smith (July 24, 1844) *London Journal of Arts and Sciences* 25: 137 (Vice-Chancellor).

Clark & Roskell v. Grimes (1851) *Morning Advertiser*, December 16, p. 7 (Marlborough St Police Court).

In re Clarke [1896] 2 Ch 38 (Court of Appeal).

Coalbrookdale Co v. John Page (1851) *Birmingham Journal*, January 25, p. 5; *Patent Journal and Inventors' Magazine* 10: 214–215 (County Court).

Cooper v. Symington (1893) 10 RPC 264 (High Court, Ch. D.).

Crosskill v. Grounsull (1844) *London Journal of Arts and Sciences* 25: 208 (nisi prius, Liverpool assizes).

Dixon v. Bessell (1850) *Morning Post*, October 2, p. 4; *Mechanics' Magazine* 53: 274 (Guildhall Police Court).

Engell & Co v. Foster & Co (May 5, 1851) *Morning Advertiser*, May 6, p. 6 (Guildhall Police Court).

Engell & Co v. Thomas and James Venables (May 24, 1851) Morning Advertiser, May 26, p. 7; *Patent Journal and Inventors' Magazine* 11:104 (Worship Street Police Court).

Evans v. Harlow (1843) Macclesfield Courier, August 5, p. 2; *London Journal of Arts and Sciences* 23: 147 (Stockport Borough).

Fox v. Evans (May 1848) *Weekly Chronicle*, May 7, p. 9; *Morning Advertiser*, May 8, p. 4; (1848) *Patent Journal and Inventors' Magazine* 4 (103): 604 (Guildhall Police Court).

Grant v. Welch, Margetson & Co (April 4, 1849) *Morning Post*, April 5, p. 8; *Morning Herald*, April 5, p. 7; (1849) *Patent Journal and Inventors' Magazine* 7: 8 (Guildhall Police Court).

Grassby v. Westerdale (1842) *Mechanics' Magazine* 36: 511 (Patrington, Yorkshire, Petty Sessions).

Gregory v. Armstrong (1851) *Morning Post*, March 10, p. 8 (Thames Police Court).

Guise v. Walsh (March 12, 1846) *Morning Post*, March 13, p. 3 (Guildhall Police Court).

Haynes v. Brown (February1848) *Morning Advertiser*, February 21, p. 4; (1848) *Patent Journal and Inventors' Magazine* 4(92):334 (Guildhall Police Court).

Hervey v. Kurtz (1848) *Morning Herald*, August 3, p. 7; *Morning Herald*, December 4, p. 6 (Rolls Court).

Holder v. Osborn (1862) *Birmingham Daily Post*, March 19, p. 3 (Birmingham Public Office 1862)

Holdsworth v. McRea (1867) L.R. 2 H.L. 380 (House of Lords).

Kennedy and Asprey v. Coombs and Finlay (February 15, 1845) *London Journal of Arts and Science* 26: 111–113 (Marlborough St Police Court).

Loveridge v. Gray, Bailey and Bartlett (January 31, 1861) *Birmingham Journal*, February 2, p. 6 (Birmingham Public Office).

Mangall v. M'Alpine (December 16–18, 1844) *London Journal of the Arts and Sciences* 25: 417 (Guildhall, Tindal CJ and Special Jury); (1846) 3 C.B. 496, 136 E.R. 198 (Common Pleas).

Margetson v. May (October 1844) *The Times*, October 2, 1844, p.8; *Morning Advertiser*, October 2, 1844, p.4; *Weekly Chronicle*, October 5, 1844, p. 6; *London Journal of Arts and Sciences* 25: 338

Margetson v. Wright (June 3, 1848) *Morning Advertiser*, June 5, p. 4; *Patent Journal and Inventors Magazine* 5(107): 59 (Guildhall Police Court); *The Times*, July 19, p. 7; *Morning Herald*, July 19; *Patent Journal and Inventors Magazine* 5: 213; (1848) 2 De G & Sm 420, 64 ER 188; (Vice-Chancellor); *The Times*, February 6, 1849 p. 7 (Queen's Bench).

M'Koy and Sidney v. Robertson, *New Times*, July 28, 1826, p. 3 (Vice-Chancellor).

Millingen v. Picken (1845), *Weekly Dispatch*, February 23, p. 4 (nisi prius); *The Times*, April 18, p. 8 (rule nisi); *Law Chronicle, Commercial and Bankruptcy Register*, April 19, p. 7; *The Times*, June 4, p. 8; *Evening Mail*, June 4, p. 7; (1845) 5 *Law Times* 216; 1 C.B. 798 (Common Pleas).

Moody v. Tree (1892) 9 RPC 333 (High Court, Q.B.D.).

In the Matter of Morton's Design (1900) 17 RPC 117.

Motte v. Lancaster (June 19, 1850) *Morning Advertiser*, June 20, p. 4; *Morning Post*, June 20, p. 8; *Patent Journal and Inventors Magazine* 9: 159–160 (Guildhall Police Court).

Motte v. Welch et al (August 29, 1850), *Morning Advertiser*, August 30, p. 4; *Morning Post*, August 30, p. 4 (Guildhall Police Court).

Muntz v. Foster (February 8–13, 1844) *London Journal of Arts and Sciences* 24: 299 (nisi prius Westminster, before Tindal CJ and a special jury).

Newall v. Webster (1844) *Mechanics Magazine* 42 (1120): 56 (Exchequer).

Nickels v. Haslam (1844) *Repertory of Patent Inventions* 4:172; 7 Man. & G. 378, 135 E.R. 158 (Common Pleas).

Pinches v. Addenbrokes (October 9–10, 1850) *London Evening Standard*, October 10, p. 4, October 11, p. 4; *Morning Herald*, October 10, p. 7; October 11, p 8; *Morning Chronicle*, October 10, p. 8; *Morning Advertiser*, October 10, p. 4; *Globe*, October 10, 1850, p. 4; *Patent Journal and Inventors' Magazine* 10:15 (Guildhall Police Court).

Pinches v. Le Challas (October 9–10, 1850) *London Evening Standard*, October 10, p. 4, October 11, p. 4; *Morning Herald*, October 10, p. 7; October 11, p. 8; *Morning Chronicle*, October 10, p. 8; *Morning Advertiser*, October 10, p. 4; *Globe*, October 10, p. 4 (Guildhall Police Court).

Pow v. Taunton (April 10–11, 1844) *London Journal of Arts and Sciences* 24: 458 (Liverpool Assizes, Rolfe B. and Special jury); 9 Jurist 1056 (Queen's Bench).

Price v. Chambers (December 31, 1847) *Morning Advertiser*, January 1, 1848, p. 4; (1848) *Patent Journal and Inventors' Magazine* 4(85):166; (Guildhall Police Court)

Robertson v. Norris (1857) *St James' Chronicle*, November 12, p. 6; *Herapath's Journal*, November 21, p. 1190, 1191 (Vice-Chancellor); *Morning Herald*, January 29, 1858, p. 7 (Lord Chancellor).

Rogers and Beedle v. Driver (1850) *Berkshire Chronicle*, March 2, p. 3; *Reading Mercury*, March 2, p. 2 (nisi prius, Berkshire Lent assizes); *Morning Herald*, March 2, p. 7 (misstating the complainants as 'Rogers and Beesley' and the judge to be Cresswell J); *Oxford Chronicle and Reading Gazette*, March 2, p. 3 (nisi prius); (1850) 16 Q.B. 102, 117 E.R. 817 (1851) 20 L.J.Q.B. 31; *Law Times* 364 (Queen's Bench).

Rubery v. Barr (November 3, 1845) *London Journal of the Arts and Sciences* 27:374 (Vice-Chancellor).

Russell v. Ledsam (June 24–25, 1844) *London Journal of Arts and Sciences* 25:44 (nisi prius, Westminster, before Baron Alderson and special jury)

Sealy v. Browne (November 16–17, 1843) *London Journal of Arts and Sciences* 23: 468 (Rolls Court).

Stead v. Williams (1843) *London Journal of Arts and Sciences* 23: 211 (nisi prius, Cresswell J.), 25: 140; (1844) *London Journal of the Arts and Sciences* 25: 140, (1844) *Repertory of Patent Inventions* 249; 7 Man. & Gr. 818, 135 E.R. 332 (Common Pleas).

Taylor v. Cowley (1868) *Aris's Birmingham Gazette*, April 23, p. 6 and April 25, p. 7 (Birmingham Public Office)

Tecalemit Ltd v. Ewarts Lts (No. 2) (1927) 44 RPC 503 (High Court, Ch. D.)

Twigg v. Smith and Kemp (November 20, 1848) *Birmingham Journal*, November 25, 1848, p. 6 (Public Office, Birmingham).

Tyler & Sons v. Sharpe Brothers (1894) 11 RPC 35 (High Court, Ch. D).

Vine & Others v. Johnson (December 28, 1843) *Repertory of Patent Inventions* 3: 118 (Worship Street Police Court).

Walker, Hunter, & Co v. Hecla Foundry (1889) 6 RPC 554 (House of Lords).

Ward v. Key (December 1, 1847) *The Times*, December 2, p. 7; *Patent Journal and Inventors' Magazine* 4(81); 61 (nisi prius with special jury).

Warner v. Woolley (March 22, 1845), *Mechanics' Magazine* 42: 215 (Guildhall Police Court).

Webb v. Hughes (April 12, 1847) *Mechanics' Magazine* 46 (No. 1236): 383; *Patents Journal and Inventors' Magazine* 2: 776 (Guildhall Police Court).

Welch v. May (October 1844) *The Times*, October 2, p.8; *Morning Advertiser*, October 2, p.4; *Weekly Chronicle*, October 5, p. 6; *London Journal of Arts and Science* 25: 338 (Guildhall Police Court).

R v. Welch (1851) 17 LT 105; 15 Justice of the Peace 338; Shipping and Mercantile Gazette, May 5, p. 4 (Queen's Bench).

Williams v. Rimell (October 1845) *Morning Post*, October 28, p. 7 (Hammersmith Police Court).

Wolferstan v. Warner (November 5, 1844), *London Journal of Arts and Sciences* 25: 340, (1845) Repertory of Patent Inventions 5: 262 (Guildhall Police Court).

Wolverson v. Law (1877) *Birmingham Mail*, May 17, p. 3 (Birmingham Public Office 1877).

Woodcroft v. Reyner (November 20, December 2–3, 1844) *London Journal of Arts and Sciences* 25: 413 (nisi prius, Tindal CJ).

Woolley v. Warner (March 22, 1845) *Morning Advertiser*, March 24, p. 4; *Mechanics' Magazine* 42 (No. 1129): 215 (Guildhall Police Court).

Wright v. Wells (May 28, 1875) *Birmingham Daily Post*, May 15, p.6; *Birmingham Daily Post*, May 29, p. 5 (Balsall Heath Petty Sessions).

Yates v. Finch (January 10, 1842), *Aris's Birmingham Gazette*, January 17, 1842, p. 3; *Mechanics' Magazine* 36: 94; *Weekly True Sun*, February 13, 1842, p. 4 (Petty sessions, Dudley).

United States

Mayo Collaborative Services v. Prometheus Laboratories, Inc., 566 U.S. 66 (2021).

Index

www.ingramcontent.com/pod-product-compliance
Lightning Source LLC
LaVergne TN
LVHW052020200926
848481LV00005B/1541
* 9 7 8 1 0 0 9 4 7 8 0 9 0 *